ORDINARY MAN
EXTRAORDINARY MISSION

ORDINARY MAN
EXTRAORDINARY MISSION

The Life and Work of
E. Stanley Jones

STEPHEN A. GRAHAM

ABINGDON PRESS / *Nashville*

ORDINARY MAN, EXTRAORDINARY MISSION:
THE LIFE AND WORK OF E. STANLEY JONES

Copyright © 2005 by Abingdon Press

Library of Congress Cataloging-in-Publication Data

Graham, Stephen A.
  Ordinary man, extraordinary mission : the life and work of E. Stanley Jones / Stephen A. Graham.
    p. cm.
  Includes bibliographical references.
  ISBN 0-687-05446-X (alk. paper)
  1. Jones, E. Stanley (Eli Stanley), 1884–1973. 2. Missionaries—India—Biography. 3. Missions—India. I. Title.

BV3269.J66G73 2005
266'.76'092—dc22

2005014436

Scripture quotations labeled NIV from *The Holy Bible, New International Version* Copyright © 1973, 1978, 1984 by the International Bible Society. Used by permission of Zondervan Publishing House. All rights reserved.

Scripture quotations labeled KJV are from the King James or Authorized Version of the Bible.

All the letters of E. Stanley Jones to Miss Nellie Logan referred to and quoted from in this book are in the E. Stanley Jones Papers, part of the Special Collections Department at Asbury Theological Seminary in Wilmore, Kentucky.

Scripture quotations labeled RSV are from the *Revised Standard Version of the Bible,* copyright © 1946, 1952, 1971 by the Division of Christian Education of the National Council of the Churches of Christ in the United States of America. Used by permission. All rights reserved.

All the correspondence between E. Stanley Jones and Ralph Diffendorfer referred to and quoted in this book are in the Methodist Archives, maintained by the General Commission on Archives and History of The United Methodist Church, at Drew University, Madison, NJ.

MANUFACTURED IN THE UNITED STATES OF AMERICA

05 06 07 08 09 10 11 12 13 14—10 9 8 7 6 5 4 3 2 1

To Bishop Jim and Eunice Mathews
and the United Christian Ashram Board
for their uncommon discernment
of God's purpose in this book
and for their steady support and encouragement
of its author

Contents

Foreword

LET ME SAY how delighted I am to be invited to write a short foreword for this book. At long last, a truly worthy and objective account of my father's life is available to readers. Of course, Stanley Jones did write an autobiography entitled *A Song of Ascents,* but this was really his spiritual autobiography. For modesty's sake alone, many things must, by definition, be left out of such a record. Then, too, one cannot write of the very end of one's own life nor can any evaluation be made. There have also been a number of doctoral dissertations produced, covering some aspects of Stanley Jones's life and work. Now, for the first time, the whole story can be told, and Stephen A. Graham has told it very well.

I must admit that I myself have felt under some obligation to tell this story and have more than once taken pen in hand to do so. Perhaps even yet I shall endeavor to give my account and appreciation of both of my parents—told as an only child can relate the tale, aided by personal letters in my possession. Meanwhile, we have this fine book.

Though Professor Graham never actually met or even heard Stanley Jones speak, you would scarcely know it as you read this volume. He shows that he has mastered the material stored in the most extensive repositories, which are found in the Lovely Lane Museum in Baltimore and in the archives of Asbury Theological Seminary in Wilmore, Kentucky, to which my husband and I gifted my father's papers in 2001. Dr. Graham's careful scholastic research has already been demonstrated in his earlier study, *The Totalitarian Kingdom of God: The Political Philosophy of E. Stanley Jones.* In the present volume, he presents the man himself, describing in detail the most incredible account of my father's wide-ranging career. For the first time, the reader is introduced to Stanley Jones's teacher and mentor: Miss Nellie Logan. It was she who saw rich promise in this boy where others saw only problems. She continued to

9

support and follow him all the days of her life. How often have I heard him sing her praises.

The story begins with my father's study at Asbury College, and his stumbling and then sturdy efforts at the work of an evangelist. It proceeds to Lucknow, India, recounting his work as a pastor and his expanding role as teller of the good news to an ever widening field—to all of India, then to other Asian lands, then back to his native land, then literally to the ends of the earth. It tells of his meeting and marrying my mother, Mabel Lossing Jones—herself a missionary possessed of many-faceted talents. It shows how he built on his rather slender academic equipment to become an insightful student of India and its many religions, as well as all world religions. He developed an almost unparalleled understanding of humankind's inner, spiritual experience. He gained a great grasp of humanity's deepest needs and pointed to the ways that Jesus Christ meets these needs.

Very early in his work, my father saw the necessity of "knowing the territory" and of becoming acquainted with the men and women who were leaders of India and other countries and seeking to understand the great issues and moments of his time. Again and again, he would move into a new cultural setting and almost immediately begin discussing with its leaders possible solutions to the problems faced by a given people. He felt obliged to see himself as having responsibility for the whole world, for as he saw it, this is precisely what a Christian is supposed to be and do. Very early, he saw that Jesus was not a stranger to any culture, nor an alien in any land.

This is a hint of the story Graham tells, for he looks over my father's shoulder, as it were, with clear discernment. Just as Stanley Jones felt obliged to speak of humanity's needs and to write more than a score of books addressing these needs, so Stephen A. Graham interprets in fascinating terms what my father lived for nearly nine decades—and finally died for.

It is my husband's and my earnest hope that other readers will find as much inspiration here as we have.

Eunice Jones Mathews

Introduction

E STANLEY JONES was one of the most widely known and universally admired Christian missionaries and evangelists of the twentieth century—a reputation richly deserved. Called as a missionary to North India in 1907 at the age of twenty-three, he served as pastor of the English-speaking Methodist Episcopal Church in Lucknow and preached as well in surrounding villages and bazaars. Later, after he married and moved to nearby Sitapur, he became the affiliated agent of the Methodist Publishing House in Lucknow, shared responsibility with his wife for the boys' school in Sitapur, and served as a Methodist district superintendent in charge of five hundred clergy and laity. As a young, enthusiastic, and supremely self-confident missionary, Jones believed that he could do it all—and do it all in his own strength. But he couldn't. After ten years of service, and nearly two years before he was due for furlough, Stanley Jones collapsed. Physically, emotionally, and spiritually exhausted, he was sent home by his bishop.

Stanley Jones knew, however, that God was not finished with him. When he returned to India in 1917, during World War I, after the end of his furlough, he found his true calling—among influential middle and upper class Indians. Even before his breakdown he had often left Sitapur to evangelize the educated intelligentsia in the urban centers of India. It was these same higher status Indians who recognized and denounced the hypocrisy of Great Britain's heroic defense of freedom and equality for itself, while denying the same rights to its colonial subjects. This was the beginning of Indian nationalism and, for Stanley Jones, the beginning of his political education.

About this time Jones met Mahatma Gandhi and learned to sympathize with the goals of the Indian nationalist movement. He visited Gandhi at his ashram or spiritual retreat at Sabarmati, corresponding with him and remaining a friend of his until Gandhi's assassination in 1948. More important than Jones's personal relationship with Gandhi, however, was his acute spiritual sensitivity to how Indian Christianity challenged the religious and cultural imperialism of Western Christianity. This was the theme of his first book, *The Christ of the Indian Road* (1925), which established the absolute moral and spiritual equivalence between Indian and Western Christianity and argued persuasively that North American and Western European Christians could and should strengthen and deepen their personal relationship with Jesus Christ by learning from their Indian brothers and sisters. *The Christ of the Indian Road* burst like a bombshell on Western Christendom. Almost overnight, E. Stanley Jones became an international celebrity. His book became a million-copy best seller and was translated into scores of languages.

Building on the success of his first book, Jones published twenty-seven more books during his lifetime, several of which sold a million-plus copies, including his two most popular collections of daily devotional meditations, *Victorious Living* (1936) and *Abundant Living* (1942). A complete bibliography of his publications lists hundreds of articles in periodicals like *The Indian Witness*, *The Christian Century*, and *The Christian Advocate*. In addition, Jones's unpublished letters, many of which are lost, number in the tens of thousands, perhaps as many as 100,000. In other words, the legacy of E. Stanley Jones, as measured by the quantity and quality of his writing, is astounding.

Jones's legacy, however, does not rest on his written words alone. Of equal importance is his personal witness for Jesus Christ. From the time he began traveling as an evangelist in India in the late 1910s, he won wide and enthusiastic recognition for his gifts as a public speaker and Christian evangelist. But because his audiences were mostly non-Christian, he spoke not in Christian churches, which Hindus, Muslims, and Sikhs were reluctant to attend, but in public halls and schools. There, on religiously neutral ground, in meetings chaired by a local dignitary who was often non-Christian, Jones addressed his listeners for an hour or more. His theme was usually a secular topic, but he always approached his subject from a specifically Christian perspective and spoke with a definite Christian focus. After his lectures he answered questions from the audience, often for several hours.

In the 1920s and 1930s his growing reputation in India preceded him as he traveled and spoke in Mesopotamia (Iraq), Palestine, and Egypt in the Middle East and in Burma, Malaya, the Philippines, China, and Singapore in East and Southeast Asia. By 1938 *Time* magazine reported that he was "the world's greatest Christian missionary."[1]

Stanley Jones was an unconventional Christian missionary evangelist who used the methods of other religions as well as secular venues to spread the gospel of Jesus Christ. In 1930 he established in North India a Christian ashram at Sat Tal (which means "seven lakes") in the foothills of the Himalayas. Drawing on his experiences at Gandhi's ashram and at Santiniketan, the ashram of the Indian poet Rabindranath Tagore, he assembled at Sat Tal, initially for two months each year, a multicultural, multiethnic, and multireligious group of men and women. The only qualification for participation in the study, prayer, and discussion of the ashram was openness to the Christian gospel and a willingness to search sincerely for God's truth together with other members of the ashram on a basis of complete equality. Jones soon duplicated the success of his Sat Tal Ashram outside of India in a Christian ashram movement that continues today in nearly one hundred locations throughout the world, under the auspices of the United Christian Ashrams.

Although Jones traveled almost constantly from the time he began his evangelistic work in India in the 1910s, he visited his native land only occasionally until the 1940s. In early 1941 he had just finished an evangelistic tour through the United States and was ready to return to India. His trunk was already on board ship in San Francisco for his scheduled departure when he received a definite word from what he called the Inner Voice or the Holy Spirit: *"I want you here."*[2] He obeyed immediately, retrieved his trunk, and, contrary to all his plans and expectations, spent six years in the United States, separated from his wife and daughter who had remained in India. He did not see his family again until after the end of World War II.

For the last four months of 1941 Jones engaged in almost nonstop "shuttle diplomacy"[3] in Washington, D.C. among the embassies of Japan, China, and Australia, the U. S. State Department, and ultimately the White House. The purpose of his strictly unofficial diplomacy was to prevent war between Japan and the United States. Few people know today how close he came to success.

He remained in the United States after the Japanese attack on Pearl Harbor not by choice but because the British government would not approve his request for a visa to return to India. Despite his friendship with Lord Halifax, the British Ambassador to the United States during the war and the former Viceroy of India, Jones was unable to persuade the British to permit him to return to his adopted homeland. The British Embassy in Washington never told him the reason for its government's decision, but since other American missionaries traveled freely between the States and India during the war, it was almost certainly Jones's outspoken support for Indian national aspirations that kept him out of India during World War II.

Beginning in the 1950s Jones spent six months of every year in India, including two months at Sat Tal and six months abroad. He used the six months outside India mostly for speaking engagements and ashrams in the United States, but also to evangelize and lead ashrams in Europe, South America, East Asia, and Africa. Throughout his long and incredibly active life, Jones remained faithful to God's call to preach the Christian gospel and to bring as many men and women as possible into a personal relationship with Jesus Christ. He maintained his position as the foremost Christian evangelist and missionary until the very end of his life. In 1964, when Jones was eighty, *Time* magazine noted that at that time only Billy Graham could rival his international reputation as a Christian leader.[4]

But what about Jones's significance today? What is his enduring legacy? The central focus of E. Stanley Jones's public and private life was the kingdom of God. This was true of his writing and speaking and of his personal relationships—relationships with his family and his colleagues, with both the wealthy and influential, and with thousands of lesser-known people who passed through his life. In an important and profound sense he rediscovered the kingdom of God for the body of Christ. He was not the only twentieth-century Christian figure to emphasize Jesus' teaching about the kingdom, but his life and work reveal the true character of the kingdom more transparently and more consistently than any of his contemporaries. Jones never claimed to be a theologian, but he left an indelible imprint on Christian theology in the lives of individuals who were transformed and whose understanding of the Christian faith was initiated or renewed by his influence. He never claimed to be a social or political philosopher, but he did have an important influence on the course of the history of the twentieth century. His colleague and later Methodist bishop J. Waskom Pickett wrote after Jones's death: "Probably no non-Indian contributed more than he to development of the strong moral and ethical sentiment that characterized Indian national leadership in the later stages of the quest for independence and in the formulation of the Constitution of India."[5]

Jones never claimed to be an educator, but through the boys' school, which his wife, Mabel Lossing Jones, operated in Sitapur, and through the scholarship money that both of them raised from their personal resources and from contributions in over fifty years of Christian missionary service in India, both Stanley and Mabel Jones left a moral and spiritual legacy in the minds and hearts of the Indian people that lives on even today.

It should be apparent that I am an unabashed admirer of E. Stanley Jones. Although I never met him in person or heard him speak, he has changed my life. I am not the same person I was when I began to research and write his biography. Jones reflects the person of Jesus Christ more directly and more clearly than any other individual I have encountered. Does his personal impact on me influence my interpretation of his life? Certainly. Does this influence prejudice my treatment of Jones or blind me to his weaknesses and shortcomings? No. Because of his steadfast and unwavering commitment to the kingdom of God, he often found himself embroiled in controversy. On some issues I support Jones wholeheartedly.

On other issues I question the wisdom of his judgment or of the judgment of the Methodist Church that sponsored him.

For example, I make no apology for Jones's early and forceful denunciation of British imperialism in India. Nor do I offer anything but praise for his hatred of racism and for his unwillingness to hold a meeting where anyone was excluded on the basis of race. But in the discussion of mass movement evangelism in chapter 2, I conclude that the Methodist Episcopal Church, and by implication Jones, missed a heaven-sent opportunity for Christian evangelism among the outcastes and lower castes of India. Moreover, I discuss in depth in chapter 10 the widespread criticism of Jones's proposal for "economic withdrawal" (in fact, a boycott) by American and British Christians in response to Japanese aggression in China, which resulted in civilian atrocities and widespread suffering in that nation. As a final example, in the same chapter I state why I think that only Jones's emotional and physical exhaustion can explain his stubborn and unreasonable criticism of the international missionary conference held at Tambaram near Madras, India, in 1938.

All biographers face the challenge of painting a complete portrait of their subjects. In the case of E. Stanley Jones there are large gaps in the information available about his life, especially information about his childhood and early family relationships. In his autobiography, *A Song of Ascents,* he states that his first genuine acceptance of Jesus Christ as his Lord and Savior at age seventeen "was the birthday of my soul. Life began there."[6] This was literally true for Stanley Jones. He rarely spoke about or reflected on his childhood and young teen years. Nevertheless, chapter 1 does narrate the events of these early years insofar as I am aware of them.

In addition, biographers must tell the life story of their subjects in a way that is both chronologically accurate and coherent. A biography written in the form of a diary would give readers little sense of the significance and interrelationship of events that may be separated by long periods of time. On the other hand, focusing on the most important events in the life of a subject without regard to the time and circumstances of their occurrence would be equally misleading. So, generally speaking, I have arranged the following chapters according to the chronology of Jones's life. However, in order to interrelate significant events that occur at different times, I often interrupt the temporal sequence of his life story. Moreover, and more important, I try to provide a historical, political, and religious context for the events of his life. A broad understanding of the Christian missionary movement in the late nineteenth and early twentieth century, of the aftermath of World War I, of the different phases of the Indian independence movement, of the origins of Japanese imperialism and militarism in the Pacific in the 1930s and 1940s, and of American domestic and international politics in the years after World War II are all essential for an accurate interpretation of the full significance of E. Stanley Jones.

I should also explain my use and acknowledgment of sources. Since I am writing for a broad audience, I have not adopted the academic convention of footnotes. However, I have provided complete information for each chapter about the sources I have used as well as occasional suggestions about additional sources for readers who want to explore Jones's life in more depth and in greater detail. In addition, a bibliography fills out the more abbreviated form of the notes.

No book is written solely by its author. As a Christian I relied primarily on God's direction and guidance in writing this biography. But, as I acknowledge in my book on Jones's political philosophy, *The Totalitarian Kingdom of God,* it was my wife, Marcia W. Graham, who first directed my attention to Stanley Jones's unique significance for both the body of Christ and American political thought. Moreover, she has continued to serve as my chief encourager and my chief critic in this biography. I am also deeply grateful to Jones's son-in-law, Bishop James K. Mathews, and to his wife and Jones's daughter, Eunice Jones Mathews. They read the manuscript in its entirety and, in the course of several long telephone conversations, offered fascinating and valuable information about Mabel and Stanley Jones and made scores of suggestions that have improved immeasurably the quality of this book.

In the task of facilitating my access to Jones's papers I thank primarily Dr. William C. Kostlevy, the former archivist, and Grace Yoder, the current archivist, at Asbury Theological Seminary, where the bulk of these papers are stored. I truly appreciate their expertise and helpfulness during my visits to Asbury. I also thank L. Dale Patterson and his staff at the Methodist Archives, located on the campus of Drew University in Madison, New Jersey. These persons were indispensable during the several days I spent reading Jones's missionary correspondence, and they were equally indispensable after I left in making photocopies and in scanning images from their files.

In the discussion of sources, which follows each chapter, I acknowledge the help of archivists at three presidential libraries—the Roosevelt Library in Hyde Park, New York; the Truman Library in Independence, Missouri; and the Eisenhower Library in Abilene, Kansas. In each case these archivists were prompt, efficient, and courteous in providing copies of materials about Jones's contact with the three presidents. In addition, I thank the staff of Krannert Memorial Library at the University of Indianapolis and especially Kim Wenning, the Head of Circulation, who handled my many interlibrary loan requests in exemplary fashion. Finally, I owe an enormous debt of gratitude to Mary Ruth Howes, who edited the content of the book on behalf of Abingdon Press. She worked tirelessly on the manuscript, checking the accuracy of the source notes and making countless suggestions to improve the clarity of my expression and to make the flow of the narrative seamless. She is also responsible for the bibliography. If there is any truth to the expression "it takes one to know one," it is certainly true of Mary Ruth. As a woman who grew up on the mission field in China, she brought a unique perspective and insight to her work on this biography. No one could have done a better job.

1

From Baltimore to Bluegrass

Well here I am safe and sound in the Bluegrass . . . of old Kentucky eating real corn pone and molasses. Glory!
      —September 11, 1903, letter to Miss Nellie Logan from Asbury College[1]

THE LETTERS OF E. Stanley Jones to Miss Nellie Logan are without doubt, I believe, the most remarkable correspondence of any twentieth-century American evangelist or missionary. For over forty years, from 1903 when he arrived at Asbury College in Wilmore, Kentucky, until the mid-1940s, Stanley Jones wrote hundreds of letters to his former first-grade schoolteacher.[2] His letters unveil much more deeply and intimately than his twenty-eight books and hundreds of published articles the mind, heart, and soul of this unique and fascinating man, the most widely known and admired and the most influential American missionary and evangelist of the first half of the twentieth century.

The relationship between Jones and Miss Nellie Logan began chronologically in a public school classroom when Stanley entered first grade. The spiritual and emotional origin of their friendship, however, came later at the altar of Memorial Methodist Episcopal Church in Baltimore. This was the most dramatic and decisive event of Stanley's life when, as a seventeen-year-old, he received Jesus Christ as his Lord and Savior. It was Miss Nellie who prayed with him at the altar. It was she who, as Jones explains in his spiritual autobiography, *A Song of Ascents,* "knelt alongside me and repeated John 3:16 this way: 'God so loved Stanley Jones, that he gave his only begotten Son, that if Stanley Jones will believe on him he shall not perish, but have everlasting life.'"[3]

Two years earlier, when he was only fifteen, Stanley experienced what he called a "half-conversion" under the preaching of a visiting English evangelist at Memorial Church. "I felt religious for a few weeks," he wrote, "and then it all faded out." But when Robert J. Bateman came to Baltimore in February 1901 to lead a series of evangelistic meetings at Memorial Methodist, Stanley said he "wanted the real thing or nothing." For two nights he listened attentively and expectantly to the evangelist's message about Jesus Christ and his gift of salvation, but his heart was not moved and his life was not changed. Finally, on the third night of the revival, before he left home Stanley prayed the most sincere and humble prayer he had ever prayed: "O Jesus, save me tonight."

When he arrived at the church, Stanley sat in a front church pew for the first time in his life and could hardly wait for the altar call after Mr. Bateman's sermon.

> When he did stop [Stanley wrote in *A Song of Ascents*], I was the first one there. I had scarcely bent my knees when Heaven broke into my spirit. I was enveloped by assurance, by acceptance, by reconciliation. . . . As I rose from my knees, I felt I wanted to put my arms around the world to share this with everybody. . . . But I have. This was a seed moment. The whole of my future was packed into it.[4]

Everything about the rest of E. Stanley Jones's life and career dramatically confirms and emphatically underscores that last statement: His whole future *was* packed into that moment at Memorial Methodist Episcopal Church in Baltimore in February 1901. Yet no one, including Jones himself, could possibly have foreseen or known

- that he would serve for seventy years as a missionary evangelist to scores of nations including India, Sri Lanka, Malaysia, Thailand, Singapore, Palestine, Egypt, China, Burma, Japan, Korea, the Philippines, Australia, Finland, the Netherlands, Holland, Sweden, South Africa, Fiji, Mexico, Cuba, Argentina, Brazil, Canada, and the United States;
- that his internationally best-selling and widely translated books would revolutionize the whole theory and practice of European and American missions to Third World nations by disentangling Christianity from Western political and cultural imperialism and would reclaim Jesus' concept of the kingdom of God in the Gospels

from a narrow and rigid individualistic interpretation and would restore the kingdom as a truly totalitarian idea embracing all personal, social, economic, and political relationships;

- that his daily devotional guides would sell more than a million copies worldwide and that his most popular book, *Abundant Living*, would still be in print nearly a quarter of a century after his death;
- that he would establish hundreds of Christian ashrams or spiritual retreats throughout the world, many of which still meet each year;
- that he would have a deep and abiding influence on government leaders and public affairs, including his friendship with Gandhi and Nehru in India and his fervent support for Indian nationalism and for Indian independence from Great Britain;
- that he would become in 1941 an unofficial negotiator among many high-level diplomats in Washington representing Japan, China, Australia, the Netherlands, and the United States, and would meet one-on-one with President Roosevelt on December 3, 1941, in an eleventh-hour, off-the-record session that came very close to postponing if not preventing the Japanese attack on Pearl Harbor;
- that he would be nominated for the Nobel Peace Prize in 1962 and would receive the Gandhi Peace Award in 1963;
- finally and most important of all, that Jones's personal Christian witness would have a life-changing impact on the millions of people throughout the world who heard him speak during his lifetime or devoured his stirring books, on the hundreds of clergy and laity in India and the United States to whom he offered personal counseling, sometimes for scores of hours, and on the hundreds of correspondents to whom he wrote tens of thousands of letters.

Jones provides an interesting postscript about Bateman in *A Song of Ascents*.[5] Bateman, he wrote,

> was on the "Titanic" when it went down. When there were not enough lifeboats for all, the men stepped back and let the women and children take them. As the ship went down, the stentorian voice of Robert J. Bateman struck up a hymn which others joined: "Nearer, my God, to thee." Only the icy waters could quench his fiery zeal.

E. Stanley Jones was born in Clarksville, Maryland, on January 3, 1884. Although he was christened Eli Stanley, he never used his first name and was always called Stanley. He grew up in nearby Baltimore with his parents, Albin Davis and Sarah Evans Jones, and with two older brothers and a sister.[6] Stanley was close to his mother but rarely mentioned his father who was, as we will see, an alcoholic. He had good relationships with his brothers and sister and was especially attached to his brother Howard, who became a prominent surgeon in Baltimore. Jones did not often speak or write about his family or about his boyhood and youth. His autobiography, however, does contain several stories of childhood experiences that shed some light on his early life.

Stanley's first memory of church, he writes,

> was when, as a little boy, I went to the Sunday school at Frederick Avenue Methodist Church, South, in Baltimore, dressed in a brand new suit. To call attention to my new suit, and me, I took a collection plate and began to pass it around before the grown-ups standing chatting. I didn't hope to get any money. I hoped to collect compliments for my new suit and incidentally for myself.[7]

This incident occurred in 1889, when Stanley was five years old. Although it is important not to read too much into this childhood event, it does reveal that from an early age, Stanley Jones did not hesitate to seek public attention and enjoyed being on center stage.

As he grew up, Stanley apparently acquired a reputation for being "mischievous," since that is the word one of his teachers, Anne Collington, used to describe him when she learned that he was going to be a preacher.

In his young teenage years Stanley's chums, as he called them, were not always a good influence on his character. One of his friends, Ras, was with Stanley at Memorial Church in Baltimore during Stanley's first conversion experience.[8] When Stanley responded to the preacher's call for salvation, he told Ras, "I'm going to give myself to Christ. Will you?"

"No," Ras replied. "I'm going to see life first."

Stanley recalled his first encounter with Ras after his genuine conversion to Christ, two years later, in 1901. "I walked up to my chum, Ras, slapped him on the back, and said, 'My, what a d___ fine day,' using the old vocabulary to express my newfound joy."

In addition to cleaning up his language, Stanley, as a new Christian, had to make other changes in his behavior. "The very next day" after his conversion, Jones writes,

> out of habit I went to the barbershop where a group used to play cards. But fortunately and providentially I picked up a pocket New Testament lying on a table in our home and took it with me. . . . As the group gathered at the card table, I went to the barber's chair and began to read the New Testament. They called to me to join them as usual in the card game. I replied: "No, I've been converted." It was a bomb. A silence fell upon the stunned group. One of them, Ras, who had refused to take the step when I took it, spoke up and said: "Well, then, read us something from that book." I knew little about "that book," but I opened it at random; and the first verse my eyes fell on was this: "What shall it profit a man, if he gain the whole world, and lose his own soul?" (Mark 8:36). I read it. Ras remarked, "That's a good one. Read some more."

One telling episode that illustrates Stanley's pre-conversion lifestyle concerns his childhood interest in homing pigeons. His desire to increase the size of his flock, he writes in his autobiography, "led me to appropriate some pigeons from someone else's flock and add them to my own." But once he became a Christian, "one of the first things" he did "was to send the price of those pigeons to the rightful owner."[9]

Another important influence on Stanley Jones was, of course, Nellie Logan. Miss Nellie's influence began well before his conversion. The Reverend Thomas S. Long, pastor of Memorial Church in Baltimore when Stanley was converted, recalled that Stanley's parents joined the church while he was pastor there and confirmed Miss Nellie's early impact on Stanley: He wrote to Miss Nellie on January 3, 1928:

> The two boys [Stanley and his brother Howard] came into the Sunday School at the time their parents joined I think—I know they came directly under your care and you had much to do with the religious life of Stanley.[10]

Miss Nellie's prayers and her personal witness both as a public school teacher and as a Sunday school teacher were crucial elements in the events that led seventeen-year-old Stanley to the altar. But he did not begin writing to Miss Nellie until he left Baltimore for Asbury College in the fall of 1903. In the intervening two years he worked for a while in the law library of the Baltimore courthouse, finding books for the lawyers who requested them and reshelving the books when they were finished. His job was a natural outgrowth of his earlier study of the law at City College in Baltimore between 1899 and 1901. Although he was apparently quite serious about his job and worked at the courthouse in the afternoon and evenings from four until eleven, he was discharged.[11] This was certainly providential. Even before he lost his job, he recalls in his spiritual autobiography, in the mornings when he was not working, "I would take my New Testament and stroll off in the woods and read it. I would find myself pressing my lips to a passage that spoke to my condition, as the Quakers would say."[12] Now that Jesus Christ had transformed his life, Stanley lost interest in his ambition to become a lawyer and spent his free time in prayer and in reading his Bible, searching for God's purpose and destiny for his life. On February 12, 1903, at Memorial Church he was licensed as a local preacher in Baltimore by the Methodist Episcopal Church.

After his discharge from the law library, Stanley worked for a year for the Metropolitan Life Insurance Company, "collecting and writing industrial insurance in a poor section of Baltimore." From this job he earned enough money not only to pay for his first year of college but also to help support his family. After that, his brother Howard, who graduated from medical school shortly after Stanley went to Asbury, "took over the support of the family" so that Stanley was free to continue his studies. During the following summers, Jones explains in his spiritual autobiography, "I . . . [made enough money] in evangelistic meetings to pay for the coming year. Thus I finished college without debt."[13]

Asbury College in Wilmore, Kentucky, was founded in 1890 by a Methodist pastor and evangelist, the Reverend John Wesley Hughes. The college was the fruit of Hughes's deep and long-felt sense of the

> need for . . . a real salvation school where religious men and women could hold their salvation; and where unsaved and unsanctified students would not only be encouraged, but urged to get saved and sanctified and prepared educationally for their work.[14]

This quotation from Hughes's autobiography reflects the school's origin in the Holiness Movement. In accordance with the doctrine of Christian perfection, which was first preached by John Wesley in the Great Awakening of the eighteenth century, the Holiness Movement[15] emphasized both salvation *and* sanctification. Originally an offshoot of Methodism in the United States after the Civil War, the movement was organized to revive and reestablish John Wesley's concept of sanctification among American Protestants. Sanctification is a "second blessing" that may occur simultaneously with or at some point after the initial transformation of Christian conversion. Conversion is arguably both a once-and-for-all experience and an ongoing or continuous reality. Today, sanctification is often referred to as the experience of being filled with the Holy Spirit. Sanctification is just as much a work of God as conversion and is both instantaneous and continuous. Sanctified believers may be filled with the presence of the Holy Spirit in an instant, but as they allow the Spirit to permeate all aspects of their life and of their relationships with others, the fruit of the Spirit should be continually and progressively manifested in personal holiness.

The Holiness Movement was such an integral and essential part of the founding of Asbury College that Hughes originally called his institution the Kentucky Holiness School. In the original announcement for the school's opening, he emphasized that "entire sanctification as a blessing received subsequent to conversion, will be taught."[16] The Holiness Movement, however, was controversial within the established denominational churches where it flourished in the latter half of the nineteenth century. The theological and ecclesiastical debate about the Holiness Movement and about the doctrine of sanctification as a second blessing became most heated within the Methodist Church at the very time when John Wesley Hughes established the Kentucky Holiness School and became its first president.

Dr. Henry Clay Morrison, a well-known Holiness evangelist and editor, and later president of Asbury College, wrote in his introduction to Hughes's autobiography that Asbury "was founded at a time when a bitter battle of opposition and persecution was being conducted against the Methodist people who professed the experience of entire sanctification."[17] Indeed, the Methodist Episcopal Church, South expelled Dr. Morrison as both a minister and a member because of his outspoken advocacy of Holiness doctrine and practice. Although Morrison's membership in the Methodist Church was later restored, his expulsion reflects the bitterness of the conflict sparked by the Holiness Movement.

There were many reasons for this opposition. First of all, there was genuine fear that the more radical Holiness leaders would form a full-blown separatist movement and split a Methodist Church still deeply and tragically divided by the issue of slavery. This fear is reflected in the fact that the bishop of the Methodist Episcopal Church, South for Kentucky refused to appoint Hughes as the president of the Kentucky Holiness School. The bishop took exception to the name of the school because, he insisted, "all Methodist schools were holiness schools."[18] Moreover, Methodist bishops and district superintendents, who were responsible for filling local church pastorates, felt threatened by the Holiness Movement, which encouraged men called to the ministry to become full-time traveling evangelists.

Stanley apparently first heard of Asbury through an advertisement in the *Pentecostal Herald*. Years later, Dr. Morrison, who edited the *Herald* before becoming president of Asbury College, was asked if he could locate the issue of the *Pentecostal Herald* in which Jones had seen the ad for Asbury. Morrison replied that it would be impossible for him to find that particular issue, but he did tell his correspondent the story of the first time he met Stanley Jones.[19] Morrison had agreed to hold a weeklong series of meetings in a large Methodist Episcopal church in Baltimore. However, when the district superintendent heard of the engagement, he told the Methodist pastor that "he would prefer to cancel the engagement." The pastor was greatly embarrassed when he wrote to Morrison and canceled the meetings. Then, Morrison continued:

> A woman who had a mission in the city asked me to give her the week I had intended for the large church. She secured a small church in a poorer part of the city and I had a gracious meeting.
> One evening after the service a handsome lad came to me and said he was called to preach and wanted to go to college, and desired to attend an institution where his spiritual life would be cultivated and where there would be nothing to hinder, but assist in his growth in grace. I recommended Asbury College. On asking the lad his name he told me he was Stanley Jones. It is quite probable that I sent him a copy of the Herald with some advertisement of the college.

In his autobiography Jones confirms Morrison's story. "Dr. H. C. Morrison . . . was holding a series of evangelistic meetings in Baltimore" and it was through him that "I became interested in Asbury."[20]

In the fall of 1903, Stanley entered Asbury and on September 11 wrote his first letter from Wilmore to Miss Nellie. "Well here I am safe and sound in the Bluegrass . . . of old Kentucky eating real corn pone and molasses. Glory!" Although he experienced some culture shock when he moved from the bustling environment of Baltimore to the tiny rural community of Wilmore, Kentucky, he was most impressed by the spiritual atmosphere of Asbury. "They don't make a turn about," he wrote, "without they have a prayer and ask God's blessing on it." Sixty-five years later, when he was in his eighties, Jones still remembered and appreciated the spiritual heritage of Asbury College. He recalls in his autobiography that although the school was well known for being conservative, it did not embrace "a cantankerous conservatism." Instead, the graduates of Asbury came from, and after graduation went back into, many different denominations, becoming "a leaven of evangelical outlook and spirit" throughout the Christian church.[21]

Before Stanley wrote this first letter to Miss Nellie, he had received a letter from her. He was so delighted to get her letter, he wrote, "that several boys made remarks about the 'smile' on his face and something about [the letter] being from his best 'girl.'"

During his first few days on campus Jones did not have a permanent place to live and found temporary housing "at a boy's room." Then, he explained to Miss Nellie,

> I waited and waited & waited (stick-to-itiveness) until my sweet Jesus just sent along the sweetest man in college. Bless His dear Name! *It's just like him.* My chum's name is "Darby."

Darby—his full name was Virgil L. Darby, a second-year student from Vilonia, Arkansas[22]—Stanley continued, was "about thirty" years old, and a "very studious" young man who had "the quiet hallelujahs." Through Darby's contacts in Wilmore, he and Jones found room and board at the home of L. L. Pickett, "the finest place to room in town." The cost of room and board at the Pickett home was only ten dollars a month. "And that isn't all," he concluded. "We have access to Bro. Pickett's library which is in our room. What do you think of that? I'll say it again *Glory to Jesus!*"

Stanley and the Pickett family became good friends. The Reverend L. L. Pickett and his wife, Ludie Day Pickett, had "about a dozen" children at the time Stanley lived there. One of them was J. Waskom who, although six years younger than Stanley, was also a beginning student at Asbury. The two "had some classes together" and became lifelong friends. Waskom also became a Methodist clergyman and a missionary to India, where he was elected a Missionary Bishop. After Stanley's death the *Indian Witness*, a weekly newspaper published by the Methodist Church in India, devoted its entire March 15, 1973, issue to Stanley Jones's life and achievements, including an article by Waskom. In it he recalled the occasion of their first meeting at Asbury.

> Stanley came to my home town of Wilmore, Kentucky, in September of 1904 [*sic*] to enter Asbury College and begin as a resident in the college boys' dormitory. This was his first experience of life away from home. His father was in service in a minor position in the city government of Baltimore, Maryland. Wilmore was then an unincorporated town, without any of the then modern advantages of any kind, and Stanley missed the relative luxury of his Baltimore home and its environs. One morning, after a restless night, he ate part of his breakfast and then was completely overcome by home-sickness. He packed his suitcase and trunk and started for the railway station. The only friend [probably Virgil Darby], to whom he revealed his purpose urged him not to act so hastily but to go to my parents' home and ask my mother to let him live with them in their moderately comfortable home. Stanley agreed to see my mother, who was the head of the Department of English in the college.
>   When I had finished playing baseball that evening and went home, my mother called me to the sitting room and told me that a young man had been there in the early afternoon saying that he would have to leave college and go home unless she could let him live with us. She replied that her home was already full and that her son Waskom had begged all year to have a room of his own and had been living in it for just one week, and she just couldn't now ask him to share it with a stranger. I asked mother who that young man was and she replied[,] "He told me that his name is Stanley Jones, but I don't know anything more about him." I had met Stanley several times, including once on the baseball diamond, and I liked him. So I replied, "If it's Stanley Jones let him come; I'll be glad to share my room with him." Thus, the next day he moved to our home, and it became his home and mine for two full years.[23]

Although Stanley was nineteen and Waskom only thirteen when Jones came to live with the Pickett family, their friendship became a deep and abiding one. As Waskom recalled shortly after Jones's death, their difference in age was "a special feature" of their relationship.

> We prayed together almost every day for an appreciable period of time. We were in the same literary society, and members of the same debating club. We exercised together, often running two or three miles several days each week.

Stanley, too, had warm and vivid memories of the two years he spent in the Pickett household. Years later, in a front-page article in the January 9,

1936, issue of the *Indian Witness*,[24] he welcomed Bishop Pickett to his new position and recalled some of his experiences in the Pickett household.

> Once the home burned down and as I looked into the burning building there was a motto upon the wall in the hallway and it was enveloped in flames, the flames making a kind of frame around it. The motto said, "Rest in the Lord." After the catastrophe was over I told Mrs. Pickett that the last thing I had seen in the house was this motto. Her smile was heavenly when she turned to me and said, "Stanley, that is exactly what I am doing. I am resting in the Lord." And everybody who knew her knew that it was beautifully true.

On another occasion everyone in the Pickett home came down with mumps, not just a slight case of mumps, but "a most virile type of mumps."

> Waskom had a very prosperous pair of jaws. I felt a lump in my jaw, showed it to Mrs. Pickett, and she said: "Stanley, you've got them. You can go downtown tonight, but it will be the last night for several weeks." But when I got back home I went to my knees and said: "Now Lord, I'm too busy to have mumps. I don't believe I'll have them." My lump faded away. Waskom was impressed. He came to me and said, "Stanley, if you will pray mine down to where you have yours, I think I could take them the rest of the way."[25]

The paths of the two friends continued to cross, since both became missionaries to India. Stanley's first assignment was to pastor the English Church in Lucknow. When he left Lucknow three years later to become a full-time evangelist, Waskom Pickett became the pastor of the Lucknow church. Jones was conducting evangelistic meetings in Madras when Pickett arrived in Lucknow. Since he could not welcome his friend in person,

> I sent him a telegram of greeting and added a scripture quotation. The numbers of the scripture verses were changed in transmission, and the passage that he got was, "For I would not have you ignorant concerning the trouble which befell me in Asia." He was puzzled at this kind of welcome![26]

As an Asbury student Stanley's routine was to rise at 5:00 A.M. in order to be ready for his first recitation at 7:30. His classes continued until noon, so that he had the afternoon and evening for study. His first-year courses included "Greek, Caesar, Rhetoric, Butler's Analogy, Church History and Ralston's Elements of Divinity." But he took part in other campus activities. As his letter of September 21, 1903, records, Stanley was involved in literary societies and led the Student Volunteer Band on campus. Topics debated by the literary societies included "Resolved that the natural wonders of the new world exceed those of the old" and "Resolved that Carrie Nation was justified in using the hatchet," and he asked Miss Nellie to send him information to help him prepare for debate on these topics.

The reference to Carrie Nation reflects the involvement of the Holiness Movement generally and of Asbury College specifically in the temperance crusade. On March 17, 1904, the famous temperance leader spoke on campus to a large crowd at Asbury Chapel. Although Jones does not refer to Carrie Nation's being at the college in any of his letters, he probably did not miss this opportunity to hear her.[27] Nine years before, the college had hosted Susan B. Anthony, one of the pioneers of the American women's movement and the leader of the National Women's Suffrage Association. Anthony spoke in the college chapel on January 11, 1895.[28]

The picture of E. Stanley Jones that emerges from his first letters to Miss Nellie is of an exuberant young man with an unquenchable thirst for learning, a young man who is on fire for Jesus Christ. His conversion two years before is an event that is still a fresh and vital part of his life. Like any adolescent, he has an insatiable appetite for new experiences, and he is eager to share the taste, touch, and smell of what he is learning with his best friend, Miss Nellie. His early letters from Asbury are full of life and energy as well as humor. But above all else, his letters are filled with enthusiasm for his Lord and Savior, Jesus Christ.

Stanley's early letters to Miss Nellie reveal other aspects of his character and personality, which were decisive factors in the formation and development of his career as a missionary and evangelist. In his letter written on January 23, 1904, he tells his friend about a comment that was made about him by "one young man" who said Stanley was "so contrary" that if he "should drown they would look for . . . [him] upstream instead of down." In his very first Asbury letter to Miss Nellie, he referred to his "stick-to-itiveness." In his letter dated November 30, 1904, he told about an incident in which his "independent spirit revolted."

> I was invited out to supper with several young ladies and what do you think? *I got into a fight*—with the devil. Several young men from Lexington were there—the flip kind—and began to talk all kinds of worldliness when they were rebuked by a young lady who said there was a *preacher* in the room (meaning me). Then they began to talk about what rascals "they" were; of course I wasn't supposed to hear for I was talking to someone else—but I heard. And oh how the fire burned within me . . . and when my chance came—well I hope it "soaked" in.

Stanley doesn't tell Miss Nellie precisely what he said to the young men from Lexington, but it must have been a sharp and perhaps intemperate remark. He did not hesitate to say to these guests exactly what he thought of their conversation. Jones may have been entirely justified in his criticism. The young men may have deserved his rebuke. But his reaction to the incident does reveal that he was bold and outspoken, that he did not hesitate to speak his mind—though it would be unfair to conclude that he was too easily provoked or that he had a quick temper. And, of course, it is important to remember that Stanley was only twenty years old and a college sophomore. His youth and inexperience certainly go a long way in explaining how he handled the situation.

President Hughes, or "Brother Hughes" as Stanley always called him in his letters, established a rigid code of discipline for Asbury College. By 1900, just ten years after he founded the school, Hughes had reduced a long list of college rules to six "Domestic Regulations." These regulations included a requirement for "strict observance of the Sabbath" as well as prohibitions against "boisterous laughing and talking," against "social visiting . . . except by permission of the faculty," and against using "tobacco, profanity, and vulgarity." Stanley was never suspected of violating any of these regulations, but he certainly violated the letter, if not the spirit, of Domestic Regulation number three: "Too much letter writing is discouraged, even to home folks, as it interferes with the best results of study."[29]

In view of the frequency and intimacy of Stanley's letters to Miss Nellie, readers may wonder whether he wrote to members of his own family. The answer is yes, but very few of these letters survive. One of Stanley's letters to his mother, however, was probably kept by Miss Nellie after Sarah Evans Jones's death because in it Stanley is remarkably prophetic about his own future. The letter is dated December 2, 1905, written from Asbury.[30]

My Dear Mother:
   "Hope deferred maketh the heart sick"—Bible. Have you experienced this on account of my delay? But mother dear I am living [Teddy] Roosevelt's "strenuous life" these days and so of course you know I write just as often as I can. Tell Miss Nellie I would have had a bad case of heartsickness if I had hoped very much for her letter to get here. Not that I had not wished & looked for it but hope like almost everything else wears out when rubbed too much. Well mother I expect before I get through with this old world I will be a "globe trotter." Do you think so? . . .

Your Loving Son
Stanley

H. C. Morrison, who, as we have seen, was instrumental in Jones's decision to attend Asbury College, was a prominent leader of the Holiness Movement[31] in the late nineteenth and early twentieth centuries. He was the president of Asbury College on two occasions, from 1910 to 1925 and from 1933 to 1942, and he founded the short-lived Holiness Union. The Holiness Union has been described by one historian of the Methodist origins of the Holiness Movement as "a loosely constructed federation of

holiness bands in Southern and Southwestern states," which was committed "to supporting independent foreign missionary activity and to nurtur-
ing converts of holiness revivals."

One of the independent foreign missionaries who received financial
support from the Holiness Union was E. Stanley Jones. In fact, Jones was
formally involved with the Holiness Movement during his second year at
Asbury. In a letter to his mother dated December 2, 1905, he describes
preparing a paper to be presented at a convention he attended. The purpose of the paper, Jones writes, was to persuade the convention "to organize a board of Missions for the whole South among the Holiness people."
When he presented his proposal to a business meeting, it was "declared
impracticable by the Pres. of the Convention." But a day or two later the
convention decided to create the very board Jones had proposed. This was
probably the same board that later sponsored Jones's early mission work in
India.

In the letter from Morrison to Dr. Robinson quoted earlier, Morrison
concludes that whether or not he sent Stanley an advertisement about
Asbury College, he

> was a fine student, received a baptism with the Spirit and claimed the expe-
> rience of entire sanctification and was a spiritual leader in the student body
> and was greatly blessed of the Lord.

The holiness background and emphasis at Asbury can be clearly seen in
Stanley's letters from the beginning of his time there. On October 5, 1903,
he describes for Miss Nellie how the Holy Spirit was moving on campus as
students went to the altar for sanctification, pardon, and cleansing. He cov-
ets the same experience for her.

> Oh Miss Nellie if you *only* had this blessing—how I do want you to get [it]
> and I'm asking God every day to make you so real hungry for it that you
> won't rest until you get it. *It's so good.* The Lord laughs all over my soul.

The implication of these words is that he himself was sanctified, receiving the second blessing by being filled with the Holy Spirit. However,
exactly when this occurred is not clear. In his autobiography Jones
describes what he calls one of "the most spontaneous, unlooked-for, and
unexpected events of my early Christian life."

> Four or five of us students [at Asbury] were in the room of another student,
> Jim Ballinger, having a prayer meeting about ten o'clock at night. I remem-
> ber I was almost asleep with my head against the bedclothes where I was
> kneeling, when suddenly we were all swept off our feet by a visitation of the
> Holy Spirit. We were all filled, flooded by the Spirit. Everything that hap-
> pened to the disciples on the original Pentecost happened to us. Here I am

tempted to tone down what really happened, or to dress it up in garments of respectability. . . . In either case it would be dishonest and perhaps worse—a betrayal of one of the most sacred and formative gifts of my life, a gift of God. . . . For three or four days it could be said of us as was said of those at the original Pentecost. "They are drunk." I was drunk with God. I say "for three or four days," for time seemed to have lost its significance. The first night I could only walk the floor and praise him. About two o'clock L.L. Pickett, the father of Bishop J. Waskom Pickett, came upstairs and said: "Stanley, he giveth his beloved sleep." But sleep was out of the question. By morning the effects of this sudden and unexpected "outpouring" had begun to go through the college and town. That morning there was no chapel service, in the ordinary sense; people were in prayer, some prostrate in prayer. No one led it, and yet it was led—led by the Spirit. For three days there were no college classes. Every class room was a prayer meeting where students and faculty were seeking and finding and witnessing. It spread to the countryside. People flocked in, and, before they could even get into the assembly hall, would be stricken with conviction and would fall on their knees on the campus crying for God—and pardon and release.[32]

Stanley does not give a date for this massive and spontaneous outpouring of the Holy Spirit. However, Professor Joseph A. Thacker quotes this same passage in his history of Asbury College published during the centennial of the school in 1990 and, on the basis of independent evidence, dates the beginning of the revival as February 18, 1905.[33] If Thacker's date is accurate, then Stanley's October 5, 1903, letter to Miss Nellie must refer to an earlier period of revival. In any case, he knew firsthand what it means to be filled with the Holy Spirit, and sincerely wanted the same thing for his good friend.

In this same letter Stanley describes some of the less serious aspects of college life, including the tricks the girls at the college played on the boys by powdering their pillows with flour and putting cockleburs and pins in their beds. About a debate on campus in which he had participated, he tells Miss Nellie that after he made his argument, "Professor Humphrey said if he could make a speech like that he would quit his job." The secret of his success in the debate, he concluded, was prayer. "I got a letter from home today and mother said she prayed for her boy—ah, that's it—*another prayed.*"

Stanley's reference to his mother, Sarah Alice Jones, is rare and unusual.[34] He does not often mention his family in these early letters. However, Miss Nellie was a good friend of his mother. In an undated letter to Stanley, Miss Nellie wrote: "While you were on a preaching tour just before your mother's death, a friend was sitting by her bedside on the evening previous to her 'going.'" The friend, although unidentified in the letter, was undoubtedly Miss Nellie herself. Mrs. Jones asked the friend not to forget Stanley.

"Will you promise to do something for *me?*" Just name it & I will do it if it is in my power to do so, answered the friend. Then she paused, looked at her friend for a few minutes and said very distinctly & deliberately, "Will you pray for him for me? I have prayed for him since a baby & more since he has been called to preach, but now I am going on to be with my Heavenly Father without seeing my boy again. . . . I would like to know that some one will be still praying for him in my stead."[35]

Miss Nellie remained faithful to her promise to Mrs. Jones. In another undated letter to Stanley she wrote,

I wonder, Stanley, if you realize how proud I am of you. . . . I have prayerfully watched [you] from the beginning, and how I rejoice in the fact that God has used & is using you so gloriously and effectively in reaching and bringing souls to Him. Every time I hear you, I wonder if your mother is listening. If so, I know she is prouder of you than I am if that could be possible.

These poignant letters reveal both Sarah Jones's love for her son as well as Miss Nellie's intimate friendship with her. Miss Nellie maintained close ties to the Jones family throughout her life. In addition to her long correspondence with Stanley, she gave regular financial support from her own income and sent contributions on behalf of various groups at Memorial Church in Baltimore to the mission work in India of both Stanley and his wife Mabel. She also wrote to Mabel and to their daughter Eunice and sent birthday and Christmas gifts to all of them.

If Jones had a strong and loving relationship with his mother, his relationship with his father, Albin Davis Jones, was more problematic. Albin Jones worked as a toll collector on U. S. Highway 40, the National Road.[36] Stanley's only public reference to his father appears in a periodical called the *Clip Sheet,* which was published by the Methodist Church Board on Temperance.[37] An article from around 1948 reports on an address that Jones gave at the Wichita, Kansas, forum to an audience of twenty-eight hundred people. In his address he responded to a sermon that had been delivered by the Roman Catholic bishop of the Wichita Diocese. The bishop had advocated moderation rather than abstinence in the use of alcoholic beverages and "had clearly implied" that he opposed prohibition. Jones responded to the bishop and made a persuasive argument for both abstinence and prohibition. He closed his address with a personal testimony about the impact of alcohol.

I don't believe I have ever mentioned this to anyone before, and I know I have never mentioned it in public but the reason for my fierce hatred for this abomination, this curse, is that my own family was struck by it. It struck my own father. Our family lost everything. My father having fallen a hopeless victim to the habit finally stopped at nothing to satisfy his awful appetite. He

sold our furniture, even our chairs and beds. He was a terrible victim. He
and his wife and his children suffered unspeakably. Now, you see why I hate
it and why I'll fight it with every breath until I die.

The emotional and spiritual impact of his father's alcoholism is dramatically underscored by Stanley's conversion experience. Reverend Bateman,
under whose preaching Stanley was saved at Memorial Methodist
Episcopal Church, was, Jones says in his autobiography, "a converted alcoholic." After hearing Mr. Bateman preach, Stanley recalled saying to himself, "I want what he has."[38] Like Bateman, he wanted more than anything
else for Jesus Christ to be his Lord and Savior. But he also wanted Jesus
Christ to deliver him from the demonic struggle against alcoholism in his
own family, just as Bateman himself had been delivered from the same
addiction.

Albin Jones's addiction to alcohol is undoubtedly the reason Stanley
does not mention his father in his spiritual autobiography, *A Song of
Ascents*, or indeed in any of his other books or articles. He did, however,
recount his mother's reaction to a very difficult time in their home.

> Perhaps the most impressive memory of my mother was one night as I came
> home at midnight from my work at the law library. I saw the door into her
> room slightly ajar. As I heard a voice in prayer, I paused to listen. The sen-
> tence I caught was this: "O God, help me to hold my family together through
> all this." "All this" was the period of calamity when disaster struck the home
> and we lost everything and had to begin all over again. She did hold the fam-
> ily together by her bravery. She lost the sight in one eye, the doctors said,
> because she refused to weep.[39]

The disastrous time Stanley writes about was undoubtedly the result of
his father's alcoholism. Mr. Jones's alcoholism also explains why, after
graduating from high school, Stanley worked at night in the Baltimore
courthouse law library to support himself and to attend law school. It was
also the probable reason for his reticence in responding to a request from
the Reverend Thomas Long, his former pastor, for an article on his childhood. In a letter dated June 30, 1932, Stanley thanks him for his request
but adds,

> I do not know what I would say for there does not seem anything to be par-
> ticularly interesting or inspiring in my boyhood. My life really began with my
> conversion so I am afraid I will have to ask you to forgive me for not com-
> plying.[40]

There is a very real sense in which E. Stanley Jones's life did begin with his
conversion. Everything that happened in his life after he went to the altar of
Memorial Church in February 1901, he interpreted through the prism of

that life-transforming experience of salvation. Once God's Holy Spirit forever changed his mind and heart by creating for him a personal relationship with Jesus Christ, his life before he accepted Christ was of little importance and, as far as he was concerned, did not exist. Even before his mother's death, Miss Nellie was a mother to Stanley. She was the one who had led him to his new life in Jesus Christ, and throughout her life she continued to give him spiritual, emotional, and financial support. In a November 18, 1913, letter Stanley calls her a "sister confessor." Much later, in the mid-1940s, in a letter written to Miss Nellie while he was bed-ridden and recovering from an operation, he said that she was simultaneously a "dear friend . . . Big Sister [and] Mother . . . for all three are in our relationship."

Stanley was an excellent student at Asbury College. On January 4, 1904, at the end of his first semester, he wrote Miss Nellie that his grades in all his courses were 94 or higher. He was especially proud of his 96 in Butler's Analogy, which was "the highest in the class."

> I feel like cracking my heels together . . . for there were three or four graduates in that class and to think that poor little me (just 20 yesterday) beat them all. *He helped.* So praise the Lord.

Stanley's academic achievement seems to have continued, eliciting praise from the Asbury faculty and administration. I have already quoted Professor Humphrey's remark about the superb quality of Stanley's argument during a student debate. Before Stanley graduated at the end of May 1907, President Hughes telephoned Jones, asking him to come to his office and to give him his "honest opinion" of his teachers. "Some I told him were excellent," he wrote to Miss Nellie, "others I said were not fit to be teachers in Asbury. I think he will change one at least." One of the most laudatory comments came from the Reverend Newton Wray, a member of the faculty at Asbury. Stanley had included Wray's name in the references he listed when he applied to the Board of Foreign Missions of the Methodist Episcopal Church to become a missionary. The Board asked Wray for his evaluation of Stanley Jones's potential for mission service. Professor Wray replied in a letter dated May 6, 1907.

> You will have a rare young man for the mission field, should you accept his application. He is *primus inter pares* as a student, and excels as a preacher and soul-winner. He knows how to prevail in prayer. . . . His work in the College, and wherever he has labored, in churches and missions, is his best endorsement. Every member of the Faculty would bear out all that I have said.[41]

Professor Wray's commendation also refers to Stanley's success as a preacher and evangelist. Stanley's application to the Mission Board stated that he had been licensed to preach as a layman on February 12, 1903, and that he had been doing evangelistic work for seven summers in addition to "preaching nearly every Sunday at College." Assuming that Stanley began his evangelistic work in the summer of 1901 after his conversion in February of that year, he includes the summer of 1907 after his graduation from Asbury in order to make a total of seven summers of evangelism. He had held camp-meetings in Virginia and Baltimore, he wrote, as well as other meetings in Virginia, West Virginia, and Kentucky, and he was holding "about 7 revival meetings during the three months of [each] summer."

In addition to his evangelistic work off campus while he was a student, Stanley often spoke on campus. Thacker notes in his history of Asbury College that in 1906 Jones was the preacher for the winter revival, which, along with the fall revival, was a regular event at the beginning of each semester.[42] At the end of the 1905–06 academic year Stanley was one of five students who gave a commencement oration on the subject of missions. His title was, "Asleep in the Crisis." He was widely admired by his fellow students. In the fall of 1906 the *Pentecostal Herald* quoted a number of Asbury students who rejoiced at the beginning of another academic year and thanked God specifically for "the finest, most spiritual and largest student body" since the arrival on campus of E. Stanley Jones in 1903.

Stanley's letters to Miss Nellie provide many descriptions of his early preaching and evangelistic work. In October 1903 during his first semester at Asbury he wrote that he and a colleague, a Mr. Spencer of Virginia, who was twenty-three years old and who planned to go to South America as a missionary, drove seven miles from Wilmore to a town where Stanley preached in a Presbyterian church. In addition, he continued, someone in Wilmore had offered him the use of a buggy if he had another opportunity to preach at that church. "It is needless to say [we] are going again, for with all these young preachers just panting to let the world see how much they know, preaching appointments are scarce."

In the same letter, however, he told Miss Nellie that at this point in his life he did not feel called to be an evangelist.

> Never mind Miss Nellie I'm not an evangelist, nor do I intend to be. I have received no call to any specific line of work and hence our waiting on Him. But whatever the verdict I say Amen.

In spite of Stanley's insistence that he had not been called to be an evangelist, his letters to Miss Nellie dated January 4 and January 23, 1904, refer to several revivals he conducted, including meetings in Shelby City and Fairview, Kentucky. At one meeting he was disappointed because the "people resisted the Holy Spirit." In spite of that, they "had about sixty saved or sanctified and a good many *poor* Christians straightening up their lives." In Shelby City, two Asbury boys were holding a meeting that had not been successful in terms of souls being saved. "They hadn't had a move [of the Holy Spirit] and they asked me to take the service that night. The Lord blessed us and three were sweetly saved." On May 12, 1904, at the end of his first year at Asbury, he wrote about his plans for the summer. He would go to "Virginia to hold five or six meetings for pastors there." His friend Brother Spencer, he added, instead of going to South America as a missionary, had received an appointment in Kansas and had "turned over his entire summer slate to me."

Stanley's account of his growing evangelistic work in his application to the Methodist Episcopal Mission Board and in his letters to Miss Nellie is confirmed by his good friend, J. Waskom Pickett. In the early 1970s Pickett wrote a short biographical article on Jones for *The Encyclopedia of World Methodism*.[43] He noted that in the summers while he was a college student, Jones "preached in campmeetings, assemblies and conventions, becoming well known as an evangelist."

At the beginning of his second year at Asbury, Stanley found it difficult to return to the schedule of classes and other campus activities. His September 28, 1904, letter to Miss Nellie describes the "fight involved to get down to work and the routine of College life." He was torn between his desire to resume his studies and the call to the ministry. "I felt that I would like to go to school & be in a revival meeting at the same time." His deep and intense passion for evangelism, which began with his conversion and continued throughout his life, is best reflected in his letter of November 5, 1904. Just as a tree bears fruit at the cost of its own life, he wrote, and just as Jesus Christ died for the sin of others and for their redemption,

> so we must die for their evangelization. When I think Miss Nellie of the possibilities of a soul *dead to everything but God and his commands* and knowing that I am responsible to God for what I am and for what I *may* be and of the souls who will *not* be saved if I do not get the power of the Holy Ghost upon me I feel like laying on my face before God and crying for power with God for souls. . . . I've told God Miss Nellie that I will have it, I must have it at any cost of suffering and He is under obligation to give this power of the Spirit to me if I pay the price. The Lord has so burdened me with this here of late that I want you and ask my other friends there to pray especially that the Spirit of intercession for souls may be on me that my life may not be fruitless. I'd rather this pen fall from my hand this moment and I die right here than not be of use to Him.

During his four years as a student at Asbury College, Stanley continued to preach and lead revival services. His letters of November 30, 1904, and August 3 and August 15, 1907, refer to meetings he held in various places in Kentucky: meetings over the Christmas holidays near Junction City; a revival in Harrodsburg; a camp meeting where he preached on his way to Chaplin to conduct another meeting; his preaching at Okolona, Kentucky, which is about ten miles from Louisville. "The class of people that were saved in the Harrodsburg meeting," he wrote, included "murderers, drunkards, etc." In Chaplin there was some confusion about exactly when he would arrive and the folk "drove eight times to the station five miles away" before they finally met him. In one of the meetings at Chaplin he says, he "preached one hour & fifteen minutes on missions." Afterward, "a young woman who supports her widowed mother gave me $20 for the cause & I felt like crying when she gave it to me."

While he was preaching in Okolona, he got a bad case of poison oak "and my eye is swollen in fearful shape," he wrote. He had been to Louisville to see a doctor who gave him a prescription but refused to charge him because he was a preacher. The doctor "must have been the son of a preacher," was his comment. His November 5, 1904, letter described what happened in one meeting at an unidentified location.

> In our meeting yesterday . . . power was wonderfully manifested nearly every one broken up and one young man . . . was completely prostrated under the burden for souls & the power of God and rolled on the floor. Glory!

At this point it would be premature to suppose that Stanley's zeal for evangelism had him completely primed and poised for being flung up on India's foreign beachhead for the missionary enterprise. In his book, *The Word Became Flesh*,[44] Jones gives this hilarious recollection of his first missionary adventure, which, he says facetiously, was "enough to dampen my zeal for missions."

> It was a home mission adventure in the mountains of Kentucky. Jim Ballinger, a singer, and I started to walk from Junction City two miles to where we were to stay for the night. It was cold and raining hard, and I was carrying two suitcases, one filled with books. As we walked along the railway tracks, to encourage my companion I called out, "Jim, I believe the stars are coming out." Just as I said it I went over the side of a steep fill. I saw stars all right! On my way down the muddy embankment I lost my two suitcases. So I had to feel over that embankment in the dark to find them. When we got near the house a gust of wind blew off my felt hat. Impossible to find it— never did, for snow covered everything the next morning. When we got to the yard a creek had arisen, so I had to take a leap toward the other bank weighted down by two suitcases. I hit somewhere near the middle! At midnight we arrived, and our host was not expecting us! When we arrived in the mountains the next day I was invited to a one-room cabin where I was to stay—and there was one bed. My host said at bedtime, "You take the far side." Then he got in and then his wife. In the morning we reversed the process! Real hospitality! I preached in a schoolhouse, and when I preached on "Thou shalt not kill" my hearers turned pale. This experience dampen my zeal? No whetted my appetite for more.

We have already indicated that Stanley's early evangelistic work was deeply influenced by the Holiness Movement, which was controversial within the Methodist Episcopal Church. The district superintendent mentioned earlier, who opposed H. C. Morrison's preaching in a Methodist church in Baltimore, was undoubtedly leery either of Morrison's leadership or of the Holiness Movement *per se,* or wary of both leader and movement. Stanley occasionally refers to this controversy in his letters to Miss Nellie. On January 23, 1904, he described what happened at an Asbury chapel program when it was announced that Morrison planned to organize a new church in Wilmore. Perhaps because of jealousy by some members of the Asbury faculty and administration, there was "an outburst of pent-up *righteous indignation* that came from the chapel platform the other morning." One administrator exclaimed, "Not another *Pentecostal Herald* [which Morrison edited and published] shall come on this campus," if Morrison were to establish his church.

In spite of such controversy, Stanley continued to support and was deeply and permanently influenced by the Holiness Movement. One of the elements of holiness doctrine, which he defended in a letter written to Miss Nellie during his last year at Asbury, is the idea that Jesus Christ would soon return to earth. He believed, Stanley wrote, that

> all the calamities in our own land, and the agitation of the powers in the East with the "falling away" that is on every hand in the Church of Christ, point to the near coming of our Lord. Do you not think so?

Miss Nellie, however, was skeptical of the Holiness Movement, and Stanley's letters respond to her criticism, especially her criticism of the experience of sanctification. Miss Nellie may well have shared the prejudice of the Methodist district superintendent who denied H. C. Morrison the opportunity to speak in the large Baltimore church. Perhaps she dreamed that her "boy" would become not a Holiness evangelist but the pastor of a local Methodist congregation, perhaps even a church in Baltimore. This may be why Stanley had told her back in October 1903, "Never mind Miss Nellie I'm not an evangelist, nor do I intend to be," in an attempt not to shatter her dream.

In the same letter in which he affirmed the apocalyptic beliefs of the Holiness Movement he also defended sanctification. In fact he wanted Miss Nellie to have the experience of sanctification for herself and offered this prayer for her:

> How I long to see you have it Miss Nellie, for which I have long been burdened in prayer knowing of what use you would be in the service of God. You have been a help (for I shall never forget your words of kindness as I knelt, broken-hearted and sinful at Memorial altar) and how I now treasure your advice and of what

service you have been to me. Thus I covet for you, both on your own account and for your usefulness in the service of the Master, a deeper experience in Him. The Lord grant it.

Another controversial issue that appears in his early letters to Miss Nellie is that of race. In his September 28, 1904, letter he tells her about the "commotion" that occurred the day before in chapel. There was an

announcement from the Pres. that they would have a certain *colored* pastor to speak on our platform. They tell me that if you shoot a gun or let a dog bark over a . . . pond you can see the alligators begin to wriggle about—that's the picture: they wriggled. My the hot southern blood flowed so fast that they announced this morning that he would not be here. The Mason and Dixon line is not yet erased from the minds of some! Oh Lord have mercy!

Stanley's letter shows how early his antiracism developed. Throughout his life racial prejudice continued to be one of the primary targets of both his public ministry and his private efforts as an informal ambassador and statesman to achieve racial reconciliation.

By the end of his senior year at Asbury, Stanley, in response to God's call, had decided to go to the mission field. In his application to the Board of Foreign Missions of the Methodist Episcopal Church, he was asked if he had "had success in winning souls for Christ." He responded,

I do not know the exact number of souls that have been blessed with a definite experience in the limited time I have been at work for the Master but it must be between 500 & 1,000. For two years I have not been out on Sunday to preach without souls finding the Lord, with the exception of one Sunday.

He did not want, however, to continue to save souls only in the United States. In reply to the question, "Do you believe that you have a special call to the foreign mission field?" he wrote,

My call was as definite almost as my conversion. The Divine acceptance was as conscious almost as the witness of my sin pardoned.

Stanley's call to the mission field was largely a product of his association with the Student Volunteer Movement at Asbury—a Christian evangelistic organization that, in the late nineteenth and early twentieth centuries, recruited thousands of American college students to go as missionaries to nations throughout the world. Because of its deep Wesleyan Holiness roots, Asbury College was as commited to foreign missions and evangelism as it was to the promotion of individual piety, sanctification, and holiness. So Asbury was a naturally fertile field for the organizational efforts of the Student Volunteer Movement. In his earliest letters to Miss Nellie, Stanley refs to his involvement in the Student Volunteer Band on campus. In 1906, during his third year at Asbury, he, along with another student, W. P. Gillis, represented the college at the Student Volunteers Convention in Nashville, Tennessee.[45] Jones recalled in his autobiography that his call from God to become a missionary was the direct result of a request by "the Student Volunteer Movement people" on campus that he give a talk on Africa. Jones agreed to speak as requested, and as he

> studied the needs of Africa preparing for that address, I became burdened— so burdened that when I was on the way to the hall where I was to speak, I went into a classroom instead. I knelt down and said: "Now, Lord, I don't want to go into that room to give a missionary address. I want a missionary to go from this meeting, and I'm not going in there until you give me one." He replied: "According to your faith, so be it unto you." So I arose from my knees and said: "All right, I'll take one." So the first thing I said to the audience was this: "Somebody is going to the mission field from this meeting." Little did I know who it would be, but I was the answer! I had prayed myself into it. Be careful how you pray; you may be the answer. From that moment I was gripped. I thought it was Africa.[46]

The Mission Board was also interested in the marital and family status of its candidates for the foreign mission field. "If single," the board asked on its questionnaire, "do you contemplate marriage?" Stanley answered,

> I contemplate marriage provided the proper person can be found. As yet I have not been able to satisfy myself that I had found one suitable to God & to me & adapted to do missionary work.

Then, concerned that his answer might give the board the impression that he was dating as many different girls as he could until he found the young lady who met all his qualifications, he added,

> This does not mean that I have gone with one young lady after another to try them, for I have not gone with anyone regularly for about 5 years.

Stanley did not in fact marry until 1911, after he had been a missionary and evangelist in India for four years. But his letters to Miss Nellie reveal that he did have romantic interests while he was a student at Asbury College. During his first two years in Wilmore, he seems to have been almost totally preoccupied with his studies and with his preaching and evangelistic work. In the same letter in which he described the "wriggling" during a chapel service when it was announced that a black pastor would speak at Asbury, he tells Miss Nellie about a "social . . . going on in town tonight." Although "the girls are going" to the social, he wrote, "I am not invited which proves the fact that they have given me up as a bad case of girl-proof."

The first hint of a serious romantic interest appears in what he wrote on September 22, 1906, during the beginning of his junior year. He tells Miss Nellie that he is now "housekeeping. Altho I was accused of being about to go into partnership with one of the young ladies in the above occupation during the summer." This young lady may be the same "Ky. girl" whom Jones referred to in his letter of November 8, 1910, written to Miss Nellie from India. He told her that the "Ky. girl & I agreed to call things off as we were not suited." In the same letter he described at length Miss Mabel Lossing, a Methodist missionary whom he met in India and whom he married the next year.

After his graduation from Asbury College on May 29, 1907, Stanley continued to preach at churches and in camp meetings and to hold revivals throughout the summer. Although he had completed his application to the Board of Missions on April 30, 1907, well before his graduation, he had had no definite word from the Board when he wrote Miss Nellie on September 20, 1907. He was still waiting to hear, he said. The board had not responded to his application even though he had written to them three times within two weeks. In the meantime he had accepted a teaching position at Asbury for that fall. In the same letter he excused his tardiness in writing to Miss Nellie by pointing out that he was teaching seven classes each day at Asbury and was also Secretary of the Faculty.

Stanley applied to the Methodist Mission Board for a position on the mission field, but then he waited for months for a reply. When he finally heard from the board, it was an offer to send him to India. At that time, in late 1907, he was already teaching at Asbury and the college wanted him to continue. Moreover, at the same time, he had an offer "from a very trusted friend" to go into evangelistic work in America.

> Here was a perfect traffic jam of wills! I had to have a clear way out. . . . So I took the letter from the Mission Board, went into my room, spread it out on a chair, knelt beside the chair, and said: "Dear Father, I've got to answer this letter [from the Mission Board], and to do so may decide my lifework. I am willing to go anywhere and do anything you want me to do. Tell me and I'll obey. What is it?" Very clearly the voice spoke: "It's India." I arose from my knees and said: "It's India."[47]

So Stanley did not complete the fall semester as a member of the Asbury faculty. His next letter to Miss Nellie, dated November 14, 1907, was written on board the British Royal Mail Steamer, *Teutonic,* a day after his departure from New York en route to Southampton, England. What happened in the meantime is best explained by Waskom Pickett in the March 15, 1973, *Indian Witness* article he wrote shortly after Stanley's death. They both graduated from Asbury in the spring of 1907 and Pickett remembered that Stanley was invited back to teach Latin and Greek, but on the eve of the opening of the new scholastic year, Stanley received a telegram from the Methodist Board of Missions inviting him to go to India to be pastor of the Lal Bagh English-speaking church at Lucknow. He accepted on condition that the college release him. Asbury agreed to release him on condition that I undertake to teach the classes that he was to have taught. He went to India, and I taught two classes in Latin and two in Greek.[48]

The experience of leaving the United States for the very first time was traumatic, as Jones recalls in his autobiography.

No one from the [Mission] board came to see me off. . . . I was given no orientation, no briefing on what to do as a missionary, no manual of instructions on how to travel. I was given a Hindustani grammar, forty pounds in British gold, a ticket to Bombay via Britain, a handshake, and sent off.[49]

He traveled second class, one of twenty-three second-class passengers on a ship whose total capacity was twelve to fourteen hundred persons. "I had my money changed to British gold," Stanley told Miss Nellie, "& nearly all my possessions were then wrapped up in a little bag—like an Italian." Anxious not to waste any time on his long voyage, he used his Mission Board book allowance to buy a Hindustani grammar for $4.15 and studied it on board the *Teutonic*. "And now," he wrote, "I am really beginning to feel like a missionary."

This voyage across the North Atlantic was Stanley's first experience at sea as well as his first trip outside the United States, and he responded with wonder and excitement.

[O]h Miss Nellie if you could stand out on that deck with me & see those great rolling waves & see the spray dash clear up over the deck your soul would go into a rapture of delight & you would about shout as I did a moment ago at the grandeur & glory of a God who can make such things.

Word spread quickly on board that among the passengers there was a missionary going to India. Stanley overheard one woman traveler say to another, "They tell me there is a missionary aboard going to India. I hope he won't get hold of me. Does he preach?" Although he was a Methodist, he conducted an Episcopal service for interested passengers on Sunday during the voyage. Like virtually everyone on board, he got seasick when the ship ran into a storm, but, he wrote Miss Nellie, he held out longer than most, including the crew.

The voyage from New York to Southampton took seven days. In Southampton he boarded the *S.S. Victoria* bound for the port city of Aden, which was then a British Colony and is now part of the Republic of Yemen. The day before arriving in Aden, the *Victoria*, a coal-fired steamer, docked in Port Said, Egypt, "the swiftest coaling station in the world," Stanley wrote. In his December 7, 1907, letter he paints a graphic picture of what he saw as the *Victoria* was loaded with coal.

> The coolies carry it from a barge up an incline in large baskets and really as you see them at night with the dim torches burning and hear their unintelligible yells & their eager running, it looks like the infernal regions in full blast.

While the ship's store of coal was being resupplied, the passengers were permitted to go ashore. Port Said was very cosmopolitan, he noted, consisting of a mixed population of Turks, English, French, and Sudanese. When the *Victoria* reached Aden, Stanley transferred to a third steamer, the *Peninsular,* which took him to Bombay.

The journey through the Middle East to India evoked a number of biblical images for Stanley. He commented on Mt. Sinai's being close to the path of his voyage. The Red Sea reminded him of the Old Testament story of the Hebrews' exodus from Egypt. His fellow missionaries aboard the *Peninsular* were also struck by their proximity to the geographical origin of so much of the Bible. Some of these other missionaries, he wrote, were "Higher-critically disposed" and did not believe that the Israelites literally crossed the Red Sea. "However," Stanley continued, given the width of most of this body of water, the Israelites "must have gone over the neck of the Red Sea for they could not have gotten over 100 miles in a single night."

His next letter to Miss Nellie, dated December 18, 1907, was written from Lucknow, in what was then the United Provinces of India. In this letter he described his arrival in Bombay and his hurried trip to Victoria Station to catch a train for the twenty-hour ride to Lucknow. On the train he shared a compartment with two male and one female Moslem passengers. The two men, he wrote, were "very agreeable & well educated" and were "ancestors of the King . . . who reigned in Lucknow before the British conquered the United Provinces." During the long trip from southwestern to central India,

> I took advantage of the opportunity & so they taught me Hindustani & then to my surprise they listened while I read the Sermon on the Mount. We became fast friends & exchanged addresses with the promise to call.

During the train ride Stanley also had his first exposure to the desperate and widespread poverty of the Indian countryside.

> Oh, Miss Nellie, I cannot describe my feelings as I came along in the train & saw the dire poverty of the people. It is simply heartrending to see them in

their hovels with nothing apparently to subsist upon. Now it is worse for we are facing a dreadful famine here [as a result of drought].

In Lucknow, Stanley was impressed by the size and the permanence of the Methodist presence in the city. His December 18, 1907, letter listed the institutions maintained by the Methodist Episcopal Church—"two colleges, two high schools, a deaconess home, a publishing plant, Hindustani mission & church and an English speaking church" in addition to the bishop's home.

Impressive as this Methodist enclave in Lucknow was, it would not be too many years before Asbury College's star graduate would begin to push through the confines of a purely denominational habitat. He would also have to disentangle himself from an eight-year stint of self-striving, self-effort, and eventual collapse brought on from wearing too many hats at once on the mission field. With his persistent invocation, "Not one step without You, Lord, but anywhere with You," resounding in his spirit, E. Stanley Jones would then go striding forth, shoulders squared, onto a global stage without borders.

If all it took in 1907 on the part of the Board of Missions to make E. Stanley Jones a *bona fide* Methodist missionary to India was arming him with "a Hindustani grammar, 40 pounds in gold, a ticket and a handshake," it would take much more than that for him to stick it out and succeed. For E. Stanley Jones to become a universal missionary, evangelist, and writer, and ultimately to soar with the "mature wisdom and insights of a spiritual giant who lived 'in Christ' for many years" would take nothing less than utter surrender to the "highest gift of God, the Holy Spirit." In that same supernatural strength he would go on to make his mark in Christendom as an unequaled illuminator and interpreter of the kingdom of God.

2

Lucknow, India:
Pastor and Evangelist

I am looking for revival & I know it is coming.
—E. Stanley Jones, December 18, 1907, letter to Miss Nellie
from Lucknow, India

T IS NO WONDER that Stanley Jones was astounded by the Methodist Episcopal establishment in Lucknow when he arrived as a twenty-year-old missionary in November 1907. At the beginning of the twentieth century, India was the "most substantial and extensive foreign mission enterprise" of the Methodist Episcopal Church, according to the official history of Methodist missions.[1]

The work in India was divided among seven annual conferences. Stanley was assigned to the North India Conference, which included territory from the Ganges River to the borders of Nepal and Tibet. The North India Conference was numerically the largest of the seven conferences and consisted of eighty-nine preaching charges. The members of these eighty-nine charges "accounted for more than half of the membership of the Methodist Episcopal Church in India." Within the North India Conference were nine districts, and within each district were a number of mission stations. Each mission station typically had many substations, each

46

one serving as the center of mission activity for the surrounding villages. This structure was similar to the structure of the other six annual conferences in India.

Taken as a whole, the Methodist Episcopal Conferences were not so much a collection of "single points of missionary organization" as "webs of evangelistic activity." At the time Jones was appointed to the North India Conference, there were approximately 170 Methodist missionaries, including married couples, serving throughout India. Between 1896 and 1919 the number of full Methodist church members in India tripled to 74,000. (These numbers should be interpreted in light of the total population of India, which in 1919 was approximately 305 million.) There was also rapid growth in the number of probationary church members (172,000 in 1919) and in the number of Sunday school pupils (167,000 in 1919). Although the number of male missionaries and of married couples appointed by the Board of Foreign Missions remained almost constant between 1896 and 1919, the number of female missionaries appointed by the Women's Foreign Missionary Society of the Methodist Episcopal Church more than doubled from 58 in 1896 to 138 in 1919. To assist these clergy, the church employed over 6,000 Indian nationals in 1919, including ordained and unordained individuals who worked as local preachers, exhorters, teachers, colporteurs, and Bible readers.

E. Stanley Jones answered God's call to go to India at a time of unprecedented growth not only in Methodist missions but also in American Protestant foreign missions as a whole. The late nineteenth and early twentieth centuries were a time of unparalleled evangelical zeal among Protestant churches in the United States, Great Britain, and other nations of the Western world. The Student Volunteer Movement (SVM), for example, which began in New England in 1886, has been called "one of the most remarkable uprisings in the history of the Christian Church."[2] Its explosive growth created an international and interdenominational organization that, up until World War II, received tens of millions of dollars in contributions for foreign missions and under whose auspices over twenty thousand young men and women left their homes and families in the United States, Canada, Great Britain, Europe, Australia, New Zealand, and South Africa and sailed to other nations throughout the world.[3]

The motto of the SVM, "The evangelization of the world in this generation,"[4] symbolizes the unlimited scope and sincere depth of the faith of these young volunteers—their faith in God and in the power of his Holy Spirit to create opportunities for them to present the gospel of Jesus Christ to literally everyone on the face of the earth. Such faith staggers the imagination of our merely human intellect and natural abilities today as much as it did in the years before and after World War I. "The evangelization of the world in this generation" was not just the motto of the SVM; it became the watchword of a much larger and more diverse group of Protestant churches and missionary organizations throughout the United States in that period. Among those who shared the supernatural faith embodied in this motto was E. Stanley Jones.

The bishop who was largely responsible for the size and strength of the Methodist Episcopal Church in India when Jones arrived was James M. Thoburn. Thoburn served as bishop from 1888 to 1908 and has been described as "a vigorous apostle of missionary expansionism." His goal was "imperial; conquest was his aim." As Thoburn himself explained to the General Conference of the church in Chicago in 1900, "In the nature of the case all our missionaries may be expected to become expansionists, in the missionary sense of that term." There is, the bishop said, "a law of spiritual life, which ever seems to prompt a living Christian organization to move onward."[5]

Sherwood Eddy lived in India from 1896 to 1911 while working for the YMCA and the Student Volunteer Movement and later traveled and preached with Jones in India and China. Dr. Eddy offers this assessment of Bishop Thoburn:

> When Thoburn arrived in India [in 1859] there were fewer than a score of Methodist communicants; when he retired in 1908 there were some two hundred thousand. From the first Thoburn was a pioneer and a trailblazer. He was a fervent evangelist with prophetic foresight, a thoughtful student, a bold administrator, and a worthy follower of the great [William] Carey [one of the very first Christian missionaries to India], who bade men expect great things from God and attempt great things for God.[6]

James M. Thoburn and E. Stanley Jones are both thoroughly typical of their generation of missionary evangelists. They were both inspired and motivated by Christ's great commission to take his gospel to all the world. Moreover, they were directed to India and, in spite of the enormous and seemingly insurmountable obstacles of traveling and living in the most primitive conditions and in spite of spiritual darkness and hostility, remained committed to the evangelization of that subcontinent throughout their lives. Thoburn and Jones were not the product of the Methodist Episcopal Board of Foreign Missions. Like so many American missionaries in the late nineteenth and early twentieth centuries, their call to India

> was spontaneous and voluntary in character and charismatically organized. It was not a campaign of churches but a movement of men and women given to the discipline of prayer and Bible study and gripped by the Spirit. Its overall aim was to make the offer of salvation in Jesus Christ known to all so that all might believe. "All should go, and go to all." There was no uncertainty about the gospel as a power unto salvation.[7]

The method of expansion employed by Methodist missionaries in India under Thoburn's direction was initially mass movement evangelism. This type of evangelism began with the conversion of individuals but relied on the family and social networks of the caste system to extend the scope of missionary activity and to spread the gospel of Jesus Christ to the mass of the Indian people. It is difficult for the Western mind to fully comprehend the all-powerful and ever-present group mentality of Indian culture and society. For American and West European missionaries who were trained in and were themselves often converted to Christianity by the individualistic method of one soul at a time, the complete identification of each Indian with his family and caste seemed to be an insurmountable barrier to effective evangelism.

Nevertheless, individual Indian men and women did become Christians under the influence of Western missionaries or of Indian converts to Christianity. The problem was that Indians who accepted Jesus Christ under these circumstances were immediately ostracized by their own families, including their spouses, and by their caste. These Indian Christians were truly alienated, not only from their group associations but also from themselves. For this reason many Indians who embraced Christianity embraced not only Jesus Christ but also the language, manners, customs, and dress of Western missionaries. Jesus Christ, of course, is not the exclusive property of any culture or society, but Indians who converted to Christianity as a result of person-centered evangelism and who adopted Western customs and attitudes became identified, in the eyes of non-Westernized Indians, not with the gospel of Jesus Christ, but with the political and religious imperialism of Great Britain. It was almost as if the British government, together with Christian missionaries, had introduced yet another caste to Indian society.

For these reasons mass movement evangelism was the Holy-Spirit-directed means of a genuine spiritual revolution in India. Here was a method that fit perfectly with the collective mentality and group-centered nature of Indian society. And, while mass movement evangelism was completely and thoroughly Christian, it was also authentically Indian. What Christian missionaries learned, as early as the middle of the nineteenth century, was that once a single Indian individual or family accepted Jesus Christ, the caste system became a powerful and effective tool for mass conversions to Christianity. Because of close family relationships within castes, one family's conversion to Christianity quickly spread to other families in the same caste and then to members of the same caste in other towns and villages. For Christian missionaries, the crucial point in this process of evangelism was the initial penetration of a caste with the gospel of Jesus Christ. Missionaries referred to this crucial point as a "break." "When breaks appeared, conversions came not in drops and driblets, but in streams and freshets, even floods." This is the origin of mass movement evangelism in India. The results were indeed dramatic. For example, in 1888 in the North India Conference of the Methodist Episcopal Church to which Jones was assigned, there were 3,121 full members and 2,899 probationary members. In just three years, by 1891, there was nearly a 300 percent increase in full membership with 8,820 full members.[8]

Although there was significant mass movement evangelism in the North India Conference of the Methodist Episcopal Church in the early twentieth century, the largest mass movements in the North India Conference occurred earlier, in the 1890s. In volume 4 of the *History of Methodist Missions,* J. Tremayne Copplestone notes that the North India Conference Reports for 1896 and 1897 were the last conference reports that documented widespread mass movement evangelism. Thereafter, growth in the membership of the Methodist Church in North India was mostly the result of child baptisms, which were associated with person-centered evangelism, rather than adult baptisms, which were characteristic of mass movement evangelism. After the 1890s, Methodists in North India were concerned primarily with assimilating and discipling those who had already been converted rather than with winning more converts through mass movements.[9] In the early twentieth century, the North India Conference inherited both the advantages and the disadvantages of its earlier mass movement campaigns.

> It inherited the benefit of access to a large reservoir of people constituting a potential source of members for the growing church. But in this reservoir accumulated a large backlog of candidates for full participation in the life of the church that the Conference never had the capability of assimilating into membership and participation according to its own standards.[10]

J. Waskom Pickett, Stanley's former housemate at Asbury College and his good friend, researched and wrote the only systematic study of mass movement evangelism in India. His 1933 book, entitled *Christian Mass Movements in India: A Study with Recommendations,* begins with a foreword written by John R. Mott, one of the cofounders, along with Sherwood Eddy and Robert E. Speer, of the Student Volunteer Movement. Mott points out that the phenomenal results of mass movement evangelism in India were not confined to the Methodist missions. He writes, "It is estimated that one half of the Roman Catholics in India are descendants of mass movement converts, and that not less than 80 per cent of the 1,800,000 Protestants are the product of mass movements."[11]

The mass movements were primarily, though not exclusively, successful among the poor and socially oppressed castes in the villages of rural India. Here, Mott observes, when the condition of villagers who heard and received the gospel of Jesus Christ is compared with their condition before they knew Jesus Christ, the

> countless transformations in individual lives and in social conditions and relationships . . . are proof positive that the living, loving Heavenly Father is brooding over these most abjectly needy and neglected of his children, creating in them hopes and aspirations for larger life and liberty, and by his Spirit moving them to will and to do.[12]

In the conclusion to his book, Pickett points out that given the caste structure and group mentality of Indian society and culture, mass movements are "for many Indian people the most natural way of approach to Christ." It is unlikely, Pickett says, that mass movement converts would have become Christians in any other way. Another advantage of mass movement evangelism over person-centered evangelism was that mass movement evangelism preserved "the integration of the individual in his group," while person-centered evangelism "unfortunately leads usually to a complete break of the convert with his group."

A third advantage of mass movement evangelism, an advantage that was especially important to Jones after his publication of *The Christ of the Indian Road* in 1925, was that mass movements "offered effective resistance to the identification of Christianity with Westernization." Individual converts to Christianity, because they completely lost their group identity, usually adopted the Western manners, customs, and dress of European and American missionaries. On the other hand, the "church of the villages, which is predominantly the church of the mass movements, is thoroughly Indian in social patterns and customs." Finally, the most important advantage of mass movement evangelism over individual evangelism is that the mass movements were far more effective in winning additional converts to Christ.

> To group-conscious people the action of a group is incomparably more important than the action of many isolated individuals, the corporate witness to Christ transcends in significance the personal witness and the most effective demonstration of the power of Christ is the transformation of a group of believers.[13]

On January 8, 1908, in his first letter to Miss Nellie after he settled into his new surroundings, Stanley wrote that at the North India Annual Conference that had just concluded, he, along with a number of his Hindustani brethren, had been ordained as deacon and elder on the same day. In the language used by Indian nationals to refer to European and American missionaries, Jones tells Miss Nellie that he is now a "full fledged 'padre sahib.'" Annual conference was conducted in Hindustani, Jones explained, among 103 full male members of the church. (The women of the Methodist Episcopal Church had a separate conference but came together with the men for the reading of appointments.) Because he had not yet mastered Hindustani, Stanley relied on an interpreter to explain what was being said. Bishops John E. Robinson and Francis Wesley Warne presided over the meetings. In Jones's words, they were "the finest bishops in the church."

Stanley was acquainted with at least one of them, Bishop Warne, in circumstances very different from the formality of Annual Conference. Bishop Warne, he confided to Miss Nellie,

> is just as simple as he can be. He forgot his bicycle lamp the other night & Bro. Meek [another new missionary] & I were lighting him home when somehow he fell behind us a little & the next thing I knew the bishop was sprawling over a rock pile.

Stanley also commented on a concert given during the conference by the high school affiliated with Isabella Thoburn College (named for Bishop Thoburn's sister who died of cholera). Comparing the concert with a similar performance in the United States, he wrote that the concert "was real good & really there is not much difference between us when Christ comes in and enlightens." He added that he really liked the way the Indian women dressed, "with their loose fitting gowns & their white head dress. It is much more modest & charming than our styles of women's dress at home!"

In the same letter Stanley told his friend that he had been asked to teach Bible to the young Indian women in the Isabella Thoburn College who were graduating that year. With respect to his living arrangements in Lucknow, he would be moving into the Methodist parsonage and would furnish two rooms there. "Bro. & Sister Meek," he explained, "are going to move in with me & take care of me."

At the same annual conference in which he was ordained, he was appointed pastor of the English Methodist Episcopal Church in Lucknow, which was also known as the Lal Bagh (Hindustani for "red garden") Church. When Jones published his spiritual autobiography, *A Song of Ascents,* in 1968 at the age of eighty-seven, he reflected on his experience sixty years earlier as the new pastor of the Lal Bagh Church. My greatest asset, he wrote, "was my colossal ignorance. . . . I had no inhibitions. All I knew was evangelism—people needed to be converted, to be changed." He went on to describe the Sunday worship services he conducted during his years at the Lal Bagh Church.

> In the morning services I would talk on the deeper life, the Holy Spirit, cleansing, for the regulars, the "saints," were present. At night the masses

would come. They packed the church, and my theme was conversion in its varying phases. I gave an altar call at each night service, and for four years every Sunday we had conversions, except for two Sundays; and on those two Sundays it was too hot for anybody to decide anything.[14]

Apparently he held evangelistic services during the week as well as on Sunday, because on February 26, 1908, he wrote to Miss Nellie that revival had already begun in his church.

We began last Sunday & the first service was one of real victory. Our long altar was filled to overflowing with seeking souls. Quite a few of the Is. Th. Col. girls were there seeking. . . . Monday night was also a night with a full altar. Tuesday we had to turn some of the benches around to make an altar rail. Tonight a good number were there also.

The revival was not limited to laymen in the Methodist Church in Lucknow. Mr. and Mrs. Meek, with whom Jones shared the Methodist parsonage, were, Jones wrote, "as happy as can be" because both of them had "entered the experience of holiness." In fact, Mrs. Meek had "become so ardent that . . . she is tackling the missionaries right & left."

Stanley's early letters from Lucknow also contain personal appeals. On February 6, 1908, he asked Miss Nellie's help in finding "a good Christian boarding house" in Baltimore for Brother Cranshaw, who was coming from India to be a lay delegate to the General Conference of the Methodist Episcopal Church to be held in Baltimore later that year. He also asked for Miss Nellie's help in soliciting money for Methodist missions in India. He sent her photographs of the kindergarten class at Isabella Thoburn College, so that she could get her Sunday school class of juniors at Memorial Church interested in sponsoring the college mission work among these young Indian children. Three years later in a letter dated November 25, 1911, he gave Miss Nellie the name of "a nice looking adorable boy of five" whom she had agreed to support. Lochan Singh was an orphan whose father was dead and whose mother was unable to support him. During the school year Lochan lived at the boys' boarding school in Sitapur operated by the Methodist Episcopal Church under the direction of Stanley's future wife, Mabel Lossing. A year later his October 24, 1912, letter told about Lochan's being sick and about his being taken from the school to the Jones's bungalow where Mabel could take care of him. Jones described him as "a lovable little chatterbox."

We can see in these early letters the start of a long and deep relationship between Stanley Jones and Methodist churches throughout the United States. Beginning with his own Memorial Church in Baltimore, Stanley, and later his wife, Mabel, sought and received financial support from a wide variety of American sponsors. Appeals for money from home were a necessity for most American Methodist missionaries in India, because the church often provided only part of their financial support. As for Jones, when he left the pastorate of the Methodist Church in Lucknow to become a full-time evangelist in October 1910, Dr. Morrison's Holiness Union in the United States paid his salary even though he remained a member of the North India Conference of the Methodist Episcopal Church. In fact, as Jones explained in his March 16, 1913, letter to Miss Nellie, "my salary is paid by the Holiness Union at home on the condition that I be free to do evangelistic work."

Throughout the half century Stanley and his wife, Mabel, served as missionaries to India, appeals for money from home were an almost perpetual preoccupation. As early as 1911 Stanley began to send "circular" letters or "round robin" letters to his friends at home.[15] Usually mailed quarterly to "My Dear Friend," or "My dear Fellow-worker," and signed, "Your Fellow-worker," "Your fellow-labourer," "Sincerely Your Brother," and, reflecting his Holiness background, "Yours Fully Saved," he typically sent the same letter to scores and eventually to hundreds of individuals and church friends throughout the United States. To save on the cost of international postage from India to the United States, he asked his addressees to circulate their copies of each letter to others who might want to support his mission work in India. In this way he was able to inform many more people about Christian evangelism in South Asia and to solicit financial support from a much broader group of Christians in North America.

Stanley needed money not only for himself, and later for his family, but also for the many Indian nationals he employed to help him in his mission and evangelistic work. In a circular letter dated August 1, 1917, written from Sitapur where he had moved after he left the Lucknow church, he confided to his supporters,

> The mission is able to give me only one-tenth of my payroll. For the other nine-tenths I am compelled to look to my old friends. You will forgive me for opening my heart thus, will you not? If each of you can sit down and send a Money Order to me here at Sitapur, or if you prefer send a check to the Mission Secretary, 150 Fifth Ave., N.Y., it will see us through this critical time and will lighten this burden on our hearts. And more, it will help us bring Christ to India.

In one of his very first circular letters, dated August 21, 1911, Stanley wrote about one of the preachers he employed. The man, he wrote, "works for a salary of fourteen rupees a month . . . the equivalent of $4.66. . . . And he must support his wife and two children from that, too!"

> Shall I tell you something of this man of God? But let me whisper it so low that the whisper will never be heard out here. He is without doubt one of the

finest workers I have ever seen. He never knows when he is tired. With an unquenchable enthusiasm he goes out in the middle of the day even when the sun is hot enough to blister one. Bazaar preaching is nerve-tearing work, but after we have been preaching for an hour or more and feel it is time to go he will ask from me the privilege of staying on and will preach alone for an hour or more longer! On Sunday he teaches in two Sunday Schools, holds three himself, preaches three or four times, and attends the general services! All this, and yet he is not expected to do preaching work at all, as he is the Manager of the Boys' Boarding School! His accounts are always correct, and the boys love and respect him. He is entirely the Lord's. Truly he is God's good man. But I cannot tell all.

Why have I told you this? Simply to let you know that it just happens that I have no support for this man.

Stanley began to preach as a traveling evangelist in India only eight months after his arrival in Bombay. On July 3, 1908, he wrote to Miss Nellie from Naini Tal, which he described as "a great deal of property" surrounding a beautiful lake in the Himalayas. "Naini," Jones tells his friend, is the name of a Hindu goddess and "Tal" means "lake."

Oh Miss Nellie I wish you could be here with me & take a stroll up these mountain sides to see the snow & the great peaks of the Himalayas. There is a beautiful lake here . . . one of the highest in the world.

The Methodist Church had only recently acquired Naini Tal after a landslide had killed hundreds of people and had built a boys' college and a girls' college on the land. During his two-week visit Stanley was asked to speak to the boys' college.

I preached at the boys school on last Sunday morning & 45 of the boys gave themselves to God. It was beautiful to see them weep before the Lord & pray out loud. I know I looked like an old Meth. itinerant as I went up the mountain with a granny apron around me, . . . & an umbrella to keep off the rain & a native boy holding on to the horse's tail with one hand thus getting a lift & switching the horse for me with the other!

After his visit to Naini Tal, he wrote, he would be traveling over a thousand miles south and west[16] to "Hyderabad Deccan South India to hold a revival meeting" before returning to Lucknow.

All of Stanley's letters reflect the consuming passion of his life—answering God's call to preach the gospel of Jesus Christ. But his early letters from India to Miss Nellie also tell the story of a young exuberant American who is living abroad for the first time in a strange land with a strange culture and who is confronted with a very difficult language; an enervating climate; and curious, exotic, and even deadly animals. In his February 6, 1908, letter he tells his friend, "Today is a Hindoo holiday & they are going by with all sorts of tinselled booths to be used in the worship of their gods." He went on to explain about the language he was learning. Hindustani is a composite language of Sanskrit, Arabic, Persian, and Indian words but also consists of two dialects—*Urdu,* which is the language of the cities and towns, and *Hindi,* which is the language of the villages and the country-side. Stanley studied Urdu with the help of his Hindu *munchi* or tutor. Part of his problem with Urdu was that he was working and preaching in both English and Hindustani churches. As he put it in his February 6, 1908, let-ter, "The Eng. work is a bad place for language study because you do not use it after you get it hence the words are so hard to retain."

During the summer of 1908, Jones admitted to his first grade and Sunday school teacher, "The language is fearfully slow in coming. It comes slowly & goes quickly." But in January 1910 he was able to tell Miss Nellie that at annual conference he had passed his language exams. Although he passed, Stanley never really mastered Hindustani.[17] In his early years, before he began his ministry to the educated classes of India, he did do some preaching in Hindustani. But after he turned to full-time evangelism among the intelligentsia, he relied almost exclusively on English. Because these sophisticated audiences usually knew English, he seldom had to use an interpreter.

In a letter to Miss Nellie about his first trip to Naini Tal, Stanley gave a bird's-eye view of his grueling travel adventures by remarking on the long train ride from Lucknow followed by a thirteen-mile trek up the mountain to the remote Himalayan wonderland. Perhaps to deemphasize the rigors this trip entailed, he commented appreciatively on the black-faced baboons he saw along the way. In a letter from Lucknow probably written during the summer of 1908, he let Miss Nellie glimpse normal everydayness, which included the keeping of several mongooses within the parsonage com-pound to control snakes. Snakes, he explained, killed at least twenty thou-sand people in India each year. Scorpions were also a menace. "The other day I was out under the tree with a blanket," he wrote on November 8, 1910, "& felt something crawling under me & soon a big black scorpion nearly as long as one's hand crawled out. *He* does take care!" Jones sprinkles other letters with occasional asides on water buffalo, ox tongas or carts, which he often used as a means of transportation, and the like.

Four years later in his October 24, 1912, letter, he told Miss Nellie about his own encounter with a snake. "The other night I was closing the front door when I heard something slapping against it. I found I had caught a very deadly snake in the crack of the door by its tail. I had him fast in the shut door." Then, turning the incident into a parable as he did so often in his daily devotional books, he wrote, "I have often overcome that other old Serpent by the shut door plan! 'When thou prayest enter into thy closet & shut the door.'"

Another chronic and disastrous event that Stanley witnessed in India was famine. As we saw at the very end of the last chapter, one of the things that most impressed him about India when he first arrived was the widespread poverty and the ever-present possibility of famine. Less than a month after his first letter to Miss Nellie from India, he was still obsessed by the human deprivation surrounding him. On January 8, 1908, he wrote, "The famine conditions are very distressing, not from what is now going on but from what is in sight unless rain comes." However, he admitted that to his Western eyes many Indians

> look so perpetually starved that you can't tell when they are really serious. The beggars sit alongside the road & tell how the baby is starving etc. But you do not really know to whom to give for there is a regular beggar caste.

Just as distressing as famine and its widespread and tragic impact on the people of India was what he was told about the method employed by some mothers in the hills of India to keep their babies quiet while the mothers worked.

> They take the child when just a few weeks or older & put them under a trough & let a little stream of water flow on top of their heads & soon being very sensitive they lapse into unconsciousness & stay that way. The water is very cold too as it comes from the melting snows of the Himalayas. Of course many of them die from it.

Finally, in this same letter to Miss Nellie, Stanley wrote about his own experience with a deadly and highly contagious disease.

> Small pox is in full swing now & I was called on to bury a man who died of small pox last week. One of the servants who waited on our table . . . has developed it & really he had it while passing things over my shoulder. I visited where some [small pox] was next door today. When they vaccinate they drive a calf to your compound & take the materials from it then as there will be no contamination with other things.

Like almost all Europeans and Americans living in British colonial India, Stanley relied on servants to perform a variety of daily household tasks. This reliance on servants, he wrote, led to the great difficulty of what he called the "servant question." Servants, he explained, steal everything, including, it is said, the sheets off your bed while you are sleeping in it. But even the problem of theft had its humorous side.

> We have to pay a man especially to watch the compound & it would tickle you to hear the medley of coughing watchmen in the compounds at night. They clear their throats in a most vociferous fashion to let the thieves know where they are.

In these early letters from India Stanley shows an obvious optimistic streak and a disciplined mind, will, and spirit. Yet while brimming with unself-consious charm, good old-fashioned naturalness, and keen receptivity to all of life, even in his correspondence to a true and deeply cared-for friend, the young missionary stayed focused on the main thing—his call and commitment to Christ.

At the same January 1910 annual conference at which he passed his language exams, Stanley also learned that he would be released in October from the Lal Bagh Church in Lucknow to become an evangelist for both Indian nationals and Europeans. He would divide his time, he wrote to Miss Nellie on January 19, 1910, between rural villages and English churches in large population centers. Although he had only been in India for two years, he was already in great demand as a preacher and had established a solid reputation in Christian communities throughout India for his gifts as a speaker and evangelist. In fact, he wrote, he had been offered an appointment as pastor of Bowen Memorial Church in Bombay, the second largest Methodist Church in India.[18] But he declined the offer, because, he wrote, "I felt God would have me in this [evangelistic] work."

Stanley left the English church in Lucknow on October 12, 1910. The church "kicked," as he put it in his November 8, 1910, letter to Miss Nellie. They petitioned the bishop several times to keep him as their pastor. But the bishop refused, deciding that Jones had been called to evangelism. Stanley's account of his leaving the Methodist Church in Lucknow is confirmed and enlarged by J. Waskom Pickett, who succeeded Jones as pastor of the church. In his March 15, 1973, *Indian Witness* article, Pickett wrote:

> After Stanley had served the church about four years, during which time he had been invited to hold services in many other cities in India, he and his bishop, the fervent Francis Wesley Warne, became convinced that he should serve a larger field. He was appointed evangelist to English-speaking people in India. I was invited to take over the pastorate of Lal Bagh Church.[19]

But there was a three-week hiatus between the time Jones left the church and the time Pickett arrived as the new pastor. During this interim Miss Helen Ingram, the deaconess, performed pastoral visits and coordinated the leadership for Wednesday evening prayer meetings. However, Pickett wrote,

> the church missed Stanley and made a sustained effort to persuade him to return as its pastor. As the deaconess took me, day after day, to call on members and friends of Lal Bagh as their new pastor, a number of members enquired whether it could not be arranged that I take the work to which Stanley had been assigned and thus open the way for him to return to them. I understood their deep satisfaction with Stanley as their pastor and sympathized with their eagerness to continue his leadership of their congregation.

But Stanley felt strongly that God wanted him to give his energies to the all-India evangelism to which his bishop had appointed him and asked his Lucknow friends to loyally accept me as their pastor. Soon I had the hearty backing of the church and in a few weeks was preaching to a full church. The membership quadrupled in my first two years and doubled again in the next two. Occasionally Stanley returned to Lucknow and was always greeted enthusiastically by the congregation he had served with such blessed results, and also by his successor as its pastor.[20]

Stanley's new responsibilities as conference evangelist were sponsored by Dr. Morrison's Holiness Union in the United States. The organization did not want to establish a new mission in India but to work with and among existing missions. Jones explained the situation to Miss Nellie in his November 8, 1910, letter.

As the N. India Conference, to which I belong, could not afford to pay my salary & then let me loose to work among all Conferences, Dr. Morrison—in the name of the Holiness Union—solved the problem by offering to support me in the evangelistic work if they would get another man for my church.

Between the time he left Lucknow on October 12 and his November 8 letter to Miss Nellie, Stanley had held evangelistic services in at least two different places, Belgaum and Bangalore. Hundreds were saved in Bangalore, but it "is the hardest place I have struck at," he wrote. "The congregation is mostly composed of British soldiers who are very hard. This regiment in particular is a difficult proposition because they lost their colors at Bunker Hill & have not forgotten it. So we Americans have a harder time winning them than other regiments."

By October of the next year, 1911, Stanley had traveled in his evangelistic work from Madras on the southeast coast of India to Arrayup in the Himalayas, from Jhansi in central India to Bombay on the west coast, Allahabad in the northwest and Karachi, which is on the Arabian Sea just south of Baluchistan. He had also been invited to speak and hold evangelistic services in Rangoon, Burma, he told Miss Nellie on October 3, 1911. A year later, on October 24, 1912, he wrote to his friend, "I am simply overwhelmed with calls in both native & English evangelistic work." At the same time he was gaining a unique perspective on Christian missions throughout India. "It is a great privilege for one gets a great view of the whole Indian field and conditions in every place are so different. It is a series of different little worlds that one enters."

Stanley's October 3, 1911, letter to Miss Nellie was written from Sitapur, a community of about forty thousand, smaller than Lucknow and about fifty miles away. The letter was written on Methodist Episcopal Mission letterhead and identified the Reverend E. Stanley Jones as Missionary in

Charge of the Sitapur Mission and as North India Conference Evangelist. Stanley moved from Lucknow to Sitapur after his marriage to Mabel Lossing in 1911, but he continued his heavy and intense schedule of evangelistic activities. And in his missionary evangelism among Indian nationals in Sitapur, he began to see the first signs of a genuine mass movement, the kind of movement that Christian missionaries in India had learned to recognize and anticipate and that, as we have seen, led to the phenomenal growth of the Methodist Episcopal Church in India in the late nineteenth and early twentieth centuries. In his June 13, 1912, letter to Miss Nellie, he wrote that an entire Hindu lower caste was on the point of becoming Christian.

> I have baptized some of their leaders and they themselves tell us that they are going to bring in the whole caste. One man said, "Sahib, if you love us the way you love these people who have just become Christians here, there is a whole village of us over there ready to accept your Christ." Love! That is what poor India needs! Among her 33,000,000 gods there is not one represented as loving.

Six months later on January 21, 1913, he explained to Miss Nellie his approach to evangelism as converting the "head men" who will then convene a council and "publicly confess that they are coming to Christ. Their people will obey them implicitly." The revival, which Jones said he had been looking for when he first arrived in India in 1907, was beginning to appear.

During these early years in India, not only were groups converted to Christianity through Stanley's ministry, like the members of a caste in a village, but there were also individual conversions. In an article written at the end of February 1912 for the *Indian Witness*,[21] he told the story of three persons who found a personal relationship with Jesus Christ in his revival meetings. The first was a "tall, slender woman of cultured intelligent face" who was brought up in the Church of England and then became a Roman Catholic. But she did not find Jesus Christ himself in either church, even though she became a Catholic nun and endured various forms of physical penance in order to find God. Finally, the woman became disillusioned with Christianity and left her convent because, she said, she was an atheist. Jones tells the rest of her story.

> She happened into our revival meetings in a certain city. God was there. She felt it. Hope fluttered in her aching breast. Several days she sought God with tears. The last night of the meetings had come. It seemed that she had lifted a tear stained face to God all in vain. She started sadly toward her home. She stopped in a shadowed place in the road and looked up at the stars and prayed: "Oh, Christ thou hast said that if we confessed Thee before men thou wouldst confess us before the Father. Oh, confess me!" Would he do it?

Glory to God He *did*! Peace came! Her heart was full! The burden? Gone!
God? Oh, so near! The past? Under the Blood! A soul had entered into rest
and that rest was sweet. That peace abides.

The second person Jones described was a doctor "all tangled up in sin
and with a hideous haunting past." While attending one of Jones's meetings, the doctor found God. After the meeting the doctor went home "and
just as usual mechanically poured out a peg." But this time it tasted strange
and medicinal.

He stood all puzzled. What could it mean? Then the thought dawned on
him. "The whiskey is changed because I am changed," and it was so! The
desire for liquor had gone! He went to the window and poured out every
drop. A changed man had made a changed whiskey. Glory!

The third person whom Jones described was a theosophist. He was "bitter and cross-grained . . . out of joint with himself, his fellow man and
God." Jones continued,

When I saw him first he was lecturing on Theosophy. He attended the meetings and was seemingly unmoved. Unknown to us he had been deeply
wounded. . . . About two o'clock in the morning . . . he said he saw the evangelist come into the room with his face pale and drawn. Coming over to him
he raised his hand toward heaven and cried "Oh, Spirit of the Living God!
Burn up sin from this heart!" He thought a moment and said "Yes" and then
fell asleep. When he awoke in the morning . . . [a] strange burning was at his
heart and a delightful sense of peace pervaded [him]. . . . [H]e said to himself, "Can this be what they call conversion at those meetings? I shall test it
and see." So he went straight to that sin that had been so dear to him. . . .
When he walked into its presence he was disgusted to the core. . . . He turned
on his heel with a shout in his soul "I'm converted!" and he was and is!

These accounts of conversion to Christianity by educated, middle-class
seekers suggest the future direction of Stanley Jones's evangelism in India.
Years before the emotional and spiritual crisis, which precipitated a nervous breakdown and an extended furlough in the United States, he was
already in 1912 beginning to hear God's call to evangelism among the
educated classes of India. This call would later bring him out of a prolonged period of depression and confusion and would establish the future
course of his ministry in India. In his October 24, 1912, letter to Miss
Nellie, he told the story of a European who had become a Hindu and had
come to Sitapur to lecture. A public discussion with Jones was arranged so
that Christianity and Hinduism could be openly debated.

I was simply chafing the bit for it [he wrote]. Well I never saw such a crowd
that gathered. All the educated people of the city were present with some of

the European officials. . . . [In the discussion the European Hindu] began to tremble & flounder about. On the offset I got him on the defensive and he never got off it. God's spirit was really present. Many Hindus & Mohammedans came to me & said that Christianity's arguments could not be answered. It was a great opportunity & a great victory for the truth. It has put Christianity in a new light before the educated people.

In later years Jones probably would have described the incident differently. In the final analysis Christianity is not an intellectual proposition that can establish its superiority over other religions by clever arguments. Christianity is true because it reveals the truth of God's love for man in the person of Jesus Christ.

In the same letter to Miss Nellie he recorded another incident in which Hindus challenged the depth and sincerity of his Christian belief and action. He was preaching in the bazaar when a man in the crowd became abusive to him and to his Christian workers. Afterward, some Hindus told the workers,

We sent that man to disturb your people. We heard your sahib say that Christianity taught people to love their enemies and we sent that man to see if you lived it. It is true for your people returned good for evil.

Stanley commented, "We kept patient and sweet" throughout the incident.

During this time Stanley made friends with a high-caste Hindu raja. The rajas were an irreplaceable and integral part of the British colonial system of indirect rule in India. In exchange for their loyalty to the British Crown, the British government in India permitted the rajas to retain their traditional authority as kings within their own districts. This system saved the British the enormous expense of conquering the whole of the Indian subcontinent and of then using British civil servants to provide basic public services for all of South Asia. Stanley had visited this particular Hindu raja on several occasions and had shared the Lord Jesus Christ with him. In his September 1, 1915, circular letter written from Sitapur on letterhead that identifies him as the district superintendent of the Lucknow district, he wrote about his most recent visit to his royal friend.

This time I was to show my magic lantern pictures of Christ's life. To get there, we began on our bicycles, took the train, went on foot, then on an elephant supplied by the Raja, then horseback, then a one-horse native vehicle called an ekka. All this in only a journey of less than fifty miles! . . . The Raja insisted on our eating before the pictures began. He was a high-caste Hindu, so all the plates in which the food was brought had to be thrown away after we had eaten from them. The plates from which we actually ate were large banana leaves. This makes a good plate, and nothing is lost when it is thrown away. When they brought some hot water in a brass vessel, for the moment I forgot and extended my finger to touch it to see how hot it was. I was called to my senses by the servant politely pulling it away before my finger reached it. Had I touched it, that valuable brass would have been useless and worse— it would have been polluted and polluting.

After the meal, crowds of people gathered from surrounding villages, because the raja had sent out the word, "The Jesus Christ man is coming." Stanley then told the story of Jesus Christ to the crowd, using the magic lantern pictures. "When the Man died on the cross," he wrote in his circular letter, "you could feel a wave of sadness go over the audience. But when He arose, they clapped their hands!" By the end of his presentation, "the great crowd around the Raja had felt the power of the message."

Stanley also learned from one of the preachers he supervised that "the Raja had been studying the Bible, and was a true enquirer." A relative of the raja, the preacher said, "was seeing Christ, and wanted to be baptised." The relative knew that becoming a Christian "would mean he must leave all, and be an outcaste. He was ready to suffer this, he said." Stanley concluded with the comment: "The leaving-all cross is heavy in India."

In addition to having many personal contacts among high-caste Indians, Stanley also developed relationships with low-caste Indians. In his August 1, 1917, circular letter, written five months after he had returned to India from a furlough in the United States, he told about a "rather interesting thing" that had occurred.

> The low caste Christians were going to have a great meeting. When the workers arrived they found that there were ropes stretched across the villages. When they enquired what it meant they said that they were to keep the high caste people out! If you knew India you would see the force of that. As if a high caste man would ever pollute himself by going into a low caste section of a village! But the remarkable thing is that when the meeting started and God's power was felt the high caste people gathered behind the ropes and one by one they ducked under, until the rope was behind them. They were ceremoniously polluting themselves because—well, because they felt they needed a heart cleansing. Their hearts got the start of their prejudices. I wonder after all whether India will not be evangelized by the out-castes. I wonder after all whether the proud Brahman will not have to "come under the ropes."

What so impressed Jones about this incident was the irony of high-caste Indians "defiling" themselves in order to accept the spiritual purity offered by Jesus Christ. Moreover, if high-caste Indians were willing to break caste barriers in order to receive the Christian gospel along with low-caste Indians, then Christian evangelization in India would mean not only the spiritual transformation of individuals but also social revolution.

As these letters and articles reveal, during these years Stanley Jones was deeply involved in both mass movement evangelism and in the more traditional and familiar person-centered evangelism. He had gone to India in 1907 in response to God's call, expecting revival. He was not disappointed. Even before he arrived in India there had been many unmistakable signs of the manifest power of the Holy Spirit in Methodist missions throughout India. Suddenly and without warning on August 4, 1905, after a message on the Holy Spirit given by Bishop Warne to a summer training school for Christian workers, a young woman stood up and testified calmly and quietly about how she had recently received the Holy Spirit for herself. What happened next can only be compared to eyewitness accounts of the eighteenth-century Wesleyan revival in Britain or of the Great Awakenings in the United States in the eighteenth and nineteenth centuries or even more apropos of the Azuza Street and Welsh revivals, which broke at about the same time as the revival in India. Bishop Warne describes the events in his own words.

> Instantly, impelled by the power of the spirit, about 150 women and girls, up to that time apparently unmoved, arose and followed her, and broke out in a roar of agony. For several hours there was such weeping, confessing, and crying for mercy, as I had never before heard among timid Indian women. In front of the altar the men, preachers, and other workers present, cried aloud for hours, under the awakening and convicting power of the spirit.[22]

Similar accounts of outbreaks of pentecostal power in boys' and girls' high schools in the North India and Northwest India Conferences are recorded in the official history of Methodist Episcopal Missions. Philo M. Buck in Meerut of the Northwest India Conference reported what he called "a tornado of grace" among both the boys and girls of his boarding schools. All the students who experienced the tornado, "although they had flocked together when the storm came, won their blessing with little or nothing of human aid."[23]

The work of the Holy Spirit in these revivals was not confined to children and youth. Under the conviction of the Holy Spirit, sinners "would fall to the floor and remain there senseless, even for hours on end. Others would kneel immobile for prolonged periods. . . . Great numbers of people engaged in paroxysms of moaning, weeping, and desperate praying." Sometimes men experienced "a violently spasmodic and convulsive twitching of the entire body," a phenomenon Bishop Warne compared to what the American evangelist Peter Cartwright called the "Jerks" during his nineteenth-century revivals on the American frontier.[24]

Another outbreak of revival occurred at the conclusion of a tent meeting held by Bishop Warne during the Philibhit District Conference in November 1906. When the bishop finished his message, approximately 300 people unleashed a veritable cyclone of prayer. Then there was silence for more than an hour. Finally, some of the men collapsed on the ground and lay there motionless and speechless for hours.

There was a general medley of weeping and praying. Then the rejoicings of the converted began to be mingled with the agonizings of the convicted. Groanings gave way to singing and rejoicing, for conviction and confession were followed by assurance of forgiveness and by inner peace and joy openly expressed.[25]

The spontaneous work of the Holy Spirit in these revivals was not ignored by the Methodist Episcopal hierarchy. During the 1904-08 quadrennium the General Conference of the church sponsored a program of spiritual renewal called Aggressive Evangelism for Methodist congregations in the United States and abroad. Responding both to the leadership of the General Conference and to the widespread moving of the Spirit among Indians who were receiving Jesus Christ as their personal Lord and Savior and were being filled with the Holy Spirit, the missionary bishops of the Central Conference in South Asia appointed in 1908 its own Commission on Aggressive Evangelism. This commission in turn promoted evangelism among the various annual conferences throughout South Asia. "The chief permanent contribution of these groups," according to the official history of Methodist missions, "was the establishment of the annual month of Aggressive Evangelism, which became a regular feature of the work on Districts throughout the India Conferences."[26]

Like most India conferences, the North India Conference to which Stanley was assigned observed its month of aggressive evangelism from mid-February to mid-March each year. When he was appointed the North India conference evangelist in 1910, and then the missionary in charge of the Sitapur Mission in 1911, Stanley felt a special responsibility for this month. He saw it as an exciting opportunity for Christian witness and conversion. But by 1915 one gets the impression that the month of aggressive evangelism had become just one more episcopal initiative among a host of required and recommended activities and observances for overburdened and sometimes exhausted missionaries.

Responding to this fatigue and lethargy, Stanley wrote a short piece for the *Indian Witness* that appeared in February 1915, as the month of aggressive evangelism was beginning.

Missionary! The details of administrative work forced on us in the mission field to make us lose touch with individual souls and their problems. Let one great word throb through this month, SOULS. Let that word stand at the threshold of all our thinking, all our planning and all our work. Let the overshadowing presence of that word make all other phases of missionary work small in comparison. We left America for souls. Are we now content to live without them? Are we willing that the missionary—the missionary should be lost in the administrator? God forbid. Then, oh, for a passionate passion until the soul shall cry out like the Master, "The zeal of thine house hath eaten me up." [Ps. 69:9 KJV] We must see a revival. Lord send it.[27]

If the vigor and success of person-centered evangelism was threatened by the bureaucratization of the routine daily tasks of Methodist missionaries in India, the unprecedented opportunity for Christian conversion and church growth presented by mass movement evangelism suffered from neglect and from the greater priority given to other ecclesiastical work by the Board of Foreign Missions in New York. Mass movement evangelism, as we have explained, was propelled and channeled by the caste structure of Indian society. The Christian conversion of the leaders of one caste in one community ignited first conversion of the other members of the caste in the same community, followed by conversions among the same caste in other communities. Unfortunately, there were not enough trained Christian teachers and leaders to disciple the flood of new converts.

> New villages turned Christian so fast, and new groups of inquirers appeared so rapidly, that the trained leaders were being steadily and automatically overwhelmed by the sheer volume of the popular and administrative demands upon their time and energies.[28]

Unlike the rapid implementation of the church's program of aggressive evangelism, the response of the Methodist Episcopal Church to the explosive growth of its new converts in India was painfully slow.[29] It was not until 1912 that the church developed any official policy on mass movement evangelism in India. Even then another three years elapsed before the Board of Foreign Missions made specific plans to allocate the money and personnel necessary to sustain Indian mass movement evangelism. These plans were largely the work of William F. Oldham, a corresponding secretary for the board, who was especially sympathetic to the peculiar problems and opportunities in the Indian mission field. However, the Board of Foreign Missions scrapped the plan shortly after it was adopted and Oldham left office in 1916. Nevertheless, the Central Conference in India continued to press its demand for more missionaries with such force and urgency that the board finally, in November 1916, established a special India Mass Movement Commission whose executive chairman was a former missionary to India, Frederick B. Fisher. Under Fisher's leadership the commission proposed and the Executive Committee of the Board approved a campaign to raise $1 million for mass movement evangelism in India. In 1917 Fisher visited India on behalf of the commission and made the following report to the Board of Foreign Missions.

> The missionaries have not exaggerated in the slightest degree when they say that hundreds of thousands are actually PRESSING toward the Kingdom of Christ. I have seen them hold them back. I have seen the struggle to provide teachers for villages of illiterate Christians. I have seen districts of sixteen thousand Christians led by just eight preachers in charge. I have seen

districts where there are as many members as there are in the New England Conference—led by just two missionaries. I tell you the task is gigantic. It takes a hero on the field to stand up before it and keep heart.[30]

But even before Fisher returned from India, two staff members who had been assigned to raise funds for the Mass Movement Campaign were reassigned to another special commission, the Centenary Commission, which was charged with making plans for the commemoration of the 1919 centennial of the Women's Foreign Missionary Society. *The History of Methodist Missions* records that

> the Mass Movement campaign was discontinued, and the office was closed. When he got back from abroad, Fisher found that even the office furniture was being used by the Centenary people. He himself was promptly caught up in Centenary work and gave little more attention to Mass Movement interests as such.[31]

Jones was probably aware of this diversion of financial resources and personnel from the Mass Movement Campaign to the Centenary Commission. However, he does not refer directly to the mission board's shift in priorities in any of his letters or articles. But he did caution his fellow missionaries in India about one potential danger of the Mass Movement Campaign. In an article written for the *Indian Witness* in 1917, which is similar to the article he wrote for the same newspaper in 1915 just before the month of aggressive evangelism, Jones said,

> Can our mass movements be run by committees? Let it be plainly said: Neither by committees in America nor in India. . . . The committee may even prove to be a hindrance, in that it may take leaders out of the mass movement, and send them over the country attending meetings, instead of leading the movement. . . . Keep that Christian spiritual, with a passion for souls, and the mass movement will go.[32]

When the centenary movement got under way in India, Jones became its chairman.[33] The evangelistic emphasis of the centenary movement had two objectives: "a hundred thousand baptisms during the Centenary. . . . [and] 200,000 heart conversions, including the 100,000 baptised from heathenism and a 100,000 from among our baptised, but unconverted Christian community."

Once Jones had explained these objectives to the readers of the *Indian Witness,* he then outlined a concrete plan of action to meet the objectives, including personal evangelism among non-Christians and unconverted Christians, the use of laymen for village evangelism, the distribution of Christian literature, and special prayers offered by students in Christian boys' and girls' boarding schools. Whether or not the Centenary

Campaign achieved its goals of 100,000 baptisms and 200,000 heart conversions in India, we do know that on November 29, 1920, the Board of Bishops of the Methodist Episcopal Church reported that the church as a whole "during 1920, had the largest increase in membership in its history; namely, 182,338." The bishops announced this achievement "with great gratitude and thanksgiving," but warned "that there must be no slackening in evangelistic zeal." Responding to the bishops' report, the North India Conference decided to make "the months of February and March a period of Intensive Evangelism" and resolved that "a real and prayerful effort be made to enlist every member of the whole Church in an effort to win at least one soul to an allegiance to Jesus Christ during the year."

In March 1921 Jones was in Southern India holding evangelistic meetings among the Syrian Christians. Southern India is the most Christian part of the country and the Syrian Christian Church, which tradition says was founded by the apostle Thomas, is one of the oldest Christian Churches in the world. But the problem with the Syrian Christian Church, Jones wrote in the *Indian Witness* reporting on the progress of the Centenary Movement in India, was that it "made friends with its environment. . . . She lost her sense of mission and commission, and so her heart died; and forms took the place of life." Jones used the experience of the Syrian Christian Church as a lesson for other Christians in India. "Our hour of opportunity has come in India. We are in the midst of the transition stage of India's history. Now is the hour to save her for Christ. And it may be now, or perhaps, never."

Jones concluded his article with the observation that Methodists in India who were seeking to fulfill the goals of the centenary movement could even learn from Muslim missionary societies. In one section of India during the year 1920, Muslim missionaries had converted 1,100 Hindus to their faith. On the other hand, Christians in the same section of India "with a fine organization and fine institutions and many paid workers, won how many? Sixty-five!" Although there were a number of differences between the Muslim and Christian missionaries in terms of their respective approaches to evangelism, there was a crucial and decisive difference.

> Every Moslem was a worker. . . . The secret was lay-workers. We must get the whole of our laity lined up in a soul-saving campaign that will not be a spasm, but a persistent effort to win at least one soul to Christ each year. Every layman every year winning a soul—this should be our aim and cry.

Did the Methodist Episcopal Church miss the leading and direction of the Holy Spirit when it closed the office of the Mass Movement Campaign for India and redirected its resources for evangelism in that nation to the Centenary Commission? Did Jones himself miss God's purpose for the church in India by not giving the mass movement campaign more whole-hearted and enthusiastic support and by becoming involved in the centenary movement? Or, was he like the sons of Issachar in 1 Chronicles 12:32? They discerned that God's anointing had been removed from Saul, and God had instead chosen David as the king of Israel. Did Jones correctly perceive the danger that both the month of aggressive evangelism as well as the broader mass movement campaign might lose their spiritual force and energy in the administrative minutiae of the committees that were organized to carry out these initiatives?

In retrospect, it seems clear that the Methodist Church in India would have been substantially strengthened and that its membership would have significantly increased if it had responded more quickly and more decisively to the spontaneous outbreaks of revival that occurred in the early twentieth century. In this sense both Jones and the Methodist Church probably missed a God-given opportunity for widespread and effective evangelism in India. On the other hand, Jones's warnings about the bureaucratization of evangelism were probably valid. But it is difficult to know whether these warnings were responsible for his not becoming more deeply involved in the mass movement campaign. However, there is one other factor that may help explain why Jones turned his attention to traditional, person-centered evangelism after the beginning of the centenary movement. This factor, whose significance Jones was one of the first to recognize, was the rise of Indian nationalism.

As early as 1917, in the same *Indian Witness* article in which he worried about the Mass Movement Campaign being run by committees, Stanley wrote that Christian missionaries "must realize" that they are bringing Christ "to a new India." "Our message," he concluded, "must be more closely associated than ever before with the legitimate national aspirations of India." In another article published in the *Indian Witness*[34] a year after he began to focus his evangelistic efforts on the educated classes of India, he said that Western missionaries, in order to influence Indians and convert them to Christianity, must present a Christianity that has "become naturalised in India." Successful evangelism begins with the missionary putting himself in the position of a potential convert and looking at the world from his point of view.

> Having sat where he sits and having obtained his standpoint and created the proper sympathetic atmosphere, we must appeal to the man not as to a Hindu or Mohammedan but as to a sinner needing Salvation and Soul-satisfaction. . . . We must appeal as man to man.

If Stanley Jones missed an opportunity for evangelism and for mass conversions to Christ when he became involved in the centenary movement, it may be because God was leading his ministry in a new direction. Perhaps God was preparing him for his work among the educated non-Christians in India by making him more sensitive to the national aspirations of the Indian people and to their desire for self-government. Instead of missing an opportunity for evangelism by turning his attention to the centenary movement, Jones may have been following the direction of the Holy Spirit. Certainly by 1925 when he published his first book, *The Christ of the Indian Road*, which revolutionized the purpose and method of Christian missions in India by making the Indian approach to Christ as authentic and as legitimate as the Western approach to Christ, Jones had established a new course for his ministry. For the remaining thirty years of his full-time ministry in India, he continued to focus his evangelism on the educated and the intellectuals of India.

3

Mabel Lossing Jones

About Miss Lossing! An interesting subject!
—E. Stanley Jones, November 8, 1910,
letter to Miss Nellie from Belgaum, India

Mrs. Jones . . . has . . . been kind of a missionary society within a missionary society.
—E. Stanley Jones, May 19, 1944, letter[1]

STANLEY JONES FIRST TOLD Nellie Logan about Mabel Lossing in
a letter from Lucknow dated January 19, 1910. Miss Nellie may not
have known Mabel personally at that time, but this letter reveals that
she was familiar with Mabel's poetry.

My other bit of news is this. I am engaged to the sweetest woman in the
world! Extravagant? Well be that as it may I will tell you about her. Do you
remember that you sent me a bit of poetry entitled "Rest Awhile Apart" by
Mabel Lossing when I was in W. Va. deciding whether I should come to India
or not? Well, that young lady is *the* young lady! She has been out here five
years & is one of our best missionaries. When Gov. [Government] wanted
some one to undertake to start the first Hindi Normal School they asked that
she might be put in charge. She made her way through college partly by writing short stories. . . . A short while ago she took very ill so now she goes home
on furlough and will return . . . to India next fall or winter. We will be married then. She is very spiritual the Lord having helped me to help her into
perfect love [holiness] last year when she was teaching here in the Isabella
Thoburn College. The W.F.M.S. [Woman's Foreign Missionary Society] will

pounce on me for stealing one of their number but what is to be done! She lived in Iowa. I hope she will run down to Balto [Baltimore] on her way out. She goes home the Pacific way.

Jones did not write to Miss Nellie again for almost eleven months. During that time she undoubtedly asked him for more information about his fiancée, because when he wrote to her again on November 8, 1910, he told her that after he first met Mabel in Lucknow, when she was teaching at Isabella Thoburn College, he had had "the privilege of leading her into holiness. Hope to have the privilege of leading her into matrimony." He and Mabel were only engaged for a month before she left on furlough.

Miss Nellie had apparently suggested that Stanley and Mabel might be on furlough at the same time and could be married in the United States. "Dear me," he wrote in exasperation in the same letter, "you talk about my taking furlough. Did you not know that we take furlough only after *ten* years?" Women missionaries who served under the auspices of the Woman's Foreign Missionary Society, as was Mabel Lossing, were eligible for furlough after five years, but those serving under the Methodist Episcopal Board of Foreign Missions "stay, if health permits until the ten years are up."

Mabel was scheduled to return to India on February 4, 1911, he wrote, and he presumed they would "be married about the 5th or 6th of Feb. in Bombay—a very quiet affair. One of the Bishops will marry us I suppose."

Miss Nellie had also apparently inquired about Stanley's physical health, since he went on to say,

> Do not worry about me physically, Miss Nellie, for I weigh six pounds more than I ever did in my life & feel excellent. I am taking care of myself for Jesus sake & for the sake of the little lady.
>
> She is going to be a great help to me I am sure & I feel she is really God's good gift. She fills up beautifully the "lacks" in my nature—which by the way are many.

Stanley's final comment to his friend in this letter about his marriage was a remarkably accurate prediction of the future course of his sixty-three year relationship with Mabel Lossing:

> Miss L. & I are going to try to be different from most other married folks in that we are going to try not to concentrate ourselves on ourselves & get self-ish & forget others.

If by not concentrating "ourselves on ourselves" and becoming selfish Jones meant that his marriage to Mabel Lossing would not interrupt or redirect the course of his career as a missionary evangelist, he was certainly correct. Mabel herself probably knew—if she was as perceptive a young bride-to-be as she revealed herself to be after marriage in the thousands of letters she would write to friends and supporters about her work—that her marriage would indeed be different. She may not have fully anticipated the number and frequency of Stanley's long absences from home during his far-flung evangelistic tours. She certainly could not have foreseen their separation during his six years in the United States during World War II while she and their daughter Eunice remained in India because the British government would not permit him to return to India. But intuitively Mabel must have known that she would have to make major adjustments to accommodate her responsibilities as a missionary in her own right, and later as a mother, to the growing demand for her husband's time and talent as a widely acclaimed preacher and evangelist.

As early as October 3, 1911, less than a year after his marriage to Mabel, Jones wrote to Miss Nellie from the Methodist Episcopal Mission in Sitapur.

> I must tell you something of ourselves. But where to begin is the question as our interests are scattered—scattered from the interest in each other to our interest in all India. So our parish is a big one. About six months I spend at home & the other six months in the Eng. [English] evangelistic work.

Mabel Lossing had gone to India in 1905, at the age of twenty-seven, two years before Stanley, sent by the Woman's Foreign Missionary Society to be a teacher. She was from Clayton in northern Iowa, a small town on the Mississippi River. Years later, in one of her duplicate letters dated August 1, 1935,[2] and addressed to "Dear Friends" throughout the United States, Mabel described her "old family home," located "at the foot of the Mississippi bluffs in Clayton, Iowa." "This home," she wrote, was "built by my grandfather nearly a hundred years ago when he came down from Canada with his young English wife." In 1910, when she was in Clayton on furlough, Mabel wrote a longhand letter, dated August 31, to Dr. Leonard, who was a corresponding secretary with the Methodist Episcopal Board of Foreign Missions in New York.[3] In it she referred to "the blanks"—the application form he had sent to her. Even though she had already served successfully as a missionary in India for five years, once she was married she could no longer be sponsored by the Woman's Foreign Missionary Society. She needed to apply to the Board of Foreign Missions and receive the board's official sanction so that she and Stanley could serve together as a married missionary couple.

Mabel responded with refreshing honesty, succinctly yet fully, to one of the questions on the Board of Foreign Missions application form.

I was brought up in the church and always [considered myself] a Christian. I never had a definite experience of conversion but I have had a number of "spiritual awakenings." The first came at 12 yrs. & as a result I joined the church.

The next came while I was at college & I made a complete surrender & became a Student Volunteer. Again, later, I sought & obtained the experience of what some call "sanctification." And in that experience I still walk—by His Grace.

I became a missionary because I was "conscious of a need that I had the power to meet"—and because I felt that if I failed to respond to that need I could not pretend to be a follower of Christ. I felt it was the only way in which I could maintain my relationship with Him "whom I loved." The way opened—my path was made plain—and I have been blessed in obeying.

Mabel Lossing's calling and commitment to God's work in India were as authentic and deep as Stanley's. Though she did not become as famous as her husband, her contribution to the education and evangelization of the children and young people of the North India Conference of the Methodist Church was unique, not merely a reflection of the work of her husband. Stanley himself gave her full credit for promoting and then taking personal charge of a new system of education for Indian boys, a system which in 1911 was a revolutionary change in elementary education in India. He explained it in his October 3, 1911, letter to Miss Nellie:

Mabel has started a new kind of school for India but quite common at home. Our mission has asked her as an experiment to open or rather change our school into a primary school for boys managed with lady teachers entirely. The ordinary Indian male teacher is very poor in the lower classes [of school]. . . . If it succeeds, the plan will be adopted in other places. It is doing finely but it is like making bricks without straw as they give us no more money. Recently our dormitories fell in. We have no others for the boys for the winter time which is coming on. But God will help us & we are going on in faith that He will see us through.

Years later on September 7, 1933, while he was on furlough in the United States, Stanley wrote to Ralph E. Diffendorfer, a corresponding secretary for the Board of Foreign Missions. He gave the following account of Mabel's ability as a public speaker.

Mrs. Jones is not known very widely as a speaker & yet she is a very remarkable speaker. In Dubuque where she spoke a great deal I was told at the close of an address, "You are good but your wife is better." And it was not said as a joke.

He went on to say that the Board of Foreign Missions should attempt to secure Mabel as a speaker while she was in the United States. "Now Mrs. J. is receiving a great many invitations to speak for the W.F.M.S. If she accepts these it will throw her influence toward the W.F.M.S. I suggest that the Board use her instead of the W.F.M.S."

In spite of the difficulties created by a lack of money and poor facilities at Sitapur, as Stanley explained them in the letter of October 3, 1911, Mabel's educational experiment was a spectacular success. In fact, less than two years after Jones described the idea to Miss Nellie, Bishop Francis Wesley Warne himself declared, "The experiment has more than exceeded our highest expectation." The bishop was such an enthusiastic advocate of Christian boys' schools run by women that on August 26, 1913, he wrote from Lucknow on official church letterhead a wholehearted endorsement of Mabel's innovative concept of education.

> The question of founding a Primary School for boys in Northern India, under the management of women, is one that I have heard debated in conferences and committees for years, and finally it was decided to try the experiment. We had no suitable property plant anywhere, but the nearest approach was in Sitapur. Rev. E. Stanley Jones, our Sitapur missionary, had just married a lady preeminently qualified for such a work. Therefore the Conference decided to open the school in Sitapur. The experiment has more than exceeded our highest expectation. We now consider the work has passed the experimental stage and has come to be a permanent and most important part of our whole educational policy for Northern India. The absence of a school-house makes it impossible for the teachers to do the work as they should. It will be a great joy and a permanent help to that excellent work, if friends can be found who will make the building of a school-house possible. I congratulate those upon whom the mantle of blessing shall fall and wish Mr. and Mrs. Jones success in securing the necessary funds to erect the much needed school-house.[4]

Mabel and Stanley no doubt used Bishop Warne's endorsement to raise money for the boys' school in Sitapur, and money continued to come in. It was Mabel, however, who assumed full personal responsibility for the school's day-to-day operation, especially during Stanley's frequent and sometimes extended absences from Sitapur. She was always burdened by the constant need for additional financial support. Even after she retired from active missionary service, she continued to be "financially responsible for the support" of the boys' school, according to an undated informational brochure written by Grace Honnell, identified in the brochure as the Missionary in Charge of the Methodist Boys' School in Sitapur.[5]

The brochure gives additional information about the school. "When the school was opened [in 1911], boys and teachers lived in mud huts." The first permanent buildings were "three dormitories, two teachers' quarters, servants' quarters and a room to be used as a hospital." The next building was a "schoolhouse with wide verandas and a spacious hall," which was added in 1915. Ms. Honnell then gives a bare-bones description of the current condition and operation of the school. "The teachers are all women. They live inside the compound, and [are] . . . in close contact with the boys who are boarders." She also provided an example of the daily chapel activities, which were conducted by the students themselves.

> This morning, for example, the second class had charge of the chapel exercises. Ten school boys represented ten boys of the Bible. Each told something of himself and then asked, "Who am I?" They were all enthusiastically recognized.

The students who were boarders at the school had a number of daily responsibilities in addition to their school work.

> The boys who live in the hostel do their own work. They are divided into five groups which rotate as each group takes its turn in cooking, drawing water, gathering fuel, cleaning rooms and cleaning the large compound. They seem to enjoy working. They have lately been weeding the garden. They put all refuse into a pit to make fertilizer. We grow about $300 worth of vegetables each year.

The boys' school enjoyed an excellent reputation in Sitapur. "Some of the best non-Christian families of the city," Honnell wrote, "send their boys and appreciate the type of education we provide. . . . Only God knows the results in lives saved, enriched and dedicated to His service."

In 1914, a daughter, Eunice, was born to Mabel and Stanley, their one and only child. Stanley had planned to be traveling outside of India around the time of the birth, but Mabel insisted that he remain with her in Sitapur. In a letter dated July 25, 1972, just six months before Stanley's death, Mabel recalled the incident.

> In these 62 years, I have only once interfered with his [Stanley's] programs & that was when he planned to accept an engagement out of the country just before the birth of our first & only!

In 1916, when Eunice was two years old, the Joneses went home to the United States on furlough. While Stanley was traveling in the East to meet relatives and friends, Mabel stayed in Clayton, Iowa. Since Stanley "could not be at home at all to help me with Eunice," she wrote to Miss Nellie on July 11, "and she is just at the most trying age, I thought it best to stop in this quiet little place until she becomes a little more subdued or I have a little more strength to manage her." Stanley had spent two days in Clayton on his way to North Dakota, Mabel told Miss Nellie, and she expected to see him again when he returned. She concluded her letter with the comment, "I hope to keep him longer this time but he has the 'wanderlust' so much developed that it is difficult to hold him."

Throughout his life Stanley continued to maintain a heavy schedule of speaking engagements. On August 3, 1967, when he was eighty-three years old, Mabel wrote to one of the officials of The United Christian Ashrams, which, as we will see, was founded by Jones to sponsor spiritual retreats in the United States and in a number of other locations throughout the world. Mabel thanked the official for sending her Stanley's itinerary. "It is not easy to keep track of him," she wrote, "but this has been his sort of life ever since we were married in 1911 & he loves it."

Back in India, when Stanley did come home to Sitapur, it was, as Eunice recalled years later, an occasion "for great rejoicing and activity." No matter how busy he was during his visits to Sitapur, Eunice knew that he would make time for her.

> Streams of visitors (both Christian and non-Christian), messengers with notes asking for interviews or invitations (there were no telephones—or electricity) filled up the daytime. I knew better than to interrupt him either in his morning devotions and writing or with afternoon visitors—for I was well aware the late afternoon was our time together and he would keep our tryst. It was our time for long walks or for bicycling together, or when I was older for tennis or badminton, in both of which he excelled.[6]

Stanley also had time for social activities with Eunice and her friends. When Eunice was sixteen, she described one such activity for "Aunt Nellie," in a letter dated February 5, 1930.

> On the 10th of January Dad took Betty and Nancy Moffatt and myself up to Allahabad to see the Kumbh Mela. The largest of its kind in 24 years. It was very interesting. We stayed with some friends there and they took us down to the Mela grounds. We were there about 6 hours, and passed nearly two miles of parading sadus which were mostly naked, also heaps of richly covered elephants.[7]

* * *

Because Stanley was so often away from home, throughout their married life Mabel took responsibility for almost all domestic matters, including finances. For example, on February 8, 1969, she wrote from her winter home in Orlando, Florida, to W. W. "Bill" Richardson, who was the general secretary of The United Christian Ashrams, about money she had received for her husband. "I am puzzled over what to do about cheques that come here for him." Mabel emphasized her point by describing a recent experience.

> After Stanley left we found a cheque for $500 in his waste basket pinned to a letter from some woman. I rushed it to him by air & hope he got it before he

took the plane. . . . You may have discovered that Stanley is better about getting money than about keeping accounts!

The gifts Stanley received for his evangelistic work were sometimes confused with gifts intended for Mabel's boys' school. On January 27, 1947, a few months after she had left her boys' school for the last time and returned to the United States, Mabel wrote to Dr. Sutherland, who was the assistant treasurer of the Board of Foreign Missions.

> Today an unsigned memo came from the B.F.M. [Board of Foreign Missions] stating "Total for Dec. $300. Amount credited to Dr. & Mrs. E.S. Jones scholarship endowment."
>
> This should be corrected. My husband has a very bad memory for business affairs. If he sees such a memo he will at once think it is something he is responsible for. Here is an instance. (private & confidential.)
>
> When I was home on my last furlough my bank in India which handled my scholarships, jumped to the conclusion that this account must be "joint" & sent the monthly statement to Stanley. He ordered it put into a Fixed Deposit for a year—to draw interest—& all my cheques to the various schools were dishonored. I had a peck of trouble over it. According to British law I could have been put in jail!
>
> *Do please* make the Board understand that our marriage relation is a private one & does not extend to scholarships. *If* he has a scholarship fund with the B.F.M. it is *on no account* to be confused with this one which has its purpose clearly defined in the contract which you gave me.[8]

Another perennial source of frustration for Mabel was Stanley's income tax returns. In her February 1969 letter to Richardson she writes,

> Every yr. (for 57 yrs) I have tried to get information from him [Stanley] for his Income Tax which he refuses to touch. He always says "Get a lawyer, if you can't do it"—as if any man on earth could do the Form with no information!
>
> When he was here, any time I could get him alone I had to try to get some necessary information from him for the Tax form. Finally by getting him to sign authorizations for me to get necessary information from his 7 accounts in 3 Banks, I think I have finally got statements that the tax man will accept. (Last year they called me to the tax office 8 times!!)

Mabel's busy schedule of activities as a missionary in her own right and as the wife of a missionary evangelist who was often away from home began shortly after her marriage to Stanley. On January 20, 1913, Mabel wrote a note to Miss Nellie, which she enclosed with Stanley's letter, thanking her for her Christmas gifts. Then she commented that Christmas was such a busy time for her and Stanley in Sitapur that "I fear we almost lose the Christmas spirit. It is certain, however, that one has no time to think of *himself.* Perhaps it is fortunate, for it keeps us from getting homesick!"

Several years later Stanley asked Mabel to write to a Dr. Walker in

Baltimore. Then he went "to the hills for a little rest before starting on another trip." Mabel wrote the letter as Stanley requested, but since he had not given her Dr. Walker's address, she wrote a cover letter to Miss Nellie, asking her to give the enclosed letter to Dr. Walker. In her letter to Miss Nellie, dated August 27, 1919, she also wrote about five-year-old Eunice, who had tonsillitis. She was having to care for her daughter because her nurse was sick. Moreover, she had "132 little boys under 12 years of age" in her school, about thirty of whom were "influenza orphans," children whose parents had died in the worldwide influenza epidemic of 1918–19. "They are having boils & sore eyes & all sorts of minor ailments. I should be in three or four places at once." In addition, she said, "it is *hot*" with the temperature in the upper 90s during the rainy season. "[O]ne feels as though one were in a Turkish bath most of the time."

Mabel concluded her letter with news about Lochan Singh, the schoolboy sponsored by Miss Nellie and other members of the Epworth League at Memorial Church in Baltimore.

> Lochan has adopted a little boy! A little boy (orphan) of 3 years was left here a few weeks ago. Lochan asked if he could be his brother. He bathes him, feeds him, sleeps with him & takes splendid care of him. I hope to get some plates for my big camera now that the war is over, so I can send you a really good picture [of Lochan].

Apparently, Mabel did not get the plates she needed for her camera because several years later she told Miss Nellie about her abortive, but amusing effort to have a photographer take a picture of Lochan.

> I am sure Lochan's face is "hoodooed"! I got a photographer at last & the large picture of Lochan he took for you looks about as much like him as I do! I have put it in the waste basket & send you these two taken with other boys —He is the exact center of the group in the small picture & is just in front of his teacher in the larger group.
>
> He had just been scolded in the small picture for not getting his hair cut when it was his turn on Sat. He explained he was driving monkeys out of my garden but he himself had no business in the garden so he got a double scolding!
>
> Then he got some boys to cut his hair & the next day appeared as he is in the larger picture without enough hair to run a comb through! If I ever get a photographer here again we will try [to photograph] Lochan again.

In another letter to Miss Nellie, written on January 26, 1921, Mabel again enclosed a letter she had written at Stanley's request, asking Miss Nellie to deliver the letter since she cannot find the address. Mabel explained that the enclosed letter was long overdue,

> but there has [*sic*] been so many other things that just could not wait. I have 149 boys just now & it takes lots of time to keep up a correspondence with

their patrons no matter how necesary or how much we enjoy it. We also have
to correspond with those who support preachers & teachers & Bible women.

Mabel also described Lochan's reaction to a book Miss Nellie had sent
him. "He was so pleased with his book. He carries it to school every day in
his bag & props it up to look at. It is difficult for him to read yet but he is
bravely trying. It will do him good."

*   *   *

There were times when Mabel took responsibility for writing the quarterly circular or round robin letters, which Stanley had begun to send to
his friends and financial supporters before he and Mabel were married.
On one occasion she agreed to tell about the boys' school. "Little did I
dream," Mabel began the letter on August 8, 1921, "of the sad story I
would have to write."

School opened July 20 and though it was boiling hot, boys and teachers
returned in good spirits and began to work earnestly.
    The following Monday I walked through the school and noticed little
Gyan was absent. I found him playing in the hostel. He said laughingly that
he had a headache and could not go to school. I sent him to bed and he ran
off still smiling.
    An hour later Miss George came running to me saying, "Gyan has just now
vomited twice and is unconscious." I started at once for the hostel and found
him dead. I tried to get a doctor but all were out. I finally decided that it must
have been a heat stroke as the day was hot beyond words. I telegraphed to
the boy's parents, who are our workers and we prepared the body for burial.
    As we worked Miss Rosaline came running and said, "Victor has vomited
and is turning cold." I hurried to him and found our lovely, plump faced,
fourth class boy as cold as death, his eyes and face sunk in, his finger nails
blue and no pulse.
    I finally succeeded in getting an Indian doctor from the jail. Before he got
there two more boys were taken. He gave a glance at the boys, said briefly:
"Black cholera," and went to work. He opened a vein in the arm, injected a tube
and gave each boy about a quart of saline injection. It was like watching a miracle to see warmth return to the body, the face fill out and consciousness
return. That night little Chunnie died before we knew he was really ill, and several others were taken down.
    My teachers, mere girls most of them, worked day and night with no
thought of their own danger and Rev. Albert Gulab and Crist Chand worked
with them. I sent telegrams to parents, tried to get the well boys off to their
homes, and segregated the orphans. The next day reports began to come in
from the boys who had gone home. James Sunder Lall who had run so hap-
pily to his train reached home safely but died at midnight. Noble Briscoe and
Solomon Har Dayal, splendid sons of our preachers, and dear little Chotte
Lall left in seemingly the best of health but were dead the next day.
    Each day brought more cases and more deaths until I felt I could bear no

more. My splendid boys, bright, clean, healthy, happy, promising little lads, who had been with me until they seemed like my own sons, snatched away while we stood helpless. I nursed the boys through 42 cases of influenza, 36 of small-pox; measles, mumps, malaria and all sorts of complaints, and we had saved them all, but this was a foe more terrible than any that had ever come our way.

The stress and anxiety of this tragedy were simply too much for Mabel. "I had not been well for several days before school opened," she confessed to her friends, "and now with the need of ten-fold strength and endurance, I collapsed." Two new missionaries in Sitapur, Dr. and Mrs. Rockey, took over the boys' school as well as Mabel's other responsibilities. Mabel telegraphed Stanley to return from Calcutta, and Miss McCartney, who was with the nearby girls' school, took Mabel and Eunice to Landour in the Himalayas. A doctor diagnosed Mabel's condition as "nervous collapse" and ordered complete rest for a month. Contributing to her illness, Mabel wrote, was "the long strain of nursing our little girl [Eunice] through typhoid last August and September and this last strain put on the finishing touches." But in spite of the devastating loss of so many of her boys at the school and in spite of her own breakdown, she testified to the depth of her commitment to the mission work in Sitapur. "I am planning to go down the first of September and gather together the scattered remnants of my flock and begin again."

A year later in a circular letter dated October 8, 1922, Mabel documented the enormous number of letters she had to write. Writing letters, she said, was "one of the bugbears of missionary life," because "it takes so much time that . . . we feel ought to be given to other things." From January to October 1922 Mabel calculated that she had "written 2,198 letters and dear knows how many post cards."

> Every patron of every boy wants to have every remittance for his support acknowledged and some patrons write three or four letters of inquiry in a year. Dozen[s] of friends of missionary work want material for missionary talks on every subject in India, from education of mass movement children to the theology of Tagore.
>
> Parents and relatives of boys must hear how they are getting along. Others write for information concerning the school or apply for work or want help, spiritual or material. I am also Secretary of the Board of Education and Chairman of the Building Committee and this requires dozens of letters in a year. Besides, there are the monthly reports to the Government and answers to communications from the Board of Missions and the Municipality, etc., etc., etc. So perhaps you will forgive me if I sometimes send a duplicate letter and if I do not write as often as you feel I should.

In addition to the letters Mabel wrote to sponsors about the physical and spiritual welfare as well as the academic progress of the boys they supported, she encouraged the boys, as soon as they could read and write, to write their own letters to their sponsors. However, because the boys were taught in their own language, Urdu, before they learned English, Mabel had to translate their letters to their sponsors into English. So the boys' letters to sponsors became another chore for Mabel.

During the hottest time of the year Mabel and Stanley often went to Kashmir for what they called a "vacation." But in fact they used the time to "try to get caught up in the correspondence." After their vacation in 1922, Mabel and Stanley returned to Sitapur for the beginning of the new school year. "I told my husband," Mabel wrote, "that I dreaded to come down this year for something always happened at the time school opened." And it did—

> this year we had a new experience. We had been having terrific rain day and night for weeks and a little creek about a quarter of a mile from our bunga- low began to rise. It kept rising until almost two feet of water flowed over our floors. We moved into the school house but that soon was flooded, too. So we moved again, this time into Mr. Hanson's house. I had just got the place cleaned up and was thinking of moving back when a second flood came. We waited for the place to dry up and seven weeks from the time we moved out we moved in again. We had just got settled when there seemed to be a cloud burst of rain. Water rose to five feet over the floors of the bungalow and three feet over the school. We did not have time to save any thing. Boys and teachers had to be rescued by Mr. Hanson and our Christian men and a squad of police through water neck deep. All my supplies of grain for the year are water-soaked and ruined—all the medicine, school books, supplies of every kind, furniture etc., etc. We have been drying out books and papers and clothes and bedding in both bungalow and school all week, and some- times I feel absolutely dismayed at our terrible loss. But God has always pro- vided in the past and He surely will again. Perhaps this is to test our faith.

On November 3, 1923, Mabel wrote a circular letter that she said might be the last one she would write from Sitapur for a while, because she and Stanley would be leaving Bombay on February 21 of the following year for furlough in the United States. Mrs. Thoburn, Mabel explained, who had taken responsibility for the boys' school during her last furlough, would take charge of the school again while she was away. Mabel also told her friends and patrons that there were floods again in Sitapur. "This time we had plenty of warning and got everything moved out." The people living in the area surrounding Sitapur, however, were not so fortunate.

> In 19 villages near Sitapur not a single house is left standing. Over an area reaching 175 miles north and south, hundreds of houses have been washed away, grain in fields and store houses destroyed, and countless animals drowned. For a country as desperately poor as India, this is indeed a great calamity.

Malaria and dengue fever are playing havoc with the poor villagers who do not have a roof over their heads. My office resembles a dispensary a good part of the day. I have given quinine and advice and sympathy until I feel almost bankrupt in all three commodities!

In that same letter, Mabel responded to friends who asked about the use of a motorcar, which she and Stanley had apparently acquired just recently. She assured these friends that the car was being put to good use and gave some examples.

Sunday. A school boy was tossed and gored by a mad buffalo. Rushed him to the hospital just in time to catch the Doctor who was leaving.

Wednesday. Mr. Jones drove 52 miles to preach at Lucknow.

Friday. Took a missionary just recovering from an operation, to an evening service and called on two people who were sick.

Saturday. Took a new missionary who had just arrived from America to the hospital to arrange for an operation for appendicitis.

Tuesday. A father sent for his son and daughter who were here in school as their mother was dying. By fast driving got them to the station in time for the only train leaving in 24 hours.

Wednesday. Went three miles to get a woman and take her to the hospital. The doctor said in another hour she would have been dead.

Later that month, in a letter dated November 28 and probably delivered by Miss Nellie, Mabel wrote to the members of the Memorial Methodist Episcopal Epworth League in Baltimore. She thanked them for their "support of a boy," and then told them what had happened to Lochan.

Lochan got very restless in school & wanted to go to work. I have put him in a Government Office for a year where he will get enough to support himself and I hope will be willing to come back and finish school. He comes to church & Epworth League every Sunday and keeps in touch with us & I hope exerts a little influence as a Christian boy in the office among about 30 Hindus.

His commanding officer is very pleased with him and even if he does not go later into definite Christian work it is a great deal to have saved a little homeless, orphan baby & cared for him until he is a good Christian young man.

Since Lochan was no longer in school, Mabel continued, she was giving a new boy to the Epworth League to support. The boy's name was John and he was the son of a Christian preacher. Even though Lochan was no longer a student in her school, he continued to be one of her "boys," and Mabel kept Miss Nellie and the Epworth League at Memorial Church in Baltimore informed about his activities. For example, she wrote to Miss Nellie on May 29, 1930,

I think you may be interested in knowing that Lochan whom you kept so long & who got so restless at the last has been with Stanley helping in the Ashram. He is his right hand man. Stanley says he does not know how he could have got on without him. He has developed a lot & is one of our family—ready to do anything—and Stanley can keep him pretty busy!

*   *   *

Mabel's letters are filled with references to her daily responsibilities. In response to a friend who asked, "I wonder what you do all day. Could you outline a day's work?" she devoted most of an undated circular letter to a long and detailed description of "a rather typical day."

5 A. M. to 6 A. M. Awoke on the roof, looked up at the sky and asked the Lord for help and guidance for the day. Had my bath and a cup of tea and a slice of toast and read a little from the Word as I ate. Made some boric lotion for a village woman who brought me her baby with sore eyes. Showed her how to use it. Took some onion seed to the garden and told the men in charge where to plant it.

6 A. M. Took prayers with the boys. Inspected the boarding house. Wrote an order for rice and salt and sent a man to the grain merchant with it. Found two boys in the sick room and investigated cause and gave each a dose of castor oil. Went into class rooms to see who was absent and why.

7 A. M. Returned to the bungalow as the health officer was waiting to see if we wanted cholera inoculations. Mail came and I answered two business letters. Village man: "My baby has had fever for five days. What shall we do." This reminds the blind man who pulls the pankah [overhead fan] to keep me cool, or perhaps I should say cooler, when I have time to sit under it! "My toe pains me very much." I look and find the nail gone and a festering sore. Clerk, "Will you please take these fees from the pupils and sign the receipts?"

8 A. M. A woman who was baptized recently, threw her arms around my feet and begged me to let her come to school long enough to learn to read. A Mohammedan official calls and asks if I have anything as good to read as *The Imitation of Christ* which he has just finished.

9 A. M. Investigated a bad odour from a school drain. Took a sick woman to the hospital. Started to write out a new time table for school as we will soon change from morning school to day school. Matron came with complaints against a teacher.

10 A. M. Took the carburator off the car to clean it.

11 A. M. An English lady who was in great trouble called for sympathy and advice.

Noon. Hot and tired. Laid down. Got up three times and decided to stay up. The cook wanted money for butter. The sweeper wanted a new broom. The mail man brought a C.O.D. parcel.

1 P. M. A note from the doctor saying that he would examine all the boys at 4 P. M. A teacher reports that the chalk is all gone. A father who wants to put his boy in school but fears Christian influence came to talk it over.

2 P. M. The pastor came to ask about some affairs connected with the church. A Hindu called to borrow a book. He is a well educated man and

getting interested in Christianity. He said, "After I read the gospel a while, I want to go out and help some one. I want to tell them of this good God. When I read the Vedas or the Puranas [Hindu religious writings] I never feel this way. Only the story of Christ effects [*sic*] me like this."

3 P. M. Cut out a dozen pair of pyjamas and sent them to Class four for their sewing period. Had lunch.

4 P. M. The Indian doctor came and we went over the physical condition of each boy. Found one case of itch and various other minor ailments. Wrote out his recommendations and ordered medicine.

5 P. M. Boy Scouts Commissioner called to see when I would have time to attend a meeting of the executive committee. He said the boys from the Mission school were the very brightest of all the boys who were enrolled as Scouts. He said, "What does your religion do to the boys? They have no business to be so superior, considering the fact that they are from our lowest classes."

An Indian Official called. He said, "I feel very discouraged over my country. Things change so slowly."

Discovered an Indian "holy man" going into the hostel. Ran after him and got him out and headed for the gate. He was dressed in a patch of cloth about the size of my hand, tied on with a string and his body was smeared with ashes.

6 P. M. A boy was brought to me for discipline for swimming in the river without permission. A man came to borrow 30 cents. A woman to beg for work. Grain merchant delivers rice and wants his pay. I make out his bill and get his signature and file the voucher.

7 P. M. An early dinner because I am alone and I want to get at the pile of unanswered letters on my desk and send a note to the little daughter [Eunice] away in Boarding School. And now I shall soon climb the stairs and look up at the stars and commit the day to Him.

One of the perennial problems of living in India, which Mabel does not mention in that account of a typical day's activities, is the problem of snakes. But her letters to Miss Nellie, like Stanley's earlier letters, do refer to the constant danger of venomous snakes. And in her duplicate letter dated September 10, 1930, she wrote about one encounter:

We are being constantly reminded in this land of God's care over us. Just as I finished the above paragraph, I reached into a cupboard that is always kept closed and locked and pulled out an account book. And clinging to it was the fresh, perfect, cast-off skin of a Russell's Viper. This little snake, whose bite would send one into eternity in 15 minutes, is hidden in there somewhere among my books and papers and five or six times today I have carelessly reached in to get something, never dreaming that there was danger. The only thing to do now is to call for one or two of the older boys and empty the cupboard at once to see if we can find the little villain.

I had intended to write you a little of the life of the boys here but the mail goes out in an hour and behind that door, within a foot of my head is that snake!

Every year, thousands of people die of snake bite. I think the figure was 47,000 last year. But in the 20 years we have had this school, although we have killed cobras and vipers on the premises and in the rooms every year, no one in our big family has ever been bitten.

Apparently, many of Mabel's friends and supporters wrote to her and asked about what happened to the snake in the cupboard, because in her next circular letter, written on January 14, 1931, she told the rest of the story.

Nearly every letter from home asks if I found that snake! You remember that I hastily closed my last letter to hunt for it. Well, we did not find it that day but that night about eleven o'clock our night watchman in making the rounds and testing the doors, nearly stepped on one at the threshold of the office door. It may or may not have been the one who left his skin for a calling card.

In the same letter Mabel wrote about other unexpected and frightening encounters with snakes in the Jones's household.

Our Eunice once had a narrow escape. She dropped down on the couch one afternoon and then decided that her head was too high. She sat up and lifted the top cushion and coiled on the pillow beneath, was one of these small brown vipers. We once found one on the stairway as we went up to bed. Another dropped from a window curtain. Another slid from the cushion of an easy chair, and still another hid in the top drawer of my desk. Surely God keeps watch over us!

The most dramatic and chilling story of a snake in the Sitapur Mission, however, appeared in Mabel's October 10, 1932, duplicate letter.

This morning, I lifted a board in Mr. Jones' room and missed a scorpion's tail by an inch. . . . We have killed several snakes and a centipede eight inches long in the bungalow, in spite of screen doors. Our most startling experience was to have a cobra six feet long jump at us!

The boys had discovered one in a store room. It was attempting to escape through an opening in the back wall. Boys inside the room prevented its retreat. Boys outside on the roof and men on the ground, all armed with long bamboo poles, were waiting for its head to emerge far enough to be hit. Miss Parks [a missionary who would take over supervision of the boys' school when Mabel went on furlough in 1933] and I stood at what we considered a safe distance, watching its wicked little eyes in the opening about twelve feet above ground. Suddenly, as though fired from a gun, it shot out straight towards us, over the heads of the men. We may be getting along in years but I am sure we broke any speed record we might have made in our younger days! It was finally killed and a few days later its mate was dispatched on our front lawn.

I often marvel at the way we escape, when every year so many thousands die in India from snake bite. . . . Truly His promises are sure that He will keep us in all our ways. When I think of how He has cared for us and our work, I feel like turning this whole letter into a testimony of praise and thanksgiving.

* * *

Mabel became well known among Christian missionaries in India for her innovative and spectacularly successful boys' school. When she was at home on furlough in 1925, she was asked for her advice about establishing a new Methodist boys' school in Bareilly, India. In a two-page, single-spaced, typed letter written on February 18, 1925, from Dubuque, Iowa, to Dr. Moss, who was probably an official with the Board of Foreign Missions in New York, Mabel gave an exhaustive and detailed account of the arguments for and against the proposed school. As a former president of the North India Board of Education for the Methodist Episcopal Church, she was thoroughly familiar with the advantages and disadvantages of another boys' school. Mabel also revealed in her letter that she had often taken in boys for her school in Sitapur from other districts that had no room in their schools or had no financial support for additional students. In fact, she wrote,

> Every year that I was at Sitapur I had to refuse many of the Bareilly boys and Philibit boys who were Christians and never had a chance to go to any school. That is one reason why I never doubted the need of a school at Bareilly.

In order to accomodate the need of these other districts for more schools, Mabel wrote, "I am willing to supervise a hostel for the [Bareilly] boys," but other arrangements would have to be made for their education. She also said that she had been asked "to take the big boys' school at Budaon," but had refused the offer for two reasons—first because there was no direct access to the school by railroad and it would be difficult for Stanley to go to and from the school. "Besides there are already two wives there who can do the work as well as I can. I am willing to do what no one else can, but not to do what some one else can do while they look on! (This is not for repitition!)"

Returning to the immediate issue of whether the Methodist Church should open another boys' school in Bareilly, Mabel concluded her letter,

> I am not at all anxious to have another boys' school. I have been tied to one for 14 years and sometimes it was an almost unbearable burden as I was nearly always alone and had my baby, too. But I am first of all a missionary and if I am given this school I will be willing to do all I can. But if the Board and Field think best not to start it it will not cause me any special grief! But please do not ask us to explain to donors why money & scholarships must be refused for so needy a situation.

As is clear from this letter, Mabel spoke her mind. She was not willing to assume responsibility as a missionary for projects while there were others who were equally capable of undertaking them but were unwilling to help. Moreover, while she would do whatever she was asked to do by the Board of Foreign Missions in New York or by the Methodist Episcopal Church hierarchy in India, she expressed some frustration with having to explain to donors who were able and eager to support foreign missions that their money could not be accepted because church bureaucrats could not agree on the organization and location of Christian boys' schools. This was by no means the only time, as we will see, that Mabel became exasperated with the Methodist Episcopal Board of Foreign Missions in New York.

The help Mabel received from the United States for the boys' school in Sitapur usually came in the form of money, but sometimes it included more direct and immediately useful assistance. While she was on furlough in Iowa in 1925, the Woman's Missionary Society at Memorial Church in Baltimore offered to make clothes for her students. Mabel responded to the offer by writing to Miss Nellie on April 23, 1925.

> I shall be very glad indeed to have a little help in fitting out my boys. I find I have a suit here & I am sending it today by parcel post. That will be better than a pattern. Any goods at all will do so long as it is washable. I use calico, gingham, muslin, plain or colored. The shirts can be made like our American shirts, too. The one I send is Indian style. They wear both kinds. But always short sleeves. . . . As it takes about 300 shirts & 300 pants a year for my school a little help is appreciated.

The Missionary Society made suits for boys, and in her first letter to Miss Nellie after she returned to India, dated January 20, 1926, Mabel thanked Miss Nellie for the clothes. The suits, she wrote,

> certainly came at just the right time. We arrived to find the school having a very hard time financially. The boys were in rags and Mrs. Thoburn sick in bed. We have had daily patching bees and the boys are fearfully and wonderfully patched up. Some times you have a hard time finding any of the original cloth on a garment! But they cover nakedness and keep out a bit of the cold wind. The first thing we had to do was to dismiss the old man who has been sewing for me at 16 cents a day for many years. I talked to the boys and they said they would make their own clothes, which was a very nice plan but it means supervision of course, and I have to give hours that I begrudge to it. Still I hope we are making character as we do it.
>
> Now about the new suits. The boys said they had never seen such beautiful clothes and they were full of ohs and ahs when I let them look at them. They handled them with the greatest of delight and revelled in the pretty colors.

Mabel was especially sensitive to the status of women in Indian society. Her boys' school staffed by women teachers was itself a direct challenge to the strict and complete separation of men and women in Indian education.

But even in Mabel's school there were strong and persistent remnants of sexual segregation. For example, on June 19, 1926, Mabel wrote to Miss Nellie about what happened when she hired a male teacher on a temporary basis.

> I have all women teachers, but because one of them got married in Feb. I had to take on a man teacher for a while. He was one of our Christian boys grown into a fine, upright worth while man. Because he was a *man* he could not, according to Indian etiquette have his class in the school-house where there were *women* teachers. So as long as I had him, his class had to meet in front of the schoolhouse.

On at least one occasion Mabel had a female student in her boys' school. A young Indian woman who converted to Christianity and was baptized had never had an opportunity to learn to read. So, Mabel explained, in one of her duplicate letters dated January 10, 1929,

> I am letting her go to school and pick up what she can, in any way she can. She sits on the floor with the boys and gets them to help her and follows the teachers around after school asking them things.

In the same letter Mabel told her friends and supporters about her visit with some Moslem women.

> Last week the old orthodox mother of one of our Mohammedan Officials came to see me with several of her daughters and grand-daughters. As we had tea together she said, "This is the first time we have ever eaten with Christians. I don't know what our relatives would say." A little later as they were getting into the carriage all covered up with huge sheets so no man could get a glimpse of them, she turned to me and said, "I want to tell you something. This is the first time in all my life that I have ever been in a home not my own." How one's heart goes out to these dear women!

Because she firmly believed that all men and women are equal in the eyes of God and because she wanted to do something to improve the degraded and inferior position of women in Indian society, Mabel taught sexual equality in her boys' school. This lesson of equality between men and women, she wrote in a circular letter on June 28, 1928, was taught by both precept and example,

> We are trying to teach our boys the equality of women and having women teachers helps. Often a little Hindu or Mohammedan boy who comes in as a day pupil and finds he has a woman teacher tries to show his contempt for her. One lad of six said to me, "Why do you give me a woman for a teacher? I want to learn something!"
>
> He is now a boy of twelve and the respect he shows his teacher is akin to reverence. He will never be able to get away from the fact that some Indian

women, and Christians at that, are intelligent, self respecting, worthy members of society.

Many Indian women shared Mabel's convictions about sexual equality. Once when she was returning to Sitapur from a tour of the schools (high schools, colleges, and vocational schools) where she had boys who had begun their education in her primary school, Mabel attended a woman's conference. She described the conference in a circular letter to friends and patrons dated February 1, 1933.

> I stopped in Lucknow to attend a few sessions of the All India Woman's Conference. It was a great gathering and we were thrilled to hear Hindu and Mohammedan ladies, some still in purdah [the Hindu practice of secluding women], urging that the purdah system be done away with; that they push female education; that they help enforce the law against child marriage; and one impassioned speaker said, "If there is an unmarried girl before me, I appeal to her to commit suttee (burn herself alive) before consenting to marry a man who has a living wife." She was vigorously applauded.
>
> One must remember, of course, that they represent only the tiniest fraction of India. But this mustard seed has life and it will grow.
>
> A Hindu woman said to me, "Behind every speaker I see a Christian who has taught and helped and encouraged."

Mabel herself was a role model for other women, not only because of the outstanding success of her radical innovation of a boys' school with women teachers, but also because of her reputation throughout the United Provinces of North India for intelligent and effective educational administration. In a duplicate letter dated April 8, 1930, she shared this public recognition of her God-given ability with her friends in the United States.

> In Feburary I was appointed a member of the District Board—a rather unusual honor for a foreign woman. This is a District of 2250 sq. miles, with a population of over a million. The roads, schools, hospitals, dispensaries etc., are in the hands of this committee of 39 members. This work gives me many points of contact with the wealthier and better educated Indian.

By 1930, of course, Stanley Jones was well known for his Christian evangelism among the intellectuals and the middle and upper classes of India. Less well known was the equally important role of his wife Mabel in educating hundreds of the boys who would later assume important Christian and secular leadership roles in Indian society. When Mabel first established the boys' school, however, her goals were much more modest. In her February 18, 1925, letter to the Board of Foreign Missions in which she stated the case for beginning another Christian boys' school in Bareilly, she explained that she first conceived of the Sitapur school as "the simplest kind of a school for the village boy. Something that would not wean him from his village home if he was found unable to profit by continuing in school." For this reason Mabel's school was a vernacular school. The language of instruction was Urdu, and the academic goal of the school was to teach the students literacy in their own language. Ordinarily only the older boys who were going on to high school were taught English. Mabel herself could only communicate in English with her head teacher because the other teachers were fluent only in their native language or dialect. The wisdom of providing this most basic form of education is revealed by Mabel's narrative of the lives of three of her former students. In her January 18, 1927, duplicate letter to friends and supporters she wrote,

> I wish I had time to tell you of the lives of some of the boys who have left us. One of you, some years ago, supported a little boy called Sundar Singh. He failed in the sixth grade and it seemed best for him to leave school. He joined the army but was unhappy. Then he came back to me and begged for another chance. We let him go to a training class for village teachers and two years later he went out to a distant village to teach. Last week I was in that district and Sundar's name is a household word. From early morning till late at night he carries on what he calls school. As the children cannot come to him he goes to them and he holds five or six schools a day in different places. His text book is the gospel of John. He is in dead earnest and a good teacher and in about eight weeks he has his boys proudly reading the Gospel in their homes and in the fields and anywhere people will listen to them. Masih Dayal, son of an ignorant and low caste coolie, is pastor of a prominent church in Bombay. Claudius Ram is in charge of a village dispensary where he acts as doctor to a large community who have no one else to turn to in case of sickness. He has married a fine Christian girl and they are showing what a real Christian home is like to hundreds of people who have little idea of anything Christian.

Many of Mabel's American patrons who sponsored boys often asked whether all her boys went into Christian work. "That is a difficult question," she responded in her October 6, 1931, duplicate letter,

> for the longer I stay in India the more I am convinced that any work done by a Christian in the spirit of Christ is Christian work as much as just preaching. Lives often speak *louder* than words. "I had heard him preach in the bazaar many times but until I saw him give drink to a bhangi (the lowest of low castes) and tie up his sore with his own hands, I did not know what he meant by his words."
>
> In these days of falling missionary income, too many preachers have had to be dismissed and have been left with no means of support. I try to have every boy learn to work with his hands. Even our smallest boys learn to cook and sew and weave beds. Older ones are sent either to industrial schools or apprenticed. And if they become Christian electricians, or carpenters, or shoe makers I do not worry. Many of our former boys are preaching and teaching and for them we thank God. But we do not know what is ahead for India.

In an undated duplicate letter Mabel mentions another former student who, although he was not a preacher, was a compelling witness for Jesus Christ.

> A Hindu spoke to me recently of a Christian shoemaker who had been one of my boys. He said, "He reads us stories from your Holy Book and they are good, but he is better than the stories. For if a thing is wrong he makes it right. He does not ask two prices for one, and his leather is good leather. Because he is such a man, we listen to get the secret."

*   *   *

In 1941, as Mabel neared the end of her active missionary service in India, she reflected on the successful careers of many of her boys. She took justifiable pride in the fact that the Christian churches in India were becoming self-supporting institutions that were no longer dependent on American churches and American Christians for leadership and financial support. On August 4, 1941, she wrote:

> Yesterday, I looked over the list of boys who have been here in school since we arrived in 1911. A great many have made good. Some are in very responsible positions in Government service; dozens are preachers and teachers; some serve in hospitals as nurses and compounders [pharmacists]; many are in business; others are electricians, radio mechanics, farmers, tailors, all decent self supporting Christian men helping to build up a self supporting Christian church. For many years now, the pastor of the Sitapur church has been entirely supported by the Christian community. They also give about as much more to benevolences. That is the ideal for all our churches. Then, if the time comes when we must leave or if mission funds are cut off, it will not be so disastrous.

During the early decades of the twentieth century, the Methodist Episcopal Church began to give its congregations on the mission field more and more autonomy. An important change in the structure and function of church government was made in 1929, a change both symbolic and substantive in terms of the increasing independence of the mission churches. This was the decision that the Central Conferences, which were the foreign missionary conferences of the Methodist Episcopal Church, could elect their own bishops. Within a year after this historic change was made, the Southern Asia Central Conference elected the first Indian bishop in Methodism, Dr. Jashwant R. Chitambar.[9] Mabel and Stanley Jones attended the Central Conference sessions in Cawnpore at which Chitambar was elected bishop. In her duplicate letter, written on January 14, 1931, after Central Conference, Mabel commented,

92

> We feel that at last the Indian Church is passing its infancy. It will need guidance for some years to come, but as the Christian Indian assumes [more] responsibility, it will free us for more work among the non-Christians, to whom we are called.

As Indian nationals took an increasingly active role in the leadership and direction of Methodist Episcopal missions in India, and as the astounding success of Christian schools like Mabel's boys' school began to be more widely recognized both in India and in the United States, Americans, especially Americans who were giving generous financial support to Christian missionaries in India, naturally wondered about the future role of Indians not only as Christian leaders but also as political leaders of their own nation. Mabel's friends and patrons often asked her about the political situation in India. But Mabel rarely responded to these requests in her duplicate letters during the 1920s and 1930s. However, her letters to Miss Nellie sometimes contain outspoken political commentary. Her June 19, 1926, letter speaks of the political and religious conflict between Hindus and Moslems that had become more important than their common conviction that British colonialism in South Asia must end immediately and that India must be given its independence.

> Hindus & Mohammedans are certainly at swords point these days. Riots everywhere. They welcome the English with open arms as their only Salvation. Quite different from their attitude a few years ago!

Several years later in another letter to Miss Nellie, dated April 15, 1931, Mabel gave her frank opinion about the prospects for Indian independence, even though she was at odds with Stanley on this issue.

> India is restless. The Mohammedans are especially so—but their wrath is against the Hindus instead of against the English. I am not as optimistic as Stanley and I do not see how the English can depart & not leave the country in the throes of civil war.

In the 1940s, Great Britain was at war in a desperate struggle for its very survival in Europe—and for its continued control of a vast colonial empire in Asia, Africa, and the Middle East. The irony and blatant moral and spiritual hypocrisy of asking Indian nationals to fight for democracy for the British in other parts of the world but for continued subjection to British imperialism in India became a persistent, growing, and dangerous source of conflict throughout India. In these years Mabel's duplicate letters contain much more political commentary than do her earlier letters to friends and supporters in the United States. There were a number of causes. Mabel was on her own in India. Stanley was not permitted by the British government to return to India from the United States during the war. Eunice had married a Methodist clergyman, James K. Mathews, who along with Eunice became American military personnel in India. In addition, several of her boys returned to India from prison camps in Burma with stories of the unspeakable cruelty of their Japanese captors. Her attitude toward the politics of Indian nationalism is best described in her July 12, 1943, duplicate lettter.

> If only the Indian leaders would get together and draw up a constitution and the Mohammedans and the Hindus would stop bickering, India could have independence at once except for control of the army and that is promised as soon as the war ends. But no. The leaders demand independence first. Then they will meet and draw up their constitution and in the meantime the country can run itself. And the Mohammedans and Hindus frankly say that they intend to fight it out and through Civil War unity will come as it did in the U.S.A. Well, enough of politics!

* * *

It is difficult to fully appreciate today the scope and depth of Mabel's commitment to her boys and to the school for which she was responsible. Indeed, it is only possible to understand the sacrifices she made in terms of her physical and emotional health, her time, the conditions under which she lived and worked, and the people and institutions with which she had to deal if we recognize and acknowledge that Mabel Lossing Jones, like her husband E. Stanley Jones, was committed above all else to her Lord and Savior Jesus Christ.

The month of May 1928 was an especially memorable month for Mabel. She revealed to her friends in a duplicate letter dated June 28, 1928, that she had had "four weeks of rather serious illness."

> The first week in May I came down with fever and an acute attack of inflammation of the larynx and wind pipe, plus quinsy. One night I fought all night long for breath and sometimes I felt I could not struggle longer. But a good doctor and a good nurse and later an operation on my throat all helped to bring me past the danger point and I am now hoping to give a few more years to India.

Moreover, the heat in Sitapur in May 1928 was especially intense and debilitating.

> I shall remember May for another reason. I have never felt the heat so much. Day after day the thermometer registered 110 in the shade and sometimes 114. Because of my throat I could not have a fan. We kept the house closed but when a door was opened the breeze that swept in was like a blast of hot air from a furnace.

Finally, Stanley was in the United States during May 1928 attending the General Conference of the Methodist Episcopal Church.

General Conference gave us a third reason for remembering May. There had been rumors in India that Mr. Jones might be considered for the Bishopric. None of us was happy over it. Our little girl wrote down fourteen reasons why she objected, one very personal reason being that she would have to leave Sitapur, her birthplace and dearly loved home.

When the Secretary of General Conference cabled me, during my illness, that Mr. Jones was elected I could only pull the sheet over my head and indulge in a very feminine cry! But after a bit there came peace and a feeling that somehow things would turn out all right. I could not understand it for in all my praying there had been the most definite conviction that my husband's work was not in the Bishopric.

And then his cable came saying that he had resigned and I knew that God had had His way. We will remain in Sitapur. I will continue the school work and Mr. Jones will remain free for the work to which God, not man, has called him.

Mabel was grateful that Stanley only accepted his election as bishop for twenty-four hours. In fact, she was certain that his resignation was an answer to her deep and sincere prayer and that his decision to continue with his evangelistic work was providential, a confirmation of God's call for him to preach the gospel of Jesus Christ. However, Stanley's faithfulness in responding to God's call meant that he and Mabel must pay the heavy price of a prolonged absence from each other and from the opportunity to be together as a family with their fourteen-year-old daughter, Eunice.

With the publication of his first book, *The Christ of The Indian Road* in 1925, Stanley became widely known and was in great demand as a speaker and preacher for Christian audiences throughout the world. After being elected bishop and then abruptly resigning in May 1928, Jones stayed on in the United States for an extended visit. Ralph E. Diffendorfer, a corresponding secretary for the Board of Foreign Missions, wrote to Mabel on November 30, 1928, about the agreement between Stanley and the board that he remain in the United States until Easter 1929.

There never was a clearer evidence of the workings of the spirit of God than is now manifest in the response to Stanley's messages here in America. It is generally agreed that no man since [Dwight L.] Moody has the hold upon American church life and thought than has Stanley.

The demand for him has been beyond that which he will ever know, for the invitations have been cleared through my desk. It would be safe to say that we could date him for evangelistic and missionary meetings of various sorts for the next year solid, including the summer.

It may be interesting for you to know that he has not yet spoken in any city where the hall has been big enough to hold the crowds of people who want to hear him.[10]

By the beginning of 1929, as she anticipated another Christmas holiday by herself, Mabel was acutely aware of her loneliness. She confided to Miss Nellie on January 17, 1929, "We are missing Stanley & feel like 'saying things' to the Mission Board!!"

During Stanley's frequent and often extended absences from Sitapur, Mabel was left in charge of their household and her boys' school and assumed all of the daily burdens these responsibilities involved. On October 6, 1931, when she was fifty-three years old and had been serving as a missionary in India for twenty-six years, she wrote to her friends and patrons in the United States describing the conditions under which she was forced to correspond.

> It isn't easy to write when one's fingers stick to the keys, and the swinging overhead punkah, which makes life partly bearable, dies down until I grow nauseated with the heat, and then comes to life with a jerk which scatters everything on the table to the four winds.
>
> The old Christian blind beggar with a blind wife and a deaf and dumb son whom we found begging in the bazaar twenty-one years ago and put at this work is growing old. But with stubborn determination he clings to his rope and refuses to surrender to a younger man.
>
> "God gave me this work to do and I will do it till I die," he calmly announced when I promised to continue his pay of $2 a month if he would stay at home. Sometimes when he dozes and I suffocate with the hot air, and then when he suddenly arouses and pulls like a hurricane over my dripping body, I wonder who will die first!

In addition to the oppressive and insufferable heat, which was a perennial problem of the plains of India for eight months of every year from March to October, Mabel had to cope with other problems which, like the heat, never went away but were sometimes worse than at other times. The need for money was one of these additional problems. In the early 1930s, contributions to Methodist Episcopal foreign missions declined rapidly, creating a financial crisis for the Mission Board. The board's response to this crisis, as Mabel explained in her October 10, 1932, duplicate letter, was to reduce all missionary salaries 35 percent beginning in September of that year. Her customary pleas for support for her boys and for Christian teachers and preachers were more urgent than ever. "Many preachers have had to be dismissed," she wrote, and "boys have had to leave school and some of our schools will probably be closed this year."

On February 9, 1933, the Joneses sailed from Bombay for their furlough in the United States. Mabel's next circular letter was written from New York on August 17, 1933.

> July 26, we sailed from Southampton and seven days later stood on deck straining our eyes for the first glimpse of America in eight years.

"This is my own, my native land," said a fellow passenger with tears in his eyes. But he had only been gone a year.

The Statue of Liberty emerged from the mist. "Why she's fat!" exclaimed a little old English lady in surprise as she looked at it for the first time. Well, perhaps she is fat but no graceful, slender Venus, no far-famed marble statue in the Vatican of Rome or the Louvre of Paris ever gives us the thrill that comes when we sight this motherly matron who welcomes us home.

"It's home again, and home again, America for me," the song keeps ringing. And yet there is India, poor, hungry, naked, poverty-striken, idol-worshipping, caste-ridden, God-searching India. . . .

But though India is ever in our hearts, it's great to be home again! India does sap the vitality of a foreigner and perhaps eight years is really too long to stay in a land so enervating. It takes too long to rebound.

But Mabel did rebound again and again. I like to think of her as still rebounding in the glory of God.

On the way to the States for their 1933 furlough, Mabel and Eunice stopped in Rome where Eunice enrolled in a Methodist mission school in order to earn some college credit before entering Oberlin College in Ohio as a full-time residential student that fall. The family was reunited for a short vacation in August in the United States before Stanley left on a speaking tour throughout the country. He returned to India in March 1934, but Mabel remained in America. In fact, she went to Oberlin with Eunice and lived in a house across the street from the dormitory. Once she had medical permission, however, she began a heavy schedule of speaking engagements across the United States. She spoke at woman's clubs, high schools, colleges, Sunday worship services, and meetings of the Methodist Episcopal Woman's Foreign Missionary Society. Mabel was gratified by the response she received from the attentive audiences who listened to her presentations about Methodist missions in India.

While she traveled around the United States, she continued to write duplicate letters to hundreds of friends and supporters, to solicit new scholarships for the Sitapur boys' school and financial support for Christian preachers and teachers. She wrote letters to maintain contact with her boys in India, who by 1933 numbered over 500, and to make sure that those who provided scholarships and support received timely information about the progress of the students and workers they sponsored.

Mabel's duplicate letters written during the mid-1930s describe her speaking tours and fund-raising activities in some detail. But the letters from this period also record her candid reflections on and critique of American society and culture from the perspective of a highly intelligent and morally perceptive observer who has returned to her native land after eight years abroad. On January 13, 1936, she wrote,

Sometimes, after a speaking trip, I come back sick at heart over our beloved land. Perhaps when we are in India we idealize America over much. . . .

Land of the free? I heard Dr. Fosdick preach in New York last month when I was there to speak at the "Bishop's Meetings" of the East N.Y. Conference. He emphasized our slavery to conformity . . . we look alike, think alike, talk alike, act alike, as alike as peas in a pod. No individuality, no independent thinking or doing. "All we like sheep" [have gone astray. Isaiah 53:6 KJV]. . . Land of the brave? Still we sit back without even a protest and accept things as they are. We seem morally paralysed. Even in churches, one sometimes senses a lethargy, a loss of morale, an acceptance of conditions of which we do not, cannot, approve as Christians but which we make no real effort to change.

If I were entertained only in Christian homes, saw only Christian people, travelled only in private automobiles, I might feel differently. But I am generally at a hotel. I travel by trains and busses. I wait in public waiting rooms. I talk with and listen to strangers. I have not been limited to one section. I have spoken in cities large and small in 22 states. And with a curiosity that is perhaps typical of a missionary, I have tried to discover what people were thinking, how they were reacting to the moral problems of the day, what they were doing—conforming, protesting or evading, ignoring.

I must confess that sometimes I have had the feeling that America should keep her missionaries at home, that Christian workers are needed too desperately here for us to share with any other land.

And then I remember that sharing is the very genius of Christianity. How could one be a Christian and disobey the command, "Go ye. . . ."

I remember the church spires in every village that I pass through. And I think of India with its thousands of villages that have never as much as heard of a church.

I read your letters and I learn what you are doing. And I think of the Hindu who laughed at the idea that his community had any responsbility for the five year old child who was starving on the street, for the sick man who lay by the roadside.

I remember that America can get to a preacher, can get to a church, can read the Bible for herself—if she wants to. But I think of the thousands to whom we have refused baptism in India because there was no missionary to explain what Christianity requires, gives and expects; no one among them who could read the Word were it given them; no preacher to teach them.

We thank God for America. Heathen though we be in spots, in rather large spots, there is still Christianity enough to transform things if it were put into action.

That Mabel Lossing Jones penned this perspicacious commentary almost sixty-five years ago does not diminish the sad fact that it continues to ring true—both for the state of Christendom in the United States and for the Indian scene.

* * *

Perhaps because of her years of difficult missionary service in India or because of her heavy speaking schedule and voluminous correspondence after she came home in 1933, Mabel was not well. She told her friends and supporters in her June 15, 1934, duplicate letter that she did not have the medical certificate required by the Board of Foreign Missions in order to return to India. Six months later on January 17, 1935, Mabel wrote to Miss Nellie from Oberlin, Ohio,

> I expected to be in Washington long before this but am still in bed. The doctor thinks I can be up by Saturday. I got up last week & went down to dinner but it didn't do me any good!! Will wait for orders next time.

In her next duplicate letter written on March 25, 1935, from Washington, D.C., where she was living with Mrs. Lum, "a delightful friend whom we knew in India," Mabel revealed that the illness that kept her bedridden in Oberlin during the winter and forced her to cancel her speaking engagements was pleurisy. In the same letter she informed her friends and patrons,

> I can accept no invitations at present. The doctors have insisted that I cancel all engagements for the spring and summer. I most deeply regret this. . . . But after a long search for the elusive germ which was suspected to be the cause of my fluctuating temperature and chronic tiredness, there seems to be general agreement that the cure is a complete rest. Since I want to get back to India some day I am trying to be obedient.

By the summer of 1935 Mabel was well enough to return to her old family home in Clayton, Iowa, where, she wrote in a duplicate letter dated August 1, 1935, "I pulled weeds, tied up grapevines, picked berries, climbed bluffs, visited the [Mississippi] river and lived outdoors." Although she planned to make a number of speeches in several different locations in the fall, she was still not in the best of health.

> I left Iowa feeling very much stronger; but my temperature continues to wobble two degrees a day and the infected ear and throat continue to pain. I am now taking electrical treatment for ear and throat and am to begin a course of treatment for latent malaria. Indian mosquitoes are very generous with malaria germs!

Mabel was able, however, to keep her schedule of speaking engagements during the fall of 1935 and reported in a November 7, 1935, duplicate letter[11] that her doctors had discovered what they believed was the source of her medical problems.

> I am very happy to say that I have started up hill physically. The "infection" so long sought has been discovered. I had no pain that seemed even remotely connected with teeth. But the last x ray revealed three that were suspicious. They were taken out and with one came a splinter of diseased

bone. The treatment was painful but the pain that I have had for about four years in nerve terminals, ears, throat etc., is nearly gone and temperature is nearly normal. Other extractions will be made after Christmas. The dentist said it was a marvel to him that I was alive with all that pus pouring into my system. Evidently God still has need of me.

For the next year and a half Mabel continued to accept invitations to speak in cities including Buffalo and Rochester, New York; Philadelphia, Scranton, and Harrisburg, Pennsylvania; and Columbus, Ohio. In fact, in her June 12, 1937, duplicate letter she reported to her friends and patrons that while she was in the United States she had "spoken over a thousand times in most of the thirty-five states east of Colorado" and had "averaged seventeen and a half letters a day," a number which "does not include the personal notes to friends."

On May 17, 1937, she wrote to Diffendorfer at the Board of Foreign Missions from Clayton, Iowa. Most of her letter was an expression of her serious reservations about Eunice's plans to travel with her father on his evangelistic tours and to act as his secretary. (Eunice did in fact accompany Stanley on some of his evangelistic tours after she took a secretarial course.) Mabel also referred to her own physical condition. She wrote that in trying to hunt

> for the infection that keeps my termperature between 96 and 99 daily and makes my throat swell till I can scarcely breathe, the last doctor ordered all my teeth out, regardless of what X rays show. The process is making me quite sick. They can only take two or three at a time before I am sick. There is evidently poison somewhere. I am spending this lovely spring between the dentist and the couch.[12]

A few days later on May 20, 1937, she wrote to Miss Nellie that she was following the doctor's orders very carefully because she wanted to return to India as soon as possible.

> I am refusing all engagements obeying the doctors much more carefully than I have ever done before, hoping to get back to India. I know it is of tremendous importance to raise funds for the work here but that is not the work "where unto I was called."

Finally, Mabel consulted specialists at the Mayo Clinic about her chronic illness. She wrote to her friends and supporters on November 5, 1937,

> Since my two weeks at the Mayo Clinic in Rochester, I feel more encouraged. They are very thorough and I was much interested to find that they did not agree with any diagnosis or treatment that has been given me since I came home! They asked me to begin my treatment by reading nothing heavier than a newspaper and by not writing a letter for six weeks. Think of it! They

seemed to think a facial nerve had gone on a rampage and told me that I would "have to exercise great patience"—as if I had not! Well, anyway, I already have a little less pain than I have had for years and I am trusting that the trouble will be cleared up.

The longer Mabel was away from India the more she missed her boys. Although she was still responsible for their financial support while she was in the United States and maintained contact with them through the boys' school in Sitapur, she knew that she could not be wholly faithful to God's call on her life until she returned to India. On July 7, 1938, Mabel wrote to Miss Nellie from Clayton about the plans of the Jones family to return to India.

> Stanley arrives in Sept. from Australia. We are counting the days—as you can imagine. We all sail Dec. 2nd on that jiggly boat the Queen Mary. Then 29 days later Bombay—Sitapur—my boys!

A month later on August 3, 1938, Mabel sent a duplicate letter expressing again her desire to return to India. Because she had heard and answered God's call to that country, she could never be happy and completely fulfilled in any other place. "The call of the need in India —the need to which we can in some degree minister—is too strong to let one who has known it, ever live in peace elsewhere."

Mabel, Stanley, and Eunice left the United States on schedule and sailed to London. From London Stanley flew to India for a conference in Madras while Mabel and Eunice continued their trip by boat. Although Mabel sprained her ankle on board ship in the Mediterranean "on a deck that had been waxed for dancing and later washed up with cold soapy water," she and Eunice arrived safely in Bombay. There they bought a Ford and drove 1,049 miles to Sitapur. In her first duplicate letter after reaching Sitapur, written on January 26, 1939, Mabel described the journey.

> On our way north from Bombay we stopped for a day at Khandwa where I spent my first years in India in charge of a girls' school. It was a great joy to see these "old girls," now mothers of splendid Christian sons and daughters, with clean, happy Christian homes and still working, many of them, as teachers and Bible women.

When she arrived in Sitapur, she continued, she felt that she had come home. "There has been a constant procession of 'old boys' telling us of their work and plans and families. It makes the years that we have given to the work seem very much worth while." In a handwritten note to Miss Nellie at the bottom of her duplicate letter Mabel added, "My visit home seems a dream. It's good to be back where I feel more worth while."

* * *

Mabel's life in Sitapur after she returned in 1939 was much the same as her life before she left in 1933. She supervised the daily operation of the boys' school, she corresponded regularly with friends who sponsored boys or Christian teachers and preachers, she gave advice and counsel and sometimes medical assistance to those who came to her for help, she served on many boards and committees both for the Methodist Episcopal Church and for the government, and she maintained her own household. Stanley was almost always away from home, either out of town or out of the country on evangelistic tours. Eunice graduated from American University and sometimes traveled with her father. She was soon to marry James K. Mathews, a Methodist missionary in India.

At the same time, Mabel's life was also different when she came back to India. She was now sixty-one years old and had endured years of painful and debilitating illness. In addition, the world was on the brink of World War II and the days of British colonialism in India were numbered. All of these events, both the unchanging routine of life in Sitapur and the changing national and international events, are reflected in Mabel's duplicate letters and in her letters to Miss Nellie.

The most striking difference, however, in her letters during the 1940s, as compared with her letters up until the mid-1930s, is her reaction to the Indian climate and to the burden of all the responsibilities she had assumed. During the early years in Sitapur, after she and Stanley were married and she had established the boys' school, she writes that the weather is a nuisance and the snakes and insects and primitive living conditions are inconvenient and troublesome. The epidemics of cholera, smallpox, and typhoid and the devastating floods are the most difficult things to endure. But the letters show that even these tragedies were overcome by Mabel's indomitable faith in God and commitment to God's call on her life to carry the good news of the gospel of Jesus Christ to the boys and young men of India. By the time she left India in 1933, however, her health was failing and the merciless heat was becoming oppressive and insufferable. Problems with insufficient scholarships for boys and dwindling funds for preachers and teachers, which had been perennial, almost routine, sources of frustration, became major crises.

These difficulties are more frequently and more prominently mentioned in Mabel's later letters, especially those written in the 1940s during her last tour of missionary service. For example, she begins her September 30, 1944, duplicate letter with this paragraph:

> Our six months of heat, exhausting, debilitating, prostrating, paralyzing, relentless and often almost unendurable, are almost over. . . . But there have

been times when dripping with perspiration, prickling with prickly heat, smarting with heat boils and sweltering through a sleepless night on the roof top, with jackals howling and bats flying and watchmen yelling and beating tin cans to keep the flying foxes from destroying the garden, and with not enough breeze to stir a feather, —there have been times when I feel like quoting a good many remarks made by poor old Job!

Mabel ended her letter with these words: "There are days when I wonder how much longer I can carry on. But underneath are the Everlasting Arms. We rest in him."

A year later on November 20, 1945, Mabel wrote to her friends and patrons, "The war is over. But our anxieties are not." She went on to say, "In January I begin the eighth year of the hardest term I have ever had in India."

In March of the following year Stanley was finally permitted by the British Government to return to India and Mabel was ready to go home. In her March 28, 1946, circular letter she told her friends and supporters,

I am not really ill but two doctors have ordered me out of the country before the extreme heat begins. They find a "tired heart," whatever that may be, and a few other odds and ends, not surprising after these long, hard years.

Although Mabel returned to the United States in 1946, she never really left her boys. In an undated duplicate letter written from Clayton, Iowa,[13] after leaving India she wrote,

6:20 am, September first, and if I were back in Sitapur, India, the bell would now be ringing for chapel and my little army of boys all washed and combed would be marching into the school assembly room. At daybreak, they had got up, made their beds, swept the floors, cleaned the yard and prepared rice and vegetables for their breakfast which would cook under the watchful eye of the matron and be ready to eat when school closed at eleven o'clock.

I, too, would have been up when the rising bell rang and after a cup of tea, I would have gone to the "sick room" to see the boys with malaria and sore eyes and boils; I would have inspected the orchard and garden and the big baskets of vegetables brought in to be sent to the boys' cook house; I would probably have seen a few sick people from the near by village and a few parents with special requests; I would have had private sessions with boys the matron had sent for discipline . . . torn clothes, dirty necks, throwing stones, even fighting, for our boys are perfectly normal boys, acting as boys do the world over.

I seem to see again the glistening whiteness of the Jasamine, catch the delicate fragrance of the Rangoon creeper that sprawls over the office window; hear the call of the wild peacock in the trees at the little river in front of the bungalow. But I remember something else! On this September morning in Iowa, breathing in the fresh, cool, sweet air, I think of the steaming, humid heat of September in India, enervating, fatiguing, prostrating; the scorpions, centipedes and deadly snakes that one must guard against; the musty smells, the mildew that overnight gathers on clothes and shoes and books. I think of the thousand and one details and problems of each day and then, though exhausted, working in the office until midnight on accounts, Government reports and letters; the sultry, sleepless, noisy nights, tucked in under a mosquito net. After more than forty years of this, could I stand it again? I doubt it. But still, if I had medical permission, I'd return by the first boat.

Mabel lived the rest of her life in the United States. She continued to maintain close contact with the boys' school in Sitapur, soliciting scholarship support for the students and keeping up to date with their activities and achievements. She spent the winter months in the home she and Stanley bought in Orlando, Florida, while in the summer she lived in her family home in Clayton, Iowa.

Mabel Lossing Jones died in May 1978, five years after Stanley's death in 1973 and shortly after her one hundredth birthday on April 3.[14]

4

Sitapur, India: Ultimate Commitment and the Growth of Vision

My head is troubling me and I must go off tomorrow for a rest in the hills. . . .
—E. Stanley Jones—August 20, 1917,
letter to Miss Nellie from Sitapur, India

SEVERAL YEARS BEFORE Mabel Jones's 1921 collapse and nervous breakdown after the long and traumatic experiences of nursing their daughter Eunice through typhoid fever and having so many of the school boys die from black cholera, there had been another breakdown in the Jones family. Stanley Jones, overwhelmed and exhausted by the burden of his own multiple responsibilities, experienced a series of collapses. The result was an early furlough for the Jones family.

Ordinarily, male Methodist Episcopal missionaries were entitled to a year's furlough after ten years of foreign mission service. Stanley had arrived in India in November 1907 and had officially assumed his duties in Lucknow after his first Annual Conference in January 1908. His first furlough, then, was due in 1918. But after "eight and a half years," Jones confessed in his spiritual autobiography, "I began to have nervous collapses, short of a nervous breakdown."[1]

The fact that he collapsed on a number of occasions is not surprising in light of the staggering responsibilities he assumed as a first-term missionary. In addition to his village work and his English evangelistic meetings, he shared with Mabel oversight of the boys' school and of other Methodist mission activities in Sitapur. As early as January 21, 1913, he wrote to Miss Nellie about oscillating "between plastering & preaching and bossing [Indian workmen] and beseeching!" because of construction that was being completed at the Mission.

Three months later on March 16, 1913, he described himself as "a house builder & contractor and labor extractor and a beater down of savages and setter of prices and settler of disputes & punisher of boys and preacher of the gospel and comforter to the persecuted few Christians and so on ad tireddom!"

The next year, at the January 1914 Annual Conference for North India, Stanley was given the additional administrative burden of supervising all the churches and clergy as district superintendent for the Lucknow district. Just after conference was over, he reported to Miss Nellie, in his January 21, 1914, letter, that he was now "the youngest D.S. in Methodism." To emphasize the scope and difficulty of the work he was adding to his job description, Jones contrasts a Methodist Episcopal district superintendent in the United States, with whom Miss Nellie is familiar, to a district superintendent in India. "A D.S. ship is a play spell at home compared to one out here." Moreover, supervising the Lucknow district was a much larger task than supervising most Methodist districts in India because, "Lucknow is the hub of Methodism in Southern Asia. Everything big is there, Colleges, Press, Large churches etc."

From the standpoint of today's stress-savvy culture, a clinical reading of Jones's bouts with "mental fatigue" would doubtless label the underlying cause as hydra-headed—a case of job-related overload. His breakdowns were in great measure triggered by spiraling pressures encountered in his new and expanding administrative responsibilities. Under these circumstances, the fact that he became seriously ill was inevitable. He recalled in his spiritual autobiography, *A Song of Ascents,*

> In the midst of this period [November 1914] I was taken down with a ruptured appendix. A British civil surgeon took me fifty miles in an army truck to Lucknow at midnight to be operated on at the Balarampur Hospital. They waited till daybreak to operate, and when I came out from under the anesthetic, the civil surgeon of Lucknow sat by my bed and told me the news: "There were too many adhesions, so we couldn't take out the appendix; we could only drain it. When you recover from this, say in six months, you can have the appendix taken out." Not very good news! But worse was to come. About ten days later I awoke with my jaws locking; I had lockjaw, tetanus. Fortunately they found some antitetanus serum—a scarcity—in Lucknow, administered it, and it was touch and go for some time as to whether I would live or die. The tetanus spasms were severe.

Stanley's close brush with death had a humorous sidelight. While he was hospitalized, Bishop Warne's daughter Edith kept her father informed about Jones's condition. When his medical status began to improve, his doctor informed Edith, "We think the backbone of the disease is probably broken." But when she wired the good news to the bishop, the telegram read, "Doctor thinks backbone diseased probably broken."

After his recovery from appendicitis and tetanus Jones assumed yet another responsibility: He became the affiliated agent of the Methodist Publishing House in Lucknow. The Methodist Publishing House, he explained in his March 5, 1915, letter to Miss Nellie, was a large operation employing about one hundred fifty people. Then in the fall of 1915, because of the death of a district superintendent, he had taken on the job of being district superintendent for another district.[2] And he also became the superintendent of the Hardoi and Rae Bareilly districts.[3] Altogether he had five hundred paid workers in four districts for whom he was responsible. The personal impact of these mountainous responsibilities for both him and Mabel he summarized briefly in his October 27, 1915, letter to Miss Nellie.

> Mabel is not very well. She needs a complete rest. She works very hard. She said she found a fitting phrase to describe me: "a chased rabbit."

A month before admitting their need for rest to Miss Nellie, he had written to Dr. W. F. Oldham, a corresponding secretary for the Mission Board in New York, about their anticipated furlough in the United States. He and Mabel would "probably leave about the first of March," 1916, "if arrangements can be made for the District work and the Press and Sitapur."[4] His physical and emotional condition must have been obvious to his superiors in India and in New York, because in *A Song of Ascents* he revealed that he "was ordered to go to America on furlough" a year and a half before the end of his first ten years of service in India.

The real source of Stanley Jones's desperate need for furlough, however, was neither physical nor emotional, but spiritual. For the first time since he heard and obeyed God's call to be a missionary and evangelist of the gospel of Jesus Christ in India, Jones began to question whether he was really fulfilling God's will for his life's work. He no longer had the inner strength he needed to perform all of the tasks he had been asked by the Methodist Church to undertake. He lacked God's reassurance, the underlying and unswerving conviction of the Holy Spirit that he was God's servant and disciple in the evangelism and mission work of North India. It was this clear sense of spiritual focus and direction that he lacked when he, Mabel, and two-year-old Eunice left India in early 1916. And it was not until after the family returned the following year that Stanley finally received

God's answer to his fervent and repeated prayer for confirmation of his call to India and for specific guidance for the future.

The family sailed east from India because of the war in Europe, stopping in Penang, now part of Malaysia, and in Singapore. In spite of the fact that several members of the crew came down with cholera, the passengers were not quarantined and the Jones family reached Hong Kong in time to catch a connecting steamer that would take them on to San Francisco via Japan and Honolulu.

The passengers had another frightening experience on the way to Japan, which Jones described in his June 1, 1916, *Indian Witness* article, "Notes Along the Way," about the voyage from India to America.

> In the Inland Sea of Japan there was a scare on board when, at dinner time, our ship smashed into a large fishing junk and sank it. The heavy mast of the sinking ship tore off part of our side-railing. In trying to get out of the way of this one, our ship ran into another one and smashed it up.

The outward physical collision of the ships during the trip reflected Jones's inward spiritual turmoil. Although he did not reveal the true state of his mind and heart in the article, years later in *A Song of Ascents* he recalled what happened on board one Sunday morning when he led a worship service. The text of his message that morning was Philippians 4:13 (KJV), "I can do all things through Christ which strengtheneth me." But, he confessed, "I was preaching beyond my experience. . . . [And] so in the midst of my address everything left me. I had to sit down—a very humiliating experience."

During his year of furlough, Stanley addressed church and missionary groups under the auspices of the Board of Foreign Missions. He also spent several months studying at Princeton Theological Seminary. It was at Princeton that he first met Toyohiko Kagawa who was also a student there. They made little impression on each other at the time, but twenty-five years later they would form a deep and lasting friendship in a mutual effort to head off war between Japan and the United States.

When it was time to return to India, however, Stanley was not ready. He had received no inner spiritual reaffirmation about God's call on his life to be a missionary evangelist to India. On board the *S.S. Korea Maru* he wrote to Miss Nellie on January 8, 1917:

> First, (and I have told no one else this) I did not want to come back to India at this time. I wanted to stay and spend a year in study.

From the time they left San Francisco, it took Stanley, Mabel, and Eunice three months to reach India. They arrived safely, Jones wrote in his first circular letter (April 3, 1917) after their return, "in spite of raiders and the ordinary dangers of the sea. A good part of the time we travelled with lights out at night, and we had one or two exciting experiences."[5]

Part of the reason their journey to India took three months was because they stopped in the Philippines for three weeks. In Manila Stanley conducted evangelistic meetings for the University students. "In the three weeks," he wrote, "we had over two hundred who came out definitely for Christ. They were practically all Roman Catholics and the picked men of the Islands studying in Manila." When the Jones family resumed their voyage, they stopped again in Singapore. Although Stanley was not able to spend as much time in Singapore as he wanted, he did give "one address to the Chinese students there and about ten of them came out for Christ in an ordinary Chapel service."

On their return to India the Jones family received an unexpected welcome, as Stanley explained in the same circular letter.

> When we arrived we found a native brass band in uniform escorting us in. Eunice, our little girl, was not used to such a racket so she promptly cried! But we were all happy to see one another again and thanked God for His mercy.

Although "Stanley got quite rested" while they were in Manila, as Mabel told Miss Nellie on a postcard dated February 20, 1917, she also wrote that "he is using up all his surplus energy holding 3 or 4 meetings daily here for the University students."[6] And after he got back to India, the nervous collapses he had experienced before he went on furlough returned. "Almost on arrival in India," Jones recalled in his autobiography, "I had to go to the mountains to recuperate." His memory is confirmed by the second circular letter, dated August 1, 1917, which he wrote to friends and supporters after his return to India.

> Since I wrote you last the hot weather has come and for the most part gone, that is, the very severe heat. I was compelled to go to the hills and get rid of a bad head. Ten years of strain has told on me and I was on the verge of a breakdown. My head refused to be goaded any longer, so I took a month's real rest. I feel grateful that God gave me the sense to do it, for I feel fit now.

But in fact Jones was not "fit," because three weeks later on August 20, 1917, he wrote to Miss Nellie,

> My head is troubling me and I must go off tomorrow for a rest in the hills again, though I just came down a little over a month ago. This weather seems too much for my thinking apparatus. So I will go off for two more weeks & not look at a book or give an address.

After his second trip to the hills to rest barely a month after his first trip, Stanley was at the end of his rope. He remembered in *A Song of Ascents,*

> When I came down the second time, I knew the game was up—I would have
> to leave the mission field and my work and try to regain my shattered health.
> It was gone.

Fortunately for Stanley, for the work of the Methodist Episcopal Church
in Central India, and for the gospel, this was not the end. Stanley's memory continued:

> In that dark hour I was in the Central Methodist Church in Lucknow. The
> Rev. Tamil David was in charge of the evangelistic services. I was at the back
> of the church kneeling in prayer, not for myself but for others, when God
> said to me: "Are you yourself ready for the work to which I have called you?"
> My reply: "No, Lord, I'm done for. I've reached the end of my resources and
> I can't go on." "If you'll turn that problem over to me and not worry about
> it, I'll take care of it." My eager reply: "Lord, I close the bargain right here."
> I arose from my knees knowing I was a well man.

This time Jones was indeed a well man. It was not until he came to the
end of his own physical, emotional, and spiritual strength and surrendered
everything to God, that he could be healed. It was only when he was utterly
helpless and freely confessed his inadequacy and turned completely and
totally to God that he heard God's voice and received the inspiration and
direction of the Holy Spirit that he so desperately needed.

The word that he received from God on his knees in the Central Methodist
Church in Lucknow was not really a new word. It was a confirmation of a previous impression that he was called to preach the gospel of Jesus Christ to the
educated and middle and upper classes of India. Even before he went on furlough, he was speaking to and receiving positive reception from elite non-
Christian audiences. Back in 1915 he had described for Miss Nellie (May 15,
1915) a lecture he had given in Sitapur for educated people

> on "The Gospel and the Gita"—the Bhagawad Gita, the most popular reli-
> gious book in India among Hindus. The head judge of the city was chairman
> of the meeting. God helped me in showing that this book gives the heart-cry
> and the Gospel gives the answer. The Spirit was present.

As soon as he returned to India from furlough, but before his transforming experience in Lucknow, he continued to hold meetings, as he wrote to
Miss Nellie in May 1917: "I have begun my work among the educated and
it is going beyond my highest anticipations."

During the following year Jones continued to speak to educated audiences. His trip to South India, he told Miss Nellie (March 16, 1918), had
been "the best trip of my life. At Vellore huge crowds packed the Town
Hall. These meetings were for educated non-Christians. There was perfect
attention & the power of the Spirit was upon the meetings."

At the end of the year he wrote a long article for the *Indian Witness* (December 4, 1918), entitled, "Evangelism among Educated Indians." Reflecting on his own experience as an evangelist to middle and upper class Indians, he offered a number of reasons why Christian evangelists and missionaries must reach the educated elite of India.

> The social, political and religious life of a nation is built around ideas. These ideas come from the brains of the thinking classes. They soon percolate down and begin to find expression in the daily lives of the masses. . . . India has built her national life around the thoughts of a few great thinkers of the past. The educated classes have taken those ideas, expressed them, interpreted them, and India lives by them today. . . . So the key man in the situation is the man who thinks. We must get to him. We must change him and his ideas. In so doing we change the people down the line to the masses.

In terms of Christian evangelism, Jones insisted, it was not the lower classes of Indian society that had been neglected, but the upper classes. Winning high-caste Indians to Christ would not only make it possible for the lower castes to accept Jesus Christ, it was also the only way to satisfy their own deep spiritual hunger.

> A hungrier class of people does not exist. Does it not show spiritual hunger, or at the very least an openness, when they [upper class Indians] will give Indian-managed municipal halls for distinctly evangelistic addresses, when they will become chairmen of the meetings, and even sign the notices that go out, as if they were calling the meetings from their side?

We must become, Jones tells his fellow missionaries, the *gurus* of the educated Indians.

What drove Stanley Jones to focus on evangelizing the Indian intelligentsia? As a missionary with only an undergraduate college degree, did he really think he had enough formal education to present the Christian gospel persuasively to Indians with advanced degrees? There is no doubt that he knew God was calling him to reach educated Indians, but he seems, at first glance, to be an unlikely messenger for such a sophisticated audience.

As we have seen, he certainly impressed the faculty of Asbury College with his remarkable intellectual ability. And anyone who has read his books knows that he was a brilliant writer. It may be that he felt his gifts and talents were not ideally suited to the typical responsibilities of Methodist missionaries in rural India in the early twentieth century. There is little doubt that he felt frustrated and unfulfilled by bazaar preaching and village work. As a young man in the very first stages of his calling and career, these negative emotions, coupled with the enormous tasks he was assigned to complete, led directly to his breakdown.

When Stanley recovered from his emotional and spiritual collapse, he prepared himself for the work of an evangelist traveling throughout India. Each year during the three months of the rainy season he researched, organized, and wrote a series of five lectures or addresses, which he gave on a weekly basis during the rest of the year. These lectures, written for educated Indian audiences and delivered in public halls and schools where Hindus, Moslems, and Sikhs felt free to attend, were more intellectually challenging by far than his previous pastoral and administrative duties in the Sitapur district. He had to read and understand Indian religious classics like the Bhagavad-Gita. He had to be well informed about current events in India and throughout the world. Moreover, he had to be acquainted with the best popular and academic thinking of philosophy and the social sciences as well as religion in the United States and Europe.

In the 1920s he organized round table conferences[7] because he felt that his lectures were "too public and professional and not sufficiently personal" to be an authentic instrument of Christian evangelism. He used the same group of local Indian leaders and officials who organized and chaired his lectures to invite about forty of "the leading men" of the cities where he lectured to participate in a round table conference. He usually suggested that the local committee invite two-thirds non-Christian and one-third Christian participants. Each invited leader who attended was simply asked to share his own religious experience. Since the conference table was round, Stanley could not sit at the head of the table nor did he control the conferences. He explained his role in *A Song of Ascents:*

> I will not sum up at the close and draw conclusions—we will simply allow the facts to speak for themselves. Nor do I comment on what each has said. I always share last, lest they be discussing what I have said.

As an evangelist who was constantly traveling and constantly preaching, Stanley also constantly talked with individuals and small groups. He wrote constantly, continuing throughout most of his life his practice of taking three months in the summer rainy season for research and writing. After 1930 when he established his first Christian ashram at Sat Tal, he invited others to join him. Over the years those months became a time for study and discussion as well as prayer and worship. And he read constantly—on trains, in railway terminals, in hotels, in the homes of his hosts. He had a voracious appetite for reading anything that would help to fulfill his calling as an evangelist to educated Indians. In his notebooks, which, along with his Bible, he carried with him everywhere, he made notes on and sometimes quoted extensively from the work of psychologists like William James, Karl Menninger, and Dale Carnegie; theologians like George Buttrick, Hendrikus Berkhof, Paul Tillich, and Albert Outler; popular religious writers like Norman Vincent Peale, Gerald Kennedy, Leslie Weatherhead, and Elton Trueblood; and historians like John Baillie, Edwin O. Reischauer, and Arnold Toynbee.[8]

One of the most important requirements for evangelizing the educated, high-caste Indians, Jones believed, was for Christians to acknowledge and identify with the way Indians think. And, as he wrote in his December 4, 1918, *Indian Witness* article, educated Indians in 1918 were primarily thinking "nationally or rather Indianly." Indian nationalism was only beginning to grow and develop in the first two decades of the twentieth century, but all Indians and especially educated Indians were becoming increasingly aware of the sharp differences between European and Western society and culture on the one hand, and Indian and Eastern society and culture on the other. Moreover, Indians were becoming more and more conscious of themselves as Indians, as a people with their own long and rich history and as a people with a distinct national identity. In this intellectual climate of nascent Indian nationalism, Christianity was identified with European and Western nations and with their customs and values. These Western customs and values were not only different from Indian customs and values, they were alien and threatening to the national aspirations of India. This "lingering suspicion" about Christianity, Jones wrote, was "openly expressed" to him by an educated Indian gentleman who said,

> We have no real objection against Christianity, but we fear that when a man becomes a Christian he is lost to our national cause; that he takes his stand on the side of the European over against Indian aspirations. That is why we fear Christianity.

Jones went on to comment that

> India is aspiring, and rightly so, for ultimate self-government in national life. Suppose it would appear to Indian educated men that Christianity is opposed to this, that it cuts across this ideal, that it stands as Priest-of-Things-as-They-Are. Could Christianity ever have any real hearing with that man? . . . Christianity must become naturalized in India to influence Indians, just as an alien must become naturalized in America, before he can hope to influence Americans. It must get behind the national spirit, guide it, control it and bless it.

His conclusion:

> The movement toward self-government in India is inevitable. It may be a long, slow, painful process, but it is inevitable. What is to be done? Sit and criticize, or get in and evangelize? Is Christianity to be the Priest-of-Things-As-They-Are, or The-Prophet-of-Things-As-They-Should-Be? . . . Will Christianity be dragged into it when too late to really influence things, or will it be led into it by wise men in order that it may lead it?

This 1918 *Indian Witness* article is Jones's first detailed discussion of the relationship between Christianity and politics. He is astutely aware of the arguments of his fellow missionaries, both European and American, that evangelizing the Indian national movement, which was pushing for democratic self-rule and independence from Great Britain, will mean disloyalty to the British colonial government of India. But the British government itself, Jones points out, had already publicly declared that its ultimate objective for India was "self-government within the Empire." Nor does Jones advocate Christian missionaries taking an active and partisan role in politics. "To enter the arena of politics" actively, Jones insists, "would limit our influence." But Christians can refrain from making and publicizing comments that would associate Christianity exclusively with Western culture and values and would deny to Indians all opportunities to identify with their own history and customs and eventually to participate in their own government. As Christians,

> we must appeal to the man not as to a Hindu or Mohammedan but as to a sinner needing Salvation and Soul-satisfaction. You appeal to him as a Hindu and all his religious national past rises up to oppose you. You appeal to him as a sinner, and all his inner cravings rise up to meet you. We must appeal as man to man.

Jones's call to take the good news of Jesus Christ to the educated classes of India was necessarily a call to speak prophetically to the political situation in India. At a time when many Indians were beginning to apply the lessons of their Western education to their own society and culture and were asking more sharply and insistently why the doctrines of freedom and equality, which were the moral foundation of government in Britain and the United States, were not also the basic principles of government in India, Jones knew that in order to reach educated Indians for Christ he would have to learn more about politics and perhaps become more deeply and personally involved in politics.

Even before 1917 when he received God's reassurance and definite instruction to take the gospel to the educated classes, Stanley's letters to Miss Nellie often referred to domestic and international politics. For instance, at the beginning of World War I, his letter of November 20, 1914, expressed concern about the loyalty of India's large Moslem population to Great Britain after Turkey had declared war against the Allies and thus against Britain.

> They [the Moslems] profess loyalty but who can tell. Our mail is all being opened & censored now. There has been a great deal of espionage so Gov. has proclaimed martial law in some cities.

114

Six months later on May 15, 1915, he noted that the war in Europe was having an effect on Christian evangelism in India. The number of baptisms during revival month in 1915 was less than the number of baptisms during previous revival months because of rumors among the lower castes that Muslims were going to rise up and murder Christians. There was thus great fear among Hindus that converting to Christianity might endanger their lives. In addition, educated Indians heard rumors that Christianity had broken down in Europe, and this obviously made Christianity less attractive to them.

Another reason for the fewer numbers of Christian baptisms in India between 1915 and 1917 was the success of the Arya Samaj. The Arya Samaj was a movement founded in 1875 by a Sanskrit scholar from Gujurat, Swami Dayanand Saraswati. Dayanand wanted to reestablish Hinduism in its pure and original form. But he also recognized the importance of education and women's emancipation and founded a number of schools and colleges. Dayanand opposed the Hindu caste system and sought to make education, instead of birth, the basis of social status. Moreover, according to the Indian historian, Ranbir Vohra, the Arya Samaj was "the first purely Indian organization that founded orphanages and widows' homes."[9]

On the other hand, the Arya Samaj was a missionary organization that promoted and supported the reconversion of Hindus who had left Hinduism for other faiths. In this sense the Arya Samaj was a radical anti-Christian sect of Hinduism. During the second decade of the twentieth century it launched a militant propaganda campaign directed toward Indians who had converted to Christianity during a mass movement that was centered in the cities of Arrah and Ballia in the Bengal Conference of the Methodist Episcopal Church. Many of the Christian converts in this Northeastern region of India were Chamars, peasants who were members of one of the poorest and most exploited castes. The leaders of the Arya Samaj were known as Samajists and used a clever and effective combination of carrot-and-stick tactics to persuade and coerce Chamar Christians to renounce their new faith and to prevent more Chamars from becoming Christian. The Samajists simultaneously promised the Chamars more stable and secure land tenure if they resisted Christian evangelism and threatened them with deprivation of their land as well as social ostracism if they converted to Christianity. It is ironic that they effectively blocked

a mass movement by utilizing the very caste patterns, devices, and pressures employed, nonviolently, by the Christian mass movement itself. The missionaries had shown that certain caste pressures could move Chamar villagers toward Christianity; the Samajists now showed that reactionary caste pressures could move them back again. Nowhere in the Methodist field was the social nature of mass-movement conversion more clearly underscored by events.[10]

This is the interpretation of the Arya Samaj offered by J. Tremayne Copplestone in his official history of Methodist Episcopal missions. Just as the Christian mass movements began with the conversion of members of one caste in one village and then spread to other members of the same caste in another village, so the Samajists spread their propaganda from village to village among the same caste members. Jones, however, wrote an article entitled, "The Secret of the Success of the Arya Samaj," in the April 15, 1915, issue of the *Indian Witness,* which disclosed another and more politically prophetic reason for the effectiveness of the Samajists in reducing conversions to Christianity. In fact, this *Indian Witness* article is Jones's first published discussion of why Christian missionaries must pay closer attention to the growing popularity of Indian nationalism. The Arya Samaj, he writes, "was born at a stragetic time—just when the national spirit began to beat in India's breast." Jones does not deny the truth of Copplestone's insight that both Christian mass movements and the anti-Christian Arya Samaj reveal the crucial importance of the caste organization of Indian society. But he is looking to the future and he sees something that Copplestone does not see.

> Now no movement will succeed in India at the present time that does not ally itself with the growing national spirit of India. We Christian missionaries must learn that lesson. We must see to it that Indian Christians are not un-Indianized. . . . What is essential is that Indian Christians remain at heart Indians. That they get into touch with Indian national aspirations, study India's national needs and get ready to have a hand in the shaping of the India of tomorrow. Political India will desperately need the steadying hand of Christian ideals.

Jones's 1915 *Indian Witness* article anticipates by several years the beginning of Gandhi's first campaign of nonviolent civil disobedience on April 6, 1919. By that time there was no question that India "desperately" needed "the steadying hand of Christian ideals." Because of the increasingly outspoken and increasingly widespread Indian demands for independence from Great Britain after World War I, the British Government in India passed the Rowlatt Acts in March 1919. The purpose of these laws was to crush subversive movements throughout India. The Rowlatt Acts

> provided for stricter control of the press, arrests without warrant, indefinite detention without trial, and *in camera* [secret] trials of political prisoners, without juries. These acts moreover denied the accused the right to know who his accusers were or to challenge the evidence on which he was being tried, while requiring ex-political offenders to deposit securities and forbidding them to take part in any political, educational, or religious activity.[11]

In response to these acts, Gandhi established himself as the new leader of India by launching throughout the country a *satyagraha,* a soul-force campaign expressed through nonviolent civil disobedience, and by calling for a *hartal*, a closing of shops and businesses, as a symbol of opposition to the repressive British measures. The *hartal* was an outstanding success for Indian nationalists, although there were some reports of violence and rioting. The worst violence, by far, occurred in the Punjab in Amritsar, the holy city of the Sikhs.

Gandhi's April 6 *hartal* was observed in Amritsar without incident. But on April 8 Gandhi was arrested. The next day a huge procession of Muslims and Hindus paraded peacefully through the city to protest his arrest. Sir Michael O'Dwyer, the British Lieutenant-Governor of Punjab, ordered the arrest and deportation without trial of two of the leaders of the procession. On April 10 a peaceful group of Amritsar protestors went to the residence of the deputy commissioner seeking the release of their leaders. Without provocation, British soldiers fired on the protestors, killing three of them and wounding many more. The result of this precipitous overreaction by the British was widespread rioting in Amritsar in which rioters set fire to buildings and looted government offices and banks. Once again, British troops fired into the crowd and there were many casualties.

The next day, April 11, control of the city was given to General Dyer, who declared, in effect, martial law. Tension was understandably high among both the British and the Indian nationalists. The nationalists planned a public meeting for April 13 in Jallianwala Bagh, a public garden in Amritsar. Coincidentally, April 13 was also Baisakhi Day, a Sikh festival that attracted many pilgrims to the city. Apparently unaware that General Dyer had prohibited the meeting, thousands of men, women, and children gathered at the Bagh.

> General Dyer decided to display the might of the British Empire by personally leading a contingent of his troops to the Bagh, and after stationing them at the only exit that the garden had, ordered them to fire on the dense, unsuspecting, unarmed crowd. After 1650 rounds of .303 bullets had been expended and the ammunition exhausted, Dyer ordered the troops to turn around and march back to their barracks.[12]

In the aftermath of the massacre there was an official investigation by the Hunter Commission, which concluded that 379 Indians had been killed. Other reliable sources, however, say that the death toll was closer to a thousand, with even more Indians who were wounded. The Jallianwala Bagh massacre did not lead to the immediate end of British rule in India. In fact, after the incident the British remained in complete civil and military control of the country. "What they lost, after Jallianwala Bagh," according to one historian, "was the moral right to rule the country."[13] Other historians have commented that General Dyer was firmly convinced that he had saved the Indian empire.[14] In fact, he had signed its death warrant. Britain's time in India was up. From that moment, for Indian nationalists, the only question was how soon they could get rid of their British rulers.

Although Jones was sympathetic to the Indian nationalist movement and appreciated the unique contributions of Indian society and culture to the history of human civilization, he was not a revolutionary. He opposed the home rule movement led by Mrs. Annie Besant. In fact, Jones said in a duplicate letter dated September 15, 1918, she was "the greatest enemy of Christianity to be found in India." Besant was a radical social activist and theosophist who was controversial both in her native England and in her adopted land of India. She attempted to organize her own movement for Indian self-government and was imprisoned by the British colonial government.[15] Her imprisonment incensed both Hindus and Moslems, Jones told Miss Nellie in his August 20, 1917, letter, and led to meetings "from one end of India to the other." His attitude toward Besant, like his initial attitude to all social and political reformers, including Gandhi, was cautious and skeptical.

Jones's hesitation about social and political change was based on his understanding and interpretation of Scripture. Mark's account of Jesus' cleansing of the temple and driving the moneychangers out of Judaism's most sacred place of worship shows that Christ did not act on impulse or without deliberation. Jesus arrived in Jerusalem the day before he cleansed the temple. He "went into the temple . . . [and] looked around at everything" (Mark 11:11 NIV). He must have seen the moneychangers at that time, but he did nothing about them until he returned to the temple the next day. Jesus had a definite word for all reformers, Jones wrote in an August 21, 1918, *Indian Witness* article entitled, "Browsings in the Scriptures."

> Let us change what has to be changed at once and then look around on all things, sleep over the matter, and then in the morning light change what we still feel should be changed. But in whatever we undertake to reform let that night intervene. . . . If we do reform in the morning, we will do it with a clearer mind and heart. Jesus was right in His method—as usual.

If Jones was cautious about social and political reform in general it was because of how he interpreted Jesus' example in the Scripture passage just referred to. Jones was also cautious about specific reforms like pacifism. He wrote in his *Indian Witness* article that there is both a "right and wrong use of military power."

> Military power usually sets Jesus at naught. It is opposed to His spirit. When John wanted to exercise force against the inhospitable Samaritans Jesus

rebuked him and said: "Ye know not what spirit ye are of." [Luke 9:55] Jesus' whole temper was against the ordinary expression of force.

But are there circumstances in which military force is justified? Jones believed that Acts 21:32 is persuasive evidence that the answer is yes. Acts 21 tells the story of Paul's tumultuous arrival in Jerusalem. Some Jews from Asia stirred up a mob from the city to seize and attack Paul, but just before Paul was killed by the mob the commander of the Roman troops arrived. "When the rioters saw the commander and his soldiers, they stopped beating Paul." This last sentence of Acts 21:32 (NIV) demonstrates, Jones believes, that Christians can use military force

> to put an end to oppression and to protect the weak. Those ruffians stopped beating Paul only when they saw the soldiers. They would not understand reason. They understood force. That is all they did understand. So force must be used.
> The only Christian position seems to be then, that military force generally is opposed to the spirit of Christ. It sets Him at naught. It can only be justified and used to stop oppression and to protect the innocent and weak.

Jones was sympathetic with the Allied effort to recruit and organize troops to fight in World War I. Initially, he considered Indian recruits for the British Army primarily as potential converts to Christianity. He wrote to friends and supporters in a duplicate letter dated June 10, 1918, that there was "a good work going on among" these recruits in Sitapur and that "[q]uite a number" had been baptized. However, he pointed out that the recruits

> need teaching, for as soon as some of them got possession of guns they formed gangs at night and went out to the villages to murder and loot. There were forty-three of these escapades in two months in the District. The Government stationed watchmen with bows and arrows to watch for the marauders. And some of the looters paid the penalty of the accurate shooting of these watchmen, too. But on one front the British Government has howitzers and out here she has men armed with bows and arrows!

In his next duplicate letter, written on September 15, 1918, he reported that he was working among the British soldiers in Poona. He was a patriotic supporter of the Allied war effort and sometimes even believed that he "should go to one of the Fronts to help do" his "bit to bring this war to a righteous close." Jones saw no incompatibility between his Christian beliefs and war. But in the end Jones felt that he could do more to help his native country and its allies by bringing the gospel of Jesus Christ to the troops. Although many of the British troops were combat veterans and "hardened men," some of them were Christians. Jones had led one of these soldiers to Christ in Lucknow.

He was the toughest man in the regiment, a prize-fighter. When converted he became one of the most ardent Christians I have ever seen. He literally gave himself to soul-winning, leading numbers to Christ. He gained two military honours for exceptional bravery. He lies in France shot through with a German bullet. God punish Kaiserism!

At the end of the war, when the armistice was signed and President Wilson announced his Fourteen Points for international peace and reconstruction, Jones believed that Wilson's program created a historic opportunity for Christianity in Asia. On December 30, 1918, he wrote a duplicate letter in which he said that Wilson's position had "done more for Christianity in the East than anything that has happened in a generation." In fact, Jones wrote,

so enthusiastic did an Englishman and I become the other day that we sat down and sent President Wilson a cablegram praying God to bless him in trying to reconstruct civilization on Christian principles and urging him to remain firm!

In the years after World War I, however, Jones became a pacifist and remained an outspoken opponent of violence and war in any form throughout the rest of his life. In the mid-1940s he recalled in *The Way*, one of his most popular (and his personal favorite) collections of daily devotional meditations, that he changed his mind about the moral justification for the use of military force because he realized that it did not protect "the innocent and the weak." In fact, Jones wrote,

I saw that innocent and guilty alike were unprotected in war—it made no moral distinctions. . . . More civilian casualties took place in this war [World War I] from wounds, famine, and disease than military casualties. War protects no one—anywhere. It does the opposite.[16]

Jones's Christian pacifism was, of course, controversial. During some of the meetings in round table conferences, Christian pacifism was a topic for discussion. At first, it was not Christians but Hindu intellectuals who challenged his insistence on nonviolence. Hindu intellectuals who attended these meetings were often familiar with the New Testament and liked to argue that Jesus' cleansing of the temple in Jerusalem proved that Christianity sanctioned the use of physical force. In response Jones pointed out that in the account of the cleansing of the temple in the Gospel of John (2:14-16), Jesus used physical force only on inanimate objects and on animals by overturning the tables of the moneychangers and by driving out the sheep and cattle with a whip. "But to the men who could understand moral force . . . [Jesus] said, 'Take them out.' On the men He did not use physical force, only moral force."[17]

Jones came to believe that pacifism simply reflects the bedrock Christian principle of love. In order to follow consistently Jesus' command for all men and women to love one another as God has loved them, they must pursue loving ends or goals, *and* they must also use only loving means to reach these goals. A Christian "cannot," Jones wrote in his 1937 book, *The Choice Before Us,* "use force as a means and dismiss it in the end desired."[18] Means and ends are morally indistinguishable. For many Christians throughout the centuries since the birthday of the church at Pentecost, and for many Christians today, this is a radical and totally unacceptable claim. Countless wars have been fought by supposedly Christian nations for supposedly Christian purposes. Jones, however, insisted that war, all war, is wrong and that Christians who attempt to justify war misunderstand the Christian gospel. At Pentecost the Holy Spirit gave Jesus' disciples and other followers new, spiritual weapons that they were to use instead of physical force. These spiritual weapons were, Jones says in *The Christ of Every Road: A Study of Pentecost* (1930), *"the weapons of inexhaustible forgiveness, unquenchable good will, and limitless love."* [19] The problem is that Christians, like Jesus' disciples at his crucifixion, withdraw in fear from appropriating the gifts of the Holy Spirit and therefore surrender helplessly to the demonic forces of violence and hatred.

War not only poisons the international and domestic politics of nations by creating a vicious and endless cycle of revenge and mutual destruction, it has led to what Jones calls "the inevitable decay" of Christianity itself. By perverting and distorting God's kingdom law of love, war immobilizes all efforts of men and women to love one another and creates a stagnant and impotent relationship between man and God. For Jones the relationship between war and Christianity creates a simple but radically important choice. "If war is right," he wrote in *Is the Kingdom of God Realism?* (1940), "then Christianity is wrong; and if Christianity is right then war is wrong."[20]

After World War I Jones consistently opposed all war. As we will learn, he was an outspoken foe of Japanese militarism in China and elsewhere. He worked tirelessly in the months preceding the Japanese attack on Pearl Harbor to prevent the war in Europe from spreading to the Pacific. And twenty-five years before the Vietnam War he warned America that its continued imperialism in Asia would inevitably lead to war.

The consequences of human disobedience to God's principle of unmerited and unconditional *agape* love for human beings and of our reciprocal duty to love God and our fellow human beings with the same *agape* love is best illustrated by the development of atomic energy. In one of his daily devotions included in *The Way,* Jones asks rhetorically about nuclear weapons, "Did a method ever reveal its inner bankruptcy so absolutely?"[21] The massive, indiscriminate physical destruction and human suffering and death caused by the use of atomic weapons so overwhelmingly outweighs any possible "good" result of their use that no one, after the tragedy of Hiroshima and Nagasaki, would argue that they should be used again. But if no conceivable end can justify using nuclear weapons as a means, the reason for abandoning them is not just their apocalyptic destructiveness. It is the inherent immorality of any use of force, however minimal.

In 1953, eight years after the United States ended the war against Japan with atomic bombs, Jones published a collection of daily devotional meditations entitled *Growing Spiritually*. In one of the meditations he recalled visiting the exact location of the Hiroshima bombing. In the granite steps of a bank building was the outline of "the body of a man who was sitting there when the bomb fell." The granite surrounding the man "was bleached by the flash" of the bomb, "but his body protected the spot" where he sat, "and it was the original dark shade." Jones recoiled at this vivid but morbid demonstration of the effect of nuclear weapons.

> Was that man my neighbor? I inwardly cried out against this thing called war—the monster that turns all our neighbors into enemies. No time now to apportion blame. The thing itself—war—must be abolished.[22]

The fact that Stanley Jones changed his mind about war and Christianity shows not that he was inconsistent but that he was growing in his receptivity to the guidance of the Holy Spirit and in his understanding of how social, political, and military affairs were just as important spiritually as an individual's personal relationship to God. What distinguished Jones from so many of his Christian contemporaries and what continues to distinguish him from many Christians today was his complete and spontaneous reliance on God's word to him. As a result of the series of nervous collapses he experienced in 1916 and 1917, he learned that he had reached the limit of his own physical, emotional, and spiritual strength. In the end he could not rely on himself; he could not even rely on his own understanding of God's clear and unmistakable word that he was called to be a missionary and evangelist to India.[23] When Stanley Jones surrendered himself completely and totally to God at Central Methodist Church in Lucknow, he no longer relied on his own resources. He relied exclusively on God's Holy Spirit. From this point on, what mattered most in his life was not human intellectual consistency but spiritual consistency and fidelity to what God told him to do.

5.

Evangelism Throughout India

Oh no, he can come home by himself![1]

—Eunice's reply to Mabel's request that
she pray for Stanley's safe return home.

IN THEIR EARLY YEARS in Sitapur, when Stanley was not traveling in evangelistic campaigns as much as he did later in the 1920s and 1930s, and when he took more personal responsibility for the operation and administration of the boys' school as well as for the supervision of Christian workers and preachers in the Sitapur district, he and Mabel often wrote joint duplicate letters to their friends and financial supporters in the United States.

Their December 1, 1917,[2] letter began with Mabel's report on the opening of school six months before in July. She emphasized how disciplined the boys were and how hard they worked each day. In addition to their school work and their daily chores of cooking, cleaning their rooms and the school compound, and mending torn clothes, they found time to earn money for charities and to do extra work around the school in order to save money on staff salaries.

"This month," Mabel wrote, the boys "have pulled weeds and gathered up dry leaves and carried bricks for ¼ cent an hour to earn money for the Red Cross in Mesopotamia [Iraq]." Moreover, in order to save the ten dollars a month, which had been used to employ a matron for the school, "the teachers volunteered to do the matron's work and the boys promised to help." The extra money was badly needed to keep the boys warm during the cold nights of northern India. "Already," she said, "the boys complain of being unable to sleep because of the cold." The bedding Mabel wanted to buy for her boys was not wool blankets or thick, warm quilts but "ticks" filled with "soft grass." This substitute for real blankets or quilts was necessary, she explained, because "the price of blankets is prohibitive." Given the harsh reality of wartime shortages there was simply no way Mabel could afford to buy wool blankets for eighty boys.

In spite of all the extracurricular activities of the boys, their academic progress, as well as the overall reputation of the school, was superlative. Mabel quoted the conclusion of the government inspector of schools who had recently visited all of the classes in her school. "I know of no school in North India as well taught or where the boys are doing so well," he had said. Her conclusion: "As this is the only boys' school in North India taught by women we believe this explains its unusual success."

While Mabel was busy with the boys' school, Stanley was beginning his evangelistic meetings for educated non-Christians. In his part of their December 1, 1917, letter he tells their friends and patrons that he had just returned from Hardoi where he held a series of meetings. "Government officials, lawyers, judges, school teachers and students . . . filled the Town Hall," where he preached the gospel of Jesus Christ. On the third night,

> I gave the opportunity of asking questions. For three hours I underwent a cross-examination from about twenty lawyers before the whole crowd. When I got through I felt like a rag. But I was a very happy one.

By December of the next year, 1918, Stanley was able to report that he had just returned from a six-week, 4,500-mile trip by rail to Allahabad, Calcutta, Madura, Palamcottah, Trevandrum, Coimbatore, Vellore, Bombay, and Ahmednagar. Since trains were extremely crowded with military personnel, he sometimes slept on the floor. In each city he ordinarily held meetings for Christians in the morning and for educated non-Christians in the evening. "In between times," he reported in his December 30, 1918, duplicate letter, "there were personal interviews with awakened souls." The evening meetings were chaired by some of the cities' most eminent men, including "a member of the Legislative Council, two Principals of Law Colleges, Professors, Judges, a General, [and] other Army Officers." "Among these chairmen," he continued, "were Parsees, Hindus, Mohammedans and Christians."

Although these meetings were held in public meeting halls, not Christian churches, and although the chairmen and audience were mostly non-Christian, Stanley described the meetings as "intensely evangelistic. The power of the Spirit breaks through these hindrances and men are brought face to face with Christ." Many educated and high-caste Indians signed cards declaring their promise to study the Bible, and a number who had signed these cards earlier were ready to convert to Christianity. During one of his meetings for non-Christians,

> a Mohammedan was a most bitter opponent. He was ready to precipitate a riot. But the Spirit of God got hold of him and he came meekly up and said that he had changed and was now our friend. In some places the crowd was so large that the public hall could not hold them. They were standing in the aisles, at the doors and around the platform. For an hour and three quarters I presented Christ and scarcely a person moved.

In 1918 Jones began to hold interdenominational evangelistic meetings sponsored by the YMCA. He relied on the Y to arrange these meetings because, as he received more and more invitations to speak, especially invitations to speak to educated non-Christian audiences, he encountered serious logistical and administrative problems. At first, his use of the Y was a purely informal arrangement, but as his involvement with the Y increased, he sought the approval of the Board of Foreign Missions in New York. In an April 15, 1919, letter addressed to Frank Mason North,[3] a corresponding secretary, Jones reminded his superior that earlier the bishop and cabinet (consisting of all the district superintendents who reported to the bishop) of the North India Conference of the Methodist Episcopal Church had "heartily agreed" that he should begin to focus his evangelism on a widespread and serious effort to reach educated non-Christians.

> When I began I felt that I should begin in a small way and gather experience and the mind of the Lord as I went. I soon saw that I was wasting a good deal of time and energy because my tours were not well planned. I have been at the mercy of calls. I have had plenty of them, more than I could accept, but the difficulty has been that I had no one to plan these tours for me. The work was necessarily interdenominational, so no official of our Church could take the matter in hand for me. I have felt the need of the backing of an inter-denominational agency, both for preparation and follow-up.

Because all mail from India to the United States was delivered by steamship in 1919, it took several months for Dr. North to receive Stanley's letter. It arrived just as North was leaving New York for a trip to the Midwest. His reply, dated July 3, 1919, was written from Columbus, Ohio. He did not flatly deny Stanley's request to be "loaned" to the YMCA, but he hoped Stanley would not take this action "without our Board and the missionaries from India now in this country having an opportunity to consider the entire situation carefully." North continued,

> With the need of our Centenary campaign before us for the immediate future on the India field, I feel strongly that we should have available all our strongest men for service. You have special fitness to lead in our campaign for the English-speaking community, whether European or Indian, and I do not think you should enter onto a course just now that might handicap us in the great campaign that the Centenary in India calls for during 1919–1920.

A month later on August 6, 1919, after the Board of Foreign Missions had received a formal request from the YMCA that Jones work with them in his evangelistic campaigns, North wrote to Jones again, endorsing and encouraging Stanley's work among educated non-Christians.

> The movement which you are able to lead in this way is so true a realization of the hopes and prayers of many who have been concerned in our Methodist work in India that we greatly desire to promote your plans in every way.

However, North continued:

> We have a feeling that in our widespread work for the lower castes in India we have laid the foundation for the very type of work which you are doing, and to many of us it seems important that you should do this in connection with your own church. This, I beg you to believe, is not due to any narrow interpretation of the task, but on the other hand indicates how broad we consider the program which the church ought to undertake.

Instead of using the YMCA to solve the problems of "arranging meetings and securing the desired hearing," North suggested that these difficulties "could be overcome by the use of a better system of making engagements and a little more money covering the expense account. Neither one of these things is beyond the power of our missionary intelligence or our missionary treasury." The bottom line was that North wanted to delay a formal response to the YMCA proposal "pending the arrival on the field of Bishop Warne and B. T. Badley," who would later become a bishop.

On September 11, 1919, Stanley replied to Dr. North.

> I shall be glad to hear what Mr. Badley and Bishop Warne have planned. If it means that I should have to spend my time among the English Methodist churches, such a programme does not appeal to me, for while it is important, it is not strategic. . . .
>
> I do not think that the matter was made perfectly plain to you. I would hardly be taken out of the Methodist work any more than I am at present. But when I go to a station it would mean that I could get all the Missions working as a unit, where I can usually get only the Methodist Mission as it is

now. As I look down my list of engagements I have for this fall I find that in eleven out of the twelve places I touch the Methodist work in that place along with the other Missions. It would not decrease my contribution to the Methodist Mission, but would include the others.

It is clear from the correspondence that the Board of Foreign Missions in New York did not accept the YMCA proposal that Stanley be loaned to them for his evangelistic work. His last word on the matter is his October 17, 1919, letter to North.

Since the Board and the Mission did not see its way clear to accept the proposition of the YMCA, I placed before them [the Bishops at Lucknow] this proposal: Would the Methodist Church be willing to do what the YMCA was willing to do . . . that I should be separated for evangelistic work among the churches in India, and among the educated non-Christians, and that the Methodist Church would pay my salary and travelling, and other expenses connected with this evangelistic work. Mr. Popley from the side of the YMCA, upon his return from furlough in October next, could manage the campaigns. He would be the contribution of the YMCA giving the interdenominational touch; I, on the other hand, would be the contribution of the Missions. We would thus combine the two elements, the Missions and the YMCA in our campaigns. In the meantime before Mr. Popley returns from furlough in England, I would give myself to the work of the Centenary Campaign.

Earlier we saw how the Board of Foreign Missions probably missed a God-given opportunity for evangelism in India when it failed to respond to the pleas of missionaries and others in the field for more resources and personnel to meet the pressing needs of the mass movements, turning its attention and efforts instead to the Centenary Campaign. In a similar way the board probably missed a providential opportunity for broader and deeper evangelism of educated non-Christians on a cooperative interdenominational basis with the YMCA when it rejected Jones's proposal made by the Y and gave greater priority, once again, to the Centenary Campaign. Although the Mission Board approved and applauded Jones's successful work among educated Indians, it did not fully appreciate the need for this work. In his October 17, 1919, letter to Dr. North, Jones emphasized the imperative necessity of reaching educated non-Christians in India.

I think our Methodist Church is beginning to realise the absolute and strategic importance of this evangelistic work among the educated non-Christians. We must put Christianity into these National Movements or we will sadly fail.

In the end Jones was forced to compromise. He did continue his evangelistic work among educated non-Christians as a Methodist missionary. And the YMCA did make arrangements for his speaking and preaching tours in India on an interdenominational basis. But, to satisfy the Mission Board, Jones also committed himself to the Centenary Campaign. Had the board been willing to accept and support his initial proposal for an ecumenical approach to taking the gospel of Jesus Christ to educated non-Christians, Jones's full-fledged efforts on their behalf would have begun earlier and he would have had more assistance from the YMCA in reaching more Indians.

The nature and format of the meetings Jones held with the cooperation of the Y were somewhat different from those he had held earlier independently of the YMCA. In his own evangelistic tours from his home in Sitapur Jones followed a consistent schedule.[4] During the summer rainy season, when travel and public speaking were virtually impossible, he took three months off for intensive study in the Himalayas, usually at Sat Tal where, as we will see, Jones established his first Christian ashram. There he carefully composed a series of five addresses, which he delivered during the rest of the year in the public halls of every city in India that had a population of at least fifty thousand. Jones visited all of these cities several times in the course of his long evangelistic career. He would stay in one city for a whole week. The five addresses were delivered Monday through Friday and each took one to one and one-half hours to give. When he needed an interpreter, the lectures lasted twice as long. After he finished speaking, he answered the audience's questions, which had been submitted in writing. Responding to these questions often took another hour or more. On Saturday Jones held meetings for Christian laymen and pastors. On Sunday he preached in a Christian church. Finally, on Sunday night he took a night train to his next destination.

When Stanley was working with the YMCA, however, he followed a different schedule. In the morning he held meetings for Christians, which in cities with missions from more than one church were interdenominational or union meetings. In the evening he had meetings for educated non-Christians. At other times he conducted interviews for interested persons. In Vellore, for example, "the large Town Hall . . . was packed" every night for the non-Christian meetings. In his June 10, 1918, duplicate letter he reported that "God powerfully gripped" the audiences.

> So many Hindus came to see me at the time appointed for interviews that I could not see them one at a time. I had to see them in groups of three and four. Most of them asked the question whether they could not [sic] be Christians without leaving their home and their all. They wanted to be secret Christians. Oh, the price these people have to pay to accept Christ!

Stanley tried to involve non-Christians as much as possible in the organization and leadership of his evening meetings. He explained to Dr. North in his October 17, 1919, letter written from Jubbalpore (Jabalpur) that in that city he had arranged for "two members of the Legislative Council, two judges, and one [man] who is the head of the Mohammedan community, a retired judge" to serve as chairmen of the non-Christian meetings. None of these men, Jones pointed out, was a Christian. The invitations for these non-Christian meetings in Jubbalpore were signed by a "leading Hindu, and a leading Mohammedan, and a Christian missionary." Furthermore, Jones made it clear beforehand that he would not "speak against any one's religion" and that "questions would be answered." Finally, he announced in advance the topics on which he would speak. In Jubbalpore he addressed the following subjects:

(1) Jesus and Democracy
(2) Can Christianity be proved?
(3) Is Jesus fitted to be universal?
(4) Who was Jesus Christ, a Conscious Pretender, One Unconsciously Deluded[,] a Good Man or the Son of God?

After the meetings in Jubbalpore and in the other cities on his tour were concluded, Stanley reported the results of his work in a circular letter dated December 15, 1919. "At Jubbalpore, the non-Christian meetings were exceptionally fine." The hall in which these meetings were held was filled every night and the meetings lasted for two and a half hours. There were also meetings for Christians in Jubbalpore and in one of these meetings "31 people arose one after the other, confessed the sin of holding grudges and settled their fusses right there." On the next stop of his tour, Delhi, Jones said that the fifteen hundred people who came to his non-Christian meetings each night were "the largest crowd in the non-Christian meetings I have had anywhere in North India." He described the atmosphere as "electric with interest."

> On the last night as I presented the Cross of Christ to the non-Christians and in the closing appeal spoke to them upon my knees, God's Spirit mightily worked. All day long between meetings there was a stream of non-Christians wanting to have personal talks with me. Many signed Cards that they would study the Bible with an open mind and prayerful heart. They will be gathered into Bible-Classes.

Another positive feature of the meetings in Delhi was the unity among Christians. Anglicans, Baptists, and Methodists all came together for Jones's meetings, "the first time these three Missions have ever united in such a way."

Jones expected that the most difficult stop on his tour would be Godhra, a city with a reputation as "a hard and bigotted place" where there had never been a city-wide Christian meeting. But when he made it clear that he would not attack non-Christians but would only present the Christian gospel, the people of Godhra cooperated fully in sending out notices and personal invitations to the meetings.

> The meetings were held in the enclosed compound of a Hindu temple in which chairs, benches, and carpets were placed. The most prominent Hindu of the city presided at the meetings and Hindu ushers showed the people to their seats and a Hindu was my interpreter. The only thing Christian about the whole affair was the address.

Suddenly, however, when Jones was three-fourths of the way through his message,

> the temple bells began to ring furiously and the conches to blow for evening worship—rather it was the time to put the god to sleep. I was non-plussed for a moment because of the racket and thought everything was spoiled, but a Hindu arose and said, "Please sit down, Sir, it will all be over in ten minutes." I sat down and people waited patiently until the din was over and I went on as if nothing had happened.

In spite of the interruption, hardly anyone in the crowd of five hundred to a thousand left the meeting and went into the temple. In fact, Jones was so well received that he was asked to stay for an additional third meeting. After each address he was garlanded by the leaders of the city, and many non-Christians visited him each day for personal conversations.

In addition to the interdenominational evangelistic campaigns Stanley conducted with the cooperation of the YMCA, he also led a number of joint campaigns in India, and later in China, with his good friend and colleague, Dr. Sherwood Eddy. Eddy (1871–1963) was the first YMCA Secretary for Asia, a position he assumed in 1890. During his lifetime he published more than thirty-five books and is remembered today as one of the outstanding American student missionary leaders and evangelists of his time. Through the Student Volunteer Movement, which Eddy helped to found (see chapter 2), thousands of American college students became Christian missionaries and millions of dollars were raised to support their evangelistic work throughout the world. Eddy spent fifteen years with the YMCA in India and beginning in 1911 served as the Y's principal evangelist in Asia. In 1921 he established the widely popular and extremely influential American Seminars, which each year brought a select group of American educators and lecturers to Europe for meetings and discussions with the continent's political, intellectual, and religious leaders. The seminars were held in England, Germany, and Russia from 1921 until World War II ended the meetings in 1939. Their immediate purpose was to encourage the American participants to return to the United States and to speak and write about what they had learned. Eddy's ultimate purpose was to use this cross-cultural exchange of ideas as a foundation for international understanding and peace.[5] Among the American participants in the seminar was E. Stanley Jones.

Stanley probably did not know Eddy personally before they worked and traveled together in India, although, as we have seen, he had become intimately acquainted with the Student Volunteer Movement while he was at Asbury. He described the evangelistic campaigns he conducted with Sherwood Eddy in articles published in the *Indian Witness* and in duplicate letters written to friends and patrons in the United States. In his August 13, 1919, article in the *Indian Witness* entitled "Notes on the Eddy Campaigns," Jones reported that he and Eddy had just completed a six-month tour in forty-three different locations.

Like the campaigns conducted with the YMCA, the Eddy campaigns included meetings for both Christians and non-Christians and were also ecumenical. In a duplicate letter dated August 6, 1919, Jones said that "all denominations" took part in the Eddy meetings "from the highly ritualistic Syrian churches and the high Anglicans all the way to the Salvation Army." For all of the churches that participated, the goal of the Christian meetings was personal evangelism, that is, the responsibility of each Christian to be an evangelist. For the non-Christian meetings Jones and Eddy developed a new approach. At a strategic point in these meetings, the speaker announced a break in the proceedings for personal conversation. For about fifteen minutes "each Christian worker turned to his non-Christian friend and did personal work with him." This format for the non-Christian meetings was well received by both Hindus and Moslems. "It took the nervousness out of the atmosphere," Jones wrote, "established points of contact and introduced the timid worker to his task." In one place there were 123 baptisms on a Sunday morning among sixteen different castes.

The most powerful and dramatic evidence of the work of the Holy Spirit in the meetings conducted by Jones and Eddy was the testimony of those who confessed and repented of their sins publicly or made professions of faith in Jesus Christ after hearing the evangelist's message. "It was interesting," Jones wrote in his *Indian Witness* article, "to see an old robber chieftan stand with folded arms and confess his sin before the audience. He had never been caught by the authorities, had been too clever."

In another report in his August 6, 1919, circular letter Jones wrote that an "astrologer who had been deceiving the people got up and confessed his sin and became a Christian." Even the high-caste educated Hindus who were unwilling to leave their homes and families, which was usually the price of openly proclaiming Jesus Christ as their Lord and Savior, were deeply moved by the Christian gospel. At one stop on this tour, Jones wrote, "we found a raja who had an embossed picture of Christ on his letter heads and had written the gospels in Telegu verse." Although this man wanted to be baptized, he had not received this sacrament because, Jones explained, "it would mean a broken home. And he could not pay the price." One student, Jones wrote in a duplicate letter dated April 30, 1919, almost paid with his life for his decision to become a Christian.

> In one of the cities as a result of the meetings a student expressed his determination to come out [for Christ]. His father was so enraged that he put poison in some food that he was going to give the son. The boy was about to eat it when the mother could not stand to see him take the poison. She took the food away from the boy. That shows the power of Hinduism. The father would rather poison his son than see him become a Christian.

In Sherwood Eddy's 1945 book *Pathfinders of the World Missionary Crusade,* he described one of Jones's public meetings for non-Christians.[6] The title of the message for the meeting was, "The What and Why of Christianity." After his address Jones invited all who were interested in knowing how to find God and in living their lives with God's help to stay for an after meeting. During that meeting Jones outlined the ten steps that must be taken by anyone who truly wants to find God.

1. Review your own life.
2. Reverse whatever is wrong in it.
3. Return to God, who is revealed in Christ.
4. Renounce yourself and your sin.
5. Restore, wherever restitution is necessary.
6. Receive God's grace and his Spirit in your heart.
7. Relate the new Christian truth to your whole life, in your own home and daily work.
8. Replenish your life by a daily quiet time of communion with God.
9. Seek release of your personality from all the manacles and graveclothes of the dead past, to free it for service for your fellow men.
10. Rejoice in God as your heavenly Father and thank him daily for his unspeakable gift of Jesus Christ.

Another place Jones and Eddy visited was the Malabar Coast, which is the southwestern coast of India along the Arabian Sea. There they saw the work of the German Basel Mission, a large and successful Christian mission, which, before World War I, had established weaving and tile-making industries for the Indian national population. During the war the German missionaries were imprisoned by the British. Jones was told that from the top of a smokestack on one of the German Mission factories the missionaries had signalled the German warship *Emden* and had passed on sensitive information. He could not confirm the truth of this story, Stanley wrote in his August 6, 1919, duplicate letter, but he did know that "there were some thoroughly godly men among" the German missionaries and that "they will be missed from India," since he did not think the British government would permit them to return after the war.

Two years later in 1921 Stanley visited the Malabar Coast again and held meetings in Mangalore, where the pre-war German missions had been. In the October 26, 1921, issue of the *Indian Witness* Jones described his visit.

> Here they started a tile factory which is sending tiles all over the eastern world. Forty-five other tile factories have been started in Mangalore from the impulse given by the Basel Mission's factory. Thus do missions stimulate economically.[7]

By far the most Christian part of India is in the south along the west coast where the Syrian Christians comprise about one-quarter of the total population. Jones and Eddy visited the Syrian Christian churches, bringing a message of spiritual renewal in an effort to motivate and energize them for evangelism. According to tradition, the apostle Thomas was the founder of the Syrian Church and, Jones explained in his May 15, 1920, circular letter, there is much persuasive historical evidence supporting this tradition. Copper plate inscriptions dating from the fifth century A.D. establish the fact that the ruler of this part of India granted Syrian Christians certain privileges that were usually given only to the highest caste Indians. These Christians accepted and enjoyed their elevated social and economic status and tolerated the heathenism that was all around them. But in spiritual terms, Jones wrote, "They vegetated. Some of the churches have not taken in a convert for 1500 years."

Jones's judgment is confirmed by Kenneth S. Latourette,[8] who was the most eminent American church historian of the twentieth century. In 1936 Latourette wrote that the Syrian Church of South India "had, in effect, become a caste." The term "Syrian" is a bit misleading since it refers not to the ethnic background of the members of the church but to their ritual, which originated in Antioch and was, until the twentieth century, conducted in the Syriac language. In the mid-nineteenth century a Syrian Christian priest was converted in a Wesleyan revival and as a result of his reforms the Mar Thoma Church was born. At the time Jones and Eddy visited the Syrian Christians, this reformed branch of the church numbered about one hundred thousand.

For a young evangelist like Jones who was brought up, converted, and trained in Wesleyan Holiness revivals in the United States, the high church ritual of the Syrian Christian Church was a real culture shock. He described the Syrian services he attended in his May 15, 1920, duplicate letter.

> There are swinging censers and chanting priests and the sign of the cross being constantly made in the service but there is a deep devotion amid it all. Many of them have become truly converted, so the combined product is like being a Roman Catholic Methodist!

Every year the Syrian Christian Church held a convention at Marramannu (Maramon) in Travancore, India. Between twenty-five and thirty thousand people attended this convention, which, Jones said, was "probably the world's largest Christian Convention." He was first invited to speak to the Marramannu Convention when he visited the meeting with Dr. Eddy in 1919, and the following year he accepted the invitation. He spoke to the largest crowd he had ever addressed. Speakers addressed the crowd from the shelter of a *pandal,* a canopy constructed from bamboo uprights and crossbars tied together with cords and covered with coconut fronds.[9] It was a good shelter from the sun, but not from the rain. The meetings were held outdoors along the bottom of a dry riverbed.

> There are no benches for the people sit right on the sand. Because of the river banks I was heard distinctly to the utmost limits of the crowds. On one side there were ten thousand women, all dressed in white; on the other side twenty thousand men. There was absolutely silence in the audience and scarcely a head would move as I presented the Gospel. The services were not run by the clock. The last Sunday morning we began at 9 and when I pronounced the benediction it was one o'clock. The two Bishops in their long purple robes, queer head dress and golden girdles sat on the platform. Below them were about fifty priests in flowing garments. The tide of power rose day by day. The meetings started on Sunday and finished on the following Sunday. On Friday morning I realized that the decisive hour had come. When I gave the invitation for those who would surrender to Christ to arise they began to rise by the thousands, and there they stood in the presence of God while His power shook them. Practically that whole audience arose at the invitation, and there were muffled, but reverent cries of Hallelujah! We kept our hand upon the situation to keep down undue excitement, but the moments were tense. Some of the priests broke and wept over their people surrendering to God. Moments like these in the Convention were great—unforgettable.

While Stanley was traveling with Sherwood Eddy, Mabel remained in Sitapur. In addition to being in charge of the boys' school, she conducted and supervised other missionary activities in Stanley's absence. Mabel began her portion of their joint duplicate letter dated April 30, 1919, with these words, "I have felt as though I had a hospital instead of a school this year." She continued,

> About five weeks ago I took a homeless, more than half-starved, little orphan lad, who had been wandering about the streets, into the school. He looked more like a skeleton than a child, but he did not seem diseased. In four days

he came down with confluent small-pox. Since then we have had 30 cases, but all have recovered and will soon be back in school.

About the same time a fond, but foolish mother gave her son some green tamarind seed. He generously shared them with 18 friends and in two days I had 18 cases of dysentery. Then a case of sore eyes infected 8 other boys and several boys came down with fever and two with measles. To top things off our little girl became very ill with tonsilitis. All the time I had fever myself and had to disobey the doctor's strict orders to go to bed.

As I took temperatures, gave medicines, washed out eyes, looked after food, tried to keep sick boys isolated, and disinfected myself several times a day before coming back to my own child, I began to wonder whether I wanted a third term in India!

What was desperately needed at the Sitapur Methodist Mission was a separate hospital building for infectious diseases. So Mabel and Stanley Jones asked their friends and patrons in the United States to each contribute $700 to build a segregation hospital not only for the students in the boys' school but also for the "5 to 20 cases outside of the school" that Mabel treated every day. The Joneses received the money they asked for because a year later in their May 15, 1920, circular letter Mabel wrote, "Last week when I discovered two cases of measles how thankful I was for a place to segregate them, thanks to your generosity."

Another problem Mabel faced in the boys' school in 1919 was the rapidly increasing number of poor village Christians whose sons had no opportunity for education of any kind. Many of these Christians had been converted in the mass movements. Mabel felt a special responsibility for mass movement children, because Methodist missionaries had brought their parents to Jesus Christ and because the children were the future of Christianity in India. "Here in India," she wrote in her portion of their December 15, 1919, duplicate letter, "we are in great danger, through the Mass Movement, of having a Christian community so ignorant and untaught that they will be a standing reproach to us if not something worse." For this reason Mabel, beginning with the 1919 school year, admitted boys from poor Christian homes. Her hope was not that these boys would become preachers or teachers or that they would be so well educated that they would be completely separated from their parents and families and live completely different lives. Rather, Mabel said, her plan was that the boys would be taught to

> read their Bibles and write a simple letter; to do enough arithmetic to keep from being cheated in buying and selling; to learn the value of cleanliness and morality. [Then they would be ready] . . . in two or three years to be bits of leaven in their degraded homes and villages.

Although Stanley was traveling in evangelistic campaigns during many months each year in the late teens and early 1920s, he continued to have a hand in many of the daily activities and responsibilities of the Sitapur Methodist Mission. One of the most pressing needs of the Christian preachers and workers for whom Stanley was responsible was the need for transportation. In his early years in Sitapur these deeply committed Indian nationals had to walk long distances every day in order to reach the villages where they preached and worked for the sake of the gospel. But in his December 1, 1917, duplicate letter Jones informed his friends and supporters in the United States, "I have bought second-hand bicycles for most of my workers. This will double their usefulness."

If Jones's workers needed rapid and reliable transportation, so did Stanley and Mabel. I have already quoted from Mabel's duplicate letters describing how she used the first automobile she and Stanley bought in India. They had received the money for the car when they were home on their first furlough. When they returned to India in 1917, however, the British colonial government prohibited the importation of automobiles into the country and there were no cars in India for them to buy. So Stanley put the money he had been given in America into a "War Loan" or savings bond to earn interest. Finally, after the end of the war he took the money from the government bond and ordered a car. In a letter to the Methodist Mission Board in New York dated April 23, 1920, Stanley reported that he expected the automobile to be delivered within a few days. In the same letter he suggested that the board could save "hundreds of dollars" by purchasing cars in the United States and then shipping them to India for missionaries. Whether or not the mission board acted on Stanley's recommendation, he and Mabel did buy their own car in India— a Willys Overland 4—and made good use of it to fulfill their myriad and widely scattered missionary and evangelistic responsibilities.

There is an interesting Jones family anecdote about the new Overland 4. Stanley picked up the car in Bombay and drove it to Sitapur. Almost as soon as he arrived home, he left for a series of meetings and the car just sat. So Mabel and another woman missionary read the instruction manual and taught themselves to drive. When Stanley returned to Sitapur, Mabel drove by herself to the railroad station to pick up her husband—to Stanley's surprise![10]

By the 1920s Mabel and Stanley Jones were beginning to experience the high watermark of Western Christian missions in the twentieth century. In his *Missions Tomorrow,* published in 1936, Kenneth Scott Latourette noted that up until the time of the Great Depression in the 1930s, the size and scope of both Protestant and Roman Catholic foreign missions were truly unprecedented.[11] Another church historian, Edmund D. Soper, was struck by the fact that Protestant mission agencies alone had spent $60 million in the year 1928 at a time when $60 million was a staggering amount of money.

The year 1928 was the end of an era in Christian missions, Soper says, an era that witnessed the largest and most explosive growth of Christian evangelism since the first century A.D.[12] It is certainly true that this unparalleled growth of American Protestant foreign missions in the late nineteenth and early twentieth centuries coincided with our nation's overseas political and economic expansion. Indeed, throughout the twenty centuries of Western Christianity, the growth of the church has generally occurred during times of political, military, and/or commercial expansion.[13] This was true during the era when Christianity expanded into the Germanic world between the fifth and the tenth century A.D. The same association of religious growth with secular political, military, and economic growth occurred again with Roman Catholic missionaries in the sixteenth century. And finally, during the eighteenth and nineteenth centuries Western Protestant churches experienced vigorous and worldwide growth at the same time that the governments in their home countries pursued a determined and sometimes bloody policy of imperial expansion.

From a purely secular point of view it is certainly possible to view the foreign missions of the United States and other Western nations in the nineteenth century as "a kind of religious foreign policy."[14] But this is not the whole story. "Missionary zeal" requires above all else "robust religious faith."[15] Secular and pagan forces do not trigger revival and fuel the engine of missionary evangelism. Rather, religious revival and the response of faithful men and women to God's call to spread the good news of Jesus Christ throughout the world are the forces that shape and direct the course of secular history. Professor Soper emphasizes that Christian missions have always been born of revival.[16] For example, in England in the eighteenth century the evangelical revival led by John and Charles Wesley and George Whitefield gave birth both to the political movements for the abolition of slavery and for prison reform as well as to the Sunday school movement. Moreover, it was the same eighteenth-century revival in England that inspired William Carey to become a missionary to India and to establish what we know today as modern Christian missions.

If the 1920s was a watershed decade for American Christian missions in general, it was also a watershed decade for the American Methodists in India. Before 1920, Methodists in India generally followed Bishop Thoburn's policy of "religious imperialism," establishing and securing Christianity and Methodist churches in competition with the traditional non-Christian religious strongholds of Hinduism, Islam, Buddhism, and Sikhism. After 1920, however, American missionaries in India confronted a new and unfamiliar force—Indian nationalism.[17] According to the official historian of Methodist missions, J. Tremayne Copplestone,

India was now a country deeply in revolution, churned up as never before by turbulent forces of nationalistic feeling and action that were to result in less than three decades more in bringing down British power and establishing the political independence of the Indian people. How was Methodism to be related to the Indian surge toward independence?—that was the question.[18]

That the Methodist Church in India was aware of the rising power of Indian nationalism and that it felt obliged to address the issue of its own political status under British colonialism in response to Indian nationalism is apparent from the resolution formally adopted by the Methodist Episcopal Central Conference of Southern Asia in 1916. The resolution, written by Bishop John W. Robinson and adopted by the conference "by a rising vote accompanied by the singing of 'God Save the King,'" expressed the Church's "deep appreciation" for "the protection and liberty our Missionaries in British India have enjoyed under the British Government." Moreover, the conference instructed its Board of Education to suggest a curriculum for Methodist schools and colleges to instill patriotism and loyalty to the British government. In fact, the resolution went so far as to

recommend the introduction into our schools of what may be termed the flag salute, in which the Union Jack shall at a convenient time each day or each week be unfurled before the assembled pupils, to be saluted by them in words, from the various vernacular areas, such as shall express in clearest form an appreciation of the blessing, the protection, the justice which is enjoyed because of it, and the pledge of loyalty and service to the King, and to the country it represents, the ceremony to be accompanied by the singing of the National Anthem in the language used by the pupils.[19]

This 1916 resolution, however, was the last such enthusiastic endorsement of British imperialism in India. At its next Central Conference in January 1920 the Methodist Church in India simply asked Bishop Warne to express to the British viceroy, who was the highest ranking British official in India, "an assurance of sincere loyalty on behalf of our people, and of our earnest desire to co-operate in any possible way for the betterment and uplift of India." By 1923 the official action of the Central Conference included no reference at all to the British viceroy or to the British government in India. Instead, for the first time the Central Conference adopted a report, submitted by its Committee on the State of the Church, that the Methodist Church support and encourage non-Christian groups in India "in such national movements as reflect legitimate aspirations." The Central Conference in 1923 even identified one of these legitimate aspirations as the "movement to obtain *Swaraj* as the ultimate goal." *Swaraj* means self-rule or independence. In later years, as the Indian nationalists led by Gandhi and galvanized by his tactics of nonviolent civil disobedience became more outspoken and more insistent in their demand for the immediate and complete independence of India from Great Britain, the term *swaraj* would acquire a more radical connotation. But in 1923 the report adopted by the Central Conference certainly implied no commitment by the Methodist Church to the revolutionary goals of Indian nationalism. Nevertheless, as Copplestone emphasizes in his history of Methodist missions, the action of the Central Conference was "the Methodists' first official gesture of sympathy with Indian nationalism."[20]

When the Central Conference met again in December 1930 in Cawnpore, it directly addressed the issue of the political situation in India. Responding to the confusion of Methodists throughout India about what their attitude toward the Indian nationalist movement should be, the conference, acting through its Committee on the State of the Church, adopted a policy of neutrality. In other words, the Methodist Church refused to ally itself with either the British government or with the Indian nationalists. The conference recognized that American missionaries could not themselves participate in political movements or political activities. Moreover, it extended this policy of nonparticipation in politics to the Methodist Church as an institution. But at the same time it acknowledged the freedom of individual Methodists, whether Indian, Anglo-Indian, or British, to participate in the political parties or political movements of their choice.[21]

The policy of neutrality, however, was not the only political position adopted by the Methodist Central Conference in 1930. In fact, the conference implicitly contradicted its own insistence on neutrality by accepting the concept of dominion status for India and by committing itself "to help in every legitimate way" to make "Dominion Status a success." Dominion status was not full independence but would have given India a greater degree of self-government within the British Empire. Whether India should be given dominion status was, in 1930, the most important and most contentious political issue in that nation. The British government had officially declared its intention to seek dominion status for India, and a number of moderate nationalist groups in India supported the British policy. But the Indian National Congress, a political party and the largest nationalist organization in India, rejected the position of the moderates and demanded full independence. Moreover, the Congress decided to boycott the round table conference, which the British government had convened in London to discuss the implementation of dominion status for India. Finally, in the midst of the political debate about dominion status, Gandhi began his second campaign of civil disobedience and noncooperation. It was at this time that the Methodist Central Conference not only pledged its support for dominion status but also voted to set aside time for intercessory prayer for the success of the round table conference. In these circumstances, as the official history of Methodist missions notes, for the Central Conference to come out . . . for dominion status was to side with the government and the co-operating moderate nationalists against the partisans of independence. This was essentially to jump into national politics with a vengeance.[22]

If the official action of the Central Conference in 1930 was openly and explicitly partisan, the episcopal address by Bishops B. T. Badley and John W. Robinson at the same conference was even more partisan. The bishops welcomed the appearance and growth of Indian nationalism but expressed their preference for dominion status instead of complete independence for India. In addition, they criticized the civil disobedience and independence movements, including specifically the Indian National Congress, and referred to their leaders as "extremists who have sought to paralyze Government through lawlessness." And, in a gesture of religious insensitivity in a nation in which religion is always divisive and often explosive, Bishops Badley and Robinson claimed that the leaders of the Indian independence movement were mostly Brahmans who wanted to perpetuate "the Hindu caste system." For this reason, along with others, the bishops concluded, the Christian Church in India could not support the independence movement in India.[23]

Although the bishops could not support the Indian independence movement, Stanley Jones did. We will see in the next chapter how Jones first met Gandhi and how this meeting as well as Jones's increasing contact with non-Western cultures in India, Mesopotamia, and China led him to a more profound revelation of the true character of the universal Christ.

6

A Widening Ministry: India, Mesopotamia, China

The present unrest is not merely political;
it has got down into the souls of the people.
—E. Stanley Jones, *The Indian Witness,* October 26, 1921[1]

STANLEY JONES FIRST met Mahatma Gandhi in 1919 and reported the results of his meeting to his friends and supporters in the United States in a circular letter written from Sitapur and dated December 15, 1919.[2]

I had an interview with the leading Indian in the whole of India. He is the idol of the people. He can turn over his hand and have a revolution or turn his other hand and stay one. He has a marvellous influence. He is outwardly a Hindu, but he has been Christianised in his conceptions. I asked what we might do in order to make Christianity naturalised, a part of the National life and make it contribute more fully to the National uplift? . . . [Ghandi] suggested four things. . . .

(1) All Christians, Missionaries and all must live more like Jesus Christ. (2) You should practise your religion without adulterating it or toning it down. (3) You should emphasise the love side of Christianity more, for love is central in Christianity. (4) You must study more sympathetically the non-Christian religions to find the good in them and to have a more sympathetic approach to them.

Before I left I read him some verses from the Bible and prayed with him. I came away with the feeling that no matter whether I agreed with his political doctrines or not, I had touched a Christianised soul. He gets his Passive Resistance doctrine from Matthew 5:38-41 [turning the other cheek]. I would like you to pray for him. Over many Hindus and Mohammedans his influence is supreme.

This meeting with Gandhi was the culmination of a gradual, but nevertheless radical and dramatic shift in Stanley Jones's own thinking about his call to be a missionary evangelist to India. As we suggested earlier, his involvement in mass movement evangelism in the first two decades of the twentieth century was limited because the Holy Spirit led him to discern, even then, that Christianity would soon face not only the traditional challenges of Hinduism, Islam, Buddhism, and Sikhism, but also the new challenge of Indian nationalism. Stanley's letters to Miss Nellie, the circular letters he and Mabel wrote to their friends and patrons in the United States, and his articles in the *Indian Witness* all reflect this transformation in his understanding of his call to India. The change was also apparent to his colleagues and associates in India. Sherwood Eddy, who was an instrument of the change in Jones's concept of Christian missions, wrote in 1945,

Stanley Jones reads widely and continuously; and he has come to grips with the social, political, and economic problems of the people of Asia. Those who have known him intimately in the Orient have watched him grow. When he began, his message was fervent but narrow, academic, and somewhat painfully orthodox. It did not take in the wide sweep of modern or social problems, nor did it link itself with the everyday human difficulties and perplexities of those he was trying to help. But as he has come into close contact with thousands of people he has seen the working of the spirit of Christ outside the so-called Christian community, he has seen "the light that lighteth every man" who is made in the image of God, and he has come to love the "other sheep" which are not of his orthodox fold.[3]

As Stanley shifted his attention from mass movement evangelism, which focused on the hundreds of millions of village peasants in the vast countryside of India, to person-centered evangelism, which directed its Christian message primarily to the educated urban elite, he became increasingly sympathetic with both the non-Christian religious sensitivities of this elite and with their growing resentment and hostility toward British imperialism. His account of his first meeting with Gandhi, however, and his statement that "no matter whether I agreed with his political doctrines or not" he had "a Christianised soul," suggests that he had reservations both about Gandhi's goal of immediate and complete independence for India and about his strategy of nonviolent civil disobedience. In fact, Jones recalled in in his autobiography,

When Gandhi was about to begin the noncooperation movement [in 1919], I was skeptical about it. I wrote him a letter begging him not to begin it. "It will mean violence and bloodshed and chaos," I said.[4]

On the other hand, in the same circular letter in which he described his first meeting with Gandhi, Stanley also emphasized Gandhi's "Christianised" conceptions and his use of the Gospel of Matthew as the moral foundation for his political campaign of passive resistance to British rule in India. Gandhi's strategy for winning Indian independence from Britain was twofold.[5] The first part of his *satyagraha* or soul-force program was nonviolent noncooperation.

Nonviolent noncooperation included the surrender of titles and honors bestowed by the British, resignation from government office, withdrawal from government-affiliated schools and colleges, and boycott of elections, law courts, and foreign goods. Civil disobedience went a step further by calling for noncompliance with British laws (for example, by not paying taxes), or even the breaking of British laws.

Nonviolent noncooperation required Indian nationalists, first of all, to withdraw from British civil, educational, and economic institutions. But at the same time, in order to provide for themselves the services that had been provided by these British institutions, nonviolent noncooperation also meant that Indians would have to establish and maintain their own national schools, arbitrate their own disputes, and develop their own local industries. Although nonviolent noncooperation could run concurrently with the second part of Gandhi's strategy, civil disobedience, Gandhi did not actively encourage the deliberate violation of British laws until 1930, after over a decade of nonviolent noncooperation.

As nonviolent noncooperation spread from one Indian province to another, and as the moral and spiritual justice of India's grievances against Great Britain gripped the mind and heart of the entire subcontinent of South Asia, Stanley became increasingly sympathetic with Indian nationalism and began to see more and more examples of Christian doctrine and practice in the tactics and goals of Gandhi and his followers.

During this time, Sherwood Eddy and Stanley were planning a year-long evangelistic campaign through the Mid and Far East, extending as far as China, Korea, and Japan, starting in September 1921. But Eddy was detained in the United States, and the trip had to be postponed for a year—and then was reduced to three months in China. But Stanley called the delay "providential." His reasons?

I do not think I should leave India at this time. The political situation has not improved since I wrote you last. The noncooperation movement is still in full swing. They desire to paralyze the British Government by refusing to have anything to do with their courts, schools, Government offices and in every way boycotting the British administration and foreign goods. It is a revolt against Western domination.

This joint circular letter, dated June 30, 1921, was written during the hottest part of the year while Stanley and Mabel were on vacation in the hills. After describing the trip he and Sherwood Eddy had originally planned, he went on to discuss the noncooperation movement. One of its most positive features, he wrote, was the nationwide boycott of government licensed liquor shops. This aspect of the movement was consistent with the longstanding Methodist opposition to the sale and consumption of alcohol. It also touched the deep wound of alcoholism in Stanley's own family. To enforce the boycott, Stanley continued, the Indian nationalists

> have unique methods: if they catch a man drinking they shave off the half side of his beard, put a necklace of old shoes around his neck, put him on a donkey and ride him through the streets with a procession of tin pans behind him and shouts of derision. This generally proves effective!

Another hopeful sign of the noncooperation movement was that the Hindus were trying to abolish "the untouchability of the lower castes. Their great leader Mr. Gandhi has even stayed with a low caste man to the scandal of the 'Holy' Brahmin. This means that the Hindus are breaking down caste and that while we [Christians] started this agitation against it, they themselves seem about to complete it."

The spirit of the Hindu caste system, which is so contrary to the egalitarian spirit of Jesus Christ who invited all persons, regardless of human status, to a personal relationship with himself and with God the Father, was very much on Stanley's mind when he and Mabel wrote their June circular letter. Stanley had recently returned from the Syrian Christian convention in Travancore where the audience each day numbered between twenty and thirty thousand. "This year we had a deeper work than ever before," he wrote, because for the first time Jones publicly confronted the problem of caste head-on. In the previous chapter we quoted the famous church historian, Latourette, who said that because the Syrian Church in South India had compromised its fidelity to Jesus Christ in order to secure its social and religious status in a Hindu-dominated culture, it had, in effect, become a caste. In past years, Stanley wrote, the Syrian Christians

> were unwilling to take into their communion the low caste people; but one day I preached the message on the worth of the individual in the kingdom of God and brought up two low caste boys at the psychological moment and placed them on the platform, put my arms around them, talked about their worth, the fact that they would grow up heathen unless the Church

responded and made them Christian. Then I stood a little Syrian boy between them and said that this boy will grow up Christian and with a chance in life, but the others would not. The Spirit of God mightily gripped the audience, so they decided to have a special meeting where the low caste, degraded Pulayas and Pariahs were brought in. They scoured the country and brought them in until the night when I spoke to them there were about twenty-five thousand in the audience. It was a great meeting and the church saw a vision of what it can do in saving these people. People at home cannot understand the caste spirit as it prevails in India. When the invitation was given one day to the nominal Christians to find conversion they responded by the thousands.

Stanley continued to work with the Syrian Christians throughout the 1920s and 1930s. At the 1923 Marramannu Convention he and Sherwood Eddy asked the Syrian Christians to accept outcastes as full and equal members of their churches. On the last Sunday morning of the convention, the question of the status of outcastes was put to a vote. The fifty priests who were present voted in favor of receiving outcastes into full communion with the church. Then there was overwhelming support from the people by a show of hands. Finally, the bishops supported the admission of outcastes into the church. In his May 25, 1923, circular letter Jones comments that the Syrian Christians

> had been [accepting outcastes] . . . spasmodically and as individuals here and there but never before as a Church. To cap it all we had an inter-caste dinner in which a hundred Syrians, a hundred outcaste Hindus, about 60 high caste Hindus, some Mohammedans and some of us sat down for an inter-caste meal. It was the first time that such a thing had ever been done in caste-ridden Travancore.

Caste, however, continued to be a problem for the Syrian Christians. Almost a decade later, Stanley reported on another visit to the Syrian Convention. "This year," he wrote in his March 29, 1932, circular letter, "all the clergy and the bishops voted" to take outcastes into their churches. Moreover, the Syrian Church launched a campaign to evangelize five thousand outcastes and to accept them into full church membership. Apparently, the campaign was successful, because Jones concluded his report on the Syrian Convention with the comment, "I have received news since then that they have been baptising them [outcastes] in large numbers already."

Back in 1921, Mabel and Stanley closed their June 30 circular letter with information about their domestic life. They were building a new house in Sitapur that was close enough to Mabel's boys' school that she could supervise her teachers and other workers in the school. Moreover, the North India Conference of the Methodist Episcopal Church had appointed Dr.

N. L. Rockey as district superintendent of the Sitapur district. Dr. Rockey's appointment relieved Stanley of the work of supervising all the Methodist preachers in the Sitapur district so that he could give more time to his ever-expanding evangelistic campaigns. "We are very happy at this arrangement," Mabel and Stanley wrote—more happy and more relieved, in fact, than their words reveal, in view of the enormous burdens that, as we have seen, had so recently led to their nervous breakdowns.

Stanley continued his evangelistic work throughout 1921, often in cooperation with the YMCA. In an article in the October 26, 1921, issue of the *Indian Witness*,[6] he reported that he had held no meetings for non-Christians in several months and was unsure "how the political temper of the country would affect the reception of the Gospel." However, much to his surprise, he wrote that when he did hold non-Christian meetings, they turned out to be "the best series of meetings I have ever had in India." The success had come, he explained, "from the very thorough preparation in each place," which was provided by Mr. Popley of the YMCA. For example, in Hyderabad Stanley spoke in Cinema Hall to "a splendid audience" of educated non-Christians, primarily Muslims. "Quite a number signed cards stating that they would study the Bible with an open mind and heart." He received a similar response in Belgaum where nearly half the audience symbolized its allegiance to Gandhi and to the cause of Indian nationalism by wearing clothes made of *khaddar* cloth. *Khaddar* was homespun Indian fabric, which was manufactured by hand on crude wooden spinning wheels or *charkas* to dramatize Indian economic self-reliance and the Indian boycott of imported British fabrics.

During the same 1921 evangelistic campaign, Stanley also held meetings for Christians. In fact, in Jaffna, Ceylon (Sri Lanka), he "had the finest gathering of Indian Christians I have seen anywhere in the East." In Jaffna he also held equally successful meetings for non-Christians.

> Here I received the most intelligent and searching questions I have received anywhere in the East. The lawyers must have sat up all night making up lists of questions. The meetings went on about three hours each night, with intense and sympathetic interest. There were a number of Hindus who declared their purpose to take their stand for Christ.

In the Indian city of Coimbatore, he held meetings for Hindu women in the Cinema for three days. He reported that at his request the Christian women shared their testimonies with the non-Christian women. "They did so with telling effect. In a kind of after-meeting with them, I asked those who would like to surrender and find a new life to hold up their hands for prayer. The large majority of them did so, and did so sincerely, I believe."

The most successful meetings of the entire evangelistic tour both in terms of attendance and in terms of spiritual impact were held in Victoria Hall in Madras. Here the Central Committee of the Christian churches had made careful arrangements for Jones's appearance.

> The crowds grew until, on the fifth and sixth nights, it was crowded to the doors. The last night, after speaking on the new birth, I asked the nominal Christians and the non-Christians who would like to find the new birth to stay for an after-meeting. There were about three hundred who stayed, of whom about one-third were Hindus. There was real power and grip in the after-meeting, as I explained how to surrender and trust; and they repeated a prayer of confession and self-committal after me. I have received word that some of these have definitely decided to come out immediately.

At the end of this 1921 campaign Stanley concluded that the political unrest throughout India which he thought might dampen the reception of the Christian gospel had in fact exposed the nation's deep spiritual hunger for the gospel. In his October 26, 1921, *Indian Witness* article, he quoted a prominent Brahmin who told him not to be disheartened by the fact that relatively few educated Indians made open professions of faith in Jesus Christ. The Brahmin referred to himself as "a Christian Brahmin," and said that he, along with many others of his caste, was trying to live his life according to "Christian principles," even though he did not have the courage to say so publicly. Moreover, in a private conversation, several Hindu nationalists who were part of Gandhi's noncooperation movement asked him, "But do not you think it is our Christian duty to help Mahommedans in this time of their difficulty?" "Our Christian duty!" he commented. "That is a little straw." Stanley was astounded that *Hindus* felt a *Christian* duty to help *Muslims*.

In the early 1920s, as he held more and more non-Christian meetings throughout India, which were increasingly attended by noncooperationists who were receptive and sometimes enthusiastic about the Christian gospel, Jones moved further and further away from the narrow and somewhat parochial constraints of his Wesleyan Holiness background and training. His divine call to preach the uncompromised gospel of Jesus Christ and to invite sinners to confess their sins and receive God's forgiveness and salvation had not changed in the slightest degree, but he was beginning to discern that God was not limited by human concepts of exactly how and to whom the gospel should be presented. When he turned his attention from mass movement evangelism among the Indian peasants and villagers to person-centered evangelism among the educated and urbanized elite, he was not inundated with Christian converts as earlier Methodist missionaries had been in the late nineteenth and very early twentieth centuries. Indeed, because the sacrifice of their social and cultural status was a price they were often unwilling to pay, many upper-caste Hindus to whom Jones

147

preached, like the prominent Brahmin mentioned above, adopted and practiced "Christian principles" without publicly professing their faith in Jesus Christ. Evangelizing middle- and upper-class non-Christians in India created a genuine dilemma for Stanley Jones. Were sympathetic and receptive audiences, like the prominent Brahmin, really "Christian," if they did not openly proclaim their Christianity?

In his article, "Through South India," in the September 20, 1922, issue of the *Indian Witness,* Jones confronted his readers with a specific and poignant question asked him by a Brahmin in Samalkot, at a non-Christian meeting in the high school.

> What would you say to a man who comes with this question, as one Brahmin teacher did at the close of this [Samalkot] meeting? "I love my wife and my wife loves me. I want to be a Christian. Shall I come out, and break up my home, and leave my wife?" Oh, for the hour when they can stay in their homes and follow Christ![7]

He concludes his article, using the language of the Christian mass movements, "the break will begin!"

In the early 1920s his meetings for the educated non-Christian elite were certainly unconventional and perhaps unique among Western missionaries in India. And his meetings presented problems, like the question asked by the Brahmin teacher, which were unfamiliar to Christian missionaries trained in evangelism during the days of the mass movements. But Stanley sensed that in spite of the difficulty of persuading elite non-Christians in India to publicly renounce their traditional faiths and openly embrace Christianity, the Holy Spirit was at work in his meetings. At Cocanada in South India he held meetings with the Canadian Baptists. His September 20 article recorded a comment made one night, when a

> leading man said a striking thing to me: "You probably are aware that there is growing up in India a Christ cult, largely apart from the Christian church and, sometimes, under its opposition. But the Christ cult is spreading fast." He expressed what I have often felt: The Holy Spirit is working far beyond the borders of the Christian church. If the church can bring Christ to India, well and good; if not, then, if He comes through other channels, we say, Amen!

These "other channels" would set Jones apart as a Christian missionary with a revolutionary way of presenting the gospel of Jesus Christ. In his first book, *The Christ of the Indian Road* (1925), he identified Gandhi, who never abandoned Hinduism, as an "irregular channel" of Christianity. Moreover, he insisted that Christ must be "disentangled" from the Western culture and traditions that had become such an integral part of the preaching of the Christian gospel in India. Now that India was engulfed in the fervor of nationalist sentiment and Gandhi had assumed the leadership of the non-cooperation movement, Christian missionaries from Western Europe and North America, instead of being greeted as selfless servants of Jesus Christ, were beginning to be seen as the agents of British imperialism. In the same *Indian Witness* article in which Jones welcomed an unorthodox "Christ cult" for India, he told what he called a "heart-breaking story" about two Europeans who killed each other in a duel in Vizagapatam in South India. The Hindus buried them where they died and, to commemorate the spirits of what the men had loved in life, the Hindus "put up a whiskey bottle and a cigar box on the tomb as their offering to the shades of the dead!" Jones concluded his article with this reflection on the story of the tomb.

> The Kingdom of God is coming to India. Christ is too great not to conquer this great people. But this ugly fact, so exaggeratedly but vividly set forth in that pathetic story, is holding back the Kingdom. If we could remove the incubus of unspiritual Europeanism, the Kingdom would burst upon us with power.

At first Jones identified "the incubus of unspiritual Europeanism" with the individual moral sins of Western civilization. His applause for the non-cooperationist boycott of British licensed liquor shops in his June 30, 1921, circular letter and his disgust at the tomb for the European duelists reflect his family's experience with alcoholism and Stanley's personal moral code, as much as they reflect his political sympathy with Indian nationalism. Nevertheless, Stanley Jones was growing in his concept of the kingdom of God. In fulfilling God's call to reach the educated elite of India with the gospel of Jesus Christ, he could not ignore the political and economic aspirations of Indian nationalism. His gospel message would have to address the injustices of British colonialism either directly or indirectly if he was going to be completely faithful to God's call to him to give his witness to the educated and often non-Christian middle and upper classes of India.

Stanley's first circular letter of 1922, dated February 20 and written while he was on an evangelistic tour, is filled with references to the rising tide of Indian nationalism and to the increasing impact of the noncooperation movement on his meetings. In this letter Jones reported that "recent months" had been a time of "political stress and anxiety," but were also "exceedingly fruitful in evangelistic work." For example, he held a series of meetings in Gujarat, which was the center of the noncooperationist movement and was where Gandhi had his headquarters. His first stop in Gujarat was in the city of Surat where, he wrote, the "response to my appeal was immediate and hearty." In Nadiad the noncooperationists were in almost complete control of the city, and the British official there advised the missionary who was making local arrangements for Jones not to have any meetings at all. But the missionary wrote to Gandhi and asked him to encourage the noncooperationists to come to the meetings. Gandhi complied with the missionary's request. Not only did the noncooperationists come to the meetings, Stanley told his American friends and supporters, but their leaders printed and signed public notices encouraging attendance at the meetings, even though "the subjects upon which I was to speak were definitely Christian."

In Bombay, as in Nadiad, there was concern about whether Jones should hold meetings at all, since there had recently been riots in the city. But in spite of the fact that "great numbers had been killed [in the riots] and race feeling was running high," the attendance at the meetings was good and increased throughout his visit to the city. But in Mainpuri there was an attempt to break up one of the meetings by force. He described what happened in his February 20, 1922, circular letter.

> A noncooperation crowd, returning from a meeting, celebrating the release of one of their leaders from jail, surrounded the building in which I was speaking and yelled "Mahatma Gandhi ki jai" [Hail to Mahatma Gandhi] most uproariously for three quarters of an hour, they stoned the building, rushed the doors and broke the locks. Some of the audience guarded the doors and I went on and finished my lecture amid the din. I was speaking on brotherhood within while brickbats were flying without.

The noncooperationist demonstrators, however, had made a mistake. They thought that Jones was holding a meeting for a group of their political opponents. On the following day the noncooperators "expressed regret" about what had happened, and he was able to conclude his evangelistic tour in Mainpuri without opposition or further incidents.

As he held meetings throughout India, Stanley was discovering that while audiences were overwhelmingly receptive to his messages about Jesus Christ, they were increasingly "bitter, resentful and antagonistic to Western civilization and to the spirit of white dominance." For the first time in over a decade of missionary service, he was beginning to realize that Western culture and traditions, which shaped and directed his presentation of the Christian gospel and which he took for granted, were, in fact, an obstacle to the dissemination of Christianity in India. He now knew that if he was going to reach India for Christ he would have to separate the gospel message from its association with Western imperialism. He would have to preach a more truly universal Christ.

Significantly, it was at this point in his ministry to the educated and intellectual elite, when he was becoming aware of the broader social and political issues of Christian missions, that Stanley began to travel outside India. In March 1922 he visited Mesopotamia (Iraq). The reason for his visit, he explained to Miss Nellie in a letter written from Sitapur on January 11,

1922, was to hold meetings "and then report on whether we [Methodists] should go into Mesopotamia as a mission and establish a station there." Bishop Warne had asked him to undertake the trip because of his contact with the Syrian Church in South India.

Stanley's first published report of his trip to Iraq appeared in the April 12, 1922, issue of the *Indian Witness* under the title, "Evangelizing in the Land of King Feisul."[8] He observed that although Mesopotamia was often "called the cradle of the human race . . . degeneracy is written over everything." In the first place, the fertility of the soil was degraded and the land could no longer support the large population that it had sustained in the past. Moreover, the prosperous cities of ancient times had been replaced by mud huts and the tents of nomadic Arabs. Nevertheless, Iraq enjoyed a degree of financial prosperity, largely because after World War I Great Britain had paid 350 million pounds "for the redemption of Mesopotamia from the hand of the Turk [who had controlled the country before the war], and incidentally to preserve the Anglo-Persian Oil Company." The problem with Iraq, he concluded, the thing that was keeping its people from achieving their true potential, was religion.

> The trouble with Mesopotamia is Mohammedanism. The "will of God" (?) is everywhere and over everything, and there seems little place for the will of man; so, the fine qualities of the Arab go to waste, either in a burst of fanaticism fighting for the cause of Allah, or are corroded by lethargy and kismet [fate]. Lift that incubus from his soul and there is no finer material in the world.

Jones began holding evangelistic meetings in Baghdad on the day he arrived in Iraq. Only a few Europeans attended his meetings, but many Asians, especially Indians, came to hear him. In fact, he discovered that there were several hundred Indian Christians in Baghdad, many of whom were members of the Indian Christian Band, which had been organized by Bishop Warne in 1920. The Band was led by an energetic group of laymen who held approximately twelve meetings each week. Through their efforts forty-nine persons had been baptized. But what was even more remarkable about the Band meetings was the fact that as many non-Christians as Christians attended. And, unlike Christians in India, Jones wrote, the members of the Christian Band in Baghdad

> all voluntarily live together in the same houses and eat the same food. In one billet, I took dinner with those living there. There were Buddhists, Hindus, Indian Christians, Burmese, and Anglo-Indians, all living joyously together. None of the Hindus seem to keep caste. Being strangers in a foreign country has driven all Indians together. Some of the Christians have [even] cremated the dead bodies of their Hindu brethren.

The meetings in Iraq that had the most powerful personal impact and left the most lasting impression on Jones were his meetings with the Assyrian refugees. Before World War I these Christian refugees had homes in Mrumiah, Persia (Iran). Many of them were converted and educated by American Presbyterian missionaries who worked in Mrumiah and had a school there. The Assyrian Christians eventually supported the Allies in the War and were led to believe that they would receive military assistance from the Russians. The Russians, however, left them to fight alone against both the Kurds and the Turks. In the end the Assyrians were forced to evacuate and fled to Baghdad. Eighty-five thousand Assyrians began the evacuation; only fifty thousand arrived in Baghdad. Unspeakable horrors occurred along the way at the hands of the Kurds. Jones wrote in the *Indian Witness,*

> It was to these people [refugee survivors] that I was privileged to speak a number of times. There would be about 800 in the audience. I have never spoken to such a responsive audience. . . . They told me that I had done them good; but, in my heart of hearts, I knew that they had done me more good than I did them.

Jones reflected on the significance of the fact that the Assyrian Christians were the descendants of the Nestorians, who were among the first Christian missionaries to Asia and China. "It may be," he said, "that God is purifying this church through these sufferings, that they may catch the fire of their ancient zeal." The example of the Assyrian Christians is one illustration of how God "turns calamities into opportunities."

He witnessed another, more personal and poignant example of God's providence during his first Sunday in Baghdad. In the audience on that Sunday,

> I saw two young ladies whom I immediately recognized as Isabella Thoburn College girls—Armenians. Later, they told me their wonderful story of how, in the early Armenian massacres of 1898, they fled with their mothers through Baghdad and Mesopotamia to India as refugees. There they have been educated; one is a graduate and the other has taken her teacher training, and now they have come back, appointed by Government to have charge of female education in Mesopotamia.

Jones undoubtedly reported the results of his trip to Mesopotamia to Bishop Warne and perhaps to the Methodist Episcopal Board of Foreign Missions in New York. But for whatever reason, the Methodist Church did not establish a mission station in Mesopotamia. Because I have not found any record of Jones's report on his trip, other than the *Indian Witness* article quoted above, we can only speculate about the reasons for the church's decision not to establish a mission in Iraq. However, we do not need to speculate about the impact of his visit on his own intellectual and spiritual development as an evangelist. His trip broadened his geographical and cultural perspective and deepened his sensitivity to and appreciation for how God was at work among Christians and non-Christians outside of India.

In terms of Stanley's growth and development as a missionary evangelist, the most important trip he took in 1922 was not his trip to Iraq, but his trip to China with Dr. Sherwood Eddy on their three-month evangelistic tour. At first, he wrote in his report of the tour for the January 17, 1923, issue of the *Indian Witness,* he had been reluctant to accept Eddy's invitation, because conditions in India were "moving toward" the acceptance of Christianity. But, even evangelists "get into ruts . . . become cock-sure," he wrote, and rely too much on "old messages and methods." For this reason he welcomed the fresh perspective of another country and a different mission field. Moreover, he was intrigued by the different intellectual traditions of India and China. India was "pantheistic and spiritual, and not very practical," while China was "agnostic and material, and intensely practical." Each nation, he thought, could learn from the other.[9]

Stanley spent the months of October and November and most of December 1922 in China with Sherwood Eddy. They were accompanied by Eddy's wife and daughter and by Eddy's brother, Dr. Brewer Eddy, secretary of the American Board of Foreign Missions. Sometimes they all traveled together. At other times they traveled separately. In each of the nearly twenty cities they visited, there was careful and thorough preparation for their Christian meetings. Unlike Jones's practice in India, the Eddy party distributed no broadcast advertising in China. Instead, Jones explained in his January 17, 1923, circular letter, written after his trip to China while on board a ship returning to India, select groups were prepared for the meetings in advance and were admitted by ticket only. Using this system, attendance at the meetings averaged about a thousand in the evening and five hundred during the day. Another difference between Christian evangelism in India and China was that in China there was no prejudice against holding meetings for non-Christians in churches. So many of the meetings were held in Christian churches.

The first city they visited in China was Peking (Beijing). There he met the leaders of the Renaissance Movement and the Anti-Christian Movement which, in January 1923, were less than a year old. In his January 17, 1923, circular letter, Jones reported that after having lunch with the Eddy party the leaders of the Anti-Christian Movement "announced to us that the movement was dead. It had died for want of a soul." The government of the Republic of China, Jones wrote, was "paralyzed through graft." The political and social turmoil, however, did not affect the enthusiastic reception of the gospel.

Those most eager for Jesus Christ in China were students. At the end of the tour Jones concluded that over three thousand Buddhist and Confucian students had made decisions for Christ. In addition, hundreds of businessmen and soldiers became Christians and another three thousand persons indicated that they wanted to become inquirers by making a conscientious effort to learn more about Christianity.

> The most remarkable experience we had was to be with General Feng, the great Christian General and Governor. Twenty years ago he was an ignorant soldier who believed that the foreigners were taking out the eyes of the children to make a medicine to send their telegrams with. He showed his contempt for Christianity by shooting holes in the sign of the Presbyterian Mission at Paotingfu. But he was touched by the way some of the missionaries died during the Boxer Uprising. He signed a card in Dr. Mott's meetings at Peking and was baptized in the Methodist Church there. He is the most outstanding character now in China. Already eight thousand of his men and one thousand of his officers have become Christians. As far as any one knows there is not one man in the twenty thousand in his army who smokes, drinks, gambles, uses opium, loots, or has a venereal disease. . . . Hundreds of others are ready for baptism but are being held off for further instruction. We had meetings each morning with his men and there were 800 or a thousand out each day, each man with his note book out taking notes from the Generals down to the youngest officers. I have never seen a more earnest set of men anywhere in the world. General Feng lives a devout, earnest life and succeeds in infusing a new spirit into his officers and men. He may be the next president of China.

While Stanley Jones spoke to audiences and asked them for personal decisions to follow Jesus Christ, Sherwood Eddy emphasized the impact of Christianity on industrial and social relations. At a time when China was industrializing rapidly and workers were ruthlessly exploited by being forced to work sixteen to eighteen hours a day in dirty and dangerous factories, Eddy persuaded many Chinese chambers of commerce to adopt resolutions which provided "(1) No employment of children under 12; (2) One day's rest in seven; (3) Safeguarding of life by safety appliances and reasonable hours of work."[10]

Thanksgiving Day 1922 was the most dangerous and exciting day of their three-month tour. Dr. Brewer Eddy and Stanley were eating their Thanksgiving dinner on board a ship en route to Foochow.

> Suddenly, a cry was raised outside and we rushed out to find that two seamen, in putting out the companion-way, were thrown into the water by the chain breaking. We turned back to try to get them, but they were lost.[11]

Later on the same day, when the ship had gone as far it could go, Jones and Eddy transferred to a launch for the last fifteen miles of their journey to Foochow. Before they arrived, the city had been a battleground between the armies of the North and the armies of the South, and the forces of Sun Yat Sen had captured Foochow. But the fighting had not yet ended. As the launch approached a Chinese government gunboat, no more than twenty yards away,

> three shots were fired into the air and three in the water in front of us. We were told in no uncertain tones to anchor nearby for the night and not move; if we did, we would be shot. There we had to stay all night in the cold, with only a steamer rug apiece and the hard floor of the wind-swept launch for a bed. All night long they kept banging away at vessels and junks to bring them in.

When they finally arrived in Foochow, they found more evidence of military and social chaos. "Each foreign house" in the city, Stanley wrote in the *Indian Witness*, "had out its national flag, as a protection against the looting of the soldiers." Moreover, because the missionaries were relatively safe from the invading armies, the Chinese friends of the missionaries left their most valuable belongings with the missionaries, whose homes were quickly filled with treasured possessions. Ironically, "China does not seem to be able to protect her own people," Jones wrote, "while foreign countries protect their nationalities at distances of thousands of miles."

Although large parts of China were in a state of political and civil turmoil in 1922, Stanley found that with respect to the Christian church China was "wonderfully open and challenging." Even in Foochow, for example, where fighting had just ended, he wrote that

> we had wonderful receptions. . . . Our Methodist work there is very strong. There were splendid audiences of a thousand girls and about fifteen hundred men students. It was a joy to speak to them. There were about three hundred decisions [for Christ].

In Amoy he spoke at Amoy University to an audience that was overwhelmingly atheist. But in spite of the fact that they did not believe in God, he found that those who came to his university meetings were "very responsive." Each evening he spoke in one of the large churches to a thousand businessmen. Because the businessmen had not participated in Bible classes before his meetings, he did not ask them to make decisions for Christ. Many of them would have declared their faith in Christ if he had asked them to do so, but, as he wrote in the *Indian Witness,* such declarations "would not be sufficiently intelligent." For this reason Stanley asked the businessmen to sign up for Bible classes, and over a hundred did so.

The Chinese city that was most responsive to Jones's presentation of the gospel was Canton. There over eight hundred people made decisions for

Christ after hearing him. On the last night of the meetings, pastors from thirty churches in Canton met with these converts to decide whether they should become church members.

The last stop on the tour was a ten-day visit to Manila, which Stanley had visited on his way back to India. Although his meetings in the Philippines were held during the Christmas holidays, he reported that several hundred people decided to become Christians.

In India Jones had preached on the person of Jesus Christ. But in China Christianity was identified with an established set of doctrines and with an institutionalized church. On many occasions the Chinese people Jones met told him that what they needed was precisely the Christ he proclaimed in India. On the other hand, what India needed was the "practical, matter-of-fact, morally earnest type of Christianity" that was the hallmark of Chinese Christians. "A cross fertilization of the two," Jones concluded in his *Indian Witness* article, "will be beneficial to both." He made a similar comment about his trip in a letter written on January 6, 1923, to Dr. Donohugh, a corresponding secretary for the Methodist Episcopal Board of Foreign Missions in New York.

> After being in this work [among the educated elite] for six years in India it has been a fine corrective to come to China where everything is so concrete. In India it is a battle of ideas and theories and in China they want something that works, they care little about ideas. It has been splendid for me to get this corrective. I am sure I will go back to India with a richer message.[12]

Stanley's 1922 trips to Iraq and China marked a decisive turning point in his career as a missionary evangelist. In extending the geographical scope of his evangelistic activities, he also extended the intellectual and spiritual scope of his messages. This process of personal and professional expansion began when he was recovering from the breakdowns he suffered in India following his first furlough in the United States. It was then that he discovered his true calling to carry the good news of Jesus Christ to the educated elite of India. But in order to reach this educated elite, Jones had to understand and appreciate how their interpretation of Christianity was twisted and distorted by its intimate association with British colonialism. For the first time in his life he questioned the relationship between his own Western culture and the basic doctrines of the Christian faith. Eventually, his questions led to his first book, *The Christ of the Indian Road* (1925), which disassociated Christianity from what he called, in his article for the *Indian Witness* in 1922, the "incubus of unspiritual Europeanism." But as he moved away from the Western cultural trappings of Christianity, he also moved away from the narrow orthodoxy of his own Wesleyan Holiness background. This does not mean that he changed in any way his understanding of the essentials of the gospel of Jesus Christ or that he compromised his presentation of that gospel in order to make it more palatable to his educated Indian audiences. But he did discover that there were many culturally distinct expressions of Christianity and that other national expressions of Christianity were just as authentically Christian as that of his own country. The personal impact of this discovery is best illustrated by the change in his relationship with Miss Nellie.

Although Stanley continued to write faithfully to his first grade and Sunday school teacher throughout her life, there was a period of at least seven years when Miss Nellie did not write to him. In a January 12, 1924, letter, Stanley told her about his plans for travel to Europe and to the United States later in the year when he would be a delegate to the General Conference of the Methodist Episcopal Church. He would also be visiting Baltimore. Then, in exasperation, he wrote,

> I am going to give you one chance for redemption. For seven years you have promised to write to me and for seven years you have failed. I know you don't want to see me [when I arrive in Baltimore] with such a delinquency hanging over your head!

But Miss Nellie failed to answer Stanley's letters, and the tone and content of his letters to her changed. In contrast to the letters he wrote while he was a student at Asbury, which reveal his deepest desires and apprehensions and often solicit Miss Nellie's advice and counsel, Stanley's letters to her in the 1920s are more matter-of-fact and do not disclose as much of his inner feelings. Nevertheless, he continued to have the highest regard for his first grade and Sunday school teacher. And he corresponded faithfully with her throughout her life.

It is impossible to give a full explanation, based on direct evidence, for the evolution of Stanley's correspondence with Miss Nellie. But circumstantial factors throw some light on the history of his relationship with her. First, in the 1920s Stanley was a married man and perhaps did not have the need for a female confidante that he had as a student at Asbury and during his first few years in India. He did, however, continue to write to Miss Nellie about his ministry to the educated middle and upper classes of India and about his meeting with Indian nationalist leaders. In his January 11, 1922, letter, for example, he mentions his contacts with Gandhi. It may be that Miss Nellie was not sympathetic with Indian nationalism or with Gandhi. And, as a longstanding and active member of the Methodist Episcopal Women's Foreign Missionary Society, she may not have understood or appreciated Stanley's new approach to missionary evangelism. Stanley recalled her reaction to *The Christ of the Indian Road* in a letter dated May 4, 1926. His book, he told her, was very popular and was selling very well. Then he wrote,

> I shall never forget your flushed face after I got through reading the manuscript [of *The Christ of the Indian Road*] to you and Mr. Robinson [the pastor of Memorial Church in Baltimore]. I could tell that you were in disagreement with a great deal of it, but you were too polite to say so.

Jones never specified what Miss Nellie disagreed with, but she probably found it provocative and controversial for the same reason that many other Western Christians and missionaries found it provocative and controversial. *The Christ of the Indian Road* was a deadly frontal assault on the cultural prejudices of most European and American Christian missionaries in the late nineteenth and early twentieth centuries. As we have seen, the Methodist Episcopal Church's own official history of its foreign missions in South Asia frankly acknowledged that Bishop Thoburn, who almost singlehandedly vastly increased the size of the church's missionary activity in India and transformed its methods and procedures, was a religious imperialist. He lived most of his life during the nineteenth century when, as church historian Kenneth Scott Latourette reminds us, the Western nations

> were invading and usually mastering the rest of the world and when, under the impact of their civilization, the other cultures were either collapsing or were being transformed. Here was an opportunity such as Christians had never before faced to give to all men a knowledge of the gospel.[13]

Christian evangelism, of course, is by its very nature "imperial" insofar as it seeks to win converts to the kingdom of God. But in the decades before World War I, when economic and political colonialism was the dominant foreign policy goal of both the major European powers and of the United States, this policy was emphatically unchristian and often anti-Christian. No amount of rationalization in terms of "manifest destiny" or "the white man's burden" can justify the brutal pursuit of national self-interest by the Western powers in the late nineteenth and early twentieth centuries. Indeed it was World War I itself that exposed and passed final judgment on the cultural and spiritual hypocrisy of the West for its longstanding policy of seizing as much economic and political power as possible over non-Western nations, while at the same time exploiting every opportunity to spread the Christian gospel of international and interracial brotherhood and equality. In the words of Nathan D. Showalter, the historian of the Student Volunteer Movement,

> When the language of crusade was employed again by evangelicals after the Great War [World War I], it was without the blessing of a Christian civilization. Christendom died in the trenches of Flanders.[14]

Unfortunately, even after the war Western Christianity generally, and Western Christian missionaries especially, were often consciously or unconsciously co-opted into becoming agents of Western imperialism. Under the guidance of the Holy Spirit, E. Stanley Jones was one of the first Western Christians to realize that in Asia, Africa, and Latin America the Christian gospel was often betrayed by being enmeshed with the economic and political self-aggrandizement of Western nations. He came to this conclusion, as we have seen, through a gradual process of prayer, study, and reflection on his own experience as an evangelist. This transformation in his understanding of how he could most effectively present the gospel to the educated classes of India emerges clearly from the book, articles, and letters he wrote in the early 1920s. He was, in effect, declaring his moral and intellectual independence from Western political and religious imperialism.

7

The Christ of the Indian Road

Man Is Man

"Oh, East is East and West is West,
And never the twain shall meet,"
So spake a son of man—and erred!
            *   *   ***

Oh, man is man, and man with man shall meet;
So taught the Son of Man, and at His feet
Bade us there learn the worth of human worth;
To see the man apart from race and birth.
    —E. Stanley Jones, *The Indian Witness,* September 13, 1922 [1]

HAS THE TIME COME that the missionaries should pack up and go home?"[2] This was the question E. Stanley Jones posed to the readers of the *Indian Witness* on August 1, 1923. His answer was that instead of packing up and going home, the missionaries should "pack up and go forward." They should continue their work, but in a new way and with a new attitude. Christians in India should maintain their ties with Christians in the West because, in the first place, Western Christianity needs the Christ of the Indian road. In Jones's words, "I believe that Indian missionaries will be necessary for the enrichment of American and European Christian life."

In 1923 the idea of sending Indian missionaries to the United States was a startling and totally unacceptable notion both to most American Christians and to most Methodist missionaries in India. But Indian Christians like Sundar Singh (1889–1929), who is often called the Saint

Paul of India,[3] were already influencing and enriching Western Christianity. Western missionaries should continue their work in India because India needed them. India needed not so much the financial and physical resources of the West as she needed the hearts and minds of Western Christians who love God and want above all else to share that love with the Indian people. Jones quoted the response of an official of the Japanese Methodist Church when asked by an American Methodist bishop whether the Japanese church wanted more money or more missionaries. The Japanese official replied, "We wish missionaries. If we have the missionaries, they will win the Christians who, in turn, will raise the money."

Jones sincerely and firmly believed that Western Christian missionaries had a vital role in the evangelization of India. After all, he himself was called by God to be a missionary evangelist to India and he committed over fifty years of his adult life to the propagation of the gospel in India. But, as we have seen, he was one of the first to recognize that the message and the methods of religious imperialism in the late nineteenth and early twentieth century were no longer acceptable to the Indian people. Indeed, he questioned whether some of the tactics of Christian missionaries were really Christian. Even before his trips to Mesopotamia and China he began to separate the essential and universal truth of Christianity from his own Western cultural heritage. These evangelistic tours in the Middle East and Far East only served to reinforce in his own mind and spirit that non-Western expressions of Christianity were just as authentically Christian as his own American understanding of Christianity.

On his return to India from his visits to Iraq and China, Stanley began to apply to his meetings in India some of the evangelistic techniques he had used so successfully in China. Instead of asking those in his audiences who wanted to become Christians to accept baptism, he asked these new Christians to pray a prayer of confession and surrender and left the matter of baptism to the conscience of each convert. Today, Christian evangelists throughout the world use the sinner's prayer, which is the same as the prayer of confession and surrender, to symbolize the conversion of a new believer. But in the 1920s the most widely accepted sign of conversion, especially among Western missionaries in non-Western nations, was baptism. So his use of the sinner's prayer was a distinct and significant departure from the practice of his Methodist missionary colleagues. As he explained to the readers of the *Indian Witness,* Christianity should emphasize Christ and his offer of forgiveness and salvation, not the ritual of baptism. To be sure, he acknowledged the importance of baptism, but he insisted that the believer's personal relationship with Jesus Christ was more important. Having sincerely repented of sin and accepted God's forgiveness and salvation, the new believer then could accept baptism into a fellowship of Christian believers. Moreover, by focusing on individual prayers of confession and repentance, evangelists avoided the suspicion that their real motive was simply to add more names to their roster of baptized Christians. Using the personal sinner's prayer "took the strain out of the meetings and the sense in the atmosphere that we had some covered motive of getting someone on the sly to profess Christianity."[4]

The Methodist Episcopal Church in India, however, continued to use statistics on the number of baptisms as indicators of the spiritual growth and vitality of the church. At the North India Conference in 1926 Jones submitted a report in his capacity as chairman of the Committee on Evangelism. He noted that 4,764 persons had been baptized into the Methodist Episcopal Church during that year. This was about the same number of persons who had been baptized in previous years. But, Jones asked in exasperation,

> All these people who are coming in, what do they do? What kind of a church are they forming? With that number added every year we ought to be setting this whole North India ablaze.[5]

"Evangelism," he suggested, had become "more imposed than inspired." Winning souls for the kingdom of God, instead of being the natural spiritual fruit of the Indian church under the leadership of Indian Christians, was a program mandated by the Board of Foreign Missions in New York and executed by its missionaries in the field. But there were Methodist congregations in the North India Conference that had made evangelism a more integral and authentic part of their own Christian witness. In Rawalpindi, for example, a certain Methodist missionary had first focused all his evangelistic efforts on bazaar preaching. He had all the best intentions and preached with great enthusiasm, but he had no positive response from his audiences and no conversions to Christianity. Then the missionary approached the local Methodist pastor and persuaded his church to be the center of evangelism for the city. The missionary submitted his own ideas about winning converts to Christianity to the authority of the local church. The result was that God's Holy Spirit was liberated to energize the laymen of the church so that each member became a missionary. There was a dramatic increase in both professions of faith in Christianity and in Christian baptisms in Rawalpindi, a Muslim stronghold in what is now Pakistan.

Stanley concluded his report to the North India Annual Conference with the following recommendation.

> I therefore suggest that in every [mission] station and in every village centre we call a meeting of all the Christians to plan the evangelistic programme for the whole year, centering that programme in the Church and subordinating

missionaries and mission agents to work that programme in conjunction with local members.[6]

By liberating the local Methodist pastor and his laymen in Rawalpindi to control and actively participate in the evangelization of their own city, the American missionary was also liberating himself from any presumption of cultural or religious superiority. Together the local church and the missionary were free from all external restraints and internal inhibitions that might keep them from proclaiming the good news of the gospel of Jesus Christ. Jones uses this example of the Methodist church and the missionary in Rawalpindi to persuade his missionary colleagues to move away from the imperialistic style of Western evangelism and to seek the direction and assistance of Indian Christians in coordinating and implementing the ministry of the church.

Largely because of his work with the intellectuals and educated classes of India, Stanley became convinced in the early 1920s that India was beginning to realize she could have Christ without Western civilization. In other words, Christ could be "expressed through India's own national genius and thought." But how, he wondered, could Western missionaries take advantage of this new Indian understanding of Christianity? His first suggestion was that missionaries should learn to appreciate why India was so attracted to Christianity. This suggestion was contained in an article entitled, "India's New Thought of Christ," published on the front page of the January 31, 1923, issue of the *Indian Witness*. Written "as a tract to non-Christians" and intended "for use in the upcoming Evangelistic campaign" during 1923, the article discussed several reasons India found Christianity attractive. The first was that "some of her greatest sons, like Mahatma Gandhi, are drawing moral and spiritual strength from Christ." Moreover, just as Jesus said he came not to destroy but to fulfill the Jewish law, so Jesus also fulfilled India's spiritual heritage.

> All the good and the true that India's teachers have taught is not destroyed in Jesus. It is rather fulfilled. . . . India, in thus drawing near to Jesus and taking Him as her Lord and Saviour is not untrue to her great past, but is really truer to it, than if she refused to make Jesus, who fulfills her past, the Lord and Master of her life.[7]

As India aspired to establish its own national and international identity in the early 1920s, it also began to develop greater appreciation for its own history and culture and greater pride in its own unique contributions to world civilization. Stanley Jones was one of the very first to realize the possibilities that this change in India's intellectual and spiritual culture created for Christianity and especially for Western Christian missionaries. But he could not fully understand the astounding scope and depth of these possibilities without experiencing the history and culture of his adopted country for himself. So, what better way to immerse himself in the ethos of India than to visit Indian ashrams? This is exactly what he did. In 1923 he spent two months at Santiniketan, the ashram of the world-famous poet, Rabindranath Tagore. Three years later in 1926 he visited Gandhi's ashram at Sabarmati.

It is no exaggeration to say that Jones's visits to these ashrams changed the course of his life. In fact, in 1930, as we shall see, he established his own ashram as a spiritual retreat for Christians modeled on his experience with ashrams in India. But this was only the first of hundreds of Christian ashrams that would eventually be established throughout the world. These ashrams are truly the work of the Holy Spirit as they continue to inspire, refresh, and renew thousands of Christians in many nations today.

Santiniketan is in West Bengal about forty miles north of Calcutta.[8] "Santiniketan is what it signifies—the Home of Peace," Stanley wrote in his *Indian Witness* article describing the ashram. Founded by the poet's father, Debendranath Tagore, the ashram sat in paradisaical natural surroundings. The reasons for the establishment of Santiniketan were religious. Debendranath Tagore was an adherent of Brahma Samaj, a reform sect of Hinduism that, beginning in the nineteenth century, advocated an end to idol worship, to caste distinctions, and to discrimination against women.[9] The abolition of idol worship was one of the things that most favorably impressed Jones about Santiniketan. He wrote in the *Indian Witness*,[10]

> There is no idolatry. On the gates, written in the marble slab, it is stated that there is to be no idolatry and no killing of animals for food or for sacrifice; or speaking against the religion of any in terms of disrespect. I have, therefore, been on a vegetarian diet since coming here, and find myself getting fat! I hope to continue it.

Jones explained that in addition to its religious and spiritual program the ashram consisted of three educational institutions—a school for boys up to university age, the Vishvabharati or International University in which Jones taught, and the agricultural section of the university that taught scientific methods of farming.

> The idea is to bring together students of all nationalities here on India's soil, where they will study each other's culture and thought with respect and sympathy, and where the international mind might be fostered. . . . I have the whole of the students of Vishvabharati who are taking English literature, and we have been studying together Benjamin Kidd's "Science of Power." This is a book that grows on me, the more I know of it. If any of my readers has not read it, then sell your coat and buy the book. It is one of the most Christian books I know.

Like all the other instructors, Jones held his classes out of doors. His class, he wrote, "was held under a large banyan tree, under a thatched cupola to keep out the rain. There are no chairs, even for the teacher; so, each one brings his mat with him, which he spreads for a seat."

In what way did Jones's stay at Santiniketan influence his understanding of Christianity and especially his understanding of the Indian expression of Christianity? He described the spiritual character at the ashram as a mixture of Christianity and of "orthodox and liberal streams of Indian thought." Although Jones sensed the real presense of "the Christian spirit," he felt that it was "held in solution, in the atmosphere of the place, but it has not been precipitated into forms of Christian expression." At Santiniketan, he did not see Indian Christianity in microcosm. What he did see was what Indian Christianity might be.

> The spirit that breathes here, the loving friendliness of every one, communion with nature, the simplicity of life and dress, and the spirituality of it all— if these were crowned with Christ, as they are now saturated with His spirit, then I begin to see what Indian Christianity would be, when it begins to gather up within itself all the best in India's past and reinterprets Christ through Indian genius and forms.

Within a few months of his visit to Tagore's ashram Jones wrote a long paper entitled, "The Influence of the Indian Heritage upon Christianity." It was read at the North India Annual Conference of the Methodist Episcopal Church and was subsequently published in three installments in the *Indian Witness*. As the title suggests, his thesis was the impact of the "social inheritance" of India's history and culture on "Christianity in the future." Every nation and culture that has adopted Christianity, he maintained, has left the distinctive mark of its customs and traditions on the Christian faith. This was a process that began as early as the first century A.D. with Saint Paul. There are real differences between the Christ of the Gospel writers and the Christ of Paul's Epistles. Beyond Paul's influence on Christianity, both Greek and Roman civilizations made unique contributions to the expression of Christianity. More recently, there have been both Anglo-Saxon and American expressions of Christianity. With respect to India's expression of Christianity, however, no particular idiom had yet emerged.

> The reason why the Indian Christian has not made any real contribution to Christian Theology is because he has been trying on the whole to think through Western forms and he is like a fish out of water here.[11]

In the last two installments of his paper in the *Indian Witness,* Stanley suggested how Indian thought and philosophy could break the narrow, rigid mold of Western Christianity. By its emphasis on intensive spiritual meditation and understanding, India liberates Western Christianity from its preoccupation with extensive thought and action, and from an ambitious and aggressive effort to re-create the world in its own image. In addition, the Indian concept of the immanence of God is a welcome and long overdue corrective to the Western fixation on a transcendent deity. The best example of the theology of transcendence in Western thought, Jones wrote, is the eighteenth century European philosophy of deism. The notion of a clockmaker god who creates the universe and winds up his timepiece by establishing predictable, scientific laws for its operation, but who then withdraws from his creation and its human creatures so that it can function independently, betrays the God of John 3:16 who is intimately involved with human beings and who loved the world he created so much that he gave his only Son for its salvation.

The Indian insistence on immanence, on the other hand, is best illustrated by the philosophy of pantheism. Pantheism or the doctrine that everything, even evil, is an expression of God is, of course, totally inconsistent with Christianity. But, Jones insisted, pantheism is a necessary corrective to Western theologies of transcendence like deism and can lead Christianity to a more biblically accurate view of the personhood of God and of God's love for all humanity. Learning the Indian lesson of the immanence of God, he wrote, "will probably bring us to something like Panentheism—every thing in God instead of Pantheism—every thing God. . . . We are not a part, but a counterpart of God."[12]

Other salient features of Indian philosophy that Jones studied were the doctrines of *karma* or fate and of the transmigration of souls. These doctrines, like pantheism, are in their strict and literal form unchristian and anti-Christian because they deny the essential Christian concept of free will. But the kernel of Christian truth in these Hindu ideas is that we reap what we sow. According to Hinduism, souls reincarnated as animals or as lower-caste men and women are suffering the punishment they deserve because of the evil things they did in their previous incarnations. Although Jones rejected the idea of reincarnation, he did believe that human choices in this life have consequences. In this sense and only in this sense the Indian ideas of karma and of the transmigration of souls underscore the necessity of God's righteousness and judgment.

Jones was fully aware that his effort to use aspects of Hindu theology to correct and enrich Western forms of Christianity might be misinterpreted. He wrote, "Let it be clearly understood that what I am speaking for is not some compromise with Hinduism or some syncretism of scattered truths." Jones did not believe that the Hindu doctrines of karma and of the transmigration of souls were true.

We need not hesitate to let our Christ stand in the stream of Indian thinking, nor should we be hesitant about letting Indians interpret Christ through their own inheritance. Only thus can Indian Christianity give a fresh and living expression.[13]

After over a decade of answering God's call to take the gospel of Jesus Christ to the intellectual elite of India, Stanley Jones discerned exactly what was happening in India, both spiritually and politically. He knew, long before most of his colleagues knew, how Indian nationalism was transforming the mind, heart, and soul of India and how Western Christianity, especially Western Christian missionaries, must respond to this transformation. He saw astounding possibilities for Christian revival and for the unprecedented growth of the church in India if the emerging indigenous leadership could be reached with the gospel. But at the same time Jones also knew that

the Christian Church, divided as it is into denominational groups and unrelated to the national life of India, is unacceptable to a large part of the educated classes of India. They are convinced of the truth as it is in Jesus, and yet dissatisfied with the Church expression of it. Many of us share with them some of the criticism, while remembering that we must share the blame, being a part of the Church.[14]

Like all the best preachers Jones was preaching first of all to himself. As he called for the church to repent and to renounce its presumption of religious and cultural superiority in India, he also confessed his own complicity in this presumption. He called for all Western Christians in India, beginning with himself, to be more sensitive to the spirit of Jesus Christ in their adopted country, even when the Holy Spirit appeared in the most unfamiliar places and in the most unexpected way. This is why he struggled so hard to discover Christian truth in Hindu theology. Although his criticism of Western Christianity is harsh, he is not so much pointing his finger at other Christians as he is pointing his finger at himself. The sharp edge of his critique of Western Christianity and of his own denomination reflects the depth and pain of self-examination. As a result of this soul searching and of his openness to God's Holy Spirit, Jones was a changed man; but the change came at a price, a price he willingly paid.

How did Western Christians, and specifically, the Methodist Episcopal Church, respond to Stanley Jones's message of a new and authentically Indian expression of their faith? Two years before the publication of *The Christ of the Indian Road* catapulted him to almost immediate national and international fame, Stanley wrote a circular letter, dated May 25, 1923,[15] informing his friends and financial supporters in the United States that he had recently taught a class of Methodist missionaries and Indian workers at the Bareilly Convention, an annual gathering of the church for study, reflection, and prayer. His topic was how to bring the "high-caste educated men to Christ." He was "doing this a good deal now," he wrote, "for many are eager to study how to reach them." Apparently there was growing interest among Methodists in India, including both American missionaries and Indian nationals, in this approach to evangelizing the intellectual elite by acknowledging and affirming the Indian expression of Christianity. But interest in his new style of missionary evangelism was not confined to India.

Almost a year later, in March 1924 Stanley, Mabel, and Eunice left India for furlough in the United States. They would not return to their home in Sitapur until November 1925. In the United States Stanley attended the General Conference of the Methodist Episcopal Church in Springfield, Massachusetts, a conference at which he was nominated for bishop but withdrew his name. There he delivered an address to the conference entitled, "With Lips of Flaming Fire."[16] He began by recalling his after-dinner conversations with Bishop Warne who had traveled to the United States on the same ship with the Joneses. The common focus of their discussions was the necessity of "a great moral and spiritual awakening" in the church. Such an awakening, he said, would be a revival. And a revival would mean "that we have to take seriously being a Christian." Speaking on the basis of his personal experience, he told the assembled delegates,

> It is possible to cross the seas and leave your home and your friends and give up your salary and everything else and yet not give up the final thing called the surrender of one's self. And some of us have realized what that means and in that extreme moment we have said, "Lord, that last thing, take it. I want nothing but that, and I choose nothing but the knowledge of God." . . . I trust that this General Conference will mean this to us, that individually we may receive our baptism of power and dedicate our lives to God and give up that last thing.

Two years later, a review of *The Christ of the Indian Road* that appeared in the *Pentecostal Herald* referred to Jones's appearance at General Conference. The author, G. W. Ridout, wrote,

> Dr. Stanley Jones made a most profound impression in America in 1924–25. At the General Conference of 1924 no missionary was listened to with intenser interest than he. When he relinquished the honor of being a Bishop he told the Conference that he did so with a clear message from the Lord that if he refused the office "the Lord would walk with him through Asia."[17]

Financial support from the United States for Jones's work in India also increased significantly during the mid-1920s. However, gifts from American donors that were earmarked for his ministry created an administrative nightmare for the Board of Foreign Missions in New York, which was responsible for disbursing them. While the Joneses were at Mabel's family home in Iowa, A. B. Moss, an official with the Methodist Episcopal Board of Foreign Missions, wrote to Stanley on October 17, 1924, about "the exceedingly important matter of the many designated gifts which are coming in for your work. The problem of relating these gifts to such items of the appropriation to India as will be for your evangelistic program is really intricate."

Moss went on to say that

> there are gifts being received labeled for "Work of E. Stanley Jones." We do not know how we are to be able to handle these to the advantage of your work and to the satisfaction of the donors unless there is a thorough understanding between you and us, and a proper provision within your budget for the inclusion of these gifts.
>
> These things are highly important, and at the rate in which gifts are coming in so designated, a good many hundreds, if not thousands, of dollars will be involved. I earnestly hope we can talk this over face to face so that we can ask questions back and forth and get a thorough understanding very soon.[18]

The problem, of course, was Stanley's own notorious lack of attention to administrative and especially financial matters. We have already referred to Mabel's letters expressing her frustration with Stanley's offhand approach to his federal income tax returns. But Moss's letter is also solid evidence of the growing American financial support for Jones's evangelistic work in India.

In early 1926 after *The Christ of the Indian Road* had been published, and after Stanley and the family had returned to India, he received good news about the success of his book in the United States. Ralph E. Diffendorfer, a corresponding secretary for the Board of Foreign Missions and a close personal as well as professional friend, wrote on January 14, 1926,

> You will be interested to know that "The Christ of the Indian Road" still continues to be one of the best sellers. We are doing all we can to stimulate it not only by general advertising but by actually using it in study conferences with ministers.

The timing of the publication of Jones's book was providential. In the mid-1920s American interest in foreign missions was at an all-time low, and financial support for missionaries was seriously jeopardized. Diffendorfer explained how he was using the book and how it was helping stimulate renewed interest in foreign missions among the Methodist clergy. In various districts of the church Diffendorfer held all-day conferences for the district superintendents and for the preachers. In these conferences he would survey the work of Methodist foreign missions based on reports from the field, and he would close by making an assignment from *The Christ of the Indian Road*. In Diffendorfer's own words,

> In this way I get messages from the fields, relate missions to the present world situation and get the spiritual dynamic and motive from your book. The combination is irresistible and I feel now for the first time in two years that I have the basis for the re-motivation for the foreign mission enterprise which is so sadly needed in our Church. The morale of the ministers is very low. It has to be reconstructed on some such basis as the above and they themselves must do it.

Diffendorfer's pessimism about Methodist foreign missions reflects the declining status of Protestant foreign missions generally in the United States after World War I.[19] Beginning in the 1920s the goals of American missionaries became more modest and the spiritual fervor of missionary organizations like the Student Volunteer Movement began to ebb. Theologically, the Protestant churches in America were weakened by the deep and often bitter conflict between fundamentalists and modernists. This conflict was primarily the result of differences among Protestants on two issues—the growing popularity of biblical criticism in seminaries based on the application of secular literary and social scientific techniques to the study of scripture, and the debate between creationists and evolutionists. The fundamentalists rejected biblical criticism and insisted upon the literal interpretation of the Bible, while the modernists embraced biblical criticism as a useful and fruitful tool for the understanding of scripture. Moreover, the modernists accepted Darwin's theory of evolution while the fundamentalists believed in the biblical account of creation as recorded in Genesis.

Jones was very much aware of the split between fundamentalists and modernists, especially within the Methodist Episcopal Church. "We have reached a crisis and we have got to get the Church on a new basis," he wrote in his March 2, 1926, reply to Diffendorfer's January 14 letter. In fact, he said, "I wrote my book with the thought in mind of holding together the two groups—Fundamentalists and Modernists—in a common cause averting a split as the other churches have experienced."

Then he referred to Ridout's recent review of *The Christ of the Indian Road* in the *Pentecostal Herald*. Ridout, Jones wrote, "has been one of the bitterest Fundamentalists in the church." But his favorable review of Jones's book "means that the 70,000 readers of the 'Pentecostal Herald' will be open to the new approach of missions. As the Fundamentalists take their cue from the 'Pentecostal Herald' it ought to be far-reaching in its effects."

In the late 1920s, in spite of the popular success of *The Christ of the Indian Road* and in spite of the Methodist Board of Foreign Missions using Jones's book to reenergize support for its ministry, foreign missions continued to decline. On November 29, 1927, Diffendorfer wrote a four-page, single-spaced letter about Jones's upcoming trip to the United States as a delegate to the 1928 General Conference. Because of his growing fame, he would be in great demand as a speaker throughout the United States. But Diffendorfer closed his letter with the comment that he hoped "to ward off the perfect deluge of invitations that will come as soon as the announcement is made that you are returning to America."

The reason for Diffendorfer's letter, however, was not the difficulty of responding to all the requests for Jones to speak while he was in the country, but the much more serious problem of the continued decline in the status of all Methodist foreign missions. This problem was so serious that he had sent Jones a cable:

PLANNING EXTENSIVE ITINERARY PLEASE MAKE NO AMERICAN ENGAGEMENTS UNTIL YOU RECEIVE MY LETTER VERY IMPORTANT

Diffendorfer hoped to organize a group that would include Jones and "outstanding nationals" from the mission field to tour the United States and encourage a renewed spirit of commitment to foreign missions in the Methodist Episcopal Church. Diffendorfer made a personal and passionate appeal to Jones as the one person who could help the Board of Foreign Missions at this critical time.

> Now my dear, good friend, you are the only man who can do this trick. The situation here is positively desperate and for the sake of the future, not only of Foreign Missions, but of the religious life of America we must pull something like this across next year and you must stand by. It is a clear, definite call from this Board for your help.

Diffendorfer's November 29, 1927, letter to Jones is convincing proof of Jones's growing reputation as a world-renowned missionary evangelist. But there is also other evidence of Jones's fame. Two years later, in 1929, the Board of Foreign Missions drafted an advertisement that appeared in Methodist publications throughout the United States. The ad read in part,

> Would you like to receive a personally written letter from time to time from E. Stanley Jones, world-famed missionary evangelist now in India? The Board of Foreign Missions of the Methodist Episcopal Church—under which Dr. Jones serves in India—has asked him to send to his numerous American friends letters on matters of special religious and missionary interest. These communications will be sent to the Board and there printed and mailed to his friends. The letters will be written as frequently as there are matters of importance; the first will probably be written in the Fall of this year. . . .
> What more stimulating and helpful and unique gift could you make to

> your own family, your friends, your pastor than a series of letters from the
> author of "The Christ of the Indian Road."[20]

Those who wanted to receive Jones's letters were asked to send $1.00 to the Board of Foreign Missions.

The first letter for distribution to the subscribers was dated September 5, 1929. Stanley enclosed this letter with a personal letter to Diffendorfer, also dated September 5, that read, "I am enclosing the first of the circular letters for the people who have paid for the privilege! I am sending to my constituency this same letter as I have always done. I do not want to lose touch with them."

In other words, the board's subscription service simply expanded the number of people who received Jones's circular or duplicate letters, letters which he and his wife Mabel had been sending to their friends and supporters in the United States for years. On October 11, 1929, shortly after Jones sent his first letter through the Board of Foreign Missions, Diffendorfer reported that "three hundred people have sent in their dollar."

One final piece of evidence for Jones's increasing popularity in the United States is the fact that during his 1928–29 visit to America he received collections in excess of $8,800 in churches and other meetings where he spoke.[21] Such amounts were unusually large for any preacher in the United States in the late 1920s. But why was Jones so popular? Why was there such widespread interest in and attention to his message? The reason, according to an editorial published in the *Christian Advocate* on January 17, 1929, was not the publication and brisk sales of his books. Nor did Jones draw large crowds because of his speaking ability. In the words of the editorial: "His vocal equipment is susceptible of vast improvement. Indeed, it is hard, physically speaking, to listen to him." Rather,

> the conclusion is inevitable that the secret of his success lies in the impression of "reality" which he gives. Mohammedans, Hindus, Christians, Agnostics, who come within range of his Spirit-filled personality feel that somehow here is a human being who lives in conscious harmony with God. If there is anything real in religion, he has it.[22]

In spite of Stanley's growing fame and influence, and the success of his books, he still felt inadequate to meet the demands that were being placed upon him. He wrote to Diffendorfer on February 6, 1925, while the family was in Iowa at Mabel's family home.

> I feel desperately the need of further study. [Sherwood] Eddy wants me to
> spend a year with him in Columbia [University] next year with a small group
> who will be given special attention by the leading men there. At the same

172

time I want to get back to India. While I am in . . . N.Y. . . . can we get together about this matter? It ought to be settled soon.

Jones did not spend a year with Eddy at Columbia, but in the summer of 1925 he did take part in the American Seminar. Originally organized and coordinated by Eddy in 1921, the seminar brought together a diverse group of American religious and social leaders to study firsthand the problems of Great Britain and continental Europe. The purpose of the seminar was to promote international understanding and goodwill between the United States and Europe. One hundred twenty-five Americans participated in the 1925 seminar. Most of them, Jones wrote in the *Indian Witness*, were pastors, but there were also "college presidents, Y.M.C.A. secretaries, professors, educational leaders, [and] social workers." Jones was the only missionary. The group sailed together from the United States to Plymouth, England. There were lectures and discussions every morning and every afternoon on board ship as they traveled. "I have never seen a more vital grappling with the problems that face us today," he commented. The members of the American Seminar interacted freely with the other passengers, and one "Russian lady, a nihilist," Jones wrote, "was beautifully converted by attending our daily sessions."[23]

When the group arrived in London, they began each day's program with a Bible hour, followed by two or three lectures, each of which concluded with an hour for questions and answers. During their stay, they heard lectures by the top British leaders of government, business, the universities, and journalism. They were also invited to receptions hosted by the Archbishop of Canterbury, the Bishop of London, and Viscount and Viscountess Astor.

From England the group traveled to Holland and to Berlin. In Germany, he reported in articles published in the *Indian Witness*,[24] the program was more carefully organized and the speakers were more thoroughly prepared than in England. In Great Britain "a good many prominent speakers spoke more or less extemporaneously. Not so in Germany. Manuscripts and carefully prepared addresses were the order." In Berlin, the members of the seminar heard presentations by outstanding political, economic, and academic leaders. Jones was among a select group from the Seminar who visited Professor Harnack, "probably the greatest living theologian." He was also among another small group from the seminar that was received by President Hindenburg.

Stanley took a week for rest in Switzerland before concluding the seminar with visits to the League of Nations in Geneva and to Paris. In Geneva the group studied the League of Nations under the auspices of the Geneva Institute of International Relations. There they were joined by a hundred men and women from England studying the League as part of the Geneva

Institute. The combined group heard lectures on international labor issues, on disarmament, on European economic reconstruction, and on the mandate system of colonial administration, which was established after World War I. Stanley also attended a reception given by the Geneva Institute. "At this reception," he wrote in the *Indian Witness*, "I had a long discussion with the head of the Political Section of the League regarding the question of the League and Race Relations. Up to this time there is no machinery in the League to deal with this delicate and difficult problem."[25]

Because of his experiences evangelizing in India, Jones was especially sensitive to the issue of race. Later, in the 1930s and 1940s, race would become an even more important problem for him as he became more personally involved in international issues. The failure of the League of Nations to confront racism, he would insist, was one of the primary causes of Japanese militarism and of the outbreak of World War II in the Pacific. Moreover, racism was also a major problem in the United States, a problem he referred to in *The Christ of the American Road* (1944) as a hesitation of American democracy to fulfill its divine potential as a nation. Indeed, throughout his long public career there is no other political question on which Jones spoke out more frequently or more passionately than the issue of racial prejudice.

When the Seminar ended, Jones traveled with a smaller group through the Balkans to Turkey. "Turkey," he wrote in an article in the December 16, 1925, issue of the *Indian Witness*, was "undergoing the most radical revolution of any country outside of Russia."[26] It was becoming Westernized, and under the leadership of Kemal Ataturk (1881–1938), the founder of the Turkish Republic in 1923, had overthrown the rule of the caliphs and transformed itself into a modern secular nation. Jones was especially impressed by the improvements in agricultural training and production, by the social revolution with respect to the position of women, and by the removal of education from the control of religious authorities.

He also sensed a new spirit of religious toleration, which extended even to the Christian Armenians. During the time of the Ottoman Empire in the late nineteenth and early twentieth centuries, Turkey had conducted several campaigns of genocide against Armenians. But now, Turkey was "willing for Armenians to be a part of their nation provided they become Turks. This they insist does not mean that they should become Moslem."[27] However, the spirit of religious toleration did not extend to the schools and colleges operated by Christian missionaries in Turkey. In all schools, Jones was told, religion could only be taught to students of the same faith. In other words, teachers of one faith could not offer religious instruction to students of another faith.

While Jones was in Constantinople, he visited a museum that had on display a block of stone taken from the Temple at Jerusalem. The inscription on the stone read, "Let no Gentile pass this point upon pain of death." Later, when he was in Jerusalem, he reflected on the significance of the inscription. Jesus, he thought, must have seen the racially prejudiced warning as he taught in the Temple.

> You can hear the break in his voice, sign of the inward pain, as he cries, "Take these things hence. It is written, 'My Father's house shall be called a house of Prayer for all nations,['] but you have made it a den of thieves." A house of prayer for all nations had been turned into a house of prejudice for the Jews. He drove them out.[28]

Like his questions about race relations, which he directed to the League of Nations staff in Geneva, his meditation on the inscription from the Temple at Jerusalem reveals his deep sensitivity to the issue of racism and to the fact that racial prejudice is fundamentally inconsistent with the gospel of Jesus Christ.

From Constantinople Jones and Eddy traveled to Ankara, the new Turkish capitol. Then Stanley traveled on his own to Jerusalem where he met Mabel and eleven-year-old daughter Eunice, who had arrived from the United States. The family spent a month together in Palestine and in Egypt. In both places Jones did some sightseeing with his family and he held evangelistic meetings. His first meeting was held at the YMCA for a religiously diverse audience. Afterward, he wrote in the *Indian Witness,*

> we noted the following in the audience: Moslems, Jews, Roman Catholics, Greek Orthodox, Marianites, Copts, Mormons, Moravians, members of the Church of England, Christian and Missionary Alliance, Episcopalians, Pentecostal Bands, Nazarenes, Methodists, Presbyterians, Church of God, Baptists, Armenians, members of the American Colony, and others not ascertained.

What gospel, he asked himself, was needed for a group composed of so many different Christians and non-Christians? His answer came as he thought about the places he had seen in Palestine where Jesus had been, and as he opened himself to the message given to him by the Holy Spirit at each of these places.

> I had sat quietly in the little synagogue at Nazareth and heard again the limpid words of the young man as he made the startling announcement: "The Spirit of the Lord is upon me, because he hath anointed me to preach the gospel to the poor. . . ." I had bowed my head and prayed that the Spirit of the Lord might be upon me also; that I, too, might preach the gospel to the poor and heal the brokenhearted. . . .
>
> I had sat by the well-side at Jacob's well in Samaria and put my fingers reverently in the grooves in the stone well-curbing worn by the ropes through

the centuries. . . . As these people from many lands and many shades of faith sat before me night after night I longed to put my bucket deep into the character and mind of Jesus and bring a crystal draught for thirsty souls. . . .

I had gone out to Gethsemane's garden at night and had the keeper let me into the garden, where I could be alone under the trees. . . . [T]he message I bore home that night was that Gethsemane's meaning is not the agony and the sweat, but its message is in the phrase, "Arise, let us be going.". . . I knew that before me sat night after night men and women who were having their Gethsemane of uncertainty about the Father's will, having hours of agony unshared by even their closest friends, and I longed to be able to tell them that prayer and surrender could bring power and poise sufficient for any looming Calvary.[29]

On another night Stanley went out of Jerusalem to Gordon's Calvary, which, he noted, is probably not the actual site of Jesus' crucifixion. But he reflected on the meaning of his visit to the site. Gordon's Calvary, he wrote,

was difficult to get into. The Moslems have built a wall around it to enclose their graves. To get to the hill I had to climb over a wall, then through a barbed-wire entanglement and up a steep way before I got to the top of the hill. As I sat there in the moonlight waiting for the meaning of Calvary to become clear, I thought how difficult we had made the cross. We have built around the cross walls of separation, placed barbed-wire entanglements of exact doctrinal statement, and have made the way incredibly steep and difficult. And yet nothing is really simpler—he gave himself for men. Love took him there for me. I sat there and took in its healing and its balm and opened my heart to accept that cross myself.[30]

After the family's visit to Egypt, they sailed for Bombay from Port Said on the *S. S. Circassia,* arriving in Bombay on October 23, 1925, more than a year and a half since they had left. The day before the ship docked, Stanley wrote to Diffendorfer, thanking him and the Board of Foreign Missions for having shown him "every courtesy & help" during his stay in the United States. He was especially grateful for the opportunity to participate in the American Seminar. The summer of 1925, he said, was "the best of my life and as useful as a University course." But, he confided to his friend and colleague,

As I face India again I am half afraid. I am not sure I can bring what the situation demands. Were it not for the power of prayer & did I not know the resources that my Father would put at my disposal I should be tempted to run away. It is no easy or light thing to be a missionary to the East now.

At first glance it might seem strange that at this point in his career Stanley Jones would doubt his own ability to return to India and resume his responsibilities as a missionary evangelist. After all, in the early 1920s he had traveled and preached in Iraq and China, he had published a best-selling book which sold 600,000 copies by 1940 and which would soon be translated into a score of languages, and he was widely known and in great demand as a speaker in both India and the United States. Even his need for additional university training, which he had expressed in his February 6, 1925, letter to Diffendorfer, must surely have been satisfied by the American Seminar. Yet his self-doubt cannot be dismissed as either false modesty or a temporary emotion.

Some of his apprehension about returning to India was based on his lack of seminary or graduate education. Although in 1920 he had been given an honorary D.D. degree from his alma mater, Asbury College,[31] and had given the commencement address there in 1925, he was acutely aware of the intellectual demands that would be placed on him in the coming years. India's educated elite were becoming more insistent that India become an independent nation. And they were probing more skeptically into the message about a Christ who was disentangled from Western culture. But on a deeper level, Stanley felt spiritually inadequate. He knew that the truth of Jesus Christ and the relevance of Christianity to Indian culture and society would be challenged when he returned to India as it had never been challenged before. In order to meet these new challenges, he needed above all the sustaining and reassuring power and presence of the Holy Spirit.

Stanley's feelings of self-doubt and personal inadequacy were reflected in the last series of meetings he had held in Egypt before returning to India. He wrote about his four-night evangelistic campaign in that country in the January 28, 1926, issue of the *Christian Advocate.*

> So when I stood before the throngs of students and others that faced me night after night, I knew my message—A Living Person. There have been times this summer when I have looked into the face of God and told Him that I could not go back to India without something big, that I refuse to face this non-Christian world without a gospel—a gospel not merely of a great Ethic or of a beautiful Character, but a gospel of Redemption.[32]

Before he returned to India, Stanley was given a genuine gospel of redemption for the non-Christian world. On the fourth night of his Egyptian evangelistic campaign after speaking to audiences of Coptic Christians, Muslims, and a few Jews and missionaries, hundreds of Copts and Muslims responded to the invitation to accept Jesus Christ as their personal Lord and Savior, and stayed for an after meeting. Of those who remained for the after meeting two hundred signed commitments to attend Bible classes.

The India to which Stanley Jones returned in October 1925 was not the same India he had left in March 1924. The noncooperation movement among Indian nationalists was gaining strength throughout the country, gathering support from more and more Indians and even from some of the British in India and of course from a few Western missionaries like Jones.

Throughout the 1920s his circular or duplicate letters make more and more references to the growing political unrest in India. Although Gandhi's first official and well publicized act of civil disobedience did not occur until he began his famous Salt March in 1930, the important transition within the Indian nationalist movement from passive noncooperation with British authority in India to active and deliberate disobedience of British law occurred much earlier. Back in May 1923, Stanley had been in Nadiad where the noncooperators were in charge of his meetings and where the nightly audiences of one thousand people were composed almost entirely of noncooperators. He wrote in his May 25, 1923, circular letter,

> The whole audience wore the white home-spun, the national costume. As they rose between the close of my address and the closing prayer they gave the nationalistic cries of "Bande Mataram" (Hail to the Motherland) and "Mahatma Gandhi ki jai" (Hail to Mahatma Gandhi), but they became perfectly quiet as I began my prayer. During the day I had long talks with the leaders of the movement. One of them had just come out of jail—political prisoner. They were most sympathetic toward Christ. They were trying to paralyze the Government of the city by refusing to pay taxes [an act of civil disobedience]. Men were moving through the city with sandwich boards on them saying "Refuse to pay the taxes. Let them sell you out. Do not strike back. Suffer. The tears of the weak will undermine the strongest wall." They were perfectly orderly.

Concerned about Gandhi's influence and the growing noncooperation movement, Stanley wrote to Gandhi on January 9, 1926, what he described as "a private note of a friend to a friend."[33] (This letter was never published either in India or the United States.) In his letter Jones was completely honest, so honest, in fact, that at the end he asked Gandhi's forgiveness "for my open frankness." He began by expressing his sincere and deep desire to visit Gandhi's ashram at Sabarmati. However, he explained that because of his heavy schedule of speaking engagements, it would probably be at least six months before he could come. "I therefore write what I wanted to talk with you." His letter continued,

> I have tried to interpret you and your message to the Western world and have been somewhat responsible for the interest that the West has in you and what you are doing. . . . We of the West have been interested in you particularly because we have seen you exemplify certain things that lie at the heart of the Gospel. I had thought that you had grasped the inner meaning of Christ and the Gospel. I find it difficult for me to hold that view now. As I have studied

your writing and watched your work . . . I have come to the conclusion that you really have missed the heart of the Gospel. . . . To me the Gospel lies in His Person. He himself is the good news. . . .

Now, Mahatmaji, I may be wrong; I hope I am. But I cannot help feeling that it is just here that your are weakest in your grasp [of Christ]. You have caught the principles but missed the Person.

Then he offered a suggestion. Since Gandhi had made it known that he was taking a year off from his public and political responsibilities as the *de facto* leader of the Indian nationalist movement in order to study, reflect, and pray at his ashram, Stanley believed that 1926 was a "providential" year for Gandhi to discover the central truth of Christianity. "My suggestion is that you go over the ground again, that you penetrate through the principles to the Person, that you then come back to us and tell us what you have found." In conclusion, he wrote,

I say these things to you not in the spirit of a mere Christian propagandist, but the fact is that we need you. We who are Christians need you. We need the interpretation and illustration which we feel you could give if you grasp this radiant Person of Jesus. The West needs you. . . . But I am frank to say to you that it is almost entirely because they have seen in you a phase of Christianity largely neglected in our Western Christianity. Their disappointment will come, as I am frank to say it has come to me, when they see that you have grasped a phase instead of an inward centre.

Gandhi replied on January 18, 1926, just over a week later.

I hasten to reply to your kind letter by return post. I appreciate the love underlying the letter and kind thought for my welfare. But my difficulty is of long standing. The matter has been presented to me before now by many other friends. I cannot grasp the position through the intellect. It is purely a matter of the heart. Saul became Paul not by an intellectual effort but by something touching his heart. I can only say that my heart is absolutely open. I have no axes to grind. I want to find truth—to see God face to face. But there I stop—

Stanley wrote a short letter to Diffendorfer on January 21, 1926, and enclosed copies of the two letters quoted above. He asked that the letters not be made public but said Diffendorfer might share them "privately with the heads of the office asking them to covenant in prayer for the revelation of Jesus Christ to come to the Mahatma. Only prayer can do it." He told Diffendorfer that he planned to spend two weeks at Gandhi's ashram in July of 1926. He closed with another appeal for confidentiality. "Above all do not publish this before any public meeting."

Diffendorfer did not reply to Jones's January 21 letter until March 26, 1926, because he had been traveling on behalf of the Board of Foreign

Missions since late December 1925. First of all, he assured Jones that he had taken "every possible caution with reference to publicity of this proposed visit of yours [to Gandhi's ashram]." He and other board staff members had entered "into their personal prayer calendars the subject of your visit." Finally, he wrote,

> We will also assemble just after Easter in a small office council, at which time I will read the correspondence to the Secretaries and Associate Secretaries and then we will join in prayer for you. I will try also to bring it to their attention again the latter part of June just before you leave for Mr. Gandhi's Ashram, so that we can remember you and him at that time.

Jones did visit Gandhi's Sabarmati Ashram for eight days in July 1926. On July 22, he wrote to Dr. John Edwards, a corresponding secretary for the board, to report the outcome of his visit. Gandhi was "greatly harassed by people from all over the world telling him where to go and what to do in religion." "My task then," he told Edwards,

> was to really present Christ to him and yet keep from precipitating a crisis that would make him take a stand on the other side and harass him still more. It was a very delicate business, but each day as we talked together we had the guidance of the living Christ, misunderstandings were removed and we led him straight to the thing to which we felt he ought to go, namely, Christian experience. . . . The basis of a lasting friendship has been laid and the way is now open for a clear impact of Christ upon his soul. The fact is he has been slipping back the last couple of years in his Christian position and outlook. I hope we have arrested that process.[34]

Undoubtedly Jones and others in India as well as the Methodist Mission Board members and staff in New York prayed fervently that as a result of Jones's visit to Sabarmati, Gandhi would receive Jesus Christ as his personal Lord and Savior. Whether these prayers were answered we do not know. But we do know that Gandhi never publicly renounced Hinduism and embraced Christianity.

So what is the enduring significance of Stanley Jones's visit with Gandhi? Certainly he established a personal relationship with Gandhi that would serve both him and Christian missions in India well throughout the years of social and political turbulence that culminated in India's becoming an independent nation in 1947. Jones visited Gandhi again, as we will see in the following chapters. And after Gandhi resumed active leadership of the Indian independence movement and in 1930 began his campaign of civil disobedience against continued British rule of India, Jones became an even more outspoken advocate of Indian independence. Indeed, after Gandhi's assassination in 1948, he wrote a book entitled, *Mahatma Gandhi:*

An Interpretation, in which he said that Gandhi's death was "the greatest tragedy since the Son of God died on a cross."[35]

Between 1926 and 1948, Jones did not change his mind about Gandhi. Gandhi was already well known throughout the world in 1926 as both the spiritual and national leader of the Indian independence movement. But as his national and international stature grew to superhuman proportions, especially in the West and especially later after his martyrdom, he became a Christ figure. What made Gandhi so emotionally and spiritually appealing as a universal Christ figure was, as Jones perceptively discerned, the fact that this Christlike person symbolized perfectly the disentangled Christ, the Christ of the Indian road who was actually the Christ of every man and woman everywhere in the world. So even though Gandhi, as far as we know, never became a Christian, Jones's personal relationship with him exerted an emphatically Christian influence not only on Gandhi but also on Nehru and on other leaders of the Indian independence movement. In addition, his honest and fruitful search for an authentically Indian expression of Christianity has left an indelible imprint on the character of Indian Christianity even today. Finally, Stanley Jones was himself changed by India and changed particularly by Gandhi. This was what made his presentation of the gospel so appealing and so compelling—his unshakable integrity grounded in God's truth that in order to evangelize others we must also be willing to be evangelized by them.

Shortly after the Jones family returned to India in October 1925, Stanley began to hold more and more round table conferences. He first mentioned these conferences in his May 25, 1923, circular letter. Round table conferences, as we saw in chapter 4, were interreligious discussion groups that Stanley held in conjunction with his evangelistic meetings for the leaders of the various religions in the cities in which he met. The term "round table" is significant because no one sat at the "head" of the table in these conferences. All religious leaders who sat at the table were represented on an equal basis. Each participant shared his personal experience with God. Stanley explained how he used round table conferences in his March 2, 1926, letter to Diffendorfer.

> [W]e are having Round-table Conferences with leading non-Christians in every place [where Jones was holding evangelistic meetings]. We invite in fifteen of the leading men and then suggest that no one argue, no one try to make a case, that we do not talk abstractly, but simply share with each other what we have found of God. We go round the circle, allowing them [non-Christians] to speak first so that they will not feel that they have to match what we say of the discovery of God through Christ.

What most impressed Stanley about these round table conferences was the fact "that the non-Christian faiths are bankrupt." Only the Christians around the table "had really realised God in any vital way." Adherents of all the other religions only hoped for a genuinely personal experience with God. Jones concluded his letter with the remark that he was taking careful notes of these conferences and that his "next book ought to be along that line."

Diffendorfer thought that Jones's round table conferences were a brilliant idea. In a letter dated April 3, 1926, he said that he was "most interested" in Jones's innovative evangelistic technique. The notes Jones was making on the conferences would be "a wonderful human document" and "a distinct contribution to the missionary enterprise all over the world." As a corresponding secretary for Methodist missions on several continents, Diffendorfer saw many opportunities for the immediate application of Jones's idea to other Methodist mission stations. In fact, Diffendorfer suggested Mexico as a country in which round table conferences would be very fruitful with the proper leadership. He quickly recognized that these conferences were really opportunities "for personal conversation—just friendly acquaintances and discussions with people of influence, regarding religion." The traditional methods of evangelism, emphasizing large open meetings led by powerful preachers who ended their messages with dramatic calls for public confession of sins and acceptance of a personal relationship with Jesus Christ, were no longer effective in many nations of the world. The situation in India and elsewhere, Diffendorfer concluded in his April 3 letter to Jones, "demands a new type of missionary, which you yourself are."

Jones's circular letters to his friends and financial supporters in the United States during the mid-1920s are filled with references to the outstanding success of his round table conferences throughout India. His April 20, 1926, circular letter reported what happened during a round table conference at Cocanada among the Telegu people, whom he described as "a very emotionally responsive people." A Hindu whom no one suspected of being a Christian revealed that after years of searching for religious truth he had finally found Christ and proclaimed that he was "an unbaptised Christian." The Hindu's testimony "moved our hearts. Since these meetings the revival has spread among the Christians of other stations round about and they are going everywhere witnessing." There was a similar response to the round table conference in Coimbatore.

> In the Round Table the deepest sense of Christ was upon us [deeper than] we had ever felt in any of these conferences. As we witnessed for Christ tears gathered in our eyes and hearts. As I left that place I went to my room and thanked God for the way Christ is capturing the heart of India.

Over a year later in a circular letter dated June 20, 1927, Jones wrote that he had spent most of the preceding two months writing *Christ at the Round*

Table. He had used his vacation time during the hottest season of the year to go "to the quiet hill station of Almora" to begin his second book. Most of the text of the book is taken from the extensive notes he had taken during the conferences. *Christ at the Round Table* provides a very detailed account of what was said at these conferences. He never identified any of the round table conference participants by name, but when a round table was organized for Jones in Madras by Charles W. Ranson (1903–88), a Methodist missionary from Ireland, Jones discovered that some of the Indians who had attended conferences were not completely anonymous. In his autobiography, *A Missionary Pilgrimage,* Ranson described what happened:

> The people who organized Jones' Madras visit asked me to convene the "round table" there as I was known to be in touch with leading Hindus. I invited about a dozen of these Hindus to my apartment to meet Dr. Jones. They were friendly and courteous; but when Jones raised questions of religion, they evaded them by promptly changing the subject. From Jones' point of view, the meeting was a flop. I was myself puzzled, because I had talked about religion with some of these men and they had spoken without inhibition. I questioned one of them later, and he said that Venkatarama Shastri, the advocate general of Madras and one of the participants, had acquired a copy of Christ at the Round Table and shown it to his friends. They saw that previous participants in these sessions, though not identified by name, were nonetheless recognizable. So they agreed ahead of time that they were not going to have their religious sentiments reproduced in print.[36]

Although Jones's round table conferences made an important contribution to the evangelization of non-Christian religious and intellectual leaders in India, it was his Christian ashrams which have made a broader and deeper impact on Christianity not only in India but also throughout the world. Jones was not the first to conceive of using the traditional Indian concept of a forest retreat for spiritual study and meditation (which is what the word *ashram* means) for Christian purposes. In his April 20, 1926, circular letter Jones reported to his friends and supporters in the United States that the first three months of 1926 were "the finest three months I have known in India." During these three months one of the places he visited was Puri.

> At Puri we visited a notable Christian leader who has set up an Ashram to make Christianity more indigenous. We encouraged him, for a blade out of the soul of India is worth a stalk of foreign transplantation.

Three years later, during the summer of 1929, Stanley had another experience with an ashram, this one in Poona, in south India, where he held very successful meetings. He described his time at the ashram in a September 5, 1929, circular letter.

I stayed with the brothers of the Christian Ashram while there. The Ashram is built on the principle of simplicity combined with a passionate Christian devotion. The brothers, European and Indian, live in little cells about five feet by seven. They wear sandals, dress in Indian home-spun, eat in Indian style with the fingers, have a sun-rise meeting each day, keep silence until 9 a.m. and also after dinner at night to bedtime, have no money, live in a brotherhood of worship of Christ and work for men. The atmosphere was joyously Christian. I loved it. I felt utterly at home. It made me very eager to hasten the establishment of our Ashram in North India. We hope to have it going by the spring.

"I am a very happy man," he wrote in conclusion. "To my very fingertips I love this struggle for the soul of a people. It has the feel of a real battle in it. I would not be elsewhere for worlds."

In a short letter to Diffendorfer, also dated September 5, Stanley said that he anticipated beginning his own ashram during the winter of 1929–30. The property for the ashram, known as the Sat Tal Estate and consisting of four hundred acres, was purchased through the private financial arrangements of "a few individuals. It looks a gift from heaven." The money actually came from Jones himself, as his son-in-law, James K. Mathews, revealed in his autobiography, A Global Odyssey.[37] Jones later gave the property to the Methodist Church in India. In the next chapter we will see how he organized and operated his Sat Tal Ashram.

While Stanley was conducting round table conferences and making plans for the establishment of his Christian ashram in the mid- and late 1920s, he continued to hold evangelistic meetings throughout India as well as in Ceylon (Sri Lanka), Burma, Malaya, Singapore, and Thailand. In the summer of 1926 he spent several months in the hill stations of India, some of them in very remote areas. In order to reach Pauri in the Garhwal district, he wrote in his July 1, 1926, circular letter, he "had to tramp three days' marches [sic] across the mountains."

The invitation to hold evangelistic meetings in Burma came from the various Christian missionary organizations that were active in that nation. In Rangoon, he spoke to what he called in his March 22, 1927, circular letter a very "cosmopolitan" crowd of over 2000, including Burmans, Chinese, Tamils, Telegus, Hindustanis, Persians, Armenians, Karens, Bengalis, Europeans, and Americans. He also held meetings in Mandalay and Moulmein and again in Rangoon where he held a final meeting for those who had signed cards during his previous visit indicating an interest in converting to Christianity.

I came away from Burma feeling that I had left a good deal of my heart with the people there. They are a most lovable people, but Buddhism left a dryness in the soul of the Burmese that we do not find among the Hindus.

Burma is spiritually dead, but they would be a wonderful people if the incubus of Buddhism could be lifted from them.

In the fall of 1927 Jones traveled to Malaya, a nation with large Indian and Chinese populations, which he referred to as "the land of opportunity."[38] As compared to India and most other Asian nations in the late 1920s, Malaya was very prosperous. The Methodist Episcopal Church had a number of mission schools throughout the peninsula, most of which were financially independent of the Board of Foreign Missions in the United States. In Kuala Lumpur, for example, Jones was astounded that one-half of the money for the new high school building for the Methodist mission school was contributed by the Chinese and Indians living in Malaya and that the other half was paid by the government. He also held evangelistic meetings and round table conferences in Kuala Lumpur. During the round table conferences Jones remarked on some of the same spiritual differences between the Chinese and Indians that he had observed in his visit to China in 1922.

The Chinese talked of his interest in religion as illustrated in his building a temple, or putting up a school; the Indian would talk of his interest in ideas, or realization of the divine. One built up a mental system and the other material things. In the interviews one could see the difference in the type of problems: the Indian would unfold his mental difficulties in regard to the gospel, while the Chinese would almost invariably locate his trouble in some question of how one should act as a Christian in some concrete relationship.[39]

After Malaya, ten days of meetings were scheduled in Singapore, most held in the YMCA. The finest group, he wrote in the *Indian Witness,* was the students in the Anglo-Chinese school.

They were alive, and when the last appeal was made 199 signed up [to declare their faith in Jesus Christ]. They were going after that one more to make it 200. A finer set of lads cannot be found anywhere in the world. In the two periods I gave them for questions they took about five hours! And they were not carping questions, but mostly questions connected with the problems of living the Christian life.[40]

The last stop on Stanley's 1927 trip was Siam (Thailand). To reach Bangkok he traveled by train for many hours "through virgin tropical forests." It was only in recent years, he wrote in his December 20, 1927, circular letter, that trains could run through these forests at night because "the wild elephants would charge them and some wrecks occurred as these mighty and proud beasts challenged the new-comers." Because Thailand was Buddhist, he did not receive the same favorable response to his

Christian messages that he had received in Malaya and Singapore, but at Bangkok Christian College there were fifty-two persons in the audience who made decisions for Christ. On the first night in the State University, the chairman of the meeting was a member of the royal family. "It was interesting to sit down with royalty and put up our gospel to them. They are folks like the rest of us."

Stanley returned to India from his long trip with the confirmation in his spirit that "the human heart is the same around the world." "We are [all] made for God," he wrote, paraphrasing Augustine, "and we rest not until we rest in Him." He also returned to India with two specific convictions about Malaya. His first was that Malaya is "one of the ripest, if not the ripest, mission field in the world. Here men have broken with the past, have little or nothing but materialism to fill the present, but they want something."[41]

His second conviction was that "our Methodist Mission, which has the ascendancy in this Peninsula, is not meeting the opportunity in an adequate way." Although he acknowledged the excellent work that the Methodist Episcopal Church was doing in Malaya, he insisted that because of the growing emigration of Chinese and Indians to Malaya and Singapore, the situation was ripe for expanded Christian evangelization and that the Methodist Church should take advantage of this providential opportunity.

During the 1920s E. Stanley Jones discovered the Christ of the Indian road. His affirmation of the non-Western expressions of Christianity as authentic parts of the Body of Christ prepared him for the challenges of the Jerusalem Conference of the International Missionary Council in 1928. While most of those at the conference concluded that criticism of Western civilization and the comparative study of all religions as morally and spiritually equal had created a profound crisis for Christian mission, he found instead an underlying unity among Eastern and Western Christians and between fundamentalists and modernists. Drawing on his experience at Tagore's Santiniketan Ashram, and on his own round table conferences, he began to develop a more culturally inclusive vision of Christianity.

As we will see in the next chapter, Jones discovered the seemingly paradoxical concept of Christ as both exclusive and universal. In 1930, at his first Christian ashram at Sat Tal during the spring and early summer, he had an opportunity to discuss these ideas and to put them into practice among a diverse group of Christians and non-Christians. At his second ashram, the topic for discussion and action was the subject of his fourth book, *The Christ of the the Mount*. At the third ashram, the subject would become of special significance for his later ministry—the kingdom of God.

Jones's discovery of the Christ of the Indian road also gave him a heightened sensitivity to the national aspirations of India. In the early 1930s, as Gandhi's campaign for Indian independence turned from passive noncooperation to active civil disobedience, Jones encountered more and more Indian nationalists at his meetings. His sympathetic understanding of Indian culture and his inclusive approach to Christianity made his messages particularly appealing to educated Indian audiences. Jones even had an opportunity, as we will see, to present the gospel of Jesus Christ to Gandhi himself.

Following the 1925 publication of *The Christ of the Indian Road,* Stanley became almost instantly famous. That, along with his travels in the United States during 1924 and 1925 as a high-profile spokesman for missions under the auspices of the Methodist Episcopal Board of Foreign Missions, made his nomination and election as bishop at the 1928 General Conference almost inevitable. Although he resigned almost as soon as he was elected, his election reflects and underscores his stature within his own denomination.

In the years leading up to World War II, Stanley would face many difficulties, both personal and professional. The financial problems of American Christian churches, especially the financial problems of overseas missions, persisted through the 1930s. In 1938, ten years after the Jerusalem Conference, he attended another international missionary conference, this time in Tambaram, near Madras, India. But at Tambaram, instead of being a voice for unity and hope, he was diametrically opposed to the position of most of the other delegates and to the position of his own Methodist Church.

Another issue he confronted again and again in his remaining years in India was the issue of religious proselytism in a nation where conversion to Christianity was a politically explosive issue. Like all Christian missionaries in India, Stanley had to decide whether he could in good conscience sign the missionary pledge, which was a commitment of his political loyalty to the British government in India. In the end, his outspoken support for Indian nationalism cost him the privilege of returning to India during World War II and separated him from his wife and daughter for nearly six years. But these problems did not diminish his growing international reputation as a missionary evangelist.

8

Crossroads and Crosscurrents

I rather dread it for they will be expecting too much from me.
—January 2, 1928, Letter to Miss Nellie on Jones's upcoming trip to the U.S.

Reasons why Daddy should <u>not</u> be Bishop.
1. Most likely have to leave Sitapur for Singapore.
2. Have to sell car. . . .
4. Have to give my Rabbits away as Singapore is to[o] civilized.
5. Have to give most of my things away as you can't cart them all.
6. Have to lose half my holidays coming & going.
7. Won't be able to see Betty, Christine etc. for years. . . .
10. Won't know anyone there & don't want to. . . .
12. Daddy turn grey hairs before his time.
13. Daddy won't be happy.
                                        —Eunice Jones (Age 14?), probably 1928[1]

THE MODERN TWENTIETH-CENTURY Christian, wrote Professor William E. Hocking in 1932, anticipates and welcomes not "the destruction" of non-Christian religions, but "their continued co-existence with Christianity, each stimulating the other in growth toward the ultimate goal, unity in the completest religious truth."[2]

This was the conclusion of the Commission of Inquiry chaired by Hocking and financed by John D. Rockefeller, Jr., to reexamine American Protestant foreign missions throughout the world. The publication of the commission's report, entitled *Re-Thinking Missions: A Laymen's Inquiry After One Hundred Years,* "burst like a bombshell upon the thinking Christian public in America."[3] Indeed, even today, seventy years after *Re-Thinking*

Missions was published, Hocking's words sound more like New Age syncretism than genuine Christianity.

By the time Hocking wrote the commission's report, American Protestant foreign missions were in a state of profound crisis. The declining financial support for Christian missions in the United States in the 1920s necessitated the drastic reduction if not elimination of hundreds of overseas mission stations. But this financial catastrophe reflected a deeper spiritual crisis in the very heart of American Christianity. World War I, fought by supposedly Christian nations against one another, had "greatly tarnished Western moral and spiritual prestige." In addition, Russia, once a proudly Christian nation, repudiated Christianity after 1917 and became an officially atheist nation. Moreover, secular humanism became increasingly popular among academicians and educated people throughout the world, including many Christian nations. So when the International Missionary Council organized a conference at Jerusalem in 1928, representing twenty-six national and international Christian bodies, the conference became the focus of several complex crosscurrents in Christianity. It "met amid widespread insecurity and instability, skepticism regarding claims of absolute truth, and immersion in material values."[4]

In his December 20, 1927, circular letter,[5] Stanley Jones wrote to his friends and financial supporters in the United States that he would leave India in March 1928 to attend the Jerusalem Conference. On January 2, 1928, he wrote to Miss Nellie that his first stop on the way to Jerusalem would be Baghdad. From Baghdad he would travel by car across the desert to Palestine. During the conference, "we will live in tents on the Mount of Olives and have our meetings in the Russian Church." Then, since he had been elected as a delegate to the General Conference of the Methodist Episcopal Church, which would meet in Kansas City in May 1928, he would continue his journey to the United States and after General Conference would conduct meetings throughout both the United Sates and Latin America at the request of the Board of Foreign Missions.[6] Mabel and Eunice remained in India, and Stanley did not see his family again until April 1929.[7]

After the Jerusalem Conference had completed its work, Stanley summarized the conclusions of the 240 delegates in an article for the *Indian Witness* entitled, "What Happened at Jerusalem?" First, he echoed the observations of the scholars quoted above. The conference met at "the most critical hour" in the history of Christian missions. The scathing criticism of Western civilization, the academic study of comparative religions suggesting that non-Christian religions are just as valid as Christianity, the "intense dislike . . . of religious imperialism"—all of these factors raised the question of whether Christian missions were obsolete and should be abandoned altogether.

189

Jones's answer to this question was an emphatic no. He firmly believed that the Jerusalem Conference marked not the end of Christian missions but the beginning of "a new creative period" for Christian missions. He found persuasive evidence for his belief in the resolution of specific conflicts within the Christian missionary movement, which, before the Jerusalem Conference, were widely assumed to be irreconcilable. Because the delegates represented a broad geographical and cultural mix of nations, he concluded that the historical, economic, and political differences between Christians in the East and Christians in the West were disappearing. In addition, the split between fundamentalists and modernists, which many commentators thought would paralyze the conference, was transcended by the common acknowledgment of the delegates that there was "something higher" shared by them all. "We were together at the feet of Christ," he wrote, and belonged to each other at a deeper level than the superficial differences between fundamentalists and modernists would suggest. He pointed out that the conference dealt with and answered the question of whether Christianity was the fulfillment of non-Christian faiths, and thus had much in common with them, or was a truly unique religion, by affirming the truth of both positions.

> A fusion took place: We saw that the Gospel was a fulfillment of the finest and noblest aspirations of the human race and that God had not left himself without witness with any people, but we saw just as clearly that there was something in the Gospel that was not merely a prolongation of other ideas, there was something more and other.

The final issue considered by the Jerusalem Conference involved the physical protection of missionaries and of missionary property. Because independence movements in India and civil war in China made this an especially sensitive issue for foreign missionaries in these countries, Stanley quoted in its entirety the conference resolution on this question.

> The International Missionary Council places on record its conviction that the protection of missionaries and missionary property should only be by such methods as will promote goodwill in personal and official relations, and that mission societies should relinquish all claim on their Governments for the armed defense of their missionaries and their property. . . .
> Finally, the International Missionary Council desires to record its conviction that the foreign missionary enterprise is spiritual and moral and not a political enterprise and its work should be carried on within two human rights alone, the right of religious freedom for all men, and maintenance by each nation of law and order for all within its bounds.[8]

The most controversial situation Jones confronted during his 1928–29 trip to Jerusalem and the United States, however, was not the matter of the protection of foreign missionaries and missionary property. It was rather the personal question of his becoming a bishop of the Methodist Episcopal Church. Whether he would accept his election to the episcopacy was a genuine crossroads both in his personal life and in his career as a missionary evangelist.

Four years earlier, in 1924, his name had been put up for election as bishop at General Conference, and he had asked that his name be withdrawn. At this 1928 General Conference in Kansas City, his name had again been proposed for election, and he had again asked that it be withdrawn. But, as he explained in *A Song of Ascents*,[9] "after twenty-two ballots there was a deadlock" between two eminently qualified candidates. To break the deadlock, someone from the floor of the conference suggested, "I believe we could elect Stanley Jones by acclamation." The presiding bishop, however, ruled that there had to be a ballot on the question of Jones's election. So the ballot was taken and Jones was elected.

But he had no inner peace. He described his spiritual and emotional turmoil in a letter dated June 6, 1928, which was written in longhand to "My Dear Folks" (probably his family in India) on stationery from The Washington Duke Hotel in Durham, North Carolina.[10]

> That night I could not sleep a wink. The next morning I knew I could not go on. I have never had such a Gethsemane as the next day. Cold sweat stood out on my brow as the inward battle went on. In the early morning I wrote out my resignation, but did not present it till night. I spoke to two people about it during the day—Diff [Diffendorfer] & Bishop Welsh. Diff. was sick over it—could not sleep either. Welsh said I must not pull out. He was strong for the organization. Welsh the man would have said resign . . . [but] the official said sacrifice yourself for the sake of the Church. . . . When we practiced going through the consecration ceremony I felt as though I was in a chain gang. It was so utterly unreal. I could not say I was called to the office & work. I felt I was deserting my work.

That evening as the Conference resumed its official work at 8:00 P.M., Stanley was still fighting the inward battle.

> When I took my place on the platform along with the bishops, my inner voice came back: "Now is the time to get out." My confidence and direction were back. I knew exactly what I should do. I walked over to the chairman, Bishop E. S. Johnson, and said: "I have a matter of high privilege to present." He asked me what it was. . . . So I put my resignation before him. He gave me the floor. I thanked the conference for the honor it had bestowed upon me, assured them of my respect for the bishops and the bishopric, ended up by saying, "But I am called to be an evangelist and a missionary, and I hereby resign as a bishop-elect of the Methodist Church." I walked out at the back of the platform, not waiting to see if they would accept my resignation.

The General Conference, of course, accepted Jones's resignation, but not without animosity and resentment directed against him for tacitly accepting his election as bishop but then abruptly resigning. In his auto-biography Jones greatly understated this animosity and resentment. But he was acutely aware of it, as his daughter Eunice revealed in an article published in *United Methodists Today* in 1975. Commenting on his refusal of the office of bishop, she wrote, "I cannot think such a decision today would cause the consternation it did then." Moreover, she continued, "Only a few close friends and his family knew his hurt."[11] Mabel, of course, was totally opposed to his becoming a bishop, as we saw in chapter 3. She knew Stanley's strengths and weaknesses better than anyone else, and she knew he was not called to be a bishop. She took the news that he had resigned with gratitude that her prayers were answered and confirmed by the specific mandate Stanley had received from the Holy Spirit.

When the General Conference of the Methodist Church concluded its business, Stanley toured the Eastern and Central United States, speaking or conducting round table conferences for pastors of different denominations during three-hour sessions in the morning and holding public meetings, which sometimes drew audiences of seven thousand at night. On April 6, 1929, he left America, sailing first to England where he spent a week. On his arrival in Liverpool he was interviewed almost immediately by both the secular and the religious press. Then he addressed the prestigious London Missionary Society. He also made radio broadcasts, which were heard throughout Great Britain, and held a service in the Liverpool Cathedral.

When his week's busy schedule in England was completed, he traveled to Marseilles where he boarded a ship for India. "My cabin mate," he wrote in his May 8, 1929, circular letter, was "a captain in the British Army" and was "converted on the second day out. It was a joy to see him after that."

In the tropics, the weather got hotter and hotter, he wrote, and "we got our sun hats and needed them."

> Bombay was hot but I knew it would be hotter as I came up through the country. On the train up I took out my clinical thermometer to see how hot it was in the compartment under the fan. The mercury straightway ran up to 108 degrees and since the thermometer would register no more it stopped there! Yesterday it was 114 in the shade and the hottest month is not yet here—June.
>
> But the missionaries and Mrs. Jones and the Indians were at the station to meet me at Lucknow and that compensated for the day of parboiling in the train.

* * *

In his December 7, 1929, circular letter Stanley informed his friends and financial supporters in the United States for the first time about his plans for a four-month ashram from April through July of 1930. He described the ashram as "a kind of forest school for meditation and prayer and thought." Although many non-Christians would be invited to participate, and the members of the ashram would live "in simplicity, in Indian style, wear Indian clothes and eat Indian food," the purpose of the ashram was Christian evangelism. "We hope," he wrote, to send the members of the ashram "back to their tasks in the plains with a new passion to make Christ a saving reality to India." This evangelistic emphasis of the ashram was, of course, more immediately relevant to Western missionaries and Indian Christians than to Indian non-Christians.

About a month after he first explained his ashram to his American friends, he and the Reverend Yunas Sinha wrote a preliminary statement for the Sat Tal Ashram (Sat Tal means "seven lakes"), which was published in the *Indian Witness* on January 9, 1930.[12] "The purpose and spirit" of Sat Tal Ashram, they wrote, was "to produce a type of Christianity more in touch with the soul of India. . . . As the location is in a hill-station we hope to have missionaries and Christian workers and laymen come to us for spiritual recuperation and to get into closer touch with the soul of India." (In fact, the previous owners of the Sat Tal Estate, Mr. and Mrs. A. C. Evans, had operated the estate as a hill-station resort before Jones acquired the property.) Eating Indian food in the ashram meant an exclusively vegetarian diet, and living in Indian style meant living as simply as possible with "few or no servants," so that almost all menial and manual work would be performed by the members of the ashram.

From ten to thirty individuals would be invited to become members of the ashram and to participate in all the activities. They would live together in a large, fourteen-room, centrally located building at Sat Tal. Other persons, who were not invited to the ashram by Jones or Sinha, were free to rent one of twelve smaller but fully furnished bungalows, which were also a part of Sat Tal. Those renting the smaller bungalows could also attend as many of the sessions of the ashram as they wanted.

A more complete explanation of the purpose of the ashram and a more comprehensive account of its program and daily schedule appeared in Stanley's July 3, 1930, circular letter, written toward the end of the first Sat Tal Christian Ashram. "We believe our gospel is universal in its very nature," he wrote, "but the forms in which it is expressed in the West are not necessarily universal." He is articulating once more the objective of his personal search for a gospel that was at once authentically Christian and authentically Indian. In other words, he believed that the gospel of Jesus Christ is both exclusive and universal. On the one hand, he knew and would not compromise in any way his belief that a personal relationship

193

with Jesus Christ is the only way to live both the abundant life now and eternal life after death. On the other hand, he was equally certain that God's offer of salvation through Jesus Christ is truly universal, given freely and graciously to everyone regardless of sex, race, nationality, or religious background. At one level, the level of purely secular logic, these two statements are contradictory. Is God's salvation the exclusive property of Christianity or do other religions offer equally valid ways of knowing God and of receiving his gifts? But on another level, the deeper level of spiritual reasoning and reality on which Jones was living, Christ is both universal and exclusive and the question of choosing among competing claims to religious truth does not arise.

Jones was certainly aware of this apparent contradiction between the exclusive and the universal Christ. For those who considered this issue to be truly problematic—and most of them were modernists within American Christianity—one way to resolve the contradiction was to identify truths common to most or all religions in an effort to define a higher and more comprehensive religious truth. This was exactly the approach of Professor Hocking, quoted earlier. But Jones knew the fatal danger of this approach. In fact, one of the reasons for his ashram, he wrote in his July 3, 1930, circular letter, was to counteract the "very definite tendency to have distinctions between religions fade out and the whole thing end in polite mush." Instead of polite mush, he wanted those who came to Sat Tal to preach a "form of Christianity" that would "be more Christian" and "closer to the New Testament" than any modernist version of the gospel, diluted and made spiritually impotent by the comparative academic study of world religions.

Twenty-five members, both Indians and foreigners, representing diverse streams of Christianity "from the High Churchman to the Quaker" were selected for the first ashram. Stanley wrote in his July 3, 1930, circular letter that "Americans, Indians, English and Anglo-Indians have lived together for these nearly four months on a basis of equality," and "as far as I know there has not been a single unkind word or clash of any type or kind." Each morning the members of the ashram rose at 5:00 and gathered for devotions on a hilltop at 5:15.

> At six fifteen we had our morning tea after which we worked around the estate to an assigned task, cutting wood, building walls on the terrace, working in the garden, etc. At eight we assembled for our group study. The first hour was occupied with a study of the New Testament. It was not a class so much as we tried to think corporately, trying to arrive at a common mind. I led this group in a study of the New Testament and Humanism. At the close of this hour we went into a study of Hinduism in some of its various phases [led by several professors and an Indian poet]. . . . After the Hindu hour we studied Islam with Dr. Titus and Prof. Subhan. . . . This ran us up to eleven

o'clock after which we had our breakfast which consisted of rice and curry, which when you become accustomed to it is very palatable. . . .

After the breakfast hour we were free to do as we liked until the music hour at 4:30 when we had classes in Indian music. . . . Our evening devotion hour was held at the lakeside at 6:15. . . . As we returned from the lake until the evening meal at 8 p.m. we kept silence. After the evening meal we read and discussed some book together until bed time.

The first year of the Sat Tal Ashram was a complete success. Many of the members were "spiritually transformed," Stanley wrote, and returned to their work renewed and refreshed. It "proved such an intellectual and spiritual tonic to many that we have decided to go on largely on the lines of last year."[13]

The next year, after the second ashram had completed three of its four months, Stanley wrote a circular letter dated June 30, 1931. The daily schedule of the second ashram, he said, was much like that of the first. "My job was carrying wood and I learned to bring it in Indian style on the head." The first group study he led focused on Jesus' Sermon on the Mount. "During the year I had written a book on the subject [his fourth book, *The Christ of the Mount*] so I have had the very great advantage of going over the manuscript with the members of the Ashram."

The most remarkable event of the second ashram was the conversion of "a rather famous swami" or Hindu religious leader. The swami

has a very large Ashram himself and has about 3000 families who take him as their guru. When he walked into the room on arrival he fell at my feet and said, "You are my guru." He took that literally and was ready to do anything I said. . . . The day came when he wanted me to baptise him. But just before the Sunday came on which he was to be baptised he revealed, as in a flash, the terrible hatred he had toward the British. . . . I told him I wanted him to be a nationalist but I could not baptise him when his heart was filled with this fierce bitterness. It was a terrible disappointment to him. He had walked hundreds of miles to get to me and here I was refusing him. The tears rolled down his cheeks. He turned to me rather fiercely and said, "How can I get rid of this hatred. Can I change my own heart?" He could not. But Christ did. Some time later he came to me and said, "You will baptise me next Sunday. The hatred is gone." It was! I have scarcely even been in such a meeting as the one in which we baptised him. Every heart there was melted.

During the third Sat Tal Ashram in 1932, Jones recorded his own testimony about a visitation of the Holy Spirit at a time of personal and family crisis. He wrote in his July 1, 1932, circular letter that during the 5:00 A.M. hour of prayer and meditation,

I was burdened about our daughter's health (for it seemed so serious that we would have to scrap all our plans for several years ahead and give ourselves to helping her to regain her health,) but in this prayer hour there came such an overwhelming assurance that she would be well that my heart sang with an absurd joy for days. Sure enough the inner Voice was true—our daughter is well. No plans scrapped.

The theme of the third ashram was the kingdom of God. Sixteen different presentations on this theme were made during the ashram. The focus on the kingdom of God is significant, because, as we will see in later chapters, this became the central message of all Stanley's writing. His profound insight into the kingdom of God as the heart of the gospel that God sent Jesus Christ to proclaim is certainly one of the most important if not the most important intellectual and spiritual legacy E. Stanley Jones left to the Body of Christ throughout the world.[14]

Six weeks after the end of his third Sat Tal Ashram, Jones had an opportunity to explain to the readers of the *Indian Witness* his belief in the importance of the kingdom of God. In an article entitled, "What Is Christianity?"[15] he first rejected several false definitions of Christianity. "Christianity has nothing to do with imperialism," because Jesus Christ would never sanction any kind of "exploitation of weaker nations by stronger nations." Moreover, Christianity, although it has its roots in the Old Testament, "is not identical with the Old Testament." Christianity transcends the divisive issue of creationism versus evolution by not requiring any specific belief about the age of the earth or the universe. Finally, Christianity is not the church. Although the church is "the finest serving institution of the world," it has done too many unchristian things to be identified as the complete and perfect embodiment of Christianity. So, what is Christianity? Jones's answer is that "Christianity is Christ." And what Jesus Christ taught was "the Kingdom of God on earth."

> This new Kingdom is that new moral and spiritual and social and economic and political world order which is knocking at the gates of things as they are. This new Kingdom will replace the present world order, both within the human heart and in the structure of human society, by a new order.

The specific and concrete meaning of this new kingdom order became the consistent and dominant theme of all the evangelistic activities of E. Stanley Jones for the rest of his life.

*   *   *

In addition to starting the ashrams at Sat Tal, Stanley eagerly resumed his heavy schedule of evangelistic meetings after his 1928–29 trip abroad. In Bangalore, he began opening his meetings in a new way—with a garden party. All the head officials came to the garden party, Jones wrote in his

December 7, 1929, circular letter, to welcome him to Bangalore. "From the prime minister down they were all there." From one of the prominent men who greeted Jones he learned that his book, *The Christ of the Indian Road*, was responsible for changing relations between South Africa and India and had facilitated the resolution of a difficult issue between the two nations— the status and rights of Indians living in South Africa. In Hyderabad (Deccan) he also began a series of meetings with a garden party. Three hundred guests, including "all the leading officials" of this Muslim state were present. The Chief Justice of the State chaired the meeting on the first night and "fez-wearing Mohammedans" packed the hall throughout his stay in Hyderabad. Garden parties were an excellent means of attracting local government and business leaders and other notables to the evangelistic meetings. Many of these prominent men who would not attend a public meeting held by Jones would attend private social functions and were thus indirectly introduced to the Christian gospel through personal conversation. Once again, Jones was led by the inner voice to adopt a new and effective method of reaching the educated upper classes of India for Jesus Christ.

In 1930 Stanley received and accepted so many invitations to speak and hold meetings throughout India that, as he wrote to his friends on December 22, he "had only about ten days at home." "It feels good," he said, "to be able to write the words ['at home'] at the top" of his circular letter.

Although he was traveling and was almost always away from Sitapur during 1930 and 1931, he continued to have domestic responsibilities. In his February 3, 1930, letter to Miss Nellie, for example, he writes about Eunice, who was then fifteen.

> We are changing Eunice from the Naini Tal school to the Mussoorie school. She will have more American girls there. There are two girls of her age living next door at the Moffatt's in Sitapur and it is a great joy to have them for they are fine play mates for Eunice. I had a lovely time with them at Christmas.

He mentioned Eunice again in his February 10, 1931, letter to Miss Nellie. He first thanked his friend for the books she had sent to all of the family.

> You were good to send those lovely books. I have seen a great many reviews of Brightmans book. Thanks so much. Eunice and Mabel will write you themselves. Eunice was away when the books came and she read them both, one yesterday and one today. She is a great reader. Today I taught her how to run the car. She does it as though born to it. There is nothing more interesting than a sixteen year old girl. She is very good at tennis, better than she is at her studies.

In the same letter Stanley discussed when he, Mabel, and Eunice would return to the United States on furlough.

> I hope to see you in 1932 though there is some difference of opinion in our family as to whether Eunice should be brought home before she finishes her high school out here. That would be at the end of 1932 while our furlough is due at the beginning of 1932. We have not decided yet.

One month later, on March 17, 1931, Jones explained his family's situation to Ralph Diffendorfer in a letter written while he was on tour in Belgaum.

> There is some doubt as to my going home in the early part of next year. Mrs. Jones and Eunice wish to be here so she can finish up her high school work here and be ready for college when she goes to home. She will finish in December 1932. They are both eager for me to stay until then.

Stanley, however, was also thinking about the General Conference of the Methodist Episcopal Church that would meet in 1932. If he stayed in India during 1932 with Mabel and Eunice, he could not be a delegate to General Conference. He asked Diffendorfer, "What do you think of this? . . . Please keep this matter of the possibility of my not going to General Conference confidential and write me what you think about it. I have not made up my mind either way."

Apparently, Stanley did not make up his mind about when he would take his furlough in the United States until January 4, 1932, two months after an impassioned plea from Diffendorfer for Jones's help in the United States in the summer of 1932. On that date he cabled Diffendorfer,

> COMING NOW WOULD MEAN TWO YEARS ABSENCE FROM EAST CAN-NOT BEAR TO LEAVE WHEN ALL LIFE MOULDS BREAKING WHEN EAST NEVER SO CONFUSED BUT NEVER SO EAGER TO RECEIVE WHAT CRIST [*sic*] OFFERS ASK AMERICA TO STAND BY

Diffendorfer had written on November 4, 1931, that "we will need your help"—

> not only next summer but for six months or more following General Conference. The conditions here in America, not only financially, but in every other way have been quite critical. . . . The local churches, colleges, hospitals, all of our mission agencies, the Federal Council of Churches, every Mission Board that I know of, both Home and Foreign—every one is struggling for an existence. If they all survive the winter we will do very well. Salaries are being reduced, budgets cut down; men are being turned away from professional positions adding to our problem of unemployment. With all this there is a panicky feeling in the atmosphere,—one which has got to

be watched very carefully. The most serious thing now that is affecting the life of our churches is the almost nationwide move to reduce pastors' salaries. It is proving very disastrous for every approach to the local church for sacrificial giving.

If, as Diffendorfer said, pastors' salaries were being reduced across the board in every Methodist conference and district, appeals for mission funds from the churches of these same pastors were likely to fall on deaf ears. At a time when the United States was in the depths of the Great Depression, the urgency and tone of crisis in Diffendorfer's letter reflected not just the clear and present danger to Christian churches and missions throughout the country but also the more widespread and more insidious danger to American society itself. Diffendorfer wrote,

Men are questioning the fundamental bases of our economic and social order and of the morality that must underlie all social life to make it stable. There is not very much danger of men seeking out religion as an opiate for the present discontent.

In other words, the moral and spiritual foundation of American society and culture was so fragile and anemic, and the Christian churches were so nearly moribund, that religion, contrary to the expectations of the Marxists, would never become a sedative for the near economic collapse of capitalism. Finally, reflecting Jones's growing fame in the United States as a missionary evangelist, Diffendorfer closed his November 4, 1931, letter with the observation that they had "dozens of requests for you already," more than six months before it was expected that he would be available for speaking engagements.

Stanley's decision to delay his furlough to the United States, like his earlier decision to resign from the episcopacy just before he was consecrated, was a genuine crossroads in his personal and professional life. He made his decision for a combination of reasons. The most important reason was probably the firm desire of Mabel and Eunice that he stay in India until Eunice graduated from high school. But there were other reasons as well. As Jones stated in his cablegram to Diffendorfer, he sensed in his mind and spirit that India in 1932 had reached the point of critical mass in terms of its receptivity to the Christian gospel. In the April 14 issue of the *Indian Witness* he wrote that the year had "been by far and away the best year I have spent in India." For the very first time in his twenty-five years in India, Jones continued, "I have really felt that I was no longer on the edges of the soul of India. I was really in."

He made a similar comment in the *Christian Advocate*[16] for which he had recently become a contributing editor: "For the first time I have felt that I have been really at grips with things this last year. I have felt that I was no

199

longer lecturing to India, but standing so close I could hear her heart beat." Although he noted that along with spiritual hunger and openness to Christianity in India there was also "more scepticism" than he had previously observed, it was "honest scepticism," an attitude that was eagerly willing to reject paganism and embrace Jesus Christ.[17] Finally, Jones wrote in a circular letter dated March 29, 1932, that as a missionary evangelist in India, "The hour of our supreme opportunity has come."

* * *

The pace of political events in India in the late 1920s and early 1930s paralleled the pace and intensity of the moral and spiritual events Jones was recording in his letters and articles. The political situation in India, like the theological confusion and controversy surrounding the Jerusalem Conference, was an important crosscurrent that had a deep and far-reaching impact on his call to reach the educated elite of India with the gospel of Jesus Christ. In 1928 the Indian National Congress made a formal declaration that if the British refused to grant full and complete dominion status to India within a year, the Congress would for the first time demand *purna swaraj*, complete independence from Great Britain. In October 1929 the British Viceroy, Lord Irwin, responded to the Congress by announcing "that the natural issue of India's constitutional progress . . . is the attainment of Dominion Status." Dominion status meant that India, like Canada and Australia, would have virtual independence as a free and equal nation within the British Empire. Significantly, however, Lord Irwin's announcement set no date for the achievement of dominion status. At its next annual meeting in December 1929, the Congress summarily rejected the British offer of dominion status at some indefinite time in the future and formally declared that its goal was thenceforth *purna swaraj*, although it disavowed violence as a means of reaching that goal. Less than three months later Gandhi began his first campaign of civil disobedience, which marked the end of the passive noncooperation phase of the Indian independence movement and the beginning of the active and deliberate violation of British law in India.

As his first act of civil disobedience Gandhi defied the British monopoly on salt.[18] He informed Lord Irwin that he and his followers would march from his ashram near Ahmedabad to Dandi, a small village on the West coast of India, and use the abundant salt on the beach there that had not been taxed or approved for sale by the British government. Gandhi and seventy-eight of his followers took twenty-four days to complete their 241-mile march to Dandi. The pace was deliberately slow so that Gandhi would attract maximum public attention. From the standpoint of the independence movement the march was a brilliant success. Thousands of Indians joined Gandhi before he reached Dandi and the national and international press gave full coverage to the march.

The British government did not immediately arrest Gandhi, but it ordered local officials to suppress the illegal production of salt. The police, apparently unrestrained in their ruthless brutality, used force without provocation against the unarmed and peaceful demonstrators who were making illegal salt. Sixty thousand Indians were arrested within a month of Gandhi's arrival in Dandi and, when Gandhi announced that he would lead the occupation of the saltworks of Dharasana, he was arrested. His arrest only served to fuel a popular uprising against the British authorities throughout India. As a result of this reaction to Gandhi's arrest, a total of a hundred thousand more Indians were arrested and the Viceroy was forced to declare martial law.

Jones's correspondence and *Indian Witness* and *Christian Century* articles in the late 1920s and early 1930s were filled with references to the developing political crisis in India. "I went to the [Indian] National Congress as a visitor," he wrote in a March 20, 1930, circular letter, while Gandhi was marching with his supporters to Dandi, "to keep my ear close to the march of events. I have to speak to India and I must know what India is thinking."

In the same letter he reported on a meeting in Allahabad with Jawaharlal Nehru, then the president of the Indian National Congress and later the first prime minister of independent India. At a dinner with Nehru, Jones had the opportunity to present the Christian gospel to him. He described Nehru as "a man of deep sincerity but of very radical views and very sceptical."

Nine months later in his December 22, 1930, circular letter, Jones told the story of what happened to Christian students at a camp near Delhi. Many of the students were enthusiastic supporters of the independence movement.

> They put up the national flag on their school building and when some of the loyalists wanted to tear it down some of them slept up on the roof for fourteen nights to protect it! We wondered how these students would respond to the message for personal decision when they were so taken up with politics. But the last day when the decisions were asked for the first one to step out was the leading nationalist and one by one these several hundred students came and stood behind me as a sign of their decision. When the giving of the invitation was over the whole of the students [*sic*] body was behind me and I had to turn around to address them. They had made it unanimous! It was one of the greatest meetings I had ever been in. It showed us that students could be nationalist and be responsive to Christ too.

For Christian churches in the United States and for Christians everywhere interested in promoting foreign missions the decisive question was what "will happen to Christianity when India gets self-government?" By 1930 almost everyone, including the British government after Lord Irwin's announcement of eventual dominion status, assumed that India would someday be an independent nation. But whether a free India would be hostile or friendly to Christianity was an unanswered question. "My own personal view," Jones wrote to an American audience in the *Christian Century*,[19] "is that only with the coming of self-government will Christ have a fair chance before the soul of India." Until the British gave India its independence the danger for Christianity was that it was the religion of India's imperial conqueror, while the traditional religions such as Hinduism and Islam were identified with patriotism. But once India was free and independent, she would reappraise her own history and culture more objectively and would embrace Christianity more willingly. He acknowledged, however, that it was easier for India to separate Christ from British imperialism than for India to separate the Christian church from British imperialism. If, as Jones had preached to educated Indians for so many years, Jesus Christ could be disentangled from Western colonialism and was therefore a truly universal man, then, he predicted, the "greatest opportunities" for Christianity were in the future. "India free will be free to choose Christ without involving national complications."

There were times in his meetings that Jones confronted Indian nationalists who were more suspicious of Christianity than the Christian students he addressed in the camp near Delhi. At the end of the evangelistic tour, which he described in his December 22, 1930, circular letter, he spoke for the first time in Assam, a state in northeast India. In the city of Sylhet in a series of meetings arranged by Welsh Calvinist Methodists the atmosphere was, Jones said, "tense with excitement."

> At this place two High School buildings had been burned down when an order came from Government that parents should sign a statement pledging their sons to take no part in the national movement. At the question time they forced me to face the issue of the attitude of Christianity toward the national movement. I did it before British officials and the leading nationalists and the heaving students. When I put our position before them and brought everything into the open they applauded the frankness with which I faced things with them. But it was a tense hour. Seldom have I felt the presence of Christ more than in that meeting. He was there! About a hundred signed up for Bible classes.

In this letter Stanley did not define exactly what he meant by "our position" with respect to the Indian national movement. But in an earlier private letter to Diffendorfer, dated July 18, 1930, he expressed his candid opinion about the independence movement.

> The national movement is going on strong. Britain must come to terms with
> it. She cannot crush it. She must meet it. The sooner the better. . . . I look
> on it as one of the cleanest movements for independence that a nation has
> ever carried on. There has been nothing like it. But this is for you, and you
> alone. Not for publication.

Through his personal contacts with both British government officials
and with Indian nationalists, and because he had won the confidence of
both sides, Stanley tried to act as a political mediator between the parties.
This would be the first of his many attempts to mediate conflict between
political opponents, first within India before independence and later
between and among many nations, including India and the United States.
After the violent suppression of Indian nationalist demonstrations by the
British in the aftermath of Gandhi's Salt March, the British convened a
round table conference in London, which the Indian National Congress
boycotted. Jones, however, tried to encourage the leaders of the independence movement not to boycott it.

He described one such attempt in his October 1, 1930, circular letter.
He was holding a series of meetings in Madras where he spoke in schools
and colleges throughout the city. At night after his lectures he met with
some of the leading Brahmins of Madras for dinner and conversation.

> There was the utmost frankness. I had seen His Excellency the Viceroy and
> had talked over the situation with him and I brought his message and out-
> look to these men. On the basis of the Viceroy's outlook I tried to urge on
> them the necessity of going to the Round Table Conference in London and
> not boycott it. I really think I was able to hold many of the moderates to par-
> ticipation. After we had exhausted the political situation—if that is possible
> in an hour or so—we turned to religion. When they found that I was inter-
> ested in their national problems they were ready to listen to anything I had
> to say on religion.

In this way Jones used his thorough knowledge of Indian culture and politics and his sympathy with Indian nationalist aspirations to share the
gospel of Jesus Christ with the leading Hindus in Madras.

The First Round Table Conference in London, which was boycotted by
the Indian National Congress, ended in failure because no credible representatives of the nationalist movement participated. So the British government changed its strategy toward Gandhi and the Congress and turned
from arrows to an olive branch. In January 1931, Gandhi and the other
Congress leaders who had been jailed in the aftermath of the demonstrations following the Salt March were unconditionally released. During the
next two months Gandhi and Lord Irwin held several face-to-face meetings. The result was an agreement by Gandhi to call off the civil disobedience movement and to attend the next round table conference and an

agreement by Lord Irwin to free all political prisoners. However, while the British pursued a conciliatory attitude toward Gandhi and the Indian National Congress, they adopted a harsh and uncompromising position toward nationalists who engaged in violence against British rule. Bhagat Singh, a leader of the radical Indian Republican Socialist Association, dropped two bombs from the visitors gallery onto the floor of the Central Legislative Assembly. Although no one was injured by the bombs, Singh was given a sentence of life imprisonment. But while he was in jail, Singh and two of his revolutionary associates were implicated in an earlier conspiracy that led to the death of an English officer in the Punjab. Although the evidence against the three was suspect, they were all found guilty of murder and were hanged on March 23, 1931.[20]

Jones commented on these important political events in his April 5, 1931, circular letter.

> Lord Irwin is a real Christian, a man of prayer and he is really interested in India. I have never talked with a man who impressed [me] with the depth of his sincerity and fineness of character. Men like him hold the British Empire together. When the announcement of the agreement [between Lord Irwin and Gandhi] was made I was in Rajkot and announced it to the audience. There were cheers, and may I add, there were tears! It seemed too good to be true.

Since then, however, two ominous events had clouded the hopeful atmosphere created by the agreement. One was the hanging of the revolutionaries. "Government should have commuted their sentences to life imprisonment," Stanley wrote, "and then they would not have been made martyrs. . . . Since their hanging the [political] situation has been set back distinctly."

The other event affected him more directly and more personally. It was a statement made by Gandhi in answer to a journalist who asked him about the status of foreign missionaries after India became independent. Gandhi's reply:

> In India under Swaraj [independence] I have no doubt that foreign missionaries will be at liberty to do their proselytising as I would say, in the wrong way; but they would be expected to bear with those, who, like me, may point out that in their opinion the way is wrong.

This statement was a "blunder," Stanley wrote in the first of two articles (June 18, 1931) in the *Indian Witness*.[21] "I do not agree with Gandhiji's position in regard to these matters." He did not think missionaries should proselytize for the sake of superficial professions of faith in Jesus Christ. The goal of Christian missionaries should be genuine conversion that, unlike proselytizing, involves a real "change in moral or spiritual character." All Christian missions, he wrote, should completely disavow proselytizing because it "smacks too much of religious imperialism." He encouraged his Methodist colleagues in India as well as other Christians to accept Gandhi's statement as a challenge to rid themselves of proselytizing and to focus their efforts on true conversion. Our goal, he concluded, is "to convert, first ourselves and then every man everywhere who is in spiritual and moral need. And that includes us all."

But there was more to Jones's disagreement with Gandhi than he revealed in his *Indian Witness* article. He told Miss Nellie in his July 9, 1931, letter,

> I have been having some interesting times with Gandhi and the national leaders. Gandhi and some of the leaders took a strong attitude of opposition to organized Christian missions. I wrote him an open letter. He saw that it was hurting his cause badly so he explained away his sharp phrases and when I saw him he took back the whole thing. At least it appeared so to me, though I am not saying that in print.

It is not clear exactly when Jones met Gandhi or precisely what they said to each other about Gandhi's opposition to religious proselytism. But Jones was deeply concerned about Gandhi's published statement on proselytism. Given his sympathy with Gandhi's Indian nationalist goals and his one-on-one relationship with Gandhi established over several years, he interpreted his criticism of proselytism as a personal rebuke. Although Gandhi never publicly retracted his statement, Jones breathed a deep sigh of relief after their meeting and, instead of embarrassing Gandhi by saying publicly that the Mahatma was no longer opposed to religious proselytism, he accepted Gandhi's earlier criticism as a challenge to Christian missions to seek true inner religious conversion and not simply proselytism.

* * *

As Great Britain began to consider seriously India's political transition from a colony in the empire to dominion status and ultimately to independence, and as she began to negotiate this transition with Indian nationalists, the paramount difficulty became the status of India's various religious communities. Before the 1930s when the British government was concerned exclusively with maintaining control of India as the crown jewel of its colonial empire, it pursued an aggressive policy of divide and conquer with respect to that country's religious groups. The British were especially successful in stimulating animosity between Hindus and Muslims as a means of preventing Indians from uniting in opposition to British rule. So when both the British government and the Indian nationalist leaders began to plan the process of India's transition to independence, the most intractable problem became securing the cooperation of both Hindus and Muslims. But the conflict was more widespread than the conflict between the two dominant religions. It also involved Sikhs and Christians as well as discord between and among the various castes of Hinduism.

Stanley, of course, was particularly concerned about the effect of independence on Christians in India. In the December 31, 1931, issue of the *Indian Witness*[22] he addressed the question of whether India after independence "would give us [Christians] the legal right to exist alongside other communities in India." The answer to this question, he wrote, was probably "yes." But the more important question for him was whether Christians in India wanted to coexist as an organized religious community on the same basis as Hinduism, Islam, and other religious communities. The answer to this question should be no. Non-Christian religious groups, he said,

> have defined themselves from others in social exclusiveness, and in a desire to gain political power according to their numbers. We would say that we do not desire religion to be used in this way. Socially, we would exclude no one except those who exclude themselves, and politically, we would say that it is organized selfishness to use religion for the gaining of political power, therefore essentially un-Christian.

Stanley's understanding of the proper role of Christianity in a free India was an integral part of his insistence that Christians should focus on conversion rather than proselytism. The mentality of proselytism, which had been encouraged by British colonial policy toward the religious communities of India, was not only un-Christian and anti-Christian but also a serious obstacle to the unity and viability of a free India.

On March 29, 1932, he wrote to his friends and supporters in the United States that the past three months had been "a period of intense national crisis." Gandhi's efforts to negotiate a settlement with the British during the Second Round Table Conference in late 1931 ended in failure. When Gandhi returned to India, he launched another campaign of civil disobedience on January 4, 1932. Almost immediately the British put Gandhi and all other important Congress leaders in jail, along with thirty-four thousand members of the Congress. By June 1932 nearly fifty thousand Indian nationalists were incarcerated without trials or hearings, and the Congress "was banned as an illegal organization."[23]

It was in this highly charged political atmosphere in early 1932 that Jones held a series of evangelistic meetings in Benares, which he described in his March circular letter.

> The chairman of the first night was the leading nationalist of the city. On the programme they printed his name "or substitute" for they were not sure he

would be out of jail that long. Sure enough by the time our meetings were held he was in jail. The next man in line to be sent to jail took his place as chairman. . . . . The last night of the meetings . . . I had a delegation wait on me asking me to postpone the meeting that night so they could come. There was to be a lathi charge [lathis were steel sheathed bamboo poles used against nationalist demonstrators] by the police on the processionists and they would have to be there to pick up the wounded (some of them were doctors) so could I please put off the meeting for they wanted to know how to find God, which was my topic that night.

Because of his speaking schedule and the local arrangements for the use of facilities in Benares, Jones could not put off the meeting as requested, but the meetings as a whole, he wrote in his circular letter, "were far better attended than any series I had ever held in Benares, even when days were quiet."

Not all Christians took the same attitude toward the political crisis in India. Some supported the Indian nationalists in their struggle for an independent India. Others supported the British government in suppressing what they considered to be "a lawless and destructive movement." In an article in the February 11, 1932, issue of the *Indian Witness*,[24] Jones quoted a resolution of the Cawnpore Central Conference of the Methodist Church, which affirmed the right of individual Christians to take different views of the political crisis in India.

While those of us who are American missionaries, whatever our opinions may be, can take no part in politics as such; and while the Christian Church cannot deliver itself into the hands of any Government, or political party or movement, nevertheless the individual Indian Christian, Anglo-Indian, or Briton who may be a member of our Church is free to partake in or to refrain from partaking in political movements as his Christian conscience may impel him to do. The Christian Church must be comprehensive enough to hold within itself men of differing political views and outlooks.

But what about Jones's own views on politics in India? "As a pacifist," he wrote in this article, his affinities were "with those who are carrying on a non-violent struggle for national self-expression." But even though non-violent civil disobedience "is closely akin to the Christian method," it is not "the highest method." He believed that the "highest method is that of negotiation and mutual agreement at a Conference." Although Britain had "given to India as good government as it is possible for one nation to give to another, and . . . no other nation . . . would have done as well," he insisted that "the continuance of the present relationship is unhealthy both for Britain and for India. It is doing good to neither."

Jones concluded by referring to himself in the third person: "The personal views of the writer" led him to decide that it would be best for him to refrain from any political stand or activity and confine himself, as an evangelist, to the work of presenting what he finds in Christ to the individual social and economic life of India, touching only indirectly the political. He feels, however, that this touch upon the political though indirect is really vital for the whole of the progress of the political depends and rests upon inner character which he believes can be renovated by his Gospel. He feels therefore that he is making a vital and needed contribution.

Stanley was quite familiar with the British government's regulation of foreign missionary organizations throughout the Empire, which required all approved missionary societies to sign a declaration that

all due obedience and respect should be given to the lawfully constituted Government, and that, while carefully abstaining from political affairs, it is its desire and purpose that its influence, insofar as it may be properly exerted in such matters, should be so exerted in loyal co-operation with the Government of the country concerned, and that it will only employ agents who will work in this spirit.[25]

He was also undoubtedly aware of what happened to Boyd W. Tucker, an American Methodist Episcopal missionary serving as the principal of Collins High School in Calcutta. Tucker was very mindful of the pledge quoted above, which was undertaken on his behalf as an "agent" of the Methodist Episcopal Board of Foreign Missions, and he did not want to embarrass the board or compromise its status in India in any way. He was sympathetic with the goals of the Indian nationalist movement and, beginning in 1923 or 1924, he had attended, but did not actively participate in, meetings of the nationalist movement. As a result, he was harassed by the British authorities and was threatened with an official complaint against him if he continued to attend Indian nationalist meetings. He then wrote a letter to his bishop stating "that he could not remain in India under such unfair restrictions." In the end Tucker was not forced by the British to resign, but his "experience with the government's representative . . . demonstrated that the missionary pledge was a very real Damoclean threat for the Mission."[26]

If Tucker's activities violated the missionary pledge, surely Jones was also in violation of the pledge. He, like Tucker, had attended Indian nationalist meetings, including a meeting of the Indian National Congress, and he had publicly expressed his support for Indian independence from Great Britain. Indeed, a literal reading of the pledge would mean that any missionary activity not "exerted in loyal co-operation with the [British] Government" violated the pledge.

Jones did not go as far in his opposition to British authority in India as another Methodist missionary, Gordon B. Halstead. Halstead was a member of the staff of Lucknow Christian College and after only a year in India "underwent . . . a deep revival of his spiritual idealism." In December 1931 he wrote, printed, and distributed copies of a manifesto "from a Christian Missionary to his fellow Missionaries and all Christians in India." There was no moral justification for Britain's holding India or "any other peoples in Bondage," the manifesto declared. It concluded, "Missionaries and Christians, I call you to battle in the name of the Christ you love—in the name of the India you desire to serve," and asked for readers to sign and return the leaflet.

Halstead's manifesto, of course, quickly came to the attention of the British authorities and he was told to either leave India voluntarily or be deported. His bishop, Bishop J. R. Chitambar, and Ralph D. Wellons, the president of Lucknow Christian College, intervened with the government on Halstead's behalf, but to no avail. The British would not accept his claim that he acted as a private individual and not as a representative of the college and the Methodist Church when he issued his manifesto. So he resigned. Because he was very popular with the students at Lucknow Christian College, they "went on strike in a period of mourning" when they learned about his resignation. The college thereupon "expelled one student activist—a Christian receiving benefits from the College and from Dr. E. Stanley Jones, the head of the Sat Tal Ashram—and warned other students who had subverted the College's discipline."[27]

Stanley intervened personally with both civil and religious officials on behalf of Halstead. In an October 31, 1935, confidential letter to the Home Member of the United Provinces Government in Lucknow,[28] Jones wrote, "I have first hand information that Prof. Halstead has changed his attitudes considerably."

> I therefore write to enquire whether . . . Government would object to his return to India, if he would sign a written statement promising to abstain from all political activity, confining himself to the social and the spiritual.

Jones gave his personal assurance that if Halstead was allowed to return to India, he would cause no further problems for the British Government, because he "would work as a member of the Lucknow Ashram [which Jones had recently established as an extension of the Sat Tal Ashram], an institution which is entirely non-political." Under this arrangement, Halstead would not return to India as a missionary under the auspices of the Methodist Board of Foreign Missions, but "I think the Board at N.Y. would stand sponsor for his behavior in the same way that it does for regular missionaries."

The Home Member's response to this letter was apparently favorable, because in a letter to Ralph Diffendorfer, dated November 5, 1935, Jones wrote that both the Home Member and the Deputy Commissioner

> said that they would have no objection to his [Halstead's] return. The Depty. Com. is the same one under whom they [Halstead and his wife] were sent home. He said that he thought Halstead was an ass for doing what he did, but that he never thought him dangerous and that if it had been left to him he would not [have] sent him home.

Jones also contacted Fred M. Perrill, the editor of the *Indian Witness*, as well as his old friend J. Waskom Pickett, who had recently been elected bishop, and Bishop Chitambar. All three, Jones reported to Diffendorfer, approved of Halstead's return to India. With his letter to Diffendorfer, he enclosed a copy of his letter to the Home Member. This would give Diffendorfer and the Methodist Mission Board an opportunity to withhold their sponsorship of Halstead before Halstead was notified of Jones's efforts on his behalf. In the end, however, the lobbying of church and government officials was unsuccessful. He wrote to Diffendorfer on January 9, 1936, "I have word from the government that they will not allow Gordon Halstead to return to India. We will therefore have to drop the matter."

Jones was not as outspoken as Halstead about his opposition to British rule in India, nor did he publicly call on other missionaries and Christians to take political action to promote the cause of Indian independence. His involvement in the Halstead incident and his knowledge of British sensitivity to political statements and activities of any kind by foreign missionaries may well have inhibited what he wrote about Indian politics in his circular letters and in magazines like *The Indian Witness* and *The Christian Century*. However, because British steps toward granting India independence in the 1930s were incremental at best and because they were completely suspended during World War II, he became an increasingly vocal opponent of British colonialism in India and finally, as we will see, came into direct conflict with the British government.

In the late 1920s and early 1930s E. Stanley Jones was a middle-aged missionary evangelist with a rapidly growing international reputation. As his public recognition increased, so did the strength of his personal relationship with God. He relied more and more exclusively on what he called the inner voice or the voice of the Holy Spirit. He began to see a world that others saw dimly and obscurely or not at all. At the 1928 Jerusalem Conference, which was held amid deep and widespread skepticism about the religious validity of Christian foreign missions, he saw not tensions and frustrations and factions among Christians but a deep inner unity, that would become the basis for renewed and expanded missionary evangelism. When his colleagues and superiors in the Methodist Episcopal Church thought they were conferring on him the highest possible honor and accolade by electing him bishop, he was led by a direct and distinct call from the Holy Spirit to decline the office in order to continue his work as a missionary evangelist. Drawing on his earlier experience with the ashrams organized and conducted by Tagore and Gandhi, he began to see in concrete physical form at Sat Tal the realization of the kingdom of God on earth. Initially because of personal and family reasons but ultimately because the inner voice led him to offer his Christian witness in India in the midst of her tumultuous nationalist movement, Jones delayed his scheduled 1932 furlough to the United States. As he continued to respond to the Holy Spirit throughout the 1930s, he found himself almost alone in perceiving the true will of God and the future meaning of the kingdom of God at a time when the world was spiraling out of control into the holocaust of another world war.

9

Ordinary Man, Extraordinary Mission

I wonder if you realize just how your influence
has penetrated the entire Christian world?
—Ralph Diffendorfer, August 4, 1932, Letter

W HILE E. STANLEY JONES was becoming, as *Time* magazine put it in 1938, "the world's greatest Christian missionary,"[1] he remained a man of humble origins, a servant and an apostle of Jesus Christ who never forgot his simple humanity. His letters reflect the fact that he routinely faced the same problems and frustrations we all encounter every day.

"I have just come back from a fruitless trip hunting my lost glasses," he wrote to Miss Nellie on July 9, 1931. "Last night they fell on this hill side from Mrs. Jones' chair as she was being carried up this mountainside. You see I have had to come to glasses at last and I suppose I will have to cut six months of time out of my life in hunting for lost glasses from time to time."

During his 1931 summer ashram at Sat Tal where, for four months, he was both the leader and an active member during the sixteen-plus-hour days, Stanley found time to meet with some Asbury students on a world tour in evangelism who were visiting for a few days. "They were lovely singers," he told Miss Nellie, spiritual and without cynicism—and they had dedicated their yearbook to him.

As the international scope of the financial crisis that first threatened Christian foreign missions in the 1920s continued to grow, and as the Great Depression jeopardized Christ's Great Commission throughout the 1930s, the impact also affected Stanley Jones. Back in September 1924, the Methodist Board of Foreign Missions faced a $4 million shortfall. Stanley was in the United States then, and wrote a front-page call to arms in the *Christian Advocate:*

> Are we willing to see the Foreign Missionary work of the Methodist Church paralyzed? Are we willing to recall missionaries from that already thin line? Are you ready to say to some of us now at home, "You cannot go back to your field?" Are we willing to sound the order to retreat at the moment of imminent triumph? . . . In Christ's name, we must not retreat.[2]

Despite Ralph Diffendorfer's desperate November 4, 1931, letter pleading with Stanley to come to the United States in 1932 and help the Board of Foreign Missions raise enough money to avert financial catastrophe, Stanley did not come until 1933. When he did arrive, he wrote another front-page editorial in the October 12, 1933, issue of the *Christian Advocate,* entitled, "SAVE OUR MISSIONS!"[3] Previous cuts in the Methodist missions budget, he pointed out, had already resulted in the recall of one-half of missionary personnel. He warned that if $225,000 additional money was not raised by October 31, 1933, further cuts would be necessary. His conclusion: "If this [missionary] movement dies, then I warn you, it will not die alone! The very existence of our Church as a living factor in moral and spiritual affairs at home and abroad is at stake."

The financial crisis of the Methodist Board of Foreign Missions came to a head in the early 1930s. But the board faced another problem, a problem more chronic than the financial crisis, and one the Methodists shared with many other foreign mission boards in the United States in the late 1920s and 1930s. This was the problem of criticism of overseas ministries. In January 1929, Jones, in response to this criticism, addressed the Foreign Missions Conference of North America in Detroit. The conference was composed of participating foreign mission boards of Christian churches in the United States and Canada. Jones was assigned to speak on the topic, "Meeting Current Objections to Foreign Missions." He began his remarks not by responding to criticism of Christian foreign missions but by frankly acknowledging their problems.

> I do not think that the mission boards at home ought constantly and continuously to try to make out a case for success. I think we ought to take the church into the heartbreaks of many of our failures. . . .

I believe that the Church can stand a little more frankness in that regard. I think you at the home base ought not to require us on the mission field to always report success. I think you ought to say to us, "Tell us about your failures, too." And don't make us write those half lies. I am serious.

My wife has said to me, "I am not quite sure that I can be a Christian and continue to write scholarship letters where they are supposed to make out angels of every last one of the whole lot.". . .

[L]et us get down off our pedestal, and tell your people that we are just ordinary folks, exactly like the kind of people that there are in the Churches from which we have come. . . . We are not super men and super women; we are just ordinary men trying to do something too big for us, something that we can't do unless we have more divine power.[4]

Six months before the Joneses went home on furlough, Stanley offered to help the Methodist Board of Foreign Missions in a small but symbolic way with its financial crisis. In a July 12, 1932, letter to Ralph Diffendorfer, Stanley told him, "I will be responsible for the travelling expenses of my family and myself from India to America on our regular furlough in January 33. . . . This is just a gift to help out in emergency for I know that the Board is hard hit."

Three months later, on October 21, 1932, a staff member of the Board of Foreign Missions responded to Jones's offer of help.

The Board yesterday through its Executive Committee gave approval for regular furlough for you and your family in 1933. It is our understanding on the basis of your letter of July 12th, that you have generously offered to pay the homecoming costs for yourself and family and the Executive Committee placed on its Minutes an expression of sincere appreciation for this gift in this emergency.[5]

While he was in the United States during 1933, Stanley took the time to explain to Dr. Morris Ehnes of the Mission Board how he collected money in his meetings. To cover the cost of his meetings, he wrote on June 10, 1933, he took a collection before he spoke. "What is left over after local expenses have been met is being sent to you." After his address he distributed cards to those who wanted to respond to what he had said.

I don't get them to sign it [a card] then and there, but ask them to take it home and think and pray about it and give it to their local pastor after filling it out. . . . It saves me from the charge of using these big meetings for purposes of money. Large givers will probably pay more after they think about it than on the spur of the moment. In the end I think it will be better.

Stanley was sensitive to the way in which collections were taken in his meetings and he was sensitive to the public image created by other events held in his name. A four dollar per plate dinner, which had been proposed for Jones to host, was too expensive, he told his friend Ralph Diffendorfer in a December 15, 1933 letter.

> The Catholic Charities had a dinner at $4 a plate in Wash. & even Mrs. Roosevelt criticized them for it. Mr. Boyd thinks it will be a pity to spoil my tour in U.S.A. by having such a dinner as you proposed at $4 a plate. I agree. If you can't get one for $1.50 or at the most $2 then I am afraid you will have to count me out.

At a time when unemployment in the United States was 25 percent and almost all families in the country were victims of the catastrophic Great Depression, Jones did not want to sponsor a dinner whose high price would exclude many Americans and that created the impression that he was unconcerned about the economic plight of millions of his fellow citizens.

Before the family went on furlough, Jones left India on July 15, 1932, for a six-month tour of the Far East. His first stop was Rangoon, Burma, where he held large meetings for several days. The Chief Justice of Burma, Jones wrote in a circular letter dated October 3, 1932, "exhorted after one of my addresses!"[6] Then he had a twelve-day visit to the Malay Peninsula, including Penang, Ipoh, Kuala Lumpur, Malacca, and Singapore. In these cities, Jones estimated, about a thousand people, most of whom were non-Christian Chinese students, signed cards professing their personal faith in Jesus Christ after his meetings. Stanley then went on to China, beginning his second visit in Hongkong, where he met Dr. Tsui of the National Christian Council who was in charge of local arrangements. The council had selected ten provincial centers in various parts of China to which it invited Christian workers for a series of evangelistic conferences. The meetings for Christian workers were held in the morning. During the afternoon and evening Jones held meetings for non-Christians who were admitted by ticket only.

After meeting Dr. Tsui in Hongkong, the first city in which Jones spoke was Peking, where he addressed an assembly of all the paid staff of the YMCA throughout China. The Y, along with other Christian groups in China, was demoralized and "somewhat shell-shocked," as Jones put it in his December 15, 1932, article for the *Indian Witness*,[7] by the anti-Christian movement that had swept across China in the late 1920s. So the YMCA, he wrote in his October 3, 1932, circular letter, "needed a new courage and new power to come back again and confront the youth of China with a spiritual programme."

Toward the end of his tour, Jones received a letter from a Western missionary at the Cheeloo School of Theology in Tsinan, Shantung, who had attended both the meetings for Christians and those for non-Christians.

The results of your meetings are notable especially in quickening and strengthening the life of Christians. That seems to me your special gift to China, rather than a message to non-Christians, though that is so much on your heart. . . . These are difficult days for us of other lands to reach out helping hands to those who are not already in our fellowship.[8]

Another provincial center Jones visited was Hankow in East Central China on the Yangtze River. There students from Hua Chung College submitted written questions they wanted him to answer. "So many [questions] were sent in," Jones wrote in his December 15, 1932, *Indian Witness* article, "that I could have spent my whole ten days doing nothing but answering those questions." In fact, when he arrived in Hankow, he was given a list of 110 questions from the students grouped into six categories—theological and philosophical; personal religious life; the Bible and science and religion; the church; social questions; and political questions.

Stanley marked on the list he was given a number of specific questions, which he probably answered in public meetings. Examples include the following.

What is the use of prayer—if any? How can we make Christianity indigenous? Explain what is God, what is life and what is conscience. How are they related? Define religion. The more we try to spread religion the worse the world becomes. Why is this? Why does God not force us to be good? If He wants us to be good will He give us the right way to do so? If there is only one God why are there so many religions? What about so-called Christians whose deeds are so unchristian? How can we answer non-Christians on this matter? Can one be a Christian without joining the Church?[9]

The category in which Jones marked the largest proportion of questions was the category of political questions. Before he visited Hankow he had been in Mukden in the north China province of Manchuria, which in 1931 had been seized by Japan. The questions uppermost on the minds of the college students were thus focused on the Christian response to the naked Japanese aggression in Manchuria.

What were your own impressions of Mukden and North China? What would be the right attitude of Chinese Christians towards the Manchurian question? Should they resist? Is there any way to solve the Manchurian problem in accordance with the will of God? What is that way? Will it get us back Manchuria? Why do the Christians of the West no[t] express their attitude to the Manchurian question? Why did Christianity start the Great War? Can Christianity really save China?[10]

Mukden, the capital of Manchuria, was clearly the most difficult place Jones visited in China. By the time of his arrival in Manchuria in the fall of 1932, the province had been occupied by the Japanese for about one year and had been renamed "Manchukuo." Chinese volunteers as well as bandits were conducting a guerilla war against the Japanese, who controlled only the major cities and the railroads, and held the rest of Manchuria in name only. In order to keep hold of the railroads, Jones wrote in the *Christian Century* on October 19, 1932, the Japanese had made each railway station "like a fortress with sandbag redoubts, trenches and Japanese soldiers everywhere." Armored trains were used to patrol the rail lines and protect them from guerilla attack.[11]

In spite of these siege-like conditions Jones held his evangelistic meetings in Mukden as scheduled. "One night," he wrote,

> seven hundred Manchukuo troops mutinied, killed their Japanese officers and burned thirteen airplanes and the arsenal. Two other bands of "volunteers" attacked the city at two other points. The battle went on for some hours. Two nights later there was worse firing. Some of the missionaries had to sit up all night with the bullets whistling around their houses. There was firing practically every night, some very near, and yet we carried on the evangelistic meetings during the day and night as though nothing were happening.[12]

Despite these circumstances, during the last night of the evening meetings for non-Christians, 250 people, most of whom were intellectuals, signed cards stating that they wanted to become Christians. But those who had sacrificed the most to attend Jones's meetings were the Chinese Christian leaders. Many of them "had come from bandit-infested regions, and they would probably lose all before getting back, and yet they carried on with cheerfulness and courage."[13]

After Mukden, Stanley returned to Peking for a series of meetings with non-Christians. There he had interviews with three influential Chinese leaders—Marshal Chiang Hsuen Liang, the leader of the Northern Armies of China and the former leader of Manchuria; the mayor of Peking; and Dr. Hu Shih, who founded the Renaissance Movement in China. He also talked with Marshall Feng, the Christian general whom he had met on his first visit to China, and with General Chiang Kai-shek, the president of China.

Toward the end of his tour, he reflected on the status of communism in that country. In the north of China, he wrote in his December 15, 1932, article for the *Indian Witness*, he thought that communism was losing influence. But after a visit to central China he was convinced that communism was spreading. The communists were successful, he thought, because of their two-pronged strategy. The first part was ruthless and was designed to instill fear in the people.

> They get a list of the estimated wealth of each man in a city they capture, they post on his door a notice that by such and such a time so much money must

be produced or his head will be off. Usually the richest man in the community has his head cut off as illustration whether he produces the money or not.[14]

But there was another part of the communist strategy. "They are teaching the people." This was "the significant thing," the thing that made communism such a threat to all of China. In addition, he learned from Chiang Kai-shek that the communists considered Christianity to be the only religious opposition that presented a serious challenge to their power. For this reason, Jones concluded, "the race is on in China between Communism and Christianity."

When Jones returned to India, he wrote an article for the January 12, 1933, issue of the *Indian Witness* summarizing the results of his meetings.[15] He described Shanghai as "the city of smouldering hate," because it was viciously and ruthlessly attacked by the Japanese. Yet the students in Shanghai were seriously interested in religion and many of them came to his meetings. The largest response to his messages came in Canton where thirty-five hundred people registered their names and addresses in order to receive tickets to his meetings, and a thousand people signed cards indicating that they had made personal decisions for Jesus Christ. Jones's statement about the success of his visit to Canton is confirmed by a letter dated December 15, 1932, which he received from George H. McNeur of the New Zealand Presbyterian Mission in that city.

> For thirty one years I have been connected with the work in this city and in the country districts around. We have never during that period had any spiritual movement which has impressed me so much as that of the past weekend. We are profoundly grateful to God for His goodness in sending you to us with His message. There was much prayer and expectation before your arrival but the fulfillment has been far greater than we dared to hope.[16]

Altogether at the end of his China tour, Jones calculated that three thousand people had decided that they wanted to become Christians. To each of them he sent a personal letter before he left China. He had sold 12,000 copies of Chinese translations of his books and 24,000 copies of a pamphlet entitled *What Is Christianity?*[17]

Stanley, Mabel, and Eunice left for their long-delayed furlough on February 11, 1933. While Mabel accompanied Eunice first to Rome and then to Oberlin, Ohio, where Eunice entered Oberlin College, Stanley toured the United States holding meetings and conferences for both Methodist and interdenominational groups. Then toward the end of 1933 he was able to arrange a personal meeting with President Roosevelt in Washington to discuss two crucial issues in the relations between the United States and the nations of the Far East, Japan in particular: first, the matter of immigration quotas; second, Japan's exclusion from the League of Nations. These two issues were the main source of Japanese grievances against the West, and because they were never resolved to Japan's satisfaction, she turned to militarism and imperialism and set in motion the events that led to World War II in the Pacific.

After World War I and the failure of Woodrow Wilson's vision for the League of Nations, the United States washed its hands of involvement in international affairs and retreated into a foreign policy of isolationism and xenophobia. This fear of foreigners and especially the racial prejudice against Asians were reflected in the restrictive immigration laws adopted by Congress in the 1920s. European immigrants to the United States were admitted on the basis of a yearly quota for each country, but immigrants from Asia were admitted on a much more restricted basis. This blatant racism was offensive to the people of all Asian nations, making it much more difficult to preach the gospel in Asia.

The other issue was the question of Japan's exclusion from the League of Nations. As the European powers consolidated and extended their colonial empires after World War I, Japan felt that its legitimate need for more territory for its large population and for more natural resources was ignored solely because it was a nonwhite, non-Western nation. Moreover, the League's rejection of Japan's request that it take a stand against racism throughout the world only served to strengthen Japan's conviction that it was being treated as an international racial pariah and that it would have to act independently to achieve its objectives in the Far East.

Stanley Jones's sensitivity to the importance of these two issues reflects his divinely guided understanding of the motives and aims of the nations of Asia in the international arena. Just as he was one of the first to perceive the spiritual power of Gandhi's noncooperation and civil disobedience movements in India and to predict that Britain would ultimately have to surrender to the superior moral power of Indian nationalism, so he was one of the first to perceive the source and depth of Japan's grievances against the West and to try to persuade the leaders of the Western nations to address these grievances.

"Had a very fine interview with Pres. Roosevelt," Stanley wrote to Ralph Diffendorfer on December 15, 1933.[18] "Asked him to put Asiatic countries on a quota basis & to offer to enter a reconstituted League, divorced from the Versailles Treaty & with Russia, Japan & Germany in it. He could help Xtian [Christian] miss. if he would do those two things. He was very responsive—said he had been thinking of those two things for some time."

Roosevelt, however, who was well known for encouraging visitors to believe that he would act on their suggestions, did nothing about changing U.S. immigration policy to admit Asians on a quota basis. (In fact, there was no basic change in American immigration policy until the

219

1960s.) Nor did Roosevelt move to reconstitute the League of Nations so that Japan could become a member.

As he came to the end of his American tour during his 1933–34 furlough, Stanley confessed to his friends and patrons across the country that when he began his tour, he was

> tired and worn from the years in India and the strenuousness of the campaign in China. At the beginning of my work here in America, I wondered if I could pull through. But I have come through stronger, I think, than when I started. I have really picked up as I have gone along, thanks to this wonderful climate and the power of prayer. God's resources are sufficient. I have laid hold on them and they have not failed me.[19]

On February 28, 1934, while his wife and daughter remained in the United States, Stanley boarded the *S. S. Manhattan* for the first leg of his journey back to India. At this point in his life he was probably ambivalent about returning to India. He was surely, as he said in the circular letter quoted above, "tired and worn from the years in India" and from "the strenuousness" of his relentless and almost uninterrupted speaking schedule. He was all too familiar with the baking heat and, during the rainy summer season, the suffocating humidity of the Indian climate. Moreover, he was returning to India alone. On the other hand, plunging into a new series of evangelistic campaigns was always an invigorating experience. Time and time again, when the obstacles to the gospel message seemed impenetrable, God made a way and confirmed once more his commission as a missionary evangelist.

It was no doubt during a time of personal reflection as he sailed toward England on the *Manhattan* that he recalled his early years in Baltimore and especially his affection for Miss Nellie. Stanley wrote to her on March 5, 1934.

> My Dear Miss Nellie:—
>
> It was beautiful of you to send that farewell note. You don't know what it meant to me. We don't correspond much, but I think of you often and always with the deepest gratitude.
>
> I can hear you say, "Now Stanley, hush." I won't! The other day I saw Blanche Thurlow—at London, Ontario, and we did nothing but talk about you for an hour. And she can talk & so can I! And every word we said was true & every word was lovely and deserved. You are one of the most wonderful women I have ever known—so fine and Christian and devoted. Memorial [Methodist Church] will never know what you mean to her until one of these days about 20 years hence you slip away to heaven. Fact!

Stanley stayed in England long enough to receive an official greeting from Charles Collett, the Lord Mayor of London,[20] and to make an address to the Missionary Demonstration in Central Hall at Westminster in London on March 9, 1934. The substance of his address was published in a British Methodist newspaper, *The Methodist Times and Leader,* and was reprinted in the April 5, 1934, issue of the *Indian Witness* under the title, "Christian Missions, Not Domination, nor Denomination, but Christ." In London, he was also the speaker at a laymen's missionary luncheon and, according to an article from another British Christian newspaper, *The Christian World,* which was reprinted in the same issue of the *Indian Witness,* he "attracted an overflowing congregation to the lunch-hour service at Wesley's Chapel."

By the time he concluded his address at the Missionary Demonstration, Stanley's self-confidence had returned as he reaffirmed his faith in Jesus Christ and his faith in his own calling as a missionary.

> I am glad that we have a message, and something that the world needs. I do not say that lightly. We must set our Savior before the world. I believe that Jesus Christ is the way of Life. If He is not a Savior I do not know who is. If He cannot redeem us we are not redeemable. I believe His hands are still out-stretched to us. I have therefore no apology to offer for being a missionary.

"England was great," he wrote to Ralph Diffendorfer from Holland on March 17, 1934. "The crowds were great & responsive. I loved them."

His host in the Netherlands was Baroness von Boetselaer, who had first met him at the Jerusalem Conference and who was largely responsible for promoting the sale of his books in Holland. In fact, the Baroness herself had written a book about Jones that she gave to Queen Wilhelmina and Princess Juliana before they heard him speak in the Hague. The queen had said that any Christian of the Indian Road was dangerous. "The Dutch have colonies!" was Stanley's comment.

He found the Dutch people *"very* responsive—youth especially." In Utrecht he had to hold two youth meetings because the hall was too small. Another day, "400 ministers came together for the first time. It was 1/3 of all the ministers of Holland."

After Jones concluded his tour of the Netherlands, Baroness von Boetselaer wrote to Diffendorfer on March 22, 1934,[21] describing the meetings and offering these comments about Stanley's visit.

> I had *some* apprehensions, if our people would *respond,* what they do not do very quickly. They are very critical, very theological, and fed-up religiously. Now I can tell you, that it has been a *wonderful* time. . . .
>
> As to the meetings, they were just wonderful. . . .The interest has been enormous everywhere. . . .
>
> We enjoyed his stay in our home immensely, my husband and I, as well as our grown-up children. Our expectations had been very high; they have been surpassed. . . .

> We thank you for your part in letting Dr. Jones come to our country. When I see a man like him I always wonder why God only makes so few of that kind! Don't you think that sometimes?

From the Netherlands Stanley began the longest leg of his journey back to India. In many ways it was the most crucial trip of his life. He traveled by train across the Soviet Union from Leningrad in European Russia to the Azerbaijan port city of Baku on the Caspian Sea. From there he went by way of Teheran and Baghdad to Bombay. In the book that he wrote shortly after his trip through Russia, *Christ's Alternative to Communism* (1935), he described the experience as a "shock," and a "terrific thud."[22] Forty-five years later in *The Reconstruction of the Church—On What Pattern?* (1970), he recalled that he was "stunned by the impact" of his visit.[23]

He found in Russia an officially atheist society that embodied a surprising number of Christian principles.[24] The contradiction was not just an intellectual puzzle it was an emotional and spiritual body blow both to his understanding of Christianity and to his association of Christianity with democratic government. But, as we saw in his report of his 1933 trip to China, he was sensitive to the spiritual power and appeal of communism. In fact, beginning as early as his ministry to the educated and intellectual classes of India, he recognized the necessity of a more holistic gospel, a gospel of both individual and social salvation. The rise of Indian nationalism and Gandhi's noncooperation and nonviolent civil disobedience movements only served to underscore more emphatically the economic, political, and social ramifications of the Christian gospel.

A few weeks before his journey through Russia, Jones had said in his address to the Missionary Demonstration in London,

> Shall we pick up the wounded in war and leave the armaments alone? Shall we redeem the drunkard and leave intact the liquor traffic? Shall we rescue the slave and leave intact the slave traffic? The answer comes as a challenge. We believe in a Gospel that will change the individual and change the national life, and bring the Kingdom of God on earth. We would say that whatever you may think about it we are out for the salvation of the individual and the nation.

Stanley was accompanied for the first part of his travels in Russia by Bishop Raymond J. Wade. After the trip Bishop Wade described their arrival to Dr. John R. Edwards, a corresponding secretary with the Board of Foreign Missions, in a letter from Stockholm dated April 13, 1934.[25] They had arrived in the Soviet Union on Easter Sunday—"the strangest Easter we have ever spent or probably will spend in our entire lives."

On the train that morning, passing through the land where they do so much to obliterate the church and religion, the first hours were employed devotionally reading the New Testament accounts of the Resurrection.

When they arrived in Leningrad about 3:00 P.M., their Intourist guide, "a very capable young lady," asked them what they would like to see. Because it was already late in the day, Wade suggested that the guide take them to the "nearest open museum." He knew from previous visits to Leningrad that directly across from the Hotel Astoria where he and Jones were staying was St. Isaac's Cathedral, which the Soviet government had turned into an Anti-Religious Museum.

"Thus it was," Wade wrote, "that on our Easter afternoon we 'did' the Anti-Religious Museum." After the tour, Stanley talked with the Intourist guide and

stated that he was ready to acknowledge that the Museum made the case pretty thoroughly against the church, and particularly against the Russian Church, but not against genuine religion. Then came the quick really eager question [from the guide], "What does your religion mean to you?" A chance for an Easter sermon.

One of the purposes of Wade's trip was to investigate the status of the Methodist Church in Leningrad. Before the Revolution in 1917, the church building was owned by the Methodist Board of Foreign Missions, but the church had been "liquidated" by the new Soviet regime. After talking with the American Ambassador in Russia, Wade recommended to Edwards that the board not attempt to maintain the property as a church. He explained that the taxes imposed by the government on churches were exorbitant, and there were too few American Methodists in Leningrad to support a church. Instead of using the property as a church, Wade suggested that the board seek reimbursement from the Russian government for the value of the property.

It is indeed ironic that while Jones was making a trip to Russia, which would forever change his life and ministry, the American Methodist Episcopal Church was in the process of withdrawing its only official presence in the Soviet Union. The Methodist historian J. Tremayne Copplestone records that throughout the 1920s and early 1930s there were several influential voices within the church who urged and pleaded with the Board of Foreign Missions to take advantage of the vast opportunities for Christian ministry in Russia. But in the end, the forces of political opposition to mission work of any kind in a communist nation prevailed and by 1940 there was no appropriation by the board for the Soviet Union. Surely the Methodist Church missed a God-given opportunity in Russia in the years between the world wars. If the church had been less distracted by its abhorrence of communism from fulfilling Christ's Great Commission, it could have established closer ties to the Russian Orthodox Church and to other Christians in Russia, and it would be in a better position now, after the fall of communism, to develop and expand its outreach in the nations of the former Soviet Union.[26]

Jones arrived in India from his trip through Russia in time for the fifth ashram at Sat Tal. In his first circular letter after he returned, dated July 5, 1934, he wrote prophetically,

> What I saw in Russia so deeply impressed me that I felt as never before, that this was the problem we would have to face in the future. I know there are two sides to the question of Russia. There is the poverty, the lack of liberty, the drive against religion. But there is another side: the enthusiasm of the people who believe that they have the truth that will hold the future; the self-sacrifice of all classes to make a new Russia in which all have a share in the good life; the sheer drive of the whole thing, all this and more, makes one feel that this is an issue that will have to be faced. We must choose, on a world scale, whether we shall make the future after the pattern of Marx or after the pattern of the Kingdom of God. I am not fair in setting them in such bold opposition, for in many places they coincide; in many things must we sit and learn from Marx. But in the end, the Kingdom of God offers something that we must take, or be compelled by the force of the pressure of circumstances to take the Russian brand of communism.

Because of Stanley's trip to Russia, the central theme of the 1934 Sat Tal Ashram was, as he put it in his July 5, 1934, circular letter, "whether we could find a Christian alternative to Marxian Communism." He described the two months of the ashram devoted to the study of this question as "glorious searching months." Within the next year he wrote and published his sixth book, *Christ's Alternative to Communism*, which was the result of his study and reflection at Sat Tal in 1934.

Christ's Alternative to Communism first of all identifies the central message of the New Testament Gospels as the kingdom of God on earth. "What . . . is the content of the Kingdom of God on earth?" This was the question Jones addressed in an article entitled "The Christian Programme of Reconstruction," which summarizes *Christ's Alternative to Communism* and was published in two long installments in the February 13 and February 20, 1936, issues of the *Indian Witness*. The content of the kingdom, he wrote, was best expressed by Jesus himself at the beginning of his public ministry when, as recorded in Luke 4:18-19, he stood up in the synagogue at Nazareth and proclaimed that he was anointed by God's Spirit to preach good news to the poor, to proclaim release to the captives, to give the recovery of sight to the blind, to set at liberty those who are bruised, and to proclaim God's year of Jubilee. This Nazareth Manifesto, as Jones called it in his later books and articles, contained not only the good news of

Jones with his students, Asbury College, 1907

Jones with Mabel, Lucknow Parsonage, 1911

Jones, second row, second from left beside Rev. and Mrs. Meek, Lucknow, India, c. 1910

Jones, front row, third from left beside Sherwood Eddy,
China, 1922

Jones with Mabel and Eunice en route to India, 1938

Jones, seated in the middle
and marked with an X,
Baghdad, 1922

Jones with Veet Singh hunting for a tiger attacking
village cattle, c. 1946

Sat Tal Ashram, Jones seated in middle in Indian garb, c. 1950

Sat Tal Ashram, probably the main building

Jones with daughter Eunice, son-in-law James K. Mathews and granddaughters Jan (left) and Ann (right), Clayton, Iowa c. 1948

Jones picking up trash at an American Ashram during Work Period, c. 1950

Jones with his Japanese interpreter, Dr. Yasumura, on Jones's left, and a Japanese pastor, c. 1950

Studio portrait of Jones, c. 1950

Jones in Vesper Service at Sat Tal Lake, c. 1950

Jones in front of his birthplace, Clarksville, Maryland, c. 1960

Jones in Finland with Mrs. Esselstrom and Erik Hellsten on Jones's left, 1963

Jones at Sat Tal, c. 1965

Jones's favorite pastime

Ralph E. Diffendorfer (1879–1951), Corresponding
Secretary, Methodist Board of Foreign Missions

Redwood Christian Ashram, August 1965.

Jones in Indian garb, c. 1965

English-speaking Methodist Church in Lucknow, India,
Jones's first appointment

Jones, Central Methodist Church, Lucknow, India, where God healed him in 1917

Jones with his notebook, late 1960s

salvation for individual souls. It was also Christ's alternative to *The Communist Manifesto* written by Marx and Engels in 1848. In order to explain the full revolutionary significance of Jesus' manifesto, Jones identified the poor as "the economically disinherited," the captives as "the socially and politically disinherited," the blind as "the physically disinherited," the bruised as "the morally and spiritually disinherited," and the year of Jubilee as "a fresh world beginning."[27]

Jones then identified Jesus' good news for each of these disinherited groups. For the poor, he said, "[t]he only possible good news . . . is that there should be no poor. Poverty can be banished." For the captives, the gospel meant "the economic means to buy culture and to buy education." And it meant liberation from race and caste as well as sexual prejudice. For the physically disinherited, Jesus brought healing and wholeness. "We do not believe that sickness is the will of God," he wrote. "Jesus never asked people to bear suffering or to accept it as God's will. . . . We believe God heals in many ways: by climate, medicine and surgery, by mental suggestion, and by the direct touch of the spirit of God upon our physical bodies."

For the bruised, Jesus' gospel meant freedom from "the inner lack of adjustment" and from the sin and pain of one's own actions. Jones often compared the laws of the kingdom of God to natural laws like the law of gravity. We are free to disobey the law of gravity, but we suffer the consequences if we disobey. The same principle applies to the moral and spiritual laws of the kingdom.

> We are free to choose our actions but not free to choose the results of these actions. We do not break the laws of God. We break ourselves upon them. We do not break them. They break us. Who has not felt within his inmost being these moral and spiritual bruises which come as a result of moral wrong doing? . . . What can take away that sense of moral inferiority, depressing guilt, and a feeling of wrongness? I know nothing except the forgiving grace of God offered to us in the nailpierced hand of Christ.

The final point of Jesus' Nazareth Manifesto, Jones wrote, was a response to communist criticism of the traditional Christian philosophy of saving society one soul at a time. The communists insisted that working from the individual to the social was much too slow and that the only real change was the result of working from the social to the individual. By contrast, the fresh world beginning of the year of Jubilee achieved its revolutionary results by working from the social to the individual *and* by working from the individual to the social. In this way, Jones thought, the kingdom of God on earth would create a new social heredity for the human race.

Beginning with the publication of his first book, *The Christ of the Indian Road* (1925), Stanley Jones recognized the contribution of each nation's social heredity to the different expressions of Christianity. Now he saw more clearly, and with deeper and broader spiritual insight, that God wanted his kingdom on earth to embrace and yet transcend all the distinctive human forms of Christianity by creating and establishing a new God-inspired and Spirit-filled humanity, all of whose relationships, both personal and social, were more thoroughly and more authentically Christian.

With the 1940 publication of *Is the Kingdom of God Realism?* he began to use the word *totalitarian* to refer to the kingdom of God.[28] His use of the word was deliberately provocative, intended to make Christians uncomfortable with conventional Christianity and to encourage them to reexamine and thereby strengthen their faith in Jesus Christ. He also used the word to contrast communism, Nazism, and fascism—which by 1940 had established brutal and repressive totalitarian regimes in Russia, Germany and Italy—with the spiritually liberating and affirming regime of the kingdom of God on earth. Like these secular forms of totalitarianism, the kingdom of God embraces every human characteristic of body, soul, and spirit and every human personal and institutional relationship. But unlike other forms of totalitarianism, the kingdom of God draws its inspiration and strength from God and is thus able to effect total and permanent change in all of these human characteristics and relationships.

Jones's articles in the *Indian Witness* begin with the question, "What is the Christian programme for reconstruction of society in general, and of the Depressed Classes in particular?" In addressing specifically the issue of how to respond to the needs of the depressed classes, he was thinking of the outcastes of India, and the work of Dr. Bhimrao R. Ambedkar. During the 1920s and 1930s Ambedkar, a Western educated government official and lawyer, emerged as the leader of the depressed classes or Harijans as they were called. (Gandhi coined the term *Harijans*, which means "children of God," to refer to the outcastes or depressed classes.) Ambedkar was born as an outcaste and became their spokesman and representative in the negotiations with the British about Indian independence. At a 1935 conference of the depressed classes in Bombay, Ambedkar called for a complete break between the Harijans and the rest of the Hindu community. He also renounced Hindu religion because, he said, it "is not good for us," that is, not good for the Harijans.[29] Finally, Ambedkar announced that he wanted to lead the Harijans out of Hindusim and into some other religion. His announcement, of course, was immediately recognized as a heaven-sent opportunity for Christianity in India.

Jones's correspondence with Diffendorfer and his circular letters between 1935 and 1938 reflect his enthusiasm about the possibility of tens of millions of outcastes becoming Christian. On November 25, 1935, he wrote to Diffendorfer that as a result of Ambedkar's announcement, "there has been a deep stir in India. All religions are bidding for them [the depressed classes]. . . . It is the most tremendous thing that has arisen in Missions in years and decades."

In the same letter, Jones reported that his good friend and colleague, J. Waskom Pickett, "has had a most satisfactory interview with Dr. Ambedkar in Bombay." Several weeks later, in January 1936, Jones informed his friends and financial supporters in the United States that Ambedkar's statement "is the most amazing challenge that has ever come before Christian Missions since the first missionaries came to the shores of this wonderful land." The sense of excitement about this once-in-a-lifetime opportunity, which filled Jones's letters, was contagious.

In his February 28, 1936, reply, Diffendorfer wrote that "what to do about the Harijan movement in India" was the uppermost thing in the board members' minds. "It is clear that we Methodists have been placed in a very peculiar relationship to this newest phase of the mass movement, quite as we were at its beginning years ago. Our church here in America trusts you and the others implicitly in the interpretation of these events."

Jones recorded his personal experience with Dr. Ambedkar in an article in the October 1, 1936, issue of the *Indian Witness*.[30] He first met Ambedkar in 1932 when they both happened to visit Gandhi at the same time while Gandhi was in jail. In order to unify the nationalist movement, Gandhi "was trying desperately" to keep the Harijans within Hinduism. In talking with Jones after he had talked with Gandhi, Ambedkar made it clear that he was interested only in social equality for the depressed classes and in the abolition of caste. Later, after Ambedkar declared that he was going to leave Hinduism and would take at least one-half of the outcastes with him, Jones saw him again at his home in Bombay. Ambedkar said that he was continuing his efforts to persuade the depressed classes to leave Hinduism and that when one-half of them were ready, he "would then move *en masse*" to another religion. Such a move, Jones noted, would involve 30 million people and would be "one of the most astonishing things that has happened in the religious world in many a century."

But suppose, he wondered, that these Harijans wanted to become Christians? "This fact gives a great deal of pause to many thoughtful Christians. Will the coming of these masses into Christianity, if they should choose that faith, mean the paganising of Christianity? It certainly might. . . . The danger is very real."

On the other hand, Jones encouraged Christians to face realistically the possibility that millions of outcastes would come into the church.

> I am just as interested in getting Christ into the collective will as in the individual will, especially if the putting of Christ into the collective will mean that the individual will accept it was [*sic*] a necessary outcome. I do not think,

therefore, that Christianity can escape this crisis by withdrawal. . . . It will evangelise the inevitable.

Five years after Jones's first interview with Ambedkar in 1932, he had another conversation (probably on June 24, 1937) with him in Bombay on his way from India to China. It "was the most important interview I have ever had with him," he wrote to Ralph Diffendorfer on July 26, 1937. Ambedkar had "said that it would be no trouble for him to decide to be a Christian if he were free to make his choice, but he is bound up with this [Harijan] movement and must move with them. He is nearer being on the Christian side than at any time I have ever known him."

Jones made confidential notes on his interview with Ambedkar and asked a missionary colleague, J. Holmes Smith, to send the notes to Diffendorfer.[31] The notes reveal that the most sensitive political issue Jones and Ambedkar discussed was the question of communal representation for the outcastes. Under the Government of India Act of 1935, which the British Parliament passed after the round table conferences failed to meet the demands of Indian nationalists, separate electorates were created for the various religious communities. These electorates then selected their representatives to the provincial and to the federal governments. The Government of India Act established the size of the electorates and the number of representatives for each electorate in accordance with the relative size of the religious communities.[32] Initially in his interview with Ambedkar, Jones reiterated his personal conviction that "communal representation was bad for the country." But then, perhaps because he was so eager to have the depressed classes become Christian, he told Ambedkar that "if they [the depressed classes] should become Christians I am sure that they would share equally any political advantage which the Christian Community would be given." "He seemed to appreciate that point," Jones commented.

On the basis of his interview with Ambedkar, Jones presented the issue of communal representation for the depressed classes to the British Government. In a letter to the Viceroy, Lord Halifax, dated February 3, 1938, and marked, "Private and Confidential,"[33] he wrote that Ambedkar had pointed out that the Government of India Act of 1935 discouraged the conversion of the outcastes to Christianity.

> If they [the outcastes] decided to embrace another faith they were blocked in large measure by the fact that they did not carry over to the new faith any political privilege they may have had. This amounts to penalizing one politically for a change of faith. This should not be.

The problem with the new Constitution established by the Government of India Act was, according to Ambedkar, that there was no provision "for

228

any change in representation if there is any considerable change in the numbers of any constituent unit. It is fixed. It should not be fixed, but should be left open to change with changes of numbers."

Moreover, providing for changes in communal representation would not introduce a new constitutional principle; it simply extended the principle already established. Ambedkar suggested that the problem could be resolved without a new Act of Parliament if the British Cabinet issued an Order in Council giving the Viceroy power "to make changes in representation where there is any considerable change in numbers in any community." Jones concluded his letter to Lord Halifax with a personal disclaimer.

> This comes from me as an individual and after having passed on the suggestion I withdraw from it as it were, and leave it in your hands to deal with as you see fit without any embarrassment of my connection with it.

Whether Ambedkar's suggestion for giving the Viceroy power to make changes in communal representation was politically feasible is open to question. The Hindu community would surely have opposed it, since Hindus had the most to lose if the depressed classes converted to Christianity. And the British Cabinet may not have been willing to risk the political consequences Ambedkar's idea would have had both in Britain and in India. But the real question for us is what Jones said in his interview with Ambedkar and what he wrote to Lord Halifax.

Jones's notes on his interview certainly reveal a new and very different attitude toward the issue of communal representation. Before the interview he consistently and emphatically opposed the concept of communal representation for India, because it established political distinctions on the basis of religion and meant that the Christian community, like the Hindus, Moslems, and Sikhs, would become another political faction. However, for Jones as a Christian evangelist, the greatest danger of communal representation was that it encouraged proselytism for political purposes instead of genuine religious conversion. So why did he accept Ambedkar's argument about the importance of communal representation for the depressed classes? And why in his letter to Lord Halifax did Jones adopt Ambedkar's idea about changes in communal representation?[34]

It may be that Jones was so anxious to have the Harijans convert to Christianity that he was willing to accommodate Ambedkar's political demands. In any event, Jones's statements in his interview with Ambedkar and in his letter to Lord Halifax were a mistake in judgment. Jones's initial cautious reaction to the possibility of tens of millions of outcastes becoming Christian is more consistent with his long-standing opposition to communal representation and to proselytism and is a more faithful reflection of his character and calling as a missionary evangelist.

If Jones responded to the Harijans' need for an alternative to Hinduism with action based on poor judgment, the Methodist Church responded quickly, but in the end inadequately, to their need for a more egalitarian and more spiritually and socially empowering religion. Shortly after Ambedkar's 1935 announcement that the depressed classes were seeking a religion to replace Hinduism, the Methodist Central Conference adopted a number of resolutions with respect to the Harijans. They began with the frank admission that "[w]hile we rejoice in the amazing possibilities which this [announcement by Ambedkar] opens before us, we are humbled that we are not better prepared for this hour."[35] When it passed these resolutions, the Central Conference probably thought it was unprepared for the Harijans because it lacked the personnel and programs to meet their expressed spiritual and physical need. And in fact what Ambedkar was asking for on behalf of the depressed classes was "Christian resources and leadership directed toward massive reconstruction of the economic, social, and political life of an entire class in the Indian population."[36] But the Methodist Church was also unprepared psychologically and spiritually to rethink its concept of the purpose and methods of Christian missions in order to make a more comprehensive response to Dr. Ambedkar.

> The Methodists proved too inflexible to be able to approach the Harijans on a sufficiently humanitarian basis; they were devotees of a form of Christian salvationism in which the prime concern was to win people to accept Christ as individual Savior. Humanitarian measures that did not lead directly to that end generally were not considered an essential part of Methodism's mission. The advent into Christianity of masses of Harijans under Ambedkar's leadership was—if it ever actually constituted a real opportunity for the Church—a lost opportunity as far as Methodism was concerned; it did not occur.[37]

Not surprisingly, the limiting mindset of Methodism in those pre-ecumenical days precluded exploring concrete ways in which linking up with other Christian denominations in India might produce a workable program for addressing the urgent social, economic, educational, and spiritual needs of the Harijans.

Was Ambedkar's search for an alternative to Hinduism on behalf of the depressed classes truly a lost opportunity for Methodism in India? Was God using Ambedkar's announcement as a way of calling Methodists to preach a more holistic gospel not focused so exclusively on individual salvation? Was this opportunity to reach the Harijans comparable to the opportunity (discussed in chapter 2) to receive and disciple the flood of outcastes who sought conversion to Christianity during the high watermark of the mass movements? If Jones's message about the kingdom of God had been more widely publicized and more willingly received, would the Methodist Church have reacted differently to Ambedkar's proposal?

Even if the Methodists had responded more favorably to the Harijans, would they in fact have come into the church? I do not think there is a definitive answer to these questions. In the long run Jones focused more of his evangelistic efforts on the educated upper castes of India than on the outcastes. Except for his interview with Ambedkar and his subsequent letter to Lord Halifax, he was generally more interested in Gandhi's announcements and proposals with respect to the nationalist movement than in Ambedkar's statements with respect to the Harijans.

On December 20, 1934, Jones wrote his last circular letter of that year, informing his friends and supporters in the United States about his activities in India since he left the ashram at Sat Tal in the middle of July. From that time until he wrote his circular letter, he said, he had been on "the long, long never-ending road . . . without any break between series" of evangelistic meetings. "I think I say each time I write that this has been the finest round of meetings I have ever had! Well, this has been the finest!"

The last six months of 1934 were significant, however, not only because of the success of Jones's speaking tour but also because of "a most important interview" he had with Gandhi on November 15. He summarized the content of the interview in an article in the December 6, 1934, issue of the *Indian Witness*.[38]

Jones interviewed Gandhi together with Professor David Moses of Hislop College in Nagpur and the Reverend S. Aldis. The three men first asked Gandhi about his proposal for village reconstruction throughout India. They wanted to know whether the proposal was "non-political and non-religious." Gandhi assured them that it was. On this basis, the three told Gandhi, the Christian community could be an active and enthusiastic partner in the process of village reconstruction. Jones then raised a question that had come up at his meeting the previous night. He asked Gandhi whether he believed in full social and religious equality and if he would "do away with caste." Jones quoted Gandhi's reply in his December 6, 1934, *Indian Witness* article.

> I would make it very plain that I would do away with inequalities in the social order, that is I would do away [with] any matter of high and low and put all on the same level. . . . I would therefore do away with caste as something which creates distinctions of high [and low] and make it occupational only.

By retaining caste as an occupational distinction, Gandhi meant that people should fulfill their *dharma* or religious duty in accordance with the Hindu concept of the talents and abilities that they possess from a previous birth. But for Gandhi every person had an equal obligation or *dharma* and no one occupation had any greater social and religious status than any other occupation.

Jones then asked Gandhi about the issue of communalism. He was concerned that there was emerging

> a separate political entity called the Indian Christian Community. Some of us deplore this fact for we do not believe that religion should be used to get political power. It is corrupted in the very process. . . . Some of us want the Christians of India to stand for India and not for the Indian Christians alone. . . . The fault for building up this communalism in India is partly ours and partly from the fact that people were not allowed to stay in their homes and be frank followers of Christ. They are put out and therefore this communalism has been built up. . . . Suppose we should say this: We are willing that the Christian community as a political entity should fade out, provided you allow people to stay in their homes and be frank, open Christians, members of a moral and spiritual organization called the Christian Church, without disability or penalty. . . . Are you willing to advocate this?

Jones recorded Gandhi's answer.

> Personally I would. If my son should become a Christian in the sense which you indicate, and there should be no brandy and cigars involved, then I would continue to hold him as an honoured member of my home and would allow him to hold his faith without interference.

Finally, Jones asked Gandhi if he would advocate his personal attitude toward conversion to Christianity for India as a whole and would "advise India to take that attitude." Gandhi replied, "I would. And moreover, if you take this attitude then most of the objections against Christianity in India will fade out."

In his December 20, 1934, circular letter Jones commented on Gandhi's reply. "This opens a wide and effectual door to the Gospel of Jesus Christ. How deeply grateful I am for this change! My soul tingles with eagerness at the prospects for a truly indigenous Christian Movement. The door is open!"

It is interesting to compare Jones's account of his November 15, 1934, interview with Gandhi after he returned to India from furlough in the United States with Gandhi's account of an earlier interview with Jones on February 4, 1933, before his furlough. Gandhi published his account of the 1933 interview in his magazine, *Harijan.*[39]

> Rev. Stanley Jones paid me a visit the other day before sailing for America. He said that in America he would be asked many questions about the campaign against untouchability and had, therefore, some questions which he wanted me to answer. I was glad of the visit and I readily answered his questions. I do not propose to reproduce the whole of our conversation and all his questions and cross-questions, but I propose to give to the readers the main questions and the substance of my answers. His first question, then, was: Why do you restrict the movement to the removal of untouchability

only? Why not do away with the caste system altogether? If there is a difference between caste and caste, and caste and untouchability, is it not one only of degree?

Gandhi answered that for him there was a very real difference in kind, not a mere difference in degree between caste and untouchability. Untouchability, he said, was "a sin against God and man." He compared it to "a poison slowly eating into the very vitals of Hinduism." Untouchability was "a hideous thing . . . [that] has stunted the growth of nearly 40 million human beings." On the other hand, the caste system was "a social institution" consisting of "trade guilds," which, he thought, had outgrown their original purpose and were "undesirable." But castes, unlike untouchability, were not "sinful" and constituted "no bar to the spiritual progress." In time, Gandhi assured Jones, the socially dysfunctional aspects of the caste system would disappear.

Another question Jones had asked concerned fasting. In 1932 and 1933 Gandhi abandoned for the most part his civil disobedience campaign and turned his attention to a campaign against untouchability and to the uplift of the untouchables. On September 20, 1932, he began a "fast unto death" to protest the discrimination by caste members against the outcastes.[40] Given the deep and seemingly impenetrable roots of the distinction between caste and outcaste, the success of Gandhi's fast was nothing short of a miracle. For the first time ever, untouchables were admitted to Hindu temples, caste members and outcastes ate together, and Hindu leaders pledged to grant full legal equality to the Harijans when India became an independent nation and wrote its first constitution. This display of unity among all Hindus, caste and outcaste, was so impressive that the British agreed to modify the terms of the communal award in the Government of India Act of 1935, giving the Harijans greater representation in the provincial and federal governments. Jones's question to Gandhi about fasting, however, involved not the political result of his fast, but its spiritual justification. "Was not your fast pure coercion?" he asked.

Gandhi answered that his fast was coercive only in the sense that it "sprang from love." He compared the coercion of his fast to the coercion of love between parents and children, between husband and wife, and between Jesus Christ and those who believe in him as their Lord and Savior. Gandhi said,

> It is the implicit and sacred belief of millions of Christians that love of Jesus keeps them from falling and that it does so against themselves. His love bends the reason and the emotion of thousands of His votaries to His love. . . . And, if all this love could be regarded as coercion, then the love that prompted my fast and, therefore, my fast [itself], was coercion, but it was that in no other sense.

Jones also attempted to act as an intermediary between Gandhi and the British government in India. In chapter 8 we saw how in 1930 Jones urged Indians in Madras to attend the round table conferences with the British in order to come to an agreement with them about the future of India. But in February of 1935 he went a step further. He suggested that Gandhi work with the British Commissioner for Rural Reconstruction in Gandhi's efforts to improve the social and economic condition of the outcastes. Gandhi replied to Jones's suggestion in a letter dated February 10, 1935.

> There is no question, so far as I am concerned, of coming into conflict with authority, or even of overlapping. I have taken up what many people consider to be a hopeless job and what many more still regard to be almost an impossible feat. So I am not likely to find in the Government a formidable competitor. And if they could take up the movement it would fill me with delight and I would still have my hands full. Lastly, if the Government would extend any help to me in the direction in which I am working, of course, I would thankfully receive it; but just at present there is that blind wall of suspicion. Therefore, as you may have seen from the papers, a circular has gone forth that their officials are not to help me in any way whatsoever, but closely watch the movement and report on its doings. I rather like this watch. That will enable me to disarm the suspicion the quickest. But whilst the suspicion lasts, I must try to live it down.[41]

When Jones received this letter from Gandhi, he wrote to the Commissioner for Rural Reconstruction in the Punjab and enclosed Gandhi's letter. On February 26, 1935, the commissioner replied and commented specifically on Gandhi's letter. His letter reveals much about the British attitude toward Gandhi and about the difficulty faced by the Indian nationalist movement in dealing with the British government.

> Mr. Gandhi takes up the most curious position. What does he mean when he says "if they could take up the movement, it would fill me with delight"? Government has been doing this work for years and years and how can Government extend help to a man who has just started on the work, has no plans, no programme and appears to be quite ignorant of the enormous amount of work already done in the field upon which he is just entering? No wonder there is a blind wall of suspicion. . . . Surely it is for Mr. Gandhi to find out what Government is doing and see whether he, as a new and ignorant recruit, can fit himself into the scheme of things and pull his weight in this big work?

Another piece of news Jones shared in his December 20, 1934, circular letter was the extension of the Sat Tal Ashram to Lucknow. The idea was that Sat Tal would continue as a summer ashram devoted to meditation and thought, while in Lucknow during the winter, active service would be added to meditation and thought. As Jones explained it six years later in the *Indian Witness*, "The Lucknow Ashram was begun to supply the applied end of the Sat Tal Ashram, the demonstration in actual corporate living of the principles of the Kingdom of God."[42]

He first outlined his plans for the Lucknow Ashram to his Methodist audience in India in a short article in the June 6, 1935, issue of the *Indian Witness*. The members of the ashram, Jones said, would provide Christian religious instruction to the seven hundred boys attending Lucknow Christian College. They would also do religious work among the thousands of other university students in the city. He proposed newspaper evangelism as another activity for the Lucknow Ashram. It would be a place where inquirers could come to study Christian doctrine and teaching. The Lucknow Ashram would also have a medical doctor among its members and would open a dispensary to provide medical care for the poor. For new missionaries who wanted to study Indian languages, the ashram would provide this opportunity during the winter months. Finally, the Lucknow Ashram would take over a small community center, which the members of the ashram would use to provide a variety of community services. The members of the ashram would be led by an American Methodist missionary from Belgaum, J. Holmes Smith. Jones was so committed to the Lucknow Ashram project that he wrote to Diffendorfer on November 22, 1934,

> I will give Jay [Smith] my salary for the next two years before his furlough in the middle of '38. I will do this on the understanding that the Board take it over then. . . . In other words I will be responsible for his salary for two years only. . . . Is that satisfactory?

Paying Smith's salary for two years, however, was only a small part of Jones's financial support for the Lucknow Ashram and for a number of other missionaries and mission projects in India. He confided to Diffendorfer in his November 25, 1935, letter,

> I am paying not only the salary of Jay Smith and family, but of all the others in the Ashram excepting those who are provided for otherwise. That means that I am providing salaries for Dr. and Mrs. Plokker, Rev. Narayan Bannerjee and his family of seven members, Mani Datt Patial and the enquirers who stay with us. Besides that I have to meet the general running expenses of the Ashram, repairs, rent, the dispensaries, the upkeep of the Ambulance and its running expenses, a social service center at Daliganj, and so on. Besides that I have given this year various sums to the N. India Conference [of the Methodist Church] amounting to several thousand rupees. In addition I must give Rs. 1500/ per year for the annuity on the Sat Tal Estate, besides repairs and running expenses there. Also for a school at Sat Tal. Also Rs. 600/ for the Institute at Sitapur, per year. I also give about Rs. 1000/ to the L.C.C. [Lucknow Christian College] for scholarships per year. Besides many smaller things. You can quite see that I have all I can do to keep these things

going. The publishing of the Fellowship [a magazine operated by Jones] costs me Rs. 1500/ per year. Then my travelling expenses. I have cut my personal expenses to a minimum, living on about Rs. 50 per month.

Unfortunately, despite Stanley's best personal efforts and extraordinary financial commitment, the Lucknow Ashram closed in 1940. It was an emotional and soul-wrenching event. "To see the child of one's heart die, and to see it die without a tear is an experience," he wrote in the April 18, 1940, issue of the *Indian Witness*.[43] He explained that the ashram was closed because it fell so far short of its original purpose.

> [W]e believed in the Ashram ideal so much that when we saw we were falling so far short of it, we were unwilling to continue something that wasn't true to what we saw in that Ashram ideal. We were unwilling to continue unless it was the real thing. We preferred closing to allowing an inadequate illustration of what we had in mind.

There was also another, more practical reason for the closing of the Lucknow Ashram. "As the head of the Ashram," Stanley wrote, "I found I was trying to do an impossible thing: be at the head of an Ashram and not live with it day in and day out. I had to choose between my evangelistic work and the Ashram work and the evangelistic work was my primary call. . . . I could not continue under these circumstances as the head of the Ashram and there seemed to be no one to take my place."

The failure of the Lucknow Ashram to apply fully the principles of the kingdom of God on earth and Jones's inability to personally supervise the ashram were the public reasons he gave for its closing in his April 18, 1940, *Indian Witness* article. But there was also another reason that Jones did not make public. In a letter to Diffendorfer dated December 17, 1939, he explained what happened when he went to the Lucknow Ashram in October of that year. J. Holmes Smith as well as several other members of the ashram had decided to organize in the United States a "League of Friendship for India's Freedom," which would promote the cause of Indian independence from Great Britain. They wanted Jones to participate in this organization. But he declined their invitation. He "pointed out the limitations of this idea," and emphasized that organizing the League of Friendship "was incompatible with the pledge which the missionary gives." At this point Smith "announced that he would probably have to break" the pledge. Jones tried to dissuade him. He wrote to Diffendorfer,

> Over a course of several months by correspondence and personal interviews we tried to keep him from doing it. We pointed out in every possible way what it would mean to the Ashram and to his missionary career. We showed

him that the probabilities were that the Lucknow Ashram would have to be closed if he went. I saw no possibility of the Ashram remaining open without his leadership.

What provoked Smith to organize the League of Friendship for India's Freedom and to decide that he could no longer keep the missionary pledge was the action of Great Britain with respect to India at the beginning of World War II. When the war began in September 1939, the British Viceroy announced unilaterally that India was at war with Germany. The Indian National Congress then asked the British government how its declared war aims of the protection of democracy and of the defeat of imperialism applied to India. The Viceroy's answer was noncommittal, promising only that there would be political discussions about the status of India after the war and inviting Indians to help mobilize public opinion in their country behind the British war effort. Indian nationalist leaders as well as Christian pacifists like J. Holmes Smith "were outraged at what they considered the imperialist hypocrisy of the British attitude." So Holmes and three other like-minded Methodist missionaries organized what they called the Kristagraha Movement and issued two manifestos denouncing Britain as hypocritical and calling for an end to its evil control of India. But in spite of the fact that "both declarations were radical in content and strongly denunciatory in tone, the [British] government registered no complaint either with the signatories or with Methodist officials."[44]

If the British government in India took no official notice of the Kristagraha Manifestos, the Methodist bishops did. According to Copplestone's *History of Methodist Missions,* Smith's bishop, John W. Robinson, "took the initiative in pressing the pledge issue upon him, indicating that he intended to cable the New York office requesting Smith's immediate recall from India."[45] According to Jones's December 17, 1939, letter to Diffendorfer, however, Bishop Robinson's reaction to the manifestos was more sympathetic to Smith's position than Copplestone makes it appear. Jones wrote,

> The matter was put up to Bishop Robinson and Bishop Robinson suggested the following possibilities: First, that Jay could break the missionary pledge and stay on in India. This he did not want to do. Second, that he could stay in India and keep the pledge. This he completely refused. Third, that he should request the Bishop to ask the Board to recall him. This he did not care to do. Fourth, that the Bishop request the Board to recall him. This the Bishop was unwilling to do. Fifth, that the Bishop ask the Board to recall him with Jay's consent. The last named was finally decided on.

Smith not only agreed to accept being recalled, he also resigned from the Lucknow Ashram. Once again, the decision was his alone. As Jones put it in another long and detailed letter to Diffendorfer dated January 28, 1940, "We . . . never asked for Jay's resignation, nor did we desire it. It was entirely his own initiative." Smith's December 3, 1939, letter of resignation, addressed to the Secretary of the Lucknow Ashram and signed by both himself and his wife Sylvia, read,

> In view of our understanding that the Ashram should be protected from the possible displeasure of the authorities due to the action of any members; and because of our decision not to be restrained, because of the missionary pledge, from exercising the fundamental Christian duty of transmitting to the people, without equivocation, what we are convinced to be God's judgments upon such momentous issues as imperialist hypocrisy and exploitation, and sanction agreement with the Archarya [leader of the Ashram, Jones] and a majority of the Staff over what we regard as compromise of a basic Christian principle, we hereby tender our resignation from membership in this Ashram, and declare that the Ashram, including its various officers and members are in no way responsible for the stand we feel in conscience obliged to take. We need not add that it is only after intensive deliberation and with great sorrow that we take this step. In spite of our deep disagreement with some of you, we shall always hold the Ashram and each of you in affectionate and prayerful remembrance.[46]

Because he had such a deep sense of personal responsibility for the Lucknow Ashram and for J. Holmes Smith as the *de facto* leader of the ashram, Jones felt obliged to explain to Diffendorfer and through him to the Mission Board both Smith's relationship to the ashram and Jones's personal relationship to Smith. His January 28, 1940, letter gives a clear and persuasive statement of the difference between himself and Smith in their approach to opposing British imperialism.

> I urged [Smith] that if the [British] Government wanted to close our institution [the Lucknow Ashram] because we were giving the full expression of our Christian convictions it could do so. It would not be a bad way to die, but I also felt that we should not commit suicide by spoiling for a fight and pushing it up under Government's nose and making them say whether or not this was breaking the pledge. Apparently Government was giving very great leeway in expression of opinion, as the British Government always does, and they did not intend to act unless there was some specific action directed against the Government. An expression of an opinion on pacifism and aggressive imperialism would not cause the Government to act. I felt that we could give our Christian position on both of these matters and that this was not against the pledge, but was in the highest interest of the Government for us to do so. I have done the above and have been perfectly free to do so.

Jones and Smith had sharp and deeply felt differences about how, as Christian pacifists, they could best oppose British imperialism and about whether they could in good conscience continue to work as Christian missionaries in India under the terms of the missionary pledge. Jones had already recognized, when he wrote to Diffendorfer in December 1939, that without Smith, he would probably have to close the Lucknow Ashram and "concentrate on Sat Tal." But Jones was not bitter and held no personal animosity toward Smith. He wrote in the same letter to Diffendorfer, "Even in my deep disagreements with Jay over the matter, I repeat that I hold him in respect and love. Deal as kindly with him as possible and anything that you can do for him will receive my gratitude."

Moreover, as Jones revealed in a February 20, 1940, letter to Dr. C. C. Morrison of *The Christian Century,* he paid the cost of the Smiths' trip back to the United States, since the Board of Foreign Missions "felt themselves in financial difficulties."[47]

The closing of the Lucknow Ashram and J. Holmes Smith's emotionally wrenching decision to leave the mission field forced Jones to examine his own position on the missionary pledge. In addition to explaining privately to Diffendorfer the differences between his opposition to British imperialism and Smith's opposition to British imperialism, he also published an article entitled, "My Position Restated" for the readers of the *Indian Witness.* He acknowledged that "there seems to be some confusion left in the minds of some as to my exact position regarding the missionary pledge." To clarify his position, he explained why he came to India in the first place. "I believe I have been called to be an evangelist," he wrote. "The calling of the evangelist is to bring people to the feet of Jesus Christ and through Him to the Kingdom of God." He had done a poor job of fulfilling his call, he confessed, "for I am proclaiming something that judges me in the very act of presenting it to others. The evangelist must be evangelized by his own evangel." Jones's call to be an evangelist was his "masterpassion." He interpreted his position with respect to the missionary pledge in terms of this fundamental commitment.

The two questions which have arisen in regard to the missionary pledge are War and Imperialism. I am interested in getting rid of war, for I am a pacifist; I have renounced war and will take no part in it. I feel it to be incompatible with the Christian way. I am also interested in India's freedom. I believe it to be the birthright of every nation to express itself in self-government. I believe it will be good for India and for Britain when the right is conceded and implemented.

I say that I am interested in getting rid of war, but not supremely. For if we should get rid of war tomorrow, the necessity for my evangel would still remain. For I believe that in a warless world men would still need Christ to meet their deepest needs.

I am interested in India's freedom, but, again, not supremely. For if India got her freedom tomorrow, I feel that she, along with the rest of the world, would still need what Christ has to offer.

While I am interested in these two things, I am supremely interested in only one thing—to bring me to the feet of Christ. On my way to my supreme task I will give my witness against war and imperialism.[48]

In his *Indian Witness* article Jones emphasized the same point that he had made earlier in his January 28, 1940, letter to Diffendorfer, namely, that as an evangelist he would not take the initiative in pressing the British government on the issues of war and imperialism. He was not, he wrote, "spoiling for a fight on these two issues," nor would he push these issues "up under the nose of Government and compel them to take notice and precipitate a crisis with me on these issues." For this reason, Jones wrote, he disagreed with the Kristagraha Manifestos because they were a diversion from what he considered to be the "main task" of the ashram. However, he continued, the British government might interpret the missionary pledge in a way that would make it impossible for him to continue his work as a missionary evangelist in India.

> If the Government of India should say that I cannot give my clear Christian witness on War and Imperialism, I should consider withdrawing from India. . . . It would depend on the Inner Call. But without a specific Inner Call I would probably withdraw. . . .
> My witnessing to my Christian convictions on War and Imperialism I feel to be entirely within my rights under the missionary pledge. To give the Christian position on this matter I believe to be not "contrary to or in diminution of the lawfully constituted authority" but in the highest interests of that authority. I believe that the Government needs to have the pressure of Christian convictions upon its conscience.

Jones did not hesitate to speak out on the issue of British imperialism when he felt compelled by his conscience and by his calling as a missionary evangelist to do so. Although he never broke the missionary pledge to do "nothing contrary to or in diminution of the lawfully constituted authority" in British India, Jones did pay a price for his political convictions when the British refused to permit him to return to India during World War II.

10

Conflict and Controversy

I think it is a great mistake for you to continue your Madras controversy. . . .
It is only fair for you to know . . . that there is little or no sympathy for your
attempt to discredit the Madras Meeting by keeping up a controversy in
which, as Dr. Cavert said to me recently, "Stanley is erecting a straw man."
— Ralph Diffendorfer, November 9, 1939, letter

THE YEARS COVERED by this chapter were a dark prelude to an even darker period in world history, the outbreak and onslaught of World War II. Due to a demonized demagogue in the person of Adolph Hitler, war erupted in Europe and soon engulfed the globe. The late 1930s chronicle a sorry legacy of entrenched global depression, seething social and political unrest, decaying old colonial imperialisms, a sinister quartet of totalitarian "isms"—communism, fascism, nazism, and a "relatively new" version of military imperialism (Japan)—not to mention a largely demoralized, ineffective, even stupefied Christendom. Amid such a rash of brutalizing "outwardisms" (as Jones would call them), is it any wonder that Stanley Jones, sensitized as he was to the sharp moral distinction between life on the lower level of "worldly reality" and abundant life on the higher level of kingdom of God reality, found his own inward spiritual equilibrium sorely tried by history's unprecedented clash and conflict, sin and death, evil and stupidity? In the process of his being awakened to and challenged by God's supreme concept and master plan, events and circumstances propelled him toward many battlefronts.

As he attempted to study and internalize, to interpret and transmit to the church and beyond what the Holy Spirit was revealing to him about this kingdom of God reality, Stanley's life was inundated with grueling travels, intensified speaking schedules, increasing ministry responsibilities in addition to his usual evangelistic work in India and elsewhere, and copious correspondence along with other written output. Consequently, during these years, not only did he struggle with tremendous "job-related" stress and strain; fatigue in body, mind, and spirit, misunderstanding; criticism; and opposition from friends, detractors, and foes, he also struggled with his own spirit. One senses that Stanley Jones was handpicked especially at this time to receive for the church this "re-presentation" of God's redemptive reign, to become impregnated with this kingdom idea, which had been there all along but had gotten misplaced, downgraded, or ignored. At this juncture, perhaps mainly subconsciously, he *knew* that this divine entrustment with the kingdom of God revelation *had* to become the most important thing there was in his life and calling. It had to be not merely *verbal* but *vital*, to put it in Jones's own words. Stanley's spiritual struggle at this time was how to give birth and expression to the kingdom of God idea, to work out what God was working within him, to protect it, to nurture it, to communicate it, to incarnate it, and, as proved to be the case, to become possessed by and obsessed with it as the Holy Spirit gave him power. If accomplishing this task of reintroducing the kingdom of God in word and deed included being *spiritually* on edge or even cranky, unreasonably insistent, emphatic, outspoken, or implacable vis-á-vis status quo churchly emphases, and/or religious trappings, so be it.

In the late 1930s, on an apocalyptic world stage looming with everything fearful and gruesome, warring and wicked, and in cooperation with Stanley Jones, surely one of Jesus' most reliable, sold-out apprentices, the Holy Spirit "launched a torpedo"—the kingdom of God. Strictly speaking, "relaunched" may not be the theological *mot juste,* since Jesus, the Word of the kingdom of "God-Become-Flesh," launched his program on earth two thousand years ago at an hour in history that was more momentous than the church has yet to grasp, to appreciate, to embrace, and to celebrate.

On January 28, 1940, in the same letter in which Stanley told Miss Nellie about J. Holmes Smith's leaving the Lucknow Ashram, he also told his good friend about his activities during the first three weeks of that month. He had been at Sat Tal, he wrote, working on his new book, *Is the Kingdom of God Realism?*

> I got a hundred and twenty-five pages finished in those three weeks which I thought wasn't bad. I also got a leopard. I have not given myself to big game

shooting in India, but when the villagers came and told me that a leopard had killed a large lungur (black-faced monkey) and begged me to kill it I consented. The leopard always comes back for a second feed the second night so the villagers built me a machan up in a tree nearby which was a bed covered with branches so that it made a little hut up there. There was just enough place to peek out at the leopard when he came. A villager and I got up in the machan at 5 o'clock in the evening and the leopard appeared twice but was very wary and each time went back. The third time he came into full view about 8:30 at night and I let go and there was a terrific roar. He rolled down under our machan to about a hundred and fifty feet below us. We did not dare to go down at night to see as a wounded leopard is a very dangerous beast, but the next morning the men found him and brought him in triumph back to the bungalow. It was a very happy set of villagers who brought him back, for the leopards ravage their cattle a great deal. The lower monkey fell into the hands of the leopard but the higher monkey through cunning and firearms got the leopard! They say the way the leopard gets the lungur is to sit down under the tree in which a lungur is found and sway back and forth with glaring eyes until the lungur with sheer fright falls out of the tree into the leopard's clutches.

Sat Tal was always a place of spiritual and physical rest and refreshment for Stanley. When he confronted the unpleasant and disappointing fact that he would have to close the Lucknow Ashram after Smith had left, he needed the solitude of Sat Tal. In the early months of 1940, he was virtually alone at Sat Tal and could spend weeks in prayer, study, and writing. One of the subjects he thought and prayed about was the problem of church unity. The lack of unity was an issue he had faced throughout his career as a missionary evangelist, but in the mid-1930s he was led by the Inner Voice to take action.

Stanley Jones felt impelled to act on the issue of church unity because of the lack of an effective Christian response to international events like the nationalist movement in India, the continued civil and military conflict in China, and the Great Depression in the United States and throughout the world. He wrote in the *Christian Century* on October 2, 1935,[1] that a sense of "fatalism" had spread to Christians of all nations.

We find ourselves drifting straight into war and yet feel helpless to avert it. . . . We feel that the problems that infest economic life are not incapable of solution, for we have the knowledge and the instruments which can produce enough for all, and yet we feel helpless in directing that knowledge and applying these instruments of production.

The source of this spiritual malaise, he thought, was the lack of unity among Christians. Even though Christians worldwide had enormous resources and "hold the balance of power in their hands," they had no instrument of collective action and their spiritual witness was unheeded.

But, "They could do anything," he wrote, if Christians of different churches and denominations would "come together."

In his round table conferences, which he began in India in the early 1920s and later held in the United States and in other nations, he shared his own Christian experiences and insights with a wide variety of Christians and non-Christians. After listening to Christians in these conferences for some fifteen years, Jones came to three conclusions about the church, which he summarized in his *Christian Century* article as unity, equality, and diversity.

First of all, "Christians are the most united body on earth—if they only knew it!" They all share the same basic faith but, ironically, "the people who are most united at the center are most divided at the circumference." In other words, the doctrine that unites Christians is much more important than the peripheral issues that separate them. Second, he wrote, God does not prefer one Christian denomination to another. "The saints are about equally distributed among all the denominations." The denominations are equal in the sense that "God accepts and uses those in any denomination who surrender to him." Finally, the expressions and manifestations of the faith and life that are common to all Christians are varied and diverse.

On the basis of these three conclusions, Stanley proposed that all Christians in the United States drop their denominational labels and become members of The Church of Christ in America. Each denomination would retain its name but would become part of the larger body—the Presbyterian branch of The Church of Christ in America, for example. Each branch would be free to have its own church polity and its own Christian creeds and doctrines, and could establish its own criteria for membership within its own part of the larger church. In this way there would be unity among all Christians in The Church of Christ in America, there would be equality among all the branches, and there would be diversity of doctrinal emphases and practices among the branches. But the real advantage of Christian unity was the greater "moral authority" with which the church would speak to the world. He concluded his *Christian Century* article by paraphrasing the closing words of *The Communist Manifesto:* "Christians of America, unite!" he wrote. "We have nothing to lose except our dividing walls."

Jones's concept of Christian unity in The Church of Christ in America is important because it reveals a number of essential components of his personal character and of his public ministry. First of all, his concept of Christian unity reflects a deep ecumenical spirit. Although he first went to India in 1907 as a Methodist Episcopal missionary, he also received financial support from the Holiness Union, an organization that crossed denominational lines. And he worked with the YMCA in both India and

China. So the development of his idea of Christian unity was a natural outgrowth of his personal experience in ecumenical ministry.

In addition, his church unity proposal reflects his insistence that Christians speak not just to individuals but also to nations and societies. The kingdom of God proclaimed by Jesus Christ is a kingdom that offers redemption for individuals both in their relationship with God and in their relationships with one another. It was in these corporate and institutional relationships, he believed, that the church was missing its opportunity to preach the gospel of Jesus Christ. One important reason that the church failed to speak forcefully and effectively to economic, social, and political issues was that it did not speak with one voice. So the proposal for The Church of Christ in America would enable Christians in the United States to take a more active role in these issues and to have a greater opportunity for successfully influencing public policy.

On another level, Jones's call for church unity responded to a specific problem he and other Christian missionaries faced on a daily basis in India. In evangelistic meetings when the preacher asked, usually on the last night of a series, for personal commitments to Jesus Christ, hundreds and sometimes thousands of people responded. But once these persons repented of their sins and professed their faith in Christ, the next issue was what church they would join. For the evangelist, of course, the question of church membership was secondary to the question of faith in Jesus Christ. But if a new convert to Christianity asked specifically which church he should join, the evangelist faced a real dilemma, a dilemma Jones attempted to resolve by proposing one church of Christ for an entire nation.

Jones himself faced this dilemma many times in India. He recalled one particular example in his October 14, 1935, circular letter.[2] The Ezhava caste in Travancore was "a very intelligent and progressive low caste" that had debated for several years whether to adopt a specific religion or to become atheists or agnostics.

> This whole caste had been once decided that it would adopt Christianity. After the momentous decision had been made a lawyer arose and asked the question. "You have adopted Christianity. May I ask you which Christianity? If you live in this section you will be Church of England, if in that you will be London Mission, in this other place Baptist. Now you are united as a caste, then you will be divided as denominations." It stopped the whole movement. A real reason for unity!

In his proposal, Stanley Jones issued a clarion call for Christian unity throughout the world and especially in the United States and India where God had called him to serve. He wanted Christians to speak with one unequivocal moral voice on public issues in the United States and Western

Europe, and he wanted Indian Christians and Western missionaries in India to have the same moral and spiritual unity. In India, the obstacles to Christian unity came from two sources—the social, economic, political, and racial differences between Western Christians and Indian Christians, and denominational differences among Christians within India. Stanley's ministry in India addressed both of these obstacles, but in the late 1930s it focused primarily on the sharply divisive issues between Western Christianity and Indian Christianity and especially on the politically explosive issues raised by the Indian nationalist movement, which, if not resolved, would be an insuperable barrier to Christian unity in India.

We have already discussed Jones's sympathy for Indian nationalism and his contacts with Gandhi and other Indian nationalist leaders as well as with the British government in an effort to promote the ultimate goal of Indian independence. He discussed one attempt to mediate between Indian nationalists and the British in his March 28, 1939, circular letter. At his visit to the annual convention of Mar Thoma Syrian Christians in Travancore State, he wrote,

> I came into a tense Travancore. I left it a year ago peaceful and calm, but now it was stirred for many had gone to jail in the non-violent movement to get Responsible Government. The Christians had joined with the Hindus in it. They had given the Government six weeks to do something, if not, the movement would begin again. I saw the Prime Minister and took the terms of the [Indian National] Congress leaders to him hoping to bring about a reconciliation. The Prime Minister was adamant. The struggle is suspended by Mahatma Gandhi for the time being, but in the end it will have to be renewed.

In addition to his acting as a personal mediator between Indian nationalists and the British government, he also hoped that his ashram, because of its multicultural and interfaith composition, would, as he put it in his July 9, 1939, circular letter, form "a bridge between the Christian movement and this new nationalist Government." By "new nationalist Government" Jones meant not a completely independent Indian government but a British-controlled government in India with substantial Indian representation.

Also in 1939 Jones had used the Lucknow Ashram as a forum for the discussion and potential resolution of the thorny problem of mission property in India. As we saw in chapter 8, the 1928 Jerusalem Conference adopted a resolution with respect to the protection of missionaries and mission property at a time when nationalist movements were beginning to become an issue not only in India but also in other parts of the world where Western missionaries were active. By 1939 far-sighted missionaries in India like Jones, who were sympathetic to the claims of Indian Christians for control of their own churches and other religious institutions, began to plan for the transfer of mission property to Indian churches. Jones wrote to Ralph Diffendorfer about his ideas on this subject in a letter dated August 1, 1939. He also met with what he called a "representative body of U.P. [United Provinces] Indian Christians" in addition to "some missionaries." This group of missionaries and Indian nationals drew up a list of proposals to resolve "the Church and Mission property question in India."[3] The first two proposals read,

> 1. That we request the various Mission Boards to transfer the ownership of the property in India now held by them to the various Indian Churches.
> 2. That, until we have a united Church, this property be transferred to a Board in each Denomination which shall hold and manage the entire property of that Denomination in behalf of the Indian Church.

These denominational boards were to be composed of a majority of Indians and a minority of missionaries and would undertake the obligation to pay any existing property debts. All money received by these boards that was not used to pay off debts was to be used not to endow local churches, but to endow "institutions which the Church is not able to support without endowment." The last proposal was that

> no missionary or Indian has any legal or moral right to claim a personal share of this [church] property. It is to be held and managed for the purposes of the Kingdom of God through the Church in India and not for the personal gain of anyone.

It is not clear exactly what happened to these proposals, but they clearly reflect Jones's views on the question of church property in India, and they were almost certainly written by Jones himself.

Jones's conviction about the absolute necessity for unity among the Christian churches was not just a topic for academic discussion and debate in his books, articles, and letters. Beginning in January and February 1936, he participated in many preaching missions in the United States that were sponsored not by the Methodist Episcopal Church or by any particular denomination, but by the Federal Council of Churches, the predecessor of today's National Council of Churches. During the first mission, the National Preaching Mission, Jones was one of eighty missioners who led meetings in twenty-five cities across the country, but he was the only missioner who held meetings continuously throughout the mission. He described his speaking schedule in his December 18, 1936, circular letter.

> The plan was to be four days in a place, two places a week, so that each place would have a Sunday either for the beginning or ending, which meant that we had to put eight days in a week. Some of the group [of missioners] would

be beginning in the new place and others ending up in the old. I usually have the task of ending up in huge mass meetings. It meant that I had to follow up in an airplane at night to catch up the next morning with the group. It was truly a man-breaking schedule for we were speaking from two to five times a day with no days of rest between for three solid months. Along about the middle I was pretty badly fagged, but I struck new Resources and came out to the end quite as fresh as when I went in. It was a miracle of God's grace and somebody must have been praying.

In the same circular letter Jones described the response to the preaching mission as "very great indeed." Christians throughout America, he reported, had "taken new heart and courage." Every place was packed out, and loudspeakers sometimes had to be put in adjoining halls or out in the open to accommodate the audiences. In Madison Square Garden in New York, he wrote, twenty thousand people attended his meeting and eight thousand remained after the meeting to make personal decisions for Jesus Christ. The preaching mission also changed the social and moral character of the cities in which it was held. Jones noted that the Roman Catholic mayor of St. Louis said that if the mission would stay in his city for another week, "he could dismiss his police force."

After Jones returned to India from his first preaching mission in the United States, he wrote an article for the April 14, 1937, issue of the *Christian Century* entitled "Afterthoughts on the Preaching Mission," reflecting on his participation in the mission during the previous year and on the role and status of evangelism in America at that time. The need for Christian evangelism, he wrote, had not changed, "but the method of approach had to be changed because the intellectual climate had changed." And the intellectual climate had changed because American culture had become more suspicious of the motives of evangelism. "We know," he wrote, "that we are being subjected to exploitation all the time."

We hear radio music, and we are not quite sure that we can enjoy it, for we know that our feelings of sympathy are being aroused so we will be in a mood to listen to the merits of Palmolive soap or something else. It puts us on the mental defensive. We bring that into the religious meeting with us. We cannot help it. We listen with an undertone of suspicion regarding the real purpose of it all. Is it to glorify the individual, to catch a man for this group, to feed a megalomania, to get money out of us?[4]

Jones concluded that evangelism in the future, in order to be effective, "must be sincerely and simply real." This is surely good advice for Christian evangelism in the United States today, which must proclaim the gospel in a culture that is supersaturated with commercialism from direct mail solicitations, telemarketers, and radio and television broadcasts. Although the intellectual climate of modern American culture may be even more

248

suspicious of the motives of Christian evangelists than it was in the mid-1930s, the need for evangelism has not changed. Many millions of Americans are still spiritually starved for the sincerely and simply real good news of Jesus Christ.

During the National Preaching Mission the missioners discovered a serious and growing gap between higher education and Christianity. So two years later, in 1938, the Federal Council of Churches, the YMCA, and the Student Volunteer Movement sponsored the University Christian Mission. This mission was led by a team of about fifteen missioners, including Jones, who visited twelve state colleges and universities in the United States in the fall of 1938. He described the program of the University Christian Mission in an article in the January 26, 1939, issue of the *Indian Witness*.[5] Beginning on Saturday night with a retreat for the local committee, the mission spent a week on the campus of each institution. On Sunday morning the mission was in local churches, and on Sunday afternoon the president of the college or university hosted a tea party so that the mission team could meet the faculty of the institution. In the mornings during the rest of the week the team visited individual classrooms at the invitation of the professors "to give the Christian interpretation of that particular subject." At noon each day there was a luncheon for the faculty. In the afternoons the mission team held seminars on various subjects, and in the evenings the team had supper in fraternity or sorority houses. After supper each evening there was a mass meeting in an auditorium.

The University Christian Mission was significant for several reasons, according to Jones. First of all, it marked the first time that public colleges and universities had invited Christians to help them achieve their educational objectives. Moreover, the purpose of the mission was openly evangelistic. And the mission team challenged both faculty and students. Finally, the mission devised a new technique for those making decisions for Christ in the mass meetings.

> In the mass meetings we would say that there were probably four classes and we would suggest:
>
> a. There were those who should go home alone and settle it with God. It would do no good for them to try to settle it publicly.
>
> b. There were those who should see somebody and talk it over personally. We told them when and where they could meet the members of the team for personal interviews.
>
> c. There were those who have questions and objections.
>
> d. There were those who would like to know the steps in finding God for they would like to take them.

In every meeting the last two groups were asked to stay after the rest were dismissed. Over the course of the mission, the number of those who stayed ranged from one hundred to two thousand people a night.

On this mission, Stanley was accompanied by his daughter, Eunice. When they returned to India, Stanley wrote a circular letter dated January 19, 1939. The mission, he said, had "squeezed out" his "last ounce of strength."

> Of course, I was dead tired, for I had been speaking three to six times a day with interviews between. I thought the trip on the Queen Mary would set me up, but it didn't. So I felt God's providence in my missing the plane in London because of bad weather. I was held up in London for a week and went to bed for 3 days complete rest. How thankful I was for them. Then the French plane took me to India in five days of glorious adventure. I arrived in Madras a week late for the Conference, but still I had a week of it. A great Conference!

The conference Jones was referring to was a conference sponsored by the International Missionary Council (IMC) in Tambaram near Madras, India. As compared with the Jerusalem Conference ten years before, the Tambaram Conference had a more orthodox theological focus.[6] It identified the "motive for missions" with the "motive for the church itself." In other words, Christian missions, like the churches that sponsored missions, proclaimed the good news of God's redemption through Jesus Christ. The task of both churches and missions was to offer the forgiveness of sins and eternal life to all who accepted Christ's sacrifice. And if churches and missions had a common motive and a common purpose, then there should be no distinction between "sending" and "receiving" churches, between Western churches that send missionaries and non-Western churches that receive them.[7] In recognition of this fact the Tambaram Conference was the first international missionary conference in which the representatives of the receiving churches and the representatives from the sending churches were equal in number.[8] Moreover, the high quality of the national leadership of the receiving churches was reflected in the outstanding character of the delegates they sent to Tambaram. After the conference Edmund D. Soper, a theologian of Christian missions, noted that many observers of the proceedings were struck by "the moral stability, intellectual alertness, and spiritual maturity of the Asiatic delegates."[9]

Stanley arrived at Tambaram, as he wrote in his circular letter, a week late. Perhaps his late arrival, coupled with the fact that he had not made a complete physical and psychological recovery from the University Christian Mission in the United States, contributed to his reaction to the conference. In any event, his evaluation of Tambaram, unlike his assessment of the Jerusalem Conference in 1928, was negative and critical, and he published his critique of the conference both in India and in the United States. His critique sparked an international debate in Christian missionary circles that was consistently vigorous and sometimes sharply worded, and continued throughout 1939. Jones felt so strongly about his position in this debate that he devoted a substantial part of his book, *Along the Indian Road* (1939), to restating and defending his argument about Tambaram.

The conference, Jones thought, missed the crucial difference between the church and the kingdom of God. By focusing almost exclusively on the human institution of the church, Tambaram came dangerously close to identifying itself with the kingdom of God. Instead of judging the church and its missionary enterprise by the kingdom standards Jesus spelled out in the Gospels, the conference accepted the church's mission work as a self-authenticating expression of Christian fellowship and a common commitment to fulfill Christ's great commission.

His views about the Tambaram Conference are best summarized in his May 31, 1939, *Christian Century* article, "What I Missed At Madras."[10]

I missed a church which started from where Jesus started, the Kingdom of God, and found instead a church which started with itself, and therefore largely ended with itself and the saving of its fellowship, dangerously near to fulfilling the statement of Jesus that he that saveth his life shall lose it. I missed finding a church which was under the conscious discipline, correction and cleansing judgment of an order higher than itself. I also missed a church that had in its hands the master conception from which it worked to all lesser conceptions. I missed a church which, while conscious of its mission as the chief instrument of the Kingdom of God, also was humble enough to rejoice that God was using other instruments to bring in the Kingdom in greater or lesser degree: the scientific movement as it is harnessed to social economic betterment, Gandhi's movement in India showing us the way to conquer by suffering and the vast movements for social and economic justice outside the church. I missed a church which said that the Kingdom of God is the hope of the church and of the world and found instead a church which said, "I am the hope of the world." I missed a church loyal to the Kingdom of God and found a church, by emphasis, loyal to its own fellowship.

Although his insistence on the crucial distinction between the church and the kingdom of God is valid and constitutes one of his most important, if not his most important, contribution to the thinking of the church, his accusation that the conference at Tambaram was unaware of this distinction and simply identified any and all Christian churches with the kingdom of God was at least exaggerated and was probably not based on a thorough and objective examination of what actually happened at the conference. The best evidence for this interpretation of Jones's critique of Tambaram is Diffendorfer's letter dated November 9, 1939.

Diffendorfer first tells Jones that he has just read the galley proofs of *Along the Indian Road*, which was written, he says, in Jones's "usual fresh, vital and gripping style." But then, in an expression of honesty and frankness that could only be the product of his deep and enduring friendship with Jones, he writes,

> One's definition of the Church and one's point of view with reference to the Kingdom have to be pretty well and clearly stated before you have any ground at all for your Madras criticism. Beyond that, however, a perusal of the Reports—I do not mean the final ones but the separate pamphlets that were printed and put in our hands at Madras—shows that that Conference did have the correct view as to the relation of the Church to the Kingdom, and there is plenty of emphasis in these reports on the Kingdom of God conception.

The real problem, as the next paragraph of Diffendorfer's letter makes clear, was that Jones was exhausted.

> A careful reading of the book [*Along the Indian Road*], however, my dear friend leads me to renew once more the suggestion which I made to you a few years ago. I make it again in the spirit of your Ashram. It is something which I would say to you if I were there and in the group—an experience which I would covet for myself, by the way. Could you not, immediately after the Preaching Mission next year, go off for a year of reading and studying without attempting to make any speeches, hold any Ashram, or write any further articles or books? I am so deeply convinced of the necessity of this that I am almost ready to say that your future place as a respected leader of Protestant Christianity depends upon your taking a little time to refresh your own mind and soul.

During 1937 and 1938 Stanley Jones became embroiled in another controversy—international politics. The situation that led to the political controversy was what happened to Shanghai, China, in July and August 1937. He was holding a series of meetings at Mokanshan, a mountain retreat west of Shanghai, when fighting broke out in the city between Chinese and Japanese troops. His experience in Mukden, Manchuria, several years earlier was child's play compared to what he found in Shanghai when he returned from Mokanshan. As usual, Jones is his own best spokesman. "The closer we got to Shanghai in the car," he wrote in his circular letter of August 18, 1937,

> the more we saw that trouble had started. They were making alternate roads around every bridge with thousands of peasants at work. When we got into the environs of Shanghai we saw trouble and more trouble. Thousands of refugees were pouring out of the section of Shanghai called Chapei which had been attacked and burnt during the last trouble. We were stopped by soldiers every few yards and then we got to the place where they told us we could not go on for the road was cut, in fact they informed us that all roads around Shanghai were cut and no one could get in. I was with Mr. and Mrs. Boynton who knew the situation so we started to try all the gates of the city. At each

place we were turned back. Soldiers were nervous and grim with their fingers on the triggers of their guns and pistols. Finally one soldier passed on us after looking at our passports with the word, "Next place Japanese". They blocked our way but finally allowed us to get through the gate. We were then in a deserted street outside the International Settlement which was barricaded against all incomers. We went from gate to gate guarded by foreign soldiers, could not get in, no orders, no key. Finally we discovered an English officer who told us to go back to the last gate and he would telephone for the Supt. of Police and he would come with a key. While we waited we could hear the rattle of the machine guns and booming of the bigger ones, war was on. When the gate rolled back and we were allowed to enter we felt we were in neutral territory, a haven of safety. Alas!

We soon found that modern war knows no safety. As we sat in the office of the N.C.C. [National Christian Council] deciding whether we should try to go on with the evangelistic campaign we looked out of the window to see what was the reason of the uproar of guns and there before our eyes, not two hundred yards away the Japanese flagship anchored inside of the International Settlement (it really had no business to be there) was being attacked by the Chinese bombers. Crash! and a great volume of smoke and flame went up. We thought the ship had been hit, but it was the wharf. We had grandstand seats for from the third story of our building we could see it all. Too close for safety. A piece of shrapnel comes through the window and spatters glass all over the Mission Treasurer's desk. Small happening compared to what was to take place. We went out into the street to find if we could go on with our campaign. The Travel Service said, No. We went out into the street again and a great mob of people had become panic stricken and swept down the street, this human tide carrying us with them. No small tide either for a million refugees had poured into the city. At the junction of the streets there was confusion. We stood for a moment at a place where in less than an hour a terrible tragedy was to occur. A Chinese airman aiming at the battleship about 400 yards away dropped a bomb on the Palace Hotel crashing down through three floors and killing about four hundred in the hotel and in the street. Forty eight hours later I went through the cordon of ropes and found pieces of reeking bodies still lying amid the debris. The Cathay Hotel opposite was also shattered. But further into the city where we had been just an hour before a worse tragedy was enacted. A Chinese bomber was killed by a Japanese bullet and in falling back with his hands upon the levers pulled the lever in death and rained death on 800 people. It fell in the center of a circle crowded with people. Dr. Rawlinson, a great missionary, stepped out of his car to see the crowd and the bomb exploded and sent a piece through his heart and he died in his wife's arms. War doesn't ask who you are. There was a huge hole in the midst of the street, but the debris had been cleaned up by the French (they got used to it in the last war), a few days later when I saw it. The fact is that I had watched that aerial battle from the place where we were living after arriving from downtown little knowing what had happened. Twelve hundred innocent gone by two bombs, and others mangled, and it was all a mistake. The fact is that the whole thing is a mistake, a hellish ghastly mistake.

In these life-threatening circumstances it is no wonder that on August 20, 1937, Frank T. Cartwright of the Methodist Board of Foreign Missions sent a telegram to Mabel Jones, who was at her family home in Clayton, Iowa.

FOLLOWING CABLE JUST RECEIVED QUOTE EVACUATING SHANGHAI MANILA INFORM FAMILY FRIENDS STANLEY JONES UNQUOTE HAVE INFORMED OUR CHURCH PAPERS.[11]

Stanley was forced to abandon his speaking schedule in China and to flee, along with hundreds of other Americans, to Manila in the Philippines. In a note to Mabel typed at the bottom of her copy of his August 18, 1937, circular letter, Stanley recounted the events of his evacuation from Shanghai. These events, even more than his firsthand encounter with war in Mukden, Manchuria, placed him directly in the path of death. As he confided to Mabel while on board the *President McKinley* in route to Manila, "One little fellow on this boat of four years said, 'Well mother this is the first war I have seen.' It is the first one I [Stanley Jones] have seen! Not anxious to see another." He went on to describe the evacuation.

> A special large launch took down about 300 people to the Pres. McKinley on which I am at the present writing. Everything was very tense as we got away to go down the river. U.S. marines stood guard on the launch. On starting they sent us all down below. Would not allow anyone on deck. We passed Japanese battleships every hundred yards and they kept firing at the Chinese as we passed. Had the Chinese replied with their field guns we would have been in serious danger. The terrible booming of their big guns not twenty five yards away as we went passed was a little shocking to those on board, but the fact is that the crowd including the women and children behaved very well indeed. No one got hysterical at all. We went down about ten miles of this and guns boomed all the way down. The Japanese gunboats had sandbags on them to keep the Chinese from sniping their marines from the river bank. We actually heard one of the snipers as we passed. The McKinley was anchored down at the mouth of the river and they had had some experience of the booming too, for the Japanese ships shot as they passed them, firing at the Chinese lines. The Chinese were trying to break through and push the J.s [Japanese] off. If they couldn't do it in the next 48 hours they had determined to retire to prepared lines to get the Japanese away from the support of the Japanese fleet which numbered about 50 vessels, I should think, perhaps more. I also saw aeroplanes dropping bombs on Chinese special places. Some of the bombs dropped down near the river bank and we could see the great clouds of earth and debris go up.

Jones got out of Shanghai at the last possible minute. By the time he arrived in Manila, even radio contact with the besieged city was impossible. Stanley wrote another personal note to Mabel on August 26, 1937, explaining that the broadcasting co. there is sending messages free to people everywhere, telling relatives that their loved ones are all right, giving instructions as to what to do, etc. I sent a message that way over to the Philippines to Tuck [a Methodist missionary and friend of Mabel and Stanley], someone picked it up and sent it to Tuck telling them I was on the McKinley.

He found Manila "twice as noisy as when we were here. There is a hustle about this city that is not seen scarcely in any city in the East and the way they blow their horns! The city is much improved and there is an air of hopefulness over everything. But they are afraid of the Japanese and frankly say so."

To give Mabel some assurance about his schedule and well-being during his stay in the relative safety of the Philippines, Stanley wrote that he planned to remain in that country until October 15, spending three weeks in the Southern Islands and three weeks in the Northern Philippines. Mabel needn't be afraid of sending mail, because letters would reach him wherever he happened to be.

Throughout the weeks of his first personal encounter with real war in China, Jones was acutely aware of the international political and moral implications of what was happening in Asia. He was shocked by the blunt honesty of the Japanese justification for their intervention in China. "Poor China," he had written to Diffendorfer on July 26, 1937, on his way to China, "If Japan would only let her alone. But one of the Japanese on this boat said to me, 'It is our Mission to bring order into China. We have given them a hundred years to set their house in order and they have not done it. Now we must do it for them. It is our Mission.'"

Stanley's reaction was that he had to *do* something about Japanese aggression in China. He concluded his August 18, 1937, circular letter with these words:

My coming here [to China] has not been in vain. I hate war with a deeper content in it now. And we are making plans as to what the next steps should be. We Christians must do something about it, or this ugly thing called militarism will destroy us as a civilization just as it is destroying these peace-loving Chinese villagers who want to be let alone.

In his next circular letter dated September 20, 1937,[12] and written from Manila, Jones told his friends and supporters that while he was being evacuated from China he wrote "an open letter to Japan" condemning its intervention in China. He had also written

an appeal to the Christians of the world for economic withdrawal from Japan. We have put out an appeal for cessation of hostilities signed by fifty leading people of neutral nations. . . . The economic withdrawal of the Christians of the world [we consider] as a moral judgment of Japan against this invasion of China. We would not wait for governments to act, but we would act as Christians across international boundary lines. . . . Certainly we must do something practical for we cannot morally condemn and economically support this cruel and senseless invasion of China.

In a sermon that Jones had preached in the Community Church in Shanghai on August 15, 1937, during a memorial service for Dr. Rawlinson, the missionary who was killed two days earlier, he quoted his open letter to Japan. Entitled "An Appeal to the Governments and People of Japan and China," the letter reads,

> The undersigned, members of neutral nations, are representative, we believe, of a vast number of Christians in many nations. Because we are deeply concerned in the highest welfare of both of these great nations, we are impelled to issue this appeal. These nations now seem to be on the verge of undisguised warfare.
>
> To us as Christians . . . the method of war for the settlement of international differences is abhorrent. It seems not only inhuman but futile. The history of modern wars demonstrates indisputably that in the end everybody loses. . . .
>
> [Our intention is] to appeal in the most urgent way to both nations to continue to seek and in the most complete and thoroughgoing way to explore the path to a peaceful and just settlement of the issues involved, without recourse to the methods of war.[13]

The catastrophic impact of modern war that Jones witnessed in China in 1937 took its personal toll on the fifty-three-year-old missionary evangelist. After six weeks of almost nonstop meetings in the Philippines he was able in mid-October to return to China to resume the heavy schedule of public speaking and personal interviews that had been interrrupted by the Japanese invasion of Shanghai. His tour of China included preaching in Hong Kong, Hankow, Changsha, Chengtu, and Chungking. Although his experience in these cities, unlike his experience in Shanghai, did not pose an immediate threat to his life, he had many close encounters with Chinese air raids. In early December 1937 he concluded his China tour and began the long journey back to India. While on board a steamer en route to Hong Kong, he wrote his "Christmas letter," dated December 9, apologizing to his good friend at the Mission Board in New York. "I am so sorry I will not be able to send a more personal letter, but I cannot reach you now except by Clipper Air Mail, and I simply haven't the time to get all my letters written—nor the strength."

> I've just come through some months of work in China and am tired. Four meetings a day on an average, and the strain of war conditions have taken a toll. . . . My, what a time I've had in China. I feel as if I had lived a lifetime in these last few months.

In spite of the physical, psychological, and spiritual toll the war conditions in China took on him, he was not discouraged, and he assured Diffendorfer that after "a day or two on the boat to India . . . I'll be alright again." However, the price he paid for his experiences in China during the latter half of 1937 was not just the consequence of his face-to-face, toe-to-toe contact with the horrors of modern war. Because of his two articles in the *Christian Century,* "An Open Letter to the People of Japan" and "An Open Letter to the Christian People of America and Great Britain," which were attempts to stop the fighting between Japan and China, he was vigorously and widely criticized by church leaders in both the United States and in the Far East. In fact, the list of those opposing the proposals in his articles, including Rufus Jones and Frederick Libby, reads like a Who's Who of American pacifists and Christian churchmen in the 1930s.

What was so controversial about Jones's proposals? Why did his efforts to end the human carnage in China ignite such vociferous opposition?

Jones's first open letter, the one addressed to the people of Japan, begins with a declaration of his affection and friendship for that nation. In support, Jones cites his personal intervention with President Roosevelt, seeking to replace the blatant racial discrimination against Japan in U.S. immigration laws with the quota system used for other nations. But then he turns to the real purpose of his letter, to address specifically Japan's policy toward China. Jones does not mince words in his outspoken and forthright condemnation of the Japanese conquest of China. This disastrous military adventure, he writes, was "the central international crime that is being committed in the world today."[14]

Jones sent a copy of his open letter along with a personal note to Arthur Jorgensen, the honorary secretary of The National Committee of Young Men's Christian Associations of Japan. In a letter dated September 22, 1937, Jorgensen responded.[15] He thanked Jones for sending him the letter and summarized the Japanese response to Jones's statements. First, he emphasized the politically explosive nature of Jones's open letter in Japan.

> The primary significance of your statement lies in its appeal to the Japanese people to break with their military leaders, and that, in the present circumstances, is about as dangerous an idea in the eyes of those who control the censorship as could be propounded. It is not exaggeration to say that no newspaper or magazine could avoid immediate and indefinite suspension, to say nothing of fines, under the new censorship regulations, were it to print your letter.

Jorgensen had "discreetly" distributed approximately twenty-five copies of the letter to "leaders of the Christian movement" in Japan. In addition, a group of fifteen people, ten Japanese and five missionaries, met on two occasions to discuss both Jones's letter and statements from other

"Christian groups and individuals in China." Summarizing the discussion, Jorgensen wrote,

> In general I think it can be said that those who have read your letter feel that it is probably a fairly accurate presentation of world opinion. At the same time you will not be surprised to learn that it contains statements and reflects attitude[s] with which there is by no means complete agreement among Japanese Christians. . . .
>
> Rightly or wrongly I think it must be said that there are few Japanese who believe that in their relations with China the way of conciliation or friendship is a practicable alternative to the way of aggression. This conclusion they deduce from the history of Chinese foreign contacts during the past century. . . .
>
> It is also felt that in your reference to the contempt and fear which Japan feels toward China you do not seem to realize the contempt which China has felt toward Japan over a long period of history. . . .
>
> I mention these few points merely to let you see how extraordinarily difficult it is to present the case from the Chinese point of view in a way that will appeal to Japanese readers as fair and unprejudiced.

Moral condemnation of Japan for its aggression in China, Jones believed, was only the beginning, not the end of the Christian response to Japan's "international crime." In his October 14, 1937, *Indian Witness* article Jones insisted that Christians "must be open to God's guidance as to how we can implement that moral judgment and make it effective." Moreover, he thought that any action taken against Japan should be a testimony "to the Christian principle of using calamity for higher ends." This redemptive principle was an integral part of Jones's concept of the kingdom of God. He wrote in his *Indian Witness* article:

> Almost everything beautiful in the New Testament has come out of some ugliness. Jesus never bore the cross, he used it. The cross was sin, and he made it into the healing of sin. . . . This gives the Christian a working philosophy of life. He is not stunned by the calamities of life. He uses them. . . . What happens to us is not really the important thing, but how we take it. The same event causes opposite results in people. Some it breaks and some it makes.[16]

A month after he published his open letter to Japan, Jones explained how he thought Christians could implement their moral judgment against Japan. In "An Open Letter to the Christian People of America and Great Britain," which was published in the *Christian Century*,[17] he called on "the Christians of the world," acting independently of their governments, "to institute an economic withdrawal from Japan." In his article Jones rejected both military intervention and various nonmilitary options. The only real choice for Christians, he concluded, was an "attitude . . . which implements good will in positive action" and "is not punitive but redemptive." Such action was necessary because the close economic relationship between Japan on the one hand and Great Britain and the United States on the other meant that all American citizens and British subjects were to some extent morally responsible for Japanese aggression in China. In his own words, "Our hands that buy and sell are stained with the blood of Chinese." Jones thought that economic withdrawal, unlike military intervention, which was a purely negative measure, would be positive and constructive and would encourage Japan to withdraw from China. Finally, he believed that economic withdrawal would be effective, and he predicted that if it was implemented, "this invasion of China would collapse in six months."

Given the depth of his personal conviction that Christians must respond to the barbarity of the Japanese invasion of China, and given the sincerity and simplicity of his compelling argument that an economic boycott of Japan was a direct application of the kingdom principle of bringing good out of evil, the telegram Jones received on September 24, 1937, from the National Christian Council of Manila left him shocked and bewildered. The telegram read,

> GREATLY DISTRESSED BY REPORT THAT YOU PLAN TO URGE BOY-COTT OF JAPANESE GOODS STOP SUCCESSFUL BOYCOTT HERE ONLY POSSIBLE BY CAMPAIGN OF HATE MAKING WAR EASY AND CLOSING DOOR TO OPERATION OF GOODWILL NOW AND LATER STOP EARNESTLY BEG YOU NOT TO MAKE APPEAL FOR BOYCOTT
>
> RUFUS JONES FREDERICK LIBBY RAY NEWTON HAROLD FEY NEVIN SAYRE CLARENCE PICKETT[18]

Three days after Jones received this cable, Frederick Libby, the executive secretary of the National Council for Prevention of War in Washington, D.C., elaborated on the points made in the telegram in a two-and-one-half page, single-spaced letter, dated September 27, 1937. Libby's argument was just as compelling as Jones's argument in his *Indian Witness* and *Christian Century* articles. Libby put the war between Japan and China in a larger international and historical context. He thought that Jones's distinction between Japan as the "aggressor" and China as the "victim" was "an oversimplification of the situation that ignored historical perspective and the economic causes of war." Libby wrote,

> Have you ever reflected upon the unequal distribution of the earth's resources? China, Japan, India and the Dutch East Indies—the four countries that comprise a considerable portion of the brown and yellow races—contain one-half the population of the earth. This half is restricted to one-seventh of the earth's area possessing few natural resources. The four

great "Haves"—the British Empire, the French Empire, the Soviet Union and the United States—have taken to themselves and control in their own interest most of the earth's natural resources and markets. The British Empire, the French Empire and Soviet Russia govern one-half the earth's surface and exploit the resources in the territory that they control. The United States does the same with the immense riches entrusted to its care. The gold and iron and oil, the cotton, the timber, the wheat and corn and oats, the tin and nickel, the gold and silver of the world are possessed for the most part by these four great Powers. By tariffs and other devices we keep the other nations from securing sufficient access to our natural wealth to permit a standard of living comparable with our own and then we exclude their goods from our markets on the charge that they employ cheap labor.

But why does Japan punish China for its dearth of raw materials and markets? Why does Italy punish Ethiopia? Why does Germany threaten Czechoslovakia? Because they are too weak to attack the powerful "Haves" and following the bad example of the "aggressors" of yesterday, they pick upon nations weaker than themselves with a view to exploiting them as the great "Haves" are doing with their empires.

Under these circumstances, it seems to me smug and hypocritical for the citizens of these four countries to join in condemnation of the aggression of today. . . .

I regard the hardness of heart manifested by the powerful "Haves" as equally culpable with the unprovoked aggression of the "Have-nots." Both are "immoral." . . .

With our minds focused on the injustice that Japan is committing in bombing unarmed Chinese civilians, we are in danger of overlooking the hidden but no less cruel injustice which we ourselves are committing in our relations with the poor and exploited peoples throughout the earth.[19]

Another critic of Jones's proposed economic withdrawal, whose opposition cut Jones more deeply because it was grounded directly in the New Testament, was Frank M. Toothaker, chairman of the Los Angeles Conference of the Emergency Peace Campaign, an organization whose goal was to keep the United States out of war. Toothaker wrote to Jones on December 2, 1937.

[M]any of us now think that, regarding the China-Japanese-World situation, you have mistaken your light. This we regret beyond words. We believe in you as much as ever, but in sorrow we cannot follow your lead.

We must part company for, as it seems to me, one chief reason. You urge us to use the coercion of a boycott before we have used the way of personal repentance, national repentance, and, to use your own phrase, "aggressive love." . . .

First, we have not repented of our racial pride, and offered fruits meet for such repentance. The Oriental Exclusion clause still stands upon our statute books, unrepealed and unrebuked. With it we have wounded the soul of Japan. Until we do this we are not in position to take the splinter out of the eye of our neighbor.

Second, we have not repented of those attitudes of imperialism, and those practices of militarism which contemplate doing exactly what Japan is now doing, and is defending on the same grounds that we defend our present naval policy. . . . Our boycott lacks, if we attempt it, the reality of moral sincerity.

Third, we have no right to demand redemptive measures from the sinner—"the aggressor",—and our withdrawal will not effect a quickening of his conscience until he sees in practice a policy of active good will on his behalf. Let our first step then be, not "quarantine" but fellowship, with economic and social implications on a wide scale. . . . Spiritually repentance will not be wrought by boycotts or blockades, but by the aggressive good will that moves, even at the midnight hour of inconvenience and of humiliation, to secure for the underprivileged peoples of our world those elements of their rightful need.

Fourth, we shall not succeed in making a boycott effective without resort to continual repetition of the story of Japan's barbarity. Merchants tell me that some have already been saying with anger that they will do no business with "those dirty Japs". On the Eastside of Los Angeles where for four years I lived near "little Japan" one is hearing much of the same talk. Theoretically, and perhaps for some elevated souls, the boycott may be waged on the high moral level you take, but for men of the common walks it will not be done. There will be hate, and hypocrisy.[20]

Although Jones was deeply affected by the sharp criticism of the telegram from the National Christian Council of Manila and the letters from Libby and Toothaker, he accepted the validity of their criticisms. He incorporated the substance of his critics' arguments in many of the letters, articles, and books he wrote after 1937. To be sure, he never retracted his proposal for an economic withdrawal from Japan by American and British Christians, but after 1937 he did put more emphasis on the historical and economic sources of Japanese imperialism in China and on the fact that the United States and Great Britain must repent of their own sins of imperialism in the Far East before they could condemn Japan for its aggression in China.

His first public response to the critics of his proposed economic withdrawal from Japan was an article published in the January 19, 1938, issue of the *Christian Century* and entitled "Apply Gandhi's Method To Japan!" In this article Jones said that he wanted to clarify "some points apparently confused in the minds of some." He reiterated that his proposal for an economic withdrawal from Japan was directed not to churches or governments in the United States and Great Britain, but to individual Christians in those nations. What he really had in mind when he proposed an economic withdrawal was "noncooperation" in the same sense that "Mahatma Gandhi . . . used the word noncooperation."[21]

The criticism that provoked the longest and the most convincing response from Jones in his *Christian Century* article was not the telegram or the letters, but rather the criticism that an economic withdrawal was ethically indiscriminate, punishing innocent Japanese women and children along with those who should be held morally responsible for Japan's war against China. Christians participating in an economic withdrawal, the critics argued, would be as much at fault as Japan itself. Jones responded that in the event of an economic withdrawal from Japan it would be Japan's leaders, not Christians refusing to trade with Japan, who were responsible for the punishment of their nation. Nor would Japanese civilians be the only innocent parties to bear the consequences of their leaders' policies in China. Jones wrote that if he took part in an economic withdrawal from Japan, "I inflict on my children an economic consequence in that I buy in a more expensive market, depriving my own children of some things."

Jones compares the argument about the innocent Japanese victims of an economic withdrawal to the argument that one "must patronize" a tavern because, if one withholds his patronage, "the innocent children of the saloon keeper will suffer." Just as the saloon keeper's children are not the issue in this case, so the innocent Japanese victims of an economic withdrawal are not the issue with respect to Japanese aggression against China. Rather, the focus of the moral question, in the first case, is the victims of alcoholic parents and spouses; in the second case, it is the victims of Japan's brutal policies in China. Jones believed that his relationship to Japan was, like Gandhi's relationship to Great Britain, one of "redemptive friendship." The unmerited suffering that Gandhi and other Indian nationalists experienced when they challenged the British government with a campaign of nonviolent civil disobedience and fasting shocked the world and defeated the injustice and evil of British imperialism in India. The British finally acknowledged the immorality of their policies in that nation and withdrew from the Indian subcontinent. In the same way Jones hoped that an economic withdrawal from Japan by British and American Christians would expose the naked barbarism of Japanese aggression in China and would encourage Japan to confess its international crimes and withdraw from China.

Jones was driven to insist on economic withdrawal from Japan as the only honest Christian response to Japan's conquest of China by the same irresistible force that compelled him to insist that the Madras missionary conference had missed its way. In both cases he was speaking and acting on the basis of his understanding of the kingdom of God. And his concept of the kingdom of God grew out of God's call to him to be a missionary evangelist. The kingdom of God not only defined his theology and his vocation; it revolutionized his life. In fact, the kingdom of God became so "totalitarian" for him that it was not just his view of reality it was reality itself. This helps to explain his reaction to the Madras conference as well as to resolve any apparent contradiction between this incident and his call to Christians for economic withdrawal from Japan. Because he was so completely and thoroughly a part of the kingdom of God and could only perceive events and circumstances from the perspective of the kingdom of God, he ignored criticism even from his closest friend in Methodism, Ralph Diffendorfer, and even when the criticism was true. There is no doubt that Jones, as Diffendorfer said, was long overdue for a sabbatical. It may also be true that by not taking time to refresh his mind and spirit he sacrificed his position as "a respected leader of Protestant Christianity." But Jones remained adamant about the failure of the Madras conference throughout his life, writing in his autobiography when he was eighty-three:

> [T]he conference chose to fasten upon the emphasis of the ecumenical church instead of the kingdom of God. I wrote an article for The Christian Century entitled "Where Madras Missed Its Way." They chose the ecumenical church as its strategy and emphasis instead of the Kingdom. I have never been forgiven by the hierarchy for that article. I cut across the prevailing accepted emphasis of the ecumenical church as the supreme emphasis. But I am unrepentant. I would do it again, and I repeat it now: Our emphasis is not and should not be the ecumenical church.[22]

Jones lived in a different world. He saw and heard things that others did not, or saw and heard only indistinctly. The kingdom of God was not, for Jones, merely a theological concept or simply a lifestyle choice, although it embraced both theology and how he lived his Christian life. The kingdom of God, which was so utterly unrealistic to most people and even to many Christians, was, in fact, more realistic than the empirical world of sensible and tangible "facts." Because he wanted above all else to live in the higher reality of the kingdom of God, and because by God's grace he was privileged to be a citizen of that kingdom on earth, he brought countless other souls into the same kingdom as fellow citizens, and achieved a degree of influence over nations and governments and over church and society, which no combination of facts and circumstances can even begin to explain. It was Jones's single-minded and acute focus on this supreme reality of the kingdom of God that led him in 1938 to write in the *Christian Century* that the Madras missionary conference confused the ecumenical church with that kingdom. And it was the same kingdom perception that led him to condemn the Japanese invasion of China and to call for an economic withdrawal from Japan. Although he did modify his initial position on this issue by putting Japanese imperialism within the larger context of Western imperialism in Asia, Jones never modified his outspoken denunciation of Japan's aggression in China, nor did he change his mind about economic withdrawal as a kingdom of God response to that aggression. However, he had not yet faced the ultimate test of his kingdom principles.

263

11

Peace:
Valiant Pursuit, Victory
Deferred

The morning my baggage was to go off on the President Harrison, which I was to catch by plane from Manila, I had a very imperative call from within: "I want you here". The Inner Voice kept sounding that for hours, and I had no alternative but to obey; so I wired San Francisco to have my baggage taken off the boat; and here I am! I feel God has something for me to do in this crisis which is upon America.
—E. Stanley Jones, Letter to Miss Nellie, March 22, 1941

DID STANLEY JONES almost single-handedly come within a hair's breadth of preventing the Japanese attack on Pearl Harbor on December 7, 1941? This is only one of the many fascinating and intriguing questions raised when one learns of his high-level but unofficial diplomacy during the last three months of 1941.

In March 1941 Stanley was completing another exhausting American evangelistic tour with the National Christian Mission. He had been speaking two to five times a day for an entire year throughout the United States. As on his previous tours with the National Christian Mission, he had come alone to the U.S. and had not seen his wife and daughter, Mabel and Eunice, for over a year. They had remained in India, and he longed to return to his home. But he suddenly encountered unexpected problems with his plan to sail back to India on the *SS President Hayes*. The ship's departure from the West Coast was delayed because of the need for repairs. Although another ship, the *President Harrison*, was scheduled to leave the United States on April 20, Jones would not complete his tour for the National Christian Mission in Los Angeles until April 24.

In a longhand letter to Miss Nellie dated March 8, 1941, written on United Airlines stationery while he was flying from Seattle to Lakeland, Florida, he talked about these complications. He had a premonition that the last-minute change of plans was providential. In fact, he may well have sensed that he would not be returning immediately to India, because he wrote to his friend, "Perhaps God is in these changes, at any rate the inner assurance is very real." When he returned to the West Coast to conclude the National Christian Mission in Los Angeles, the Holy Spirit confirmed his premonition on the very morning (March 20, 1941) that his baggage was to be put aboard ship for India. As he recalled in his autobiography, *A Song of Ascents,*[1]

> I was in Los Angeles in 1941 ready to go back to India. I was awakened in my hotel room about four o'clock with the inner voice saying: "I want you here." It persisted. I struggled with it: "Lord, I can't. The National Christian Mission is over. My work is done. My wife and daughter are in India. I haven't seen them for over a year (as it turned out, it was to be six years). The boat with my trunk is leaving San Francisco today (I was to pick it up in the Philippines). I do not see how I can stay." But the voice was persistent: "I want you here." After fighting with it for two hours I succumbed, said I would obey.

As soon as Western Union opened its telegraph office in Los Angeles, he sent a short telegram to Ralph Diffendorfer.

GUIDANCE POSTPONE INDEFINITELY RETURN INDIA WRITING ABOUT PLANS STANLEY JONES.

Diffendorfer apparently also had a premonition that Stanley would not be returning to India as scheduled, because on the very next day, March 21, he sent an air mail special delivery letter: "Your telegram has been received," he wrote, "and we are not at all surprised at your decision." Diffendorfer was not surprised, both because his own Inner Voice told him Stanley might well stay in America and because of Stanley's activities earlier in the year. In an undated circular letter, he had told Diffendorfer that he had interrupted a series of meetings on the Pacific Coast to go to Washington, D.C. There he discovered the source of the war mentality that was engulfing the nation.

> I had been told that while 80-85% of the people of the country did not want war, about 80-85% of the newspaper men and the officials at Washington felt that war was inevitable. And they, rather than the people, would decide the matter. The outlook in Washington was one of fatalism.

As an alternative to war, Jones suggested in his letter that the United States "should be the mediator of a new world order based upon equality of opportunity." He had proposed his idea to a luncheon meeting of business and professional men in Washington. Then he met with a group of congressmen and proposed the same idea. The congressmen believed that the nation was in "a race against time," and that if war was to be averted, action would have to be taken "in the next thirty days for by that time the decision would be made." Jones had also scheduled a meeting with Roosevelt, but because of the President's busy schedule, he had to submit his idea in writing. However, he had met with Felix Frankfurter, an associate justice of the U.S. Supreme Court. Frankfurter, Jones had been told, "was the brains behind the whole thing," meaning that Frankfurter had the ear of the President. In fact, Roosevelt's secretary had arranged for the interview, which began on an unexpectedly negative note. Jones wrote,

> It proved to be . . . stormy . . . for the first ten minutes, at least on the part of the Justice. For he blew up at the idea that he had any influence in the Government, that it was all false, that he did not see the President for months, that he had practically "taken the veil" when he became a Supreme Court Justice. I accepted his statement and then asked if I could put it before him as a citizen, to which he assented. After I presented my seven points he said very slowly, "Well, you and I are not very far apart on the goal. But I believe that Germany must be defeated first for only then would they listen." I suggested that whether they listened or not we must hold this position to keep it alight within our own hearts and broadcast it. To which he agreed. . . . We parted friends.[2]

While he was in Washington Jones had also presented his concept of the United States as the mediator of a new world order to various peace groups and in a public evangelistic meeting.[3] In these meetings, as in the earlier meetings with the business and professional men, with the members of Congress, and with Justice Frankfurter, Jones had "the sense of God unfolding this whole thing with our simply following the gleam." "In each case," he wrote in his circular letter, "the initiative came from someone else. . . . It seemed as though God was doing it and we were just following the gleam."

Because of Stanley's peace efforts described in this circular letter, Diffendorfer was not surprised by Stanley's decision not to return to India in March 1941. And Stanley himself surely knew, even before his March 20 telegram, that his meetings and speeches on behalf of peace were a piece of unfinished business infinitely more important than his return to India.

In the summer of 1941 he received final confirmation of his instructions from the Inner Voice when he and Dr. Toyohiko Kagawa, the famous Japanese Christian leader, were speakers at the same conference in Lake

Geneva, Wisconsin.[4] Kagawa told him that the Japanese ambassador in Washington, Admiral Kichisaburo Nomura, was not a member of the war party in Japan. The war party wanted to resolve the escalating tension between Japan and the United States by going to war. Instead, Kagawa insisted, Nomura sincerely wanted peace. He strongly urged Stanley to visit Nomura and suggest to him an idea that could reduce or end Japanese imperialism in the Pacific. Kagawa's idea was that New Guinea, the world's second largest island (after Greenland), which was sparsely populated but richly endowed with natural resources, be given to Japan. If Australia and the Netherlands, countries which at that time controlled New Guinea, could be persuaded to give up the island, then there would be a real basis for peace in the Far East.

Now Stanley knew more fully why the Inner Voice would not let him return to India and what he was to do in the United States.

> So I went to Washington, going out, like Abraham, not knowing whither I was going. . . . From September til December 7, Pearl Harbor day, I took off three days each week to go to Washington to see what we could do to head off the war. I would have evangelistic series in different parts of the country from Sunday to Wednesday and then go to Washington from Thursday to Saturday. Dr. O. G. Robinson, a Methodist pastor, set up the interviews in my absence and sat in at all the interviews except those with the President.[5]

During the rest of the summer after his meeting with Kagawa, while he waited for Washington life to resume after summer vacations, Stanley continued his attempts to keep the United States out of war.[6] His proposal for the United States to mediate a new world order was printed in the *Congressional Record,* was read by the Secretary of State, was sent to approximately 100,000 Christian ministers, and spawned two grassroots movements—the Mediation Committee and the Churchman's Campaign for Peace through Mediation. He also completed a full schedule of evangelistic meetings throughout the United States, spoke at the World Sunday School Convention in Mexico City in July, and led three summer ashrams—at Occidental College in California (where he began the practice of an all-night prayer vigil), at Blue Ridge, North Carolina (where "our Negro friends were received on the basis of complete equality"), and at Saugatuck, Michigan.[7]

All these meetings were not mere interludes between his political and unofficial diplomatic efforts to prevent war between the United States and Japan. His hurriedly written note to Miss Nellie of July 17, 1941, illustrates how his activities worked together. While he was in Mexico City speaking at the World Sunday School Convention, he wrote, "Josephus Daniels, the Amer. Ambassador came to my mtgs. twice & I had lunch with him yesterday." In another letter, written a week later to Mrs. O. G. Robinson,[8] he described Daniels as so "interested" in and "sympathetic" with his ideas for peace in the Pacific, that he "sent a copy of my memorandum to the President in his diplomatic bag." In other words, Jones used the occasion of his visit to Mexico City, a visit made for a religious purpose, to promote peace between Japan and the United States. As he explained to his friends and patrons in a circular letter dated September 13, 1941,

> I shall . . . give any message I have to give to America within the framework of my evangelistic meetings; for I shall not allow anything to keep me from my central call—an evangelist.

Jones published two accounts of his activities in Washington between September and December 1941, the first in December 1945 just after the end of the war in a periodical, *Asia and the Americas;* and the second twenty-three years later in his autobiography, *A Song of Ascents.* While most Americans during and after World War II willingly believed that "a united Japan undertook world conquest, with no inhibitions and no internal opposition,"[9] the truth, as Jones learned during the last three months of 1941, was more complicated. He was convinced that the diplomatic personnel at the Japanese Embassy in Washington

> were not playing a double game, pulling the wool over our eyes while the Japanese in Japan were getting ready to strike. They were of the peace party and were trying desperately to find a basis for peace and were brokenhearted when the negotiations broke down and war broke out.[10]

After the war Jones found convincing evidence among both Americans and Japanese to support his conclusion that there was a genuine Japanese peace party that was sincerely committed to finding a way to avoid war with the United States in the Pacific. General Douglas MacArthur told him, "I agree with you; they [the Japanese] knew nothing of what was going to happen at Pearl Harbor." Similarly, Admiral Nomura told him,

> We had no notion of Pearl Harbor. We thought the crisis meant that diplomatic relationships were going to be broken, or that the Japanese fleet was going to Southeast Asia, a crisis spot, but of Pearl Harbor we knew nothing.

Finally, on the basis of his personal contact with Roosevelt, Jones was persuaded that the President himself "wanted peace, at least in the Pacific."[11]

During the last few months of 1941, however, there was in the United States no public recognition of a peace party in Japan. Instead, diplomatic relations between the United States and Japan deteriorated rapidly as the United States put an embargo on the sale of oil to Japan, froze Japanese assets in United States banks, and ordered American nationals living in

Japan to leave that country. Moreover, in September 1941, Dr. Kagawa, as a prominent Japanese citizen, was ordered to leave the United States. Shortly after he arrived in Japan, Kagawa sent an urgent cable to Jones.

SITUATION VERY SERIOUS HERE. SEE PRESIDENT ROOSEVELT IMMEDIATELY. GET HIM TO AVERT CATASTROPHE IN PACIFIC. AM WORKING WITH UNFAILING FAITH AT THIS END.[12]

Jones was not able to see Roosevelt in September 1941, but in the meantime he pursued the idea, first suggested by Kagawa, that New Guinea be given to Japan as a place to settle its surplus population and as a source of badly needed natural resources. In Washington, Jones approached the Australian minister, Richard Gardiner Casey, with this idea. Casey, Jones recalled in his autobiography, was "very sympathetic" and agreed that there must be an alternative living space for the densely populated Japanese islands. "If we don't do it now," he told Jones, "we will have to do it in ten years."[13] He suggested that Jones take the idea to the U.S. State Department. Stanley did so, but in his presentation to the State Department, he added the proposal that the United States pay both Australia and the Netherlands $100 million as compensation for those people living in New Guinea who would be displaced by the Japanese. Although two former American high commissioners to the Philippines, Paul V. McNutt and U.S. Supreme Court Justice Frank Murphy, supported the proposal, the State Department told Jones that it "could not very easily take up the question of the disposal of the property of other nations." Jones also approached the Dutch minister in Washington with his idea, but the Dutch were even more emphatically negative than the State Department. The Dutch minister told Jones, "No part of the Dutch Empire is for sale!"[14]

Although neither the United States nor Australia nor the Netherlands accepted Jones's proposal to give New Guinea to Japan in order to satisfy Japan's need for land and raw materials and to end her imperial ambitions in the Pacific, Jones was undeterred and continued to pursue his idea after the war. He even raised the question with General MacArthur during the American occupation of Japan. MacArthur's response was positive, as Stanley remembered in *A Song of Ascents*. MacArthur told him,

I've fought all over that country [New Guinea], and it is the most lush, undeveloped country in the world. The Japanese, being the best farmers of the world, could make a paradise out of it. They could support fifty million people on it where now it has a million and a quarter. The Japanese are the only people who could develop it. But don't say anything about this until the peace treaty.[15]

So Jones waited for a more propitious time to pursue his idea of giving New Guinea to Japan. In the early 1950s, John Foster Dulles (who would become the American Secretary of State under President Eisenhower) visited Japan to negotiate a peace treaty between Japan and the United States to formally and officially end World War II in the Pacific. On that visit, Jones met with him and once again suggested transferring New Guinea into Japanese hands. He described Dulles's reaction in *A Song of Ascents*.

> I saw him [Dulles] and presented to him the New Guinea proposal. His reaction: "That is a very interesting proposal." He called for a map of the Pacific to see where New Guinea was! He asked me to write a memorandum for Allison, who was an expert on Japan. I did, and I sent a copy of it to Mr. Casey, now the Foreign Minister of Australia.[16]

Although Jones did not receive a favorable response to his memo at the time of Dulles's visit to Japan in the early 1950s, he never abandoned his idea of giving New Guinea to Japan. In 1959, when he was conducting his sixth tour of Japan after the end of the war, he wrote to Casey on April 11, arguing that giving New Guinea to Japan, especially if the grant were made under the auspices of the United Nations, would strengthen the security of Australia.

> Suppose New Guinea should be given to Japan under the United Nations. That would mean that Japan would be allotted by peaceful means what she could not obtain by war. That would convince her people that peaceful democratic means are preferable to force and war.
>
> It would add to the security of Australia. For the whole of the United Nations would guarantee that Japan would go no farther. That would be far better for the security of Australia than to have a disgruntled Japan at a distance, resenting the fact of comparatively empty countries, unutilized and undeveloped while her own country is at the bursting point.
>
> Real statesmanship looking ahead will, by wise and generous moves, head off another explosion in the Far East. I hope, Mr. Casey, that you will be the statesman who will be sufficiently far-sighted and decisive enough to rise above local prejudices and fears and lay the foundation for peace for generations to come. . . .
>
> As I see it, Mr. Casey, you are the one man who could do most to solve this festering problem. You may have been brought to the kingdom for such a time as this.

Although he had been favorable to Jones's idea in 1941, almost two decades earlier, Casey was now a part of the government of Australia, acting more directly under the Prime Minister and speaking as a politically responsible official. Casey responded to Jones's letter on May 31, 1959.

> As you are aware there have been many changes in the world situation since my meeting with you in 1941, not the least signficant being the war of

aggression waged by Japan during which Australian cities were bombed and Australia's security was most acutely threatened.

It is not the policy of the Australian Government to acquiesce in any scheme which would lead to the settlement of large numbers of Japanese in New Guinea or other areas situated close to Australia. To do so would be completely at variance with the strong feelings which the Australian people hold on this matter and which have been reflected in numerous public statements by spokesmen of all parties represented in the Australian Parliament.[17]

Back in 1941, Jones's dogged insistence that giving New Guinea to Japan was the key to lasting peace in the Far East was certainly the most controversial proposal he made in his tireless efforts to prevent war between the United States and Japan. It was not the only proposal or attempt to bring peace. The possibility of success seemed remote indeed on October 15, 1941, when the Japanese government led by Prince Konoye fell and was replaced with a government led by Admiral Hideki Tojo, an outspoken militarist and member of the militant war party. But this apparent setback did not discourage Jones, who redoubled his attempt to bring peace to the Pacific. And when the Japanese government sent Saburu Kurusu as a Special Envoy from Emperor Hirohito to Washington in a last-minute effort to avoid war with the United States, Jones saw his chance.

According to a *Washington Post* reporter, "With Kissinger-like anonymity, Dr. Jones shuttled between President Roosevelt and special envoys who, he said, were sent to Washington by the Japanese emperor in an effort to forestall war."[18] He now asked the Japanese in Washington whether they would participate in a peace conference with China under the auspices of the United States if the United States would lift its oil embargo against Japan. The Japanese responded to Jones with an enthusiastic yes. Encouraged by this reply, he immediately forwarded his idea to the U.S. State Department, to President Roosevelt, and to Lord Halifax, the British Ambassador to the United States whom Jones had known in India when he was the British Viceroy. Unfortunately for Jones and for the prospect of peace, however, on November 26 the United States gave to Ambassador Nomura and Special Envoy Kurusu a memorandum that the Japanese could only interpret as an ultimatum. The memo, in effect, required immediate capitulation to four American demands: "Get out of the Axis, get out of China, get out of Indo-China and equality of trade in the Far East."[19] These demands were, of course, intolerable to the Japanese, even to the members of the peace party. The only remaining opportunity for peace, and by the end of November it was only the faintest glimmer of hope, was for a spokesman for the Japanese peace party to serve as a personal emissary to President Roosevelt himself.

Roosevelt scheduled a personal audience with Nomura and Kurusu on

November 28, 1941, at 2:30 P.M. At about noon on November 28 Mr. Hidenari Terasaki, the Counsel of the Japanese Embassy in Washington, implored Jones to talk with Roosevelt before the 2:30 meeting. Jones immediately telephoned Marvin H. McIntyre, the President's secretary, but was told that the President's schedule was already filled. However, McIntyre offered to transcribe a memo, which Stanley dictated over the telephone, and to give it to Roosevelt before his 2:30 meeting with Kurusu and Nomura. The memo read in part,

> Don't compel us [Japanese] to do things but make it possible for us to do them. If you treat us in this way we will reciprocate doubly. If you stretch out one hand we will stretch out two. And we can not only be friends, we can be Allies.

On the next day, November 29, Nomura and Kurusu were "obviously delighted" with Jones's memo and told him that it was the basis for their "whole conversation" with Roosevelt.[20]

Convinced that they could put their complete confidence in Jones, Nomura and Kurusu then asked Jones to fly to Warm Springs, Georgia, where the President had gone for a few day's rest. They had a message they wanted Jones to give to Roosevelt, a message so secret that they permitted Jones to write only part of it and even the written part was not typed but was in Jones's own handwriting. Nomura and Kurusu would only permit Jones to give the most sensitive part of their message to Roosevelt orally and in person. Although arrangements were made for Jones to take a special plane to Warm Springs to deliver the Japanese message, events in Washington forced Roosevelt to cut short his stay in Georgia and to return to the capital on December 1. The President read the written part of Jones's message on behalf of the Japanese "on the way to the White House."[21]

In the meantime, because Jones knew of nothing more he could do immediately in the interests of peace, he fulfilled a prior commitment for evangelistic meetings in Thomasville, North Carolina. But he interrupted his meetings when he learned of the extreme urgency of his delivering the most secret part of his message to Roosevelt in person. I wrote about what happened next in my book, *The Totalitarian Kingdom of God.*[22]

> Jones returned to Washington on Wednesday, December 3 and telephoned the President's secretary who said that Roosevelt responded favorably to Jones' written message. Jones recalls that when he told the secretary about the unwritten part of his message, it "was arranged that I see the President at once, 'off the record.'" Arriving at the East Gate of the White House to avoid the curiosity of reporters, Jones met Roosevelt and told him that the Japanese he had been dealing with were desperate to find a way to avoid war with the United States. Jones' confidential message from the Japanese was an

urgent plea for the President to send a cable directly to the Emperor of Japan.

A direct appeal to the Emperor himself was the last chance for peace. Although Hirohito rarely intervened in the policies of his government, when he did speak out, his authority was unquestioned and his decision was final. So Jones gave Roosevelt in person the unwritten part of his message. Roosevelt replied that he had already considered a personal message to the Emperor but that he did not want to offend the Japanese special envoys by going "over their heads to the Emperor." Jones then pointed out that the request for the President to contact Hirohito came directly from the envoys themselves. In that case, Roosevelt responded, "that wipes my slate clean. I can send it." However, Roosevelt explained, he could not exchange cablegrams one-on-one with Emperor Hirohito. But he could, he told Jones, cable Mr. Joseph C. Grew, the American ambassador to Japan, who had a diplomatic right of access to the Emperor. The President's cable to Hirohito, of course, would be sent in the utmost secrecy. But, in order to put pressure on Japan to take his offer of peace seriously, Roosevelt told Jones, "if I don't get an answer in twenty-four hours I will give it to the newspapers and force a reply."[23]

Roosevelt was as good as his word. He sent a cable to Ambassador Grew on December 5. The newspapers were given word of the cable on December 6 and published stories about the President's message on December 7. Unfortunately, however, the "records of Ambassador Grew show that the cable did not get to the Emperor until after the attack upon Pearl Harbor."[24]

In *A Song of Ascents,* Jones entitles his chapter on his attempt to mediate peace between Japan and the United States, "Guidance—An Adventure in Failure." Certainly he failed to prevent the outbreak of war in the Pacific in 1941. But his autobiography does not reveal the depth of Jones's disappointment. Toward the end of November, just two weeks before Pearl Harbor, he wrote to the Robinsons from Dayton, Ohio, where he was holding evangelistic meetings. During the train trip to Dayton, Jones wrote, "I received an overwhelming conviction that a way was going to be found to prevent war with Japan." However, in the devastating aftermath of Pearl Harbor he had second thoughts. On December 8, 1941, at 10 a.m. Jones, who was then in Pittsburgh, wrote again to his good friends the Robinsons, "Rob" and "Dar" as he called them, in Washington.

Today my Scripture was "His words make peace for the nations" (Habbakuk 9). I still believe it, in spite of!
   I do not know how to interpret my experience of the train to Dayton. Perhaps it was assurance of God's approval in what I was doing & I thought it an assurance of peace in [the] Pacific.

> In any case my soul is at peace in Him—I've not been unduly depressed—sorrowful of course—yet always rejoicing.
>
> God's best to you beloved people. You have wrought valiantly & well. We were not defeated—our very attempt was the victory.

Then he added a postscript that reflects his sense of disappointment and failure as well as his self-doubts.

> P.S. I still believe that if our Gov. had acted quickly on the New Guinea proposition we could have headed off the Japanese war party. I believe the Japanese at Wash. were sincere, don't you?

Four days later on December 12, 1941, Jones wrote once again to the Robinsons who had been absolutely indispensable to him not only in arranging and participating in his meetings in Washington during the last three months of the year, but also in providing emotional support and spiritual encouragement throughout his endless round of meetings.

> Thank you so much for your lovely letter and for Dar's. You two have been the deepest consolation to me during the whole matter. To know that our love has bound us together closer than ever through this failure is a joy deeper than words. . . .
>
> I was never so convinced as now that the Christian way is utter realism. . . . I dare say that those who thought that an affair with Japan would be a weekend affair are now seeing their ghastly mistake. It is going to be a hard grim struggle and may take years.

Knowing that the Christmas holidays would be especially difficult for Stanley, the Robinsons offered him the temporary use of the vacant apartment of a friend in Washington. Jones was grateful for the offer, but concluded his December 12 letter by saying,

> I feel I must stay here [in New York] during these holidays. I am afraid that Washington would break my heart just now when I remember how we trudged from place to place trying to head off what has happened.

Did Stanley Jones mistake his fervent personal goal of peace with Japan for the Inner Voice of God's Holy Spirit? Or did God have a larger and more important goal for him, a goal which transcended the immediate and desperate need for peace in the Pacific? The answer lies in the content of his proposal for peace. Chastened by the criticism of his call for American economic withdrawal from Japan in the late 1930s, he now viewed the causes of Japanese aggression within the larger context of the long history of Western imperialism in Asia. The immediate cause of Japanese militarism was that nation's need for more land and more natural resources. But the deeper and contributing causes of its policy of armed conquest were its racially motivated exclusion from the distribution of the spoils of war by the Allies after World War I and the discriminatory immigration policies of the United States toward all Asian nations, including Japan. For this reason Jones exhorted the United States and its leaders to seize the moral high ground. By proposing a practical solution to Japan's obvious need for more land and natural resources, the U.S. would be making an implicit confession of its own wrongdoing in Asia. In other words, behind Jones's proposal for giving New Guinea to Japan was the moral and spiritual principle he articulated in his March 19, 1941, *Christian Century* article, calling on the United States to act as the mediator of a new world order based on equality of opportunity.[25]

Stanley Jones never abandoned his call from God to be a missionary evangelist. Christian evangelism was always his primary task. But as the geographical scope of his call grew beyond India to encompass most of the globe, he became increasingly certain that the gospel of Jesus Christ must be not merely the good news of salvation for individuals; it must also be the good news of salvation for society. This is why, beginning with the 1940 publication of *Is the Kingdom of God Realism?* Jones referred to the kingdom of God as "totalitarian."

We have already examined the first applications of Jones's concept of the kingdom of God to politics in his Christian critique of British imperialism in India and in his proposal for economic withdrawal from Japan. But in 1941 he began to think of the kingdom of God as a universal idea, as the foundation for Christian mediation of political disputes throughout the world. To be sure, when Jones wrote his *Christian Century* article in early 1941, he was preoccupied with the growing tension between the United States and Japan. But the article's proposal that the United States should act as a mediator is based on the kingdom principle of Ephesians 2:15-16 (NIV, emphasis added), which states that the purpose of Jesus' death and resurrection was to "create *in himself* one new man . . . and in this one *body* to reconcile . . . [all] to God through the cross." In this scripture passage Paul is focusing on Jesus' death and resurrection as the means of reconciling specifically Jews and Gentiles to God. Jones zeroes in on Paul's definition of Jesus as a mediator between enemies who creates within himself one new entity from the conflicting parties. Just as Jesus through the cross created within himself the means of reconciling all humanity to God, so the United States could act as a mediator to reconcile conflicting nations, like Japan and China, by persuading both parties "to change and thus come to a third position, beyond each and yet gathering up the truth in each."

But was persuading the Netherlands and Australia to give New Guinea to Japan and convincing the United States to give $100 million as

275

compensation for their loss a sensible proposal? To a secular critic today Jones's proposal may seem "unrealistic." Indeed, from a secular point of view, the very notion of using the kingdom of God to solve political problems is wholly "impractical," even bizarre. Jones was fully aware of this criticism, as his book title, *Is the Kingdom of God Realism?* makes clear. He responded to the criticism that the kingdom of God was unrealistic by asserting that the kingdom was, in fact, the only ultimate reality. What secular "realists" unthinkingly assume to be real—the empirical world of modern science and technology and, in the sphere of international relations, the supremacy of national self-interest and power politics—is actually only a part, and a subordinate and inferior part, of reality. Jones not only imagined the superior reality of the kingdom of God; he lived, preached, and, as we have seen, conducted unofficial international diplomacy in the kingdom of God.

In his efforts to mediate peace between the United States and Japan, he began not with the so-called realistic assumption of the international balance of power in the Pacific, but with the moral truth that both nations had legitimate grievances against each other. The United States was justifiably concerned about Japanese aggression in the Far East, especially Japan's indiscriminate killing of civilians in China. On the other hand, Japan had every reason to be outraged at its racially prejudiced treatment by the World War I Allies and by the United States itself in its immigration laws. By applying the kingdom of God principle of creating a new entity out of both parties, Jones sought to mediate the dispute of the United States and Japan, first by accepting the truth of each nation's position and then by developing a third truth that transcended and yet retained the truth of both the United States and Japan. To mediate their disagreement, Kagawa first suggested and Jones later proposed the third and higher truth of giving New Guinea to Japan. The most credible evidence for the realism of this proposal is the fact that Jones persuaded so many high-ranking officials in so many nations to seriously consider if not accept it as a way to end Japan's imperialism in the Pacific.

There is a very moving footnote to Stanley Jones's efforts to prevent war between Japan and the United States. Stanley was in Tokyo in 1947 and was able to meet with Nomura, Kurusu, and Terasaki, the three Japanese diplomats with whom he had met in Washington in 1941. Terasaki's American wife, Gwen, recalled Jones's visit with her husband in March of 1947. As her husband came out of the Imperial Palace,

> he caught sight of an oddly familiar figure alighting from a taxi on the street below. The man was of medium build and carried himself with military erectness; as he turned from the cab he started briskly up the steps and his handsome head of snow white hair came into full view. It was Stanley Jones, whom

we had not seen since early December nearly six years before. The two men recognized each other at the same time. They fell into each other's arms and stood on the steps of the Palace weeping.

As soon as it could be arranged, Dr. Jones and Terry [Terasaki] met for dinner. With profound wistfulness they talked of the past, of what could be done to help Japan recover, and of how to prevent a recurrence of the tragedy they had so nearly avoided.

How nearly they had come to averting the tragedy of war in the Pacific Stanley learned for the first time in his luncheon with Terasaki.

Terry informed Jones that the Emperor had told him that if he had received the cablegram from Roosevelt a day sooner he would have stopped the attack. What poignant memories my husband and his American comrade shared that night![26]

12

Closed Door to India

We reaffirm and proclaim that we believe in democracy.
We would define democracy as equality of opportunity.
—E. Stanley Jones's Proposed Pacific Charter, August 10, 1942[1]

HOW STANLEY JONES arrived in the United States in 1940, under the guidance of the Inner Voice, is just as dramatic a story as how he was led to stay in 1941. He told the story in his autobiography, *A Song of Ascents.*[2]

> Mr. E. V. Moorman wrote me in India, saying that if I would transplant the Christian Ashrams into America, he would pay the bills for setting them up. The Department of Evangelism of the Federal Council of Churches, under Dr. Jesse M. Bader, undertook to set them up if I would be willing to conduct them. I agreed. The first one was to be held in Saugatuck, Michigan, in July, 1940.

As Stanley made his travel plans, everything seemed to be in place for his timely arrival in the United States. But then quite unexpectedly, while he was at the Sat Tal Ashram in May, the Inner Voice said, "It's all right. I'll get you there safely and on time." He soon discovered why he would need

278

God's help getting to Michigan. Because of the war in Europe his travel plans were canceled. When he learned that a ship was going from Bombay to New York by way of South Africa, he booked a passage, even though the ship was not scheduled to arrive in New York until ten days after the opening of the ashram in Saugatuck. He simply trusted the Inner Voice.

On the long voyage he worked on his book, *Is the Kingdom of God Realism?* In Capetown, South Africa, the captain of the ship told the passengers that the ship would have to stop in Trinidad for fresh water. When Stanley looked at a map and saw that Pan-American Airlines had a route through Trinidad to Miami, he wired Dr. Bader, who made a plane reservation for him. In Trinidad, he caught the plane to Miami. From there he took a train for Chicago where he was met by a pastor who, on the day the ashram was to open, took him by car to Saugatuck. Stanley tells the rest of the story in his autobiography.

> But when we got within twenty miles of Saugatuck, going down a hill the car careened this way and that and drew up just this side of disaster. The brakes were gone! We had to go back five miles to a garage. The garageman worked on it for three hours. I watched the clock as the deadline approached for getting there "on time." Just as it came, the garageman came out from under the car and said: "I've got it." We jumped in the car and drove the twenty miles, and just as we turned into the campground, the bell was ringing for the opening of the Ashram. "Safely and on time"! I simply could not have thought out that route beforehand. It had to be God's guidance and God's intervention, or it just could not have happened.

The Inner Voice, which directed Stanley when he left India in 1940 and which prevented him from returning to India in 1941, continued to guide him throughout World War II. In his first circular letter written after Pearl Harbor, he told his friends and patrons in the United States that he did not regret his efforts to keep America out of the war. "I am not sorry for what I tried to do at Washington," he wrote. "We failed, but we failed gloriously. If I had it to do over again, I would do the same."[3]

For Christmas Day 1941, Stanley prepared a Christmas message that was probably broadcast by radio, though there is no information about its broadcast.[4] "Amid the crash of things," he said, "something solid, unshakable remained. My world of real value was intact—the center of my faith—Christ—was unscathed."

Even though he acknowledged in his December 26, 1941, circular letter that the war prevented him from going back to India and that the war "interns Mrs. Jones and my daughter and son-in-law in India for the duration of the war," he went on to conduct four ashrams during the summer of 1941 and was at work on his new book, *Abundant Living.*[5] This book, a collection of one-page devotional meditations for each day of the year, was published in 1942 and became his single most popular title. It is significant that *Abundant Living* was completed during wartime. Despite "these dreadful days of war," Jones wrote in his December 26, 1941, circular letter, "Christ still rules, and I was never so sure as now that His way is the way of complete realism." He had begun writing the book in the fall of 1941, and he had told his friends in his September 13, 1941, circular letter that it was rooted in his previous book, *Is the Kingdom of God Realism?* "I am trying," he wrote, "to put that book into techniques of applied living."[6]

Stanley wrote to Miss Nellie on March 7, 1942, that when the war began he had thought he would "have to hibernate & write books." But in fact he was having "fine meetings" throughout the United States. "I've never had a better hearing & response." By April 20, 1942, he was able to report to his friends and patrons that during January and February he had spent a week in each of the following places—Paducah, Kentucky; South Bend, Indiana; Wheeling, West Virginia; Johnstown, Pennsylvania; San Angelo, Texas; Hagerstown, Maryland; Canton, Ohio; and Duluth, Minnesota. These meetings were part of the National Christian Mission sponsored by the Federal Council of Churches. Following that, he held his own evangelistic meetings in other cities through the end of June. In July he began to hold his Christian ashrams. In his August 29, 1942, circular letter he reported that during June 1942 he spoke at the Pastor's School in Dallas and at the National Education Association in Denver. And he had spoken at several Japanese American camps on the West Coast. These internment camps, or "relocation" camps as they were called, were established by the U.S. military after Pearl Harbor, pursuant to executive orders from President Roosevelt and acts of Congress. All Japanese Americans on the West Coast, regardless of citizenship or loyalty to the United States, were ordered to leave their homes and report to internment camps for the duration of the war. After Jones spoke to the camps at Santa Anita and Pomona, California, he wrote, "I have never felt the breathless silence of a spiritual craving more deeply in any meeting anywhere in the world."

His August 29, 1942, circular letter also briefly described plans for the resettlement of Japanese American Christians from the internment camps to other locations throughout the country. According to the plan, individual churches would agree to sponsor one or more Japanese American families, to support the families until they became self-sufficient, and to include them within their fellowship. "If the churches would do this," he wrote, "it would demonstrate to the world that the Christian fellowship is unbroken, even amid war-time." Throughout July and August 1942 he exchanged letters with a number of individuals and organizations in an ultimately unsuccessful effort to move Japanese Americans out of the internment camps and reassimilate them into American society.

Stanley first proposed that churches throughout the United States take responsibility for the resettlement of Japanese Americans in a July 10, 1942, letter to his friends Dr. and Mrs. O. G. Robinson, written during his ashram at Occidental College in Los Angeles.[7] He had also suggested the idea to some prominent Quakers. He proposed that the American Friends Service Committee, a well-known and highly regarded Quaker social service agency, carry out the resettlement of Japanese Americans under the sponsorship of the Federal Council of Churches. Over the next month Jones wrote letters to and received letters from the Protestant Church Commission for Japanese Service and the Home Missions Council of North America. Some of his correspondents asked whether the resettled Japanese Americans might become the victims of mob violence. Others asked whether the government, specifically General DeWitt, the U.S. Army General in charge of the internment camps, would permit the resettlement of Japanese Americans. But the question that challenged his proposal most directly was raised by Mark A. Dawber of the Home Missions Council of North America in his letter of August 6, 1942.[8] Dawber pointed out that the most difficult obstacle to the resettlement of the Japanese Americans was the problem of how to create "a general public opinion favorable to the American Japanese."

> And now I bring the challenge to you. Will you be willing to give some time to campaign across this country in the interest of creating such a public opinion and Christian attitude?

Four days later on August 10, 1942, Jones responded to Dawber. He said that after discussing Dawber's suggestion with Jesse Bader of the Federal Council of Churches, he and Bader agreed that he should not cancel the engagements he had made for the rest of the year. He could, however, take up the challenge of creating a public opinion that would be favorable to the resettlement of Japanese Americans "through the engagements which I now have."

> Combining it [Dawber's challenge] with an evangelistic series would in many ways be more effective, because after preparing the people spiritually I could say that one of the things that they could do at the close of this series of evangelistic meetings would be as churches and communities to take in these Japanese and help them to resettlement. . . . I shall be most happy to do everything I can in regard to this matter, for it is upon my heart in a real way. I think that the Christian Church has one of the greatest opportunities ever presented to it.

Unfortunately, the church did not respond to the opportunity to give its Christian witness by participating in the resettlement of Japanese

Americans, who remained in the internment camps throughout the war. Because of their ethnic heritage, they were the targets of public resentment and hostility for many years after the war. In fact, it was not until 1988 that Congress finally appropriated money to compensate the survivors of the internment camps for their loss of property and liberty.

Another controversial public issue Jones confronted in 1942, an issue whose significance he was one of the very first to recognize and which would become especially important in his next book, *The Christ of the American Road* (1944), was the issue of racial equality. In his August 29, 1942, circular letter he reported that at his Blue Ridge, North Carolina, Ashram, "we had four members of the colored race as part of our Ashram fellowship and they made very distinct contributions." Earlier in the summer, he had written to Mrs. O. G. Robinson on June 1.

> I had two days in Jackson, Mississippi under the auspices of the Negroes. They had a public meeting at night with twenty-five hundred Whites and fifteen hundred Colored in the municipal auditorium. There were two Bishop Greens presiding and neither one was green. One was White and the other Black.[9]

Perhaps because of these interracial meetings, a Methodist pastor in Texas wrote to the World Service Agencies of The Methodist Church in Chicago on November 23, 1942. He was "desperately sincere and in deep distress," he said, and asked the Board of Missions why it had sent Jones

> into the deep south with his out-spoken advocacy of bitter opposition to the Jim Crow law here? It is my humble opinion that his views are not sane and he is a liability to the cause of missions and world service. . . . He tends dangerously toward Communism, Socialism and especially social equality between all races.
>
> The laymen to whom we look for money are asking serious questions. . . . It is my humble judgment that the Socialists and Communists are using the negro as a blind as a means of advancing their cause in the south and Dr. E. Stanley Jones is one of the chief aids to this cause now.

The World Service Agencies office gave the letter to Jones. An angry Stanley Jones waited over two weeks, until December 12, 1942, to respond.[10] "I have waited to answer your letter," he began, "until I could be sure I could give a Christian reply."

> You ask why I should come to the South? I was born in the South and educated there—may I not visit my home land?
>
> You say that I am guilty of an "outspoken advocacy of bitter opposition to the Jim Crow law here." If that is a crime then I plead guilty. If to ask for equal rights for citizens of the American democracy is a crime, then I'm guilty of that crime.

You say: "He tends dangerously—toward social equality between all races." If to do so is a crime against Democracy and Christianity then again I plead guilty and glory in that guilt. The crime it seems to me is to be on the other side. It is treason against Democracy and against the Christian faith to advocate inequality of treatment of races. . . .

If I should be kept back from India permanently, which God forbid, then I should consider seriously giving the balance of my working days to help the Negroes of America to an equal status in our democracy and to their fullest development as a people. For the color question has become a world question. . . . The attitude which you symbolize is pushing the colored majority of the world straight into an alliance against the white minority of the world. . . .

You suggest that I "tend dangerously toward Communism." My reply is simple: I have written a book entitled: "Christ's Alternative to Communism." In it I advocate neither Socialism, nor Communism, nor any other "ism," but I advocate the Kingdom of God on earth. If that is treason, make the most of it.

Of all that Stanley Jones wrote and published on the issue of racial equality, he never wrote anything that was more providentially inspired, more perceptive, or more prophetic than this letter.

During the summer of 1943, Stanley wrote to Miss Nellie about "a great meeting" he had had in Chicago

with the Negroes. . . . The Negroes in that great meeting were deciding whether they would embark on civil disobedience of Jim Crowism across the country. They decided not to have it as a mass movement but to pick out a few places, Richmond, Washington, New York, Chicago, and have only trained disciplined volunteers who would disobey the Jim Crow laws and then take the consequences. . . . I was the only white speaker and they took my message wonderfully. I hope I helped to turn them into non-violent channels.

Stanley does not identify the meeting at which he spoke nor the African American organization that was deciding to conduct a campaign of civil disobedience against Jim Crow laws. In light of the fact that the American civil rights movement did not begin boycotts, freedom rides, and sit-ins until the late 1950s and early 1960s, the meeting he attended was truly remarkable. Equally remarkable is the fact of his participation in the meeting and his advocacy of nonviolence, anticipating his role in the civil rights movement as the man from whose book, *Mahatma Gandhi: An Interpretation*, Martin Luther King, Jr., learned about Gandhi's philosophy of nonviolent civil disobedience.

Stanley Jones's outspoken advocacy of racial equality was rooted in his concept of the kingdom of God. For him the laws of the moral universe were the principles of the kingdom of God applied to human behavior. And the first law of the moral universe is equality. We are all created with equal moral dignity by God; therefore, we should all have equal moral dignity in the eyes of one another. God created human beings to live and interact in a world governed by these laws of the moral universe. When we obey these laws, we cooperate with God in the purposes of his human creation and we reap the abundant fruit of living in harmony with both God and man. But when we knowingly disobey these laws, we resist God's purposes and reap the bitter fruit of living in tension and conflict with ourselves, with others, and with God. This is why he insisted on racial equality.

If racial issues were only beginning to become the focus of public attention in the United States in 1942, they were already the focus of international attention because of World War II. As we saw in chapter 11, Jones had keen insight into the racial dimension of the sources of Japanese imperialism in the Pacific. If the laws of God's moral universe demanded racial equality for African Americans and other ethnic minorities within the United States, the same laws demanded racial equality for all people throughout the world. Moreover, it was the insistence on racial equality that consistently guided Stanley Jones in his tireless efforts in late 1941 to keep the United States out of a war with Japan. Although he did not succeed in that effort, he did not abandon the kingdom principle of racial equality. In the summer of 1942, he was particularly concerned about racial equality among the World War II Allies. He wrote to President Roosevelt on August 10, 1942, that

> British imperialism is in danger of entangling the Indian situation into hopeless knots. . . . The Tory mind hopes that by some juggling of chance they may still be left in possession of India. In this they are dreadfully mistaken. India will get freedom with or without the consent of Britain. It would be far better to give consent than to have it wrung from her.

Because the United States was so closely tied to Great Britain during the war, he suggested to Roosevelt that the two nations jointly issue "a Pacific Charter declaring their aims in the Pacific." If Britain would not join America in the charter, then, he said, the United States should proclaim the charter on its own to separate herself from British imperialism.[11]

Jones enclosed the Pacific Charter with his letter to the President. It was modeled on the Atlantic Charter that Roosevelt and Churchill had already drawn up in 1941 for postwar Europe and that became the basis for NATO. The first paragraph of the Pacific Charter stated that it applied to "all the areas not specifically covered by the Atlantic Charter. In other words, this Charter supplements the Atlantic Charter and gives our position for the world as a whole." The charter went on to proclaim its belief in democracy, which it defined as "equality of opportunity." Moreover, equality of opportunity should apply to "all areas of life," including political, social, economic, and religious institutions. On the basis of these democratic principles the Charter supported "the liquidation of imperialism" at the "earliest possible" date. Instead of imperialism and denial of equality, the Charter proposed "a new world order," which would consist of

1. Equality of access to the raw materials of the world . . . [and] equitable access to the markets of the world.
2. Equality of opportunity for immigration. . . .
3. A more equitable distribution of opportunity for settlement of surplus populations in the less occupied portions of the world.
4. The free, unhampered opportunity for all peoples to decide their own destiny.
5. Where there are undeveloped peoples, not yet in a position to decide their own destiny, the period of preparation would be a world responsibility; carried out through some form of world organization or government.
6. Equality of opportunity for the greatest possible development of all peoples in all areas of life. . . .

In short, we stand for a world order based on mutual aid—a welfare economy instead of a power economy.

The first three points listed above refer directly, as we saw in chapter 11, to Jones's efforts to prevent war between the United States and Japan. The remaining points refer more generally to the gross maldistribution of wealth and resources between the poor nations and the rich nations of the world. As we will see later, his proposal of a new world order based on the kingdom of God principle of equality of opportunity, or a more equitable distribution of opportunity, would inspire and shape the formation and implementation of his vision of the postwar world.

These ideas, of course, were controversial at the time Jones first proposed them, and many of them are still controversial today. But in 1942 what was even more controversial than the Pacific Charter in terms of America's wartime alliance with Great Britain was Jones's written proposal in his August 10, 1942, letter that Roosevelt "bring pressure to bear upon Britain to give India an offer of freedom now." From the standpoint of a "political realist," the status of India within the British Empire was too sensitive an issue with the British Conservative Party and with its leader, Winston Churchill, who was then prime minister, for a political pragmatist like Roosevelt to bring pressure on Britain to give India its independence.

Jones did receive an official response to his proposed Pacific Charter from the U.S. Department of State, to whom he sent a copy of the Charter. Maxwell M. Hamilton, the chief of the division of Far Eastern Affairs in the State Department, thanked Jones for his ideas and then wrote,

Your letter to the President and the proposed "Pacific Charter" have been read with interest and have been brought to the attention of other interested

285

officers in the Department. We shall of course give careful thought to the contents of the proposed "Pacific Charter" in connection with our studies of the problems to which it relates.[12]

This reply from the State Department is too easily dismissed as a polite but bureaucratic way of saying, "Thanks, but no thanks." The Atlantic Charter itself declared universal respect for the right of all people to choose their own form of government and for the restoration of the right of self-government to all people who had been forcefully deprived of this right. But when the question was raised whether the Atlantic Charter applied to India, Churchill made it clear in a speech to the House of Commons in September 1941 that the answer was no. Later, after the United States entered the war, Roosevelt brought pressure on Churchill to give India more freedom and responsibility so that it could have a more independent role in the war effort.[13] So Jones's letter to Roosevelt and his proposed Pacific Charter may well have had an important role in motivating the American President to give the Atlantic Charter a truly global significance while simultaneously exposing British moral and spiritual hypocrisy in applying the Atlantic Charter to white, Western nations but not to nonwhite, non-Western parts of its own empire.

Some months later, on January 5, 1943, Jones wrote to Roosevelt again. Churchill's statement that the Atlantic Charter did not include India, he said, meant that "the political battle of the East has already been lost." But, he continued, "the situation may yet be saved," and Roosevelt was "the only man who can save it." What the President had to do, he wrote, was to give clear and convincing support to the "Britain of Democracy," but at the same time to denounce the "Britain of Empire." Otherwise, he warned, the United States must be "prepared to go to war every twenty-five years to rescue that Britain of Empire from the wars in which imperialism involves her." Jones was concerned not just about India but, on the basis of the kingdom of God principle of universal equality of opportunity, about the nonwhite majority populations of Asia, Africa, and Latin America. By not specifically rejecting Churchill's announcement, Roosevelt would lose the support of all the colonized people of the globe, and he would lose not just their support of the Allied cause in World War II but also their friendship and support after the war. For this reason, Jones concluded, Roosevelt "must face the fact with Mr. Churchill that Britain cannot expect to keep the sympathy and goodwill of America, or even her help in this war, if Empire is to determine her foreign policy."[14]

The ultimate source of Jones's concept of a new world order was the kingdom of God. But a more immediate source was his own Methodist heritage. In a chapter included in the book *Christian World Mission* published by the Commission on Ministerial Training of the Methodist Church after the war, Jones traced the origin of his thinking and praying about a new world order to the very core of John Wesley's contribution to Christianity—his ideas of the warmed heart and the world parish.[15] The warmed heart, of course, refers to Wesley's experience at Aldersgate in London, when his heart was "strangely warmed" and his life forever transformed by the infilling of the Holy Spirit. The world parish, on the other hand, refers to the global reach of Wesley's evangelical zeal in the aftermath of his encounter with God at Aldersgate. In Jones's chapter for *Christian World Mission,* using Wesley's idea of the world parish and reflecting on his own missionary experience, he wrote,

> The conception of one half of the world saved, and the other half lost, the half that is saved going out after the half lost, is a misconception. We are all lost without God. We are not only going to them because they are in need; we need what they can give us. The tide is now beginning to flow back. In the days to come we shall want these men whose hearts have been touched with the grace of God to come and help us in the uncompleted task of evangelization.[16]

There was a third contribution of Methodism to Christianity—church union. Like the first two contributions, Jones said, church union also had its origin in Wesley, specifically in Wesley's statement, "If your heart is as my heart, give me your hand." Church union, Jones argued, was the "next great test within Christendom."[17]

For Jones, of course, church union in 1946 was hardly a new issue. As we saw in chapter 10, he first addressed the need for Christian unity in the mid-1930s. Only if the various Christian churches and denominations conquered the stubborn persistence of their divisive doctrines and competitive ministries, he had written in 1935, would the infinite spiritual power of the body of Christ be harnessed and speak with one clear, effective, and unequivocal moral voice to the social, economic, and political problems of the day. The need for Christian unity was certainly urgent before World War II, but during the war the need was truly desperate, as people longed for what he called "a vast world reconstruction." World reconstruction, however, was impossible "without a mighty moral and spiritual impulse behind it,"[18] and that impulse, Jones knew, could only be spearheaded by the Christian church. But the question remained, how could the churches unite? What would they have to do in order to speak God's word to the world?

In three articles published over a six-month period between December 1942 and June 1943 in the *Christian Century* and in the *Christian Advocate,* Jones explained that there were three ways of uniting American Christians.[19] One was amalgamation, the second was federation, and the third was federal union. He modeled these three forms of ecumenical polity on the history of the American states and on their various efforts to create a United States of America.

Using arguments that he would spell out more clearly and in more detail in *The Christ of the American Road* (1944), he explained that amalgamation of the states was never seriously considered by the framers of the U.S. Constitution. After all, amalgamation is exactly the policy that King George III had tried to enforce when the states were British colonies, and amalgamation was precisely what Americans fought the Revolution to defeat. So, in reaction to British colonialism, the first but short-lived American national government was based on the Articles of Confederation, which established a league of friendship, or what Jones calls a federation, among the sovereign and independent states. But just as the League of Nations, which was created to maintain international peace after World War I, did not work because "each constituent nation refused to surrender any sovereignty to the League," so the Articles of Confederation lasted for less than a decade and ended by calling for another convention to establish a more viable national government. The Articles of Confederation failed, Jones said, for the same reason that the League of Nations failed. They both violated the "law of the kingdom of God: 'He that saveth his life shall lose it.'"[20] On the other hand, what has made the third form of unity such an outstanding political success in the United States is its conscious or unconscious reliance on this kingdom law. The United States was successfully created at the Constitutional Convention only because the individual states were willing to surrender some of their sovereignty to a new national government.

Applying this political history of the American states to the Christian churches of the United States, Jones argued that neither amalgamation nor federation would be any more successful among churches than it had been among the states. Amalgamation relied too heavily on "a desire for unity," while federation relied too heavily on "a desire for local autonomy and self-expression." Federal union was the only way to combine these desires in a proper balance. He called the federal union of the various American denominations "The Church of Christ in America." The same principle of federal union, he thought, should be applied internationally to "The Church of Christ" consisting of Christian churches throughout the world. Jones was encouraged that within the United States the Federal Council of Churches had taken an important step toward federal union, but in order to be a true executive arm of The Church of Christ in America, its power would have to be substantially increased. He was also encouraged that the World Council of Churches had been created just before World War II, even though it would not be able to function, even in an advisory role, until after the war.[21]

In his second *Christian Century* article, "Federal Church Union—A

Reply," published in June 1943, Jones responded to various criticisms of his proposal for federal union of the Christian churches. At the beginning of the article he clarified the origin of federal union by explaining that it was not "my proposal; it was proposed to me."

> I was walking across the veranda of a mission house in India about six years ago, not thinking about church union at all, when suddenly there it was—the whole proposal, full bloom. It seemed to be "given," from a source outside myself.[22]

Jones was fully aware that this assertion of divine guidance by the Inner Voice might make the concept of federal union appear to be "sacrosanct and beyond criticism." But in fact, he wrote, "I make no such claim, for at best it would go through a very faulty human channel." What he did claim, however, was that God's initiating federal union gave him "an inner poise and detachment about the whole matter." In other words, he knew that, as a fallible human being, his expression of God's revelation to him was probably imperfect and incomplete and he was therefore open to criticism and suggestions. But, because federal union was really God's idea, not Stanley Jones's idea, he knew that he was not ultimately responsible for its adoption and implementation or its rejection. This sense of poise and detachment, as he put it, was important. It enabled him to endure scathing and sometimes slanderous criticism, the kind he had received over his decision to resign from the episcopacy, as well as after his outspoken attack on the Madras Conference, and over his proposal for economic withdrawal from Japan. This same poise and detachment continued to be invaluable for the remainder of his life and ministry.

As he spoke to many different groups in different settings throughout 1942, more and more people asked why he remained in the United States and did not return to India. One explanation, which he heard from several sources, was that the British Government had refused to give him a visa to return to India. In fact, the British had given him a visa before the Inner Voice guided him to stay in the United States, and as far as he knew, the visa was still valid. Nevertheless, in order to resolve any public misunderstanding, he asked Ralph Diffendorfer, in a letter dated January 18, 1943, whether he should issue a statement about the reasons for his remaining in America. Three days later, on January 21, Diffendorfer responded that he had taken Jones's letter to the monthly meeting of the administrative committee of the Division of Foreign Missions of the Methodist Church and that the committee had accepted his letter as a request for an extension of his furlough. The committee then issued a public statement, which was released to the religious press throughout the United States, that Jones's furlough was extended until January 1, 1944.

The statement continued,

> This action was taken in view of the many continued requests for the services of Dr. Jones in preaching missions in the United States and neighboring countries. . . . Furthermore, the military situation in India is such now as to render it quite probable that no large meetings for the discussion of public issues could be held in that country.

In the latter part of 1942, in response to the requests for his services as a preacher and evangelist, Jones spoke in Williamsport, Pennsylvania, to all the public school teachers, to the supervisors, executives, and heads of departments of all the industries in the city, and to all the luncheon clubs of the city. In addition, he reported in his first circular letter of 1943, dated January 22, that he spoke to a youth conference in Georgetown, Texas, and held meetings in a Unitarian Church sponsored by the Ministerial Association of Quincy, Massachusetts. In the same letter Jones also told his friends and financial supporters that he was collecting material for his next book, *The Christ of the American Road,* which would "interpret the kind of Christianity emerging out of American civilization." By the end of February 1943 his schedule of meetings and interviews was beginning to affect his health. Jones wrote to Diffendorfer from Eugene, Oregon, on February 26,

> For 10 days I have been skirting pneumonia. The doctors begged me to give up and go to the hospital but I told them I had not missed an engagement in 25 years, so they allowed me to go on, on the condition that I would whisper into the microphone. I have carried on a whispering campaign but I have come through and am well again. My health and my itinerary were both kept intact.

While he was on the West Coast, Jones reported to Mrs. Robinson in Washington in a letter dated April 1, 1943, that he had made a radio address from Los Angeles to the Japanese internment camps, that he had spoken on India to the presitigous Commonwealth Club in San Francisco, and that he had addressed 3,000 prisoners at San Quentin Prison. On April 16 he wrote his second circular letter for 1943. He was excited about the success of *Abundant Living* because after only four and one-half months since publication there were 150,000 copies of the book in print. And he was beginning to receive testimonies from people whose lives had been changed by reading the book.

> The other day a business man who had not been in church in eighteen years, told me he was converted by Abundant Living and the place that he happened to open to—of all places—was the page on the use of tobacco. It got him! He read the rest and was converted—soundly so.

In the same circular letter, he told about speaking to students at the University of Tennessee in Knoxville where the entire student body attended his meeting and where "nearly all of them" stayed "for an after meeting for personal decision." He also spoke to three thousand students at Oregon State University in Corvallis, Oregon, on Sadie Hawkins Day. Despite the fact that the students dressed "in the most outlandish, rube costumes" and that the "beginning of the Assembly was rocking with fun and frivolity," two minutes after he began to speak, the students "were in pin drop silence and they never moved for three quarters of an hour as I presented Christ." Finally, he reported that he spoke to the Breakfast Club in Los Angeles and to the High School in Hollywood and that he was invited to speak to the State Legislature in Nevada.

Jones spent the month of June 1943 in Mexico, holding evangelistic meetings in Monterrey, Saltillo, Aguacalientes, Guadalajara, Mexico City, and Chihuahua. His companion and interpreter for these meetings was Mr. Bais-Camargo, the secretary of the Evangelical Churches of Mexico. Because, under Mexican law, religious meetings could only be held in churches, Jones spoke mostly in evangelical churches. On June 30 at the end of his tour he wrote to his good friends the Robinsons that the churches where he spoke were "packed out" and that "almost all" who attended stayed for after-meetings. In Mexico City about twelve hundred people came to his meetings each night. "When I would ask only [for] those who wanted to make a personal surrender to Christ," he wrote in his August 30, 1943, circular letter, "about eleven hundred of them would stay!"

Despite the prohibition on holding religious meetings outside churches, Jones did speak in the Labor Temple, in the Masonic Temple, to the Rotary Club, and in a government college. The college meeting, he told the Robinsons, was "one of the most important mtgs. I've had in Mexico— a straight out Xtian [Christian] presentation." And it was

> interesting for many of the professors were supposed to be Communists and religion was supposed to be banned from Government institutions. But I spoke on "What may a modern person believe?" and . . . when I finished they applauded and applauded even until I was walking down the aisle and out of the door. It showed what those students wanted—they wanted something to live by!

Before he left Mexico, he visited what he called in the August 12, 1943, issue of the *Indian Witness* "the most astonishing thing in nature I've ever looked at"—a new volcano. In just four months it had erupted from the ground to a mountain of two thousand feet. When Jones went to the volcano, most of the dust and ashes had already been spewed out and lava was flowing over the countryside surrounding the mountain. He was able to

291

observe the volcano from the edge of the lava flow, which he described as "an advancing wall about 30 to 50 feet high. At the base of this wall the lava was red hot." In addition to the lava flow, Jones wrote, there were "spectacular outbursts" from the top of the volcano in the form of "red hot rocks," some of which were "treble the size of a piano."

> When these explosions took place the earth beneath your feet would tremble at the mighty convulsion. . . .
> We stood there for an hour in the dark, our faces lighted up from the glow of the lava and the continuous fireworks with the tongues of flame licking the sky—our hearts filled with an unutterable awe.

Back in the United States from Mexico, Stanley led four ashrams during July and August 1943 and in the fall resumed his demanding schedule of evangelistic meetings. In October the Prohibition Party approached Jones about the possibility of his being their presidential candidate in 1944. Edward E. Blake, the Chairman of the Prohibition National Committee, wrote to him on October 21, 1943, and asked him if he could attend the party's convention in Indianapolis in November. "[I]f our Convention wanted to draft you as a candidate for president," he asked, "would you be willing to accept?" Jones replied on November 1 in a letter written on the stationery of Hotel Frontier in Cheyenne, Wyoming. He was "deeply grateful" for Blake's offer and he felt "completely unworthy."

> But in weighing the matter, I am afraid that I cannot get inner consent to have you place my name in nomination. I am deeply interested in prohibition and believe in it, but in view of my interest in world reconstruction, I could not make it the central issue by running under the banner of the Prohibiton Party. I think the supreme issue is world reconstruction of which prohibiton is a corollary.

In Jones's January 16, 1944, circular letter he summarized his activities during the last three months of 1943. For two weeks he conducted evangelistic campaigns in the Japanese internment camps in Rivers, Arizona; Poston, Arizona; Manzanar, California; and Topaz, Utah. He also visited Canada and, for the first time, Cuba. He spent two weeks in Cuba, holding meetings in Havana, Pinar del Rio, Cardenas, Matanzas, Santa Clara, Camaguey, Holquin, and Santiago de Cuba.

> I found Cuba the most open and responsive to an evangelical Gospel of any Latin country. In Habana they gave us the magnificent hall of the Asturian Club for our evangelistic meeting—the most magnificent hall I have ever spoken in, either in East or West, really a marble palace.

Among the places in the United States where Jones held meetings in the latter part of 1943 were the University of Tennessee in Knoxville and Berea College in Kentucky. In several of his meetings, he arranged for the Reverend Paul Turner, an African American lawyer and minister, to lead the music. Jones concluded his circular letter by outlining some of his plans for the coming year. But after the four summer ashrams he was not sure what he would do. He wrote, "And then? I do not know. Will it be India? I hope so, and yet it is not clear." He was anxious to return to India. He felt that he had completed the task the Inner Voice had directed him to undertake in 1941—trying to maintain peace between Japan and the United States before the war by applying kingdom of God principles, and by using these same principles trying to prepare his native land for a new world order based on equality of opportunity after the war. But in order to return to India, he would first need the permission of the British government.

On February 11, 1944, Jones wrote to the British Passport Control Office in New York City, saying that he wanted to return to his "missionary work." His ministry among the "educated Hindus and Moslems . . . presents peculiar problems," he wrote.

> After my addresses I have a question period and am asked all sorts of acute questions. I must be free to express my moral convictions, among them my conviction of the right of India to self-government. . . .
>
> I pledge you that I would take no part in politics as such. But I must be free to express my deepest convictions. Would I be allowed this freedom?
>
> As I see it, this would not be in violation of the missionary pledge "to do nothing contrary to or in dimunition of the lawfully constituted authority," since it has been the declared intention of the constituted authority to give India self-government.
>
> If I am allowed to return under these conditions, I would endeavor to be a reconciling influence between Britain and India and between Indians themselves.

There was a difference of opinion within Methodist Mission Headquarters about the wisdom of Jones's letter. His good friend and fellow missionary in India, Murray Titus, felt that he should have simply asked the British for permission to return to India without explaining the special circumstances—that in the course of his public meetings he would have to address the politically sensitive issue of Indian independence. But Stanley felt that he had done the right thing. "My dear Murray," he wrote on February 18, 1944, he found it

> very difficult to get an inner consent to go back to India . . . without any clarification of my position. . . . If they let me go back after reading my letter then the situation is clear for them and clear for me. . . . It would give them

an opportunity to clarify their position and also clear my conscience. I therefore feel that I must go on with this letter.

The British government took its time in responding to Jones's February 11 request. "No reply as yet," he wrote in his second circular letter of 1944, dated April 17. While he waited, he wrote to Lord Halifax, the British Ambassador to the United States, and enclosed a copy of his February 11 letter to the Passport Control Office. Halifax replied on March 30.

> Dear Doctor Jones,
> Thank you very much for your letter, enclosing a copy of the letter you wrote to the British Passport Control Office in New York.
> I hope you are well—I often remember our meeting in India.
> Yours sincerely,
> Halifax

Finally, on April 29, 1944, Jones was able to write to Diffendorfer, who was then attending the quadrennial General Conference of the Methodist Church in Kansas City, that he had received a letter that day from the British Passport Office stating that "the authorities regret that they are unable to accede to your request for a visa at this time." The British response was "not entirely unexpected," he wrote, but he was clearly disappointed.

> While, of course, this is something that is not easy to take, nevertheless I find myself able to take it, going on without bitterness and without resentment. I have nothing but the deepest love and respect for the British people as such. But here we are up against a system which shows its essential nature. But I must not comment any further.

After Diffendorfer discussed Jones's letter with Murray Titus, who was also at General Conference, Titus wrote to Jones suggesting that his letter to the British Passport Office was a "tactical mistake." In his May 10 response, Stanley wrote,

> I am not yet convinced that it was [a tactical mistake], for if they had refused me the visa on a straightout request, without a letter of explanation as to the basis on which I wanted the visa, it would have left me in a far worse position than I am now in. This leaves me in a morally advantageous position for they turn me down on the basis of this letter.

Titus's last word was his May 17 letter.

> I certainly do agree with you that if we go on the assumption that the Passport Office would have refused an ordinary request to return to India in any case, then you are in a better position as matters stand now than if you

had not put up your case as you did. The only thing that we will never know is whether the Passport Office would have actually refused a visa for you to return to India, if you had put up a simple request to return without any conditions. However, since you felt that this was for you impossible without making your position clear, we must honor your judgment in the matter and go on from this point in full accord.

Perhaps because of lingering uncertainty about whether the British might have permitted him to return to India if he had not included any conditions in his request, Jones wrote to Lord Halifax again on June 1, 1944.

As you perhaps know, the authorities have refused to give me a visa to return to India. I am not sure what this means. As I see it, it may mean one of two things. (1) It may mean that this is simply a war measure, taken because of war expediencies. The phrase "at this time" makes possible that interpretation. (2) It may mean that there is no place in India for an American missionary who asks for the freedom to express his moral conviction regarding India's right to self-government when asked by Indians, although that missionary pledges himself to take no part in politics and further pledges that he would strive to be a reconciling influence between Britain and India and between Indians themselves—such a missionary would not be wanted.

In other words, Jones wanted to know why he had been denied a visa to return to India. He closed his letter expressing "my deep appreciation of you and your Christian spirit." Six days later on June 7 Lord Halifax replied:

I am making some enquiries into the question of your Visa to return to India and as to why it has been refused. I shall hope to write to you further in the course of a few days.

Lord Halifax's inquiries apparently took longer than he anticipated because it was not until July 8 that Jones received a letter from the British Embassy in Washington. The letter, signed by Ronald I. Campbell, read

In the absence of the Ambassador in England I am writing to you about the question of your journey to India.

I am glad to be able to assure you that your first interpretation of the words "at this time" is correct. I have ascertained that, should you renew your application at an appropriate moment later on, that is to say at the end of the war, the Government of India will be ready to reconsider their present decision.

But Jones was still not satisfied. He wrote again to Lord Halifax on September 8.

I am glad to be assured at this point, that the refusal of the visa was a measure taken because of the exigencies of war. That clears the matter somewhat. But not fully.

I am puzzled at this point: If this refusal of the visa is a war measure, then one would expect that all American missionaries would be refused visas to India during the war. But some are granted visas and allowed to go back. . . .

On the face of it, then, it would seem not to be a war measure, but a matter of the views on political issues in India of the missionaries concerned. Is that the point at issue?

All I asked for was the privilege of stating, when asked, that I believed in the moral right of India to self-government. Is that the point on which my visa was refused?

I shall await your further word. I need not tell you that I hope it can be clarified satisfactorily, for I have no taste nor desire for controversy, particularly on such an important issue with those with whom otherwise I have so much in common.

A month later, on October 5, Lord Halifax replied to Jones.

I had hoped after your earlier letters that you would not have been dissatisfied with the assurance that the Government of India's action in refusing you a visa was a temporary war measure.

I had understood this to be the point with which you were principally concerned, and that this is the attitude of the Government of India is plain from the fact that they have expressed their willingness at the end of the war to reconsider their decision.

I can of course understand that this decision should be a disappointment to you, but I think you would on your side appreciate that the Government of India, like other Governments, must reserve to itself the right of taking decisions in these matters, and also of deciding whether or not to discuss the reasons. There is, therefore, I am afraid, nothing which I can usefully add to Sir Ronald Campbell's letter of July 8.

This is a truly extraordinary exchange of letters—for several reasons. First, Jones's initial request for a visa is extraordinary because he insisted that he be able to speak openly on the issue of Indian independence if he was permitted to return to India. Had Jones simply asked for a visa without moral conditions, he might well, as Murray Titus suggested, have gone back to India before the end of the war. It is also extraordinary because of Jones's determination to discover the reason for the denial. Even after Sir Ronald Campbell had clarified the denial by explaining that the phrase, "at this time" meant that the British government would reconsider Jones's request after the war, Jones was still not satisfied. In the end the British would not give Jones a reason for their refusing him a visa. Since, however, they did permit other American missionaries to return to India during the war, the reason they denied Jones's request is almost certainly because they knew he would speak out against British imperialism and for Indian independence.

Finally, the extraordinary character of Jones's correspondence with the British Government springs from the clarity with which he adhered to his concept of the kingdom of God and from the consistency with which he applied it. All persons are equal in God's sight because all are created equally in God's own image. Therefore, all persons are endowed by God with equal moral dignity and with the right to be treated by others on the basis of equality. This fundamental tenet of the kingdom of God means that all individuals are entitled to equal opportunity in the pursuit and acquisition of economic, political, and social advantages and resources. Jones could not in good conscience return to India and fail to speak against the fundamental injustice of British imperialism in that country. He would betray his calling as a missionary evangelist and his lifelong commitment as an advocate of the kingdom of God if he did not articulate in unmistakable terms the moral bankruptcy of Great Britain's denial of every individual's God-given equality in India. This is why Jones was so dogged in his pursuit of the reason for the British Government's denial of his request for a visa to return to India. This is also why he was so appalled by Churchill's limitation of the Atlantic Charter to white European nations and why he proposed a Pacific Charter to guarantee the global application of the kingdom principle of equality.

The same kingdom principles of equality and equal opportunity motivated Jones to propose that Christian churches in the United States take responsibility for the resettlement of the Japanese Americans who were displaced from the West Coast after Pearl Harbor. Certainly the federal government, by forcefully evacuating and relocating these Americans, most of whom were loyal citizens, denied them equal rights and opportunities. Finally, he insisted on the same kingdom principle of equality in his own meetings in the United States. His acute sensitivity to God's hatred of racial discrimination led him to condemn this form of inequality long before it became the dominant domestic issue in the nation.

In the same way that kingdom of God principles motivated Jones to oppose British imperialism in India, to propose a Pacific Charter as a guarantee of equality for all people everywhere, to advocate church leadership in the resettlement of Japanese Americans, and to implement racial equality in his own meetings, so kingdom principles were also the foundation for his ideas for federal union of the Christian churches. Self-surrender, of course, is the key to Jesus' expression and embodiment of the kingdom of God in the New Testament. But while most evangelists restrict the application of self-surrender to personal morality and spirituality, Jones was more holistic and expanded this kingdom principle to corporate relationships between and among human institutions. He did not give a full explanation of how the concept of losing one's life in order to save it applied to political institutions until he wrote about federal union at length in *The Christ of the American Road* (1944). But in the late 1930s and early 1940s Jones did apply the idea of federal union to the problem of church unity. Theological and doctrinal differences among Christians not only weakened the church spiritually, they also weakened the moral voice of the church in speaking out on economic, social, and political issues. In the 1950s and 1960s, as we will see in subsequent chapters, Jones's call for federal union of the Christian churches resonated with more and more American Christians until he found himself the leader and spokesman for a nationwide grassroots movement.

13

Toward Indian Independence

Forgive this personal word in a semi-official letter. But last night I dreamed that you and I were talking about the matter of my visa to return to India when I said to you, "At heart I'm really a conservative," to which you replied, "Then I'll recommend the granting of your visa."
I am now writing in hopes of making that dream come true!
— E. Stanley Jones, August 27, 1945, letter to Lord Halifax[1]

WHEN THE BRITISH government denied him a visa to return to India, Stanley Jones had no immediate public comment. But privately he did not hesitate to express himself frankly and openly to his friends and to ask them for their reactions to the decision. "The British are adept in the art of diplomacy," he wrote to Murray Titus, on October 12, 1944, "and there is no beating them at this game. . . . But at least, they didn't dare say that the reason I put, was the reason for the refusal. They took refuge in secrecy."[2]

Five months earlier, on May 18, shortly after the British first informed him that he could not return to India "at this time," J. Waskom Pickett, Jones's colleague and one of his closest friends, wrote him that they "should try to get this reversed and to insure your return to India." Pickett's comment, however, was not just the product of his deep friendship and personal sympathy for Jones. His very next sentence read, "I am eager that this [decision] should not be permitted to cause new antagonism against Great Britain in the U.S.A."[3]

What prompted Pickett to include domestic and international politics in his letter was an article Jones had just published in the *Christian Century* entitled "Gandhi and Christian Missions." Jones had written, "A prominent missionary is quoted as saying that Gandhi is 'Enemy Number One' of the Indian Christians."[4] Pickett asked, "Is it possible that you were referring to me as 'the prominent missionary'?" He also wondered if the *South Carolina Advocate,* a Methodist newspaper in South Carolina that had attributed the statement to Pickett, was Jones's source in his *Christian Century* article. The statement in the South Carolina newspaper, Pickett explained, was not accurate. "What I had said was that depressed classes leaders in India called Gandhi the public enemy number one of their people." He added, "[Y]ou are not fully cognizant of the situation as it has unfolded in India since you were last there."

On May 31, Jones replied in a three-page single-spaced letter.[5] He was "especially grateful" for Pickett's support of his desire to return to India. "I want to get back to India, Waskom," he wrote, "for my heart is there. But I don't want to work in a mouse-trap. I must be free to express my convictions. If not, then I prefer to stay here and do what I can from this angle."

The tone of the rest of the letter is that of a stern lecture on the evils of British imperialism in India and on the perilous future of Christianity in an independent India. When he expressed his deepest convictions and when he was fully convinced that he was being guided by the Inner Voice, Stanley did not let friendship inhibit his frankness.

> I was troubled, Waskom, over the clipping sent to me from the S.C. Advocate. It seemed to me, Waskom, that you were leading the missionary movement into a head-on collision with the national forces of India working for freedom. That would mean that the missionary movement would have no part in a free India. . . .
> [T]he future belongs to nationalist India and not British Imperialism. If you back British imperialism, you are backing the wrong horse. Its day is about to be ended as far as India is concerned. A part of our job, as I see it, is to help the Indian Christians to orient themselves to that free India in which they will have to live and function.

At the end of his letter, to reassure his friend that he did not intend his broad categorical declarations as a personal attack, Stanley wrote,

> I am sorry, dear Waskom, to have to be at seeming odds with you on so vital a question. I love and admire you and have stood by you. But your attitude has troubled me. . . .
> Forgive me if I've seemed over-blunt. I love you deeply even amid this disagreement and shall continue to do so. But I've bared my heart to you.

Clearly, Jones's heart was in India. But he did not return to his adopted land until January 1946. "In the meantime," as he informed his friends and patrons in a circular letter dated September 4, 1944,

> I shall try to be a missionary to my own people and shall continue to speak in behalf of India's freedom while here in America, where it counts more than if I were in India. I shall get back to India for India is bound to get her freedom.[6]

Although domestic politics was not the focus of Jones's efforts to be a missionary to his own people, the letters he wrote during the presidential election year of 1944 do reveal his political views. For example, on August 8, 1944, just after the conclusion of the Democratic National Convention in Chicago, he wrote to Vice President Henry A. Wallace on behalf of his Northeast Christian Ashram at Lake Winnipesaukee, New Hampshire. Wallace, an outspoken liberal, was dropped from the Democratic ticket by the Convention and was replaced by the more moderate Harry Truman. (This, of course, was a fateful decision, because Roosevelt died in 1945 shortly after he was inaugurated for his fourth term.) Jones's letter to Wallace expressed his dismay at the Democrats' failure to renominate the Vice President.

> This is just a note to say that a group of us here, representing many denominations and many states of the Union, have asked me to express to you our profound sorrow that you were not re-nominated for the Vice Presidency. We feel that a tragic blunder has been made. . . .
> We, therefore, would reiterate our faith in you and in the part you are going to play in the re-making of the world. Perhaps God can use you more greatly in some other position than that of Vice President.[7]

Wallace replied a week later, on August 14, 1944:

> Knowing your background, I am sure you will agree with me when I say my defeat at Chicago will probably bring me a greater opportunity than my victory.

Jones's disillusionment with the Democratic Party may be the reason he wrote to his friends Rob and Dar Robinson on November 2, 1944, "I am not voting for anybody because I did not register. Thomas [Norman Thomas, the Socialist candidate for president] would be the only man I could honestly vote for."[8]

*   *   *

Certainly the strangest political incident of Stanley Jones's long and eventful career was a truly bizarre chain of events culminating in his being visited by two FBI agents in early February 1944. The incident involved not only Jones and the FBI agents but a confidential FBI informant; FBI Director J. Edgar Hoover; Harry L. Hopkins, special assistant to Franklin D. Roosevelt; and President Roosevelt himself.

A letter from Stanley to the President, dated December 30, 1943, provides the background for this most unusual combination of circumstances.[9] He had written on behalf of a diverse but representative group of Christian ministers who met in Washington "for a three days period of meditation and prayer to face together the issues that profoundly affect humanity in these days of crisis." His letter continued,

> We would share with you Mr. President, a deep concern. Our wide contacts through this country have revealed to us a growing feeling that the starving of Europe, especially the children in occupied countries, should be fed. . . . There is the further growing conviction that the one thing that is blocking the feeding of these starving people is the attitude of those in authority in Britain. This fact is causing a growing strain on the good relationships of Britain and America; the truth is that it is endangering those relationships. . . .
>
> [W]e appeal to you, Mr. President, to use the power of your position and influence to get food speedily to these starving millions. We are convinced that in doing so you will be backed by the conscience of this country.
>
> We feel that you, and you alone, hold the key to this situation. We trust, Mr. President, you will use that key.

Even before Roosevelt received Stanley's letter, the FBI was receiving information from a confidential source about Jones's involvement in political activities.[10] On December 9, 1943, Hoover wrote to Harry Hopkins informing him about a mimeographed letter dated October 27, 1943, and addressed, "Dear Ashram Comrades." It was written by John J. Handsaker, a minister of the Christian Church in Portland, Oregon, to the Reverend Archie Matson of Ketchikan, Alaska. In his letter to Hopkins, Hoover attached the following excerpt from Handsaker's letter.

> A few days ago [Handsaker had written] I received a letter from Brother Stanley in which he made the following comment: "A friend of mine was taking dinner with the President and Mrs. Roosevelt. He turned to Mrs. Roosevelt and said, 'Why is it we are not feeding the starving of Europe? Is it because we don't want to or is it because we can't?' Her reply was, 'I don't know, I will ask my husband.' So she turned to him and said, 'Franklin, Mr. Sonso [So-and-so?] asks the question, why are we not feeding the starving of Europe? Is it because we can't or is it because we don't want to?' His reply was, 'Nothing has created more strain between us and Mr. Churchill than this question, it had brought us almost to the breaking point. If the country will force my hand in the matter I shall be very glad. This is confidential and must not be quoted in any written statement, but I pass it on to you as it is an invitation to bring pressure to bear upon the administration.'"

Hoover's letter identified "Brother Stanley" as E. Stanley Jones, "a rather well-known missionary who spent a number of years in India." He also quoted Handsaker's advice to Matson to "keep up your pressure on Washington and help force the President's hand." Hoover's letter to Hopkins was delivered by special messenger.

In response to Hoover's letter, Hopkins sent a short typewritten memo, dated December 20, 1943, to Grace Tully, Roosevelt's secretary. The memo read,

> Dear Grace:
> Will you please show this to the President and return it for my files when he has finished with it.
> H.L.H.

Two days later, on December 22, Roosevelt replied to Hopkins.

> I do not know what you are going to do about this but the fact remains that the conversation as reported between Mrs. Roosevelt and myself at a dinner party is not true.
> F.D.R.

On the basis of this memo from Roosevelt, Hopkins wrote to Hoover on December 30 that the President

> has advised me that the conversation, as reported between Mrs. Roosevelt and himself at a dinner party, was not true.
> I don't quite know what you can do about it, but something may occur to you.
> Cordially yours,

Finally, on January 10, 1944, Hoover reported to Hopkins what he had done.

> In view of the information set forth in your letter, the individuals concerned are being appropriately contacted in order that the falsity of the story may be brought to their attention and in order that they will not be in the position of continuing to unknowingly disseminate such false statements.

This was the series of events and documents that resulted in the FBI's visit to Jones. He told the Robinsons about the visit of the two agents in a letter dated February 14, 1944.

> Their mission was this: We do not come officially, they began, but we have heard that the statement has been made that the President said there is a difference between him & Mr. Churchill re the feeding of the starving of Europe & that this statement was made at an interview or dinner party. We

have heard that the statement came from you. We have checked up on the story and the White House says that there is no difference of opinion between Mr. Roosevelt & Mr. Churchill & that no such statement was ever made, and that the interview never took place. So we have come in a friendly way to inform you of this. They were very nice friendly young men, one of them a Methodist Youth Fellowship youth.

I told them where I got the story, from you, Dar, & [I] told them that you got it, I think, thru Dorothy Datzer, and she from Clarence Pickett & that C.P. was the person from whom it came. And that it was all seemingly very straight. I told them I would check up with you & Clarence P. Frankly, I think this is one of those double-faced transactions which is rather characteristic. He [Roosevelt] did say it to C.P. & then when there was danger of something coming between him & Churchill he denies it. Am I right?

In the interview he said he wished the American people would force his hand so we could get food across. When they began to do it, then he pulled back by a denial.

Jones's last written reference to the FBI incident, as far as I know, was his February 21, 1944, letter to Mrs. Robinson.

I think the F.B.I. men . . . came from, as the boys said, the White House, so I am puzzled about it.

I did wrong in using the story publicly; but if the President wanted pressure to be brought upon him to force his hands, then I do not see why it could not be used to do so. However, it was a mistake to use it in public. Perhaps the best thing to do is to say nothing about it and let it rest. I shall not use it again in public.

I do not know from the letters and memos I obtained from the Asbury Seminary Archives and from the Franklin D. Roosevelt Library whether Clarence Pickett was, as Jones suspected, the source of the story about the alleged disagreement between Roosevelt and Churchill. More important, we will probably never know whether the report Jones received about the conversation between Franklin and Eleanor Roosevelt was true. But it is certainly possible that Churchill, on the basis of wartime necessity, opposed shipments of food to hungry people in occupied Europe. And it is also possible that Churchill and Roosevelt disagreed on this issue and that Roosevelt deliberately leaked this fact at the dinner party with Mrs. Roosevelt in order to encourage public opposition to Churchill's blocking food shipments and to strengthen his hand politically in dealing with the British.

The FBI visit to Jones in early 1944 was not Jones's last personal contact with the agency. On May 27, 1944, L. R. Pennington, an FBI employee, wrote a memo complaining about a speech he heard Jones make on the previous day at the Daughters of the American Revolution (DAR) Hall in Washington, D.C. Pennington reported that Jones in his address said that the FBI had "thoroughly investigated" all Japanese "released from Japanese Relocation Centers and gave their blessing on the release." After Jones's speech Pennington informed Jones that the FBI did not investigate all Japanese released from relocation centers, the agency merely checked the names of those released by the War Relocation Authority to determine whether FBI files contained any information detrimental to these individuals. Pennington, in order to make certain Jones understood the distinction, wrote to Jones on June 8, 1944. Eleven days later, on June 19, Jones acknowledged Pennington's letter. Jones thanked Pennington for his letter and wrote, "the matter is now quite clear. The FBI does not recommend people for relocation, it simply checks up on them."

Pennington, however, was not convinced that the issue was "quite clear," so he wrote to Jones again on July 6. Pennington said, "I am afraid you do not as yet quite understand the limitations on the activities of the Federal Bureau of Investigation with reference to the release of Japanese from War Relocation Centers." Once again, Jones wrote to Pennington on July 22 and thanked him for his letter. Then, with a bit of subtle sarcasm, Jones said, "I am glad that you have patiently explained the matter to me. I read your letter to a Japanese-American to let him know your view-point. He seemed to quite understand it."

Pennington, of course, was sensitive to Jones's implication that the FBI had investigated the loyalty of Japanese Americans released from relocation centers. Japan, after all, was at that time the mortal enemy of the United States, the treacherous aggressor of Pearl Harbor, the nation that in 1944 was still killing thousands of American soldiers, sailors, and marines in the bloody island-hopping campaign that eventually ended World War II in the Pacific.[11]

* * *

Although Stanley did occasionally become involved in domestic politics during the course of his evangelistic work in the United States, more typical of his activities in the mid-1940s are the events and accomplishments he reported in his September 4, 1944, circular letter. "It has been the best year of my life," he wrote, "the very best." Two months after *The Christ of the American Road* was published on June 15, the first edition of 50,000 copies sold out and another edition was being printed. Moreover, by September 1944, sales of *Abundant Living* had passed the 300,000 mark. But more gratifying to Jones than the commercial success of his books were the testimonies of his readers. A Chinese bishop sent word that Generalissimo Chiang Kai-shek read a page of *Abundant Living* every day for his devotions. In addition, a doctor told Jones that he gave 250 copies of *Abundant Living* to his patients—"instead of a purgative!"[12]

Stanley was now collecting material for a new book of daily devotional meditations, he wrote, and was "itching to get at it," although it would not be published until 1946. The book entitled, *The Way*, would become his personal favorite. Finally, assuming that he would soon be able to return to India, he outlined in the same circular letter a proposed schedule of activities "for the next ten years." For six months of each year, from January until June, he would be in India. He would hold evangelistic meetings between January and April and would be at the Sat Tal Ashram during May and June. Then for the next six months of each year, from July through December, he would be in the United States, leading ashrams in July and August and conducting evangelistic campaigns from September until the end of the year. Once the British government permitted him to return to India, this tentative plan was, in fact, the schedule Jones followed for most of the rest of his life.

In his next circular letter, dated December 30, 1944, Stanley highlighted two series of evangelistic meetings, one in London, Ontario, Canada, and the other in St. Louis, Missouri.[13] With respect to the Canadian meetings he wrote,

> I have never had quite such splendid preparation as they made at London. For instance, twenty leading laymen called on the firms and factories of the City and asked the heads of these organizations to do three things: (1) Will your firm sponsor the Mission, allowing the use of the name as sponsor? (2) Will you send a personal invitation to all of your employees? (3) Will you, as head of the firm, come to a luncheon of laymen? They presented a luncheon ticket then and there. Of the two hundred and eight firms called on, one hundred and seventy seven agreed to the three propositions; even a brewery was willing to sponsor the Mission, but we drew the line there!

The St. Louis meetings were unique because they were the only mission he had held that was devoted exclusively to high school students. He had often spoken to high schools in the United States as part of a broader city-wide mission, but St. Louis was the first city in which Jones focused his evangelistic meetings on teenagers. In eight days, he reported, he visited sixteen high schools and spoke to approximately twenty-five thousand students. "Probably half of them," he wrote in his circular letter, "were under no real religious influence." On December 13, 1944, he wrote to Miss Nellie that on that day he "spoke to three thousand [students] in two assemblies, one colored and the other white." Between his public addresses, he spent hours in interviews, sometimes one-on-one, sometimes with two or more, and sometimes with an entire classroom of students.

Two other outstanding events of 1944 for Stanley Jones were meetings he held in Columbus, Ohio, and Buffalo, New York, for the creation of an organization that became the Association for the Realization of a United

Church in America. His leadership was the inspiration for the meetings, and his concept of federal union was the focus of the discussion. In a letter dated December 18, 1944, sent to those who had attended the two meetings, he summarized the outcome of the meetings, including the decision that he would serve as temporary president of the organization until "a leading layman" could be found to serve as president. In addition, both meetings decided that federal union would be the basis of the organization's efforts to establish one united Christian church in the United States. The Buffalo meeting unanimously adopted a statement of the purpose of the organization.

> We commit ourselves to the general principle of Federal Union as offering the most promising plan for the realization of a United Church in America, but we advocate that the whole matter be studied for a year before the formulation of a stated plan to be presented to the denominations and other units for possible action.[14]

One of the people Jones hoped would attend the Columbus meeting was his good friend, Dr. O. G. Robinson. Unfortunately, "Rob," as Stanley called him, could not attend. But Stanley did write to Rob after the meeting in a letter dated November 2, 1944, informing him briefly about the result of the meeting and asking him for suggestions for "suitable officers." As we will see in the following chapters, the Columbus and Buffalo meetings were the beginning of a grassroots movement in the United States to unite the various Christian denominations into one church organized on the basis of Jones's kingdom of God principle of federal union.

While Jones was in St. Louis conducting the mission for high school students, he also attended a meeting conducted by two officials from the U.S. State Department "to acquaint the public with Dumbarton Oaks." Dumbarton Oaks was the site of an international conference at which the United Nations was first proposed as a world organization committed to maintain peace after World War II. In a letter dated December 15, 1944, Jones wrote to Rob Robinson that he applauded the purpose of the meeting. "[I]t is fine to have them [the State Department] going around this way. It is the first time democracy of the State Department has come to the country. This augurs well for the future." Approximately fifty people representing some twenty organizations attended the meeting.

After discussing the Dumbarton Oaks proposals, the State Department officials asked for a vote on three questions. The first question was, "Do the proposals go too far?" No one, Jones said, agreed with this question. The second question was, "Are the proposals correct as they are?" "Two hands went up," Jones reported. Finally, when the last question was asked, "Does the Dumbarton Oaks proposal not go far enough?" Jones wrote, "The whole of the rest of the company of about fifty people put up their hands." He concluded, "I think the State Department people must have had a jolt."

If the State Department officials in St. Louis received a jolt when almost everyone at the meeting agreed that the Dumbarton Oaks proposals did not go far enough, the Secretary of State, Edward R. Stettinius, must have been knocked off his feet by a letter he received from Jones shortly after the St. Louis meeting. The letter, dated December 18, 1944, and written just three days after his letter to Rob Robinson, pointed out "just one defect" in the Dumbarton Oaks proposals discussed in St. Louis. "As the proposals now stand the whole thing seems a military alliance between five nations with a padding of democracy around it. That is not collective security—it is five nations telling the world what to do."[15]

The five nations Jones refers to are the five World War II Allies—the United States, the United Kingdom, France, Russia, and China. Under the Dumbarton Oaks proposals, these nations became the five permanent members of the United Nations Security Council. Each of the five had the right to veto any action, including military action, taken by the Security Council. The problem with giving ultimate power to these five nations, Jones explained, was that "no five nations are good enough or wise enough to boss the world."

> As I see it there is only one thing that can save the proposals and make them acceptable to the mass of mankind: Let it be inserted in the proposals that these powers vested in the Security Council are temporary, for the duration of the disturbed period following the war; that as soon as practicable, say within five years following the war, the powers of the Security Council will be transferred to the [General] Assembly; that security will then be a world responsibility; that these five powers will, like the rest, be amenable to the Assembly.

According to the Dumbarton Oaks proposals, Jones insisted, the five permanent members of the Security Council would appear to the world to be exactly what they were, namely, five nations "grasping world power under the guise of keeping the world at peace." There would be no real peace under these proposals unless the five nations became "amenable to something beyond themselves. They must lose their lives to find them again." Jones was especially concerned about the effect of the proposals on the scores of nations, including India, who were subject to European imperialism.

> To have five nations, amenable to nothing but themselves, dominating the world perpetually and in doing so freezing the status quo with its imperialisms, is anything but a pleasant prospect. Rather it can be looked forward to only with dread, for the peace they imposed would be a sullen, resentful, dangerous peace.

Jones concluded his letter with a personal appeal to Secretary Stettinius.

> I trust, Mr. Stettinius, you will be courageous enough to insist upon this fundamental change. If so, you may completely change the complexion of the world situation. Now it is dark and foreboding.

On January 25, 1945, Leo Pasvolsky, special assistant to the Secretary of State, replied on behalf of Stettinius.[16] He welcomed the "opportunity to answer the questions which you ask and to endeavor to remove the doubts and fears which you express over certain aspects of the Proposals." In response to Jones's blunt criticism that the proposed international organization was really a military alliance disguised as a peace-keeping body, Pasvolsky said,

> The primary purpose of the Proposals is to create a system not for the use of force but for the collaboration of all peace-loving states in the pacific settlement of disputes and in the promotion of human welfare. . . . In their security provisions the Proposals merely recognize the fact that certain states, because of their extraordinary resources and capacities, necessarily and inevitably have the primary responsibility for maintaining international peace and security. . . . The Proposals do not add to the military and economic strength which these states already possess; they merely provide a mechanism by which this strength may be used for the benefit of all peace-loving states.

Pasvolsky's letter is a serious, thoughtful, and reasoned response to Jones's critique of the Dumbarton Oaks proposals. However, he does acknowledge that the five permanent members of the Security Council do "receive . . . new powers" insofar as they have "special responsibilities for the maintenance of international peace and security." And this, of course, is the whole point of Jones's criticism. But on a deeper level Paslovsky and Jones have radically different perspectives on the world. Paslovsky speaks from the "realistic" perspective of things as they appear to the purely secular mind. Jones speaks on behalf of the ultimate reality of the kingdom of God. Jones knew that no organization would maintain international peace if it sacrificed God's intention for the so-called collective security of the world as defined by the victorious World War II Allies. Just as no man or woman can enjoy the full and abundant blessing of a personal relationship with Jesus Christ unless he or she renounces sin and dies to the slavery of selfishness, so no nation or people can experience true peace and genuine cooperation with its neighbors unless it renounces self-interest by voluntarily giving up some of its sovereignty to an international organization whose ultimate allegiance is the kingdom of God as revealed by Jesus Christ.

* * *

In 1945, Stanley planned a trip to Latin America. He would hold evangelistic meetings in Mexico, Costa Rica, Panama, Peru, Chile, Argentina, Uruguay, and Brazil. He had visited Mexico and Cuba in 1943. That was when evangelical Christianity was not popular, and he "could get a public hearing only by being advertised as a friend of Gandhi and Tagore."[17] Now, in 1945, even with the increased interest in Christian evangelism, there were serious questions about whether he should go to Latin America at all. One problem was explained in a December 28, 1944, letter written by George P. Howard, the contact person for his local arrangements in Uruguay.[18] Howard wrote,

> On the part of one or two of our national leaders there was a little hesitancy regarding the advisability of Dr. Jones' visit just now. This applies especially in countries like Argentina and Peru where the Roman Catholic church is making much of the argument that Protestantism is a foreign or imported religion. . . . [P]ossibly it might be better for him to wait for the above reason until 1946 in the hope that Catholic aggression would be less violent by that time.

The other problem was the timing of this proposed visit. It coincided with the San Francisco Conference at which the Dumbarton Oaks proposals were finalized, and there had been talk that Stanley should attend. While he was in São Paulo, Brazil, at the end of his South American tour, Murray Titus wrote to him on May 31, 1945,

> I am sure your work down in South America will bear much fruit and be a means of better understanding between the people down there and the United States. It is a shame, however, that this trip coincided with the San Francisco Conference, for I am sure you would have been able to make a real contribution there as a consultant from the Federal Council of Churches.[19]

In an *Indian Witness* article, Jones referred to "a certain amount of pressure" being put on him not to go to Latin America because of the San Francisco Conference.[20] Did Jones miss an opportunity to influence the structure and substance of the United Nations by not attending the San Francisco Conference? Did the Inner Voice speak through Titus and perhaps others when they urged Jones to organize his Latin American tour around the conference? We do know that an organized group of Protestant churches "did influence the final wording of the Charter of the United Nations"[21] with respect to the protection of religious beliefs. If Jones had been in San Francisco, would the Christian churches have had a greater voice in the language of the charter or even in the organization and powers of such basic institutions as the Security Council and the

General Assembly? These are intriguing questions for which we have no definitive answers. But the questions do suggest that Jones's presence at the San Francisco Conference might have been an important influence at this crucial formative stage of the United Nations.

In the end Stanley did not regret his decision to go ahead with his Latin American trip. He arrived, he wrote afterward in his *Indian Witness* article, "at the right psychological moment," when there was a spiritual vacuum that only evangelical Christianity could fill. Two factors created this vacuum: first, the end of the war in Europe (VE Day was celebrated while he was in Argentina) followed by an uncertain peace; second, the religious and intellectual skepticism that was the result of the authoritarian control of the Roman Catholic Church. The more important factor, however, was the Catholic Church.

> Latin America is just as religious as North America, except among the intellectuals. The difference is in the kind of God. The God mediated through the Roman Catholicism of Latin America has weakened the character of the people. The church has refused to allow them to think or act independently. This has produced a mentality of spiritual and intellectual subservience.[22]

Moreover, spiritual and intellectual subservience created political subservience. He noted that except for Uruguay there was hardly a genuine democracy in Latin America. "Why? Because the church has been a dictatorship." For example, at the time of his visit, the most repressive dictatorship in Latin America was probably in Argentina. Stanley described in his *Christian Century* article what happened on his first day in Buenos Aires.

> Fifteen minutes after we reached the hotel in Buenos Aires two volleys of shots sounded in the street below. We ran to the window and saw the mounted police charging the crowds. The official report said two killed and seven wounded, but the people say there were seventy killed. A reign of terror was on. . . .
>   For Argentina is a suppressed nation—suppressed by a fascist-minded, jittery government resting on bayonets.[23]

Because of this identification of political with religious dictatorship in Argentina and elsewhere in Latin America, and because of the deep and widespread opposition to both forms of repression, Jones found an exciting opportunity for evangelical Christianity. Instead of being the religion of Yankee imperialism, Protestantism, and especially evangelical Protestantism, was becoming the religion of personal freedom and political democracy. This new intellectual and spiritual climate opened the door for Christian evangelism in almost every place he visited. He mailed a hurried handwritten note on hotel stationery to Murray Titus from Santiago, Chile, on April 29, 1945.[24]

I'm having a grand time. I haven't time to give a detailed description. . . . But today I spoke in the Municipal Theatre here in Santiago—first time ever given to Evangelicals. Mayor present & read address of welcome. Twice as many tickets asked for as accomodation—packed out. The address was broadcast—first time that [was] ever done for the Evangelicals, so they say. It was broadcast from 10-12 A.M.—2 hrs.! music & all. Marvellous attention & response. Thus it goes.

Stanley maintained a very hectic pace on this trip. "At one place," he wrote in July, toward the end of it, "I found they had me down for eight addresses one day—I took six. In several other places I took seven! But I came out at the end of the series fresh and well." What sustained him through these pressing and ceaseless demands on his time were, first of all, the inner resources of the Holy Spirit. But Jones was also strengthened by the sense that Latin America was at the brink of a genuine revival. He wrote in his October 25, 1945, *Indian Witness* article,

The stage is set, psychologically and physically, for the greatest period of advance the [evangelical] movement has ever dreamed of—possible Reformation movement that may run through Latin America. . . . I came from Latin America with a great hope in my heart—a hope that this young Evangelical Church now come of age, may be great enough and Christian enough and united enough to meet its hour of great opportunity.[25]

* * *

When World War II ended with the surrender of Japan in August 1945, Stanley was more than ready to return to India. Since the British government had said that it would reconsider his request for a visa after the war, he wrote to Sir Girga Shankar Bajpai, who was then handling requests for visas to India, in the latter part of August 1945. He also wrote to Lord Halifax on August 27, asking him to support his request for a visa. He received further encouragement from Mr. Rhys Davies, a member of Parliament in the Labour Government of Britain, who was visiting the United States and giving lectures across the country. Jones met Davies and explained his request for a visa to return to India. He wrote to Diffendorfer about Davies's reaction.

He was very interested in the matter of my being deprived of the visa to go back to India. He said the matter was being suppressed in England, that it would have raised a great storm had it been known. . . . He said if no attention was paid to it, he would raise the matter in Parliament.[26]

In November 1945 Stanley finally received the permission he had been seeking.[27] M. Ahmad, the second secretary for the Agent General for India in Washington, wrote to him on November 16 that "the Government of India have now agreed to the grant of a visa to you to return to India." However, on the same day Ahmad also wrote to Diffendorfer that the government of India was not

> able to accept his [Jones's] construction of the pledge which enjoins non-participation in political affairs and which requires the abstention of Dr. Jones from the public propagation of his views on Indian politics. They have requested the Agent General to point out that under the arrangements for the entry of foreign Missionaries into India the Mission is responsible for the observance of the undertaking by Dr. Jones.[28]

In other words, regardless of Jones's statement of the conditions under which he would return to India, it was the Methodist Division of Foreign Missions and not Jones who was accountable for his pledge "to do nothing contrary to, or in diminution of, the authority of the lawfully constituted" government of India. When Jones replied to the agent general for India on November 26, he thanked him for the visa to return to India, but then added,

> The Government of India have granted my visa, for which I am grateful, while differing from my position. I shall reciprocate and accept the visa and faithfully abide by the conditions under which it is granted, while differing from the position of the Government of India.

Jones pointed out to the agent general that he had not asked for the right to publicly proclaim his "views on Indian politics." He would, he said, refrain from taking part in politics in India and would endeavor "to be a reconciling influence between Britain and India and between Indians themselves," but he would insist on the right to say, when asked in his public meetings, that India had the moral right of self-government. Jones concluded his letter to the agent general by saying that he had asked the secretary of the Methodist Division of Foreign Missions to sign the missionary pledge on his behalf.

Whether Jones returned to India under his own conditions or under conditions imposed by the British, the point is that he went back to his adopted homeland. He told his friends and patrons in a circular letter on January 3, 1946, that he had booked passage on a ship sailing from New York on January 10. "These have been great years I have spent in my native land," he wrote, "and I am not sorry that I have spent them here to do what I could to help America find God in this crisis." He had obeyed the instructions of the Inner Voice in March 1941 to give up his plans for India and to remain in the United States to express God's kingdom reality and to apply it to the catastrophic "unreality" of World War II.

Although his circular letter stated that he would sail from New York on January 10, he may have left earlier, because he wrote to Miss Nellie in a handwritten postscript on January 7,

> I am on board ship & about to sail. I'm going through some letters & found your letter unsent. So sorry. But it was Providence that I found it. I will send it off with the pilot. We are about to leave.
>
> The ship [is] so large & thus there are four in the cabin—three of us are missionaries & one a Parsee doctor. Four doctors—2 medical & 2 divinity in one cabin!

On his arrival in India Stanley was delighted to be reunited with his family. But he was almost immediately on his own again. Mabel's poor health would not, as we learned in chapter 3, permit her to remain in India. Not long after Stanley's arrival, when she had found suitable leadership for the boys' school, she returned to the United States, where she continued to support her boys through scholarship funds, which she administered. Jones's daughter and son-in-law also returned to the United States in 1946. James K. Mathews was a Methodist pastor and missionary in India, and could have served as a chaplain in the armed services during World War II. Instead he chose to join the U.S. Army Quartermaster Corps in India, because he wanted to live under the same hardships that other American military personnel endured. In 1946, after Eunice and James's return to the U.S., James became the secretary for India for the Methodist Division of Foreign Missions in New York.

Stanley's first circular letter after he returned to India (March 30, 1946) recorded his astonishment that the country in which he had arrived "was not the India I left five and a half years before. It was rocked with strife and conflict and filled with bitterness and hate." What had happened since 1940 to make his beloved adopted country so different that he no longer recognized it? The most obvious answer is the war. But how had the war affected India and how had it affected the relationship between Great Britain and India? Did the war help or hurt India's long struggle for independence?

In February 1946 the British government in London announced that three cabinet ministers would go to India to draft a plan for self-government.[29] At this point the biggest obstacle to self-rule was not the intransigence of the British but the deep and often violent conflict between Hindus and Muslims. The leader of the Muslim League in India was Muhammad Ali Jinnah. Originally an Indian nationalist who supported the Indian National Congress and its goal of Indian independence, Jinnah by the late 1930s became "a bitter Muslim communalist" whose goal was the creation of a separate Muslim state independent of both Great Britain and Hindu India.[30] Jinnah and the Muslim League, of course, finally achieved their goal with the creation of Pakistan. But Gandhi and the leadership of the Congress Party only accepted the partition of Pakistan from India after years of incessant and bloody communal violence between Hindus and Muslims. So, the primary task of the British cabinet mission in 1946 was to accommodate both Hindu and Muslim demands within the framework of self-government. The mission proposed a national government for British India whose powers would be limited to defense, foreign affairs, and communications. All other government powers would be held and exercised by semi-independent provinces. Special provisions for communal issues were made in both national and provincial governments so that the interests of both Hindu-majority and Muslim-majority areas would be protected.

The cabinet mission was also charged with setting up an interim government, which would supervise the selection of a constituent assembly to write the permanent constitution for a free India. Unfortunately, because Muslims and Hindus could not agree on the composition of the interim government, the Muslim League withdrew from the cabinet mission negotiations, and Jinnah established August 16, 1946, as "Direct Action Day, when Muslims were to begin their struggle for Pakistan." The result, in the words of one Indian historian, "was the biggest and bloodiest outbreak of communal violence under the British regime" up to that time.[31] Over the next few months some twelve thousand people were killed, and many more were injured or lost their homes as the violence spread from Calcutta to East Bengal and Bihar.

Finally, on February 20, 1947, the British government in London announced that it would transfer power to an independent India no later than June 1948. The government also announced the appointment of Lord Mountbatten as the new viceroy to supervise the political transition. However, in view of the unresolved tension between Muslims and Hindus, the British in the end did not really transfer power, they simply abandoned it. Mountbatten worked quickly to prepare for independence, dividing the Indian subcontinent into three parts—India, West Pakistan, and East Pakistan. (Today East Pakistan is Bangladesh and West Pakistan is Pakistan.) He set an early date in 1947 for independence, August 14 for Pakistan and August 15 for India. But as the day of independence approached, violence erupted in a fury of ethnic cleansing along the borders of India and Pakistan. In Muslim-majority districts the Muslims attacked the minority Hindus. In Hindu-majority and Sikh-majority districts Hindus and Sikhs attacked the minority Muslims. This time the result of the communal violence was a genuine holocaust with hundreds of thousands killed and with an estimated 10 million refugees. Professor Ranbir Vohra in his *The Making of India* gives this assessment of the continuing impact of communalism in India.

Theoretically, communalism, having fulfilled its purpose, should have died with the birth of Pakistan. Unfortunately, it continued to flourish. In fact, one can conclude that communalism, more than anything else, has thwarted the process of nation building in the independent nation-state of India.[32]

When Jones arrived in India in early 1946, these political developments, especially the Hindu-Muslim issue, had an immediate and direct effect on his work. On April 12, 1946, he wrote to Jinnah, speaking as one who was "detached both from the Indian and the English side of things" but who was "deeply interested in the finding of a solution of the present problems." He proposed "a possible way out" of the impasse between Hindus and Muslims, which was in many ways quite similar to the British cabinet mission plan. First, he suggested that the Congress Party accept "the principle of Pakistan." Second, he suggested an agreement between India and Pakistan to form what was essentially a federal union with respect to "defence, foreign affairs and other areas of mutual interest." Then with respect to matters peculiar to India and peculiar to Pakistan, Jones recommended the creation of two constituent assemblies, one to draw up a constitution for India and the other to draw up a constitution for Pakistan. At the end of his letter he asked Jinnah whether he would accept his suggestions "in whole or in part," emphasizing that his ideas were "entirely" his own and concluding that "I represent no one but myself, except perhaps the millions who desire that a solution may be found that India may go on to an orderly progress." Jinnah's April 27, 1946, reply was noncommittal. He thanked Jones for his letter and said that he had read the suggestions "with great interest." However, Jinnah continued, "I hope you will understand, it is not possible for me to discuss them by means of correspondence."[33]

This was not Jones's last contact with Jinnah. Later, in 1947, as India moved into the last months of British rule, Jones tried one last time to break the deadlock between Hindus and Moslems. But in 1946, during the remainder of his six months' stay in India, he focused his efforts on evangelistic meetings and on his Sat Tal Ashram. Jones spoke in many of the places where he had spoken before the war, including Lucknow, Hyderabad, Travancore at the Syrian Convention, Vellore, and Madras. In all of these places, he wrote in his March 30, 1946, circular letter, "My theme is always Christ, no matter where I begin. And we have the message which India so deeply needs."

During his six months in the United States in 1946, Jones, as usual, conducted public meetings throughout the country and in the summer led his Christian ashrams. On September 29, 1946, he wrote to his daughter and son-in-law about his meetings in South Bend, Indiana, and Troy, Ohio.[34] In Troy, he said, the city did something interesting & effective. They signed up 1200 people who would buy & read Abundant Living as prep. for the Mission. Everyday the newspaper carried a reading from it & the pastors spoke on it once a month. That made the people ready. This in a town of 12,000 was good.

"We have had a grand mission here," he wrote from Oklahoma City to his son-in-law, on November 22, 1946.

We opened with 5000 the first night, and a grand after-meeting. Last night, on Youth Night, there were about 4000 out. All through the week every meeting seemed to be vital. These Oklahomans are marvellous people. For the first time in the history of the city the Negroes and Whites mingled freely in the auditorium and in the church. Last night nearly one-half of those in the choir were colored—a sight for the gods to behold—and the universe didn't seem to fall in.

Other places where Jones spoke in 1946 include York, Pennsylvania; Huntington, West Virginia; the University of Kentucky at Lexington; Indianapolis, Indiana; Mason City, Iowa; Philadelphia, Pennsylvania; Toronto, Canada; Newark, New Jersey; El Paso, Texas; Kansas City and St. Louis, Missouri; and Redlands, California. In some of these places he took along a visitation evangelism team that would go out in the city and make personal calls to win people for Christ.

In his last circular letter for 1946, dated December 30, Jones told his friends and patrons that when he returned to India he would begin some construction at Sat Tal. One of the new buildings would be a sanatorium. The purpose of the sanatorium, as he explained it earlier to Diffendorfer on July 28, 1946, was to provide for those who needed both spiritual and psychiatric help. He already had the money for the building in the form of a memorial for E.V. Moorman, who had financed Jones's first ashrams in the United States. Moreover, he believed he had found the right doctor for the sanatorium, Dr. John Plokker, a Dutch physician who had earlier served as the ashram doctor at Sat Tal. Finally, Jones explored another proposed development for Sat Tal as a place where selected individuals from East and West could come together to discuss and suggest solutions for India's many problems.

Later in the summer Jones discussed with Diffendorfer the possibility of attending a meeting of a committee of the International Missionary Council in the summer of 1947. The purpose of the committee meeting was to consider a five-year plan for evangelism throughout the world. The committee wanted Stanley "present for the entire meeting," Diffendorfer wrote to Jones on August 20, 1946. "This seems to us to be a first claim upon your time." On September 11 Diffendorfer wrote again that "the time is ripe for inaugurating a world-wide evangelistic campaign" and that

317

"yours is certainly one of the minds that should be engaged in this project." Jones replied on October 23, from Mason City, Iowa. "You have put me in a very difficult position," he wrote, "for it is a hard decision to make."[35] The problem was that he already had four ashrams scheduled for the summer of 1947, and he was reluctant to interrupt them for the IMC committee meeting. However, he did offer to attend part of the meeting. In a November 29 letter to Diffendorfer, he said that "two types of persons" would probably attend the meeting—those "who could help out in the mapping out of general programs" and those who would be responsible for "detailed planning." Jones said that he "would belong to the first type" and could attend that phase of the meeting.

Stanley, however, did not fully understand the purpose and format of the committee meeting. Diffendorfer's last letter to Jones on the matter, dated December 5, explained that

> what they [the committee] are doing is to give ample time to the consideration of the present world situation and then wait to see if the Holy Spirit will work upon the group and call them out to a great program of Evangelism in order to meet this need. Thus, it may not be until the end of the conference when such a proposal will emerge.
>
> I may say that the committee is more disappointed than I can possibly tell you that you do not find it possible to be present throughout the entire session of the council.

One is tempted to ask whether Jones's decision to stick to his schedule of summer ashrams instead of attending the IMC committee meeting was a mistake. Certainly the meeting, coming less than a year after the end of World War II, was crucial for the future of Christian missions throughout the world. Jones, as we know, had for years tried to prepare his missionary colleagues in India for the inevitable coming of independence in that country. Other nations in Asia and Africa had experienced or would soon experience similar nationalist movements. Jones's forty years of experience in India together with his international reputation as the leading Christian evangelist in the world would have been invaluable for the IMC in the summer of 1946. Had he attended the committee meetings, he might have had a deeper and more widespread impact on the future of Christian missions.

On January 5, 1947, Jones returned to India for his annual six months' visit. He knew before he left that it would be an eventful and decisive time for the future of the country. In his December 30, 1946, circular letter he wrote, "I go back to a disturbed India, but to an expectant and an awakened India, a glorious India in which to work. I fairly tingle at the thought of it!" He traveled to India by plane on the first TWA air service from New York to India. Although there were several stops along the way, it took only forty-eight hours to reach India, a considerable savings in time compared with any form of surface transportation. Air travel, however, did have some drawbacks. As Jones explained in his circular letter, "It is not easy to decide what to take and what not to take when only 65 lbs. [of luggage] are allowed and that for six months' absence!" Then, in typical Jonesian fashion, he added, "Your wealth is to be judged not by the abundance of your possessions but in the fewness of your wants!"

In his personal letters from India, Stanley remarked often about the short time of his flight from New York. He must have referred to his trip in a letter to Gandhi because of what Gandhi wrote in reply on February 20, 1947.[36] Gandhi began his letter, "Dear Dr. Stanley Jones, It almost appears as if you had never gone to America." Air travel, he observed, "effectively reduced distances" even more than trains and ships. "Nevertheless," Gandhi observed in a remark that was thoroughly characteristic of his suspicion of scientific technology, "I am not satisfied that it has increased the real happiness of mankind."

The important subject of Gandhi's letter, however, was not air travel but communal violence. He wrote from the Noakhali district of East Bengal located about 70 miles south of Dacca and 140 miles east of Calcutta. Here, and in nearby Bihar, violence flared after Jinnah announced that August 16, 1946, was Direct Action Day for Muslims who wanted to create a separate nation of Pakistan. Gandhi did what he could to stop the violence, traveling to some of the most troubled areas and applying his doctrine of *ahimsa*. *Ahimsa* is both a Hindu and Jainist concept of nonviolence, which means not just the rejection of physical violence but also "actively returning good for evil." Gandhi believed in the power and effectiveness of *ahimsa* to overcome the hatred and bloodshed of communal violence. He "went to Noakhali, to try to bring peace by his presence," say Read and Fisher in *The Proudest Day*.[37]

> You have kindly referred to my tour in Noakhali [Ghandi wrote]. The result is in God's hands. You have mentioned Bihar in the same breath. I do think that the Bihar crime was much greater than that of Noakhali in magnitude. Man became brute, I hope temporarily only, in both the places. But I haven't yet seen the light leading me to Bihar. If I can see that, I should have no hesitation in going there. I am in constant touch with the ministers and the people of Bihar. So far as I can see there is real repentance. But I cannot positively swear that I am not being misled. Immediately I feel the call, I should interrupt my work in Noakhali and hasten to Bihar. All I can say today is that I am on the watch. One thing I would add. I have come here to put my Ahimsa to test. I have no misgiving as to the effect of Ahimsa. But I am fully conscious that I may not know the whole technique and may not even be living up to what I do know. Therefore I have submitted myself for examination here. Hence if that examination demands my presence in Bihar I shall go.

Like Gandhi, Jones was in close touch with the savage violence that accompanied India's tumultuous and troubled road to independence. He reported in an April 1, 1947, circular letter that the day after he spoke in Lahore, the capital of the Punjab, "the disturbances began which have resulted in over two thousand deaths and a great deal of arson and loot[ing]." Jones also spoke in Calcutta where, in the months preceding his visit, some four thousand had died in the Hindu-Muslim riots. But in the very midst of the death, destruction, and chaos he found hope. While caste and communal loyalties brought India to the brink of civil war in cities like Calcutta and Lahore, Jones found that caste differences were disappearing in other places. When he spoke in a college founded by Dr. Ambedkar, the famous leader of the outcastes, he was astounded, he reported, that of the college's thirteen hundred students "only 55 . . . are outcastes; the rest are caste Hindus. This is a great change." Because he saw the violence around him from the perspective of the kingdom of God, Jones, unlike Gandhi, was not burdened by a sense of personal responsibility for the sporadic genocide that was occuring all around him. Looking back on his first three months in India during 1947, he concluded his April 1 circular letter: "I find myself coming to the conclusion that I have had the greatest hearing and response I have had in the forty years I have been in India."[38]

But if Jones's kingdom perspective spared him Gandhi's personal agony about the chaos and human carnage in India, that same perspective made him acutely sensitive to the spiritual and symbolic significance of Gandhi as the father of his country. On April 14, 1947, he wrote to his daughter Eunice and her family that he had recently gone back to Sabarmati, where Gandhi had his ashram, and had stayed in the same room where he had stayed for ten days years earlier when Gandhi was there. It was from Sabarmati, he recalled, that Gandhi had

> left on his salt march on Mar. 12, [19]30, saying that he would not come back to the Ashram until he had independence. He set out with a stick and courage to make war with empire. And he has won and will come back next year with his independence. That will be one of the greatest homecomings in human history.[39]

Jones assumed that India would gain its independence in 1948. Like almost everyone else, including the most well-informed observers both in India and abroad, he underestimated the speed of political events over the next few months. The bold and decisive action of the new viceroy, Lord Mountbatten, caught both the nationalist leadership in India and much of the British government in London by surprise. But before he left his Sat Tal Ashram at the end of June for his annual six-month tour of evangelistic missions and speaking engagements in the United States, Jones was deeply and intimately involved in negotiations with the top political leadership of the Congress Party and of the Muslim League, including both Nehru and Jinnah. As we will discover in the next chapter, these negotiations focused on two issues—breaking the deadlock between Hindus and Muslims over Pakistan and the status of Christian missionaries in independent India.

14

In the Aftermath of War:
Hopes and Disappointments

The night before I took plane to leave India, I asked Mahatma Gandhi for "a message to America from this new India that is coming into being." He replied: "I cannot speak of this new India until I see it in the flesh and blood. I am like the disciple who said, 'I will not believe until I put my hand in His side and feel the wound prints.' So I cannot speak of it or even believe in it until I see it."
— E. Stanley Jones, *The Christian Century,* July 17, 1946[1]

I AM SEATED OUT on the veranda of Mr. Chas. Thomas' house where I am staying," Stanley wrote in a family letter from Dehra Dun, a mountain retreat in the north of India on April 14, 1947. "Bishop Badley occupies a half of the house. I am taking meals with him. As usual he is talking about the Methodist past. I never saw anyone who dwelt so much upon the sayings and doings of the Methodist pioneers. I am afraid I am more like: Let the dead bury the dead and let's go preach the Kingdom! But it takes people like that to hold the past to the present."[2]

His next family letter, dated April 28, 1947, was written from the YMCA in New Delhi to keep them up to date on the fast-breaking events in India and on his hectic schedule of interviews with the top nationalist political leaders in the country. "I have so much to tell you," he wrote, "that I think I had better write it on the typewriter." He went on to quote the words of the new leaders of India as they answered the question that was his first concern: the status of missionaries after independence. Would missionaries, he asked

India's emerging political leadership, be welcomed or tolerated in an independent India?

Chakrovarti Rajagopalachari, a prominent Congress Party leader from Madras who succeeded Lord Mountbatten as Governor-General of India after independence, said that missionaries would be "welcomed and with gratitude if they come in the spirit of humble service." Abul Kalam Azad, a Muslim and Indian nationalist who was President of the Congress Party before independence, and an important minister after independence, told Jones,

> The word "tolerate" should not be used. We will welcome you and welcome you gladly in the making of the new India. The only question at issue is mass conversions. Concerning the right of individual conversion when there is a change of inner conviction there can be no two ideas. Apart from mass conversions there is no issue and you will be welcomed and gladly welcomed in this new India.

Finally, Jawaharlal Nehru, who would soon be Prime Minister of India, said, "We will welcome anyone who throws himself into India, identifies himself with us."

The most exciting news Stanley shared with his family, however, was his meeting with Jinnah. He asked the leader of the Muslim League not about Christian missionaries but about Pakistan. "If the Congress will concede Pakistan will you be willing to say that you will enter a union with India?" Jones asked him.

> After combating with me for a long time he suddenly changed and said: "If the Congress will concede Pakistan, I will say that I will enter a union with India." "And mean it," I asked. "Yes, and mean it," he replied. I could scarcely believe my ears. It was the very thing which the Congress had offered and he had turned it down. And here he was accepting it.

Jones enthusiastically told the unbelievably good news to Patel, to Nehru, and to Lord Mountbatten. He also wrote letters with the same information to Gandhi and to J. B. Kripalani, who was then President of the Congress Party, among others. Kripalani responded to Jones in a letter dated May 5, 1947.[3]

> Thank you for your letter of the 28th April. If you can get, what you say in your letter Mr. Jinnah is prepared to do, in writing, there will be no difficulty from our side to the proposal you suggest. Let him say, that in different areas, not necessarily provinces, he is willing to abide by the decision of the majority; we on our part are willing to say that in those areas where the majority of population desire to have Pakistan, with or without federation, they might have it. I hope it will be possible for you to get from him a statement to this effect.

Stanley concluded his April 28 family letter with this comment, "God apparently used me in this crisis to get him [Jinnah] to say it." Just as he was sure that God had called him to remain in the United States in 1941 to use his best efforts to prevent war with Japan, so he was now confident that God had placed him in India at the critical moment before independence. God had given him the high-level contacts he needed to resolve the issue of Pakistan so that the entire subcontinent of South Asia could become the single nation of India.

But on May 5, 1947, Stanley wrote another family letter[4] to say that the story of his meeting with Jinnah had "a sequel—a sad one!" Jinnah changed his mind!

Jones was doubly embarrassed, not only because of Jinnah's abrupt and inexplicable about-face, but also because of all of those whom he had informed in good faith that Jinnah had accepted the Congress position on Pakistan. On May 12, 1947, Jones wrote to Jinnah, documenting the entire unhappy sequence of events. He recalled that Jinnah agreed with the Congress on Pakistan in their April 26 conversation.

> This was important news, obviously given to me to pass on. If not to be passed on it would have no meaning. So I passed it on to certain people concerned.
>
> When someone asked me what you mean by "union," I wrote to you on April 27th, asking for clarification—was it federal union you meant by union?
>
> You can realize the moral shock which came to me when you wrote in reply: "I regret that you have entirely misunderstood me. No suggestion came from me, except that you made suggestions which, I thought were thoroughly impracticable and contradictory in terms."
>
> Since I had raised false hopes, however dim, in the minds of those to whom I passed on your word to me, I was bound to send them your second word.[5]

If Jones was devastated by the "moral hurt and disillusionment" (as he put it in his May 12, 1947, letter to Jinnah) of Jinnah's duplicity, he was greatly encouraged by the results of two missionary conventions he attended before he returned to the United States at the end of June. Both conventions addressed the important issue of the role and status of Christian missionaries in independent India. And both conventions under Jones's leadership adopted "A Missionary Declaration," which welcomed the advent of a free India and pledged missionary support for the new government. He reported on the first convention, held at Kodaikanal, in his May 5, 1947, family letter. He reported on the second convention, held at Landour, Mussoorie, in a letter dated June 5, 1947, written to his daughter and son-in-law. The Landour Declaration read in part:[6]

> We are grateful that this independence is coming into being with the consent and cooperation of Britain. We believe that this amicable separation will

mean that these two nations will be bound together by closer ties in the future.

We are aware of the difficulties ahead, but we are more aware of the possibilities. We pledge ourselves to help in every legitimate way in the solution of those difficulties and in the realization of those possibilities. . . .

We would be servants of Christ and of India and would identify ourselves with the people of this land—their sorrows our sorrows, their joys our joys and their successes our successes.

We regret that the political life of the country is organized on a communal basis. If the Christian community has been compelled to accept communal representation, it does so with no inner belief in its validity and we are convinced that it will be the first to repudiate it if another and better basis is found.

We believe in the inherent right of individuals and groups to outer conversion where there is inner conversion, but we have no desire now nor have we had any desire in the past, to build up communal power for political ends through religious conversion. We think it debasing to religion and to politics to use a moral and spiritual movement for political ends.[7]

We pledge ourselves to support in every legitimate way the lawfully established government set up to serve the interests of the people. We will give it the best we have. We hope that the government will feel free to call on us to help make India the land of our hopes and prayers.

On June 5, 1947, Jones wrote to Diffendorfer from Sat Tal saying how delighted he was with the two missionary declarations.

It means everything to the Christian movement to have had this done. We have sent copies to the national leaders and to the daily press. Kripalani, the Pres. of the Congress, thought it a wonderful statement and asked for a copy. The editor of the Harijan [Gandhi's newspaper] asked for a copy for that paper.

On May 17, 1947, after the first week of his Sat Tal Ashram Jones wrote another family letter.[8] "The crowd is slow in coming up," he said, "but by the end of next week we will have more than we can accommodate." In the meantime, he continued, "I have been swimming each day. With swimming . . . I have been getting rid of some of my surplus flesh. Have lost five pounds in a week. That will not matter. It is to the good."

He had begun writing another book of daily devotional meditations, he told his family. But *The Way to Power and Poise* was not published until 1949. His work on this book was interrupted on January 30, 1948, by the tragic assassination of Mahatma Gandhi. Jones expressed his reaction to Gandhi's death in a statement written while he was on a plane leaving Delhi for a series of evangelistic meetings in Colombo, Ceylon (Sri Lanka).

I am on a plane leaving Delhi for Madras and Colombo. I was in Delhi only 14 hours, and yet those 14 hours were the most tragedy-packed and hope-inspiring I have ever experienced. I had asked a friend to arrange an interview with Mahatma Gandhi but I found on arrival that the only chance I had to see him would be to go to his daily prayer meeting. If I could get a taxi I could just make it, but owing to an engagement later I decided against it. I came near witnessing a tragedy second only to the crucifixion of the Son of God.

In a way I am grateful I was spared that, but I am more deeply grateful for what I saw as I looked into the soul of a grief-stricken nation. Never have I seen anything so spontaneous as the grief and sorrow that seized the soul of India, as in a moment. . . . Everybody was stunned as if by the dropping of an atom bomb. . . .

When we gathered at the radio to hear Jawahar Lal's [Nehru's] and Vallabhbhai Patel's addresses strong men wept, soldiers among them. How could they do otherwise, for these two iron men who had gone to jail without a quiver or murmur were so shaken they could not speak except in broken sentences? Shops closed, bazaars closed, everything closed as by a silent, inexorable command. . . .

A Hindu whispered to me, "And this is Friday too." I pick up my paper and find this: "He came to a Christlike end, is the universal comment." An editorial in the Hindu of Madras says: "He was the second savior." [9]

What delayed Jones's work on *The Way to Power and Poise*, however, was not Gandhi's death itself, but a telegram that he received from his publisher, Abingdon Press in Nashville, Tennessee. The telegram read,

HOW QUICKLY CAN YOU PRODUCE MANUSCRIPT FOR MAHATMA GANDHI BIOGRAPHY STRESSING SPIRITUAL GENIUS AS WELL AS THE GREAT STORY PREFER BOOK 160 TO 224 PAGES CAN ARRANGE SIMULTANEOUS PUBLICATION HERE AND LONDON SHOULD HAVE FINE RECEPTION IN ALL COUNTRIES[10]

Jones's immediate reaction to this message was negative. "When the cable came from the publishers in America," he explained in the foreword to the book he eventually wrote, "I put it aside as impossible. I never write a book by request. It must come as a result of an inner urge which I cannot put aside. I felt no such inner urge about this." But after thinking and praying about it, he decided that

I could lay an honest tribute at the feet of the great little man. And could do it with my whole heart. To have won an evangelist to a whole-hearted affection amid the clash of thirty years is no small conquest. But in the end he had conquered me. This book is a sign of that conquest.[11]

On May 3, 1948, just over two months after Jones received the telegram from Abingdon Press, he wrote to his son-in-law that he had finished the manuscript of his book on Gandhi and had mailed it to his publisher. "I have enjoyed this writing," he said, and "I am glad they asked me to write it."[12] In

the same letter he reported that he was proceeding with his plans for opening the sanatorium in Lucknow, which would provide both psychiatric and
spiritual healing for missionaries and for others in need of this combination
of therapy. His motivation for the sanatorium was influenced by his own
emotional and spiritual breakdown at the beginning of his ministry, and by
his long experience as a counselor to a wide variety of individuals whom he
met in his evangelistic meetings, his round table conferences, and his
Christian ashrams. The sanatorium would be located on the property of the
former Deaconness Home, which he had originally purchased for the
Lucknow Ashram. It was here that Jones would establish the Nurmanzil
(Palace of Light) Psychiatric Center, the first psychiatric center in India,
which continues to operate as a Christian institution today. Finally, he
reported that two new buildings, a doctor's home and a dormitory that
would house up to twenty-four men, were being completed at the Sat Tal
Ashram.[13]

Jones returned to the United States at the end of June 1948 for his
summer ashrams. They were, he wrote in a circular letter on September
30, 1948, "the best we have had in the nine years of Ashrams."[14] When the
ashrams ended, Jones spent five days in Clayton, Iowa. There at Mabel's
family home he relaxed and resumed his writing on *The Way to Power and
Poise*. After "getting a few days of quiet," Jones told his friends and financial supporters, he began to speak on behalf of his Crusade for a United
Church. This Crusade began in 1947 and was the outgrowth of his meetings in Columbus, Ohio, and Buffalo, New York, in 1944 to create a federal
union of Christian churches in the United States.[15]

In spite of the steadfast support of those who attended the Buffalo and
Columbus meetings, the idea of federal union did not ignite broadscale
grassroots involvement until Jones held his Northeast Ashram in Lake
Winnipesaukee, New Hampshire, in the summer of 1944. When Harvey
Kazmier, an estate trustee from Boston who was attending the ashram,
heard Jones talk about federal union, it became the defining moment in
his life. From that point on he was possessed by an unquenchable passion
to put Jones's concept of federal union into practice among the Christian
churches in America. Kazmier's passion was so contagious that he convinced a small group of friends to join him. Together they approached
Jones and persuaded him that only with his personal leadership would
their dream have any possibility of becoming a reality.

And so in the fall of 1947, Jones agreed to sacrifice thirty days of his time
to speak in thirty cities on behalf of federal union among American
churches. For Jones, who was then sixty-four, this schedule of speaking
approximately three times in each of the thirty cities was nothing unusual.
But for Kazmier, who was twenty years younger, and who accompanied
Jones throughout the crusade, it was too much.

In a long feature article on the crusade in the *Saturday Evening Post,* Hartzell Spence wrote that Jones

> breezed through the schedule without so much as pouches under his eyes. Midway, however, Mr. Kazmier began to break down, and turned to Doctor Jones for aid. That day Doctor Jones had made three speeches and a radio address; had undertaken two newspaper interviews; had led two conferences and shaken 2000 hands, all on a reserve of four hours' sleep from the previous night.
> "How do you do it?" Mr. Kazmier asked.
> "Do what?"
> "Keep going. I'm about dead."
> "I feel fine," the missionary answered.
> "I know," Kazmier went on, "but look at me"
> "You must surrender yourself to this crusade," he advised Kazmier. "Then your strength will come from without, and your own stamina will not be sapped. If I leaned only on my own strength, I would be ten years dead."[16]

The Crusade for a United Church was sponsored by the Association for a United Church of America, which rented a forty-dollars-per-month office in Brookline, Massachusetts, and had a small volunteer staff supervised by Kazmier, who served as executive director. The association solicited pledge cards, memberships at $1.00 per year, and additional financial support from individuals who were interested in church union. By early 1948, the *Saturday Evening Post* reported, the association was receiving between three and four thousand new pledge cards each week, cards that promised personal prayer and commitment to federal union. In Youngstown, Ohio, Jones said that the purpose of the crusade was "to so saturate the soul of the church with the demand for unity that this saturation will be precipitated into action."[17] At first he was skeptical about the results of the crusade.

> How would the Crusade be received? We did not know. It was a leap in the dark. But we hadn't gone very far when we discovered that we were uncovering something already there—dim but wanting expression. We were putting into words the thought of many hearts.[18]

Jones was convinced that the crusade was a response to a genuine movement of God in America. "A movement of the Spirit is on," he wrote in his September 30, 1948, circular letter at the end of the second year of the crusade, "and the amazing thing is that although we are presenting the most controversial subject possible—union of the churches—we have not left behind a controversy or a split condition in any local situation. It has been healing. Only the Spirit of God could have produced that."

While Jones received virtually unanimous support for federal union from the laymen to whom he presented his idea of one Church of Jesus

Christ in America, the response of clergymen and church officials was decidedly mixed. One critic of his crusade, Dr. Truman B. Douglas, wrote an article for the *Christian Century* entitled "Federal Union Is Not Enough," in which he argued for what Jones called amalgamation or "one undifferentiated church with the same ordination, the same rites and ceremonies, the same church government." In response to Douglas, Jones argued that the only form of church union that had any chance of success was a union rooted in man's fundamental spiritual nature.[19] Or, as the *Christian Science Monitor* put it in an editorial during the first year of Jones's crusade, "The more spiritual Christians become, the less they will find themselves divided by material things."[20] But man's spiritual nature was ambivalent, Jones insisted, because it contained "two contradictory urges or instincts—a desire for union with the whole and a desire for local self-government, for self-expression."[21]

The problem with Douglas's proposal was that it reflected only the human desire for union. This partial and inadequate expression of human nature ignored the historical and spiritual roots of the American denominations. Jones correctly and astutely perceived that God "raised up" each denomination "to emphasize neglected or muted truth."[22] No plan for uniting the Christian churches in the United States that consolidated or assimilated all the denominations, so that the unique spiritual truth of each church was ignored or forgotten, would survive. Dr. Douglas's argument for total church union was valid and persuasive insofar as it was based on the spiritual hunger of all Christians for fellowship with one another, but it was incomplete because it neglected the other face of the human spirit, the desire for independence and autonomy. Jones believed that Paul's first letter to the Corinthians (12:12-14 RSV), in its famous analogy of the church to the various parts of the human body, provided the best description of how Christians should be joined together. The physical body is both "one" and "many" just as man's spirit craves both unity and independence.

The enthusiastic response of laymen to Jones's Crusade for a United Church confirms the fact that he had indeed heard from the Inner Voice when he proposed his plan for federal union. During the second year of the crusade in the fall of 1948 he wrote in his September 30 circular letter that "the people are beginning to see what it is all about, beginning to see that it can really happen and that it is possible *now*." For Jones, of course, it was "a long-awaited dream come true."

The best evidence for the spontaneous nature of the public response to his Crusade for a United Church is the informal polls of audience opinion about federal union, which were first conducted in 1948. Jones emphasized the fact that he "did not ask for audiences to vote but they themselves demanded it from the floor." He listed the results of these polls in his September 30 circular letter.[23]

City	Approximate Attendance Votes	Against Federal Union
Cedar Rapids, IA	2500	2
Enid, OK	3000	2
San Antonio, TX	4000	11
Houston, TX	3000	2
Memphis, TN	1500	2
Champaign-Urbana, IL	2800	3
Louisville, KY	2000	6

The most heated and formidable opposition to federal union came from clergy who were deeply concerned about the issues of apostolic succession and reordination. The Roman Catholic Church would not permit anyone but a Catholic priest to administer the sacraments because only Catholic priests were legitimate successors to Saint Peter, whom Christ called the "rock" upon which "I will build my church" (Matthew 16:18 NIV). On the other hand, many Protestant churches would not accept the ordination of the Roman Catholic Church. To overcome this problem, clergy who were sincerely interested in some form of church union suggested an "extension of authority" instead of reordination. Jones, however, opposed such extensions of authority, which would be required by one denomination before it would accept the ordination of another denomination, because they were really reordination under another name.[24] The problem with reordination, like the problem with rebaptism, was that the church requiring it refused to accept the validity of the first ordination or baptism. Only with Jones's proposal for federal union did each branch of the Church of Christ of America have the authority to establish its own rules for ordination and baptism as well as for other sacraments and practices. With respect to fundamental doctrine he believed that all Christian churches could accept Peter's confession, "You are the Christ, the Son of the living God" (Matthew 16:16 NIV). This would satisfy basic human need for spiritual unity as well as the need for a unique Christian identity. On other issues Jones thought that the denominations should agree to disagree.[25]

* * *

Jones's zeal and enthusiasm for a federal union of the Christian churches in the United States sprang directly from the reality of the kingdom of God in which he lived. As a kingdom principle federal union had a solid scriptural basis in the New Testament. We have already mentioned the concept of self-surrender as key to both the political relationship between states and nation in the U.S. Constitution, and between individual denominations and the United Church of America. But there is also another New Testament foundation for the higher kingdom reality of federal union. It is found in Paul's letter to the Ephesians (2:15-16) in which he says that Christ through his suffering, death, and resurrection created a new being out of both parties. We discussed this idea earlier with respect to Jones's mediation between Japan and the United States in the months preceding the Japanese attack on Pearl Harbor. There we saw how his coming within a hair's breadth of preventing Pearl Harbor vindicated the kingdom reality of a new man out of both parties. Now, in the case of his Crusade for a United Church, Jones wanted to help create a new and higher humanity, the United Church of America, out of the conflicting and lesser truths of the various denominational churches.[26] He recognized and applauded the unique and invaluable contribution of the individual churches to the Body of Christ. But these individual truths were at once incorporated into and transcended by the more ultimate truth of the kingdom of God, which was embodied in Jones's proposed federal union of all the churches. The question remains, however, did his Crusade for a United Church succeed in the same way that his attempt to mediate the hostility between Japan and the United States so very nearly succeeded?

Between 1947 and 1954, Jones led the Crusade for a United Church by devoting one month each fall to mass meetings in nearly five hundred cities throughout the United States. Over this seven-year period some two hundred fifty thousand people sent in cards to the Association for a United Church of America, pledging their support for federal union. This strategy to develop massive grassroots support for federal union among rank and file church members deliberately bypassed the church hierarchy. But beginning in October 1952 in Buck Hill Falls, Pennsylvania, Jones met with denominational leaders. As he explained in an article in the *Christian Century*,[27]

> We said to these denominational leaders that we had our eyes on them from the beginning and that we knew they were the people who would be the most important people in the final decisions about union of the churches. I also told them that if they would take federal union and implement it, as far as I was concerned I would say, "Now, Lord, let thy servant depart in peace." I could go back to my evangelistic work with a lighter conscience. They could carry on from there. But if not, I had no choice but to continue this grassroots movement till something happened.

Jones did indeed continue his grassroots movement for federal union, primarily in the form of his writing, because he was convinced that the overwhelming response he received during the Crusade for a United Church was a mandate from the people. But from the standpoint of the American churches actually forming a federal union modeled on the kingdom of God principles of self-surrender and of a new humanity out of both parties, nothing ever happened. Jones's last published work on federal union was an article in the May 21, 1970, issue of the *Indian Witness* and his book *The Reconstruction of the Church—On What Pattern?* which also appeared in 1970.[28] But even before the article and the book were published, there were definite signs that the Crusade for a United Church was losing its grassroots support. On May 12, 1966, Allister R. MacKay, the associate treasurer of the association, wrote to Jones in India to say that Harvey Kazmier, the executive director of the association, was in the process of closing his office in Boston and moving the association's records and equipment to his home in Newton, Massachusetts. MacKay gave Jones his frank opinion.

> The way things shape up at the moment, it looks very much as if the work of the Association could not extend too far into the future. Such contributions as are received in response to our mailings are very small and many of the larger ones have dried up altogether.[29]

Nevertheless, Jones continued to advocate and press for acceptance of his plan for federal union of the Christian churches in the United States, even after he suffered a crippling stroke in December 1971. In March 1972, he wrote a letter to his fellow United Methodists who had been elected delegates to the quadrennial General Conference of the Church, which would meet in Atlanta.

> As I am not a delegate to this General Conference and am unlikely to be sent to either of the next two, I would like at this time to place before you an alternative, and in the view of many, a vastly superior prospect for a united church. I refer to Federal Union. The enclosed pamphlet sets the matter forth in some detail. Federal Union provides for a maximum expression of unity and at the same time for a legitimate expression of the diversity embodied in the principal denominational traditions in Protestantism.[30]

Jones's fellow Methodists, however, did not act on his proposal.

It is fair to ask why Jones's Crusade for a United Church apparently failed. On the whole, as we have suggested, the reaction of the clergy and of church officials to his proposal for federal union of the churches was, at best, lukewarm, a response that persisted into the late 1960s. The attitude of Bishop Richard Raines of The United Methodist Church in Indiana is typical. On February 17, 1967, Raines wrote to Harvey Kazmier about Jones's plans to be the featured speaker at the School of the Prophets at DePauw University in the late summer of that year. This was an annual event at which Methodist clergy in Indiana met for study and fellowship. Raines, who was much beloved by Methodists in Indiana but was ecclesiastically conservative, said in his letter to Kazmier, "I would hope that Dr. Jones would be the preacher to preachers and not speak on the general subject of federal union."[31] It may be that clergy felt threatened by federal union. They may have been fearful about how federal union would affect their position and status within their denominational churches. Or perhaps Jones's strategy of enlisting the support of the laity in mass meetings before he presented his plan to clergy was a mistake. If he had made his proposal for federal union to clergy and laity simultaneously, his Crusade for a United Church might have been more successful. In any case, Jones's ideas for a federal union of Christian churches in the United States were not adopted and implemented.

But was his crusade a failure? Jones never changed his mind about federal union, nor did he abandon the concepts of self-surrender and of a new humanity out of both parties on which federal union was based. Both of these concepts continued to be key components of his thinking, writing, and acting on behalf of the kingdom of God. As we will see in the next chapter, they were woven into the very fabric of his Christian ashrams.

* * *

When Stanley went back to India in 1949, he spent only a short time in his adopted homeland during the first six months. The rest of the time, he reported in a circular letter dated May 27, 1949,[32] he spent in Burma; Singapore; Kuala Lumpur, Malaya; Bangkok, Siam (Thailand); the Philippines; Japan; Korea; and China. Altogether, he spent four months in the Far East—"the most eventful four months," he wrote, "of my not uneventful life." The "crux" of the trip, he said, was Japan. It was his first trip to that country, which had only a tiny minority of Christians. He went to Japan, Jones wrote in the *Indian Witness* on July 7, 1949,[33] "with inner hesitation." Even though Kagawa had written to him that "Japan was ripe for Christianity," Jones "was more than sceptical." However, after he had been in the country for only a short time, he reported to the Methodist Division of Foreign Missions in New York, "As you see I'm here! And how!"[34] Jones was overwhelmed by the sincere and spontaneous warmth of his reception by the Japanese. Part of the reason for this enthusiastic greeting, he admitted, was the newspaper stories, published before his arrival, stating that in an effort to prevent war between Japan and the United States in 1941 he had been an intermediary between the Japanese embassy in Washington and Roosevelt. Jones wrote in the *Indian Witness*, "This publicity made for a favorable reception. But it couldn't account for the response. There was something deeper."

At the time of Jones's visit, Japan was still rebuilding from the vast and catastrophic physical, psychological, and moral destruction of the war, and the country was still under U.S. military occupation. World War II and its aftermath had left a profound political and spiritual vacuum in Japan. The "whole basis of her spiritual life had crashed," Jones wrote in the *Indian Witness,* "the belief in the near divinity of the Emperor and of the Japanese people themselves as descended from [the] Sun Goddess and of their superiority and destiny to rule." It was this state of spiritual collapse that Jones believed was the deeper reason for his warm and enthusiastic reception in Japan. The eminent church historian Kenneth Scott Latourette confirms Jones's assessment of the opportunity for Christian evangelism in Japan after World War II.

> The years which immediately followed Japan's surrender appeared unusually propitious for acquainting the Japanese with the Christian message. Thousands were adrift emotionally and were searching for an answer to life's deepest questions. The foundations on which the super-nationalists had based their adventures in East Asia and which had depended on high-powered propaganda had crumbled. What spiritual resources had enabled the Americans to overpower Japan?[35]

Stanley described what happened when he arrived at the Tokyo airport in February 1948 in his letter to the Methodist Divison of Foreign Missions.

> Photographers rushed up to me and [a] reporter said straight off: "All Japan is talking about Christianity, what have you to say about it?" I replied that I favored it! . . . I was whisked through the Customs and taken over by a G.I. and driven to Yokohama where I was to address an audience of military people and "dependents." Got there exactly on time—8:30: Church full and good many decisions—straight off and an American audience. The G.I. called out to the airport guard: "V.I.P." and when I asked what it meant had it interpreted: "Very Important Person." . . . they took me to Tokyo where I stayed at G.H.Q. [General Headquarters] hotel—Imperial Hotel.

In other words, Jones got the red carpet treatment from the American military in Japan. But there was an element of irony in his status as an American citizen in a nation occupied by American soldiers. After his first night's stay in Tokyo, he took a military train for Nagoya. He had to receive a "special permit to have a Japanese, my interpreter, Mr. Yassumura, ride in [the] train with me. But he cannot eat in [the] dining car."

In Nagoya his first meeting was held in a church that had been built by Church World Service to replace one that was destroyed in the bombing. The pastor did not encourage him to ask for signed cards indicating personal commitment to Jesus Christ because, the pastor said, "They won't write their names in public." But in spite of the pastor's skepticism Jones received 120 signed cards in an audience of 450 people, half of whom were non-Christian.

One of the real highlights of his tour of Japan was Hiroshima, where he held a prayer meeting on the exact spot where the atomic bomb fell. Jones described what happened in Hiroshima in his letter to the Division of Foreign Missions.

> It is nothing less than a miracle that in Hiroshima we could receive such love and response after what happened to that city. But in the three meetings there were 450 who signed cards, saying they want to become Christians. The largest meeting was in the school hall with 1000 people there. We had a prayer meeting at the place where the bomb fell with newspaper photographers taking the picture and it was in the paper the next day, with the remark I made in big headlines: "I feel like falling on my knees."

Another event in Hiroshima vividly underscored the spiritual significance of Jones's visit.

> A pastor walked over to me in the pulpit and before the audience said, after I had spoken on using calamity and sorrow, "Sir the fire of the Holy Spirit is burning in the hearts of the people. It is our new beginning." The fire of an atom had left this city a cinder, but the fire of the Holy Spirit burning in the hearts of the people would rebuild that city and the country on better foundations, for it was the fire of a creative love. I bet my life on the fire in the hearts of the people against the fire released from an atom—it will outlast the other and recreate the world.[36]

Altogether Jones visited sixteen cities on the three main islands of Japan—Honshu, Kyushu, and Hokkaido. In these cities approximately eight thousand non-Christians signed cards affirming their personal belief in Jesus Christ and their desire to grow in their new Christian faith. The climax of Jones's tour of Japan, both spiritually and personally, was his series of meetings in Tokyo. He met and talked not only with Nomura, Kurusu, and Terasaki, whom he had not seen since before the war, but also with General MacArthur, the commander of the American occupation force in Japan, and with Emperor Hirohito.

On March 23, 1949, shortly after he concluded his visit to Japan, Jones wrote to the Robinsons, who had arranged and participated in most of his meetings in Washington in the months preceding Pearl Harbor. They, especially Rob, knew Nomura, Kurusu and Terasaki, and they were just as devastated as Jones was when the Japanese attacked Pearl Harbor. He was anxious to reassure his good friends that the "work we did at Washington has borne fruit in Japan." Admiral Nomura, the Japanese Ambassador to the United States in 1941, was on the platform with Jones when he spoke to a crowd of three thousand in Hibiya Hall in Tokyo. "I paid a tribute to his peace efforts at Washington," Jones wrote to the Robinsons, "and the crowd applauded."[37] After the meeting Nomura told Jones privately that if

Roosevelt's cable to the Emperor had been sent a week earlier, "it might have headed off the war." Jones also visited Kurusu who was recovering from a stroke. Kurusu agreed with Nomura that had Roosevelt's cable been sent a week before, "it might have changed the whole course of history." In his letter to the Division of Foreign Missions, Jones quoted Tojo's comment to Kurusu, "If that cable had come a week earlier this war need not have taken place." Kurusu also gave Jones a copy of his memoirs with this inscription,

> To Dr. Stanley Jones who offered invaluable assistance to us during the negotiations in Washington, 1941. If his plans had been accepted in time, the course of world history would have been entirely different—no war, hot or cold.

What was even more gratifying for Stanley than Kurusu's confirmation of and appreciation for his role in trying to prevent war between Japan and the United States was Kurusu's decision to become a Christian. Kurusu promised to be baptized when Jones returned to Japan.

On March 18, 1949, Jones was given "an Imperial audience by invitation of the Imperial Household."[38] When he arrived at the Emperor's palace, he was met by Terasaki, the third Japanese official whom he had dealt with in Washington in 1941. Terasaki was the Emperor's interpreter and advisor at the time of Jones's interview with Hirohito. He showed Jones the letter Jones had written to him on December 10, 1941. "This letter," he told Jones, "kept me alive spiritually during the war." Jones quoted the letter in his *Indian Witness* article.

> Dear Mr. Terasaki:
>
> Words cannot express my sorrow that things have turned out the way they have. I am perfectly sure that your group at Washington sincerely and earnestly tried to avert this hour. It is not your fault that the war party won. You did your best.
>
> This is just a note of deep appreciation for what you and Mr. Kurusu and Admiral Nomura have done in the cause of better relationships between our countries. You failed, but you have the satisfaction of knowing that you did your best.
>
> This is to pray that God's grace may be with you in the dark hours and days ahead. Please give my best regards to Mrs. Terasaki and say to her that I shall uphold you both with prayer.[39]

Jones talked with Hirohito for three-quarters of an hour. It is revealing of Jones's character and commitment as a Christian that he did not ask the Emperor about Roosevelt's eleventh-hour telegram. Instead, as he wrote to the Robinsons:

I suggested to the Emperor the possibility of his becoming a Christian. He said I had raised a very serious question, that he had great respect for Christianity, but since most of his people are Shintoists, this had to be taken into consideration. He could not have said otherwise under the circumstances, as several court officials were present. Terasaki had told him of our work at Washington and of my work in Japan and he thanked me for both and invited me to come back. What the Emperor said is not for quotation.

The topic of Christianity was also the focus of Jones's interview with General MacArthur. He wrote to the Division of Foreign Missions,

Saw MacArthur and had nearly an hour with him. I got up three times to leave but he wouldn't let me go. Told him of the [evangelistic] campaign, greatly delighted. Asked him what message to America and he said: "Where you sent one missionary, now send a hundred. This is the greatest opportunity the Church in the world has faced in 500 years. How long the door may be open is uncertain, probably ten years."

Jones also discussed with MacArthur the idea of giving New Guinea to Japan. MacArthur liked the idea. In fact, Jones told the Robinsons, he "waxed eloquent over its possibilities." But he cautioned Jones not to pursue his proposal until a peace treaty formally ending the war between Japan and the United States was negotiated.

Jones concluded his letter to the Robinsons with the comment, "My month in Japan was the most fruitful I have ever spent in my life." It was fruitful to Jones personally because finally, eight years after he tried so desperately to prevent war between Japan and the United States, he saw the unfolding of God's purpose for him in Japan. Although he did not stop an American war in the Pacific in 1941, his efforts on behalf of peace reopened the door to Christian evangelism in Japan after the war. But, like MacArthur, he knew that the window of opportunity for Christianity would not remain open indefinitely. The greatest danger was that the glowing embers of evangelism, which Jones ignited in early 1949, would not have sufficient strength and support to burst into the flames of genuine revival. He wrote in his *Indian Witness* article,

The weakest spot is the follow-up period. The churches are simply not prepared for this heavy responsibility which has suddenly been placed upon them. . . . The whole church must be mobilized. And help from Christians everywhere must be brought to Japan.[40]

Japanese Christians also knew they would need help in order to give guidance and encouragement to those who had signed cards in Jones's meetings.

On the night of March 18, a few hours before Jones left Japan, Michio

Kozaki, the chairman of the National Christian Council of Japan, which was the official sponsor of Jones's evangelistic tour, presented Jones with a statement of the council's sincere and deep appreciation for his work in that country.

> It is really a marvellous thing that you could bring about such a wonderful result, even in such a brief span of time, since you arrived in Japan. You have come at this opportune time and struck the keynote of the Movement to Christianize this country, and have shown us the way of God in the power of His Gospel, to our great encouragement.
>
> We shall now pledge ourselves to attend to the follow-up work, in order to reap the souls you have awoken to seek after truth, so that your work thus initiated may not be in vain. . . .
>
> Taking advantage of this opportunity, we wish you will convey our heartfelt greetings to the American Churches and Mission Boards, telling them all about the actual situation as you saw it, together with our deep gratitude for what they have done for us, ever since the close of the war.
>
> We wish further that the American Churches will come to help us in the cause, so that we may be able to meet this great challenge of the day.[41]

Jones's 1949 tour of Japan was only the first of many trips to that nation. He was certain that the Inner Voice of the Holy Spirit had directed him to Japan and that his evangelistic meetings there were an integral part of God's call to proclaim the good news of Jesus Christ. Moreover, after Jones began his tour and saw the deep spiritual hunger of the people, he developed a strong personal bond with the Japanese, which reinforced his sense of a divine commission to take the gospel to Japan. The Japanese in turn were deeply grateful for Jones's visit. Michio Kozaki concluded his letter of appreciation to Jones,

> Our prayer will follow you wherever you are that God may bless you richly in your physical and spiritual strength, and that you may render the most invaluable service for the up-building of His Kingdom in this bewildered world.
>
> Now we bid you farewell.
>
> God bless you!

It might be argued that the challenge of the Christian evangelization of Japan was a lost opportunity, since the Japanese Christian community is even today a relatively small group, but this interpretation ignores God's design and God's timing for the evangelization of Japan. We still do not know the full purpose and meaning of Jones's work in Japan, but we do know that the spontaneous enthusiasm of his reception confirms the genuine spiritual need of the people. He responded to that need in 1949 and in his subsequent visits. Moreover, the fact that he continued to receive thousands of decisions for Christ even after the end of the American military occupation of Japan supports the view that his success was not dependent on the Japanese desire for help to rebuild their country after World War II. Of course, it is true that Christians in America and elsewhere, perhaps because they were weary of war and weary of Japan, did not respond fully to the spiritual challenge of the evangelization of Japan. And it is also true that Japan, instead of constructing a broad new spiritual foundation for its people, tended to focus its psychic and spiritual energy on rebuilding its devastated economy. Nevertheless, Jones was doing the work of the kingdom of God in Japan and the result of his work is still bearing spiritual fruit in Japan and throughout the world.

While Jones was primarily concerned about the future of Christianity in Japan, he was also concerned about the political and military presence of his own country in Japan. He wrote in his *Indian Witness* article,[42]

> Personally I hope the Americans will not stay too long, for this is not good for the Americans. They are beginning to like the privileged position they occupy—the best of homes and hotels; the best of the railroad equipment for the Allied trains, first class being given to them and second and third to the Japanese; a roped-off lane separates them from the Japanese in the railway stations; plenty of clean and efficient servants for the homes; good meals in the military establishments at 40 cents a meal and above all a people at their beck and call. . . . From this privileged position they have come to teach the Japanese people democracy. This is a heavy handicap. It may result in this situation teaching them imperialism. Many like it so well they come back. I hope this unnatural relationship soon ends for the sake of the Japanese who are being weakened by too much dependence, and especially for the sake of the Americans in whom the imperialistic mind is in the making.

This warning about imperialism echoes Jones's earlier warning, which he gave in 1945. At the conclusion of his first published account of his role in trying to maintain peace between Japan and the United States, Jones wrote,

> If we continue to police the Pacific as an overlord in that area, then there would be no lasting peace; and we shall be hated as few nations have been hated. Another war would be inevitable, likely in less than 25 years.[43]

In view of the United States's tragic involvement in the long and bloody Vietnam War, this statement is both ominous and remarkably prophetic. Jones's accurate prediction is even more remarkable, given the fact that it was made four years before he saw the first evidence of an imperialistic attitude in the American occupation of Japan and before the international role of the United States in the postwar world became clear. His perception of things to come in the Pacific is further evidence that he was responding to the Inner Voice when he began making regular visits to Japan in 1949. Nothing other than divine guidance could have led him to make his prophetic warnings about the disastrous consequences of an American policy of imperialism in the Far East.

At the end of his tour of Japan in March 1949, Stanley visited and spoke in public meetings in two other Asian countries—Korea and China—before returning to India. He wrote about his visit to China in the July 14, 1949, issue of the *Indian Witness*.[44] By April 1949, the communists under Mao Zedong already controlled large parts of the country, and before Jones left China, they took over Nanking, the Nationalist capital of China, one of the last strongholds of Chiang Kai-shek. Jones's host in China was the National Christian Council, which, in spite of the precarious position of the Nationalist government, encouraged him not to confine his meetings to the coastal cities but to venture inland. "You will probably be the last one in from the outside," the council told Jones, "before the Bamboo Curtain goes down. They will need you especially."[45]

Responding to this request, Jones held evangelistic meetings in Shanghai, Nanking, Chengtu, Amoy, and Canton. "In each place," he wrote, "I was just a step or two in front of the Communist flood." The reason for the ultimate victory of the communists over the Nationalists was really very simple, as Jones verbalized it in *The Way to Power and Poise*. "The Kuomintang said they would put in land reforms—after the civil war. The Communists redistributed the land as a part of their war. They won."[46] But what puzzled Jones was the public reaction among both Christians and non-Christians that the communist takeover was inevitable. He said in his *Indian Witness* article, "In every place I was there was no will to resist, only a passive waiting to be taken over."

> Why has this swing in thought taken place so universally, for from Nanking to Canton it is the same? The answer seems to be that the Kuomintang Government has completely lost its grip on the people. I never heard one defender. Why? Well, it started out to be a radical, revolutionary movement—a movement that would sweep out feudalism and social and economic abuses from China. Then it stalled, became conservative, then reactionary, then corrupt. It lost its moral drive and purpose. . . . The Communists were the only driving force at hand. They stepped in to take over the revolution where the Kuomintang had morally abdicated. They were the only broom at hand and God uses available brooms even when He cannot approve of them.[47]

God obviously disapproved of the ruthless tactics of any-means-justifies-the-end of seizing control of China, which was practiced by the communists. Moreover, he could never approve of the outspoken atheism of Chinese communist philosophy and policy, nor would he sanction the idolatry of the communist party that was encouraged by its leadership or the later idolatry of Mao himself. But God does use whatever means are available, including spiritually indifferent and even evil means, to accomplish his purposes. However, if he does employ less than good means, he does not leave them untouched by his presence. Indeed, this is what Jones called in his *Indian Witness* article "the genius of the Christian faith," which is the power of "transformation." "Jesus took the worst thing that could happen to him, namely, His death, and transformed it into the best thing that could happen to the world, namely its redemption."[48] But this analysis of God's transforming power in Jesus Christ does not answer what was for Jones the central question about the new communist China—would Christianity survive as an evangelical force under the new regime? His answer was conditional. If Christianity did survive, it would "have to re-examine its message and emphasis," because Chinese Christianity, like Western Christianity in the twentieth century, was distorted by the philosophy of individualism. To correct this distortion, Jones predicted,

> Collectivism will probably drive it [Christianity] to rediscover the Kingdom of God—its central message. If so, then the Church in China will discover something more radical than communism—something that gathers up the good in individualism and the good in collectivism and goes beyond each and gives us a society where you love your neighbor (the truth of collectivism) as yourself (the truth of invidualism). . . . Christianity is not anti-capitalist or anti-communist, as such—it is anti-evil whether that evil be in capitalism or in communism. It must not be identified with either, but must stand on its own ground—the Kingdom of God—an "unshakable Kingdom."[49]

The kingdom principle Jones articulated in his *Indian Witness* article is, of course, the familiar principle of a new man out of both parties. Just as Jesus reconciled Jews and Gentiles through his death on the cross and at the same time transformed Jews and Gentiles by taking the truth of each and creating a new person who transcended them both, so Chinese Christians, if they were to continue to proclaim the gospel with a spiritual fervor that would attract new Christians, would have to reconcile individualism and collectivism and proclaim the kingdom of God that incorporated individualism and collectivism but also transcended them both. This new, distinctively Chinese Christianity would not only survive and prosper under communism; it would "enrich world Christianity." In other words, Jones was exhorting Chinese Christians to discover and proclaim the Christ of the Chinese road.

I am reminded here of the encounter that former Bishop Leroy Hodapp had with an avowed atheist instructor at Indiana University in the early 1960s. The remarkable account of this public debate between Hodapp and the professor is documented in E. Carver McGriff's history of Indiana Methodism, *Amazing Grace.*

> Hodapp allowed the professor to carry on at great length, producing his erudite quotations and presenting his overwhelmingly persuasive argument for atheism. Or so the man thought. When he was done, Hodapp thanked the professor for his forthright approach. Then Hodapp stated that while he disagreed and believed most profoundly in the existence of God and in the Bible, he realized that no one can be persuaded by argumentation. But what he did propose was this: "Since you and I both want to see the ills of our society overcome, and since both of us wish very much for the welfare of everyone in our community, can we join hands—you from your admirable insights from the field of science, me from my insights of my religion—and can we then join our energies, each according to our understanding, in making this world a better place?" Point, set, and match to Hodapp.[50]

It may be mere flight of fancy to attempt a parallel between Hodapp's adroit approach and the implied direct challenge Jones desired for the Chinese Christians vis-a-vis communism. In 1949 or before, had the Chinese church leaders boldly offered to work with the communist leaders—along the disarming lines Bishop Hodapp proposed to the outspoken Indiana University professor—to meet head-on the staggeringly unjust social and economic realities that drove the revolution, it is conceivable that Christianity, at least as a provoking barb in the side of communism, could have had a grudging, softening influence and effect on the course of the communists and the revolution. Stranger things have been known to happen.

Jones's spiritual insight into the Chinese character was not confined to the Christian community in that country. With amazing accuracy he predicted the political future of Chinese communism. Communism began in China, he said, with the lofty ideals of sweeping away bribery and corruption as well as feudalism and other forms of injustice. But in time communism "will probably taste power and prosperity and be corrupted by both and will need an inner dynamic for the re-making of moral character and an incentive for altruism."[51]

Within a few years of assuming absolute power in China, Mao Zedong was searching frantically for an inner dynamic to sustain the revolutionary zeal of the Communist Party and to transform China more quickly from a peasant society to a modern industrialized state. The inner dynamic he developed and implemented was The Great Leap Forward, which turned out to be a great failure and was followed by the even more ambitious and more catastrophic Cultural Revolution. Whether China will yet find the inner dynamic of the kingdom of God, as Jones hoped, remains to be seen.

Jones returned to India on May 4, 1949. As he reflected on his four-month tour of East Asia, his deepest satisfaction came from his visit to

Japan. There he was exhilarated by the personal and spiritual bond he formed with the Japanese people, and by the exciting new opportunities for Christian evangelism in that country. But in China, although he was optimistic about the survival and vitality of Christianity, he was deeply concerned about the political future of that nation. The success of Mao Zedong and of his Communist Party in seizing control of the world's most populous nation was a stern warning to the leaders of other developing nations who were threatened by communism. And, of course, he was especially concerned about the threat of communism in India. On May 15, 1949, he wrote a long and didactic letter to his friend, the new Prime Minister of India, Jawaharlal Nehru.[52] In his letter Jones first outlined the reason for the failure of the Nationalists in China and for the success of the communists. Because the Kuomintang Party, which began as "a revolutionary movement," he wrote, "slowed down, stalled, turned reactionary, and finally corrupt . . . the Communists . . . stepped in to complete the revolution." Jones continued his letter,

> The question that has begun haunting my mind since my return [to India] is this: Will the Congress go the way of the Kuomintang, for many of the same reasons, and will the Communists then step in and try to complete the revolution in India? I hope and pray not, for I look on the Congress and its leaders as the brightest spot in Asia. You have done magnificently. But will your revolutionary movement now slow down with its taste of power? Will it hesitate about getting the land back to the people, spending too much time on terms? Every hour counts now. And will the Congress tolerate or turn a blind eye to the bribery and corruption among the lower ranks of officials? . . .
>
> If the Congress can answer these questions in the right way and with decisiveness, then the country can be saved from Communism. . . .
>
> The Congress must complete the revolution which it has nobly begun, but which seems to some of us to be in danger of slowing down, perhaps stalling. . . . I look on the Congress as the noblest political movement of our century, and I am eager that it be the instrument of a completed revolution. But I remember being in China at a period when the Kuomintang seemed as secure and promising as the Congress does today. Its failure must not be repeated in India.
>
> I have unburdened my soul to you, for I believe in you and the Congress so profoundly that I have dared risk rushing in where angels fear to tread.

Nehru was a lifelong Indian nationalist and socialist and was committed to the same goals of redistributing land and of eliminating corruption that Jones discussed in his letter. As far as I know, he did not respond immediately to Jones's letter. Three years later, however, he did respond to another letter Jones wrote to him. On May 20, 1952, Jones wrote to Nehru and enclosed a copy of an article published in the May 21, 1952, issue of the *Christian Century*,[53] in which he referred to his May 15, 1949, letter. This letter, Jones wrote in his *Christian Century* article, had so impressed Nehru that he had sent it "to all his cabinet ministers and to all state governors."

On May 29, 1952, Nehru responded to Jones's statement by stating that he had "sent a quotation from" Jones's letter "to some of the members of our Government." But his primary concern was Jones's assertion in the *Christian Century* that "[c]orruption among officials [in India] continues."[54] "[W]hat has amazed me," Nehru wrote to Jones, "is your reference to corruption. I cannot imagine where you got your facts from about this."[55] Nehru was especially sensitive to the allegation of continued corruption among government officials, because he had tried so hard to wipe it out.

Whatever the truth about the extent of corruption in postindependence India, this exchange of letters between Jones and Nehru clearly underscores Jones's support for and personal identification with the goals of the Indian nationalist movement. Moreover, Nehru had great respect for Jones as a friendly critic of his government, and readily accepted his warning about the danger of the government's losing the inner dynamic of its revolutionary spirit. Even Nehru's sharp retort to Jones's suggestion of the persistence of official corruption confirms Jones's international prestige and influence, and the weight that his suggestion carried both in India and in the United States.

By 1949 we can clearly identify a genuine turning point in Jones's long career as a missionary evangelist, both in America and abroad. His six-year stay in the United States during World War II, prolonged by the British government's refusal to give him a visa to return to India until after the war, was the longest period of time he had spent in his native land since he first left America for India in 1907. During this time Jones became more broadly and more deeply involved in the religious and political affairs of the United States than he had ever been before.

The other event that makes 1949 a turning point in Jones's career is his trip to Japan and China. In Japan the spiritual seed he had so carefully sown in Washington in 1941 before Pearl Harbor finally bore fruit when the Japanese people opened their arms to him and opened their hearts to the good news of Jesus Christ.

After World War II Jones announced that he would spend six months of each year in the United States and six months in India. However, as his message of the kingdom of God resonated in the hearts of more people in more nations of the world, God began to call Jones to sacrifice some of his time in India and the United States in order to share the good news with those who hungered for Jesus Christ in other parts of the world. His vision became more global as he responded to a genuinely universal spiritual need. However, the top priority in Jones's schedule each year was his Christian ashrams, a subject to which we now turn.

15

Christian Ashrams

So the Ashram has become my home. It is an unbreakable fellowship,
for it does not depend on meeting together as a group,
but it depends on meeting together in him.

—E. Stanley Jones, *A Song of Ascents*[1]

IN AUGUST 1940 CLARENCE E. HILL, a staff reporter for the *Kansas City Star,* visited Jones's first Christian ashram in America in Saugatuck, Michigan. The Sunday, August 11, edition of the newspaper carried his story about the Saugatuck Ashram.[2] The ashram, Hill wrote, was held in a secluded, "heavily-timbered camp on the edge of [a] . . . resort village on the shore of Lake Michigan." Then he described the physical setting of the camp and the appearance of the leader of the ashram.

> The camp is on a high hilly plot overlooking a wide expanse of beach of Lake Michigan and there each morning the day begins with prayer, meditation and song, with the gentle lash of the waves as a background.
>
> The deep blue, fog-like mist hanging far out over the seemingly endless expanse of water and penetrated only by the rays of the morning sun, hushes the gaiety of the children and the adults speak in undertones as they make their way through the sand to the meeting place in the shadow of a huge, roughly-hewn cross marking the altar of the outdoor chapel.
>
> Again the Biblical background is brought vividly to mind as Dr. E. Stanley

Jones, Methodist missionary to India and moving spirit of the ashram dressed in native Indian costume, his feet covered only by the strips of sandals, plods slowly to the mound of sand upon which he sits with legs crossed in the manner of an Indian teacher, to lead the service.

For Stanley Jones, who traveled constantly and was able to visit his wife and daughter for short periods of time only infrequently, his ashrams were indeed his home. From the time he established his first ashram at Sat Tal in 1930 until his death in 1973, nothing was closer to his heart than these Christian spiritual retreats. Jones's ashrams are perhaps his most important and his most enduring contribution to the Body of Christ. Even more than his books and articles, which inspired millions of readers; his public evangelistic meetings in which thousands were led to a personal relationship with Jesus Christ; his interviews and counseling sessions, which reoriented the lives of thousands more on the basis of the principle of self-surrender—his ashrams transformed those who participated in them. Referring to the men, women, and children who attended the Saugatuck Ashram, Clarence Hill concluded, "To them the kingdom of God is real."

This is the key to the success of Jones's Christian ashrams: They embodied the kingdom of God. Although Jones founded the Sat Tal Ashram and later led the Christian ashram movement in America and throughout the world, the real leader or *guru* of the Christian ashrams was Jesus Christ. This central focus on Christ meant that Jones, just like the other members of the ashram, was accountable first of all to God. But as a Christian community the members of the ashram, including Jones, were also accountable to one another. The members of the ashrams, Jones liked to say, were the kingdom of God in miniature because they accepted God's love for them through Jesus Christ and they shared that love with each other.

In his spiritual autobiography, *A Song of Ascents,* Jones traced the origin of his Christian ashrams to the Wesleyan class meetings he attended at Memorial Methodist Episcopal Church in Baltimore after he was converted. In these weekly meetings the members shared "their experiences with God," both positive and negative. For Jones the class meetings were an opportunity for growth and development in the Christian faith. "Everyone," he said, "needs a close-knit fellowship to which he is responsible and which is responsible for him."[3] But Jones did not fully recognize the need for group discipline and group accountability in his calling as a missionary evangelist until 1930.[4] Then he drew on his experience at the ashrams established by Tagore and Gandhi to create a Christian ashram at Sat Tal. The word *ashram* comes from two Sanskrit words, *a* meaning from and *shram* meaning hard work. So an ashram is a retreat from hard work, usually in an outdoor or forest school under the guidance of a *guru* or teacher.[5]

Sat Tal was an ideal location for an ashram because it consisted of approximately four hundred acres with a number of lakes, including Panna (Emerald) Lake, and was situated at an elevation of five thousand feet in the foothills of the Himalayas. The name *Sat Tal* means "seven lakes," and there is an Indian legend about the origin of the name. Eunice Jones Mathews, Jones's daughter, learned about the legend from the wife of the previous owner of the Sat Tal estate, Mrs. A. C. Evans, who recorded this account of the legend.

> In the beginning Sat Tal seems to have been considered a holy place inhabited by gods, and we may suppose goddesses also. There were seven sacred hilltops round about the valley and there is a very charming legend which may account for the suitable name the valley bears.
>
> A poor native woman was picking up dry twigs and small branches with which to cook her food when she suddenly saw, under a tree, an old man who appeared to be very ill. She went and spoke to him. "Daughter," he replied, "I am very ill and am dying from thirst. Have mercy and bring me water to drink." She said, "O Stranger, the spring is far from here and I have nothing in which to bring you water."
>
> The old man, however, seemed to her so ill that she hurried down the hill to the nearest spring and laboured up again with as much precious water as she could retain in her cupped hands. This she did seven times. Her efforts seemed to revive the old man who said to her, "O daughter, you have done well. For each handful of water you have brought me a lake will be formed amongst these hills." And so Sat Tal owes its origin to a god and a kind woman.[6]

Stanley and Mabel had spent several summers at Sat Tal while it was operated as a summer resort by Mr. and Mrs. Evans, a retired British engineer and his wife. When the Evanses became too old to maintain Sat Tal as a resort, they sold the property to Stanley who, using the profits from the sale of his books, paid them an annuity until Mrs. Evans died in 1947. Together with the Reverend Yunas Sinha, an Indian Christian minister, and Ethel Turner, a retired missionary from the London Missionary Society, Stanley established a Christian ashram at Sat Tal as "a vacation with God" during May and June, the two hottest months of the year.[7] Reflecting on the ashram in a statement that was published (after Stanley's death) in 1980 for the fiftieth anniversary of its founding, Jones recalled the early years at Sat Tal.

> So in the Sat Tal Ashram we determined to live in simplicity, in Indian dress and with Indian food. The framework of our thinking . . . [was] as Indian as possible. As we expected to have Hindus join us, the food was vegetarian. For our meetings and meals we sat on mats on the floor, ate out of brass vessels, sang a Hindi grace set to a beautiful Sanskrit tune, left our sandals at the door and tucked our feet up under us as we sat in meditation.[8]

Although the concept of an ashram has a Hindu origin, and although the members of the Sat Tal Ashram practiced an Indian lifestyle, this does not mean that the ashram subordinated Christ to India's culture and religion. Instead, the spirit of the ashram, Jones insisted, was always that "reverence for India and her genius will only be exceeded by our reverence for Christ, and His way, and His truth."[9] It is also a mistake to assume that Jones's Christian ashrams were a syncretism or combination of Hindu and Christian ideas, or that his ashrams were eclectic, picking and choosing among Christian and non-Christian concepts. Jones said that the best word to describe Christian ashrams was "assimilation."

> The Christian faith, being life, assimilates. Like the plant which reaches into the soil and picks out things akin to its own nature, takes them up into the purpose of its life, but transforms them according to the laws of its own being, so the Christian faith reaches into the culture of every nation and takes out things which can be assimilated into its purpose, but in doing so makes something entirely different.[10]

Moreover, unlike Hindu ashrams, which were organized around the personality of their human leaders, for example, Tagore and Gandhi, Christian ashrams were organized around Jesus Christ, who became their *guru.*

In a pamphlet entitled, "What Is an Ashram?"[11] which was written by Jones and distributed by The United Christian Ashrams, an organization incorporated by Jones in 1957 after his Christian ashrams became a worldwide movement, he explained that ashrams were one of many group movements designed to restore *koinonia* or fellowship to the church. *Koinonia* refers to the type of fellowship created among the believers by the coming of the Holy Spirit as described in Acts 2:42 (NIV)—"They devoted themselves to the apostles' teaching and to the fellowship, to the breaking of bread and to prayer." The church, Jones emphasized, grew out of *koinonia*, but it was not the same as *koinonia.* In his own words, "This Koinonia became the soul out of which the body, the Church, grew. It was the organism out of which the organization, the Church, emerged."

Christian ashrams were one attempt to re-create the original understanding of fellowship in the church, but they were not the only way or even the best way. "Only Jesus Christ is the Way." And because all Christians "have one thing in common," namely, Jesus Christ, "[e]veryone who belongs to Christ belongs to everyone who belongs to Christ." In order to establish this fellowship as the kingdom of God, which Jones called "God's redemptive invasion of us," Christian ashrams had to remove barriers, both external and internal. External barriers included differences in nationality (especially at Sat Tal), denominational differences, age differences, socioeconomic differences, and gender differences. But the most difficult barriers are internal. As Jones explained in his spiritual autobiography,

> [T]he biggest barriers are within us—fears, resentments, self-preoccupation, guilts, impurities, inferiorities, jealousies, and emptiness. These are the things that separate us from one another, from ourselves, and from God.[12]

The first task of a Christian ashram, if it is to establish a genuine *koinonia* by receiving the redemption of the kingdom of God, is to confess these internal barriers so that their demonic power can be broken and that they may be replaced by the fruit of the Holy Spirit. For this reason Jones always opened his ashrams with the "Morning of the Open Heart." In this meeting the members of the ashram responded to the questions, "Why have you come? What do you want? What do you really need?"[13]

One of the most moving experiences I have had in doing the research for this book is reading the meticulous, handwritten notes Jones made in his notebooks as members of each ashram he attended responded to these questions. (His notebooks, which he always had with him, contain a wide variety of materials, including meditations, notes for sermons and addresses, and summaries of key passages of books he read.) These notes reveal Jones's disciplined and conscientious attention to what the members of his Christian ashrams shared during the "Morning of the Open Heart." But on a deeper spiritual level, the notes disclose how profoundly important the ashrams were to Jones personally and how essential they were to God's call on his life as an evangelist. As the members of the ashram opened their hearts to one another and to God, the inner barriers of fear, resentment, jealousy, and so forth, began to fall. Then at the end of the ashram, during a meeting which Jones called the "Overflowing Heart" and which he also carefully recorded in his notebooks, the members testified to what God had done in their lives. Here was concrete evidence of the transforming power of *koinonia* among fellow believers in Jesus Christ. Here was the kingdom of God in miniature.

In 1984, on the 100th anniversary of Stanley Jones's birth, the Reverend Dr. Roberto Escamilla, a Methodist pastor who accompanied Jones while he was leading ashrams in South America and who acted as his interpreter, recalled Jones's sensitivity to what the members of the ashrams shared during the meetings of the "Open Heart" and the "Overflowing Heart."

> During the "Open Heart" and "Overflowing Heart" experiences, he took copious notes as he did in all other Ashrams. Everything people would say was important. He wanted literal translations of what was being said and not just the highlights. He would watch the faces and expressions of people and attempt to penetrate into their emotional conditions even though he did not understand what they were saying.[14]

Another Christian who functioned as Jones's interpreter in a country half a world away from South America, and in a language very different from Spanish, confirms Escamilla's assessment of Jones's spiritual sensitivity. Sabrow Yasumura served as Jones's interpreter in Japan. After traveling with Jones for three months in 1953 Yasumura wrote,

> [W]hen I think of good interpretation, I realize that it demands a depth of spiritual experience on the part of the interpreter in order to transmit the power of the speaker. For transmitting the Christian message means transmitting not only the logical statement of truths, but also spiritual power. If I may borrow the term used by Dr. Jones, it requires a full surrender in order that God's own reality may be revealed to the hearers. Here I am utterly far from being anywhere near to Dr. Jones in his experiences. Not only in his words but in his everyday life, his wonderful sense of surrender and his faith in the abiding presence of the Holy Spirit so permeate his life that he is utterly free in his Christian living. There is nothing formal or artificial about his morning devotions. There is no long praying and no repetition of vain words. Just a quiet, unhurried hour of meditation over a passage in the Bible and communion with the living Christ in a most unpretentious manner, and yet almost every day he talked about some new discovery in the Bible passage.[15]

Jones's ashrams not only provided a disciplined fellowship, which gave him a sense of belonging and a source of accountability, they also tested his sensitivity to the Inner Voice and his obedience to God's direction as well as the integrity of his message. In the early ashrams at Sat Tal, Jones often used his book manuscripts or his ideas for evangelistic addresses as the basis for group discussion. "If the response was faint or unsatisfactory or just not what it ought to be," he wrote in *A Song of Ascents,* "the message was quietly laid aside or interred." Later, when his ashrams became an international movement, Jones tailored his ashram messages according to the needs expressed in the "Morning of the Open Heart." What he was doing in his ashrams, he said, was not "preaching, but prescription. The patients had described their symptoms in the Open Heart, and now I had to give in my addresses the prescription for the cure."[16]

In order to provide a spiritually effective cure, Jones had to correctly discern God's word for the members of the ashram, but he also had to practice what he preached. The most compelling evidence that he did indeed rightly perceive God's will, and that he was in fact a living example of his sermons, is the testimony of thousands of those who, during the sessions of the "Overflowing Heart," told how the internal and external barriers in their lives had been broken and how their relationships to God, to themselves, and to others were forever changed.

This evidence by those who knew Jones as a public figure in his ashrams is confirmed by those who knew him on a more personal basis. His son-in-law, James K. Mathews, wrote of Stanley Jones after his death,

I never saw him lose his temper; nor heard him speak ill of anyone; nor even a hint that he was discouraged or depressed. He kept up a regular and systematic devotional life—simply disappeared for an hour or so morning and evening for his Quiet Time. He was constantly at work; constantly reading, writing, studying, counseling, replying to extensive correspondence. Yet he had time for his grandchildren and to be nice to visitors in our home. We were aware of his constant helpfulness to others. We saw him send out checks for scholarship aid to students, to the needy, to those who were suffering some hardship. He gave away all his "book money"—the royalties amounting to more than a million dollars from his books. He was in private what he was reputed to be in public. I have never seen his like.[17]

Another person who knew Jones well and who often gave her Christian witness before he spoke at ashrams was Mary Webster Tattersall. She wrote that when she first heard him preach on March 19, 1950, in Peoria, Illinois,

I saw also the Lord, as Isaiah did, high and lifted up, and His Presence filled the Church, and my heart also. There were a thousand people present, but he spoke as if I were the only one! . . . After being in his presence only one hour and a half, he had brought me into His Presence. . . .

Later, I was privileged to serve as a part-time secretary to him in some of his overseas missions. Many people treated him as if he were a "seven-day-wonder," a saint or a spiritual superman; but I noticed that God had given him a remarkable balance that kept him from forgetting that he was simply a man whom God had chosen to work through because of his willingness to be used. He possessed a "spiritual transparency" that let you see not him, but see Jesus through him! . . .

Brother Stanley was like inlaid linoleum; not like congoleum with the pattern just stamped on top, but the same from top to bottom. He was Christian all the way through![18]

Between the time of the "Morning of the Open Heart" and the concluding session of the "Overflowing Heart" the members of the ashram confronted and attacked external barriers to Christian fellowship. One of these barriers was the distinction between manual workers and white-collar workers. In order to break down this barrier of occupational and class status, Jones included in the daily schedule of his ashrams a work period during which each member performed some kind of manual labor. In his spiritual autobiography he described the origin of the work period in the Sat Tal Ashram.

We gave the servants we have at the Ashram a holiday once a week and asked for volunteers to do their jobs, including the sweeper who cleaned the latrines, in those early days by hand, since we had no flush latrines. To do his work would make the person who did the work a sweeper, the lowest caste, in the eyes of the Brahmin and other Hindus. The first day we gave the vacation I volunteered to do the sweeper's work along with several others. When a Brahmin convert was hesitating to volunteer, I asked him when he was going to volunteer. He shook his head and said: "Brother Stanley, I'm converted, but I'm not converted that far."[19]

Later, after Sat Tal acquired indoor plumbing and his Christian ashrams became an international movement, Jones described his new responsibility during the daily work period.

> My job has been to pick up paper, so they usually provide me with a sharp stick and a bag. The consequence is I have become paper conscious. I see paper everywhere. I feel an almost irresistible impulse to pick it up. Some places in Denmark, Holland, and Scandanavia were so clean I had difficulty in keeping my job.[20]

After leading the Sat Tal Ashram for ten years, from 1930 to 1940, Jones transplanted his Christian ashrams to the United States. With the financial help of Mr. E. V. Moorman and with the administrative assistance of Dr. Jesse Bader, the executive secretary of the Department of Evangelism of the Federal Council of Churches, Jones held his first American ashram, as we have seen, at Saugatuck, Michigan, in August 1940. In 1957, in order to promote greater independence and greater local responsibility among the ashrams, which were growing rapidly in many nations throughout the world, the ashram movement was incorporated in the state of Texas as American Christian Ashrams. (In 1961 the incorporation papers were amended to change the name to United Christian Ashrams, the name which the organization still bears today.) Jones's Christian ashrams were so successful that by the time he published his spiritual autobiography in 1968 there were one hundred ashrams throughout the world, including ashrams in Canada, Puerto Rico, Mexico, Spain, Uruguay, Peru, Bolivia, Brazil, Argentina, Chile, Israel, Japan, India, Burma, Korea, Taiwan, the Philippines, Indonesia, Malaysia, Singapore, Germany, the Netherlands, Norway, Spain, Sweden, Denmark, Finland, the Belgian Congo (Congo), Nigeria, and Southern Rhodesia (Zimbabwe).[21]

As the ashrams grew in number and in diversity of locations, nationalities, and languages, Jones recognized the need for a single organizational structure to preserve the integrity of their Christian spiritual focus, while at the same time accommodating the different national and cultural expressions of the common search for a deeper and more meaningful *koinonia*. In his *Song of Ascents* he depicted the overall structure of the ashram as a pyramid with numbers of people increasing from top to bottom. At the apex of the pyramid was the head of the ashram, Jesus Christ. Just below Christ were The Three (later The Four), followed by The Seven, The Twelve, The 120, The 500, The Church, and finally The Kingdom of God. Some of the numbers had biblical significance: The Twelve, for example, were the same as the number of Jesus' disciples, and The 120 reflect the number in the Upper Room at Pentecost.[22]

In terms of authority and responsibility, The Seven were comparable to a board of directors with ultimate power over the policy, personnel, and property of the United Christian Ashrams. The Three were an executive committee of The Seven and in 1968 consisted of Jones; Dr. J. T. Seamands, a faculty member at Asbury Theological Seminary; and the Reverend Dr. William E. Berg, the pastor of a large Lutheran congregation in Minneapolis. The Twelve were not a single group but many groups of twelve, each of which was in charge of one ashram. The Twelve consisted of nine local representatives plus The Three. The 120, whose actual number varied with the size of each ashram, were the Family Meeting, a feature of the United Christian Ashrams first used in the United States. The Family Meeting was held each day and included all members of the ashram in an informal session during which criticism and suggestions for improvement of the ashram were openly discussed. As the authoritative body of the local ashram, the Family Meeting approved the selection of the Twelve, who functioned as a continuing group between meetings of the ashram. The 500 Brethren were the Ashram Associates, who committed themselves to support all the ashrams financially as well as through prayer and active service. The Church, although near the bottom of the pyramid, was what Jones called "the home of us all" and an integral part of the United Christian Ashrams. It is important to remember that Jones never intended his ashrams to compete with the various Christian churches, and, in fact, they never have.

In his pamphlet, "What Is an Ashram?" Stanley explained:

> The Ashram is deeply Christ-centric and deeply Church-centric. We are not trying to pull people away from the churches and absorb their loyalty and love apart from the churches. We are trying to make the Ashram a permeative movement in the life of the churches to make better pastors, better officials and better members by making better persons. Finally, at the bottom of the pyramid was the kingdom of God, "the ultimate loyalty of us all."

As we have seen (see chapter 14), Jones first acquired continuing staff assistance in 1947 when Harvey Kazmier volunteered to help organize the Crusade for a United Church. In the early years of the ashram movement in the United States, Jesse Bader of the Federal Council of Churches served as an administrative assistant for Jones not only in scheduling his ashrams but also in organizing his preaching and evangelistic missions. In 1960, because of the rapidly growing momentum of the ashram movement, Jones asked William W. Richardson, an insurance executive and active layman in the United Church of Christ who had served as general secretary of the New England Ashram, to become general secretary of all the ashrams. Richardson served in this capacity for fifteen years until two years after Jones's death. He worked on a volunteer basis with his "'tent making' or financial remuneration" coming from his insurance agency.[23] After his retirement in 1975, Richardson documented the growth of the United Christian Ashrams during his tenure as general secretary. "It is interesting to note," he wrote, "that our budget in 1963 was $8000, moving up to $80,000 in 1975. Our mailing list jumped from 2500 in those early years to 10,000 in 1975."[24]

Jones remained actively involved in every aspect of the United Christian Ashrams throughout his life. But in December 1971, while in Oklahoma City for a speaking engagement, he suffered a stroke that severely impaired his speech, sight, and physical mobility. He was transferred to the Boston Rehabilitation Hospital, and because of his illness was unable to attend the annual meeting of the UCA Board of Directors (The Seven) scheduled to be held in Orlando, Florida, in January 1972. He did, however, manage to communicate to Eunice and Jim Mathews and to Mary Webster Tattersall, who had been serving as his secretary, the contents of a memorandum for the board meeting. Although he lived for another year after the board meeting, his January 3, 1972, memo was, in effect, his last will and testament for the Christian ashram movement. The memo read in part:

> It is my earnest desire that the Ashram movement be kept open theologically, spiritually and practically as for my whole life I have attempted to be and do: evangelical and evangelistic, in the sense of being responsive to and obedient to the whole Gospel, commending it to all mankind; ecumenical, transcending all denominational and sectarian division; inclusive, with equal participation of all without respect to race, nationality, class, age or sex; perpetually relevant to the times and the real needs of humankind; committed to Christ and his Kingdom, individually and corporately; guided by the Holy Spirit, together with the combined wisdom of the concerned and committed fellowship.[25]

For Jones the Christian ashrams were the consummate expression of the kingdom of God. They embodied all the distinctive features of his thinking, preaching, writing, and action. Beginning at Sat Tal, Jones's ashrams embraced non-Western expressions of Christianity and by their openness to different races, cultures, traditions, and customs drew all who shared in their fellowship to the feet of Jesus Christ. His ashrams were evangelical in the broadest sense, proclaiming the good news of God's saving and redeeming power through Jesus Christ not only to individuals but also to society as a whole

It was in this evangelically broad sense that Jones enjoined The Seven in his January 3, 1972, memo to obey "the whole Gospel" and to remain always "relevant to the times and the real needs of humankind." Nothing short of the totalitarian kingdom of God, in the best sense of the term, could fully and adequately respond to the universal human need for personal and for corporate salvation. Social, political, and economic issues were therefore an integral part of the thought, discussion, and prayer of Jones's Christian ashrams. In addition, his ashrams were consistently ecumenical, reflecting the interdenominational nature of his own work as a missionary evangelist and drawing on his deep conviction, grounded in the New Testament Gospels and Epistles, that the Body of Christ must be one. Jones insisted that his ashrams be open to all Christians, from Roman Catholics to Pentecostals.

Jones also insisted that Christian ashrams must be racially and gender inclusive. He was one of the very first American evangelists to include African Americans in his public meetings. In fact, he refused to hold meetings where African Americans or any other racial or ethnic group was excluded, a policy he extended to the ashram movement. At the risk of being overly repetitive, it is no exaggeration to emphasize again how egalitarian the ashrams were meant to be, simply because Jones so strongly adhered to the kingdom-derived plank of equality of opportunity. Parenthetically, as one reads about and closely examines the spirit, the intent, and the scope of the ashrams, one detects the rich blend of Christianity's spiritual and theological emphases down through the ages, characteristics that were so bedrock to and exemplified in Christ's life and ministry, namely: *holiness, compassion, contemplation, evangelistic zeal,* and *charismatic and incarnational* (full dimensional) *living.*[26] Finally, just as Jones himself relied on the Inner Voice as the final authority for his personal decisions and actions, so the Holy Spirit guided the decisions and actions of each ashram as discerned by the collective wisdom of the *koinonia.* In each aspect or element of his Christian ashrams, Jones acted on the basis of the concepts of self-surrender and of a new man out of both parties, which were foundational to the kingdom of God. In order to be fully part of a Christian community, each member of the ashram had to surrender himself or herself to God and to the other members of the ashram. Self-surrender in this dual sense created from the diverse members of the ashram new men and women in Christ who lived transformed lives in the kingdom of God.

16

The Last Years

As the years come and go I feel less and less that I'm doing things —
I'm just letting God do things through me.
　　　　　　—E. Stanley Jones, December 22, 1951, circular letter[1]

I read your "Song of Ascents" last week. My heart tells me to write and say how grate-
ful I am that you have kept interpreting Jesus Christ all these years to all the world. It
seems to me that Christ has somebody who stays with him through thick and thin every
century, when the devil tries his best to make the world forget or deny his divinity, and
that you are the man he used this century. They must have you very very high in the
estimation of heaven.
　　　　　　—Frank C. Laubach, November 18, 1968, letter to E. Stanley Jones[2]

IN EARLY 1953 STANLEY JONES was in Japan for his third evangelistic
tour since the end of World War II. As he planned his itinerary for the
rest of the year in India and the United States, he wondered if the government of India would permit him to return. And when he was permitted to return to lead the annual spring ashram at Sat Tal, he "came to
India," he said, "for the first time in . . . forty-six years of connection with
her with a feeling that I was not wanted."

What had happened to make him feel unwelcome? India was, after all,
as he often said, his "adopted homeland," where he had his second conversion experience, where he met and married his wife, Mabel, where
their only child, Eunice, was born, and where he had poured out his heart
and soul for nearly half a century to fulfill God's call to him to proclaim
the good news of Jesus Christ. The cause of his concern was a newspaper
article he read in Japan reporting on a parliamentary debate in India
about the status of missionaries. It was so "painful" to read, Stanley said

afterward, that in response he wrote an "Open Letter" to the Government of India.[3] He did not publish the letter but sent it "to some of the national leaders of India for a personal reply."

The "Open Letter" does not refer specifically to what was said in the parliamentary debate, but it almost certainly reflects renewed suspicion on the part of the government that Christian missionaries were the agents of Western imperialism and that the religious conversions that missionaries sought would upset the fragile political balance between the Hindu majority and the various minority religions in India. It is indeed ironic that Stanley Jones, who for so many years spoke out so directly and so forcefully on behalf of India's right to be free, was now, as a Christian evangelist, suspected of the crime of neocolonialism. The open letter is a bitter reflection of his dismay and his sense of personal betrayal. Because he had insisted on his moral right "to speak of the right of India to freedom" while it was under British rule, Stanley wrote, he "was kept out of India by the British authorities for five years during the war." He had paid a high price to advocate India's right to independence, but now all his efforts on behalf of his beloved India were being swept aside by self-serving demagogues.

After India became an independent nation in 1947, the new Republic of India had increasingly denied visas to Western Christian missionaries seeking admission to that country. The government's most serious continuing concern was proselytism. A good example of this official concern was a later report, made in 1956, by a committee appointed by one of the state governments of India, the government of Madhya Pradesh. According to church historian Kenneth Scott Latourette, the report

> had high praise for missionaries for establishing schools, hospitals, dispensaries, orphanages, and institutions for the handicapped. It commended them for elevating the neglected classes to a better social position, for improving the status of women, and for stimulating many social and religious reforms in Hindu society. But it objected vigorously to changing the religious orientation of Indians and charged that non-religious inducements were offered to produce conversions, especially among the hill tribes and the depressed classes. It accused missionaries of mixing in politics. It maintained that missionaries were placing obstacles to the creation of the secular welfare state which was the goal of the Republic of India. It recommended, among other measures, that the large influx of foreign missionaries be checked, that missionaries whose primary object was "proselytization" be asked to withdraw, that the Indian Christians establish a united church in India which would be independent of foreign support and control, that the use of medical or other professional services to effect conversions be prohibited by law, that the employment of any means to induce individuals to change their religious faith should be absolutely interdicted, that the circulation of literature for religious propaganda be not permitted unless with government approval, and that no non-official agency be allowed to obtain foreign assistance except through government channels.[4]

To be sure, this report was not adopted by the national government, but it does reflect the widespread concern about Christian missionaries in India that had sparked the parliamentary debate back in 1953 that Jones found so profoundly disturbing.

In reply to the abhorrence of proselytism, Jones's "Open Letter" made the distinction, which he had often made in the past, between proselytism or merely changing religious labels and genuine conversion. He did not believe in proselytism; instead, he had committed his entire life to Christian conversion.

> I want to produce conversion in everybody, East and West, beginning with myself. For I believe that this fact of moral and spiritual conversion is a prime necessity for life everywhere and a strong, progressive national life cannot be built unless there is a moral undergirding by this moral and spiritual change. Hence I think I am contributing a nation-building element, a very necessary element in both East and West. For the outer structure of life depends on that imponderable thing called character. If the character breaks the confidence breaks, if the confidence breaks the country breaks. One of your outstanding national leaders, a Hindu, said as a chairman of one of my meetings: "Our problem has not changed—it is not to gain independence, but to retain it. For this we need changed character. There is no doubt that the impact of Christ upon the framework of human nature produces miracles of changed character. As such we welcome it."

After explaining how his pursuit and practice of genuine Christian conversion, by changing human character, had made a vital and absolutely necessary contribution to the success of the world's largest democracy, Jones demanded to know, first of all, whether he would be permitted to return to India. He explained that he wanted to return to the United States at the end of June and then come back to India for a four-month evangelistic tour sponsored by the National Christian Council and for two months at the Sat Tal Ashram. "Will I be allowed to do so?" he asked. If the government did permit him to return to India, he wanted to know under what conditions. In language he could have taken verbatim from his exchange of letters with the British government about their permitting him to go back to India after World War II (see chapter 12), Jones concluded his "Open Letter,"

> I need not tell you that I have no desire to enter India by a side-door of compromise and then continue my work [under] another guise. I want to enter the front door of my adopted land with a plain understanding and I hope, with a welcome. And I hope that welcome will be also extended to my missionary brothers and sisters who take my same general attitudes. I know of no land in the world, outside the Communist countries, where I am not welcome—and welcome as an evangelist. I should hate to think that the land of my adoption would be the exception and that I would have to skirt this land in the future and go to other lands.

The replies Jones received were encouraging and reassuring. In his June 17, 1953, circular letter he wrote that he received responses from almost all of the officials to whom he sent it.[5] The "consensus of replies," he said, "was that if evangelistic missionaries would do evangelistic work in the spirit and outlook in which I was doing it there could be no objection." With this clarification he felt he was "apparently free to carry on" his "evangelistic work." One of the reassuring replies was from Chandra Bhal,[6] whose brother had given him a copy of the "Open Letter." Bhal wrote:

> I do not think you need worry over what individual members say in the course of a debate in Parliament, even if they be members of government. Unless the government passes any definite order against mission work, I think you can just ignore individual expressions of opinion.

He received another reply from Sri Prakasa, the Governor of Madras,[7] who wrote:

> You know my own sentiments towards Christian endeavour in India. I have made no secret of my feelings of gratitude and respect for all that they have done and sought to do. . . . I am therefore sorry that any incident should have occurred which has resulted in your feelings of despondency for the future. I do hope that you will be able to shake that feeling off, and that we shall do nothing which should give you the idea that we are not conducting ourselves as a free and great people should.

Prakasa then explained some of the reasons for Indian animosity toward Western missionaries, reasons with which Jones was thoroughly familiar. In the past, Prakasa wrote, the British had used "missionaries as their collaborators in the imperialistic game." Moreover, many Indians suspected that "foreign missionaries were taking too great an interest in the internal politics" of India. Because of this history of strained relationships between India and Christian missionaries, Prakasa appealed to Jones to use his "great innate capacity for influencing others for good" and to

> tell missionaries in India to have nothing any more to do with politics, but to devote themselves entirely to their evangelistic work. I have no doubt that there would be no trouble at all, if that were so. . . . Everybody is most anxious—honestly anxious—that all religions should have equal place in the land, and that all persons—whatever their religious calling may be—should have all the advantages of being the citizens of the country.

In conclusion, Prakasa offered his personal support and encouragement.

> So far as I am concerned, you may be sure I shall use whatever little influence I possess, in favour of all that you wish. It is a great and noble task you

have undertaken, and I have no doubt more and more persons will help and not hinder in the good work.

After this exchange of letters with Indian government officials, Stanley did not again question his right to remain in India or to conduct evangelistic campaigns in the country. Throughout the 1950s, however, he felt obliged to speak out on a number of issues that were the source of continued opposition to Christian missions in India. One of these was the decision of the United States in 1954 to give military aid to Pakistan.[8] The decision was made when Kashmir, a region lying between India and Pakistan and claimed by both nations, was becoming a serious and volatile issue. In his June 26, 1954, circular letter, Stanley wrote that, during the first six months of that year in India,

> I had to work against the background of U.S. military aid to Pakistan, a grave mistake. Two armies are drawn up in Kashmir awaiting a settlement of the Kashmir question and to give military aid to Pakistan meant giving arms to a belligerent and was an unfriendly act to India. So India interpreted it. We have lost a great fund of good will India had for us. The American missionaries in India, being at hand, were made the whipping boys. An anti-missionary agitation has been carried on in the newspapers and in some government circles. It was amid this atmosphere I carried on my work among the educated classes.

He felt so strongly that the decision by the United States to give military aid to Pakistan was wrong that he published an outspoken article in the November 11, 1954, issue of the *Christian Century*.[9] Indians were enraged, he wrote, at the United States taking sides in their bitter dispute with Pakistan. Because of this anger, Jones, together with "a group of Indians and missionaries" at Sat Tal, felt obliged to draw up a statement "[t]o clarify the position of Christian missions in India." The statement summarizes and reaffirms many of the principles that Jones had developed and articulated during his long missionary career in India: Social services should not be used by missionaries as "baits" for conversion to Christianity; the Christian gospel is not for "any particular nation," but for everybody; proselytism but not genuine conversion should be rejected; missionaries "*should have no political or financial connections with the government of the country from which they come,* and they should take no part in the politics of the country to which they go"; no missionary should attack any person's religion; and the property and institutions of foreign missions "should be transferred as quickly as possible to responsible bodies of indigenous Christians."

Another problem in the 1950s that complicated the relationship between Christian missionaries and the Republic of India was the denial of visas and the delay in granting visas to American missionaries. On April 7 and 8, 1958, Stanley and the Reverend H. A. Townsley conducted interviews with three top government officials about this problem—Jawaharlal Nehru, the prime minister; Govind Ballabh Pant, the home minister; and Rajendra Prasad, the president.[10] Prime Minister Nehru agreed that, in general, relations between missionaries and the government "were better." Jones then explained why, after the war, the number of missionaries in India had increased from approximately twenty-five hundred to about five thousand. The increase came not from "the old line missions," like the Methodists, but from "the marginal groups, the independent groups." The established missions, he said, were Indianizing as fast as possible; for example, all four Methodist bishops, 93 percent of the district superintendents, and the heads of almost all Methodist institutions were Indian. So, Jones concluded, when the traditional missions asked for a missionary to be admitted to the country, it was because there was a real need for the missionary. Again, he cited a personal example with his Nurmanzil Psychiatric Center, which needed expert personnel from abroad. Jones and Townsley made similar points in their interviews with the Home Minister and the President and felt afterward that they had made definite progress in resolving the problem of visas for Christian missionaries and especially Methodist missionaries.

The anti-American and anti-Western attitudes Jones encountered in India after independence came to a climax in the mid-1950s, but at no time did they prevent him from conducting evangelistic missions or from leading his Christian ashrams. At the beginning of the decade, as he prepared to leave the United States for India, he wrote to his friends and financial supporters on April 30, 1950, about his plans for the coming year. As soon as he arrived in India, he said, he hoped to see the Premier, Prime Minister Nehru, and other government officials about the opening of the Nurmanzil Psychiatric Center. Then he would speak in a series of evangelistic meetings in Shillong and Darjeeling before the beginning of the Sat Tal Ashram. In July he would return to America for five summer ashrams, followed by public meetings throughout the country on behalf of the Crusade for a United Church during September, and finally by evangelistic missions from October through December. In addition, by September he planned to begin work on a new devotional book, *How to Be a Transformed Person*.

> I hope to have it completed in the early summer of 1951 and it should be out by November—two years after the last one. I'm spacing my babies now about two years apart. More birth-control? Perhaps!

In his next circular letter, dated October 15, 1950, he reported that he had completed most of the schedule outlined in his April 30 circular letter. "Sandwiched in between other engagements," he wrote, "I went to Washington to see if we could do anything to head off another world war." He anticipated another world war because he feared that the Korean War might well escalate into a much wider and more deadly conflict. India, acting on behalf of developing nations and nations that were not aligned with either the United States or the Soviet Union, had made a proposal for ending the war. Stanley thought this proposal might actually work, and it was the proposal that he went to Washington in the fall of 1950 to promote. In a period of two days he had seen twenty-five members of Congress, spent an hour with officials of the State Department, and testified for fifteen minutes before the House Foreign Affairs Committee. On September 1 he had a fifteen-minute appointment with President Truman. The purpose of his visit, he wrote in his October 15 circular letter, was to urge Truman "to go to the U.N. Assembly in person and make a dramatic appeal for peace around the India proposal." In terms of the final results, Jones's "15 minutes" in the "sun" of President Truman might as well have been fifteen seconds. Jones's papers contain no further word on the outcome of this meeting.[11]

In chapter 14 we saw how deeply Stanley was moved by his first visit to Japan in 1949. Because he was welcomed so warmly, and because the Japanese responded so enthusiastically to his Christian messages, he resolved to return to Japan every other year. He made his second visit to Japan in 1951, a trip he called "the event of the year—perhaps of my life." In three months he visited forty-one cities, he wrote in his June 1, 1951, circular letter, and collected 21,390 cards signed by Japanese who wanted to become Christians after they heard him speak. Two years earlier he had identified the biggest obstacle to Christian evangelism in Japan as the lack of effective follow-up by the Japanese churches after his evangelistic messages. For this reason, on his 1951 trip, he took with him Dr. H. H. McConnell of the Department of Evangelism of the National Council of Churches (formerly the Federal Council of Churches) in the United States to instruct pastors and lay leaders in the techniques of visitation evangelism.

Another highlight of his second visit to Japan was a second interview with Emperor Hirohito. "Knowing that I am an evangelist you would probably know what I would say to him [the Emperor]." In other words, Jones witnessed to him again, as he had first witnessed to him in 1949, about Jesus Christ. Once again Hirohito graciously declined Jones's invitation to become a Christian. "He was very cordial," Jones wrote, "and invited me back to Japan."

In 1953 Jones made his third visit to Japan, speaking in seventy-two cities and receiving approximately thirty-four thousand decision cards during his three-month tour. Why, he wondered in articles published in the *Indian Witness* and *Christian Advocate*, did he continue to be so successful as a

Christian evangelist in Japan, even after the end of the American military occupation? The reason he succeeded, he wrote in the June 11, 1953, issue of the *Indian Witness*,[12] was that his experience in India made him thoroughly familiar with the "desire to please an occupying power." Just as he had learned to disentangle Christianity from Western imperialism in his early years in India, so in Japan he dissociated Christianity from the American postwar occupation. He frankly admitted, however, that some of the success he and other Christian evangelists experienced immediately after the end of the war was due to the occupation, and that when the occupation ended, the attendance of non-Christians at Christian churches would decline. But he also knew that the deeper reason for the fluctuating success of Christianity in Japan was the continued "moral and spiritual chaos" among the people of that nation.

As Jones analyzed the significance of the 34,000 decisions for Christ that he received during his 1953 evangelistic tour of Japan, he "had no illusions as to what this really meant." In 1951 he estimated that only about one-quarter of those signing decision cards actually joined a Christian church. In 1953 he tried to determine the reason for this disparity.

> Where did the fault lie? With the evangelist—was his message and his method too shallow? It brought great searching of heart and I tried to deepen my message and my method. Or did the fault lie with the Christian Church? Had it lifted its sights from being a small sect on the borders of Japan's life to the winning of a nation to Christ?

Part of the reason for the disparity, as Jones certainly knew, was endemic to Christian evangelism itself. The evangelist is not a pastor who disciples and nurtures converts in the Christian faith and life. His job is simply to bring non-Christians to the feet of Jesus Christ as sinners in need of the salvation that only Christ can give. It is then the responsibility of local pastors to test the sincerity and depth of the decisions for Christ made in response to the good news proclaimed by the evangelist. In this narrow sense evangelism in itself is almost always insufficient. Only very rarely will 100 percent of those responding to an evangelical message of the gospel of Jesus Christ become faithful members of a Christian congregation. Nevertheless, Jones wanted to do better as an evangelist and he wanted the Japanese churches to do better also.

"I had the temerity," he wrote, to tell Japanese Christians "that the Church in Japan is a pastor's church, organized around the pastor." And pastor's churches produce weak laymen who contribute little or nothing to Christian evangelism. He found that not only laymen but also women and young people were excluded from full participation in the life of the Japanese churches. There were churches where the women cannot have a meeting without the pastor being present to pray the prayer, read the scripture and preach a sermon! The consequence is that some of the strongest Christian women are functioning outside the Christian Churches. And the young people! I asked a Sunday morning congregation how many of them were above forty and four held up their hands. And yet young people are not given official responsibility in the Churches till they are forty!

In 1955 Jones made his fourth trip to Japan.[13] The peace treaty formally ending World War II in the Pacific had been signed, and the American military occupation had ended. But there were still political tensions between the United States and Japan. They were the result of the new international conflict that was rapidly polarizing almost all the nations of the world—the Cold War. In spite of the peace treaty, some American troops remained in Japan, not to supply personnel and provisions for UN military forces during the Korean War, but to maintain "internal security" in Japan.[14] There was a shred of plausibility for the continued American military presence in Japan, because Japan officially renounced rearmament in its constitution and therefore had virtually no military forces available in the event of civil unrest or natural disasters. But the real reason for U.S. troops remaining in Japan was the threat of communism.

The fear of communism, and especially Chinese communism, was so great in the United States that all available military resources were marshaled against the "red menace" in Asia. In fact, there was strong American support for the rearmament of Japan as a dependable bulwark in East Asia against the rising communist tide. Moreover, the Eisenhower administration developed a policy of massive nuclear retaliation against the Soviet Union in the event of armed conflict between the United States and Russia. In order to implement this policy, the United States proceeded with a highly controversial series of hydrogen bomb tests in the Pacific. Japan, as the only nation in which nuclear weapons have ever actually been used, vehemently opposed the development of the hydrogen bomb and was at best uneasy about the U.S. military forces that remained on its soil and about being drawn into the Cold War as a stronghold of anti-communism.

It was in this anti-American political climate that Jones made his biennial evangelistic tour of Japan.[15] But his Japanese hosts knew his outspoken views on international politics too well to let the policy of the American government stand in the way of his preaching missions. So in the late 1950s, unlike his early years in India, he did not have to waste much time in disentangling Christianity from American and Western imperialism. Instead, he concentrated his efforts on the obstacles to evangelism within the Japanese church. The biggest problem, as we have seen, was the lack of effective lay participation. So beginning in 1959, in addition to using the expertise of Dr. McConnell in the practice of visitation evangelism, Jones also invited Mary Webster (later Tattersall) to be part of the team.

Mary Webster's life was changed, as I mentioned in chapter 15, when she heard Stanley Jones preach in Peoria, Illinois, in 1950. After she wrote to him about her experience, he invited her to attend the Texas Ashram later that year. In 1951, she first shared her testimony in another ashram. Then tragedy struck the Webster family.[16]

> Three weeks later [she wrote in a *Transformation* article after Stanley's death], my family and I were involved in a head-on collision, in which my husband, sitting beside me, was killed. When the news of this reached Brother Stanley, he immediately wrote me a letter, half fatherly and half ministerial. From the hospital room I answered it and told him how victoriously Jesus was dealing with it and with me, never dreaming that any eyes but his would ever see the letter! Later, he used it in a book to help others who go through the sorrow of death to turn themselves and their grief over to Jesus that He might turn their sorrow into joy.

After her husband's death, Mary Webster began to share her witness on a regular basis at ashrams. "Brother Stanley knew the art of moving over to let someone else serve the Lord, even though he knew he could do it better. So in his great humility, he began to train me in Lay Evangelism by letting me witness before he spoke."

In the June 18, 1959, issue of the *Indian Witness*[17] he explained how she helped to encourage lay evangelism.

> We have tried to meet this need by bringing as a part of our team this year, Mary Webster, an untrained, but effective lay witness. It was an eye-opener to many who have been brought up under the tradition that only the theologically trained could be used to win converts, to see an untrained farmer's wife used of God to win intellectuals and non-intellectuals by the simple power of witnessing, including some pastors themselves.

Another problem Jones encountered in Japan was the problem of teaching Christianity as a form of "information instead of transformation." Too often, he wrote in the *Indian Witness*, the Japanese were "taught to know about Christ, instead of to know Christ." In order to overcome this problem, Jones took with him to Japan Dr. Thomas Carruth,[18] the head of the Prayer Life Movement in the Methodist Church, who would later be one of The Four in the United Christian Ashrams. The final member of Jones's evangelistic team in Japan in 1959 was Dr. Melvin Evans, who headed an organization in the United States called Democracy in Action. Evans, a labor-management expert, intended Democracy in Action "to change human relations by changing the lives of management." Because of Japan's rapidly growing, "almost miraculous" postwar industrialization, Jones invited Evans "to come to Japan and put his movement into Japanese industrial relations." The result, Jones reported in the *Indian Witness,* was that Evans's movement

> has taken root and is proving very effective in Christianizing industrial relations. One head of a large business concern said to me: "My men are no longer mad at me," and when I asked him, "Why?" he replied: "Because I am no longer mad at them."[19]

Jones held six ashrams in Japan in 1959 and saw the fruit of a practice he had introduced there four years earlier in his Christian ashrams—the three-finger salute symbolizing the oldest known Christian confession of faith, "Jesus Is Lord!" By 1959, the salute as a form of both greeting and farewell had spread from Japan to Korea, India, Africa, and America. Jones commented, "I have never seen a simple thing become so effective."[20]

* * *

On January 3, 1954, Stanley Jones was seventy years old. His friends, he wrote in a circular letter on January 9, 1954, "conspired to surprise me with a Commemoration dinner." The dinner was not a complete surprise, however, because he had learned of plans for the event some months before.

> I said beforehand to a friend that I would rather take a whipping than go, but after I got there I saw they were honoring me only to the degree I was honoring Christ. So I sat there handing on to the feet of Jesus everything that came. It ended up in being more like an evangelistic meeting than a Commemoration dinner. It really did! A bound volume of a thousand letters from friends everywhere is a treasure I shall never forget. A second volume is in the making. A dozen other dinners were held in various parts of the country simultaneously. All this didn't go to my head, but, to my knees.

Jones attended one more birthday celebration at Sat Tal, which was delayed for six months until he arrived in India for the ashram. Moreover, because of his age, he was officially retired by the Methodist Divison of Foreign Missions on June 30, but he wrote to the Division,

> You may retire me as an active missionary of the Board of Missions, but you cannot retire me as a missionary. That goes on—I trust till my last gasp.[21]

Nine years later, and four days after his seventy-ninth birthday, Jones wrote to his friends and financial supporters on the letterhead of Huntington Court Methodist Church in Roanoke, Virginia. He had celebrated his seventy-ninth birthday, he said, "in Durham, N.C., in a Negro church, and blew out 79 candles with one puff. So I have some breath left!"[22] The next year, 1964, would be the occasion of his eightieth birthday. He continued to enjoy an extraordinary international reputation. In fact, *Time* magazine reported in its January 24, 1964, issue that Jones's "fame overseas as an American evangelist is matched only by Billy Graham."[23]

Building on the outstanding success of Jones's seventieth birthday parties, W. W. "Bill" Richardson, the general secretary of the United Christian Ashrams, organized eight American birthday dinners for Stanley's eightieth birthday, beginning on December 30, 1963, in Chicago and ending on January 14, 1964, in San Francisco.[24] For the celebrations as a whole, and in each of the cities where the dinners were held, prestigious political and religious leaders chaired a group of committees, which had responsibility for the series of gala events. These leaders included United States District Judge and former Governor of Minnesota Luther W. Youngdahl and Bishop Gerald H. Kennedy. But far and away the biggest celebration of his eightieth birthday was held at the Mar Thoma Syrian Church in south India, where seventy-five thousand gathered to commemorate his half-century of missionary evangelism in India and to present him with a beautiful ivory box as a precious gift marking the occasion.

*   *   *

As he reflected on his long and distinguished career as a missionary evangelist, Stanley began to think about his spiritual legacy and about the enduring significance of his life for the kingdom of God. Back in the fall of 1953, while he spent a week with Mabel in Clayton, Iowa, he "began to toy with the idea of writing on my Autobiography," he reported in his January 9, 1954, circular letter. "The toying became a trying and before I knew what was happening I was writing on it." However, when he attempted to continue writing his autobiography in early 1954, the Inner Voice stopped him and directed him to work instead on another collection of daily devotional meditations. This book, entitled *Mastery*, his eighteenth book, was published in 1955.

In January 1956, just before leaving the United States for six months in India and Southeast Asia, Jones spoke in the Arena in Norfolk, Virginia, to an audience of four thousand, one-third of whom were African Americans. He was grateful for the meeting, he said in a circular letter, because "I knew that the first thing they would ask me in the East would be: 'What is America going to do about segregation?'" After the meeting Jones could answer the question by saying that "the two races were going to work this thing out together under God."[25]

On his way to India he spent a week in Cairo where he held meetings in the Evangelical Church. Back in India, he conducted a series of meetings for non-Christians in Gorakhpur, Belgaum, and Madurai, and then spoke at the Syrian Christian Convention in Maramon followed by two more series of meetings in Punjab and Gujarat. Finally, before the beginning of the Sat Tal Ashram, he went to Burma and Malaya. In Burma he held a number of meetings in Rangoon and an ashram in the mountains at Kalaw. Here the Karen rebels, who were Christians, were leading an insurgency against the government. A Karen girl who "had been four years with the rebel forces in the jungles," he reported in his 1956 circular letter, came to the ashram and "was transformed." In addition, he said, he "wrote a letter to the four Karen Christian leaders who are still in the underground rebel forces urging them to give up this useless and disastrous struggle and come out and cooperate" with the government.

At the beginning of 1957, while he was on board a plane flying from Chicago to San Francisco, Jones outlined his schedule for the rest of the year. He would spend three months in Japan, he wrote in his January 28 circular letter,[26] followed by two weeks in Korea, before leading the Sat Tal Ashram in India. Then he would return to the United States for six ashrams during July and August. During September, he would speak on behalf of the Crusade for a United Church, and he would complete the year with one-week evangelistic missions in fourteen different cities across the country. But the big news of the previous six months, Jones wrote, was that he had finished his new book of daily devotional meditations, *Christian Maturity*, and that it would be published by Abingdon in September 1957. Finally, Jones said, his next book would not be a collection of devotions but "a regular type book" on the topic of conversion. Such a book was needed because "only about a third of church members know what conversion is by first-hand experience." Jones solicited from the readers of his circular letter "instances of striking conversions" that he could use in his new book "with or without names."

The year 1958 marked a new and important phase of his ministry. He would hold evangelistic meetings in Central Africa among the people of the Belgian Congo. It was remarkable that at seventy-four, when most working people have retired, he was expanding his evangelistic work into another continent and adding to his already overcrowded schedule of meetings and ashrams. His experience in Africa brought back memories of his student days at Asbury when he first "volunteered to be a missionary" and "volunteered to go to Africa." Africa, he said in his January 25, 1958 circular letter, "was my first love."[27]

At the time Jones visited the Belgian Congo, Africa was just beginning to break the chains of European colonialism. Ghana, a British possession, had become independent in 1957. Based on his long experience in India, Jones predicted that news of Ghanaian independence will be sent out and that news will spread and permeate and stir clear through Africa. You cannot suppress the demand for human freedom. It is innate. Wise colonialists will prepare for it and welcome it and further it. Only thus will they hold their position. There is no other way.

Jones was witnessing the rising political tide of nationalism in Africa, but he also witnessed a rising spiritual tide. In Wembo Nyama in the Central Congo, he held a five-day ashram primarily for the missionaries. In Lodja, also in the Central Congo, Jones encountered what he called in his January 25, 1958, circular letter "a very remarkable spiritual awakening." The Africans, he wrote, "spend whole nights in confessing their sins publicly." Jones found the sins they confessed "startling," for they included cannibalism, witchcraft, idolatry, and adultery. He continued his account of the revival,

> There is a great deal of emotion connected with this, but it is at heart very ethical. Lives are changed. Belgian officials having investigated the movement say that it is sound, that people are better citizens, illicit distilling of liquor is stopped and crime goes down, the schools are better. One offical asked that fifty Christian workers be sent to another tribe where there has been no Christian work. They cannot change the people by governmental processes, only a change from within can do it. . . . The new converts stand before the altar and out of gratitude to God pledge themselves to win their families, their village, their tribe and the neighboring tribes. In large measure this movement is in the hands of Africans under the guidance of the Spirit. The missionaries are not leading it.

In Elisabethville in the Belgian Congo, Stanley spent four days and spoke sixteen times. The most noteworthy event in that city occurred in the three-thousand-member Methodist Church. "The crowds responded in great numbers," he reported, "when the invitation to personal surrender was made." The missionaries told him, "We have never seen such response. You treat them [Africans] not as children as the rest of the visitors do, but you respect their mentality and they respond."

Jones's excitement about the moving of the Holy Spirit in the Belgian Congo was confirmed by Alexander J. Reid, a district superintendent in the Central Congo Conference of the Methodist Church, who thanked Jones for his visit, especially for his ashram. He wrote to Jones on February 25, 1958.

> In behalf of the Central Congo Conference of the Methodist Church, I want to express to you our deep and lasting appreciation for your visit to us during the past month. Your messages and your life have so exalted Christ that our folks who were there for the week can never be the same. Profound changes have already taken place in the lives of a number of our missionaries, as well as our African people who were there.[28]

Reid also confirmed the popularity of Jones's three-finger salute, "Jesus Is Lord!" among the Africans. He noted in his letter that when he traveled 150 miles north of Lodja, where Jones had been so astounded by the spiritual awakening, he was greeted with the salute. "Now day by day we see them saluting each other and giving for their parting word the same salute."

In the 1960s, as Jones approached his 80th birthday, he continued to introduce his circular letters by saying that his most recent ashram or his most recent evangelistic mission or the events of the past year taken as a whole were "the best ever." In addition, because he was an international celebrity in Methodist and Christian evangelical circles, Jones continued to schedule almost nonstop public meetings and ashrams, sometimes speaking four or five times a day. However, the pace of his writing and speaking showed clear signs of slowing as he grew older. His circular letters had for decades been written four times a year as a vital part of his ministry and an indispensable means for maintaining personal contact with his friends and financial supporters. By the late 1950s, however, he wrote only twice a year, and the letters no longer contained the rich color and textured descriptions of his wide and varied activities, which had been so characteristic of his earlier quarterly letters. Moreover, he was no longer able to complete his heavy schedule of speaking engagements by himself. He needed the help of Dr. McConnell, of Mary Webster, of Dr. Evans, and later of others, in part because of the growth of the ashram movement. There were more ashrams meeting at the same time in different places and in different countries, and he had to rely on others to lead some of them in his absence. But Stanley was also feeling the effects of his age and welcomed the assistance of friends, family, and colleagues. In spite of his age, however, his physical health was remarkably vigorous throughout the 1960s, and he maintained his lifelong practice of traveling, speaking, and writing on an almost perpetual basis. The only serious threat to his health was a mild form of diabetes, which he successfully controlled by diet.[29]

As his Christian ashrams multiplied geometrically so that it was physically impossible for Stanley to lead each of them in person, he was enormously gratified not only to see and applaud what he had begun and nurtured so carefully but also to watch them expand independently of his supervision. In 1964 he wrote a circular letter from New York at the end of a six-month trip that included holding ashrams in India, Japan, Hong Kong, Thailand, the Philippines, Finland, and Sweden.[30]

> The thing that impressed me most about these Ashrams across the world is the fact that while we can stimulate them in the beginning, and I talk about "we" as some of us who have founded the Ashram Movement, nevertheless we are not indispensable. The Ashrams can go along without us. . . .

The point that I'm trying to make is that this movement when it puts its roots into a situation should be self-sustaining, self-supporting, and self-propagating. We believe that the Ashram Movement has the possibility of being the center of spiritual awakening for the whole of the Christian Movement.

Five years later when he had to cancel his appearance at one of his ashrams, the wife of the director of the ashram wrote to him that "things are going very well indeed without you." Jones said his response was, "Amen."

So this may throw you back on the resources of the Holy Spirit and spread the movement more widely through the laity. There comes a time when movements must go down to their basic bed-rock and perhaps this is the time for the Ashram Movement to do that. It may be that you will depend on God and yourselves more than ever and make the Ashram Movement a power for revival in this country.[31]

*   *   *

In 1960 Stanley made his second trip to the Belgian Congo, visiting again and holding ashrams at Wembo Nyama in the Central Congo and at Kapanga in the Southern Congo. The paramount chief in Kapanga, who was chief of 1,500,000 people, was converted during the ashram. "He was baptized at Easter," Jones wrote in a January 1961 circular letter addressed to "My dear Ashram Friend,"

and has been visiting the U.S.A. under the State Department on a goodwill tour. When asked over the T.V. "What is your faith?" he put up his three fingers: "Jesus is Lord."[32]

Since the time of his first visit to the Belgian Congo, the nation had become independent and he hoped that "the Ashram experience" would help prepare both missionaries and Africans for the "period of upset." This period of upset was in no way confined to the former Belgian Congo. The social and spiritual upheavals that accompanied the political transition to independence, as European colonialism crumbled throughout Africa and Asia, came to a dramatic, almost apocalyptic climax in 1965 as Jones traveled in these troubled continents. In Southern Rhodesia (Zimbabwe) a television reporter asked him,

"You are going to all the trouble spots of the world—Rhodesia, Congo, Nigeria, Indonesia, Malaysia, India—why?" I replied that the trouble spots are the possibility spots. The Chinese have a word for "crisis" made up of two characters—"danger" and "opportunity." In every crisis there is opportunity, so I go to see if I can help in that opportunity. Of course it did seem a foolhardy adventure, but I felt "the pressure of the Spirit," the call of God, so went and it has proved that the adventure was of God.[33]

Stanley wrote these words on April 27, 1965, from Penang, Malaysia, to his ashram comrades. The first stop on his four-month tour, he reported, was Southern Rhodesia, "where a white civilization is trying to stem the tide of a rising black nationalism." Here Jones spoke on Christ creating within himself a new man out of both parties, which, in the case of Africa, would be a new continent composed of Western achievements in science and technology together with African political leadership. While he was in Southern Rhodesia, he confronted the racism of the white minority by holding a healing service in a Christian ashram where "black men laid their hands on the heads of white people—never done before—and they were healed!" Jones next visited the Congo (his third trip), a destination that "horrified" the whites of Southern Rhodesia, because for them the Congo "is the symbol of red ruin." The outcome of the conflict between communist and noncommunist forces in the Congo was unclear in 1965, at the time of Jones's trip to that country, but he believed that Congolese Christians were "the cement that held the country together." The prime minister of the Congo, Moise Tshombe, with whom Jones had prayer, agreed with Jones's assessment, telling him, "Apart from the church I see no solution of the problems of the Congo."

Jones concluded the African leg of his 1965 tour in Nigeria, where he visited five different cities, held an ashram, and, because of the presence of a large proportion of Christians among the officials of the national government, concluded that Nigeria was "the most progressive and hopeful of African democracies." Indonesia, however, was a very different story. Under the leadership of Sukarno, the country was in a state of constant anti-American and anti-Western ferment. When Jones visited Indonesia, Sukarno was exploiting this anger about colonialism, not only to unite his people against the West but also to unite them in support of his territorial ambitions in neighboring Malaysia. Jones commented in his April 27 circular letter,

> I left Indonesia with a pang—a pang because the Indonesians are a lovely people and here they were being herded by an irresponsible dictator into a war with Malaysia—over an imaginary issue—Neo-Colonialism in Malaysia.

Jones's next stop was Malaysia, whose land and resources Sukarno coveted. Stanley described Malaysia in a June 1965 circular letter[34] as "a paradise" compared with Indonesia.

> We have an Ashram at Port Dickson which is the nearest spot to Indonesia and the spot where guerillas are sent over to invade Malaysia. They are told

they will be welcomed with open arms as liberators instead of being shot down. But we went on with the Ashram as though nothing were happening. Many were transformed.

The final destination of Jones's 1965 far-flung series of ashrams and evangelistic meetings in the trouble spots of the world was, he said, "in perhaps the most troubled spot of all." He described his arrival in this most troubled nation in a December 2 circular letter to his fellow Ashramites.[35]

> As our plane came down into Los Angeles the pilot said that fires were raging in a section of Los Angeles. He pointed out the billowing smoke. We thought it was an ordinary fire—it was Watts, a racial conflagration, symbol of the pent up angers.

Later, in the deep South, Jones confronted the American dilemma of racism again, this time in Decatur, Alabama, where blacks and whites together faced the harsh realities of racial discrimination from the standpoint of their common faith in Jesus Christ. With the recent memory of the Watts riots burned into his spirit, Stanley expected that he "was going into the caldron." Actually his meetings at an interracial dinner for pastors and their wives, and other civic and religious leaders were entirely peaceful and exhibited a commitment to resolve racial problems through patience and love.

* * *

I would be remiss if I did not reemphasize here what an enormous debt the American civil rights movement owes to E. Stanley Jones. Almost entirely unknown today is the fact that Martin Luther King, Jr., learned about Gandhi's theory and practice of nonviolent civil disobedience from Jones. In *A Song of Ascents* Stanley wrote,

> I thought my book Mahatma Gandhi, an Interpretation was a failure. It did not seem to dent the Western world with its emphasis on armaments. But when I saw Dr. Martin Luther King, he said: "It was your book on Gandhi that gave me my first inkling of nonviolent noncooperation. Here, I said to myself, is the way for the Negro to achieve his freedom. We will turn this whole movement from violence to nonviolence. We will match our capacity to suffer against his physical force; and we will wear our opponents down with goodwill." "Then my book was not a failure," I replied. "No, if we can keep the movement nonviolent," he answered.[36]

King, of course, insisted without exception on nonviolence in his campaigns and demonstrations for racial equality, even when confronted with the most extreme and frightening provocation. And with amazing consistency the marches and protests he led were, in fact, nonviolent. But King's discovery of Gandhi's tactics from Jones's writings is only the beginning of Stanley Jones's role in the American civil rights movement. In *The Christ of the American Road* (1944), over a decade before the beginning of the civil rights movement in the mid-1950s and nearly a quarter of a century before the signing of the landmark Civil Rights Act of 1964, Jones made an astounding prediction. Unless effective measures were taken to end racial discrimination in the United States, he said,

> then Negroes, probably joined by whites, may have to resort to non-cooperation, by picking out certain unjustices and then, through volunteers trained in nonviolent methods, refusing to obey these specific injustices and taking the consequences of that civil disobedience.[37]

The origin of Jones's prediction was his concept of the kingdom of God. Fundamental and absolutely essential to the kingdom of God was, as we have seen, the fact that all persons are equal in God's eyes and therefore should be equal in the eyes of one another. This God-centered idea of equality, he argued in *The Christ of the American Road*, was embodied in Jefferson's phrase in the Declaration of Independence, that "all men are created equal." But this highest form of equality had not yet been achieved in American society. For this reason Jones believed that the soul of America was an unfulfilled dream.

> America is a dream—unfulfilled. A dream of equality of opportunity, of privilege and property widely distributed; a dream of a place where class is abolished and where a man is a man, a place where race and birth and color are transcended by the fact of a common brotherhood that will be a new beginning for the race as a whole, a place where all our gifts and resources are held not for ourselves alone but as instruments of service for the rest of humanity—that is the dream.[38]

The dream of America could not and would not be fulfilled until the United States overcame what Jones called the hesitations of American democracy. Among the seven hesitations he discussed in *The Christ of the American Road*, the most important by far—the hesitation that he felt most keenly and that motivated not only his opposition to British imperialism in India and his opposition to Japanese imperialism in Asia, but also his abhorrence of racial discrimination in the United States—was the hesitation to grant racial equality.

The stubborn persistence of racial discrimination of any kind, public or private, is much more than a temporary obstacle to the fulfillment of the dream that is America. For Stanley Jones, racism was an act of spiritual treason against the kingdom of God. Racial prejudice is such a serious sin and has such far-reaching social and political consequences that it creates, in fact,

two Americas. One is the America of freedom, the lover of liberty, the believer in democracy. That America I love. Under God, it has my complete loyalty. But there is another America—and it is not sectional; it is found in both North and South—which would deny that freedom and democracy and would have us say, "With liberty and justice for all white people." That America I do not love. It does not have my loyalty. For this is a false America, a traitorous America, and a greater danger to our democracy than Hitlerism. For it is Hitlerism right in our own midst.[39]

The publication of these words in 1944, when the United States and her allies were locked in a life and death struggle with Hitler, must have fueled a firestorm of criticism. He certainly made himself appear traitorous in the eyes of many of his fellow Americans. However, as I put it in *The Totalitarian Kingdom of God,*

Jones was not blinded by patriotism. If, as he accurately predicted at the very beginning of the war, the United States emerged as a superpower after the war, it could not assume the role of moral and spiritual world leadership implied in the Declaration of Independence as long as its own hands were stained with the blood of racism.[40]

During World War II when almost no one questioned the glaring and monstrous hypocrisy of asking African Americans to sacrifice their very lives overseas for a nation that defiantly refused to give them any meaningful form of equality at home, Jones knew he had to speak the truth to those in power. In April 1942, he was in Columbia, South Carolina, for a series of meetings. On his last night in the city, April 29, Jones spoke in the First Presbyterian Church. April 29 was also primary election day in Columbia for the office of mayor. Since the Democratic Party was the only viable political party at that time, winning the Democratic nomination for mayor in the primary was tantamount to election. The week before the primary the city election board purged from the roll of eligible voters all African Americans. Jones knew about the board's action, and before his message at the First Presbyterian Church he read an "Obituary for Democracy" to the audience. According to a story in the *State* newspaper, which was carried on the front page on April 30, 1942, Jones said,

Democracy died today in the city of Columbia when suffrage was denied citizens of this state, the only reason being the color of their skins.
Ballot boxes will be henceforth draped in black as a sign of mourning for those whose eyes can see.[41]

The irony of Stanley Jones's visit to the state where the Civil War began was not lost on George Green, the reporter who covered Jones's meeting for the *State*. Green began his article,

> Standing in the shadow of an old brick stockade at Senate and Assembly streets where Charles Logan threw Negro slaves he was holding for sale some 80 years ago, Dr. E. Stanley Jones, one of the foremost religious leaders of the day, last night hurled a challenge to the people of Columbia and South Carolina to give the Negro "the simple, fundamental right to vote" and "equal opportunity in every realm of life."[42]

In his address at the Presbyterian church Jones connected the issue of racism to the war effort in a way that few South Carolinians or indeed few Americans had even considered. Green continued his article,

> "Every injustice done to the Negro in America is picked up by the Japanese and exploited for all it is worth," Doctor Jones, who has spoken at Columbia churches and schools since Sunday, argued. "Everything that happens here on a racial issue goes through the bazaars of the East. This matter, then, is not a local issue. It has been suddenly thrust into the world arena and the matter cannot be dodged any longer."[43]

Stanley Jones's realization that racial equality was a primary and integral principle of the kingdom of God was not a lesson that he learned gradually from his decades of experience in Asia, where the United States was always viewed through the lens of racial differences and racial discrimination. Rather, soon after his dramatic and life-changing conversion experience in Baltimore as a young teenager, one of the first spiritual and social evils God sensitized him to was the evil of racism. In his autobiography he recalled that his brand-new relationship with Jesus Christ demanded that he treat African Americans with respect and dignity, even if it painfully embarrassed the very person who had prayed so earnestly for his conversion and who knelt with him at the altar of Memorial Church to lead him to Christ in a prayer of confession and repentance—his dear friend and teacher, Miss Nellie.

> I was in a streetcar with my beloved teacher of early years, Miss Nellie Logan, in Baltimore. The car was full, and when a Negro woman got in and had to stand, I got up from my seat, touched my hat, and gave her mine. My school-teacher companion blushed, and a twitter ran through the car. I was giving a Negro my seat! And I touched my hat in the process! I was touching my hat in salutation to a rising race, though I didn't know it then. That was over sixty-four years ago, and I had just committed myself as a new Christian to a reverence for people and their possibilities, apart from race and color and status.[44]

Almost as close to Jones's heart as Miss Nellie was Asbury College. As a faithful alumnus and member of the Board of Trustees of the college, he learned in early 1959, "with deep sorrow of heart" (to use his own words), while he was in Japan, that the trustees had voted to make the institution racially segregated. Jones wrote to Dr. Johnson, the president of Asbury, on February 19, 1959, from Tokyo.

> I find myself in a serious dilemma. I have believed in Asbury College and want to be loyal to it. But Asbury College as a deliberately segregated institution is something else. It is something else & something essentially different. It grew up in a social order where the issue of segregation was not raised. It was taken for granted. But now it has chosen by deliberate choice to be a segregated institution.[45]

Jones knew he had no choice but to resign from the board of trustees.

* * *

As we have seen, the inspiration for Stanley Jones's concept of equal opportunity was the phrase, "all men are created equal" from the Declaration of Independence. Another inspiration for the same idea was the concluding phrase of the Pledge of Allegiance, "with liberty and justice for all." He felt so strongly about the application of this idea to American public policy, both at home and abroad, that he wrote to President Eisenhower on December 26, 1956.[46]

> I believe that our national destiny is to take that last portion of the pledge of allegiance to the flag: "with liberty and justice to [*sic*] all" and apply it to all at home, to set our own house in order. And then go out into the world situation and apply it there . . . to all men everywhere.
>
> The social revolution is on, especially in the East. Subject nations are throwing off imperialisms and colonialisms. Man is on the march. The Communists did not produce that social revolution—they have betrayed it. They have turned it into channels of tyranny and compulsion. We must rescue it and turn it into channels of freedom and democracy. . . .
>
> I believe, Mr. President, that America, after having been under a cloud, is now emerging to its greatest opportunity for assuming the leadership of this social revolution. Two things have given us this opportunity: First, the Suez Canal issue allowed us to stand out on our own ground, with our feet extricated from suspicions of alliance with decaying imperialisms and colonialisms. It has left us free to be true to our destiny of entering the world situation and especially the Eastern situation with the outlook and driving force of "with liberty and justice for all." Second, Prime Minister Nehru's visit now has apparently cleared the way for that entrance "with liberty and justice for all," for many suspicions have apparently been cleared up. So from our side and from their side the way is clear, clearer than it has ever been.
>
> I believe, Mr. President, that God is matching you against this opportunity.

Armed with that simple phrase "with liberty and justice for all," you can assume a moral leadership in this social revolution. If you do, Communism will not get a look in.

I pray that you may be led, not to seek for allies of America, but to ally yourself with this rising social revolution and humbly and prayerfully and courageously lead it.

Eisenhower was eager to accept Jones's suggestion, and two weeks later, on January 11, 1957, the President responded to his letter.[47]

Dear Dr. Jones:
Thank you very much for your letter.
As I read it, I find that I concur in most, if not all, of the ideas you present—and I am particularly delighted that you find such an enthusiastic reception of your message "with liberty and justice for all." Frankly, it is a message I have been trying, though perhaps in an entirely inadequate way, to make the central theme of most of my speeches and documents that have to do with world affairs.
I enclose a copy of a speech I made just yesterday before the assembled Congress of the United States and which, for that reason, has already gone all over the world. While other subjects are dealt with, I am sure that you will find implicit in it the basic idea of equality for all.
I shall look for opportunities to use the particular expression in quotations.
Sincerely,

Three years later, during the last year of his second term as President, Eisenhower received another letter from Jones. On May 25, 1960, Frederic Fox, a special assistant to Eisenhower, responded to Jones's letter on behalf of the President.[48] Fox recalled Jones's earlier correspondence with Eisenhower. "As he wrote you a few years ago, the President continues to make that great phrase, 'with liberty and justice for all,' the central theme of his life and work." Fox then quoted from a speech Eisenhower had recently made to the American Civil Liberties Union in which he had used the phrase first suggested by Jones. Finally, Fox wrote that the President's words about liberty and justice for all were "backed up by concrete action in domestic and foreign affairs—for example, in the signing of the Civil Rights Act of 1960 and in the signing of the Food-for-Peace agreement with India this month." For both of these historic pieces of legislation Eisenhower received inspiration from the concluding phrase of the Pledge of Allegiance, "with liberty and justice for all." This phrase, of course, was at the very heart of Jones's concept of the kingdom of God.

Just as troubling to Jones as the Watts riots, which he saw from the air as he approached Los Angeles in 1965, was the new God-is-dead "theology." In that same year he was invited to speak at Emory University where Dr. Thomas J. J. Altizer, the leader of the God-is-dead movement, was a member of the faculty. Jones's December 2 circular letter described what he said to the assembled students and faculty at Emory. Perhaps remembering the obituary for democracy, which he had read twenty-three years earlier in Columbia, South Carolina, he told them,

> I hear there has been a death since I was last here. If the person who announced it will say, "As far as I am concerned, God is dead," I will accept it. The students roared.

Jones also met with Altizer for an hour in order to more fully understand the source and significance of his unique theology. After the interview Jones wrote down his reaction:[49] Altizer had simply "theologized his own emptiness of God." The God-is-dead movement, he wrote, "is the queerest movement I have ever come across in all my days, and I deal a great deal with wacky movements but this is a really wacky one." From the standpoint of Christianity, Jones wrote, the most incomprehensible aspect of Altizer's ideas was his insistence that although God is dead, Christ is alive and real and should be the object of personal faith and belief. Jones simply noted,

> A Godless Christ is unthinkable but that is what they are presenting, that God is dead and Christ is alive, but if you find Christ you find God, and He is very much alive the moment you find Christ.

Jones despaired of this new theological movement, but with his typical evangelical zeal completely undiminshed by the fact that he was eighty-one years old, he concluded that the God-is-dead philosophy "opens up a tremendous mission field to present a living God found in a living contact with a living Christ."

If age was no obstacle to Jones's opening a fruitful new mission field among the avant-garde thinkers who declared that God is dead, it was also no obstacle for the continued geographical expansion of his Christian ashrams. The next site for a new ashram, he hoped, would be Galilee in Israel.[50] Traveling with the Reverend Don Saylor, a Lutheran pastor from Columbus, Ohio, who had taught pastoral counseling at the Sat Tal Ashram, and with Sister Lila, a Greek Orthodox nun who was very active in the ashrams, Jones flew from Delhi to Galilee in early 1966 to locate suitable property. However, in July 1967 Jones reported in a circular letter,[51]

> After a month in India at the Sat Tal Ashram I intended to stop in Galilee to see about the site the Israel government is offering us on the bluff overlooking the lake [Sea of Galilee]. But four days before war [the Six Day War] broke out I was awakened by the Inner Voice saying, "Cancel." So I cabled the Finnish lady in Galilee: "Cancelling trip." War broke out the day before I was to have arrived in Tel Aviv!

But this was not the end of the story. Although Jones never established a permanent Christian ashram in Galilee, he did, in the last year of his life, lead a World Ashram Congress in Jerusalem. The Reverend William E. Berg, Brother Bill Berg, who was one of The Three of the United Christian Ashrams, testified about the miracle of Jones's participation in the World Ashram Congress.[52]

> I believe in miracles. The World Ashram Congress, held in Jerusalem in June of 1972, was a miracle of God.
> In January of 1972, I stood with Jim and Eunice Mathews, Bill Richardson, and Gordon Hunter at the bedside of Brother Stanley in the Boston Rehabilitation Hospital. He was paralyzed on one side and was suffering from gravely impaired speech and sight. Doctors had predicted that he would not walk or lecture again.
> I recall saying that day, "Brother Stanley, you have often said that you were going to keep going until the boiler bursts. But I believe that there is still life and fire in the old boiler and that God isn't through with you yet."
> Five months later Brother Stanley came to Jerusalem after a number of lectures in India. The fires of his burning heart spread a magnificent glow far and wide. He attended every Congress session, morning and evening, plus several afternoon sessions, one session of the International Committee and numerous consultations and planning sessions.
> In his key-note address on "Jesus is Lord," he said, "This is one of the happiest moments in my life, if not the happiest."
> In his closing message, his valedictory to his world family which was a most moving and memorable address, Brother Stanley, with brilliant clarity and Holy Spirit power, reviewed the foundation of the Ashram movement and its basic principles. Surrounded by members of the International Committee in the YMCA auditorium platform in East Jerusalem, Brother Stanley officially turned the Ashram over to his World Partners. Speaking from his wheel chair and bound by many physical infirmities, he was the living symbol of liberation and deliverance. With the laying on of hands we prayed for the healing of Brother Stanley, and God answered with a spectacular healing of the spirit in Brother Stanley and in many other lives.
> He then prayed for us. Brother Samuel Kamalesan of India sang "How Great Thou Art." There was not a dry eye in the assembly as Rilla Carlson led us in singing the Lord's Prayer. Hands were held high. Brother Stanley raised up and stood with the rest of us. When the crescendo was reached, "Thine is the Kingdom and the Power and the Glory," Heaven came down and overwhelmed us. On that mountain top, we caught a glimpse of the Promised Land.

*　*　*

Up to the very end of his life Stanley remained keenly interested in public affairs and international events. On December 24, 1971, just two weeks after he suffered a stroke in Oklahoma City and while he was recovering in Boston, Jones wrote to Indira Gandhi, the Prime Minister of India. The background of his letter was the tense and difficult relationship between the

United States and India that developed because of conflict between India and Pakistan. Pakistan, which was divided into Pakistan and East Pakistan in 1947 when both India and Pakistan became independent nations, was never really one country. Geographically, East Pakistan was situated north of the Bay of Bengal between India and Burma and was a thousand miles away from Pakistan, which was north of the Arabian Sea between India and Afghanistan. Politically and ethnically, there were deep-seated differences between the two, which came to a head after the 1970 national election in Pakistan. The Pakistani government was unwilling to accept the result of the election because the Awami League Party, which campaigned for regional autonomy in East Pakistan, won a majority of the votes. Instead of accepting Sheikh Mujibur Rehman, the leader of the Awami League Party, as the new prime minister, Pakistan put him in prison and took military action to suppress the movement for autonomy in East Pakistan. As a result, an estimated one hundred thousand were killed in Dhaka, the capital of East Pakistan, and ten million refugees fled from East Pakistan to India.[53]

Jones's letter to Indira Gandhi, however, dealt not with the relationship between Pakistan and East Pakistan, but with the relationship between India and Pakistan and between India and the United States. The United States, along with China, had sold arms to Pakistan for a number of years. If India began a war against Pakistan to protect the interests of East Pakistan, the question was whether the United States would support India or Pakistan. Henry Kissinger, who was President Nixon's national security advisor, answered this question while he was in Delhi a few days before his secret trip to Beijing to establish a new relationship between the United States and the People's Republic of China. If there was a war between India and Pakistan, Kissinger said, and if China intervened on the side of Pakistan, the United States would not come to the aid of India. In the end, the policy of the United States did not affect the resolution of the conflict between India and Pakistan. Pakistan, on December 3, 1971, made a pre-emptive air strike against India. India responded by invading both East Pakistan and Pakistan. Pakistan surrendered to India, which then withdrew all its forces from East Pakistan so that Rehman could establish a government in the new independent nation of Bangladesh.

It was in these circumstances that Jones wrote to Mrs. Gandhi.[54] His primary concern, he said, was

> to effect attitudes in the United States with regard to Southern Asia. How many times during these days have my thoughts and prayers been directed toward my beloved India and her people among whom I have been privileged to move for nearly seventy years. Their pains have been mine and their achievements have been cause for my deepest pride. Especially have I been praying for you that you may be sustained under the crushing responsibilities you must bear.

I cannot tell you how distressed I have been at the unwarranted and unwise attitude of our President and our State Department. Please believe me when I assure you that this does not represent the real attitude of most Americans and of none, I believe, who are well-informed about issues in Southern Asia. . . .

I know you were most reluctant to have to resort to force of arms. In this also admirable restraint has been shown and the armed phase of the conflict has been mercifully short. I know the road ahead will not be easy but, with your many other admirers, I am confident that you will be given a sure and steady hand for your leadership.

Indira Gandhi responded on January 5, 1972.

Thank you for your letter. A large number of American citizens have written to me. I am grateful for your support of India's action and for the sympathy you have shown for the democratic struggle of the people of Bangladesh. This is proof, if proof were needed, of the American people's love of liberty and justice.

With every good wish for 1972,

In 1972 after the end of the war between India and Pakistan, Pakistan's Prime Minister, Zulfiqar Ali Bhutto, went to India to obtain the release of Pakistani prisoners of war. While he was in India, Bhutto also reached an agreement with Indira Ghandi that neither country would resort to war to settle their dispute over Kashmir and that the issue would be resolved bilaterally without the intervention of any third party.

When Jones returned to India after beginning rehabilitation from his stroke in Boston, he was taken to the Clara Swain Hospital in Bareilly where he continued his recovery. On July 4, 1972, he wrote to Mrs. Gandhi congratulating her on the agreement she had negotiated with Pakistan.[55]

Nothing has on this trip, over recent days, given me so much real satisfaction and joy as your magnificient achievement in the treaty renouncing force in the settlement of questions between India and Pakistan. You have done a magnificient bit of statesmanship. We are very proud of you and your achievements. This puts India back into the leadership of the search for world peace. We hope you will undertake that task as nobly as you have undertaken this one. It will fulfill India's destiny. I shall pray for you and thank God for you.

Jones concluded his letter by referring to the excellent medical care he was receiving in an Indian hospital. Indira Gandhi responded to Jones on July 11, 1972.

Dear Dr. Jones,
I have your letter of July 4.
Thank you for your kind words about the Simla Agreement. As you know,

we have always stood for normal and friendly relations with Pakistan. This is the first time that there has been any response. One can only hope that this new mood will enable us to work towards a lasting peace.

I am glad that you have made some progress. My good wishes for your speedy and complete recovery.
Yours sincerely,

The other international issue with which Jones was involved during the last years of his life was the Vietnam War. Among his papers at the Asbury Seminary Archives is a January 18, 1966, letter from Richard I. Phillips, the acting assistant secretary for public affairs with the U.S. State Department.[56] Phillips's letter is a reply to an earlier letter Jones had sent to President Johnson about a proposal for peace in Vietnam that had been made by the President of India, Dr. Radhakrishnan. Phillips thanked Jones for his interest and stated that the United States had "been in contact with the Indian Government" with respect to Radhakrishnan's proposal. "We find his suggestion interesting and believe there is much in it that might be acceptable." Like many proposals for peace in Vietnam in the 1960s, however, Radhakrishnan's ideas did not lead to an immediate end to the war. Three months later on March 16, 1966,[57] Jones informed his friends and financial supporters in a circular letter that on February 4, the day of his arrival in India, he had had interviews about Vietnam with "the three most important people in India . . . Mrs. Indira Gandhi, the Prime Minister; Mr. Nanda, the Home Minister; and Dr. Radhakrishnan, the President of India." Jones was hopeful that the efforts then being made by India to broker peace between the United States and Vietnam would be successful. His last public word on the issue of Vietnam was a January 7, 1973, letter to President Nixon, written just two weeks before Jones's death. It was not a personal letter from Jones to the President, but a letter written on Sat Tal Ashram letterhead and signed by nineteen members of the ashram, including Jones. The letter deplored "the continued bombing of Vietnam" and called on the President "to cease immediately the bombing of Vietnam and seek a peaceful and human solution to this war."[58]

* * *

On January 28, 1967, Stanley included in a circular letter news that the manuscript for his spiritual autobiography was finally complete.[59] It was his third attempt to write an autobiography.

The first time I tried [in the mid-1950s] to write a regular biography, saw the outer events of my life were not sufficiently important to record, abandoned it. Wrote a spiritual autobiography, 560 pages, went over it, felt it wasn't good enough, scrapped it and began over again. I finished it in 1966. Now I think

> it is what I wanted to say but my only question is, did I say too much? It is 700 pages!

The manuscript was published in 1968 under the title *A Song of Ascents.* Although Jones was eighty-three when he finished his autobiography, he wrote and published three more books—*The Reconstruction of the Church—On What Pattern?* (1970), which described his detailed plans for a federal union of the Christian churches; *The Unshakeable Kingdom and the Unchanging Person* (1972), which is his most complete statement of his concept of the kingdom of God; and *The Divine Yes,* which was completed with the assistance of his daughter Eunice Mathews and Mary Webster Tattersall after he suffered a stroke and was published after his death in 1975. Jones began working on *The Divine Yes,* he said in an October 1971 circular letter, in the fall of that year. He had a premonition that this book "may be my last though I'm not always sure but I would like to go out with a resounding yes on my lips for Jesus is the yes."[60]

In October and November of 1971, Jones led another evangelistic campaign in Japan, with Mary Webster. They traveled to more than forty-five major cities, and Stanley spoke 154 times. During these two months approximately six thousand Japanese accepted Christ for the first time or rededicated their lives to Christ. When the campaign ended, Stanley returned to the United States and stopped in Oklahoma City for an ashram at a Roman Catholic seminary. On December 8, shortly after midnight, he suffered a stroke. Several months later, Stanley recalled what happened.

> Everything was lovely and I went to bed in peace. But during the night, I awoke to go to the bathroom and found I was paralyzed. The left side of my body was completely paralyzed, but the right side was intact. In struggling to get back to bed, I collapsed in the middle of the floor and my arm fell around my aluminum suitcase. I stayed there for several hours in complete collapse, but somehow the right side of my body worked and I was able to get back into my bed with a great deal of effort and prayer.
>
> From about two o'clock a.m. until 7 a.m. I was alone and utterly helpless, since there was no phone in my room. At 7 a.m. there was a knock at the door, but I was unable to answer it. I was on the first floor and the window was opened partly, so they were able to climb in and help me.[61]

After spending some time in the intensive care unit of Baptist Memorial Hospital in Oklahoma City, he was flown to Massachusetts General Hospital in Boston shortly before Christmas, since his daughter Eunice and her family lived in nearby Brookline. After two weeks he went to the Boston Rehabilitation Hospital, where he made a partial recovery from his stroke. Although the doctors concluded that Jones would not walk or lecture again, he proved them wrong. As we have mentioned, he attended the

World Ashram Congress in Jerusalem and then underwent five months of rehabilitation in the Clara Swain Hospital in Bareilly, India. In December, he went to Sat Tal where he wrote to his ashram brothers and sisters, "I am improving in my walking. The most steps I have taken in one day are one thousand five hundred fifty six steps."

On January 15, 1972, while Stanley was recovering from his stroke in Boston, he wrote to The Seven of the United Christian Ashrams.[62]

> I do not know what the future holds, but I know who holds the future. I am ready to be healed, as the prayers of so many are insisting, but I am also ready not to be healed. God will either heal me or give me power to show the Victory. I'm the same person and I belong to the Unshakable Kingdom and the Unchanging Person. I haven't had a blue hour since it happened. Victory, victory, victory. I will not bear it but use it. I have preached Victory in Jesus for over 60 years, and now I will demonstrate it in my own body and continue to love and praise Him in the process. In the meantime, I am going on, going on, and thank you for all your prayers in my behalf.

David N. Henderson, a close friend, recorded this account of the last weeks of Jones's life in India.[63]

> The days were full of activity. Two hours every morning were devoted to corrections and additions to the rough draft of his last book—The Divine Yes. When the book was sent to his daughter for final revision we read aloud from The Christ of the Indian Road and other books. In the mid-afternoon he exercised his legs by taking laps around the Ashram. Every evening he would announce his progress. Doctors in Boston had told him he would never walk again. With the support of the staff of Clara Swain Hospital in Bareilly he paced off a thousand steps a day. He maintained a vital interest in all that was going on around the world. The newspaper was read to him daily. He was particularly grieved by the earthquake in Nicaragua and the bombing in Vietnam. Every evening he listened to several chapters of the Gospels and spent 30 minutes to an hour in meditation. Brother Stanley was thoroughly human. He had his likes and dislikes. However, he had time for everyone and was visibly irritated when people tried to butter him up or take advantage of him for personal gain. Much to the dismay of those responsible for accounts, he forgave endlessly. At the end others tightened his girdle and led him where he did not wish to go. He passed his last weeks in a deep poignant solitude. By his own account he "never had a blue hour."
>
> My last moments with Brother Stanley were as he was being removed to Bareilly with a worsening lung infection. "I want you to follow the doctor's orders," I teased. "You follow His," he answered. Till the end he never ceased diverting attention from himself to his Lord.

Stanley Jones died on January 25, 1973, shortly after his eighty-ninth birthday, surrounded by his immediate family and close friends. His heart was buried in India, his adopted homeland, for that was truly where his "heart" was. The rest of his body was cremated and the ashes interred in the Bishops' Lot at Mount Olivet Cemetery in Baltimore, after a service of recognition and praise at Memorial United Methodist Church. As a part of the service a small kneeling altar, built in part from the wood of an earlier altar where Stanley had knelt to receive Jesus Christ as his personal Savior, was placed at the divided chancel in the church.[64] With this service of tribute celebrating his life and witness as a unique and profoundly eloquent advocate for the kingdom of God, whose testimony and influence were unparalleled in the twentieth century, Stanley's life had come full circle.

* * *

Jones's spiritual transparency, which I have referred to elsewhere throughout this book, is the most common personal comment I have seen about him in the hundreds of books and articles and the thousands of letters I have read in researching his life and its enduring significance. No account of his relationship with world political leaders, including Indira Gandhi and Dwight Eisenhower; no assessment of the transforming power of his twelve postwar visits to Japan on both Christians and non-Christians; no narration of the outpouring of love, affection, and adulation by VIPs in the series of dinners held on his seventieth and eightieth birthdays in both the United States and India; and no recognition of his pivotal, but neglected role in the American civil rights movement can ever fully reflect the character and charisma of E. Stanley Jones. In the end all any Christian has to give to anyone else is just who he is in Christ. In the case of Stanley Jones, what he had to give was such a nearly perfect reflection of Jesus Christ that thousands of people who read his books, heard him speak, or had the privilege of a private interview or conversation with him during his ashrams or in the time he made available between evangelistic meetings were forever transformed by their encounter with him. It is the testimony of these witnesses, more than anything I can say as a secondhand observer and commentator, that enshrines and will preserve through the ages the legacy of E. Stanley Jones. What follows is a small sampling of the hundreds, probably thousands of letters from men, women, and children on whom he made an indelible and permanent impact.[65]

In 1938 as Mabel and Stanley Jones prepared to leave India for the United States, they received a letter from Vasanti Asirvatham dated June 23 and entitled "From the Children of India." Written in pencil in large block letters, which were then traced over in ink, Vasanti wrote to the Joneses on behalf of the children of Sat Tal.

> Grown ups in Sat Tal and other parts of India have a big brother in Dr. Stanley Jones, but we children of India like to think of him as a loving "uncle" as well as a "big friend" to all of us little folks in India. Right here, in

Sat Tal, our uncle Stanley has many friends whose ages range from 2 to 60 or 70.

I am speaking for all his tiny nephews and nieces of India. Uncle Stanley, we should like to tell you that you have won our hearts by your friendly spirit.

We wish you the best voyage, a successful tour which will bring bountiful blessings to all whom you meet, and a speedy return to India and Sat Tal in particular.

Five years earlier, in 1933 Jones received a letter dated July 12 from Pacific Palisades, California, and signed by sixty Disciples of Christ missionaries. The letter read,

As a token of our affection and evidence of our deep concern that you may be enabled to continue your missionary career, to write, and to speak for years to come, we, the undersigned, agree to bear you and your loved ones to the throne of God for at least the ensuing year. We have all been personally benefited by your extraordinary addresses. Through them we have been led to love the Saviour more, we have been encouraged to apply ourselves more diligently to our tasks, and we have been reassured and cheered with the hope of coming victory.

We are members of the Disciples of Christ, and the Intercessory Fellowship which includes a large number of our missionaries of all lands.

To this some sixty of us have signed our names as here.

On March 21, 1941, the Reverend Richard H. Bowling, the pastor of First Baptist Church in Norfolk, Virginia, a black congregation, wrote to Dr. Jesse Bader, who arranged Jones's preaching missions in the late 1930s and early 1940s. Bowling enclosed with his letter a contribution for Jones's work.

Here is a small token of appreciation from the First Baptist Church of Norfolk for the great work being done by Brother Stanley, I came near saying "in India," but I realize I should say "in all the civilized world."

I could only wish it were many times the amount the check indicates. However, it does give an American Negro congregation a chance to reach across racial lines in extending the cause of Christ. So, here it is with all our best wishes for many more years of life for one of the world prophets of the present day.

Another letter Jones received in 1941 was written by Richard A. Heim, a young pastor in Lincoln, Nebraska, who shared a family tragedy. Heim's letter was dated March 3 and was addressed to "E. Stanley Jones, on Some Boat, Somewhere on the Pacific." His letter read in part,

On Feb. 11th we said goodbye to our four year old son, and gave him back to the One Who sent him, thankful for the happy hours that he brought. Four years ago we named him Stanley Conwell, hoping that in some strange way he might possess some combination of the powers of yourself, and Russell H. Conwell. . . . Now we let it rest there, believing that His will has been done—but understand it, we just can't. Now I think I know a little more about what it cost God to give his only son, for Connie was our only child . . . that is, of our very own. . . . We have a little girl that we had adopted, just the same age. . . .

Preaching since that time has not been easy. Not that God is any less real, or any less wonderful, or that this civilization needs the redemptive power of the Gospel any less. But to keep the eyes dry and the voice steady while handling things sacred and tender has some times been beyond me, I must confess.

I must tell you about a strange thing that happened. On the first day that the Doctors told us that they were certain of the diagnosis, leukemia, and that medical science knew of absolutely nothing to help us, things were so that I could not share that information with anyone. Mrs. Heim was not physically able to take such a blow just then. But on that day I went into the sanctuary of the church, after having locked all the doors. I knelt at the altar and prayed as sensibly as I possibly could pray, asking God to perform His will in a perfect way. I stayed there till I was nearly exhausted, and then I said, "Now God, I'll keep still; and I'll wait while you talk to me." Well, I waited . . . and I waited, listening with ears and heart both. But never a sound; never a feeling. And after a long time I arose to go. Then I got the surprise of my life. For the first time I discovered that my eyes were dry, and I no longer trembled, and that I was calm in my heart. Maybe that's the way He answers sometimes.

Well, some time, if you have a moment to spare, drop a line to a couple young folks who named their son after you, and then lost him.

Mildred G. Gregory, a medical doctor, who attended the Blue Ridge Ashram in August 1940, wrote to Jones on March 16, 1941.

I shall never forget your first appearance at the Ashram. When, after a preliminary service in the hall, with a downpouring of rain outside, we saw you coming in, your presence was brighter than sunlight. Throughout that Ashram you shed a light that must have penetrated into each one there. I know I have been different since then—convinced that the light of Jesus Christ that you radiate is a reality that I want in my life. It seems like a long, slow process with me, for barriers of self-will, pride and fear of being thought righteous continually show up. I do realize that the most encouragement comes from helping someone else to turn to the Christ-way of life.

A high school girl in Rangoon, Burma, Doreen Wason, wrote to Jones on January 17, 1949, a day after he spoke in her school.

Dear Mr. Jones,

Just one of the kids who put up her hand after listening to you at the U. C. High School on the 16th.

Please write a few words which will remind me of the promise we made over there so that I can stick it in my autograph book.

Thank you so much. I do hope your cold is better and that you will visit Burma again.

During one of Jones's National Preaching Missions, Christine Landfear of Geneva, Ohio, heard him speak in Cleveland. When Jones learned about her testimony, he asked her to put it in writing. So Landfear wrote to him on October 30, 1936. I quote at length from her letter because her story is so poignant.

Dear Dr. Jones,

First let me identify myself. Never having seen my name you could not recognize it, yet you know me. I attended your addresses on three evenings in Cleveland when the "National Preaching Mission" was there. I am the girl who was in bed a year and had the entire situation changed upon reading your book Christ and Human Suffering.

Now that you know who I am, I will continue. I would not be writing this had you not asked me to, yet many times I have wanted to tell you how much you have given to me. As I said in Cleveland, your life and your books have changed my life. . . .

Christ and Human Suffering came to me at a time when I needed it badly. I had been out of high school scarcely a year and was trying to earn enough to go to college. It seemed that just as I had been thrust in the sunlight of life, the rains came and drenched my wings. After a throat infection of a months' duration, the doctor told me rheumatic fever had left me with a heart leakage. If I was ever to hope to live an active life again I must stay in bed for from three months to a year.

I then read your book for the first time. It came like a light in the darkness of night. Later when I was able to sit up a little, I read the rest of your books. My heart worked fairly well in bed but could not stand the strain of much walking around. I got up a little several times but had to go back to bed. It was only when I told God if He wanted me there, I would stay there the rest of my life, that I began to improve. Needless to say, I am all right now. It was study of your book that brought me to the place where I could really mean this.

May God prosper the "National Preaching Mission," and your work in the service of mankind.

After Stanley's death, Cyril Thacore, who knew him throughout his years in India, wrote about some of his experiences:

When I first saw and heard Dr. Stanley Jones, I was a high school student in Ahmedabad. The year, I think, was 1921 or 1922. This was his first visit to the city which had been in the forefront of the movement for freedom launched vigorously two or three years previously. As the home of Mahatma Gandhi Ahmedabad had provided the main current of the political life of the country, and men like Vallabhbhai Patel were emerging as the strong leaders of the movment. Dr. Jones was to address public meetings in the city lecture hall which for years had been the scene of the political nurture of the citizens of Ahmedabad, particularly the youth. His addresses were to be on such topics as "The Karma and the Cross" and "The Way, the Truth and the Life." No such themes had ever been presented to the educated non-Christians of the city before, and, as in other parts of the country, Christianity was looked upon as a foreign religion or a religion of the foreign rulers. There was apprehension on the part of the small Christian community of the city as to how the meetings would go.

But contrary to all fears, each night the hall was packed to overflowing, and Dr. Jones established a rapport with his hearers at the very first of the six meetings he was to address. His attractive person and bearing, his brilliance and humour, his eloquence and mastery of phrase, his partiality for the cause of Indian freedom, his appreciation of the points of view of others, and his presentation of the essential Christ free from western trappings set the audience wondering at the entirely new approach he was making. The question hour at the end of each address was eagerly looked forward to and even those who came to scoff went away pondering on the great issues Dr. Jones had presented. Such was the popularity he won in six days, that the citizens asked him to give a seventh address—on the Kingdom of God—after which he was given a most touching farewell with garlands and speeches. . . .

During his visit to Ahmedabad, after he had spoken in the Presbyterian Church on a Sunday morning, I wanted to talk with him. He readily agreed, and giving up riding in the car with his host, he walked about a mile with me across the Ellis Bridge talking and praying as we went along. . . .

My wife and I had the honour of being invited to the ceremony at which the Gandhi Peace Award was made to Dr. Jones at the Community Church in New York on November 7, 1963, at 8:00 p.m. We had arrived that same afternoon from India. I had the privilege of reading a message for the occasion from the Indian Embassy in Washington. . . .

In these days just following his passing, there will be many and varied estimates of the life, work and influence of Dr. Jones, in an attempt to gather together the many facets of the personality of this man of God. The one I would hold above many is in the words of Paul Tillich used in estimating St. Paul's appeal. Adapted, it would read: To the man who longed for God and could not find him; to the man who wanted to be acknowledged by God and could not even believe that he is; to the man who was striving for a new imperishable meaning of his life and could not discover it—to this man Dr. Jones spoke.

In the fall of 1965 Jones spoke to the students of Hamline University in St. Paul, Minnesota. After his visit Frank Dreisbach, the chaplain of the university, wrote to Jones on September 28.

It is not often that a campus such as ours is put on the spot the way you put us on the spot. You brought a group of six hundred students to the point of taking Christ seriously. One cannot measure the vast effect which forcing such a decision can produce in the lives of so many people. It was not merely what you said—there is something about you yourself which inspires reconciliation between men and God.

There was indeed something about Stanley himself that reconciled man to God. He, more than any other twentieth-century thinker, writer, or preacher, rediscovered the kingdom of God and its crucial role in our relationship to God through Jesus Christ. But it was not just what he wrote and published and preached about the kingdom that brought men, women, and children to the foot of the cross of Christ. It was the man himself. There is an amazingly consistent simplicity in the life of E. Stanley Jones. In the complex web of the innumerable events and achievements of his long and incredibly active life there is a single, simple thread. And that thread is his spiritual transparency. Stanley Jones's character reflected the living reality of Jesus Christ so perfectly that others were drawn immediately into intimacy with God.

In 1957 Stanley Jones made this statement in a conference address on the Wesleyan movement:

> It doesn't take much of a man to be a Christian, but it takes all there is of him. It doesn't matter how much you've got; it matters much how much he's got of you.[66]

God certainly had all of E. Stanley Jones—and that was enough to change the world.

17

The Legacy of
E. Stanley Jones

E. STANLEY JONES CAST a long and impressive shadow across the tumultuous years of the twentieth century. No written account of his life can do justice to the man or to what he was able to accomplish once he was fully surrendered to Jesus Christ. The preceding chapters, therefore, have only sketched a portrait of Stanley Jones and of his long and fascinating life—one that is comprehensive but not exhaustive.

The most salient and spiritually significant characteristic of Stanley Jones, as we suggested at the end of chapter 16, was the transparent clarity and persuasiveness of his personal witness for Christ. One of his favorite scriptures was 2 Corinthians 5:17-18, that "if anyone is in Christ, he is a new creation" and that "God, who reconciled us to Himself through Christ . . . gave us the ministry of reconciliation" (NIV). For Stanley Jones, this passage contains the whole gospel of Jesus Christ. God makes us new creations through our acceptance of the death and resurrection of Christ, a sacrifice that reconciles us once and forever to God. But salvation through the blood of Christ is only the beginning of God's plan. Those who are saved through Christ bear the responsibility of sharing God's ministry of reconciliation and of bringing others into a personal relationship with Christ. There are no better or more accurate words to describe Jones the man, and the nature of God's call on his life. As an evangelist, of course, his primary commitment was to carry on the ministry of reconciliation by winning souls to Christ. But he was a minister of reconciliation in more than one sense.

Like most Christians, Stanley Jones did not learn the secret of self-surrender until he had tried to fulfill his calling in his own power. After his nervous breakdown and his taking an early furlough from his missionary duties in Sitapur at the insistence of his bishop, Jones finally knelt at the back of Central Methodist Church in Lucknow, knowing that he was unable to continue his work in India, and confessed to God, "I'm done for." But God, speaking through the Inner Voice, replied, "If you'll turn that problem over to me and not worry about it, I'll take care of it." Jones quickly and eagerly replied, "Lord, I close the bargain right here." He got up off his knees, realizing at last that he was, as he recalls in his autobiography, "a well man." And so began his true ministry of reconciliation.[1]

Even before his breakdown Jones was traveling as an evangelist beyond Lucknow and Sitapur and speaking in public halls and schools instead of in Christian churches, in order to reach the educated classes of India with the gospel of Jesus Christ. But he was not just reconciling individual Indians to God through Christ, he also reconciled the whole Western missionary enterprise to non-Western expressions of Christianity. By persuading Western Christians that they could learn from Asian and later African Christians, he reconciled the Western church to a richer and deeper experience in the kingdom of God and to a more complete and more responsible commitment to kingdom purposes throughout the world.

In India there was still another dimension to Stanley Jones's ministry of reconciliation. His work with educated, English-speaking Indians brought him into direct and frequent contact with the leaders of the Indian national movement, including Gandhi himself. Although he did not, as we have seen, go as far as some of his Methodist missionary colleagues in sympathizing with Indian nationalists and actively participating in Indian politics, he could not be silent about the brutality and injustice of British colonialism in India. Transcending cultural differences between Western and non-Western Christians meant that Western Christians must first repent not only of their religious imperialism but also of their political imperialism. He knew that Christianity had no real chance in India as long as it was simply the religion of the colonial oppressors. So, in fulfilling his call as a minister of reconciliation, he began to expand the scope of the kingdom of God to embrace not just personal relationships between man and God but also interpersonal relationships, which are the substance of social, economic, and political institutions.

In India before 1947, his first task was to reconcile Indian nationals with their British overlords. Only when India achieved true independence would the Christian gospel message, that all men and women are equal in the eyes of God, be completely free of hypocrisy. Stanley Jones was one of the first Western Christians to call for Indian independence from Great Britain. As we saw at the very end of chapter 2, his contribution as a non-Indian to the strong moral character of the Indian national leaders who supervised India's transition to independence and the formulation of her own constitution was probably unequaled.

Jones began to appreciate more deeply the political and economic dimensions of the kingdom of God when he embarked on his next major ministry of reconciliation—reconciling Japan and China. Excluded from the Versailles peace process by the European powers for what it perceived to be racial reasons, Japan felt that its imperial conquests in Asia were both morally and politically justified. Because his experience in India had sensitized him so acutely to racism and imperialism, Stanley Jones sympathized with the Japanese, and especially with their need for more land and resources for their growing population. However, he could in no way justify Japan's naked aggression in China or its savage and wholesale destruction of civilian lives and property. To stop Japanese imperialism in China and to reconcile the two major nations of East Asia, he proposed his controversial economic withdrawal by Christians in the United States and Great Britain. His proposal, of course, did not stop Japanese aggression, but the failure of his idea to be adopted or implemented did not stop Jones. His understanding of Japan's national aspirations and his personal contacts with the Japanese embassy in Washington led to the most dramatic episode in his ministry of reconciliation—his dogged efforts to reconcile Japan and the United States in 1941.

Although almost forgotten today, his personal but unofficial diplomacy in the months leading up to Pearl Harbor formed the basis for another phase of his ministry of reconciliation, his evangelism in Japan after World War II. In a nation that is still today overwhelmingly non-Christian, Jones's postwar preaching missions in Japan were probably the most successful of any Christian evangelist and, for Jones personally, they were, next to his work in India, the most gratifying of all of his evangelism efforts outside the United States.

If the birth of Jones's revelation that the kingdom of God was both personal and interpersonal, both individual and corporate occurred in his early years in India, and if the growth and development of that revelation came with his experiences in China and Japan both before and after World War II, the full maturity of the revelation came after his long journey across the Soviet Union in 1934. Ironically, it was in the world's first politically totalitarian state, with its officially atheist ideology, that Jones discovered the only genuine totalitarianism—the kingdom of God—a discovery that dominates the next phase of his ministry of reconciliation.

Two books he wrote in the 1940s, *Is the Kingdom of God Realism?* (1940) and *The Christ of the American Road* (1944), define the totalitarian nature of the kingdom and elaborate the specific and concrete meaning of that kingdom for the religious, social, economic, and political life of the United States. In order for individuals to be reconciled to one another across racial, sexual, age, and socioeconomic class lines in the same way that God reconciled all men, women, and children everywhere to himself through Christ, the hesitations of American democracy to fulfill the promise of the Declaration of Independence that "all men are created equal" would have to be destroyed and removed in all individual and collective relationships.

In the 1950s and 1960s, as Jones divided his time between India, the United States, and the rest of the world, he combined the ministry of reconciliation, based on his mature understanding of the totalitarian kingdom of God, with the ministry of reconciliation, based on his youthful zeal for personal evangelism after his recovery from the emotional and spiritual breakdown in his early years. Only Holy Spirit–inspired motivation and resources for proclaiming the good news of Jesus Christ can explain the virtually nonstop schedule of preaching missions, meetings, conferences, and ashrams that Jones maintained for sixty-five years until he was in his mid-eighties.

The ministry of reconciliation, however, that ignited the most spontaneous, the most geographically and culturally diverse, and the most enduring response was the ministry that remained closest to his heart up until the time of his death in 1973—the Christian ashrams. In these spiritual retreats, which Jones adapted from his experience in non-Christian ashrams in India, people of all faiths, all racial and ethnic backgrounds, all ages, and both sexes came together at the foot of the cross. Jones's ashrams were never merely tools to proselytize pagans. But in the end he found, as all authentic Christian evangelists know, that most people come to Christ and grow in Christ through witnessing personally the difference Christ has made in the lives of others. And what better venue is there for genuine Christian conversion than the outdoor, rural, small-group setting of a Christian ashram?

So, what is the legacy of E. Stanley Jones? How can we summarize his enduring contribution? Part of the difficulty of answering this question is that the man doesn't fit neatly into traditional categories of religious figures. We have described him properly as an evangelist and missionary. In fact, he was, I believe, the outstanding American evangelist and missionary of the twentieth century. Richard J. Foster, a popular and best-selling contemporary writer, defines six streams or traditions of the Christian faith—the contemplative, the holiness, the charismatic, the social justice, the evangelical, and the incarnational.[2] Stanley Jones, according to Foster, is part of the holiness tradition, along with such other leaders as the early church Father Tertullian; the Cistercian monk Bernard of Clairvaux; the French philosopher and mathematician Blaise Pascal; the founder of Methodism, John Wesley; and the twentieth-century Christian martyr Dietrich Bonhoeffer. Certainly Jones's conversion as a teenager in Baltimore and his education at Asbury College, as we saw in chapter 1, were very much part of the Wesleyan Holiness movement. But Foster's categories, as he freely admits, are not mutually exclusive. Many Christian leaders fit into more than one category. Stanley Jones, for example, could easily be a member of the evangelical stream, since he always described his own life as his response to God's call to be an evangelist. Moreover, because of his deep commitment to and involvement with social and political issues, he could also be classified as part of the social justice tradition. Finally, his ashrams are a perfect illustration of the incarnational stream of Christianity.

The fact that Stanley Jones has not been treated seriously in academic studies of American Protestant Christianity and church history is puzzling, but it probably stems from the fact that he was not seminary trained and that he did not speak or write for a narrow audience of scholars. He wrote and spoke instead for the widest possible audience, including university faculty in religious studies—for clergy, for laity who ranged from middle-class professionals and business people to blue-collar hourly workers, as well as the unchurched who might fall into any of the preceding categories. Jones would not today be classified as a theologian, although he was, in the words of his son-in-law, Bishop James K. Mathews, a "spiritual genius" whose work on the kingdom of God, on social and political ethics, on the role of the Holy Spirit, and on the function of the church clearly merits serious attention by scholars.[3]

Jones himself, referring to the twentieth-century division between fundamentalism and modernism in American Christianity, said that he was neither a fundamentalist nor a modernist. And in his spiritual autobiography he recalls that "[a] conservative journal discussing the question 'Is Stanley Jones a Modernist?' came to the conclusion that 'he has a fundamental soul with a modern mind.' Perhaps," Jones concludes, "that describes it!"[4] In other words, he defies classification because he refused to accept or use the conventional categories employed to differentiate American Christians. Instead of defining and articulating a fixed set of religious assumptions or principles in order to identify his own Christianity and to distinguish himself from other Christians, Stanley Jones appealed simply and directly to the person of Jesus Christ. Jesus Christ was the focus of his entire life as a missionary and evangelist. Jones poured his body, soul, and spirit into his personal witness for Christ and he did so with such honesty, clarity, and conviction that he transformed the lives of thousands who heard him or interviewed him in person, read his books, or participated in his ashrams.

Because of Jones's spiritual transparency, even his severest critics revered his personal witness for Jesus Christ. Reinhold Niehbur, Jones's contemporary and, along with Karl Barth and Paul Tillich, one of the foremost Christian theologians of the twentieth century, classified Jones as a romantic and sentimental Christian liberal and called Jones's book, *Christ's Alternative to Communism,* the "most perfect swan song of liberalism."[5] What Niebuhr meant by liberalism was the modernist approach to Christianity that optimistically, and for Niebuhr unrealistically, assumed that the kingdom of God could, through the conscientious and sincere efforts of committed Christians, be literally established on earth. According to Niebuhr, Jones and other liberals ignored or underestimated the power and persistence of human sin and of the widespread evil that was the result of that sin. But if Niebuhr rejected what he called Jones's liberal theology, he nevertheless had nothing but respect and admiration for Jones the man. Robert McAfee Brown recalls that when he was one of Niebuhr's students at Union Theological Seminary during World War II, he, along with other students, often visited Dr. and Mrs. Niebuhr, who held an "open house" in their home on Thursday evenings. Brown writes,

> On one such occasion there was a sharp and typically polemical discussion of pacifism in general and the pacifism of E. Stanley Jones in particular. It centered on the "naivete" of Christian pacifists who assumed, in the midst of World War II, that pacifism would still "work." Niebuhr was sharing in the discussion with his accustomed vigor when all of a sudden he stopped, and in a very different tone of voice said, "But who am I to pass judgment on Stanley Jones? He's one of the great Christian saints of our time."[6]

Jones was indeed regarded and treated as a saint, especially in the later decades of his life. He was never entirely comfortable with the label, but he never took the opinions of others, either positive or negative, too seriously. Through the direction of the Inner Voice and the power of the resurrected Christ, he simply remained faithful to God's call on his life to be a missionary and evangelist. In the end he must be judged not by academic criteria or by what he accomplished for the Methodist Church or by his influence on political leaders or by his impact on the history of the twentieth century, but by his steadfast loyalty as a citizen of the kingdom of God.

Notes

Introduction

1. *Time,* December 12, 1938, p. 47.

2. *A Song of Ascents,* p. 194.

3. Marjorie Hyer, "Dr. E. Stanley Jones, Evangelist, Dies," *The Washington Post,* January 26, 1973, p. B4. Hyer wrote about Jones's efforts to prevent war between Japan and the United States: "With Kissinger-like anonymity, Dr. Jones shuttled between President Roosevelt and special envoys who, he said, were sent to Washington by the Japanese emperor in an effort to forestall war."

4. *Time,* January 24, 1964, p. 34.

5. J. Waskom Pickett's biographical article on Jones appears in *The Encyclopedia of World Methodism,* vol. 1, p. 1275.

6. *A Song of Ascents,* p. 27.

1. From Baltimore to Bluegrass

1. Stanley Jones's letters to Miss Nellie Logan are at Asbury Theological Seminary in Wilmore, Kentucky. Unless otherwise identified, all of Stanley Jones's letters referred to and quoted from in this chapter are his letters to Miss Nellie. All the italicized portions of these letters are emphasized in the originals.

2. According to a letter Jones wrote to his friends and financial supporters on December 22, 1951, Miss Nellie died earlier that year.

3. *A Song of Ascents,* p. 27.

4. Ibid, pp. 27-28. The section of the altar rail where Jones was converted at Memorial Methodist Episcopal Church in Baltimore was made into a prayer desk and was dedicated at a special service at the church on May 24, 1931. This information is in the Asbury Seminary Archives.

5. *A Song of Ascents,* p. 40.

6. James K. Mathews, "The Legacy of E. Stanley Jones." I found the full names of Jones's parents in the Asbury Seminary Archives.

7. *A Song of Ascents,* p. 26.

8. Stanley's encounters with chum Ras after his conversion are described in *A Song of Ascents*, pp. 34, 35.

9. Ibid, p. 63.

10. Thomas Long's letter to Nellie Logan is in the Asbury Seminary Archives.

11. Jones discloses the fact that he was fired from his law library job in one of his notebooks. These notebooks, which are now among his papers at Asbury, contain a variety of materials, including notes on books he read and extensive notes on personal testimonies he recorded at his Christian ashrams. In a notebook dated 1952–54 is a page entitled, Notes on Autobiography. Point number six includes the words, "*Discharged* from law library" (emphasis in original).

12. *A Song of Ascents*, p. 44.

13. Stanley refers to working for an insurance company and earning money from evangelistic meetings to pay for his education at Asbury on pp. 64 and 65.

14. John Wesley Hughes's statement as to why he founded Asbury College is quoted in Joseph A. Thacker, Jr., *Asbury College: Vision and Miracle*, p. 9.

15. For general information about the Holiness Movement, I relied on Mark A. Noll, *A History of Christianity in the United States and Canada*, pp. 378-81, and on Grant Wacker's article, "The Holiness Movement," pp. 332-35.

16. Hughes's announcement for the opening of Asbury is from Thacker, p. 12.

17. The quotation from Morrison's introduction to Hughes's autobiography is from Thacker, p. 16.

18. Ibid, p. 19.

19. The query about the Asbury College advertisement in the *Pentecostal Herald* came from Dr. Orris G. Robinson, a Methodist pastor and close friend of Jones. Morrison replied in a letter dated April 5, 1937, which is in the Asbury Archives.

20. *A Song of Ascents*, p. 65

21. Ibid, p. 67.

22. For the full name and hometown of Virgil Darby, Jones's first roommate at Asbury, I am indebted to Professor Art McPhee of the Associated Mennonite Biblical Seminary in Elkhart, Indiana.

23. J. Waskom Pickett, "The Promising Young Stanley," p. 2.

24. Jones, "We Welcome Bishop J. Waskom Pickett."

25. *A Song of Ascents*, p. 343.

26. Ibid, p. 344.

27. Thacker, p. 32.

28. Ibid, p. 29.

29. Ibid, p. 24.

30. Jones's letter to his mother is in the Asbury Seminary Archives.

31. The information about the Holiness Union comes from Charles Edwin Jones, *Perfectionist Persuasion: The Holiness Movement and American Methodism, 1867–1936*, p. 93.

32. *A Song of Ascents*, pp. 68-69.

33. Thacker, pp. 51-52.

34. Jones never talked about his mother much, but he was probably referring to his mother's death when he addressed the 120th Annual Meeting of the Board of Foreign Missions of the Methodist Episcopal Church at Mecca Temple in New York City on November 15, 1938. "The greatest ordination I ever had," he told the group, "was from a dying woman. She put her hands on my head and prayed that I might be an evangelist that I might preach this good news." This quotation is from page 21 of a stenographic record of Jones's address, which is in the Methodist Archives.

35. Miss Nellie's undated letters to Stanley Jones are in the Asbury Seminary Archives.

36. James K. Mathews and Eunice Jones Mathews, "Stanley Jones—as Father (and Father-in-Law)," p. 8.

37. The *Clip Sheet* article on Jones's experience with alcoholism in his family is in the Asbury Seminary Archives.

38. *A Song of Ascents*, p. 27.

39. Ibid, pp. 72-73.

40. Jones's letter to Reverend Long is in the Asbury Seminary Archives.

41. Professor Wray's letter of recommendation and Jones's application to the Mission Board are in the Methodist Archives.

42. See Thacker, pp. 65, 67, 68.

43. "E. Stanley Jones," in Harmon, ed., pp. 1275-76.

44. *The Word Became Flesh*, p. 325.

45. Thacker, p. 66.

46. *A Song of Ascents*, pp. 71-73.

47. Ibid.

48. Pickett, "The Promising Young Stanley," p. 2.

49. *A Song of Ascents*, p. 75.

2. Lucknow, India: Pastor and Evangelist

1. The official history of Methodist missions referred to in this chapter is J. Tremayne Copplestone, *History of Methodist Missions*, Vol. 4: *Twentieth Century Perspectives*. The passages I quote and the information I paraphrase may be found on pages 777, 779, and 785-86.

2. Edmund D. Soper, *The Philosophy of the Christian World Mission*, p. 12.

3. Statistics on the number of student volunteers who went abroad as missionaries between 1886 and 1945 can be found in Nathan D. Showalter, *The End of a Crusade*, p. 182. Financial information about SVM budgets can be found on pages 114ff.

4. Showalter, p. 2.

5. Copplestone, p. 787.

6. Sherwood Eddy, *Pathfinders of the World Missionary Crusade*, pp. 84-85.

7. Norman A. Horner, ed., *Protestant Crosscurrents in Mission: The Ecumenical-Conservative Encounter*, p. 20.

8. Copplestone, p. 789.

9. Copplestone, pp. 840-41.

10. Copplestone, p. 841.

11. John R. Mott, "Foreword," J. Waskom Pickett, *Christian Mass Movements in India*, pp. 5, 7.

12. Ibid.

13. The quotations from the conclusion of Pickett, *Christian Mass Movements . . .* appear on pp. 330, 331, 332, 333. In another book on Christian mass movements in India, written for a popular audience, *Christ's Way to India's Heart* (p. 40), Waskom Pickett emphasized again the superiority of mass movement evangelism in India over the traditional person-centered evangelism, which is more appropriate for Western than for Asian Christianity.

> We are persuaded that the quality of faith and experience is very much better in the areas where group or mass movements have taken place than in areas where converts have been won by independent, individual decisions.

14. *A Song of Ascents,* p. 80.

15. The circular letters or round robin letters referred to in this chapter are part of the E. Stanley Jones Papers at Asbury Theological Seminary. At the height of his popularity, at least a thousand people received Jones's circular letters. (From a telephone interview with Bishop James K. Mathews, October 30, 2000.)

16. The approximate distance from Naini Tal to Hyderabad Deccan in South India is 1000 miles according to the map on page xvi of Anthony Read and David Fisher, *The Proudest Day.*

17. I learned from Jones's son-in-law, James K. Mathews, that Jones never really mastered Hindustani. (From a telephone interview, October 30, 2000.)

18. Bowen Memorial Church in Bombay, which wanted Stanley as its pastor, would continue to have close family connections for the Jones family. Mabel and Stanley Jones were married in Bowen Memorial Church, and their son-in-law, James K. Mathews, later became pastor of the church.

19. Pickett, "The Promising Young Stanley," pp. 2-3.

20. Ibid.

21. "Some Remarkable Conversions," pp. 167-68.

22. Bishop Warne is quoted in Copplestone, p. 842.

23. Philo Buck is quoted in Copplestone, p. 845.

24. Ibid, p. 842.

25. Ibid.

26. Other information and quotations about the revival among adults appear in Copplestone on pages 846-50 passim.

27. Jones, "The Revival Month—Some Thoughts."

28. Copplestone, p. 822.

29. My account of how the Methodist Episcopal Board of Foreign Missions responded to mass movement evangelism in India is based on Copplestone, pp. 824-29.

30. Ibid, p. 829.

31. Ibid, p. 831.

32. "The Lucknow Dasehra Convention," *The Indian Witness,* August 22, 1917, p. 571.

33. My discussion and the quotations from Jones about his involvement in the Centenary Campaign are based on the *Indian Witness* articles in the following issues: February 25, 1920, p. 154; January 26, 1921, p. 71; and March 2, 1921, p. 175.

34. "Evangelism among Educated Indians," *The Indian Witness,* December 4, 1918, p. 786.

3. Mabel Lossing Jones

1. Jones's letter to a "Miss Holler" is in the Methodist Archives.

2. Unless otherwise noted, all of Mabel Lossing Jones's letters, both personal and circular, are with the papers of E. Stanley Jones in the Asbury Seminary Archives.

3. Mabel's August 31, 1910, letter to Dr. Leonard is in the Methodist Archives at Drew University in Madison, New Jersey.

4. Bishop Warne's letter endorsing the boys' school in Sitapur is among the E. Stanley Jones Papers at Asbury Theological Seminary.

5. The brochure about the Sitapur Boys' School, written by Grace Honnell, is from the Methodist Archives. The brochure itself is undated, but Mabel's March 28, 1946, duplicate letter informs her friends and patrons that Honnell will be assuming on-site supervision of both the boys' school and the nearby girls' school when Mabel returns to the United States. The brochure was date-stamped as being received by the Methodist Archives on May 12, 1949.

6. Eunice Jones Mathews's description of her father's homecomings at Sitapur is from her article, "E. Stanley Jones—as Father (and Father-in-Law)," p. 7.

7. Eunice's February 5, 1930, letter to Miss Nellie is with the E. Stanley Jones Papers at Asbury Theological Seminary.

8. Mabel's January 27, 1947, letter to Dr. Sutherland is in the Methodist Archives.

9. On the Central Conferences of the Methodist Episcopal Church electing their own bishops and the election of Dr. Chitambar, see Copplestone, p. 872.

10. Diffendorfer's November 30, 1928, letter to Mabel is in the Methodist Archives.

11. Mabel's duplicate letter of November 5, 1937, is in the Methodist Archives.

12. Mabel's May 17, 1937, letter to Diffendorfer is in the Methodist Archives.

13. Mabel's undated duplicate letter after leaving India is in the Methodist Archives.

14. I am indebted to Bishop and Mrs. James K. Mathews for the information about the last years and death of Mabel Jones. (From a telephone interview, October 5, 2004.)

4. Sitapur, India: Ultimate Commitment and the Growth of Vision

1. The quotations in this chapter from *A Song of Ascents* appear on pp. 85, 83, 84-85, 86-87, 88, 89.

2. Letter to Miss Nellie of October 21, 1915.

3. Jones refers to his superintendency of the Hardoi and Rae Bareilly districts in *A Song of Ascents,* p. 85.

4. Jones's September 27, 1915, letter to Dr. Oldham is in the Methodist Archives.

5. Unless otherwise noted all the duplicate or circular letters referred to and quoted from in this chapter are in the Asbury Seminary Archives.

6. Mabel Jones's postcard to Miss Nellie is with the Papers of E. Stanley Jones at Asbury Theological Seminary.

7. The information about the round table conferences comes from *A Song of Ascents,* pp. 236-37. The best source of information about the origin, development, and content of Jones's round table conferences is his second book *Christ at the Round Table.*

8. Jones's reading list comes from his notebooks in the Asbury Seminary Archives, some of which are undated. The dated notebooks containing examples of his reading are for 1949–50, 1950–54, 1955, 1967, 1968–69.

9. Ranbir Vohra, *The Making of India: A Historical Survey,* p. 111.

10. The quotation and preceding information about the Arya Samaj is from Copplestone, pp. 808-10.

11. The discussion of the Rowlatt Acts and the events leading up to the Jallianwala Bagh massacre comes from Vohra, pp. 134-35.

12. Ibid, p. 135.

13. Ibid, p. 143.

14. See, for example, Read and Fisher, p. 9.

15. For general information about Annie Besant, I relied on Read and Fisher, pp. 10-21 and 185-86, and on Vohra, p. 139.

16. *The Way,* p. 329.

17. *The Word Became Flesh,* p. 352.

18. *The Choice Before Us,* p. 128.

19. *The Christ of Every Road: A Study of Pentecost,* p. 191. The emphasis in the quotation is in the original. The further discussion is from p. 197.

20. *Is the Kingdom of God Realism?* p. 251.

21. *The Way,* p. 326.

22. *Growing Spiritually,* p. 304.

23. The discussion of Jones's pacifism is based on my book, *The Totalitarian Kingdom of God: The Political Philosophy of E. Stanley Jones,* pp. 143-48.

5. Evangelism Throughout India

1. Quoted by Stanley in *A Song of Ascents,* p. 83.

2. Unless otherwise noted, all of Stanley and Mabel Jones's duplicate letters referred to or quoted in this chapter are with the Papers of E. Stanley Jones at Asbury Seminary.

3. The correspondence of Stanley Jones and Dr. Frank North quoted from and referred to in this chapter is in the Methodist Archives.

4. I am indebted to Jones's son-in-law, Bishop James K. Mathews, for information about Jones's schedule when he was conducting evangelistic campaigns on his own from Sitapur. (From a telephone interview, October 30, 2000.)

5. I obtained biographical information about Sherwood Eddy from his autobiography, *Eighty Adventurous Years,* including the dust jacket, and from an article about Eddy written by Susan Billington Harper in the *Biographical Dictionary of Christian Missions,* pp. 193-94.

6. See Eddy's *Pathfinders of the World Missionary Crusade,* pp. 273-74.

7. Jones's comment about the tile factories established by the German missions in Mangalore appears in the *Indian Witness,* October 26, 1921, p. 825.

8. Latourette discusses the Syrian Christian Church in *Missions Tomorrow,* p. 181.

9. I obtained information about the construction of the *pandals* used at the Maramon Convention in an October 30, 2000, telephone interview with Bishop James K. Mathews.

10. Mabel's learning to drive the Overland 4 was related to me by Bishop Mathews in a telephone interview, October 30, 2000.

11. Latourette, *Missions Tomorrow,* p. 12.

12. Soper, p. 11.

13. For the discussion of the relationship between Christian church growth and political, military, and economic expansion, I am indebted to Hocking, *Re-Thinking Missions,* p. 10.

14. Showalter, p. 184.

15. Ibid, p. 183.

16. Soper, p. 123.

17. Copplestone, p. 1131.

18. Ibid, p. 1132.

19. Ibid.

20. Ibid, p. 1133.

21. Ibid, p. 1134.

22. Ibid.
23. Ibid.

6. A Widening Ministry: India, Mesopotamia, China

1. Jones, "Evangelism through South India," p. 825
2. Unless otherwise noted, all of Jones's circular letters referred to or quoted in this chapter are in the Asbury Seminary Archives.
3. For the evolution of Jones's preaching see Eddy, *Pathfinders of the World Missionary Crusade,* pp. 274-75.
4. *A Song of Ascents,* p. 136.
5. For Gandhi's two-part strategy for Indian independence see Vohra, pp. 147-48.
6. Jones's October 26, 1921, article is "Evangelism through South India." The quotations are from pp. 825, 828.
7. The quotations from "Through South India," are from p. 629.
8. The quotations from Jones, "Evangelizing in the Land of King Feisul," are from pp. 241-42.
9. Jones, "Evangelistic Work in China," *The Indian Witness,* January 17, 1923, p. 45.
10. Ibid, pp. 45-46.
11. Jones continued his report, "Evangelistic Work in China," in the January 31, 1923, issue of the *Indian Witness.* The quotations and material appear on p. 85.
12. Jones's letter to Dr. Donohugh is in the Methodist Archives.
13. Latourette, *Missions Tomorrow,* p. 91.
14. Showalter, p. 185.

7. The Christ of the Indian Road

1. These are the first two stanzas of Jones's poem, which was published on page 1 of the *Indian Witness* on September 13, 1922. At the end of his poem Jones added this note: "Kipling, in his poem, grants that strong individuals of East and West may meet, but declares that East and West themselves are permanently divided till God's great judgment-seat. Against this view these lines protest."
2. Jones, "Forward to the New Situation," *The Indian Witness,* August 1, 1923, p. 533.
3. For Sundar Singh as the Saint Paul of India, see *Renovare Devotional Readings,* Vol. 1, November 19, 1990, p. 1.
4. Jones, "Evangelism in South India," *The Indian Witness,* April 4, 1923, p. 234.
5. Jones, "Evangelism, Imposed or Inspired," p. 739.
6. "Evangelism, Imposed or Inspired," p. 740. Jones was not the only American Methodist missionary in India who questioned the emphasis of the church on baptism. The following quotation is from Bishop Frederick B. Fisher's episcopal address at the beginning of the Central Conference in 1928, quoted in Copplestone, p. 1151.

> Christianity in India is slowly coming to realize that it is insufficient merely to uproot individuals from their religious groups, out of their old social order, away from their economic inheritance, by means of the mysterious rite which we call Baptism. No one can expect this ceremony to act as a charm to keep men from future sin. Baptism is

only the beginning of our responsibility. . . . It is not the numbers that we seek. It is the highest possible Christian character.

7. "India's New Thought of Christ," p. 82.

8. Read and Fisher, p. 154.

9. The information about the Brahma Samaj is from Vohra, pp. 109-10.

10. "My Stay at Santiniketan," *The Indian Witness,* September 5, 1923, p. 621. A similar account was published as "In Tagore's 'House of Peace,'" *The Christian Advocate,* March 13, 1924, pp. 319-20.

11. The quotations from "The Influence of the Indian Heritage upon Christianity," December 19, 1923, are from pp. 909 and 910.

12. "The Influence of . . . ," December 26, 1923, p. 928.

13. "The Influence of . . . ," January 2, 1924, p. 11.

14. "The Present Religious Situation in India," an unpublished typescript, p. 23. The date, December 3, 1924, appears in longhand above the title on p. 1. The manuscript is in the Methodist Archives.

15. All of Jones's circular letters referred to or quoted in this chapter are in the Asbury Seminary Archives.

16. Jones's address to the 1924 General Conference of the Methodist Episcopal Church was published in the June 26, 1924, issue of the *Christian Advocate.* The quotations are from pp. 803 and 804.

17. G. W. Ridout's review of *The Christ of the Indian Road* is entitled "A Remarkable Book by a Remarkable Man," p. 2. Jones was nominated for bishop at the 1924 General Conference but withdrew his name from consideration.

18. The correspondence of A. B. Moss and E. Stanley Jones is in the Methodist Archives.

19. For general information on the declining interest in and support for foreign missions in the United States after World War II, see Showalter, p. 185.

20. The subscription advertisement is in the Methodist Archives.

21. The report (dated February 9, 1929) of collections received in Jones's meetings is in the Methodist Archives.

22. Editorial, *The Christian Advocate,* January 17, 1929, pp. 67-68.

23. The information and quotations about the American Seminar are from Jones, "The American Seminar," August 19, 1925, p. 511.

24. "The American Seminar II: A Word About Germany," September 2, 1925, p. 545.

25. "Studying the League at Geneva," p. 3. Jones's November 12, 1925, circular letter also contains information about his participation in the American Seminar.

26. "Turkey's Remarkable Revolution," p. 787.

27. Ibid, p. 788.

28. "Evangelizing Where the Good News Was Born," p. 197.

29. Ibid.

30. Ibid, p. 198.

31. He would later receive honorary doctorates from Syracuse and Duke.

32. "Evangelizing in the Land of the Pharaohs," *The Christian Advocate,* January 28, 1926, p. 105.

33. The correspondence of E. Stanley Jones and Mahatma Gandhi is in the Methodist Archives.

34. The correspondence of E. Stanley Jones and John Edwards is in the Methodist Archives. Jones made a brief public reference to his meeting with Gandhi in the December 1, 1926, issue of the *Indian Witness* in an article entitled, "A Year of Evangelism," p. 757.

35. *Mahatma Gandhi: Portrayal of a Friend,* p. 11. This 1983 publication is a reprint of *Mahatma Gandhi: An Interpretation,* published in 1948.

36. Charles W. Ranson, *A Missionary Pilgrimage,* p. 48. Jones's September 15, 1927, circular letter does refer to his being in Madras and to his meeting with "[s]everal of the leading Hindus, among them the Advocate General." However, Jones does not mention the reluctance of these Hindus to discuss religion.

37. James K. Mathews, *A Global Odyssey,* p. 359.

38. Jones reported on his trip to Burma, Malaya, Singapore, and Thailand in two *Indian Witness* articles, both entitled, "Malaya: Where Opportunity Beckons."

39. "Malaya: Where Opportunity Beckons," October 26, 1927, p. 684

40. "Malaya: Where Opportunity Beckons," November 23, 1927, p. 750.

41. Ibid, p. 751.

8. Crossroads and Crosscurrents

1. Eunice's list of reasons her father should not be bishop is in the Asbury Seminary Archives.

2. Hocking, p. 44.

3. Soper, p. 215.

4. Horner, p. 31.

5. All Jones's circular letters quoted in this chapter are in the Asbury Seminary Archives.

6. I have found no account of Jones's 1928 visit to South America.

7. "What Happened at Jerusalem?" *The Indian Witness,* May 2, 1928.

8. Six years later Jones referred to the Jerusalem Conference in an address he gave to the Missionary Demonstration in London on March 9, 1934. Responding to the criticism of Western missionaries being agents of Western imperialism, he said, "I believe that the last of this kind of thing was swept away at the Jerusalem Conference." His address was published in the April 5, 1934, issue of the *Indian Witness* in an article entitled, "Christian Missions, Not Domination, nor Denomination, but Christ." In the same address he explained the circumstances in which the resolution about military protection of missionaries and missionary property was passed at the Jerusalem Conference.

9. *A Song of Ascents,* p. 210.

10. Jones's June 6, 1928, letter to his family is in the Asbury Seminary Archives.

11. Eunice Jones Mathews, "My Father, E. Stanley Jones," p. 25.

12. Jones and Sinha, "The Proposed Ashram at Sat Tal (A Preliminary Statement)," pp. 27, 28.

13. "Sat Tal Ashram," *The Indian Witness,* January 15, 1931, p. 40.

14. The paper Jones delivered to the 1932 Sat Tal, which formed the basis for much of the ashram's discussion of the kingdom of God, was entitled, "The Kingdom of God in the New Testament." It was published along with other papers delivered at the ashram in *The Message of the Kingdom of God: Sat Tal Ashram Essays 1932.* In the light of his later and more coherent and systematic treatments of the kingdom of God, *Is the Kingdom of God Realism?* (1940) and *The Unshakeable Kingdom and the Unchanging Person* (1972), Jones's 1932 paper is a fascinating prototype of his radical reinterpretation of the New Testament Gospels.

15. "What Is Christianity?" August 18, 1932, p. 515.

16. "A Mesage to the Methodist Church," *The Christian Advocate,* April 14, 1932, p. 391.

17. *The Indian Witness,* April 14, 1932, p. 233.

18. My account of Gandhi's 1930 Salt March is based on Vohra, pp. 156-58.

19. "Christianity and Self-Government in India," *The Christian Century,* September 3, 1930, pp. 1058, 1060.

20. My account of the failure of the First Round Table Conference and of the agreement after the Conference between Lord Irwin and Gandhi is based on Vohra, pp. 158-60.

21. "To Proselytize or Convert—Which?" June 18, 1931, p. 387.

22. "To Proselytize or Convert—Which?" December 31, 1931, p. 838.

23. Vohra, p. 161.

24. "The Christian and the Present Crisis," *The Indian Witness,* February 11, 1932.

25. Quoted in Copplestone, p. 1136.

26. The information and quotations about Boyd W. Tucker are from Copplestone, pp. 1136-37.

27. Copplestone, pp. 1139-40.

28. Jones's October 31, 1935, letter to the Home Member of the United Provinces Government is in the Methodist Archives.

9. Ordinary Man, Extraordinary Mission

1. "One Hope," *Time,* December 12, 1938, p. 47.

2. "The Facts Themselves Are the Alarm: A Plain Word for a Critical Hour," *The Christian Advocate,* September 25, 1924. Jones wrote several other similar articles in *The Christian Advocate:* "The World's Whispering Gallery," November 13, 1924; "A Message to the Church," October 11, 1928.

3. October 12, 1933, *The Christian Advocate,* p. 961. Financial problems continued to burden the Methodist Church. In 1934 the General Commission on Benevolences of the Methodist Episcopal Church, South, published a book by Bishop Arthur J. Moore entitled *The Sound of Trumpets.* The book included a chapter by Jones entitled, "Is It Worth While?" an exhortation on the importance of supporting Christian missions. Jones's conclusion (p. 75): "Is it worth while being a Christian? Then if it is, is it not worth while offering others the privilege of being Christian?

"If we hold our peace, will not the stones cry out?"

4. "Meeting Current Objections to Foreign Missions," Leslie B. Moss, editor, *The Foreign Missions Conference of North America 1929,* pp. 131-32.

5. The correspondence between Jones and the Board of Foreign Missions referred to and quoted from in this chapter is in the Methodist Archives.

6. Jones's circular letters referred to and quoted from in this chapter are in the Asbury Seminary Archives.

7. Jones's *Indian Witness* article is entitled "The Situation in China."

8. The letter from a missionary at Cheeloo School of Theology is dated October 17, 1932, and is in the Asbury Seminary Archives. The missionary's first name appears to be Luella, but the last name is illegible.

9. The list of 110 questions submitted by Hua Chung College students in Hankow is in the Asbury Seminary Archives.

10. Ibid.

11. "What I Saw in Manchuria," *The Christian Century,* p. 1267.

12. Ibid., p. 1268.

13. Ibid.

14. "The Situation in China," *The Indian Witness,* December 15, 1932, p. 793.

15. "Notes on the China Tour," *The Indian Witness,* January 12, 1933, p. 26.

16. The December 15, 1932, letter from George H. McNeur of the New Zealand Presbyterian Mission is in the Asbury Seminary Archives.

17. Jones reported these figures to Diffendorfer in a letter dated December 19, 1932.

18. This interview with President Roosevelt probably occurred on December 12, 1933, on a visit with a group of missionaries. Roosevelt's appointment book for that day indicates that he met with foreign missionaries at 12:30 p.m. Although the Franklin D. Roosevelt Library does not have a list of missionaries attending the meeting, it is fair to assume that Jones's December 15, 1933, letter to Diffendorfer refers to the December 12 meeting. I am indebted for this information to Raymond Teichman, Supervisory Archivist for the Franklin D. Roosevelt Library in Hyde Park, New York. (Email to the author dated July 13, 2000.)

19. From his February 3, 1934, circular letter.

20. A copy of the Lord Mayor of London's greeting is in the Asbury Seminary Archives. The greeting is a handwritten message on a Post Office Telegraph form dated March 7, 1934.

21. Baroness von Boetselaer's March 22, 1934, letter to Diffendorfer is in the Asbury Seminary Archives.

22. *Christ's Alternative to Communism,* p. 34.

23. *The Reconstruction of the Church,* p. 118.

24. There was in Soviet Russia an organization called the Union of the Militant Godless. (See Sherwood Eddy's autobiography, *Eight Adventurous Years,* p. 142.) However, even the efforts of this organization did not succeed in completely suppressing religion in Russia.

25. Bishop Raymond J. Wade's April 13, 1934, letter to Dr. Edwards is in the Asbury Seminary Archives.

26. My statement that the Methodist Church missed a real opportunity for ministry in Russia is based on Copplestone, pp. 1002-15.

27. The quotations about the content of the kingdom of God and the Nazareth Manifesto in this and the following paragraphs are from his February 13, 1936, *Indian Witness* article, pp. 101-3.

28. Jones first used the word *totalitarian* to refer to the kingdom of God on page 53 of *Is the Kingdom of God Realism?*

29. Ambedkar's statement is quoted in Copplestone, p. 1153.

30. Jones's first meetings with Ambedkar are recorded in his article "The Significance of the Ambedkar Movement in India," *The Indian Witness,* October 1, 1936, (reprinted from *The British Weekly*), p. 630.

31. Jones's "Notes on an Interview With Dr. Ambedkar" are in the Methodist Archives. The notes state that the interview occurred "on the morning of June 24th"; the year was probably 1937.

32. The reference to the Government of India Act of 1935 is based on Vohra, pp. 162-64. The discussion of the law in this chapter is somewhat oversimplified. Under the Act, members of the depressed classes voted in both general and special constituencies, women had special constituencies from which they elected representatives on a communal basis, and in Punjab and Bengal the percentage of seats reserved for Hindus, Muslims, and Sikhs was different from the percentage of seats they received elsewhere in India.

33. Jones's February 3, 1938, letter to Lord Halifax is in the Methodist Archives.

34. Jones's support for communal representation in the hope that Ambedkar would bring the outcastes into Christianity is inconsistent both with his own earlier

opposition to communalism and with resolutions adopted by the Central Conference of the Methodist Episcopal Church in India. See Copplestone, pp. 1147-48 for a discussion of the Central Conference position on communalism, as expressed in repeated resolutions adopted in the 1920s and 1930s—that "it desired an electoral system that would unite India rather than divide her into suspicious and warring religious groups"(Copplestone, p. 1147).

35. Copplestone, p. 1153.

36. Ibid, p. 1154.

37. Ibid, p. 1155.

38. "An Interview with the Mahatma," pp. 774-75.

39. Gandhi's account of his February 4, 1933, interview with Jones appears in *The Collected Works of Mahatma Gandhi*, Vol. 53, pp. 257-59. Gandhi originally published his report of the interview in *Harijan* on February 11, 1933.

40. My account of Gandhi's fast unto death and its consequences is based on Vohra, pp. 162-63.

41. Gandhi's February 10, 1935, letter to Jones and the Commissioner's February 26, 1935, letter to Jones are in the Asbury Seminary Archives.

42. "Announcement Concerning the Lucknow Ashram," *The Indian Witness*, June 6, 1935, p. 862.

43. "The Closing of the Lucknow Ashram," pp. 248-49.

44. Copplestone, p. 1141.

45. Ibid, p. 1142.

46. The Smiths' December 3, 1939, letter of resignation is in the Asbury Seminary Archives.

47. Jones's February 20, 1940, letter to C. C. Morrison of *The Christian Century* is in the Asbury Seminary Archives.

48. All the quotations from Jones's article on the missionary pledge, "My Position Restated," are from *The Indian Witness*, April 11, 1940, p. 233. Jones, unlike Smith, did not seek confrontation with the British authorities. His cautious attitude toward politics is also reflected in his October 14, 1935, letter to Diffendorfer. He discussed his travel plans for the coming year, including his participation in the first preaching mission (described in chapter 10) in the United States sponsored by the Federal Council of Churches. Diffendorfer had suggested that Dr. Julius F. Hecker travel with Jones during the mission. Hecker, a Russian-born Methodist Episcopal minister assigned to the New York East Conference, had expressed "outspoken sympathy with the objectives of the Russian Revolution" (Copplestone, p. 1004). Jones's October 14 letter to Diffendorfer questioned the wisdom of including Hecker in the preaching mission. He wrote,

> I am wondering if this [having Hecker travel with the mission] would not deeply prejudice our mission in the minds of the people, at least a great portion of them. I would have no personal objections, but I wonder if it would be wise strategy. Please let me have your thoughts about it. I have not heard from him, so I do not know his position. But he is a convinced Marxian Communist. What effect did he have in U.S.A. on his last tour?

10. Conflict and Controversy

1. "Christians of America Unite," *The Christian Century*, October 2, 1935, pp. 1235, 1237. Jones proposed a similar plan for unity among the Christian churches

in India. See his articles on this plan in the *Indian Witness:* "Some Thoughts on Church Unity," April 25, 1935, pp. 261-62; "More Thoughts on Church Unity," May 16, 1935, p. 309; "The Church of Christ in India," September 26, 1935, p. 613; "Church Union in India," October 24, 1935, pp. 680-81; and "The Next Great Step: Unite!" May 6, 1937, pp. 275-76.

2. Unless otherwise noted, all of Jones's circular letters referred to or quoted in this chapter are in the Asbury Seminary Archives (including the letter of August 18, 1937, with personal notes to Mabel).

3. The undated list of proposals drawn up by a representative group of Indian Christians and missionaries for the disposition of mission property is in the Methodist Archives.

4. "Afterthoughts on the Preaching Mission," p. 483.

5. "The University Christian Mission in America." On the Christian interpretation of a subject, see p. 51. On the technique for decisions for Christ, see p. 52.

Before arriving in the United States for the University Mission, Jones visited Australia, New Zealand, the Fiji Islands, and Hawaii. He went to Australia at the invitation of the World Christian Endeavor Convention in Melbourne and of the United Missionary Council of Australia. In Australia he spoke in Perth, Adelaide, Melbourne, Geelong, Ballarat, Newcastle, Canberra, Maitland, Warwick, Toowoomba, Brisbane, and Sydney. In New Zealand he spoke in Auckland. In Fiji he spoke in Suva "in a church where the bones of the missionary Baker, who had been killed and eaten by the cannibals, were buried." Jones noted that at the time of his visit all of the Fiji Islands were Christian, "90% of them being Methodists! . . . What hath God wrought!" Finally, in Honolulu Jones recorded a message that was later broadcast by radio throughout Hawaii. This information and these quotations are from Jones's September 29, 1938, circular letter.

6. On the Tambaram Conference, see Scherer, "Ecumenical Mandates for Mission," in Horner, p. 34.

7. The terms "sending" and "receiving" churches are from David J. Bosch, *Transforming Mission,* p. 465.

8. The fact that the sending and receiving churches sent the same number of delegates to Tambaram is in Stephen Neill, *A History of Christian Missions,* p. 386.

9. On the high quality of the Asiatic delegates, see Soper, p. 13. Despite the sense of equality between delegates from sending churches and delegates from receiving churches, one of the leaders of the conference "found it necessary to remind the delegates . . . that the 'younger' churches are the fruit of missionary labor, not the *possession* of mission societies." Bosch, p. 465.

10. "What I Missed at Madras," p. 707. Jones responded to criticism of his negative assessment of Tambaram not only in this *Christian Century* article but also in a long letter to the editor of the *Indian Witness* in its March 23, 1939, issue, p. 181.

11. Frank T. Cartwright's telegram about Stanley's evacuation from Shanghai is in the Methodist Archives.

12. Jones's September 20, 1937, circular letter is in the Methodist Archives. Jones published an account of his evacuation from China in "From the War Zone," September 9, 1937, *The Indian Witness,* pp. 563-64.

13. Jones's "Appeal to the Governments and People of Japan and China" is included in his October 14, 1937, *Indian Witness* article, "The Christian Attitude in the China War Crisis," pp. 643-44. Another account of what he experienced in China appears in the January 6, 1938, issue of the *Indian Witness* in an article entitled, "Dr. Stanley Jones in China," pp. 5-6.

14. The "central international crime," is from "An Open Letter to the People of

Japan," p. 1133. The depth of Jones's revulsion at the Japanese attack on China was, in part, the result of letters he exchanged with Madame Chiang Kai-shek, a Christian and the wife of Generalissimo Chiang Kai-shek, the leader of the Chinese Nationalist forces. Although I have not found Jones's letter to Madame Chiang, the Methodist Archives does have a copy of her letter to him, dated September 13, 1937, and signed, Mayling Soong Chiang. Her letter begins with accounts of Japanese atrocities in various places in China. Then she wrote,

> I have felt that we Christians . . . are not living up to our Christian beliefs if we see such brutalities going on and do nothing. . . . The utter silence of the foreign powers in the face of this catastrophe and their seeming indifference bewilder me. When I saw your Ambassador last week I asked him whether America is interested in seeing or in helping Japan browbeat China. It was of course undiplomatic of me to ask such a thing, but our people, and I myself also, cannot understand why America said absolutely nothing to Japan when the 1932 Chapei affair already showed so clearly what Japan's game was. . . . Japan of course takes the silence of the powers as approval of her methods.
>   I am having the statements [in Jones' letter] translated to the Generalissimo and I feel certain that they will hearten him in the terrifically difficult task now confronting our country.

15. When he reached Rangoon, Burma, on his return trip to India from China, Jones wrote a circular letter dated December 22, 1937, summarizing the events of his journey, which is in the Asbury Seminary Archives, as is Arthur Jorgensen's letter of September 22, 1937.

16. "The Christian Attitude in the China War Crisis," *The Indian Witness*, October 14, 1937, pp. 643, 644.

17. The quotations about Jones's proposed "economic withdrawal" from Japan are from his article, "An Open Letter to the Christian People of America and Great Britain," *The Christian Century*, November 10, 1937, p. 1387. My discussion of this letter and of Jones's earlier open letter to the people of Japan is based on my book, *The Totalitarian Kingdom of God*, pp. 73-74.

18. The telegram from the National Christian Council of Manila is in the Asbury Seminary Archives.

19. Frederick Libby's September 27, 1937, letter is in the Asbury Seminar Archives.

20. Frank M. Toothaker's December 2, 1937, letter is in the Asbury Seminar Archives.

21. "Apply Gandhi's Method to Japan!" *The Christian Century*, January 19, 1938, pp. 75-77. My discussion is based on my book, *The Totalitarian Kingdom of God*, pp. 75-77.

22. *A Song of Ascents*, pp. 54-55.

11. Peace: Valiant Pursuit, Victory Deferred

1. *A Song of Ascents*, p. 194.

2. Jones's undated circular letter about his peace efforts in Washington in early 1941 is in the Methodist Archives. The quotations about the war mentality in Washington, about his meetings with congressmen and Justice Frankfurter, and about Jones following the gleam are all from this circular letter.

3. Jones spelled out his idea about the United States as the mediator of a new world order in "What Is America's Role in This Crisis?" *The Christian Century*, March

19, 1941, pp. 388-90. I discuss the content of this article in more detail in *The Totalitarian Kingdom of God,* chapter 7, "The Totalitarian Kingdom and a New Man Out of Both Parties," pp. 99-109.

4. *A Song of Ascents,* pp. 194-95.

5. Ibid.

6. When Jones's decision to stay in the United States became public knowledge, he issued a statement in response to "a good deal of misunderstanding as to just why and for what purposes I am staying in America." The statement listed four reasons for his decision to remain in the United States.

> First, I am here because the Inner Voice, upon which I depend in times of crisis, clearly said, "I want you here". . . .
>
> Second, I am here primarily for evangelistic work.
>
> Third, within the framework of that evangelistic work I shall endeavor to help to hold the Christian Church together in spite of differences over the Christian position regarding war. . . .
>
> Fourth, I hope it may be possible to get together in our own country those differing fundamentally on the issue of pacifism and after prayer and counsel to come to a common mind on a Christian program of national and world reconstruction.
>
> I hope, though it may appear a fond hope, that we may be able to replace in some measure the present warmindedness of America with a consideration of this program of reconstruction, as a means of ending the war and of laying the foundations of a new beginning among nations.

This undated statement, which was probably issued as a press release by the Methodist Episcopal Church, is in the Asbury Archives.

7. The information and quotations about Jones's activities before September 1941 are in his September 13, 1941, circular letter in both the Asbury Seminary and the Methodist Archives.

8. Jones's July 23, 1941, letter to Mrs. O. G. Robinson is in the Asbury Seminary Archives, as is all the correspondence between Jones and the Robinsons.

9. Jones, "An Adventure in Failure: Behind the Scenes Before Pearl Harbor," *Asia and the Americas,* December 1945, p. 609.

10. *A Song of Ascents,* p.195.

11. The statements of General MacArthur and Admiral Nomura, and the attribution to President Roosevelt are in *A Song of Ascents,* p. 196. Throughout chapter 11, I rely on the discussion in chapter 6, "The Totalitarian Kingdom in Crisis: Jones as an Unofficial Ambassador of Peace," of my book, *The Totalitarian Kingdom of God,* pp. 87-98.

12. Kagawa's cablegram is quoted in Jones's article "An Adventure in Failure," p. 610.

13. *A Song of Ascents,* p. 198.

14. "An Adventure in Failure," p. 611.

15. *A Song of Ascents,* pp. 198-99. Jones's memory of his discussion with MacArthur is confirmed by a letter he wrote to Dr. and Mrs. Robinson from Seoul, Korea, on March 23, 1949 (in the Asbury Archives).

> I saw MacArthur, had a long talk with him, and found him very sympathetic toward the idea of New Guinea for Japan's surplus population. He waxed eloquent over its possibilities but thought we should not raise the question now until the peace treaty. I tried three times to go but he would not let me.

16. *A Song of Ascents,* p. 200. There is in the Asbury Archives a letter from Dulles to Jones, dated February 9, 1951, written from Tokyo. It acknowledges Jones's letter of February 6 as well as a memorandum Jones had enclosed. Dulles said that he "had already spoken to Mr. Allison about New Guinea in accordance with our conversation." Dulles concluded his letter with an invitation. "If you are in Tokyo," he wrote, "please come to the reception we are giving at the Imperial Hotel Saturday from five to seven." It is interesting to note that during World War II, Dulles was the chairman of a Commission to Study the Bases of a Just and Durable Peace. The commission was appointed by the Federal Council of Churches and, according to church historian Kenneth Scott Latourette in *Christianity in a Revolutionary Age* (vol. 5, pp. 112-13), it

> placed much emphasis upon the importance of creating the United Nations. Its findings were presented to officials in Washington to acquaint them with the facets of thought for which it could speak. . . . Dulles later said that it was his association with the Commission which led him to accept the task of negotiating the treaty of peace with Japan—an assignment which he undertook before becoming Secretary of State—and to make it a document embodying the spirit of forgiveness rather than of hate.

17. Jones's April 11, 1959, letter to R. G. Casey, the Australian Minister for External Affairs, and Casey's May 31, 1959, response are in the Asbury Archives.

After President Truman relieved MacArthur of his command during the Korean War, Jones pursued the idea of giving New Guinea to Japan with the new commander, General Matthew B. Ridgway. Jones wrote to Ridgway on May 1, 1951. I have not been able to find Jones's letter, but the Asbury Archives has a copy of Ridgway's reply dated May 15. The General wrote,

> Although the solution you propose [to the problem of Japan's surplus population] is not within the scope of my authority to recommend or implement, the policy since the early days of the occupation relative to the emigration of Japanese has been extremely liberal and permits any Japanese national on an individual case-by-case basis to emigrate from Japan to any country which will permit Japanese nationals to enter as permanent residents.
>
> Since your proposal has been communicated to Mr. Dulles, it may be expected that Mr. Dulles will give it due consideration to the extent that such consideration is feasible.

18. Marjorie Hyer, "Dr. E. Stanley Jones, Evangelist, Dies," p. B4, January 26, 1973. The quotation summarizing the United States' November 26 ultimatum to the Japanese is from Jones's "Asia and the Americas" article, p. 614, as are also the quotations of the memo to FDR, and the Japanese response to their meeting with FDR and the quotation about FDR reading the written part of Jones's secret message on behalf of the Japanese on the way to the White House.

19. "An Adventure in Failure," p. 614.

20. Ibid.

21. Ibid.

22. *The Totalitarian Kingdom of God,* p. 94. Within the quotation is another quotation from Jones's "An Adventure in Failure," p. 614. My account of Jones's unofficial diplomacy during the last three months of 1941 relies heavily on *The Totalitarian Kingdom of God,* pp. 91-95.

23. All of the quotations about Jones's meeting with Roosevelt are also from "An Adventure in Failure," p. 614.

Jones's account of his meeting with FDR is confirmed by several pieces of evidence. The Franklin D. Roosevelt Library in Hyde Park, New York, has a record of Jones's meeting with FDR beginning at 12:15 p.m. on December 3, 1941. However, the Library does "not have any documents relating to [the content of] this meeting." This statement from Raymond Teichman, the Supervisory Archivist of the Roosevelt Library in a letter to me dated February 3, 1998, confirms Jones's statement that his meeting with FDR was off the record. Moreover, on Sunday December 7, 1941, the *New York Times* reported in a front-page story that on December 6 "President Roosevelt made a personal appeal to Emperor Hirohito of Japan."

24. After the war Gwen Terasaki, the American wife of Hidenari Terasaki, the Counsel of the Japanese Embassy in Washington, published an account of her life, *Bridge to the Sun*, in which she confirmed Jones's recollection of his efforts to prevent war between the United States and Japan. Pages 65-69 discuss Jones's role as a mediator.

Leonard Mosley in his biography, Hirohito: Emperor of Japan, pp. 249-51, also relies on Mrs. Terasaki's account of Jones's role. However, he incorrectly identifies Jones as "a Wesleyan minister" (p. 249). Mosley believes that if Roosevelt's telegram to Hirohito "had reached its destination, it might have worked" (p. 260). He explains:

> Arriving in good time, it [Roosevelt's telegram] could not have failed to have produced a positive reaction from Hirohito. His zeal for peace was such that he would undoubtedly have ordered his armed forces to pause.

Joseph C. Grew, the American Ambassador to Japan in 1941, wrote in his memoirs, *Turbulent Era: A Diplomatic Record of Forty Years 1904–1945*, that he was unable to deliver Roosevelt's message directly to Emperor Hirohito. Grew's account of receiving and trying to deliver the President's telegram appears in Vol. II, pp. 1249 ff. After the war, in hearings before a joint committee of Congress investigating the attack on Pearl Harbor, Grew "stated that he believed the Japanese military authorities held up the delivery of the President's message to him in order to delay its presentation to the Emperor" (Vol. II, p. 1250, n.7).

25. "What Is America's Role in This Crisis?" p. 388. For a more complete discussion of Jones's concept of a new entity out of both parties, based on Ephesians 2:15-16, see chapter 7, "The Totalitarian Kingdom and a New Man out of Both Parties," in my book, *The Totalitarian Kingdom of God*, pp. 99-109.

26. Gwen Terasaki, *Bridge to the Sun*, pp. 215-16.

12. Closed Door to India

1. "A Proposed Charter for the Pacific Area," Asbury Seminary Archives.

2. *A Song of Ascents,* pp. 192-93.

3. Unless otherwise noted, all of Jones's circular letters referred to or quoted from in this chapter are in the Asbury Seminary Archives.

4. An incomplete typescript of his Christmas message is in the Asbury Seminary Archives. Although it is undated, it focuses on the aftermath of Pearl Harbor and must have been written for Christmas 1941.

5. *Abundant Living* was a sequel to Jones's first collection of daily devotions, *Victorious Living* (1936). He explained the purpose of his daily devotional books in an October 14, 1935, letter to Diffendorfer:

> I am going to try to serve three purposes through it [*Victorious Living*]: 1. As a book of Daily Readings for personal devotions. 2. A book for group studies. I will try to arrange my materials so that it can be used on a weekly basis, that is, the daily readings could be grouped in groups of seven. 3. I hope to make it such a living whole that it can be read straight through as an ordinary book.

6. Jones's September 13, 1941, circular letter is in the Methodist Archives.

7. The July 10, 1943, letter to Miss Nellie and all the correspondence between Jones and the Robinsons quoted in this chapter is in the Asbury Archives.

8. The correspondence between Mark Dawber and Stanley Jones is in the Methodist Archives.

Other correspondence about Jones's proposal for the resettlement of Japanese Americans, including his July 16, 1942, and August 7, 1942, letters to Dr. Sam Cavert and Dr. Roswell Barnes of the Home Missions Council of North America; Jones's August 5, 1942, letter to Dawber; and a July 28, 1942, letter written to Jones by Gordon K. Chapman of the Protestant Church Commission for Japanese Service are also in the Methodist Archives.

9. In a June 30, 1943, letter to the Robinsons, Jones refers to his plans to go to Chicago "on July 4 to speak to 2500 Negroes."

10. The Texas Methodist pastor's November 23, 1942, letter to the Methodist World Service Agencies and Jones's December 12, 1942, reply are in the Methodist Archives.

11. Jones's August 10, 1942, letter to President Roosevelt and his proposed Pacific Charter are both from the Asbury Seminary Archives.

12. The dates of Jones's letter to Maxwell Hamilton and Hamilton's reply on behalf of the U.S. State Department (which are in the Asbury Archives) are problematic. Hamilton's letter is dated June 26, 1942, and refers to Jones's "June 10" letter to Roosevelt and to Jones's "June 12, 1942" letter to the State Department. If the date of his August 10, 1942, letter is accurate, then apparently Jones had written earlier letters on the same subject to both the President and to the State Department.

13. Churchill's stating that the Atlantic Charter did not apply to India and Roosevelt's bringing pressure on Churchill with respect to India is based on Vohra, p. 171.

14. Jones's January 5, 1943, letter to Roosevelt is in the Asbury Archives.

15. Jones, "The Price of Ultimate Victory," in Anderson, ed., *Christian World Mission*, pp. 263-69.

16. Ibid, p. 265.

17. Ibid, p. 267.

18. Jones, "Church Federal Union—Now!" *The Christian Century*, December 16, 1942, p. 1554.

19. Jones's articles are "Church Federal Union—Now!" *The Christian Century*, December 16, 1942; "Is Church Federal Union the Answer?" *The Christian Advocate*, January 14, 1943; "Federal Church Union—A Reply," *The Christian Century*, June 16, 1943.

20. The quotation about the League of Nations not surrendering sovereignty and violating the law of the kingdom of God is from Jones's article, "Is Church Federal Union the Answer?" *The Christian Advocate*, January 14, 1943, p. 42.

21. The quotation about the desire for unity and the desire for autonomy is from "Church Federal Union—Now!" *The Christian Century*, December 16, 1942, p. 1554.

22. The quotations from Jones's second *Christian Century* article appear on p. 713.

13. Toward Indian Independence

1. Jones's August 27, 1945, letter to Lord Halifax, is in the Methodist Archives.

2. Jones's October 12, 1944, letter to Murray Titus is in the Asbury Archives.

3. J. Waskom Pickett's May 18, 1944, letter is in the Asbury Archives.

4. "Gandhi and Christian Missions," *The Christian Century*, May 3, 1944, p. 553.

5. Jones's May 31, 1944, letter to Pickett is in the Methodist Archives.

6. Jones's September 4, 1944, circular letter is in the Methodist Archives.

7. Jones's August 8, 1944, letter to Henry Wallace and Wallace's August 14, 1944, letter are in the Asbury Archives.

8. Unless otherwise noted, all the correspondence between Stanley Jones and the Robinsons is in the Asbury Archives.

9. Jones's December 30, 1943, letter to Roosevelt is in the Asbury Archives.

10. The following documents relating to this incident, from which I quote, are in the Franklin D. Roosevelt Library in Hyde Park, N.Y.: J. Edgar Hoover's December 9, 1943, letter to Harry L. Hopkins with attached excerpts from Handsaker's October 27, 1943, letter to Matson; Hopkins's December 20, 1943, memo to Grace Tully; Roosevelt's December 22, 1943, memo to Hopkins; Hopkins's December 30, 1943, letter to Hoover; and Hoover's January 10, 1944, letter to Hopkins.

11. L. R. Pennington's May 27, 1944, memo, his letters dated June 8 and July 6, 1944, as well as Jones's letters of June 19 and July 22, 1944, are all from FBI files released to the author under a Freedom of Information Act request by David M. Hardy, Chief, Record/Information Dissemination Section, Records Management Division of the Federal Bureau of Investigation (FOIPA No. 1001925-000).

12. In his September 4, 1944, circular letter Jones made this comment about his books—"I love the writing after I get started, and I love to turn the proceeds from the books over to the work of Christian Missions in India." One example of Jones's generosity to Indian missions is contained in Murray Titus's July 11, 1944, letter to Jones (in the Methodist Archives). Titus's letter explains the allocation by the Methodist Division of Foreign Missions of a $30,000 gift from Jones.

13. Jones's December 30, 1944, circular letter is in the Asbury Archives, as are the other circular letters quoted in the rest of the chapter (unless noted otherwise).

14. Jones's December 18, 1944, letter to the attendees of the Columbus and Buffalo meetings is in the Asbury Archives.

15. Jones's December 18, 1944, letter to Edward R. Stettinius is in the Asbury Archives.

16. Leo Pasvolsky's January 25, 1945, letter to Jones is in the Asbury Archives.

17. Jones, "What I Found in Latin America," Part II, *The Christian Century*, July 25, 1945, p. 859.

18. George P. Howard's December 28, 1944, letter to Dr. A. W. Wasson of the Divison of Foreign Missions of the Methodist Church, is in the Methodist Archives.

19. Murray Titus's May 31, 1945, letter to Jones is in the Methodist Archives.

20. Jones, "Report on Latin American Evangelistic Tour," *The Indian Witness,* October 25, 1945, p. 242.

21. Hartzell Spence, "Can He Unite the Protestants?" *The Saturday Evening Post,* December 4, 1948, p. 203.

22. Jones, "What I Found in Latin America," *The Christian Century,* July 18, 1945, p. 833.

23. Jones, "What I Found in Latin America," Part II, *The Christian Century,* July 25, 1945, p. 858.

24. Jones's April 29, 1945, letter to Murray Titus is in the Methodist Archives.

25. Jones, "Report on Latin America Evangelistic Tour," *The Indian Witness,* October 25, 1945, p. 242.

26. Jones's letter to Diffendorfer about Rhys Davies's support for his request for a visa to India is undated, but it was probably written in mid-November 1945. It is in the Asbury Archives.

27. In the latter part of 1945 Jones visited and spoke in Puerto Rico. His January 30, 1946, *Christian Century* article, "What About Puerto Rico?" pp. 138-40, summarizes the highlights of his visit and gives his impressions about the Commonwealth.

28. M. Ahmad's November 16, 1945, letters to Jones and Diffendorfer and Jones's November 26, 1945, reply are in the Methodist Archives.

29. The following discussion of political events in India after World War II is based on Vohra, pp. 164-89.

30. Ibid, p. 167.

31. Ibid, p. 183.

32. Ibid, p. 188.

33. Jones's April 12, 1946, letter to Jinnah, and Jinnah's April 27, 1946, reply, are in the Asbury Archives.

34. Jones's September 29, 1946, letter to his daughter and son-in-law, and his November 22, 1946, letter to his son-in-law are in the Methodist Archives.

35. Jones's October 23, 1946, letter to Diffendorfer is in the Asbury Archives.

36. Gandhi's February 20, 1947, letter to Jones is in the Asbury Archives.

37. The information about the Noakhali district of East Bengal, and the quotation about the reason for Gandhi's visit to Noakhali are from Read and Fisher, pp. 403, 404. The meaning of *ahimsa* is also from Read and Fisher, p. 143.

38. Jones's April 1, 1947, circular letter is in the Asbury Archives.

39. Jones's April 14, 1947, letter to his daughter, Eunice, and her family is in the Methodist Archives.

14. In the Aftermath of War: Hopes and Disappointments

1. Jones, "I Saw a New India Rise," *The Christian Century,* July 17, 1946, p. 891.

2. Jones's April 14 and April 28, 1947, family letters, are in the Methodist Archives.

3. Kripalani's May 5, 1947, letter to Jones, is in the Asbury Archives.

4. Jones's May 5, 1947, family letter is in the Asbury Archives.

5. Jones's May 12, 1947, letter to Jinnah is in the Asbury Archives. Jones published two accounts of his efforts to resolve the conflict between Hindus and Muslims over Pakistan. One was chapter 4, "The Coming Into Being of Pakistan," in *Gandhi: Portrayal of a Friend,* pp. 42-50. The second, an abbreviated account, is in *A Song of Ascents,* pp. 318-19.

6. I quote most of the Landour Declaration from Jones's June 5, 1947, family letter, which is in the Methodist Archives.

7. In 1946 and 1947 Jones published three articles about the politically sensitive issue of religious conversion and communal representation. The first, "Opportunities for the Church Facing Indian Nationalism," appeared in two parts: in the August 1, 1946, issue of *The Indian Witness,* pp. 1, 3, and in the August 15, 1946, issue, pp. 195, 197. The second, "Which Way Will Free India Go?" was published in the August 7, 1946, issue of *The Christian Century,* pp. 959-61. The third, "Report on the New India," was published in the April 30, 1947, issue of the *Christian Century,* pp. 555-56.

8. His June 5, 1947, letter to Diffendorfer and his family letters dated May 17, 1948, and February 6, 1948, are from the Methodist Archives.

9. Jones's first published response to Gandhi's death appeared as a letter to the editor in the February 18, 1948, issue of the *Christian Century* entitled "Gandhi's Death—the Indian Reaction," p. 209. Within a week of Gandhi's death Jones wrote to his family in America, which now included Mabel, who had finally returned home, as well as his daughter Eunice and son-in-law Ken. His letter was written from Colombo, Ceylon (Sri Lanka), and was dated February 6. Jones described the immediate reaction to Gandhi's murder.

> For some days the radio gave nothing except speeches about Gandhi from national leaders. . . . But none of the ideas of Hinduism fitted Gandhi. So they set them aside and quietly adopted Christian ideas. Instead of Karma, the suffering was vicarious. Instead of Gandhi entering Nirvana they wanted him to come back & guide them. . . . [One leader] in her speech over the radio said, "This is the third day. He must rise again & come back & lead us." Instead of transmigration they wanted him back in [their] presence immediately! . . . They wanted him to come back as Gandhi and have his presence lead them. None of the Hindu ideas fitted. Only Xtian [Christian] ideas ruled their thinking. The Xtian Scriptures quoted a lot.

10. The telegram from Abingdon Press appears to be dated February 20, 1948, and is from the Asbury Archives.

11. Jones, "Foreword," *Gandhi: A Portrayal of a Friend,* pp. 5, 8.

12. Jones's May 3, 1948, letter to his son-in-law is in the Asbury Archives.

13. *A Song of Ascents,* pp. 325-26.

14. Jones's September 30, 1948, circular letter is in the Asbury Archives.

15. Some of the information about Jones's Crusade for a United Church and the Association for a United Church of America is from what appears to be a form letter on association letterhead dated October 30, 1947, in the Asbury Archives.

16. Hartzell Spence, "Can He Unite the Protestants?" p. 205.

17. Ibid.

18. Jones's being skeptical about the results of the crusade is from an undated six-page typescript entitled "The Crusade for a United Church—What Did It Reveal?" which is in the Asbury Archives.

19. Jones's response to Douglas was, "Is Federal Union a Halfway House?" *The Christian Century,* July 14, 1948.

20. Quoted in Spence, p. 206.

21. "Is Federal Union a Halfway House?" p. 705.

22. Ibid, p. 706.

23. An article Jones wrote for the January 26, 1950, issue of the *Christian Advocate,* "Is the Movement for Federal Union Waning or Waxing?" reports the results of independent polls "taken in places not reached in the crusades" (p. 102).

The polls, which were conducted by a University of Illinois professor and by an Oklahoma oil company executive, concluded that 85 percent of those questioned favored federal union over church councils, mere federation without any surrender of sovereignty, or complete amalgamation.

24. My discussion of Jones's argument against reordination is from his "Re-ordination or Right Hand of Fellowship?" *The Indian Witness,* January 20, 1949, pp. 43-44.

25. Jones, "On What Basis Should the Churches Get Together?" *The Indian Witness,* June 23, 1949.

26. Jones explicitly refers to the concept of a new man out of both parties in one of his *Indian Witness* articles on federal union entitled, "Is Federal Union The Way Out?" published in two parts, January 26, 1956, p. 28; February 9, 1956, pp. 43-44.

27. "Federal Union of Churches," *The Christian Century,* June 10, 1953, p. 691.

28. Jones's *The Reconstruction of the Church—On What Pattern?* was written toward the end of his life. Also, one chapter of his autobiography, *A Song of Ascents,* is devoted to church union—"Will the Church Sing a New Song?" pp. 271-88. His last *Indian Witness* article on federal union, "A Last Minute Call to Reconsider Church Union," was published in the May 21, 1970, issue. In this article Jones (p. 157) explained that his strategy for federal union among the Christian churches in India was similar to his strategy for federal union in the United States.

> When it came to union of the churches in India, I let my views be known, and then I took the inner attitude: "Now let the churches decide. . . ." Here, I made a mistake. My friends, who want union of the churches . . . have accused me of letting them down and the cause of Branch Union. As I have watched the increasing doubts, and even bitterness about merger I have felt I should make this last minute appeal for the adoption of Federal or Branch Union.

29. Allister MacKay's May 12, 1966, letter to Jones is in the Asbury Archives.

30. Jones's March 1972 letter to the delegates to the United Methodist General Conference is in the Asbury Archives.

31. Bishop Raines's February 17, 1967, letter to Harvey Kazmier is in the Asbury Archives.

32. Jones's May 27, 1949, circular letter is in the Asbury Archives.

33. His article in the July 7, 1949, issue of *The Indian Witness* (reprinted from Jones's publication, *Fellowship*), is entitled, "The Greatest Christian Opportunity on Our Planet": Jones's hesitation, p. 507; advance publicity, p. 508; the crash of Japan's political spiritual life, p. 508.

34. Jones's letter to the Methodist Division of Foreign Missions is part of a five-page document entitled, "Letters from Dr. E. Stanley Jones" (in the Methodist Archives), a composite record of his experiences in Japan dated February 25 and March 4, 10, 19, and 22, 1949.

35. Latourette, *Christianity in a Revolutionary Age,* Vol. V: *The Twentieth Century Outside Europe,* p. 437.

36. "The Greatest Christian Opportunity," p. 508.

37. Jones's March 23, 1949, letter to the Robinsons is in the Asbury Archives.

38. Jones received permission to enter the Imperial Palace Grounds from the General Headquarters of General MacArthur, the Supreme Commander for the Allied Powers in Japan. This information is from a memo dated March 12, 1949, in the Asbury Archives.

39. Jones's December 10, 1941, letter to Terasaki is from Jones, "The Greatest Christian Opportunity," pp. 508, 510. The weak spot of Japanese evangelism, ibid, p. 508.

40. Ibid, p. 508.

41. Michio Kozaki's letter to Jones is in the Asbury Archives.

42. "The Greatest Christian Opportunity," pp. 510-11.

43. Jones's "An Adventure in Failure: Behind the Scenes Before Pearl Harbor," p. 616.

44. "As the Bamboo Curtain Goes Down," *The Indian Witness,* July 14, 1949, pp. 523-24.

45. Ibid, p. 523.

46. *The Way To Power and Poise,* p. 190.

47. "The Greatest Christian Opportunity," p. 524.

48. Ibid, p. 523.

49. Ibid, p. 524.

50. E. Carver McGriff, *Amazing Grace,* p. 114.

51. "The Greatest Christian Opportunity," p. 524.

52. Jones's May 15, 1949, letter to Nehru is in the Asbury Archives.

53. Jones, "India at the Polls," *The Christian Century,* May 21, 1952, p. 615.

54. Ibid, p. 616.

55. Nehru's May 29, 1952, letter to Jones is in the Asbury Archives.

There is support for Jones's statement that corruption was a real problem in India after independence. In 1964 he wrote two articles in the *Indian Witness* on the problem of corruption: "Three Vultures Over the House of the Lord," March 19, 1964, addressed the problem of corruption in the Methodist Church in India. Jones wrote (p. 96) that in "the struggle for position in the church, bribery sometimes . . . [is] used to get support." More specifically, he noted, "I am told on good authority that personal and church money is being used to buy votes and influence elections to church offices." Jones concluded with a call for the Methodist Church in India to "observe a day of fasting and prayer and humiliation" to overcome the problem of corruption and bribery.

The second article, "The Nation's Call to Christians," *The Indian Witness,* July 16, 1964, dealt with the more general problem of both private and public corruption in India. Jones noted (p. 129): "Those who rejoice in the progress India has made since" independence "have had that rejoicing tempered by an ominous fact," namely the continued problem of corruption. There is no better evidence for the stubborn persistence of corruption than the fact that seventeen years after independence, the Union Home Minister of the new government of India, formed by Prime Minister Shastri after the death of Nehru, "pledged to eradiate corruption in public life over which he is responsible, or resign at the end of two years."

15. Christian Ashrams

1. *A Song of Ascents,* p. 234.

2. Clarence Hill, "An American Gandhi Leads Christian Campers in Religious Revival on Michigan's Sands." A copy of his article is in the Asbury Seminary Archives.

3. *A Song of Ascents,* p. 40. About Christian ashrams assimilating, p. 221.

4. Ibid, p. 42.

5. Ibid, p. 220.

6. Eunice Jones Mathews learned about the legendary origin of Sat Tal from Mrs. A. C. Evans, the wife of the previous owner. She recounts the legend in her article "Historical Sketch of Sat Tal," included in *Sat Tal Ashram Golden Anniversary 1930–1980*, an 88-page magazine published on the fiftieth anniversary of the Sat Tal Ashram. (The publication is located in the Asbury Archives.). The quotation is from page 8. Mathews notes: "It is hard to find all seven [lakes] nowadays. Three are quite evident: Ram Tal, Sita Tal and Panna Tal. During the rainy season, with a healthy imagination, one can discern all seven lakes of varying size.

7. *A Song of Ascents*, pp. 214-15.

8. *Sat Tal Golden Anniversary 1930–1980*, p. 2.

9. Ibid, p. 5.

10. *A Song of Ascents*, pp. 221.

11. *What Is an Ashram?* an undated pamphlet, is in the United Christian Ashram (UCA) Archives at Asbury Theological Seminary.

12. *A Song of Ascents*, p. 224.

13. Ibid.

14. Roberto Escamilla, "As I Remember Brother Stanley," *Transformation*, Winter 1983, p. 21. The magazine is in the Ashram Archives at Asbury Seminary.

15. Sabrow Yasumura, "Three Months' Tour with E. Stanley Jones," p. 222.

16. *A Song of Ascents*, pp. 233, 234.

17. James K. Mathews, "E. Stanley Jones—as Father (and Father-in-Law)," p. 9.

18. Mary Webster Tattersall, *Transformation*, Winter 1983, p. 14.

19. *A Song of Ascents*, pp. 216-17.

20. Ibid, p. 223.

21. For information about the history and administration of Jones's Christian ashrams, I relied on a five-page document prepared by the Special Collections Department of Asbury Theological Seminary as an introduction to the records of the United Christian Ashrams. This introduction, written in July 1991, states that up to that time, in addition to the ongoing local ashrams, there had been eight international ashrams in the following locations—Jerusalem (1972), which Jones attended, Israel and India (1974), Japan (1978), Sat Tal (1980), Finland (1982), United States (1986), Korea (1988), and Canada (1990). Another international ashram was held at Sat Tal in 2000 to commemorate the 70th anniversary of the first ashram.

22. *A Song of Ascents*, pp. 231-32.

23. William W. Richardson, "Reminiscing," p. 27.

24. Ibid, p. 26.

25. Jones's January 3, 1972, memo to The Seven is in the UCA Archives at Asbury.

26. On the blend of historical emphases, see Richard J. Foster's superb treatment of these traditions of Christian faith in his book, *Streams of Living Water,* 1998.

16. The Last Years

1. Jones's December 22, 1951, circular letter is in the Asbury Archives.

2. Frank C. Laubach's November 18, 1968, letter is in the Asbury Archives.

3. Although I have not found Jones's "Open Letter" to the Government of India among his papers at either Asbury or the Methodist Archives, there is a copy of the letter in appendix E (pp. 292-95) of C. Chacko Thomas's Ph.D. dissertation, *The Work and Thought of Eli Stanley Jones With Special Reference To India.*

4. Latourette, *Christianity in a Revolutionary Age,* Vol. V, p. 302. In the same volume (p. 303, n. 6) Latourette quotes the policy of the national government in India with respect to giving visas to missionaries: "In 1955 the Government of India said that visas were to be granted to new missionaries only if the applicant had outstanding qualifications or special experience; that they would normally be given for the return to India of missionaries who had been in the country five years or more; that new missionaries would not be admitted to border or tribal areas; and that to enter new centres missions must have its permission."

5. Unless otherwise noted, all of Jones's circular letters are in the Asbury Archives.

6. Chandra Bhal's May 30, 1953, letter is in the Asbury Archives.

7. Sri Prakasa's June 19, 1953, letter is in the Asbury Archives.

8. With respect to the United States's decision to give military aid to Pakistan, see my *The Totalitarian Kingdom of God,* p. 46.

9. "Christian Missions in Today's India," pp. 1362, 1363.

10. The interviews Jones and the Reverend H. A. Townsley conducted with Nehru, Pant, and Prasad are from an eight-page typed record made after the interviews on the basis of Jones's notes and memory together with commentary by Townsley. The record is among Jones's papers in the Asbury Seminary Archives.

11. The Harry S. Truman Library does not have any record of the content of Jones's conversation with the President, but in the files of Matthew J. Connelly, who was a member of Truman's staff, there is a schedule of Truman's appointments for September 1, 1950. Connelly apparently provided Truman with the following information about his noon appointment.

> Dr. E. Stanley Jones (Requested by Senator Graham of North Carolina. Dr. Jones is famous Methodist Minister and Missionary in Asiatic field, mainly India; author of several Asiatic books, most famous being Christ of the Indian Road. Has long been interested in world peace. Wants to talk to the President about Asiatic situation with special reference to India)

12. Jones's article in the June 11, 1953, issue of the *Indian Witness* is entitled, "Evangelism in Japan after the Occupation," pp. 189, 190. His article in the September 24, 1953, issue of the *Christian Advocate* entitled "Let's Give the Japanese Christ" is essentially the same as his *Indian Witness* article.

Jones also published articles in the *Christian Century* about his trips to Japan: "Japan Open to Christianity," April 20, 1949, pp. 492-93; "Report from Japan," June 13, 1951, pp. 710-11.

13. For a report on Jones's 1955 trip to Japan see "Will Japan Go Christian," in the *Christian Advocate.*

14. See "Evangelism in Japan after the Occupation."

15. During the 1950s, Jones became a target of the infamous U.S. House Un-American Activities Committee. The committee had actually begun to investigate him as early as 1939. For the full story see my *The Totalitarian Kingdom of God,* p. 160, n. 9.

16. Mary Webster Tattersall, "In Loving Remembrance of Brother Stanley," in *Transformation.*

17. Jones, "The Seven Main Needs of the Christian Movement in Japan," June 16, 1959, p. 195.

18. "The Seven Main Needs . . . ," p. 195.

19. Ibid, 196.

20. Ibid.

21. Jones quotes from his letter to the Methodist Division of Foreign Missions in his January 9, 1954, circular letter (in the Asbury Archives).

22. Jones's January 7, 1963, circular letter, in which he wrote of celebrating his 79th birthday in an African American church in Durham, N.C., is in The United Christian Ashram Archives at Asbury.

23. *Time,* January 24, 1964, p. 34.

24. For information about Jones's 80th birthday dinners, I relied on a press release issued by the Methodist Division of Foreign Missions, which is among his papers at Asbury, and on W. W. Richardson's article "Reminiscing."

25. The circular letter I quote with respect to Jones's integrated meeting in Norfolk, Virginia, is undated, but the content of the letter suggests that it was written in 1956. The letter is among Jones's papers at the Asbury Archives.

26. Jones's January 28, 1957, circular letter is in the Asbury Archives.

27. Jones's January 25, 1958, circular letter is in the Asbury Archives. There is another letter from Jones at Asbury dated May 1958 and addressed, "My Dear Ashram Friend." The content of this letter is much the same as his January 25, 1958, circular letter, although it does contain some additional information for the American ashrams.

28. Alexander J. Reid's February 25, 1958, letter to Jones, is with Jones's papers at Asbury.

29. Jones discusses his diabetes in *A Song of Ascents,* pp. 335-37.

30. Jones's 1964 circular letter is among his papers at Asbury. The letter is typed but undated. However, the date "1964" is written in longhand at the top of the letter.

31. Jones's August 1969 circular letter about his canceling his appearance at an ashram is in the Ashram Archives at Asbury.

32. Jones's January 1961 circular letter addressed to his ashram friends is in the Ashram Archives at Asbury.

33. Jones's April 27, 1965, circular letter, written on United Christian Ashram letterhead, is in the Ashram Archives at Asbury.

34. Jones's June 1965, circular letter, which repeats much of the April 27 circular letter, is in the Ashram Archives at Asbury.

35. Jones's December 2, 1965, circular letter is in the Ashram Archives at Asbury.

36. Jones's conversation with Martin Luther King appears on pp. 259-60 of *A Song of Ascents.* King's acknowledging his reliance on Jones's *Mahatma Gandhi: An Interpretation* is confirmed by an exhibit in the Martin Luther King Museum in Atlanta. An upstairs display shows King's copy of Jones's book, which is marked in King's handwriting: "Chap. VII" and "p. 98 very imp." Chapter VII of Jones's book is entitled, "The Center of Gandhi's Contribution—Satyagraha." *Satyagraha* means "truth force" or "truth power." On page 98 Jones discusses Gandhi's philosophy of suffering and Gandhi's willingness to admit mistakes. There is a photograph of the museum display in the Asbury Archives.

37. *The Christ of the American Road,* p. 180.

38. Ibid, p. 60.

39. Ibid, pp. 77-78.

40. *The Totalitarian Kingdom of God,* p.116.

41. George Green, "Stanley Jones Charges Columbia Has Written Her 'Obituary for Democracy,'" *The State,* April 30, 1942, p. 9.

42. Ibid, p. 1.

43. Ibid, p. 9. Jones's own account of his being in Columbia appears in *A Song of Ascents*, pp. 256-57. However, he remembered the incident as occurring "in the thirties."

44. *A Song of Ascents*, p. 256.

45. Jones's February 19, 1959, letter to the president of Asbury College is among his papers at the Asbury Archives.

46. There is a copy of Jones's December 26, 1956, letter to President Eisenhower in the Eisenhower Library in Abilene, Kansas.

47. Eisenhower's January 11, 1957, reply is in the Eisenhower Library and is also among Jones's papers at Asbury.

48. Frederic Fox's May 25, 1960, letter to Jones is also in the Eisenhower Library and at Asbury.

49. Jones's notes on his personal conversation with Altizer are a two-and-one-half-page typescript among his papers at Asbury. The notes are undated, but based on the fact that he visited Emory in 1965, Jones probably interviewed Altizer and made his notes on the interview at about the time of his visit to Emory.

50. Jones first mentioned a possible ashram in Galilee in his June 1966 circular letter written from Rimforsa, Sweden, which is among his papers at Asbury.

51. Jones's July 1967 circular letter is in the Asbury Archives.

52. Bill Berg, "Miracle at Jerusalem: Excerpts from Brother Bill Berg's World Ashram Congress Report," p. 12.

After Jones suffered a stroke in Oklahoma City on December 7, 1971, W. W. "Bill" Richardson, as General Secretary of the United Christian Ashrams, issued special bulletins on the status of Jones's health. Richardson sent copies of these bulletins to about 75 ashram leaders throughout the world. Altogether he issued 11 special bulletins, beginning on December 8, 1971, and ending on January 25, 1973, the day after Jones died in India.

53. My account of the conflict between Pakistan and East Pakistan and between Pakistan and India is taken from Vohra, pp. 234-36.

54. Jones's December 24, 1971, letter to Indira Gandhi and Gandhi's January 5, 1972, reply are among Jones's papers at Asbury.

55. Jones's July 4, 1972, letter to Indira Gandhi and Mrs. Gandhi's July 11, 1972, response, are in his papers at Asbury.

56. Richard I. Phillips's January 18, 1966, letter is with Jones's papers at Asbury.

57. Jones's March 16, 1966, circular letter is in the United Christian Ashram Archives at Asbury.

58. The collective letter of January 7, 1973, from the Sat Tal Ashram is in the Ashram Archives at Asbury.

59. Jones's January 28, 1967, circular letter is in his papers at Asbury.

60. Jones's October 1971 circular letter is among his papers at Asbury.

61. The facts and quotation about Jones's stroke are from an undated two-page typescript entitled "For Transformation Magazine," and from a letter dated Eastertide 1972, addressed to his ashram brothers and sisters. Both documents are in the Asbury Archives.

62. Jones's January 15, 1972, letter to The Seven is in the United Christian Ashram Archives at Asbury.

63. David N. Henderson's account of the last weeks of Jones's life is dated December 17, 1973, and is attached to a note signed by Lawrence W. Henderson. The note indicates that the account is a transcription of an audio tape made by David Henderson. Both documents are among Jones's papers at Asbury.

64. The information about Jones's memorial service and burial is from J. C. McPheeters's article "E. Stanley Jones Translated," p. 3.

65. All the letters from which I quote at the end of this chapter are from Jones's papers at Asbury.

66. The quotation from Jones's address on the Wesleyan movement is taken from what appears to be a transcript of a recording he made at the Kenlake Conference, which was held at Kenlake State Park in Kentucky on January 8-11, 1957. The transcript is among Jones's papers at Asbury.

17. The Legacy of E. Stanley Jones

1. *A Song of Ascents,* p. 89.

2. See Foster, *Streams of Living Water,* p. 60. There is a brief biography of Jones on p. 338.

3. Bishop Mathews's statement that Jones was "a spiritual genius" was made in a telephone interview on June 17, 2002.

4. *A Song of Ascents,* p. 92.

5. Niebuhr's criticism of Jones's *Christ's Alternative to Communism* appears in Niebuhr's *An Interpretation of Christian Ethics,* p. 162.

6. "Reinhold Niebuhr: A Study in Humanity and Humility," in Nathan A. Scott, Jr., ed., *The Legacy of Reinhold Niebuhr,* p. 1.

Bibliography

Books by E. Stanley Jones

Abundant Living. Nashville: Abingdon, 1942.
The Choice Before Us. New York, Cincinnati, and Chicago: Abingdon, 1937.
Christ at the Round Table. New York & Cincinnati: Abingdon, 1928.
The Christ of Every Road: A Study of Pentecost. New York, Cincinnati, and Chicago: Abingdon, 1930.
The Christ of the American Road. Nashville: Abingdon, 1944.
The Christ of the Indian Road. Nashville: Abingdon, 1925.
The Christ of the Mount: A Working Philosophy of Life. Nashville: Abingdon, 1931.
Christ's Alternative to Communism. Nashville and New York: Abingdon, 1935.
Growing Spiritually. New York and Nashville: Abingdon, 1953.
In Christ. A Festival Book. Nashville: Abingdon, 1980.
Is the Kingdom of God Realism? New York and Nashville: Abingdon-Cokesbury, 1940.
Mahatma Ghandi: Portrayal of a Friend. Nashville: Abingdon, 1983. Reprint edition of *Mahatma Ghandi: An Interpretation.* Nashville: Abingdon-Cokesbury, 1948.
The Reconstruction of the Church—On What Pattern? Nashville: Abingdon, 1970.
A Song of Ascents: A Spiritual Autobiography. Nashville and New York: Abingdon, 1968.
The Unshakable Kingdom and the Unchanging Person. Nashville: Abingdon, 1972.
Victorious Living. Nashville: Abingdon, 1936.
The Way. Nashville: Abingdon-Cokesbury, 1946.
The Way to Power and Poise. New York and Nashville: Abingdon-Cokesbury, 1949.
The Word Became Flesh. New York and Nashville: Abingdon, 1963.

Articles by E. Stanley Jones in *The Indian Witness*

"The American Seminar," August 19, 1925, pp. 511-12.
"The American Seminar, II: A Word about Germany," September 2, 1925, p. 545.
"Announcement Concerning the Lucknow Ashram," June 6, 1935, p. 862.
"As the Bamboo Curtain Goes Down," June 14, 1949, pp. 523-24.

426

"Browsings in Scripture," August 21, 1918, p. 544.

"The Christian and the Present Crisis," February 11, 1932, pp. 86-87.

"The Christian Attitude in the China War Crisis," October 14, 1937, pp. 643-44.

"Christian Missions, not Domination, nor Denomination, but Christ," April 5, 1934, pp. 210, 212.

"The Christian Programme of Reconstruction," February 13, 1936, pp. 101-3; February 20, 1936, pp. 118-20.

"The Church of Christ in India," September 26, 1935, p. 613.

"Church Union in India," October 24, 1935, pp. 680-81.

"The Closing of the Lucknow Ashram," April 18, 1940, pp. 248-49.

"Dr. Stanley Jones in China," January 6, 1938, pp. 5-6.

"Evangelism among Educated Indians," December 4, 1918, pp. 785-87.

"Evangelism, Imposed or Inspired," November 24, 1926, pp. 739-40.

"Evangelism in Japan after the Occupation," June 11, 1953, pp. 189-90.

"Evangelism in South India," April 4, 1923, p. 234.

"Evangelism through South India," October 26, 1921, pp. 825, 828.

"Evangelistic Work in China," January 17, 1923, pp. 45-6; January 31, 1923, p. 85.

"Evangelizing in the Land of King Feisul," April 12, 1922, pp. 241-42.

"Evangelizing Where the Good News Was Born," March 31, 1926, pp. 197-98.

"Forward to the New Situation," August 1, 1923, p. 533.

"The Greatest Christian Opportunity on Our Planet," July 7, 1949, pp. 507-8, 510-11.

"India's New Thought of Christ," January 31, 1923, pp. 81-82.

"The Influence of the Indian Heritage upon Christianity," December 19, 1923, pp. 909-10; December 26, 1923, pp. 927-28; January 2, 1924, pp. 5-6, 11.

"An Interview with the Mahatma," December 6, 1934, pp. 774-75.

"Is Federal Union the Way Out?" January 26, 1956, p. 28; February 9, 1956, pp. 43-44.

"A Last Minute Call to Reconsider Church Union," May 21, 1970, pp. 157-58, 160.

"Malaya: Where Opportunity Beckons," October 26, 1927, pp. 683-84; November 23, 1927, pp. 750-51.

"Man Is Man" (a poem), September 13, 1922, n. p.

"More Thoughts on Church Unity," May 16, 1935, p. 309.

"My Position Restated," April 11, 1940, p. 233.

"My Stay at Santiniketan," September 5, 1923, pp. 621-22.

"The Nation's Call to Christians," July 16, 1964, p. 229.

"The Next Great Step: Unite!" May 6, 1937, pp. 275-76.

"Notes Along the Way," June 1, 1916, pp. 426-27.

"Notes on the China Tour," January 12, 1933, p. 26.

"Notes on the Eddy Campaigns," August 13, 1919, p. 517.

"On What Basis Should the Churches Get Together?" June 23, 1949, pp. 475-77.

"Opportunities for the Church Facing Indian Nationalism," August 1, 1946, pp. 1, 3; August 15, 1946, pp. 195, 197.

"Re-ordination or Right Hand of Fellowship?" January 20, 1949, pp. 43-44.

"Report on Latin America Evangelistic Tour," October 25, 1945, p. 242.

"The Revival Month—Some Thoughts," February 4, 1915, p. 96.

"Sat Tal Ashram," January 15, 1931, p. 40.

"The Secret of the Success of the Arya Samaj," April 15, 1915, pp. 284-85.

"The Seven Main Needs of the Christian Movement in Japan," June 16, 1959, pp. 195-96.

"The Significance of the Ambedkar Movement," October 1, 1936, pp. 630-31.

"The Situation in China," December 15, 1932, p. 793.

"Some Remarkable Conversions," February 27, 1912, pp. 167-68.

"Some Thoughts on Church Unity," April 25, 1935, pp. 261-62.

"Studying the League at Geneva," September 16, 1925, p. 3.

"Three Vultures over the House of the Lord," March 19, 1964, p. 96.

"Through South India," September 20, 1922, p. 629.

"The Proposed Ashram at Sat Tal (A Preliminary Statement)," January 9, 1930, pp. 27-28. (Co-authored with Yunas Sinha.)

"To Proselytize or Convert—Which?" June 18, 1931, p. 387.

"To Proselytize or Convert—Which?" December 31, 1931, p. 838.

"Turkey's Remarkable Revolution," December 16, 1925, pp. 787-89.

"The University Christian Mission in America," January 26, 1939, pp. 51-52.

"We Welcome Bishop J. Waskom Pickett," January 9, 1936, pp. 17-18.

"What Happened at Jerusalem?" May 2, 1928, pp. 283-84, 288.

"What Is Christianity?" August 18, 1932, pp. 515-16.

"A Year of Evangelism," December 1, 1926, pp. 757-58.

"A Year's Pilgrimage," April 14, 1932, pp. 231-33.

Other Articles and Publications by E. Stanley Jones

"An Adventure in Failure: Behind the Scenes Before Pearl Harbor," *Asia and the Americas*, December 1945, pp. 609-16.

"Afterthoughts on the Preaching Mission," *The Christian Century*, April 14, 1937, pp. 483-85.

"Apply Gandhi's Method to Japan!" *The Christian Century*, January 19, 1938, pp. 75-76.

"Barbed Wire Christians," *The Christian Century*, November 24, 1943, pp. 1364-66.

"Christian Missions in Today's India," *The Christian Century*, November 10, 1954, pp. 1362-63.

"Christianity and Self-Government in India," *The Christian Century*, September 3, 1930, pp. 1058, 1060.

"Christians of America Unite," *The Christian Century*, October 2, 1935, pp. 1235-37.

"Church Federal Union—Now!" *The Christian Century*, December 16, 1942, pp. 1554-56.

"Evangelizing in the Land of the Pharaohs," *The Christian Advocate*, January 28, 1926, pp. 104-6.

"The Facts Themselves Are the Alarm: A Plain Word for a Critical Hour," *The Christian Advocate*, September 25, 1924, p. 1161.

"Federal Church Union—A Reply," *The Christian Century*, June 16, 1943, pp. 713-14.

"Federal Union of Churches," *The Christian Century*, June 10, 1953, pp. 690-91.

"Gandhi and Christian Missions," *The Christian Century*, May 3, 1944, pp. 553-55.

"Gandhi's Death—The Indian Reaction," *The Christian Century*, February 18, 1948, p. 209.

"I Saw a New India Rise," *The Christian Century*, July 17, 1946, pp. 889-91.

"In Tagore's 'House of Peace,'" *The Christian Advocate*, March 13, 1924, pp. 319-20.

"India at the Polls," *The Christian Century*, May 21, 1952, pp. 615-17.

"Is Church Federal Union the Answer?" *The Christian Advocate*, January 14, 1943, pp. 42-43, 59.

"Is Federal Union a Halfway House?" *The Christian Century,* July 14, 1948, pp. 705-7.

"Is It Worth While?" in Moore, *The Sound of Trumpets,* pp. 65-75.

"Is the Movement for Federal Union Waning or Waxing?" *The Christian Advocate,* January 26, 1950, pp. 6-7.

"Japan Open to Christianity," *The Christian Century,"* April 20, 1949, pp. 492-93.

"The Kingdom of God in the New Testament," *The Message of the Kingdom of God: Sat Tal Ashram Essays 1932* (Calcutta: Y.M.C.A. Publishing House, 1933), pp. 11-38.

"Let's Give the Japanese Christ," *The Christian Advocate,* September 24, 1953, pp. 6, 7, 29, 31.

"Meeting Current Objections to Foreign Missions," in Moss, ed., *The Foreign Missions Conference of North America 1929,* pp. 129-40.

"A Message to the Church," The Contributing Editor's Page, *The Christian Advocate,* October 11, 1928 p. 1231.

"A Message to the Methodist Church," *The Christian Advocate,* April 14, 1932, p. 38.

"An Open Letter to the Christian People of America and Great Britain," *The Christian Century,* November, 19, 1937, pp. 1386-88.

"An Open Letter to the People of Japan," *The Christian Century,* September 15, 1937, pp. 1131-33.

"The Present Religious Situation in India." Unpublished article in the Methodist Archives, handwritten date of December 3, 1924.

"The Price of Ultimate Victory," Anderson, ed., *Christian World Mission,* pp. 263-69.

"Report from Japan," *The Christian Century,* June 13, 1951, pp. 710-11.

"Report on the New India," *The Christian Century,* April 30, 1947, pp. 555-56.

"What About Puerto Rico?" *The Christian Century,* January 30, 1946, pp. 138-40.

"What I Found in Latin America," *The Christian Century,* July 18, 1945, pp. 833-34.

"What I Found in Latin America, Part II," *The Christian Century,* July 25, 1945, pp. 858-60.

"What I Missed at Madras," *The Christian Century,* May 31, 1939, pp. 704-8.

"What I Saw in Manchuria, *The Christian Century,* October 19, 1932, pp. 1267-68.

"What Is America's Role in This Crisis?" *The Christian Century,* March 19, 1941, pp. 388-90.

"Which Way Will Free India Go?" *The Christian Century,* August 1, 1946, pp. 1, 3.

"Will Japan Go Christian?" *The Christian Advocate,* June 26, 1956, pp. 6, 23, 27.

"With Lips of Flaming Fire," *The Christian Advocate,* June 26, 1924, pp. 803-4.

"The World's Whispering," *The Christian Advocate,* November 13, 1924, pp. 1387-88.

Other Books and Articles

Anderson, William K., editor. *Christian World Mission.* Nashville: Commission on Ministerial Training of the Methodist Church, 1946.

Berg, William E. "Miracle at Jerusalem: Excerpts from Brother Bill Berg's World Ashram Congress Report," *Transformation,* Spring 1973.

Bosch, David J. *Transforming Mission: Paradigm Shifts in the Theology of Mission.* American Society of Missiology Series, No. 16. Mayknoll, N.Y.: Orbis Books, 1991.

429

Brown, Robert McAfee. "Reinhold Niebuhr: A Study in Humanity and Humility," in Scott, *The Legacy of Reinhold Niebuhr.*

Copplestone, J. Tremayne. *History of Methodist Missions.* Vol. 4: Twentieth Century Perspectives. New York: Board of Global Ministries of the United Methodist Church, 1973.

Eddy, Sherwood. *Eighty Adventurous Years.* New York: Harper & Bros., 1955.

————. *Pathfinders of the World Missionary Crusade.* New York and Nashville: Abingdon-Cokesbury, 1945.

Escamilla, Roberto. "As I Remember Brother Stanley: A Tribute to E. Stanley Jones," *Transformation,* Winter 1983. *Transformation* was published between 1961 and the present by the United Christian Ashrams. This issue is a book-length magazine celebrating the 100th anniversary of Jones's birth.

Foster, Richard J. *Streams of Living Water.* San Francisco: HarperSan Francisco, 1998.

Gandhi, Mahatma. *The Collected Works of Mahatma Gandhi,* Vol. 53 (January-March 1933). Ahmedabad: Government of India, 1971.

Graham, Stephen A. *The Totalitarian Kingdom of God: The Political Philosophy of E. Stanley Jones.* Lanham, Md.: The University Press of America, 1998.

Green, George. "Stanley Jones Charges Columbia Has Written Her 'Obituary for Democracy,'" *The State,* April 30, 1942, pp. 1, 9.

Grew, Joseph C. *Turbulent Era: A Diplomatic Record of Forty Years 1904-1945.* Edited by Walter Johnson. Boston: Houghton Mifflin, 1952.

Harmon, Nolan B. ed., *The Encyclopedia of World Methodism.* Nashville: United Methodist Publishing House, 1974.

Harper, Susan Billington, "Sherwood Eddy," in Gerald H. Anderson, ed., *Biographical Dictionary of Christian Missions.* New York: Simon & Schuster Macmillan, 1998, pp. 193-94.

Hill, Clarence. "An American Gandhi Leads Christian Campers in Religious Revival on Michigan's Sands." *Kansas City Star,* August 11, 1940.

Hocking, William E. *Re-Thinking Missions: A Laymen's Inquiry After One Hundred Years.* New York and London: Harper & Brothers, 1932.

Horner, Norman A., ed. *Protestant Crosscurrents in Mission: The Ecumenical-Conservative Encounter.* New York and Nashville: Abingdon, 1968.

Hyer, Marjorie. "Dr. E. Stanley Jones, Evangelist, Dies." *The Washington Post,* January 26, 1973, p. B4.

Jones, Charles Edwin. *Perfectionist Persuasion: The Holiness Movement and American Methodism, 1867-1936.* ATLA Monograph Series No. 5. Lanham, MD and London: Scarecrow Press, 1974.

Latourette, Kenneth Scott. *Christianity in a Revolutionary Age: A History of Christianity in the Nineteenth and Twentieth Centuries.* Vol. V. *The Twentieth Century Outside Europe.* New York and Evanston: Harper & Row, 1962.

————. *Missions Tomorrow.* New York: Harper & Row, 1936.

Mathews, Eunice Jones. "Historical Sketch of Sat Tal," *Sat Tal Ashram Golden Anniversary 1930–1980,* pp. 8-11.

————. "My Father, E. Stanley Jones," *United Methodists Today,* June 1975.

Mathews, James K. *A Global Odyssey.* Nashville: Abingdon, 2000.

————, and Eunice Jones Matthews. "Stanley Jones—as Father (and Father-in-Law)," *Transformation,* Winter 1983.

McGriff, E. Carver. *Amazing Grace: A History of Indiana Methodism 1801-2001.* Franklin, Tenn.: Providence House, 2001.

McPheeters, J. C. "E. Stanley Jones Translated," *The Herald* (March 7, 1973), p. 3.

Moore, Arthur J. *The Sound of Trumpets.* Nashville: General Commission on Benevolences, Methodist Episcopal Church South, 1934.

Mosley, Leonard. *Hirohito: Emperor of Japan.* Englewood Cliffs, N.J.: Prentice-Hall, 1966.

Moss, Leslie B., ed. *The Foreign Missions Conference of North America 1929.* New York: Foreign Mission Conference of North America, 1929.

Mott, John R. "Foreword," in Pickett, *Christian Mass Movements in India.*

Neill, Stephen. *A History of Christian Missions.* 2nd ed. New York: Penguin, 1986.

Niebuhr, Reinhold. *An Interpretation of Christian Ethics.* New York: Living Age Books, 1956.

Noll, Mark A. *A History of Christianity in the United States and Canada.* Grand Rapids, Mich.: Eerdmans, 1992.

"One Hope," *Time,* December 12, 1938.

Pickett, J. Waskom. "The Promising Young Stanley," *The Indian Witness,* March 15, 1973.

———. *Christian Mass Movements in India: A Study with Recommendations.* New York, Cincinnati, and Chicago: Abingdon, 1933.

———. *Christ's Way to India's Heart: Present Day Mass Movements in Christianity.* New York: Friendship Press, 1938.

———. "E. Stanley Jones," in Harmon, ed., *Encyclopedia of World Methodism.*

Ranson, Charles W. *A Missionary Pilgrimage.* Grand Rapids: Eerdmans, 1988.

Read, Anthony and Fisher, David. *The Proudest Day: India's Long Road to Independence.* New York and London: W. W. Norton 1997.

Renovare Devotional Readings. Wichita, Kan., Vol. 1, No. 19, 1990.

Richardson, William W. "Reminiscing," *Transformation,* Winter, 1983, pp. 25-26.

Scherer, J. A. "Ecumenical Mandates for Mission," in Horner, ed., *Protestant Crosscurrents in Mission.*

Scott, Nathan A., Jr. *The Legacy of Reinhold Niebuhr.* Chicago: University of Chicago Press, 1974.

Showalter, Nathan D. T*he End of a Crusade: The Student Volunteer Movement for Foreign Missions and the Great War.* ATLA Monograph Series, No. 44. Lanham, Md. and London: The Scarecrow Press, 1998.

Soper, Edmund D. *The Philosophy of the Christian World Mission.* New York and Nashville: Abingdon, 1943.

Spence, Hartzell. "Can He Unite the Protestants?" *The Saturday Evening Post,* December 4, 1948.

Terasaki, Gwen. *Bridge to the Sun.* Chapel Hill: University of North Carolina Press, 1957.

Thacker, Joseph A., Jr., *Asbury College: Vision and Miracle.* Nappanee, Ind.: Evangel Press, 1990.

Thomas, C. Chacko. *The Work and Thought of Eli Stanley Jones With Special Reference to India.* Unpublished Ph.D. dissertation. Ames: University of Iowa, 1955.

Vohra, Ranbir. *The Making of India: A Historial Survey.* Armonk, N.Y. and London: M.E. Sharpe, 1997.

Wacker, Grant. "The Holiness Movement," *Eerdman's Handbook to Christianity in America.* Grand Rapids, Mich.: Eerdmans, 1983.

Webster Tattersall, Mary, "In Loving Remembrance of Brother Stanley," *Transformation,* Winter 1983, pp. 14-15.

Yasumura, Sabrow. "Three Months' Tour with E. Stanley Jones," *The Japan Christian Quarterly,* Summer 1953.